Real Estate Principles

FOURTH EDITION

BRUCE HARWOOD

Real Estate Principles

FOURTH EDITION

A RESTON BOOK
Prentice-Hall
Englewood Cliffs, New Jersey

This book is dedicated

to the reader's success in the field of real estate

ADDRESS EDITORIAL CORRESPONDENCE TO:
Real Estate Editor, College Division
Prentice-Hall
Englewood Cliffs, N.J.   07632

ADDRESS ORDERS TO:
Prentice-Hall
200 Old Tappan Road
Old Tappan, N.J.   07675

COVER PHOTOGRAPH BY GEORGE WHITELEY, PHOTO RESEARCHERS

Library of Congress Cataloging-in-Publication Data

Harwood, Bruce M.
    Real estate principles.

    "A Reston book."
    Includes index.
    1. Real estate business—United States.   I. Title.
HD1375.H38   1986   333.33'0973   85-28132
ISBN 0-8359-6603-8

A Reston Book
Published by Prentice-Hall, A Division of Simon & Schuster, Inc.
Englewood Cliffs, New Jersey 07632

© 1977, 1980, 1983, 1986 by Prentice-Hall, Englewood Cliffs, New Jersey   07632

1   3   5   7   9   10   8   6   4   2

PRINTED IN THE UNITED STATES OF AMERICA

CONTENTS

v

LIST OF ILLUSTRATIONS & TABLES

Is your goal a full-time or part-time career in real estate? Do you own or plan to own your home or an investment property? Are you a student of real estate desiring to broaden your knowledge of this subject? If you answered "Yes" to one or more of these, the contents of this book will be of immense help to you.

In this book you will learn about real estate brokerage, appraisal, financing, contracts, closings and investing. Additionally, you will learn about land descriptions, rights and interests, fair housing, taxes, leases, condominiums, zoning, careers and licensing and the use of computers in real estate. You will find particularly valuable the attention given to such timely topics as a real estate agent's liability and professional obligation to buyers and sellers, brokers who represent buyers, advance fee listings, errors and omission insurance, foreclosure and time-sharing. Included throughout the book are numerous examples from actual practice, including important decisions in several recent court cases.

Throughout this book emphasis is placed on an easily readable style of writing that will take you by the hand and lead you through the chapters in a pleasant and enjoyable experience. You will find emphasis placed on explanations that combine "how" things are done in real estate with "why" they are done. Numerous tables, sketches and diagrams will help you to visualize real estate rights and interests, financing techniques, appraisal methods, closing statements and map reading. Simplified, plain English examples of real estate documents are used so their key elements can be easily identified and not lost in a maze of legal language. Warranty deeds, grant deeds, quitclaim deeds, trust deeds, title insurance policies, promissory notes and mortgages are among the documents so treated.

Starting with Chapter 2, key real estate terms are listed and defined at the beginning of each chapter in addition to being explained in the chapter. Correspondingly, you will find end-of-the-chapter vocabulary reviews plus questions and problems to test your comprehension of the material just read. Also presented at the end of each chapter are additional readings you may wish to use in furthering your real estate education.

The appendices of this book contain easy-to-understand residential construction illustrations plus sample questions typical of those found on real estate license tests. You will also find a real estate math review and answers to the chapter-end vocabulary reviews, questions and problems. Lastly, there is a combined index and glossary that allows you to simultaneously find a short definition of a word and a page reference for further information.

Your author completed his undergraduate work in real estate at the University of California, Berkeley, in 1963. Upon graduation, he became a salesman in a Los Angeles real estate office. In 1965 he became a broker and completed his Masters in Business Administration at UCLA with a major in urban land economics. In 1972 he completed doctoral studies in Business Administration, with a specialization in finance and real estate, at the University of Colorado. He has taught real estate at the college level in Florida, Colorado, California and Hawaii. His real estate principles textbooks, the first published in 1977, bring together a combination of real estate field experience, teaching experience in both day and evening programs, and writing experience.

Criticisms of and suggestions for improving this book are welcomed. They should be sent to the Real Estate Editor, College Editorial Department, Prentice-Hall, Englewood Cliffs, N.J. 07632.

ACKNOWLEDGMENTS   *A personal thanks to the following people who by written correspondence, telephone calls or personal meeting have helped to shape this book:* Floyd Adashek, Otis T. Amory, Merlin Bauer, Sandy Berens, Mark Brothers, A.L. Bocchini, Arthur Bowman, Sandra Cece, Tom Cook, John Cornelius, Robert Coulthard, Wallace Dean Davis, Keith Donaldson, Brunell Ellis, Jack Ellis, Barney Fletcher, Stephen Guice, Jr., Charles Haley, Allan Harvie, John W. Hill,

Lynn Hoover, Anne Hruby, Ed Jutzi, F. Jeffrey Keil, Jack Kessinger, Jay Lamont, Cecil Lawter, David Lawter, Frank Lembo, Tom Lynch, Ben Marilla, John Marshall, Jr., Roger Meade, Don Moseley, Susan Moseley, Allen Natella, Gene Padgham, Leonard Palumbo, Linda Phillips, Lee Frew Platt, Hugh Prichard, Judith Rachap, John Reilly, Phil Sapp, Rudy Schmidt, Malcolm Searle, Carolyn Shea, Morris Sleight, Martie Stegall, Jean Tate, Hugo Weber, Jr., Wayne Weeks, A.P. Werbner, Dorothy Whetstone, Yvonne Whitney, Kathleen Witalisz, and Michael Witt.

NOTE TO READERS

The author anticipates that as many women will read this book as men. However, it would make the sentences in this book harder to read if "he and she" and "his and her" were used on every possible occasion. Therefore, when you read, "he," "his," or "him" in this book, please note that they are being used in their grammatical sense and refer to women as well as men.

*   *   *

The forms in this text are for information *only* and are not intended for use as legal documents. In such matters, an attorney should be consulted.

Introduction to Real Estate

Welcome!

Real estate is an exciting business. But it is also a demanding one since it requires that one know the ethical and business principles fundamental to the successful selling and buying of real property. There are some who say that the only way to learn these principles is by experience. That can be extremely time-consuming and costly, no matter how good a teacher experience is. A more logical approach is to learn a substantial portion of this complicated body of knowledge from experts already at work in the field. Then personal experience can be acquired. With that combination in mind, this book has been written to provide you with an understanding of the basic principles and business fundamentals of real estate. Emphasis is placed on an easily readable presentation that combines explanations of "how" things are done in real estate with "why" they are done.

HOW TO READ THIS BOOK

At the beginning of each chapter (2 through 23) there is a list of the new "Key Terms" that you will learn, along with brief definitions. Read these before starting the chapter. In the body of the chapter these terms, along with other terms important to real estate, are set in **boldface type** and given a more in-depth discussion. At the end of each chapter is a vocabulary review plus questions and problems. These are designed to help you test yourself on your comprehension of the material in the chapter you've just read. The answers are given in Appendix H in the back of the book.

At the back of this book is a combined index and glossary. This will help reinforce your familiarity with the language of real estate. When you use this index and glossary you will receive a short definition followed by a page reference for more detailed discussion.

A unique feature of this book is its simplified documents. Deeds, mortgages and title policies, for example, are usually written in legal language and small type that defies comprehension by anyone except a lawyer. In the chapters ahead, you will find simplified versions of these documents, written in plain English and set in standard size type. The benefit to you is that you will come away with an understanding as to what is actually inside these important real estate documents.

Another special feature of this book is the wide margin on each page. Besides its eye appeal, it is helpful for locating subject headings and it provides a handy place for your study notes.

TRANSACTION OVERVIEW

Figure 1:1 provides a visual summary of the real estate transaction cycle. It is included here to give you an overview of the different steps involved in the sale of real property and to show how the steps are related to each other. The chapter where each step is discussed is also shown. Whether your point of view is that of a real estate agent, owner, buyer, or seller, you will find the chapters which follow to be informative and valuable.

Chapter Organization

Great care has been taken in organizing this text so as to build your knowledge of real estate. For example, land description methods and rights and interests in land are necessary to sales contracts, abstracts, deeds, mortgages and listings and therefore are discussed early in the text.

In Chapter 2 you will find such topics as metes and bounds and tract maps. You will also find a discussion of what is real estate and what is not, and how land is physically and economically different from other commodities. Having described real estate, the next logical step is to look at the various rights and interests that exist in a given parcel of land. In Chapter 3 you will see that there is much more to ownership of land than meets the eye! In Chapter 4 we look at how a given right or interest in land can be held by an individual, by two or more persons, or by a business entity. Included in this chapter are discussions of joint tenancy, tenancy in common and community property.

Chapters 5 and 6 deal with the process by which the ownership of real estate is transferred from one person to another. In particular, Chapter 5 discusses deeds and wills, and Chapter 6 deals with how a person gives evidence to the world that he

AN OVERVIEW OF A REAL ESTATE TRANSACTION   **Figure 1:1**

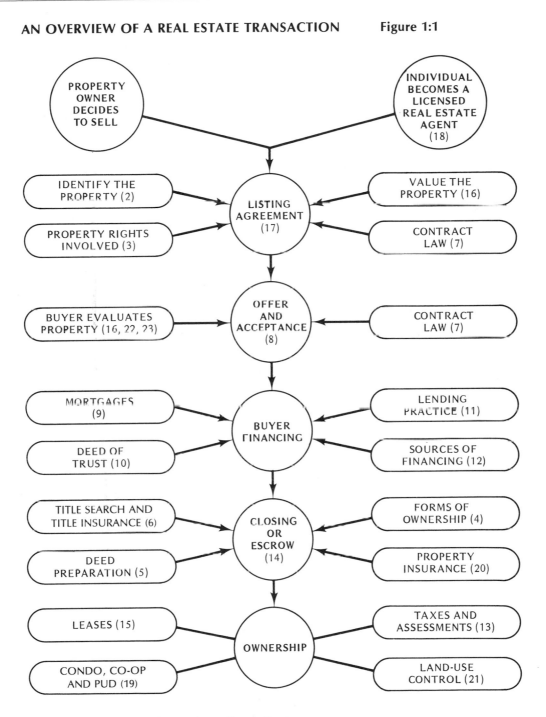

NOTE: Numbers in parentheses refer to Chapter Numbers.

possesses a given right or interest in land. Abstracts and title insurance are among the topics included.

In Chapters 7 and 8 we turn to contract law and its application to offers and acceptances. Because so much of what takes place in real estate is in the form of contracts, you will want to have a solid understanding of what makes a contract legally binding, and what doesn't.

Chapters 9 through 12 are devoted to real estate finance. In Chapter 9 mortgages and the laws regarding their use are explained. Chapter 10 covers the deed of trust and is intended for readers in those states where the deed of trust is used in place of a mortgage. Amortized loans, points, FHA and VA programs, loan application and mortgage insurance are discussed in Chapter 11. Mortgage lenders, the secondary mortgage market, due-on-sale clauses, adjustable rate mortgages and financing alternatives are covered in Chapter 12.

In Chapter 13 we see how property taxes and assessments are calculated, and Chapter 14 explains title closing and escrow. Chapter 15 deals with leasing real estate and includes a sample lease document with discussion. Chapter 16 explores the language, principles and techniques of real estate appraisal.

In Chapter 17 we examine the relationship between real estate agents and buyers and sellers. Special emphasis is placed on the duties and obligations of brokers to their clients and on fair housing laws. The chapter following that deals with real estate license law requirements, how a salesperson chooses a broker and professional ethics.

The remaining chapters of this book deal with a number of individual and specialized real estate topics. Chapter 19 explores the condominium, cooperative and planned unit development forms of real estate ownership. Included is a look at how they are created and the various rights and interests in land that are created by them including timesharing. In Chapter 20 we take a brief and informative look at property insurance. As an owner of real property you should know how to insure against financial loss due to property damage and public liability.

Zoning, land planning and deed restrictions are covered in Chapter 21. These are important topics because any limitation on a landowner's right to develop and use land can have a substantial effect on its value. Chapter 22 explores several pertinent and timely relationships between the value of real estate and the condition of the United States economy. The final chapter, Chapter 23, is an introduction to the opportunities available to you as a real estate investor. Topics include tax shelter, equity build-up, what to buy and when to buy.

Following the final chapter are several appendices which you will find useful. There are compound interest, present value and measurement conversion tables. (Amortization and loan balance tables are located in Chapter 11.) There is also an appendix containing construction illustrations to help acquaint you with construction terminology. Still other appendices contain sample questions typical of those found on real estate licensing examinations administered by the Educational Testing Service, the American College Testing Program and Assessment Systems, Inc. These three firms write and administer real estate license exams in three-quarters of the states. Additionally, you will find a short real estate math review section plus the answers to the quizzes and problems found at the end of Chapters 2 through 23.

The contents and organization of this book are designed for persons who are interested in real estate because they now own or plan to own real estate, and for persons interested in real estate as a career. It is to those who are considering real estate as a profession that the balance of this chapter is devoted.

CAREER OPPORTUNITIES

Most persons who think of real estate from the career standpoint see only the real estate agent who specializes in selling homes. This is quite natural as home selling is the most visible segment of the real estate industry. Selling residential real estate is how most people enter the real estate business, and where most practicing real estate licensees make their living. Selling residential property offers a good way to experience whether real estate sales appeals to you, or whether residential property is the type of property in which you wish to specialize.

Residential brokerage requires a broad knowledge of the community and its neighborhoods, an understanding of real estate principles, law and practice, and an ability to work well with people. Working hours will often include nights and

RESIDENTIAL BROKERAGE

weekends as these times are usually most convenient to buyers and sellers. A residential agent must also supply and drive his or her own automobile—one that is suitable for taking clients to see property.

In only a few real estate offices are new residential salespersons given a minimum guaranteed salary or a draw against future commissions. Therefore, a newcomer should have enough capital to survive until the first commissions are earned—and that can take four to six months. Additionally, the salesperson must be capable of developing and handling a personal budget that will withstand the feast and famine cycles that can occur in real estate selling.

A person who is adept at people relations, who can identify clients' buying motives and who can find property to fit, will probably be quite successful in this business.

COMMERCIAL BROKERAGE

Commercial brokers, also called income property brokers, specialize in income-producing properties such as apartment and office buildings, retail stores and warehouses. In this specialty, the salesperson is primarily selling monetary benefits. These benefits are the income, appreciation, mortgage reduction and tax shelter that a property can reasonably be expected to produce.

To be successful in income property brokerage, one must be very competent in mathematics, know how to finance transactions and keep abreast of current tax laws. One must also have a sense for what makes a good investment, what makes an investment salable and what the growth possibilities are in the neighborhood where a property is located.

Commission income from commercial brokerage is likely to be less frequent, but in larger amounts than from residential brokerage. The time required to break into the business is longer, but once in the business, agent turnover is low. The working hours of a commercial broker are much closer to regular business hours than for those in residential selling.

INDUSTRIAL BROKERAGE

Industrial brokers specialize in finding suitable land and buildings for industrial concerns. This includes leasing and developing industrial property as well as listing and selling it. An industrial broker must be familiar with industry requirements such as proximity to raw materials, water and power, labor supplies and transportation. An industrial broker must also know about local building, zoning and tax laws as they pertain to possible sites, and about the schools, housing, cultural and recreational facilities that would be used by future employees of the plant.

Commissions are irregular, but usually substantial. Working hours are regular business hours and one's sales efforts are primarily aimed at locating facts and figures and presenting them to clients in an orderly fashion. Industrial clients are usually sophisticated business people. Gaining entry to industrial brokerage and acquiring a client list can be slow.

FARM BROKERAGE

With the rapid disappearance of the family farm, the farm broker's role is changing. Today a farm broker must be equally capable of handling the 160-acre spread of farmer Jones and the 10,000-acre operation owned by an agribusiness corporation. College training in agriculture is an advantage and on-the-job training is a must. Knowledge of soils, seeds, plants, fertilizers, production methods, new machinery, government subsidies and tax laws are vital to success. Farm brokerage offers as many opportunities to earn commissions and fees from leasing and property management as from listing and selling property.

PROPERTY MANAGEMENT

For an investment property, the property manager's job is to supervise every aspect of a property's operation so as to produce the highest possible financial return over the longest period of time. The manager's tasks include renting, tenant relations, building repair and maintenance, accounting, advertising and supervision of personnel and tradesmen.

The current boom in condominiums has resulted in a growing demand for property managers to maintain them. In addition, large businesses that own property for their own use hire property managers. Property managers are usually paid a salary, and if the property is a rental, a bonus for keeping the building fully occupied. To be successful, a property manager should be not only a public relations expert and a good bookkeeper but also at ease with tenants, handy with tools and knowledgeable about laws applicable to rental units.

RENTAL LISTING
SERVICES

In some cities there are rental listing services that help tenants find rental units and landlords find tenants. Most compile lists of available rentals and sell this information to persons looking for rentals. A few also charge the landlord for listing the property. The objective is to save a person time and gasoline by providing pertinent information on a large number of rentals. Each property on the list is accompanied by information regarding location, size, rent, security deposit, pet policy, etc.

Especially popular in cities with substantial numbers of single persons are roommate listing services. These maintain files on persons with space to share (such as the second bedroom in a two-bedroom apartment) and those looking for space. The files will contain information on location, rent, male or female, smoking or nonsmoking, etc. Most roommate and rental listing services have been started by individual entrepreneurs and are not affiliated with real estate offices. Depending on the state, a real estate license may or may not be required.

REAL ESTATE
APPRAISING

The job of the real estate appraiser is to gather and evaluate all available facts affecting a property's value. Appraisal is a real estate career opportunity that does not require property selling; however, it does demand a special set of skills of its own. The job requires practical experience, technical education and good judgment. If you have an analytical mind and like to collect and interpret data, you might consider becoming a real estate appraiser. The job combines office work and field work, and the income of an expert appraiser can match that of a top real estate salesperson. One can be an independent appraiser, or there are numerous opportunities to work as a salaried appraiser for local tax authorities or lending institutions.

GOVERNMENT SERVICE

Approximately one-third of the land in the United States is government owned. This includes vacant and forested lands, office buildings, museums, parks, zoos, schools, hospitals, public housing, libraries, fire and police stations, roads and highways, subways, airports and courthouses. All of these are real estate and all of these require government employees who can negotiate purchases and sales, appraise, finance, manage, plan and develop. Cities, counties and state governments all have extensive real estate holdings. At the federal level, the Forest Service, Park Service, Department of Agriculture, Army Corps of Engineers, Bureau of Land Management, and General Services Administration are all major landholders. In addition to outright real estate ownership, government agencies such as the Federal Housing Administration, Veterans Administration and Federal Home Loan Bank employ thousands of real estate specialists to keep their real estate lending programs operating smoothly.

LAND DEVELOPMENT

Most new homes in the United States are built by developers who in turn sell them to homeowners and investors. Some homes are built by small-scale developers who produce only a few a year. Others are part of 400-home subdivisions and 40-story condominiums that are developed and constructed by large corporations that have their own planning, appraising, financing, construction and marketing personnel. There is equal opportunity for success in development whether you build 4 houses a year or work for a firm that builds 400 a year.

URBAN PLANNING

Urban planners work with local governments and civic groups for the purpose of anticipating future growth and land-use changes. The urban planner makes recommendations for new streets, highways, sewer and water lines, schools, parks and libraries. Emphasis on environmental protection and controlled growth has made urban planning one of real estate's most rapidly expanding specialties. An urban planning job is usually a salaried position and does not emphasize sales ability.

MORTGAGE FINANCING

Specialists in mortgage financing have a dual role: (1) to find economically sound properties for lenders, and (2) to locate money for borrowers. A mortgage specialist can work independently, receiving a fee from the borrower for locating a lender, or as a salaried employee of a lending institution. The ease with which mortgages can be bought and sold has resulted in many individuals opening their own mortgage companies in competition with established lending institutions. Some mortgage specialists also offer real estate loan consulting for a fee. They will help a borrower choose from among the numerous mortgage loan formats available today, find the best loan for the client and assist in filling-out and processing the loan application.

SECURITIES AND SYNDICATIONS

Limited partnerships and other forms of real estate syndications that combine the investment capital of a number of investors to buy large properties have become popular over the past 25 years. The investment opportunities and professional management offered by syndications are eagerly sought after by people with money to invest in real estate. As a result, there are a number of job opportunities connected with the creation, promotion and management of real estate syndications.

COUNSELING

Real estate counseling involves giving others advice about real estate for a fee. A counselor must have a very broad knowledge about real estate—including financing, appraising, brokerage, management, development, construction, investing, leasing, zoning, taxes, title, economics and law. To remain in business as a counselor, one must develop a good track record of successful suggestions and advice.

RESEARCH AND EDUCATION

A person interested in real estate research can concentrate on solutions to applied questions such as improved construction materials and management methods or to economic questions such as "What is the demand for homes going to be next year in this community (state, country)?"

Opportunities abound in real estate education. Nearly all states require the completion of specified real estate courses before a real estate license can be issued. A growing number of states also require continued education for license renewal. As a result, persons with experience in the industry and an ability to cause understanding to occur when they teach are much sought after as instructors.

FULL-TIME INVESTOR

One of the advantages of the free-enterprise system is that you can choose to become a full-time investor solely for yourself. There are a substantial number of people who have quit their jobs to work full time with their investment properties and who have done quite well at it. A popular and successful route for many has been to purchase, inexpensively and with a low down payment, a small apartment building that has not been maintained, but is in a good neighborhood. The property is then thoroughly reconditioned and rents are raised. This process increases the value of the property. The increase is parlayed into a larger building—often through a tax-deferred exchange—and the process is repeated. Alternatively, the investor can increase the mortgage loan on the building and take the cash he receives as a "salary" for himself or use it as a down payment on another not-too-well maintained apartment building in a good neighborhood. This can also be done with single-family houses. It is not unusual to find individuals who have acquired several dozen rental houses over a period of years.

Other individual investors have done well financially by searching newspaper ads and regularly visiting real estate brokerage offices looking for underpriced properties which can be sold at a mark-up. A variation of this is to write to out-of-town property owners in a given neighborhood to see if any wish to sell at a bargain price. Another approach is to become a small-scale developer and contractor. (No license is needed if you work with your own property.) Through your own personal efforts you create value in your projects and then hold them as investments.

Property owners dealing with their own property are not required to hold a real estate license. However, any person who for compensation or the promise of compensation lists or offers to list, sells or offers to sell, buys or offers to buy, negotiates or offers to negotiate either directly or indirectly for the purpose of bringing about a sale, purchase or option to purchase, exchange, auction, lease or rental of real estate, or any interest in real estate, is required to hold a valid real estate license. Some states also require persons offering their services as real estate appraisers, property managers, syndicators, counselors, mortgage bankers or rent collectors to hold real estate licenses.

If your real estate plans are such that you may need a license, you should skip ahead to Chapter 18 and read the material there regarding real estate licensing.

LICENSE REQUIREMENTS

ADDITIONAL
READINGS

At the end of each chapter you will find a list of additional readings. These are included to give you a cross-section of written materials you may find valuable in furthering your real estate education. Because of space limitations, not all real estate books, booklets and periodicals currently available are listed in the additional readings. A visit to your local library and bookstores will undoubtedly produce additional real estate material not listed here and each year brings new titles.

"A Self-Evaluation Quiz" by **Ron Riggins.** (*Real Estate Today*, Nov/Dec 84, page 28). Article and three-page quiz to help determine your potential for success in real estate. Looks at competence, professionalism, determination and attitude.

Guide to the ACT Real Estate License Examinations by **John Ellis** and **John Beck.** (Prentice-Hall, 1984, 339 pages). This is a combination text and workbook designed for real estate salesperson and broker applicants. Over 750 sample exam questions with answers. Also available in separate books for the ETS and ASI real estate exams.

In Search of Excellence by **Thomas Peters** and **Robert Waterman, Jr.** (Harper and Row, 1982, 360 pages). Valuable and interesting reading for anyone planning to go into business, including real estate, and be successful.

Real Estate Principles for License Preparation, 3rd ed. by **Dennis Tosh** and **Nicholas Ordway.** (Reston, 1984, 416 pages). Includes every subject tested and has over 1,100 practice questions and problems with explanations. Available in both ACT and ETS versions.

Real Estate Programs. (National Association of Realtors, 1984, 318 pages). This is a guide to real estate courses offered at universities, colleges and junior colleges in the United States. Includes school names and addresses, course titles, scholarship availability, degrees offered and program goals (license preparation, continuing education, general education, professional training, theory, analysis, etc.). Updated periodically.

Real Estate Resource Book, 4th ed. by **Bruce Harwood** and **John Ellis.** (Reston, 1986, 360 pages). Contains over 1,400 practice questions with answers. Keyed to the chapters in the book you are now reading.

The Language of Real Estate, 2nd ed. by **John W. Reilly.** (Real Estate Education Co., 1982, 630 pages). This single-volume reference book contains over 2,200 of the most frequently encountered real estate terms. Includes basic definitions, examples and cross references.

Nature and Description of Real Estate

Fixture: an object that has been attached to land so as to become real estate

Improvements: any form of land development, such as buildings, roads, fences, pipelines, etc.

Meridians: imaginary lines running north and south, used as references in mapping land

Metes and bounds: a method of land description that identifies a parcel by specifying its shape and boundaries

Monument: an iron pipe, stone, tree or other fixed point used in making a survey

Personal property: a right or interest in things of a temporary or movable nature; anything not classed as real property

Real estate: land and improvements in a physical sense as well as the rights to own or use them

Recorded plat: a subdivision map filed in the county recorder's office that shows the location and boundaries of individual parcels of land

Riparian right: the right of a landowner whose land borders a river or stream to use and enjoy that water

What is real estate? **Real estate** or **real property** is land and the improvements made to land, and the rights to use them. Let us begin in this chapter by looking more closely at what is meant by land and improvements. Then in the next chapter we shall focus our attention on the various rights one may possess in land and improvements.

LAND

Often we think of land as only the surface of the earth. But, it is substantially more than that. As Figure 2:1 illustrates, land starts at the center of the earth, passes through the earth's surface, and continues on into space. An understanding of this concept is important because, given a particular parcel of land, it is possible for one person to own the rights to use its surface **(surface rights),** another to own the rights to drill or dig below its surface **(subsurface rights),** and still another to own the rights to use the airspace above it **(air rights).**

Figure 2:1

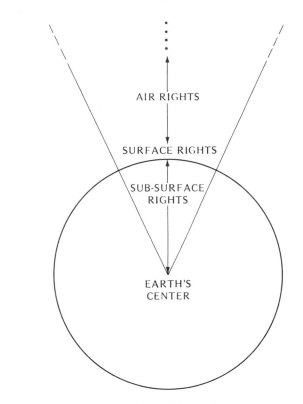

Land includes the surface of the earth and the sky above
and everything to the center of the earth.

IMPROVEMENTS   Anything affixed to land with the intent of being permanent is considered to be part of the land and therefore real estate. Thus houses, schools, factories, barns, fences, roads,
pipelines and landscaping are real estate. As a group, these are
referred to as **improvements** because they improve or develop
land.

Being able to identify what is real estate and what is not is
important. For example, in conveying ownership to a house,
only the lot is described in the deed. It is not necessary to describe the dwelling unit itself, or the landscaping, driveways,
sidewalks, wiring or plumbing. Items that are not a part of the
land, such as tables, chairs, beds, desks, automobiles, farm machinery, and the like, are classified as **personal property;** if the

right to use them is to be transferred to the buyer, there must be a separate **bill of sale** in addition to the deed. Broadly speaking, personal property is everything that is not real property and vice versa.

When an object that was once personal property is attached to land (or a building thereon) so as to become real estate, it is called a **fixture.** As a rule, a fixture is the property of the landowner and when the land is conveyed to a new owner, it is automatically included with the land. The question of whether an item is a fixture also arises with regard to property taxes, mortgages, lease terminations and hazard insurance policies. Specifically, real estate taxes are based on real property valuation. Real estate mortgages are secured by real property. Objects attached to a building by a tenant may become real property and hence belong to the building's owner. Hazard insurance policies treat real property differently than personal property.

FIXTURES

Whether or not an object becomes real estate depends on whether the object was affixed or installed with the **intention** of permanently improving the land. Intention is evidenced by four tests: (1) the manner of attachment, (2) the adaptation of the object, (3) the existence of an agreement, and (4) the relationship of the parties involved.

The first test, **manner of attachment,** refers to how the object is attached to the land. Ordinarily, when an object which was once personal property is attached to land by virtue of its being imbedded in the land or affixed to the land by means of cement, nails, bolts, etc., it becomes a fixture. To illustrate, when asphalt and concrete for driveways and sidewalks are still on the delivery truck, they are movable and therefore personal property. But once they are poured into place, the asphalt and concrete become part of the land. Similarly, lumber, wiring, pipes, doors, toilets, sinks, water heaters, furnaces and other construction materials change from personal property to real estate when they become part of a building. Items brought into the house that do not become permanently affixed to the land remain personal property; for example, furniture, clothing, cooking utensils, radios and television sets.

Manner of Attachment

Adaptation of the Object

Historically, the manner of attachment was the only method of classifying an object as personal property or real estate, but as time progressed, this test alone was no longer adequate. For example, how would you classify storm windows, which for a few months of the year are temporarily clipped or hung in position? For the answer, we must apply a second test: **How is the article adapted** to the building? If the storm windows specifically fit the windows in the building, they are automatically included in the purchase or rental of the building. Another example is the key to a house. Although it spends most of its useful life in a pocket or purse, it is nonetheless quite specifically adapted to the house and therefore a part of it.

Existence of an Agreement

The third test is the **existence of an agreement** between the parties involved. For example, a seller can clarify in advance and in writing to his real estate broker what he considers personal property and thus will take when he leaves, and what he does not consider personal property and thus will leave for the buyer. Likewise, a tenant may obtain an agreement from his landlord that items installed by the tenant will not be considered fixtures by the landlord. When it is not readily clear if an item is real or personal property, the use of an agreement can avoid later argument or a court case.

Relationship of the Parties

The fourth test in determining whether an item of personal property has become a fixture is to look at the **relationship of the parties.** For example, a supermarket moves into a rented building, then buys and bolts to the floor various **trade fixtures** such as display shelves, meat and dairy coolers, frozen-food counters and checkout stands. When the supermarket later moves out, do these items, by virtue of their attachment, become the property of the building owner? Modern courts rule that tenant-owned trade fixtures do not become the property of the landlord. However, they must be removed before the expiration of the lease and without seriously damaging the building.

Ownership of Plants, Trees and Crops

Trees, cultivated perennial plants and uncultivated vegetation of any sort are considered part of the land. For example, landscaping is included in the sale or rental of a house. If a tenant plants a tree or plant in the ground while renting, the tree or plant stays when the lease expires unless otherwise agreed by both landlord and tenant. Plants and trees in movable pots are personal property and not generally included in a sale or lease.

Annual cultivated crops are called **emblements** and most courts of law regard them as personal property even though they are attached to the soil. For example, a tenant farmer is entitled to the fruits of his labor even though the landlord terminates the lease part way through the growing season. When property with harvestable plants, trees or crops is offered for sale or lease, it is good practice to be clear in any listing, sale or lease agreement who will have the right to harvest the crop that season. This is particularly true of farm property where the value of the crop can be quite substantial.

APPURTENANCES

The conveyance of land carries with it any appurtenances to the land. An **appurtenance** is a right or privilege or improvement that belongs to and passes with land but is not necessarily a part of the land. Examples of appurtenances are easements and rights-of-way (discussed in Chapter 3), condominium parking stalls and shares of stock in a mutual water company that services the land.

WATER RIGHTS

The ownership of land that borders on a river or stream carries with it the right to use that water in common with the other landowners whose lands border the same watercourse. This is known as a **riparian right.** The landowner does not have absolute ownership of the water that flows past his land but may use it in a reasonable manner. In some states, riparian rights have been modified by the **doctrine of prior appropriation:** the first owner to divert water for his own use may continue to do so, even though it is not equitable to the other landowners along the watercourse. Where land borders on a lake or sea, it is said to carry **littoral rights** rather than riparian rights. Littoral rights allow a landowner to use and enjoy the water touching his land provided he does not alter the water's position by artificial means. A lakefront lot owner would be an example of this.

Ownership of land normally includes the right to drill for and remove water found below the surface. Where water is not confined to a defined underground waterway, it is known as **percolating water.** In some states a landowner has the right, in conjunction with neighboring owners, to draw his share of percolating water. Other states subscribe to the doctrine of prior appropriation. When speaking of underground water, the term **water table** refers to the upper limit of percolating water below the earth's surface. It is also called the **groundwater level.** This may be only a few feet below the surface or hundreds of feet down.

LAND DESCRIPTIONS   There are six commonly used methods of describing the location of land: (1) informal reference, (2) metes and bounds, (3) rectangular survey system, (4) recorded plat, (5) assessor parcel number, and (6) reference to documents other than maps. We shall look at each in detail.

INFORMAL REFERENCES   Street numbers and place names are informal references: the house located at 7216 Maple Street; the apartment identified as Apartment 101, 875 First Street; the office identified as Suite 222, 3570 Oakview Boulevard; or the ranch known as the Rocking K Ranch—in each case followed by the city (or county) and state where it is located—are informal references. The advantage of an informal reference is that is is easily understood. The disadvantage from a real estate standpoint is that it is not a precise method of land description: a street number or place name does not provide the boundaries of the land at that location, and these numbers and names change over the years. Consequently, in real estate the use of informal references is limited to situations in which convenience is more important than precision. Thus, in a rental contract, Apartment 101, 875 First Street, city and state, is sufficient for a tenant to find the apartment unit. However, if you were buying the apartment building, you would want a more precise land description.

METES AND BOUNDS   Early land descriptions in America depended heavily on convenient natural or man-made objects called **monuments**. A stream might serve to mark one side of a parcel, an old oak tree to mark a corner, a road another side, a pile of rocks a second corner, a fence another side, and so forth. This survey method was handy, but it had two major drawbacks: there might not be a convenient corner or boundary marker where one was needed, and over time, oak trees died, stone heaps were moved, streams and rivers changed course, stumps rotted, fences were removed and unused roads became overgrown with vegetation. The following description excerpted from the Hartford, Connecticut, probate court records for 1812 illustrates just how difficult it can be to try to precisely locate a parcel's boundaries using only convenient natural or man-made objects:

> Commencing at a heap of stone about a stone's throw from a certain small clump of alders, near a brook running down off from a rather high part of said ridge; thence, by a straight line to a certain marked white birch tree, about two or three times as far from a jog in a fence going around a ledge nearby; thence by another straight line in a different direction, around said ledge and the Great Swamp, so called; thence . . . to the "Horn," so called, and passing around the same as aforesaid, as far as the "Great Bend," so called, and . . . to a stake and stone not far off from the old Indian trail; thence, by another straight line . . . to the stump of the big hemlock tree where Philo Blake killed the bear; thence, to the corner begun at by two straight lines of about equal length, which are to be run by some skilled and competent surveyor, so as to include the area and acreage as herein before set forth.*

The drawbacks of the above outmoded method of land description are resolved by setting a permanent man-made **monument** at one corner of the parcel. This monument will typically be an iron pin or pipe 1 to 2 inches in diameter driven several feet into the ground. Sometimes concrete or stone monuments are used. To guard against the possibility that the monument might later be destroyed or removed, it is referenced by means of a connection line to a nearby permanent reference mark established by a government survey agency. Other parcels in the vicinity will also be referenced to the same permanent reference mark.

Permanent Monuments

---

*F. H. Moffit and Harry Bouchard, Surveying, 6th ed. (New York: Harper and Row, 1975). By permission.

The surveyor then describes the parcel in terms of distance and direction from that point. This is called **metes and bounds** surveying, which means distance (metes) and direction (bounds). From the monument, the surveyor runs the parcel's outside lines by compass and distance so as to take in the land area being described. Distances are measured in feet, usually to the nearest tenth or one-hundredth of a foot. Direction is shown in degrees, minutes and seconds. There are 360 degrees (°) in a circle, 60 minutes (') in each degree and 60 seconds (") in each minute. The abbreviation 29°14'52" would be read as 29 degrees, 14 minutes and 52 seconds. Figure 2:2 illustrates a simple modern metes and bounds land description.

Note in Figure 2:2 that with a metes and bounds description you start from a permanent reference mark and travel to the nearest corner of the property. This is where the parcel survey begins and is called the **point of beginning** or **point of commencement.** From this point in Figure 2:2, we travel clockwise along the parcel's perimeter, reaching the next corner by going in the direction 80 degrees east of south for a distance of 180 feet. We then travel in a direction 15 degrees west of south for 160 feet, thence 85 degrees west of south for 151 feet, and thence 4 degrees, 11 minutes and 18 seconds east of north for 199.5 feet back to the point of beginning. In mapping shorthand, this parcel would be described by first identifying the monument, then the county and state within which it lies, and "thence S80°0'0"E, 180.0'; thence S15°0'0"W, 160.0'; thence S85°0'0"W, 151.0'; thence N4°11'18"E, 199.5' back to the p.o.b." Although one can successfully describe a parcel by traveling around it either clockwise or counterclockwise, it is customary to travel clockwise.

The job of taking a written land description (such as the one just described) and locating it on the ground is done by a two-person survey team. The survey team drives a wooden or metal stake into the ground at each corner of the parcel. If a corner lies on a sidewalk, a nail through a brass disc about one-half inch wide is used. (Look closely for these next time you are out walking. At construction sites you will see that corner stakes often have colored streamers on them.) The basic equipment of a survey team includes a compass, a transit, a sight pole or rod, a steel tape and a computation book. A transit

DESCRIBING LAND BY METES AND BOUNDS   **Figure 2:2**

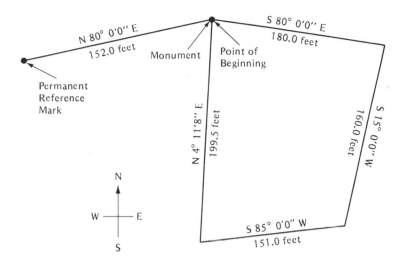

consists of a very accurate compass plus a telescope with cross hairs that can be rotated horizontally and vertically. It will measure angles accurately to one second of a degree. The sight pole is about 8 feet high and held by the rodman, the second member of the survey team. Marks on the sight pole are aligned by the surveyor with the cross hairs in the telescope. A 100-foot steel tape of special alloy to resist expansion on hot days is used to measure distances. For longer distances, and especially distances across water, canyons, heavy brush, etc., surveyors use laser beam equipment. The beam is aimed at a mirror on the sight pole, bounced back and electronically converted to a digital readout that shows the distance to the pole. Handheld computers now perform many of the angle and distance computations necessary to a survey.

Compass Directions

The compass illustrated in Figure 2:3A shows how the direction of travel along each side of the parcel in Figure 2:2 is determined. Note that the same line can be labeled two ways depending on which direction you are traveling. To illustrate, look at the line from *P* to *Q*. If you are traveling toward *P* on the line, you are going N45°W. But, if you are traveling toward point *Q* on the line, you are going S45°E.

Figure 2:3   **METES AND BOUNDS MAPPING**

(A) NAMING DIRECTIONS FOR
A METES AND BOUNDS SURVEY

(B) MAPPING A CURVE

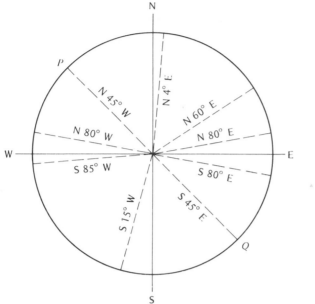

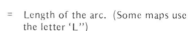

A = Length of the arc. (Some maps use the letter 'L')

R = Radius of the circle necessary to make the required arc (shown here by the broken lines)

Δ = Angle necessary to make the arc, i.e., the angle between the broken lines

Moving in a clockwise direction from the point of beginning, set the center of a circle compass (like the one shown above) on each corner of the parcel to find the direction of travel to the next corner. (*Note:* Minutes and seconds have been omitted above for clarity).

Curved boundary lines are produced by using arcs of a circle. The length of the arc is labeled L or A; the radius of the circle producing the arc is labeled R. The symbol Δ (delta) indicates the angle used to produce the arc (see Figure 2:3B). Where an arc connects to a straight boundary or another arc, the connection is indicated by a small circle or by a dot as shown in Figure 2:3B.

Bench marks are commonly used as permanent reference marks. A bench mark is a fixed mark of known location and elevation. It may be as simple as an iron post or as elaborate as an engraved 3¾" brass disc set into concrete. The mark is usually set in place by a government survey team from the United States Geological Survey (USGS) or the United States

Coast and Geodetic Survey (USCGS). Bench marks are referenced to each other by distance and direction. The advantages of this type of reference point, compared to stumps, trees, rocks and the like, are permanence and accuracy to within a fraction of an inch. Additionally, even though it is possible to destroy a reference point or monument, it can be replaced in its exact former position because the location of each is related to other reference points. In states using the rectangular survey system or a grid system (discussed shortly), a section corner or a grid intersection is often used as a permanent reference mark. As a convenience to surveyors, it will be physically marked with an iron post or a brass disc set in concrete.

The **rectangular survey system** was authorized by Congress in May 1785. It was designed to provide a faster and simpler method than metes and bounds for describing land in newly annexed territories and states. Rather than using available physical monuments, the rectangular survey system, also known as the **government survey** or **U.S. public land survey,** is based on imaginary lines. These lines are the east-west **latitude** lines and the north-south **longitude** lines that encircle the earth, as illustrated in Figure 2:4. A helpful way to remember this is that longitude lines run the long way around the earth.

RECTANGULAR SURVEY SYSTEM

SELECTED LATITUDE AND LONGITUDE LINES SERVE AS BASE LINES AND MERIDIANS

Figure 2:4

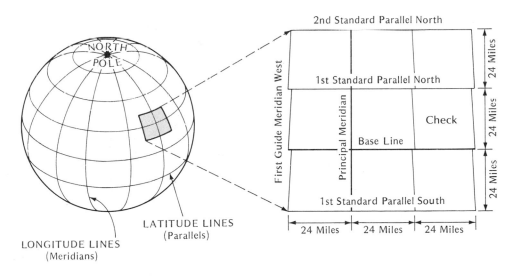

Certain longitude lines were selected as **principal meridians.** For each of these an intercepting latitude line was selected as a **base line.** Every 24 miles north and south of a base line, **correction lines** or **standard parallels** were established. Every 24 miles east and west of a principal meridian, **guide meridians** were established to run from one standard parallel to the next. These are needed because the earth is a sphere, not a flat surface. As one travels north in the United States, longitude (meridian) lines come closer together, that is, they converge. Figure 2:4 shows how guide meridians and correction lines adjust for this problem. Each 24-by-24-mile area created by the guide meridians and correction lines is called a **check** or **quadrangle.**

There are 36 principal meridians and their intersecting base lines in the U.S. public land survey system. Figure 2:5 shows the states in which this system is used and the land area

Figure 2:5   **THE PUBLIC LAND SURVEY SYSTEMS OF THE UNITED STATES**

for which each principal meridian and base line act as a reference. For example, the Sixth Principal Meridian is the reference point for land surveys in Kansas, Nebraska, and portions of Colorado, Wyoming and South Dakota. In addition to the U.S. public land survey system, a portion of western Kentucky was surveyed into townships by a special state survey. Also, the state of Ohio contains eight public land surveys that are rectangular in design, but which use state boundaries and major rivers rather than latitude and longitude as reference lines.

Figure 2:6 shows how land is referenced to a principal meridian and a base line. Every 6 miles east and west of each principal meridian, parallel imaginary lines are drawn. The resulting 6-mile-wide columns are called **ranges** and are numbered consecutively east and west of the principal meridian. For example, the first range west is called Range 1 West and abbreviated R1W. The next range west is R2W, and so forth. The fourth range east is R4E. *Range*

Every six miles north and south of a base line, township lines are drawn. They intersect with the range lines and produce 6-by-6-mile imaginary squares called **townships** (not to be confused with the word township as applied to political subdivisions). Each tier or row of townships thus created is numbered with respect to the base line. Townships lying in the first tier north of a base line all carry the designation Township 1 North, abbreviated T1N. Townships lying in the first tier south of the base line are all designated T1S, and in the second tier south, T2S. By adding a range reference, an individual township can be identified. Thus, T2S, R2W would identify the township lying in the second tier south of the base line and the second range west of the principal meridian. T14N, R52W would be a township 14 tiers north of the base line and 52 ranges west of the principal meridian. *Township*

Each 36-square-mile township is divided into 36 one-square-mile units called **sections.** When one flies over farming areas, particularly in the Midwest, the checkerboard pattern of farms and roads that follow section boundaries can be seen. Sections are numbered 1 through 36, starting in the upper-right *Section*

Figure 2:6   **IDENTIFYING TOWNSHIPS AND SECTIONS**

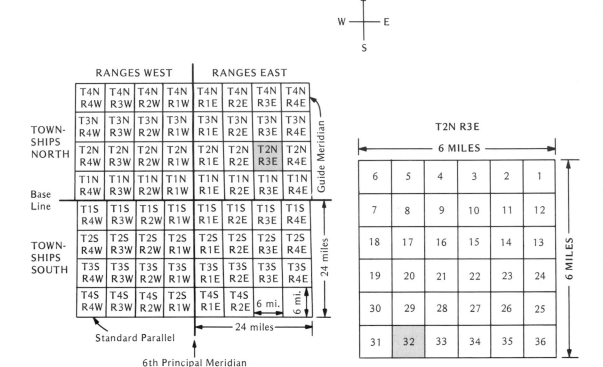

IDENTIFYING TOWNSHIPS   TOWNSHIP DIVIDED INTO SECTIONS

corner of the township. With this numbering system, any two sections with consecutive numbers share a common boundary. The section numbering system is illustrated in the right half of Figure 2:6 where the shaded section is described as Section 32, T2N, R3E, 6th Principal Meridian.

Acre   Each square-mile **section** contains 640 acres, and each **acre** contains 43,560 square feet. Any parcel of land smaller than a full 640-acre section is identified by its position in the section. This is done by dividing the section into quarters and halves as shown in Figure 2:7. For example, the shaded parcel shown at Ⓐ is described by dividing this section into quarters and then dividing the southwest quarter into quarters. Parcel Ⓐ is described as the NW¼ of the SW¼ of Section 32, T2N, R3E, 6th

SUBDIVIDING A SECTION   Figure 2:7

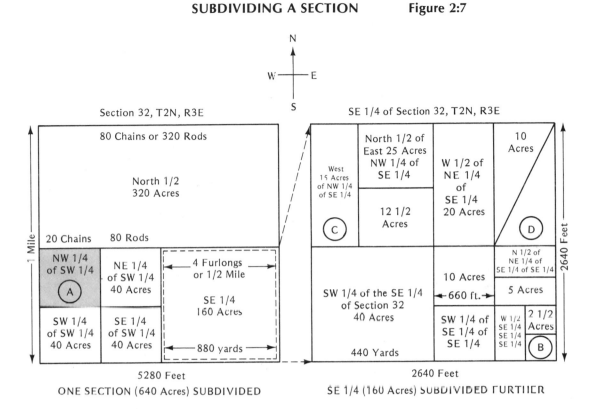

Section 32, T2N, R3E

ONE SECTION (640 Acres) SUBDIVIDED

SE 1/4 of Section 32, T2N, R3E

SE 1/4 (160 Acres) SUBDIVIDED FURTHER

P.M. Additionally, it is customary to name the county and state in which the land lies. How much land does the NW¼ of the SW¼ of a section contain? A section contains 640 acres; therefore, a quarter-section contains 160 acres. Dividing a quarter-section again into quarters results in four 40-acre parcels. Thus, the northwest quarter of the southwest quarter contains 40 acres.

The rectangular survey system is not limited to parcels of 40 or more acres. To demonstrate this point, the SE¼ of section 32 is exploded in the right half of Figure 2:7. Parcel Ⓑ is described as the SE¼ of the SE¼ of the SE¼ of the SE¼ of section 32 and contains 2½ acres. Parcel Ⓒ is described as the west 15 acres of the NW¼ of the SE¼ of section 32. Parcel Ⓓ would be described in metes and bounds using the northeast corner of the SE¼ of section 32 as the starting point. When locating or sketching a rectangular survey on paper, many people find it helpful to start at the end of the description and work to the beginning, i.e., work backwards. Try it.

Not all sections contain exactly 640 acres. Some are smaller because the earth's longitude lines converge toward the North Pole. Also, a section may be larger or smaller than 640 acres due to historical accommodations or survey errors dating back a hundred years or more. For the same reason, not all townships contain exactly 36 square miles. Between 1785 and 1910, the U.S. government paid independent surveyors by the mile. The job was often accomplished by tying a rag to one spoke of the wheel of a buckboard wagon. A team of horses was hitched to the wagon and the surveyor, compass in hand, headed out across the prairie. Distance was measured by counting the number of wheel turns and multiplying by the circumference of the wheel. Today, large area surveys are made with the aid of aerial photographs, sophisticated electronic equipment and earth satellites.

In terms of surface area, more land in the United States is described by the rectangular survey system than by any other survey method. But in terms of number of properties, the recorded plat is the most important survey method.

RECORDED PLAT   When a tract of land is ready for subdividing into lots for homes and businesses, reference by **recorded plat** provides the simplest and most convenient method of land description. A **plat** is a map that shows the location and boundaries of individual properties. Also known as the **lot-block-tract system, recorded map** or **recorded survey,** this method of land description is based on the filing of a surveyor's plat in the public recorder's office of the country where the land is located. Figure 2:8 illustrates a plat. Notice that a metes and bounds survey has been made and a map prepared to show in detail the boundaries of each parcel of land. Each parcel is then assigned a lot number. Each block in the tract is given a block number, and the tract itself is given a name or number. A plat showing all the blocks in the tract is delivered to the county recorder's office, where it is placed in **map books** or **survey books,** along with plats of other subdivisions in the county.

Each plat is given a book and page reference number, and all map books are available for public inspection. From that

LAND DESCRIPTION BY RECORDED PLAT   **Figure 2:8**

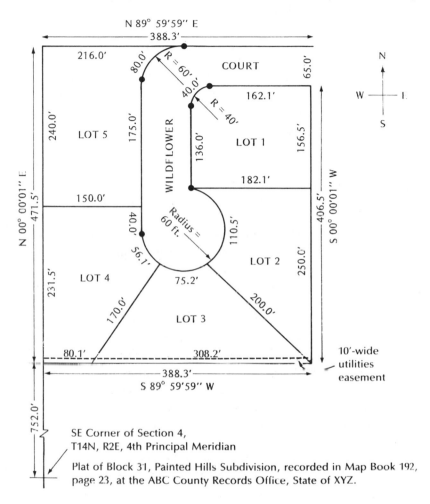

point on, it is no longer necessary to give a lengthy metes and bounds description to describe a parcel. Instead, one need only provide the lot and block number, tract name, map book reference, county and state. To find the location and dimensions of a recorded lot, one simply looks in the map book at the county recorder's office.

Note that the plat in Figure 2:8 combines both of the land descriptions just discussed. The boundaries of the numbered lots are in metes and bounds. These, in turn, are referenced to a section corner in the rectangular survey system.

ASSESSOR'S PARCEL
NUMBERS

In many counties in the United States, the tax assessor assigns an **assessor's parcel number** to each parcel of land in the county. The primary purpose is to aid in the assessment of property for tax collection purposes. However, these parcel numbers are public information and real estate brokers, appraisers and investors can and do use them extensively to assist in identifying real properties.

A commonly used system is to divide the county into map books. Each book is given a number and covers a given portion of the county. On each page of the map book are parcel maps, each with its own number. For subdivided lots, these maps are based on the plats submitted by the subdivider to the county records office when the subdivision was made. For unsubdivided land, the assessor's office prepares its own maps.

Each parcel of land on the map is assigned a parcel number by the assessor. The assessor's parcel number may or may not be the same as the lot number assigned by the subdivider. To reduce confusion, the assessor's parcel number is either circled or underlined. Figure 2:9 illustrates a page out of an assessor's map book. The assessor also produces an assessment role that lists every parcel in the county by its assessor's parcel number. Stored and printed by computer now, this roll shows the current owner's name and address and the assessed value of the land and buildings.

The assessor's maps are open to viewing by the public at the assessor's office. In many counties, private firms reproduce the maps and accompanying list of property owners and make them available to real estate brokers, appraisers and lenders for a fee.

Before leaving the topic of assessor's maps, a word of caution is in order. These maps should not be relied upon as the final authority for the legal description of a parcel. That can come only from a title search that will include looking at the current deed to the property and the recorded copy of the subdivider's plat. Note also that an assessor's parcel number is never used as a legal description in a deed.

ASSESSOR'S MAP   **Figure 2:9**

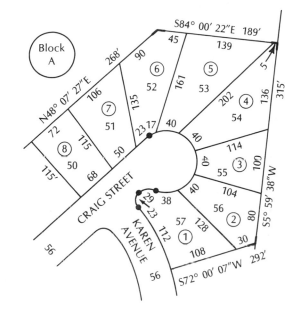

Assessor's Map
Book 34
Page 18

Assessor Parcel Numbers
shown in circles

Lots 50 through 57 of
Tract 2118, filed in
Recorded Maps, Book 63,
page 39.

The tax assessor assigns every parcel of land in the county its own
parcel number. For example, the westernmost parcel (Lot 50) in
the map would carry the number 34-18-8, meaning Book 34,
Page 18, Parcel 8.

Land can also be described by referring to another publicly
recorded document, such as a deed or a mortgage, that contains
a full legal description of the parcel in question. For example,
suppose that several years ago Baker received a deed from
Adams which contained a long and complicated metes and
bounds description. Baker recorded the deed in the public
records office, where a photocopy was placed in Book 1089,
page 456. If Baker later wants to deed the same land to Cooper,
Baker can describe the parcel in his deed to Cooper by saying,
"all the land described in the deed from Adams to Baker recorded in Book 1089, page 456, county of ABC, state of XYZ, at
the public recorder's office for said county and state." Since
these books are open to the public, Cooper (or anyone else)

*REFERENCE TO
DOCUMENTS OTHER
THAN MAPS*

could go to Book 1089, page 456 and find a detailed description of the parcel's boundaries.

The key test of a land description is: "Can another person, reading what I have written or drawn, understand my description and go out and locate the boundaries of the parcel?"

GRID SYSTEMS

Several states, such as North Carolina and Connecticut, have developed their own statewide systems of reference points for land surveying. The North Carolina system, for example, divides that state into a grid of 84 blocks, each side of which corresponds to 30 seconds (one-half of one degree) of latitude or longitude. This establishes a **grid system** of intersecting points throughout the state to which metes and bounds surveys can be referenced. State-sponsored grid systems (also called coordinate systems) are especially helpful for surveying large parcels of remote area land.

VERTICAL LAND DESCRIPTION

In addition to surface land descriptions, land may also be described in terms of vertical measurements. This type of measurement is necessary when air rights or subsurface rights need to be described—as for multistory condominiums or oil and mineral rights.

A point, line or surface from which a vertical height or depth is measured is called a **datum.** The most commonly used datum plane in the United States is mean sea level, although a number of cities have established other data surfaces for use in local surveys. Starting from a datum, **bench marks** are set at calculated intervals by government survey teams; thus, a surveyor need not travel to the original datum to determine an elevation. These same bench marks are used as reference points for metes and bounds surveys.

In selling or leasing subsurface drilling or mineral rights, the chosen datum is often the surface of the parcel. For example, an oil lease may permit the extraction of oil and gas from a depth greater than 500 feet beneath the surface of a parcel of land. (Subsurface rights are discussed more in Chapter 3.)

An **air lot** (a space over a given parcel of land) is described by identifying both the parcel of land beneath the air lot and the elevation of the air lot above the parcel (see Figure 2:10A). Multistory condominiums use this system of land description.

AIR LOT AND CONTOUR LINES   **Figure 2:10**

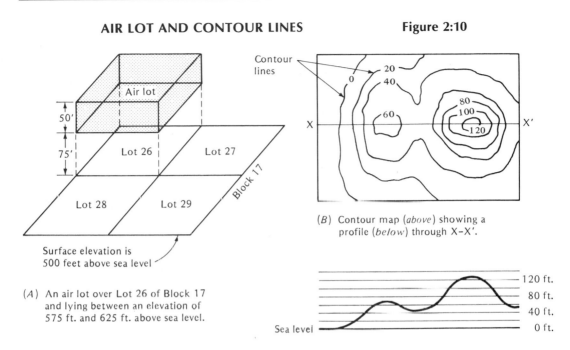

(*B*) Contour map (*above*) showing a
profile (*below*) through X–X'.

(*A*) An air lot over Lot 26 of Block 17
and lying between an elevation of
575 ft. and 625 ft. above sea level.

Contour maps (topographic maps) indicate elevations. On
these maps, **contour lines** connect all points having the same
elevation. The purpose is to show hills and valleys, slopes, and
water runoff. If the land is to be developed, the map shows
where soil will have to be moved to provide level building lots.
Figure 2:10B illustrates how vertical distances are shown using
contour lines.

In talking about subdivisions there are several terms with *LOT TYPES*
which you should be familiar. All of these are illustrated in Figure 2:11. A **cul de sac** is a street that is closed at one end with a
circular turnaround. The pie-shaped lots fronting on the turnaround are called **cul de sac lots.** A **flag lot** is a lot shaped like a
flag on a flagpole. It's a popular method of creating a buildable
lot out of the land at the back of a larger lot. A **corner lot** is a lot
that fronts on two or more streets. Because of added light and
access, a corner lot is usually worth more than an **inside lot,**
i.e., a lot with only one side on a street. A **key lot** is a lot that
adjoins the side or rear property line of a corner lot. The key

Figure 2:11   **LOT TYPES**

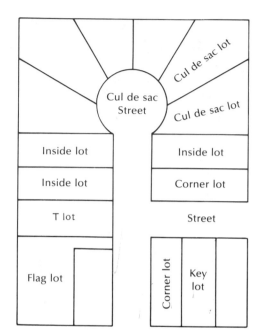

lot has added value if it is needed by the corner lot for expansion. A **T lot** is a lot at the end of a T intersection as shown in Figure 2:11.

PHYSICAL   The physical characteristics of land are immobility, inde-
CHARACTERISTICS   structibility and nonhomogeneity. This combination of charac-
OF LAND   teristics makes land different from other commodities and
                    directly and indirectly influences man's use of it.

Immobility   A parcel of land cannot be moved. It is true that soil, sand,
                    gravel and minerals can be moved by the action of nature (ero-
                    sion) or man (digging); however, the parcel itself still retains its
                    same geographical position on the globe. Because land is **im-
                    mobile,** a person must go to the land; it cannot be brought to
                    him. When land is sold, the seller cannot physically deliver his
                    land to the buyer. Instead, the seller gives the buyer a docu-
                    ment called a deed that transfers to the buyer the right to go
                    onto that land and use it. Because land is immobile, real estate
                    offices nearly always limit their sales activities to nearby prop-

erties. Even so, a great deal of a salesperson's effort is used in traveling to show properties to clients. Immobility also creates a need for property management firms, because unless an owner of rental property lives on it or nearby, neither land nor buildings can be effectively managed.

Land is **indestructible,** that is, durable. Today one can travel to the Middle East and walk on the same land that was walked on in Biblical days. Most of the land that we use in the United States today is the same land used by the American Indians a thousand years ago.

Indestructibility

The characteristic of physical durability encourages many people to buy land as an investment because they feel that stocks and bonds and paper money may come and go, but land will always be here. Although this is true in a physical sense, whether a given parcel has and will have economic value depends on one's ability to protect his ownership and on subsequent demand for that land by others. That is, physical durability must not be confused with economic durability.

The fact that no two parcels of land are exactly alike because no two parcels can occupy the same position on the globe is known as **nonhomogeneity** (heterogeneity). Courts of law recognize this characteristic of land and consequently treat land as a **nonfungible** (pronounced non·fun'je'ble) commodity; that is, nonsubstitutable. Thus, in a contract involving the sale or rental of land (and any improvement to that land), the courts can be called upon to enforce specific performance of the contract. For example, in a contract to sell a home, if the buyer carries out his obligations and the seller fails to convey ownership to the buyer, a court of law will force the seller to convey ownership of *that* specific home to the buyer. The court will not require the buyer to accept a substitute home. This is different from a homogeneous or **fungible** commodity which is freely substitutable in carrying out a contract. For example, one bushel of No. 1 grade winter wheat can be freely replaced by another bushel of the same grade, and one share of General Motors common stock can be substituted for another, as all are identical.

Nonhomogeneity

Although land is nonhomogeneous, there can still be a high degree of physical and economic similarity. For example, in a city block containing 20 house lots of identical size and shape, there will be a high degree of similarity even though the lots are still nonhomogeneous. Finding similar properties is, in fact, the basis for the market-comparison approach to appraising real estate.

ECONOMIC
CHARACTERISTICS OF
LAND

The dividing line between the physical and economic characteristics of land is sometimes difficult to define. This is because the physical aspects of land greatly influence man's economic behavior toward land. However, four economic characteristics are generally recognized: scarcity, modification, permanence of investment (fixity), and area preference (situs, pronounced sī'tus).

Scarcity

The shortage of land in a given geographical area where there is great demand for land is referred to as **scarcity.** It is a man-made characteristic. For example, land is scarce in Miami Beach, Florida, because a relatively large number of people want to use a relatively small area of land. Another well-known example is 2-mile-wide, 13-mile-long Manhattan Island in New York City, where more than a million people live and twice that number work. Yet one need only travel 25 miles west of Miami Beach or into central New York State to find plenty of uncrowded land available for purchase at very reasonable prices. The sheer quantity of undeveloped land in the United States as seen from an airplane on a cross-country flight is staggering.

Land scarcity is also influenced by man's ability to use land more efficiently. To illustrate, in agricultural areas, production per acre of land has more than doubled for many crops since 1940. This is not due to any change in the land, but is the result of improved fertilizers and irrigation systems, better seeds and modern crop management. Likewise, in urban areas, an acre of land that once provided space for five houses can be converted to high-rise apartments to provide homes for 100 or more families.

Thus, although there is a limited physical amount of land on the earth's surface, scarcity is chiefly a function of demand for land in a given geographical area and the ability of man to make land more productive. The persistent notion that all land is scarce has led to periodic land sale booms in undeveloped areas, followed by a collapse in land prices when it becomes apparent that that particular land is not economically scarce.

Land use and value are greatly influenced by **modification,** that is, improvements made by man to surrounding parcels of land. For example, the construction of an airport will increase the usefulness and value of land parallel to runways but have a negative effect on the use and value of land at the ends of runways because of noise from landings and takeoffs. Similarly, land subject to flooding will become more useful and valuable if government-sponsored flood control dams are built upriver.

Modification

One of the most widely publicized cases of land modification occurred near Orlando, Florida, when Disney World was constructed. Nearby land previously used for agricultural purposes suddenly became useful as motel, gas station, restaurant, house and apartment sites and increased rapidly in value.

The fact that land and buildings and other improvements to land require long periods of time to pay for themselves is referred to as **fixity** or **investment permanence.** For example, it may take 20 or 30 years for the income generated by an apartment or office building to repay the cost of the land and building plus interest on the money borrowed to make the purchase. Consequently, real estate investment and land-use decisions must consider not only how the land will be used next month or next year, but also the usefulness of the improvements 20 years from now. There is no economic logic in spending money to purchase land and improvements that will require 20 to 30 years to pay for themselves, if their usefulness is expected to last only 5 years.

Fixity

Fixity also reflects the fact that land cannot be moved from its present location to another location where it will be more valuable. With very few exceptions, improvements to land are also fixed. Even with a house, the cost of moving it, plus building a foundation at the new site, can easily exceed the value of the house after the move. Thus, when an investment is made in real estate, it is regarded as a **fixed** or **sunk cost.**

Situs or **location preference** refers to location from an economic rather than a geographic standpoint. It has often been said that the single most important word in real estate is "loca-

Situs

tion." What this means is the preference of people for a given area. For a residential area, these preferences are the result of *natural* factors, such as weather, air quality, scenic views and closeness to natural recreation areas, and of *man-made* factors, such as job opportunities, transportation facilities, shopping and schools. For an industrial area, situs depends on such things as an available labor market, adequate supplies of water and electricity, nearby rail lines and highway access. In farming areas, situs depends on soil and weather conditions, water and labor availability, and transportation facilities.

Situs is the reason that house lots on street corners sell for more than identical-sized lots not on corners. This reflects a preference for open space. The same is true in apartments; corner units usually rent for more than similar-sized noncorner units. In a high-rise apartment building, units on the top floors, if they offer a view, command higher prices than identical units on lower floors. On a street lined with stores, the side of the street that is shaded in the afternoon will attract more shoppers than the unshaded side. Consequently, buildings on the shaded side will generate more sales and as a result be worth more.

It is important to realize that, since situs is a function of people's preferences and preferences can change with time, situs can also change. For example, the freeway and expressway construction boom that started in the 1950s, and accelerated during the 1960s, increased the preference for suburban areas. This resulted in declining property values in inner city areas and increasing land values in the suburbs. Today, historic rehabilitation and a desire to live closer to work are drawing people back to downtown areas.

VOCABULARY REVIEW

Match terms **a–v** *with statements* **1–22.**

a. *Acre*
b. *Appurtenance*
c. *Assessor's parcel number*
d. *Base line*
e. *Bill of sale*
f. *Contour lines*
g. *Cul de sac*
h. *Datum*
i. *Emblements*

j. *Fixture*
k. *Flag lot*
l. *Government survey*
m. *Lot-block-tract*
n. *Meridian*
o. *Metes and bounds*
p. *Monument*
q. *Quarter-section*
r. *Riparian rights*

s. *Section*   u. *Township*
t. *Subsurface rights*   v. *Water table*

1. An object that has been attached to land so as to become real estate.
2. Contains 36 sections of land.
3. The depth below the surface at which water-saturated soil can be found.
4. A survey line running east and west from which townships are established.
5. Contains 640 acres of land.
6. The right of a landowner to use water flowing past his land.
7. An iron pipe or other object set in the ground to establish land boundaries.
8. A survey line that runs north and south in the rectangular survey system.
9. Annual crops produced by man.
10. A horizontal plane from which height and depth are measured.
11. A numbering system to aid in the assessment of property for tax collection purposes.
12. A system of land description that identifies a parcel by specifying its shape and boundaries.
13. A land survey system based on imaginary latitude and longitude lines.
14. Includes the right to mine minerals and drill for oil.
15. Lines on a map that connect points having the same elevation.
16. Land description by reference to a recorded map.
17. 43,560 square feet.
18. Contains 160 acres of land.
19. A right or privilege or improvement that passes with land.
20. A document that shows the transfer of personal property.
21. A street that is closed at one end with a circular turnaround.
22. A lot shaped like a flag on a pole.

QUESTIONS AND PROBLEMS

1. Is the land upon which you make your residence described by metes and bounds, lot-block-tract, or the rectangular survey system?
2. On a sheet of paper sketch the following parcels of land in Section 6, T1N, R3E: (a) the NW¼; (b) the SW¼ of the SW¼; (c) the W½ of the SE¼; (d) the N17 acres of the E½ of the NE¼; (e) the SE¼ of the SE¼ of the SE¼ of the NE¼.
3. How many acres are there in each parcel described in number 2?

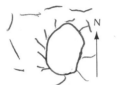

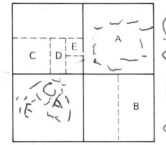

4. Describe the parcels labeled A, B, C, D and E in the section shown in the margin.

5. Using an ordinary compass and ruler, sketch the following parcel of land: "Beginning at monument M, thence due east for 40 feet, thence south 45° east for 14.1 feet, thence due south for 40 feet, thence north 45° west for 70.7 feet back to the point of beginning."

6. If a landowner owns from the center of the earth to the limits of the sky, are aircraft that pass overhead trespassers?

7. Would you classify the key to the door of a building as personal property or real property?

8. With regard to your own residence, itemize what you consider to be real property and what you consider to be personal property.

9. With regard to riparian rights, does your state follow the doctrine of prior appropriation or the right to a reasonable share?

10. What effects do you think changes in the location of the magnetic north pole would have on surveys over a long period of time? How would earthquakes affect bench marks?

ADDITIONAL READINGS

"Boundary Disputes: Is the Broker on the Line?" by **Jeffrey Krivis**. (*First Tuesday*, Sep 84, page 19). Article points out the broker and seller can be liable if there were misleading statements or concealments.

"Land for All: A History of U.S. Real Estate to 1900" by **John McMahan.** (*Real Estate Review*, Winter 76, page 78). A fascinating four-part history of American real estate speculation and development before the year 1900.

Real Estate Law, 8th ed. by **Robert Kratovil** and **Raymond Werner**. (Prentice-Hall, 1983, 650 pages). Chapter 2 discusses land and its elements, Chapter 3 is on fixtures and Chapter 5 deals with land descriptions.

Real Estate Quick and Easy by **Roy Maloney**. (Dropzone Press, 1983, 336 pages). A guide to real estate purchase and ownership. Profusely illustrated to help the reader see the points being made.

Real Estate Securities and Syndication Picture Dictionary by **Edward** and **Darlene Hooper.** (Hooper, 1984, 336 pages). Contains 1,008 cartoon-illustrated real estate and real estate syndication terms. Both entertaining and educational as the cartoons reinforce the definitions.

Surveying: Principles and Applications by **Barry Kavanagh** and **Glenn Bird.** (Reston, 1984, 640 pages). Two-part text covers both introductory and advanced surveying. Includes latest in instrumentation and computation systems.

Rights and Interests in Land

Chattel: an article of personal property

Easement: the right or privilege one party has to use land belonging to another for a special purpose not inconsistent with the owner's use of the land

Eminent domain: the right of government to take privately held land for public use provided fair compensation is paid

Encroachment: the unauthorized intrusion of a building or other improvement onto another person's land

Encumbrance: any impediment to a clear title, such as a lien, lease or easement

Estate: one's legal interest or rights in land

Fee simple: the largest, most complete bundle of rights one can hold in land; land ownership

Lien: a hold or claim which one person has on the property of another to secure payment of a debt or other obligation

Title: the right to or ownership of something; also the evidence of ownership, such as a deed or bill of sale

Early man was nomadic and had no concept of real estate. Roaming bands followed game and the seasons, and did not claim the exclusive right to use a given area. When man began to cultivate crops and domesticate animals, the concept of an exclusive right to the use of land became important. This right was claimed for the tribe as a whole, and each family in the tribe was given the right to the exclusive use of a portion of the tribe's land. In turn, each family was obligated to aid in defending the tribe's claim against other tribes.

As time passed, individual tribes allied with each other for mutual protection; eventually these alliances resulted in political states. In the process, land ownership went to the head of the state, usually a king. The king, in turn, gave the right (called a feud) to use large tracts of land to select individuals, called lords. The lords did not receive ownership. They were tenants of the king, and were required to serve and pay duties to the king and to help fight the king's wars. It was customary for the lords to remain tenants for life, subject, of course, to the defeat of their king by another king. This system, wherein all land ownership rested in the name of the king, became known as the **feudal system.**

The lords gave their subjects the right to use small tracts of land. For this, the subjects owed their lord a share of their crops and their allegiance in time of war. The subjects (vassals) were, in effect, tenants of the lord and subtenants of the king. Like the lord, the vassal could not sell his rights nor pass them to his heirs.

Allodial System   The first major change in the feudal system occurred in 1285 when King Edward I of England gave his lords the right to pass their tenancy rights to their heirs. Subsequently, tenant vassals were permitted to convey their tenancy rights to others. By the year 1650, the feudal system had come to an end in England; in France it ended with the French Revolution in 1789. In its place arose the **allodial system** of land ownership under which individuals were given the right to own land. Initially, lords became owners and the peasants remained tenants of the lords. As time passed, the peasants became landowners either by purchase or by gift from the lords.

When the first European explorers reached North American shores, they claimed the land in the name of the king or queen whom they represented. When the first settlers later came to America from England, they claimed the land in the name of their mother country. However, since the feudal system had been abolished in the meantime, the king of England granted the settlers private ownership of the land upon which they settled, while retaining the claim of ownership to the unsettled lands.

Claims by the king of England to land in the 13 colonies were ended with the American Revolution. Subsequently, the U.S. government acquired the ownership right to additional lands by treaty, wars and purchase, resulting in the borders of the United States as we know them today. The United States adopted the allodial system of ownership, and not only permits but encourages its citizens to own land within its borders.

GOVERNMENT RIGHTS   Under the feudal system, the king was responsible for or-
IN LAND   ganizing defense against invaders, making decisions on land use, providing services such as roads and bridges, and the gen-

eral administration of the land and his subjects. An important aspect of the transition from feudal to allodial ownership was that the need for these services did not end. Consequently, even though ownership could now be held by private citizens, it became necessary for the government to retain the rights of taxation, eminent domain, police power and escheat. Let us look at each of these more closely.

Under the feudal system, governments financed them-selves by requiring lords and vassals to share a portion of the benefits they received from the use of the king's lands. With the change to private ownership, the need to finance govern-ments did not end. Thus, the government retained the right to collect **property taxes** from landowners. Before the advent of income taxes, the taxes levied against land were the main source of government revenues. Taxing land was a logical method of raising revenue for two reasons: (1) until the Indus-trial Revolution, which started in the mid-eighteenth century, land and agriculture were the primary sources of income; the more land one owned, the wealthier one was considered to be and therefore the better able to pay taxes to support the gov-ernment; (2) land is impossible to hide, making it easily identi-fiable for taxation. This is not true of other valuables such as gold or money.

Property Taxes

The real property tax has endured over the centuries, and today it is still a major source of government revenue. The major change in real estate taxation is that initially it was used to support all levels of government, including defense. Today, defense is supported by the income tax, and real estate taxes are sources of city, county and, in some places, state revenues. At state and local government levels, the real property tax pro-vides money for such things as schools, fire and police protec-tion, parks and libraries. To encourage property owners to pay their taxes in full and on time, the right of taxation also enables the government to seize ownership of real estate upon which taxes are delinquent and to sell the property to recover the un-paid taxes.

The right of government to take ownership of privately held real estate regardless of the owner's wishes is called **emi-nent domain.** Land for schools, freeways, streets, parks, urban

Eminent Domain

renewal, public housing, public parking and other social and public purposes is obtained this way. Quasi-public organizations, such as utility companies and railroads, are also permitted to obtain land needed for utility lines, pipes and tracks by state law. The legal proceeding involved in eminent domain is a **condemnation proceeding,** and the property owner must be paid the fair market value of the property taken from him. The actual condemnation is usually preceded by negotiations between the property owner and an agent of the public body wanting to acquire ownership. If the agent and the property owner can arrive at a mutually acceptable price, the property is purchased outright. If an agreement cannot be reached, a formal proceeding in eminent domain is filed against the property owner in a court of law. The court hears expert opinions from appraisers brought by both parties, and then sets the price the property owner must accept in return for the loss of ownership.

When only a portion of a parcel of land is being taken, **severance damages** may be awarded in addition to payment for land actually being taken. For example, if a new highway requires a 40-acre strip of land through the middle of a 160-acre farm, the farm owner will not only be paid for the 40 acres; but will also receive severance damages to compensate for the fact that the farm will be more difficult to work because it is no longer in one piece.

An **inverse condemnation** is a proceeding brought about by a property owner demanding that his land be purchased from him. In a number of cities, homeowners at the end of airport runways have forced airport authorities to buy their homes because of the deafening noise of jet aircraft during takeoffs. Damage awards may also be made when land itself is not taken but its usefulness is reduced because of a nearby condemnation. These are **consequential damages,** and might be awarded, for instance, when land is taken for a sewage treatment plant, and privately owned land downwind from the plant suffers a loss in value owing to foul odors.

Police Power   The right of government to enact laws and enforce them for the order, safety, health, morals and general welfare of the public is called **police power.** Examples of police power applied to real estate are zoning laws, planning laws, building, health and fire codes and rent control. A key difference between police power and eminent domain is that, although police power restricts how real estate may be used, there is no legally recognized "taking" of property. Consequently, there is no payment to an owner who suffers a loss of value through the exercise of police power. A government may not utilize police power in an offhand or capricious manner; any law that restricts how an owner may use his real estate must be deemed in the public interest and applied evenhandedly to be valid. The breaking of a law based upon police power results in either a civil or criminal penalty rather than in the seizing of real estate, as in the case of unpaid property taxes. Of the various rights government holds in land, police power has the most impact on land value.

Escheat

When a person dies and leaves no heirs and no instructions as to how to dispose of his real and personal property, or when property is abandoned, the ownership of that property reverts to the state. This reversion to the state is called **escheat** from the Anglo-French word meaning to fall back. Escheat solves the problem of property becoming ownerless.

PROTECTING OWNERSHIP

It cannot be overemphasized that, to have real estate, there must be a system or means of protecting rightful claims to the use of land and the improvements thereon. In the United States, the federal government is given the task of organizing a defense system to prevent confiscation of those rights by a foreign power. The federal government, in combination with state and local governments, also establishes laws and courts within the country to protect the ownership rights of one citizen in relation to another citizen. Whereas armed forces protect against a foreign takeover, within a country deeds, public records, contracts and other documents have replaced the need for brute force to prove and protect ownership of real estate.

FEE SIMPLE

The concept of real estate ownership can be more easily understood when viewed as a collection or bundle of rights. Under the allodial system, the rights of taxation, eminent domain, police power and escheat are retained by the government. The remaining bundle of rights, called **fee simple,** is

Figure 3:1   **THE FEE SIMPLE BUNDLE OF RIGHTS**

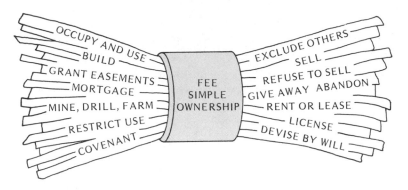

Real estate ownership is, in actuality, the ownership of rights to land.
The largest bundle available for private ownership is called "fee simple".

available for private ownership. The fee simple bundle of rights can be held by a person and his heirs forever, or until his government can no longer protect those rights. Figure 3:1 illustrates the fee simple bundle of rights concept.

The word **estate** is synonymous with bundle of rights. Stated another way, estate refers to one's legal interest or rights in land, not the physical quantity of land as shown on a map. A fee simple is the largest estate one can hold in land. Most real estate sales are for the fee simple estate. When a person says he or she "owns" or has "title" to real estate, it is usually the fee simple estate that is being discussed. The word **title** refers to the right or ownership of something. All other lesser estates in land, such as life estates and leaseholds, are created from the fee estate.

Real estate is concerned with the "sticks" in the bundle: how many there are, how useful they are, and who possesses the sticks not in the bundle. With that in mind, let us describe what happens when sticks are removed from the bundle.

Whenever a stick is removed from the fee simple bundle, it creates an impediment to the free and clear ownership and use of that property. These impediments to title are called encumbrances. An **encumbrance** is defined as any claim, right, lien, estate or liability that limits the fee simple title to property. An encumbrance is, in effect, a stick that has been removed from the bundle. Commonly found encumbrances are easements, encroachments, deed restrictions, liens, leases and air and sub-surface rights. In addition, qualified fee estates are encumbered estates, as are life estates.

The party holding a stick from someone else's fee simple bundle is said to hold a claim to or a right or interest in that land. In other words, what is one person's encumbrance is another person's right or interest or claim. For example, a lease is an encumbrance from the standpoint of the fee simple owner. But from the tenant's standpoint, it is an interest in land that gives the tenant the right to the exclusive use of land and buildings. A mortgage is an encumbrance from the fee owner's viewpoint but a right to foreclose from the lender's viewpoint. A property that is encumbered with a lease and a mortgage is called "a fee simple subject to a lease and a mortgage." Figure 3:2 illustrates how a fee simple bundle shrinks as rights are removed from it. Meanwhile, let us turn our attention to a discussion of individual sticks found in the fee simple bundle.

An **easement** is a right or privilege one party has to the use of land of another for a special purpose consistent with the general use of the land. The landowner is not dispossessed from his land, but rather coexists side by side with the holder of the easement. Examples of easements are those given to telephone and electric companies to erect poles and run lines over private property, easements given to people to drive or walk across someone else's land, and easements given to gas and water companies to run pipelines to serve their customers. Figure 3:3 illustrates several examples of easements.

There are several different ways an easement can come into being. One is for the landowner to use a written document to specifically **grant** an easement to another party. A second way is for an owner to reserve (withhold) an easement in the deed when granting the property to another party. For example, a land developer may reserve easements for utility lines when selling the lots and then grant the easements to the utility companies that will service the lots. Another way for an easement to be created is by government condemnation, such as when a government flood control district purchases an easement to run a drainage pipe under someone's land.

EASEMENTS

**REMOVING STICKS FROM THE FEE
SIMPLE BUNDLE**

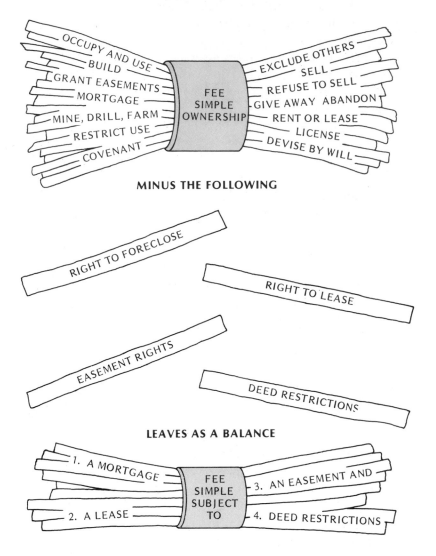

Note that the fee simple bundle shrinks as an owner voluntarily removes rights from it.

It is also possible for an easement to arise without a written document. For example, a parcel of land fronts on a road and the owner sells the back half of the parcel. If the only access to the back half is by crossing over the front half, even if the seller

COMMONLY FOUND EASEMENTS   Figure 3:3

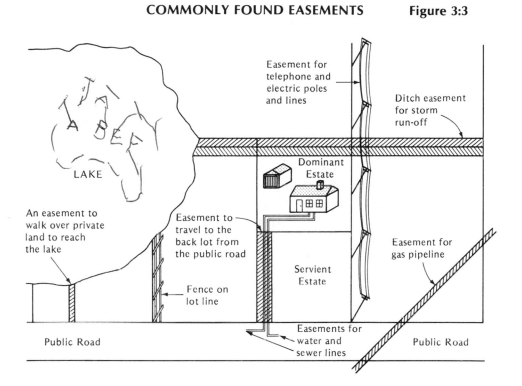

did not expressly grant an easement, the law will generally protect the buyer's right to travel over the front half to get to his land. The buyer cannot be landlocked by the seller. This is known as an **easement by necessity.** Another method of acquiring an easement without a written document is by constant use, or **easement by prescription:** if a person acts as though he owns an easement long enough, he will have a legally recognized easement. Persons using a private road without permission for a long enough period of time can acquire a legally recognized easement by this method.

In Figure 3:3, the driveway from the road to the back lot is called an **easement appurtenant.** This driveway is automatically included with the back lot whenever the back lot is sold or otherwise conveyed. This is so because this easement is legally connected (appurtenant) to the back lot. Please note that just as the back lot benefits from this easement, the front lot is burdened by it. Whenever the front lot is sold or otherwise

Easement Appurtenant

conveyed, the new owners must continue to respect the easement to the back lot. The owner of the front lot owns all the front lot, but cannot put a fence across the easement, or plant trees on it, or grow a garden on it or otherwise hamper access to the back lot. Because the front lot serves the back lot the front lot is called the **servient estate** and the back lot is called the **dominant estate.** When one party has the right or privilege, by usage or contract, to travel over a designated portion of another person's land, it is called a **right-of-way.**

Although the law generally protects the first purchaser through the doctrine of easement by necessity, it is nonetheless critical that any subsequent purchaser of back lots and back acreage carefully inspect the public records and the property to make certain there is both legal and actual means of access from a public road to the parcel. It is also important for anyone purchasing land to inspect the public records and the property for evidence of the rights of others to pass over that land, for example, a driveway or private road to a back lot or a pathway used by the public to get from a road to a beach.

Easement in Gross

An **easement in gross** differs from an easement appurtenant because there is a servient estate but no dominant estate. Some examples will illustrate this: telephone, electricity and gas line easements are all easements in gross. These easements belong to (attach to) the telephone, electric and gas companies, respectively, not to a parcel of land. The servient estate is the parcel on which the telephone, electric and gas companies have the right to run their lines. All future owners of the parcel are bound by these easements.

Although utility easements are the most common examples of easements in gross, the ditch easement for storm runoff in Figure 3:3 is also one. It will most likely be owned by a flood control district. Note that utility and drainage easements, although legally a burden on a parcel, are consistent with the use of a parcel if the purpose of the easement is to provide utility service or flood control for the parcel. In fact, without these services, a parcel would be less useful and hence less valuable.

It is also possible to grant an easement to an individual for his or her personal use. In Figure 3:3, a landowner has given a friend a personal easement in gross to walk over his land to reach a choice fishing area on the lakeshore. An easement in gross for personal use is not transferable and terminates with the death of the person holding the easement. In contrast, the holder of a commercial easement, such as a utility or flood control easement, usually has the right to sell, assign or devise that easement.

Party wall easements exist when a single wall is located on the lot line that separates two parcels of land. The wall may be either a fence or the wall of a building. In either case, each lot owner owns that portion of the wall on his land, plus an ease ment in the other half of the wall for physical support. Party walls are common where stores and office buildings are built right up to the lot line. Such a wall can present an interesting problem when the owner of one lot wants to demolish his building. Since the wall provides support for the building next door, he must leave the wall, and provide special supports for the adjacent building during demolition and until another building is constructed on the lot. A party wall is an easement appurtenant.

Party Wall Easement

Easements may be terminated when the necessity for the easement no longer exists (for example, a public road is built adjacent to the back half of the lot mentioned earlier), or when the dominant and servient estates are combined (merged) with the intent of extinguishing the easement, or by release from the easement holder to the servient estate, or by lack of use (aban donment).

Easement Termination

The unauthorized intrusion of a building or other form of real property onto another person's land is called an **encroach- ment.** A tree that overhangs into a neighbor's yard, or a build ing or eave of a roof that crosses a property line are examples of encroachments. The owner of the property being en croached upon has the right to force the removal of the en croachment. Failure to do so may eventually injure his title and make his land more difficult to sell. Ultimately, inaction may result in the encroaching neighbor claiming a legal right to continue his use. Figure 3:4 illustrates several commonly found encroachments (overleaf).

ENCROACHMENTS

Figure 3:4   **COMMONLY FOUND ENCROACHMENTS**

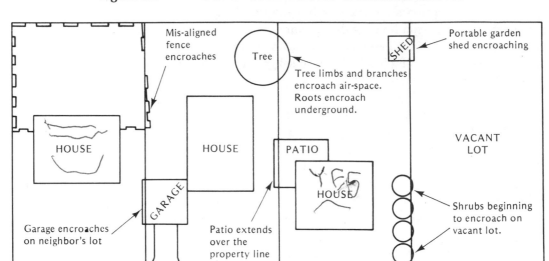

Most commonly found encroachments are not intentional but are due to poor or nonexistent planning. For example, a weekend garden shed, fence, or patio project is built without surveying to find the lot line, or a tree or bush grows so large it encroaches upon a neighbor's land.

DEED RESTRICTIONS   Private agreements that govern the use of land are known as **deed restrictions** or **deed covenants.** For example, a land subdivider can require that persons who purchase lots from him build only single-family homes containing 1,200 square feet or more. The purpose would be to protect those who have already built houses from an erosion in property value due to the construction of nearby buildings not compatible with the neighborhood. Where scenic views are important, deed restrictions may limit the height of buildings and trees to 15 feet. A buyer would still obtain fee simple ownership, but at the same time would voluntarily give up some of his rights to do as he pleases. As a buyer, he is said to receive a fee simple title subject to deed restrictions. The right to enforce the restrictions is usually given by the developer to the subdivision's homeowner association. Violation of a deed restriction can result in a civil court action brought by other property owners who are bound by the same deed restriction.

LIENS   A hold or claim that one person has on the property of another to secure payment of a debt or other obligation is called a

lien. Common examples are property tax liens, mechanic's liens, judgment liens and mortgage liens. From the standpoint of the property owner, a lien is an encumbrance on his title. Note that a lien does not transfer title to property. The debtor retains title until the lien is foreclosed. When there is more than one lien against a property, the lien which was recorded first usually has the highest priority in the event of foreclosure. Property tax liens are, however, always superior to other liens.

Property tax liens result from the right of government to collect taxes from property owners. At the beginning of each tax year, a tax lien is placed on taxable property. It is removed if the property taxes are paid. If they are not paid, the lien gives the state the right to force the sale of the property in order to collect the unpaid taxes.

Property Tax Liens

Mechanic's lien laws give anyone who has furnished labor or materials for the improvement of land the right to place a lien against those improvements and the land if payment has not been received. A sale of the property can then be forced to recover the money owed. To be entitled to a mechanic's lien, the work or materials must have been provided under contract with the landowner or his representative. For example, if a landowner hires a contractor to build a house or add a room to his existing house, and then fails to pay the contractor, the contractor may file a mechanic's lien against the land and its improvements. Furthermore, if the landowner pays the contractor, but the contractor does not pay his subcontractors, the subcontractors are entitled to file a mechanic's lien against the property. In this situation, the owner may have to pay twice.

Mechanic's Lien

The legal theory behind mechanic's lien rights is that the labor and materials supplied enhance the value of the property. Therefore the property should be security for payment. If the property owner does not pay voluntarily, the lien can be enforced with a court supervised foreclosure sale.

Mechanics (contractors), materialmen, architects, surveyors and engineers are among those who may be entitled to the protection of mechanic's lien laws. All mechanic's liens attach and take effect at the time the first item of labor or material is furnished, even though no document has been filed with the county recorder. To preserve the lien, a lien statement must be filed in the county where the property is located and within 20 to 120 days (depending on the state) after labor or material has been furnished. This is called **perfecting the lien.**

Whenever improvements are made to the land, all persons (including sellers under a contract for deed and landlords) may be held to have authorized the improvements. As protection, an owner can serve or post notice that the improvements are being made without the owner's authority.

A lender planning to finance a property will be particularly alert for the possibility of mechanic's liens. If work has commenced or material delivered before the mortgage is recorded, the mechanic's lien may be superior to the mortgage in the event of foreclosure.

Judgment Lien

Judgment liens arise from lawsuits for which money damages are awarded. The law permits a hold to be placed against the real and personal property of the debtor until the judgment is paid. Usually the lien created by the judgment covers only property in the county where the judgment was awarded. However, the creditor can extend the lien to property in other counties by filing a **notice of lien** in each of those counties. If the debtor does not repay the lien voluntarily, the creditor can ask the court to issue a **writ of execution** that directs the county sheriff to seize and sell a sufficient amount of the debtor's property to pay the debt and expenses of the sale.

Mortgage Lien

A **mortgage lien** is created when property is offered by its owner as security for the repayment of a debt. If the debt secured by the mortgage lien is not repaid, the creditor can foreclose and sell the property. If this is insufficient to repay the debt, some states allow the creditor to petition the court for a judgment lien for the balance due. (Mortgage law is covered in more detail in Chapter 9.)

Voluntary and Involuntary Liens

A **voluntary lien** is a lien created by the property owner. A mortgage lien is an example of a voluntary lien; the owner voluntarily creates a lien against his/her property in order to borrow money. An **involuntary lien** is created by operation of law. Examples are property tax liens, judgment liens and mechanics' liens.

A **special lien** is a lien on a specific property. A property tax lien is a special lien because it is a lien against a specific property and no other. Thus, if a person owns five parcels of land scattered throughout a given county and fails to pay the taxes on one of those parcels, the county can force the sale of just that one parcel; the others cannot be touched. Mortgages and mechanic's liens are also special liens in that they apply to only the property receiving the materials or labor. In contrast, a **general lien** is a lien on all the property of a person in a given jurisdiction. For example, a judgment lien is a lien on all the debtor's property in the county or counties where the judgment has been filed. Federal and state tax liens are also general liens.

Special and General Liens

The party holding the lien is called the **lienor.** Examples of lienors are mortgage lenders, judgment holders and tax authorities. The party whose property is subject to the lien is called a **lienee.** The terms "lienor" and "lienee" apply whether the lien is voluntary or involuntary, specific or general.

Lienor, Lienee

A **qualified fee estate** is a fee estate that is subject to certain limitations imposed by the person creating the estate. Qualified fee estates fall into three categories: determinable, condition subsequent, and condition precedent. They will be discussed only briefly as they are rather uncommon.

QUALIFIED FEE ESTATES

A **fee simple determinable** estate indicates that the duration of the estate can be determined from the deed itself. For example, Mr. Smith donates a parcel of land to a church so long as the land is used for religious purposes. The key words are "so long as." So long as the land is used for religious purposes, the church has all the rights of fee simple ownership. But, if some other use is made of the land, it reverts back to the grantor (Mr. Smith) or someone else named by Mr. Smith (called a **remainderman**). Note that the termination of the estate is automatic if the land is used contrary to the limitation stated in the deed.

A **fee simple subject to condition subsequent** gives the grantor the *right* to terminate the estate. Continuing the above example, Mr. Smith would have the right to reenter the property and take it back if it was no longer being used for religious purposes.

With a **fee simple upon condition precedent,** title will not take effect until a condition is performed. For example, Mr. Smith could deed his land to a church with the condition that the deed will not take effect until a religious sanctuary is built.

Occasionally, qualified fees have been used by land developers in lieu of deed restrictions or zoning. For example, the buyer has fee title so long as he uses the land for a single-family residence. In another example, a land developer might use a condition precedent to encourage lot purchasers to build promptly. This would enhance the value of his unsold lots. From the standpoint of the property owner, a qualification is an encumbrance to his title.

LIFE ESTATES

A **life estate** conveys an estate for the duration of someone's life. The duration of the estate can be tied to the life of the **life tenant** (the person holding the life estate) or to a third party. In addition, someone must be named to acquire the estate upon its termination. The following example will illustrate the life estate concept. Suppose you have an aunt who needs financial assistance and you have decided to grant her, for the rest of her life, a house to live in. When you create the life estate, she becomes the life tenant. Additionally, you must decide who gets the house upon her death. If you want it back, you would want a **reversion** for yourself. This way the house reverts back to you, or if you predecease her, to your heirs. If you want the house to go to someone else, your son or daughter for example, you could name him or her as the **remainderman.** Alternatively, you could name a friend, relative or charity as the remainderman. Sometimes a life estate is used to avoid the time and expense of probating a will and to reduce estate taxes. For example, an aging father could deed his real estate to his children but retain a life estate for himself.

Prohibition of Waste

Since a life estate arrangement is temporary, the life tenant must not commit **waste** by destroying or harming the property. Furthermore, the life tenant is required to keep the property in reasonable repair and to pay any property taxes, assessments and interest on debt secured by the property. The life tenant is entitled to income generated by the property, and may sell, lease, rent or mortgage his or her interest.

Although the life estate concept offers intriguing gift and estate planning possibilities, the uncertainty of the duration of the estate makes it rather unmarketable. Thus, you will rarely see a life estate advertised for sale in a newspaper or listed for sale at a real estate brokerage office.

Statutory estates are created by state law. They include **dower,** which gives a wife rights in her husband's real property; **curtesy,** which gives a husband rights in his wife's real property; and **community property,** which gives each spouse a one-half interest in marital property. Additionally there is **homestead protection,** which is designed to protect the family's home from certain debts and, upon the death of one spouse, provide the other with a home for life.

STATUTORY ESTATES

Historically **dower** came from old English common law in which the marriage ceremony was viewed as merging the wife's legal existence into that of her husband's. From this viewpoint, property bought during marriage belongs to the husband, with both husband and wife sharing the use of it. As a counterbalance, the dower right recognizes the wife's efforts in marriage and grants her legal ownership to one-third (in some states one-half) of the family's real property for the rest of her life. This prevents the husband from conveying ownership of the family's real estate without the wife's permission and protects her even if she is left out of her husband's will.

Dower

In real estate sales, the effect of dower laws is that, when a husband and wife sell their property, the wife must relinquish her dower rights. This is usually accomplished by the wife signing the deed with her husband or by signing a separate quitclaim deed. If she does not relinquish her dower rights, the buyer (or even a future buyer) may find that, upon the husband's death, the wife may return to legally claim an undivided ownership in the property. This is important if you buy real estate. Have the property's ownership researched by an abstracter and the title insured by a title insurance company.

Roughly the opposite of dower, **curtesy** gives the husband benefits in his deceased wife's property as long as he lives. However, unlike dower, the wife can defeat those rights in her

Curtesy

will. Furthermore, state law may require the couple to have had a child in order for the husband to qualify for curtesy.

Because dower and curtesy rights originally were unequal, some states interpret dower and curtesy so as to give equal rights while other states have enacted additional legislation to protect spousal rights. To summarize, the basic purpose of dower and curtesy (and community property laws) is to require both spouses to sign any deed or mortgage or other document affecting title to their lands, and to provide legal protection for the property rights of a surviving spouse.

Community Property

Eight states (Arizona, California, Idaho, Louisiana, Nevada, New Mexico, Texas and Washington) subscribe to the legal theory that during marriage each spouse has an equal interest in all property acquired by their joint efforts during the marriage. This jointly produced property is called **community property.** Upon the death of one spouse, one-half of the community property passes to the heirs. The other one-half is retained by the surviving spouse. When community property is sold or mortgaged, both spouses must sign the document. Community property rights arise upon marriage (either formal or common law) and terminate upon divorce or death. Community property is discussed at greater length in Chapter 4.

Homestead Protection

Nearly all states have passed **homestead protection laws,** usually with two purposes in mind: (1) to provide some legal protection for the homestead claimants from debts and judgments against them that might result in the forced sale and loss of the home, and (2) to provide a home for a widow, and sometimes a widower, for life. Homestead laws also restrict one spouse from acting without the other when conveying the homestead or using it as collateral for a loan. Although dower, curtesy and community property rights are automatic in those states that have them, the homestead right may require that a written declaration be recorded in the public records. As referred to here, homestead is not the acquiring of title to state or federally owned lands by filing and establishing a residence (see Chapter 5). Additionally, "homestead protection" should not be confused with the "homestead exemption" some states grant to homeowners in order to reduce their property taxes (see Chapter 13).

A homeowner is also protected by the Federal Bankruptcy Reform Act of 1979. A person who seeks protection under this act is entitled to an exemption of up to $7,500 of the equity in his/her residence. Also exempt is any household item that does not exceed $200 in value.

In a carryover from the old English court system, estates in land are classified as either **freehold estates** or **leasehold estates.** The main difference is that freehold estate cases are tried under real property laws whereas leasehold (also called non-freehold or less-than-freehold) estates are tried under personal property laws.

FREEHOLD ESTATES

The two distinguishing features of a freehold estate are (1) there must be actual ownership of the land, and (2) the estate must be of unpredictable duration. Fee estates, life estates and estates created by statute are freehold estates. The distinguishing features of a leasehold estate are (1) although there is possession of the land, there is no ownership, and (2) the estate is of definite duration. Stated another way, freehold means ownership and less-than-freehold means rental.

As previously noted, the user of a property need not be its owner. Under a leasehold estate, the user is called the **lessee** or **tenant,** and the person from whom he leases is the **lessor** or **landlord.** As long as the tenant has a valid lease, abides by it, and pays the rent on time, the owner, even though he owns the property, cannot occupy it until the lease has expired. During the lease period, the freehold estate owner is said to hold a **reversion.** This is his right to recover possession at the end of the lease period. Meanwhile, the lease is an encumbrance against the property.

LEASEHOLD ESTATES

There are four categories of leasehold estates: estate for years, periodic estate, estate at will, and tenancy at sufferance. Note that in this chapter we will be examining leases primarily from the standpoint of estates in land. Leases as financing tools are discussed in Chapter 12 and lease contracts are covered in Chapter 15.

Also called a tenancy for years, the **estate for years** is somewhat misleadingly named as it implies that a lease for a number of years has been created. Actually, the key criterion is

Estate for Years

that the lease have a specific starting time and a specific ending time. It can be for any length of time, ranging from less than a day to many years. An estate for years does not automatically renew itself. Neither the landlord nor the tenant must act to terminate it, as the lease agreement itself specifies a termination date.

Usually the lessor is the freehold estate owner. However, the lessor could also be a lessee. To illustrate, a fee owner leases to a lessee who in turn leases to another person. By doing this, this first lessee has become a **sublessor.** The person who leases from him is a **sublessee.** It is important to realize that in no case can a sublessee acquire from the lessee any more rights than the lessee has. Thus, if a lessee has a 5-year lease with 3 years remaining, he can assign to a sublessee only the remaining 3 years or a portion of that.

Periodic Estate   Also called an estate from year-to-year or a periodic tenancy, a **periodic estate** has an original lease period with fixed length; when it runs out, unless the tenant or the landlord acts to terminate it, renewal is automatic for another like period of time. A month-to-month apartment rental is an example of this arrangement. To avoid last minute confusion, rental agreements usually require that advance notice be given if either the landlord or the tenant wishes to terminate the tenancy.

Estate at Will   Also called a tenancy at will, an **estate at will** is a landlord–tenant relationship with all the normal rights and duties of a lessor–lessee relationship, except that the estate may be terminated by either the lessor or the lessee at anytime. However, most states recognize the inconvenience a literal interpretation of "anytime" can cause and require that reasonable advance notice be given. What is considered "reasonable" notice is often specified by state law.

Tenancy at Sufferance   A **tenancy at sufferance** occurs when a tenant stays beyond his legal tenancy without the consent of the landlord. In other words, the tenant wrongfully holds the property against the owner's wishes. In a tenancy at sufferance, the tenant is commonly called a **holdover tenant,** although once the stay exceeds the terms of the lease or rental agreement he is not actually a tenant in the normal landlord–tenant sense. The landlord is entitled to evict him and recover possession of the property, provided the landlord does so in a timely manner. A tenant at sufferance differs from a trespasser only in that the original entry was rightful. If during the holdover period the tenant pays and the landlord accepts rent, the tenancy at sufferance changes to a periodic estate.

Figure 3:5 provides an overview of the various rights and interests in land that are discussed in this chapter and the previous chapter. This chart is designed to give you an overall perspective of what real estate includes.

OVERVIEW

A **license** is not a right or an estate in land, but a personal privilege given to someone to use land. It is nonassignable and can be canceled by the person who issues it. A license to park is typically what an automobile parking lot operator provides for persons parking in his lot. The contract creating the license is usually written on the stub that the lot attendant gives the driver, or it is posted on a sign on the lot. Tickets to theaters and sporting events also fall into this category. Because it is a personal privilege, a license is not an encumbrance against land.

LICENSE

A **chattel** is an article of personal property. The word comes from the Old English word for cattle, which, of course, were (and still are) personal property. Chattel is a word more often heard in a law office than in a real estate office. Occasionally you will see it used in legal documents, such as in the case of a **chattel mortgage,** which is a mortgage against personal property.

CHATTELS

You will better understand real estate law when you understand its roots. Most American law originally came from early English law through English colonization of America. Additionally, Spanish law, via Spain's colonization of Mexico, can be found in Arizona, California, Idaho, Nevada, New Mexico, Texas and Washington. Lastly, old French civil law, by way of the French ownership of Louisiana, is the basis for that state's law. In all three of these, the law that came to America

LAW SOURCES

Figure 3:5   **RIGHTS AND INTERESTS IN LAND**

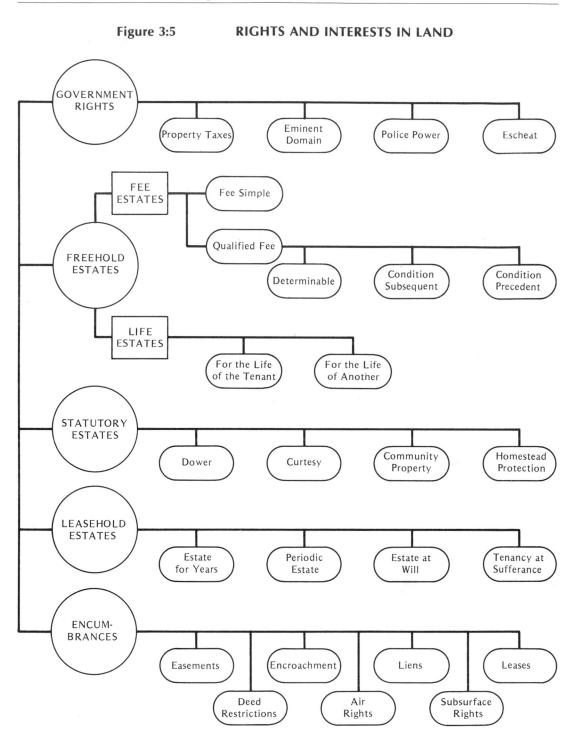

was from predominently agricultural economies. Consequently, there has been much legal modification over the years
by legislatures and courts.

You will also find it helpful to understand the difference   *Common Law*
between common law and statutory law. **Common law** derives
its authority from usage and custom over long periods of time.
Thus the concepts of fee simple estates, qualified fee estates,
life estates, leasehold estates, mortgages, air rights and subsurface rights, for example, grew out of usage over hundreds of
years. Individual court decisions (called **case law**) also contributed to the development of common law in England and the
United States.

Statutory law is created by the enactment of legislation.   *Statutory Law*
Examples of statutory laws are laws enacted by state legislatures that require the licensing of real estate agents. Zoning
laws and building codes are also statutory laws as they have
their source in legislative enactment. Federal and state income
tax and local property tax laws are statutory laws.
Sometimes common law concepts are enacted into statutory law. For example, many statutory laws pertaining to leasehold estates and the rights and obligations of landlords and
tenants have come directly from common law. Additionally,
statutory laws have been passed where common law was held
to be unclear or unreasonable. For example, old English law did
not provide equality in property rights for both spouses. Modern statutory laws do provide equality.

Let us conclude this chapter by combining what has been   *PICTORIAL SUMMARY*
discussed in Chapter 2 regarding the physical nature of land
with what has been covered in this chapter regarding estates
and rights in land. The results, diagrammed in Figure 3:6 and
3:7, show why real estate is both complicated and exciting at
the same time. A single parcel of land can be divided into subsurface, surface and airspace components. Each of these carries
its own fee simple bundle of rights which, in turn, can be divided into the various estates and rights which we discuss in
this chapter.
To more clearly convey this idea, let us turn our attention
to Figure 3:6. In parcel A, the fee landowner has leased the bulk

Figure 3:6   CROSS SECTION OF ESTATES AND RIGHTS IN LAND

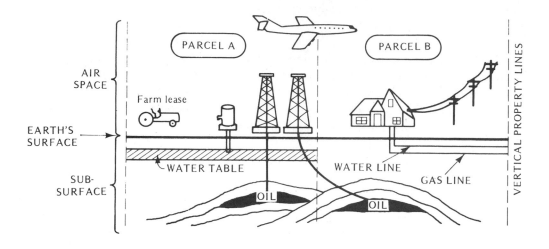

of his surface and air rights, plus the right to draw water from his wells, to a farmer for the production of crops and livestock. This leaves the fee owner with the right to lease or sell subterranean rights for mineral, oil and gas extraction. With a single parcel of land, the fee owner has created two estates, one for farming and another for oil and gas production. With the minor exception of the placement of the well platforms, pumps and pipes, neither use interferes with the other and both bring income to the landowners. The farmer, in turn, can personally utilize the leasehold estate he possesses or he can sublease it to another farmer. The oil company, if it has leased its rights, can sublease them; if it has purchased them, it can sell or lease them. A variation would be for an oil company to buy the land in fee, conduct its drilling operations, and lease the surface to a farmer. In the public interest, the government has claimed the right to allow aircraft to fly over the land. Although technically a landowner owns from the center of the earth out to the heavens, the right given aircraft to fly overhead creates a practical limit on that ownership.

Surface Right of Entry   In parcel B, the fee simple landowner has leased or sold the right to extract oil and gas from beneath his land. However, no

CROSS SECTION OF ESTATES AND   Figure 3:7
RIGHTS IN LAND (*continued*)

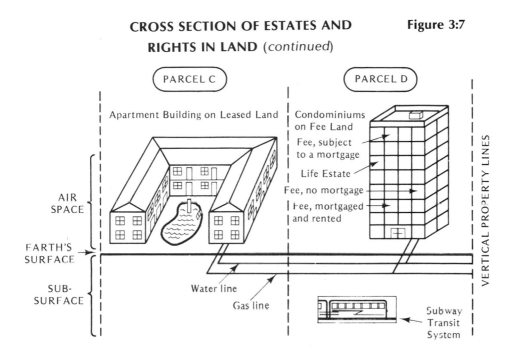

surface right for the purpose of entering and drilling has been leased or sold. Thus, the oil company must slant drill from a nearby property where it does have a **surface right of entry.** The remaining rights amount to a full fee estate in the surface and airspace. However, use of those rights is subject to zoning laws and building codes that restrict what can be built. Deed restrictions may include additional limitations on the type of structure that can be built. Also, the government claims airspace rights for passing aircraft, as it does over all land within its borders. Just above and beneath the surface, easement rights have been granted to utility companies for electric, telephone, water and gas lines.

Despite the fact that this homeowner's bundle of rights is not complete, what he does have is quite suitable for a home site. Recognizing this, lenders will accept the owner's offer of this house and lot as collateral for a loan. This might not be the case if the oil company had a surface right of entry. The noise, odor and fire hazard of a working oil well next to a house would considerably reduce its value as a residence.

Land Lease   In parcel C shown in Figure 3:7, the fee owner has created
an estate for years by a long-term lease of his land to an investor, who has subsequently constructed an apartment building
on the land. This estate gives the building owner the right to
occupy and use the land for a fixed period of time, most often
between 55 and 99 years. In turn, the building owner rents out
apartment units on a monthly or yearly basis. The rights to any
mineral, oil or gas deposits can either be included in the lease
or reserved by the landowner. At the end of the lease period,
the reversion held by the owner of the fee estate entitles the
owner to retake possession of the land, including the buildings
and other improvements thereon.

Condominium Lots   In parcel D, fee simple air lots have been sold to individual
apartment owners in a condominium apartment building. The
owner of each air lot has a fee simple bundle of rights and is
free to mortgage it by taking the foreclosure "stick" out of the
bundle and giving it to a lender in exchange for a loan. Also,
the owner can lease the unit to a tenant, thereby creating a
leasehold estate and a reversion.

Condominium owners as a group usually own the surface
of the land upon which the building rests, any airspace not
used as air lots and the subsurface. In parcel D, the owners
have either sold, leased or granted to a transit authority the
right to build a subway line under this parcel. Underground
rights of this type are very important in cities with subsurface
transportation networks and will continue to be so as more
cities open underground mass transit systems.

An alternative to fee owners granting a subsurface right for
underground transportation lines is for the line owner to own
the fee interest in the entire parcel, use the subsurface position
for its tracks, and sell or lease the use of the surface and airspace above. In Chicago and New York City, for instance, railroads have sold or leased surface and air rights above their
downtown tracks for the purpose of constructing office buildings and convention halls. Passenger trains run just below the
surface, while new buildings occupy the space above.

Match terms **a–x** with statements **1–24**.

a. *Allodial*
b. *Chattel*
c. *Common law*
d. *Dominant estate*
e. *Easement*
f. *Easement appurtenant*
g. *Eminent domain*
h. *Encroachment*
i. *Encumbrance*
j. *Escheat*
k. *Estate*
l. *Estate for years*

m. *Freehold estate*
n. *Inverse condemnation*
o. *Lessor*
p. *Lien*
q. *Life estate*
r. *Mechanic's lien*
s. *Party wall*
t. *Periodic tenancy*
u. *Right-of-way*
v. *Special lien*
w. *Statutory law*
x. *Voluntary lien*

1. A lease with a specific starting and ending date and no automatic renewal provision.
2. A charge or hold against property to use it as debt security.
3. A leasehold estate that automatically renews itself unless cancelled.
4. An article of personal property.
5. The unauthorized intrusion of a building or other improvement upon the land of another.
6. Any impediment to clear title.
7. The right of government to take property from private owners, who in turn must be compensated.
8. A real property ownership system that allows land to be owned by individuals.
9. One's legal interest or rights in land.
10. A lawsuit by a property owner demanding that a public agency purchase his property.
11. The reversion of property to the state when the owner dies without leaving a will or heirs.
12. One who holds title and leases out property; the landlord.
13. A right or privilege one party has in the use of land belonging to another.
14. Law based on custom and court decisions.
15. Law created by the enactment of legislation.
16. A lien purposely created by a property owner.
17. A lien on a specific property.
18. Lien rights for suppliers of labor or materials.
19. The parcel that benefits from an easement across another person's land.
20. An easement attached to a parcel of land and included with that parcel whenever it is conveyed.
21. An estate indicating actual ownership of land.
22. An estate for the duration of someone's life.
23. A wall located on a property boundary line.
24. The right to travel over a portion of another's land.

QUESTIONS AND
PROBLEMS

1. Distinguish between freehold and leasehold estates in land.
2. Under what conditions is it possible for an easement to be created without there being specific mention of it in writing?
3. What steps have been taken by your state legislature to recognize the legal equality of married women in real estate ownership?
4. What three European countries provided the basis for real estate law in the United States?
5. From the standpoint of possession, what is the key difference between an easement and a lease?
6. What is an encumbrance? Give three examples.
7. In your community, name specific examples of the application of police power to the rights of landowners.
8. If your state has a homestead protection law, how much protection does it offer and what must a person do to qualify?
9. Technically speaking, a 99-year lease on a parcel of land is personal property. However, from a practical standpoint, the exclusive right to use a parcel of land for such a long period of time seems more like real property. Do the laws of your state treat a 99-year lease as real or personal property?

ADDITIONAL
READINGS

Hidden Fortunes by **Albert Lowrey.** (Simon and Schuster, 1983, 368 pages). This is an entry-level real estate investment book covering such topics as how to borrow, how to buy, buying at foreclosure sales, auctions, price versus terms, sharing ownership and syndication.

How to Survive While Realestating by **Marvin Myers** and **Alison Myers.** (M&M Productions, 1985, 63 pages). Contains 55 humorous cartoons about real estate that both teach and entertain.

Land Rush by **Mark Stevens.** (McGraw-Hill, 1984, 290 pages). An entertaining visit into the world of powerful and well-connected real estate brokers and developers both residential and commercial.

Real Estate Law by **Marianne Jennings.** (Kent, 1985, 657 pages). Chapters 2 through 6 deal with rights and interests in real estate. Includes freehold, nonfreehold, easements, subsurface rights and fixtures. Court cases used as examples.

The Allen and Wolfe Illustrated Dictionary of Real Estate by **Robert Allen** and **Thomas Wolfe.** (Wiley, 1983, 266 pages). Defines over 3,000 terms from real estate and allied fields. Includes maps, charts, graphs and tables.

The Smart Investors Guide to Real Estate, 3rd ed. by **Robert Bruss.** (Crown, 1984, 270 pages). Emphasis is on the do-it-yourself investor with a small amount to invest. Author is a nationally syndicated real estate columnist.

4

Forms of Ownership

KEY TERMS

Community property: spouses are treated as equal partners with each owning a one-half interest
Concurrent ownership: ownership by two or more persons at the same time
Estate in severalty: owned by one person; sole ownership.
Joint tenancy: a form of property co-ownership that features the right of survivorship
Limited partnership: composed of general partners who mainly organize and operate the partnership and limited partners who provide the capital
Right of survivorship: A feature of joint tenancy whereby the surviving joint tenants automatically acquire all the right, title and interest of the decreased joint tenant
Tenancy by the entirety: a form of joint ownership reserved for married persons; right of survivorship exists and neither spouse has a disposable interest during the lifetime of the other
Tenants in common: shared ownership of a single property among two or more persons; interests need not be equal and no right of survivorship exists
Undivided interest: ownership by two or more persons that gives each the right to use the entire property

In Chapter 2 we looked at land from a physical standpoint: the size and shape of a parcel, where it is located and what was affixed to it. In Chapter 3 we explored various legal rights and interests that can be held in land. In this chapter we shall look at how a given right or interest in land can be held by one or more individuals.

When title to property is held by one person, it is called an **estate in severalty** or **sole ownership.** Although the word "severalty" seems to imply that several persons own a single property, the correct meaning can be easily remembered by thinking of "severed" ownership. Sole ownership is available to single and married persons. However, in the case of married persons, most states require one spouse to waive community

SOLE OWNERSHIP

69

property, dower or curtesy rights in writing. Note that marriage does not automatically convert a person's separate property to marital property. Businesses usually hold title to property in severalty. It is from the estate in severalty that all other tenancies are created.

The major advantage of sole ownership for an individual is flexibility. As a sole owner you can make all the decisions regarding a property without having to get the agreement of co-owners. You can decide what property or properties to buy, when to buy and how much to offer. You can decide whether to pay all cash or to seek a loan by using the property as collateral. Once bought, you control (within the bounds of the law) how the property will be used, how much will be charged if it is rented and how it will be managed. If you decide to sell, you alone decide when to offer the property for sale and at what price and terms.

But freedom and responsibility go together. For example, if you purchase a rental property you must determine the prevailing rents, find tenants, prepare contracts, collect the rent and keep the property in repair; or you must hire and pay someone else to manage the property. Another deterrent to sole ownership is the high entry cost. This form of real estate ownership is not possible for someone with only a few hundred dollars to invest.

Let us now turn to methods of **concurrent ownership,** i.e., ownership by two or more persons at the same time.

TENANTS IN COMMON   When two or more persons wish to share the ownership of a single property, they may do so as **tenants in common.** As tenants in common, each owns an **undivided interest** in the whole property. This means that each owner has a right to possession of the entire property. None can exclude the others nor claim any specific portion for himself. In a tenancy in common, these interests need not be the same size, and each owner can independently sell, mortgage, give away or devise his individual interest. This independence is possible because each tenant in common has a separate legal title to his undivided interest.

Suppose that you invest $20,000 along with two of your friends, who invest $30,000 and $50,000, respectively; together you buy 100 acres of land as tenants in common. Presuming that everyone's ownership interest is proportional to his or her cash investment, you will hold a 20% interest in the entire 100 acres and your two friends will hold 30% and 50%. You cannot pick out 20 acres and exclude the other co-owners from them, nor can you pick out 20 acres and say, "These are mine and I'm going to sell them"; nor can they do that to you. You do, however, have the legal right to sell or otherwise dispose of your 20% interest (or a portion of it) without the permission of your two friends. Your friends have the same right. If one of you sells, the purchaser becomes a new tenant in common with the remaining co-owners.

Wording of Conveyance

As a rule, a tenancy in common is indicated by naming the co-owners in the conveyance and adding the words "as tenants in common." For example, a deed might read, "Samuel Smith, John Jones, and Robert Miller, as tenants in common." If nothing is said regarding the size of each co-owner's interest in the property, the law presumes that all interests are equal. Therefore, if the co-owners intend their interests to be unequal, the size of each co-owner's undivided interest must be stated as a percent or a fraction, such as 60% and 40% or one-third and two-thirds.

In nearly all states, if two or more persons are named as owners, and there is no specific indication as to how they are taking title, they are presumed to be tenants in common. Thus, if a deed is made out to "Donna Adams and Barbara Kelly," the law would consider them to be tenants in common, each holding an undivided one-half interest in the property. An important exception to this presumption is when the co-owners are married to each other. In this case, they may be automatically considered to be taking ownership as joint tenants, tenants by the entirety or community property depending on state law.

No Right of Survivorship

When a tenancy in common exists, if a co-owner dies his interest passes to his heirs or devisees, who then become tenants in common with the remaining co-owners. There is no **right of survivorship;** that is, the remaining co-owners do not acquire the deceased's interest unless they are named in the deceased's last will and testament to do so. When a creditor has a claim on a co-owner's interest and forces its sale to satisfy the debt, the new buyer becomes a tenant in common with the remaining co-owners. If one co-owner wants to sell (or give away) only a portion of his undivided interest, he may; the new owner becomes a tenant in common with the other co-owners.

Co-owner Responsibilities   Any income generated by the property belongs to the tenants in common in proportion to the size of their interests. Similarly, each co-owner is responsible for paying his proportionate share of property taxes, repairs, upkeep and so on, plus interest and debt repayment, if any. If any co-owner fails to contribute his proportionate share, the other co-owners can pay on his behalf and then sue him for that amount. If co-owners find that they cannot agree as to how the property is to be run and cannot agree on a plan for dividing or selling it, it is possible to request a court-ordered partition. A **partition** divides the property into distinct portions so that each person can hold his proportionate interest in severalty. If this is physically impossible, such as when three co-owners each have a one-third interest in a house, the court will order the property sold and the proceeds divided among the co-owners.

"What Ifs"   The major advantage of tenancy in common is that it allows two or more persons to achieve goals that one person could not accomplish alone. However, prospective co-owners should give advance thought to what they will do (short of going to court) (1) if a co-owner fails to pay his share of ownership expenses, (2) if differences arise regarding how the property is to be operated, (3) if agreement cannot be reached as to when to sell, for how much and on what terms, and (4) if a co-owner dies and those who inherit his interest have little in common with the surviving co-owners. The counsel of an attorney experienced in property ownership can be very helpful when considering the co-ownership of property.

JOINT TENANCY   Another form of concurrent ownership is **joint tenancy.** The most distinguishing characteristic of joint tenancy is the right of survivorship. Upon the death of a joint tenant, his interest does not descend to his heirs or pass by his will. Rather, the entire ownership remains in the surviving joint tenant(s). In other words, there is simply one less owner.

To create a joint tenancy, **four unities** must be present. *Four Unities*
They are the unities of time, title, interest and possession.

Unity of time means that each joint tenant must acquire his or her ownership interest at the same moment. Once a joint tenancy is formed, it is not possible to add new joint tenants later unless an entirely new joint tenancy is formed among the existing co-owners and the new co-owner. To illustrate, suppose that *A, B* and *C* own a parcel of land as joint tenants. If *A* sells his interest to *D*, then *B, C* and *D* must sign documents to create a new joint tenancy among them. If this is not done, *D* automatically becomes a tenant in common with *B* and *C* who, between themselves, remain joint tenants. *D* will then own an undivided one-third interest in common with *B* and *C* who will own an undivided two-thirds interest as joint tenants.

Unity of title means that the joint tenants acquire their interests from the same source, i.e., the same deed or will. (Some states allow a property owner to create a valid joint tenancy by conveying to himself, or herself, and another without going through a third party.)

Unity of interest means that the joint tenants own one interest together and each joint tenant has exactly the same right in that interest. (This, by the way, is the foundation upon which the survivorship feature rests.) If the joint tenants list individual interests, they lack unity of interest and will be treated as tenants in common. Unity of interest also means that, if one joint tenant holds a fee simple interest in the property, the others cannot hold anything but a fee simple interest.

Unity of possession means that the joint tenants must enjoy the same undivided possession of the whole property. All joint tenants have the use of the entire property, and no individual owns a particular portion of it. By way of contrast, unity of possession is the only unity essential to a tenancy in common.

The feature of joint tenancy ownership that is most widely *Right of Survivorship* recognized is its **right of survivorship.** Upon the death of a joint tenant, that interest in the property is extinguished. In a two-person joint tenancy, when one person dies, the other immediately becomes the sole owner. With more than two persons as joint tenants, when one dies, the remaining joint tenants are automatically left as owners. Ultimately, the last survivor becomes the sole owner. The legal philosophy is that the joint tenants constitute a single owning unit. The death of one joint tenant does not destroy that unit—it only reduces the number of persons owning the unit. For the public record, a copy of the death certificate and an affidavit of death of the joint tenant is recorded in the county where the property is located. The property must also be released from any estate tax liens.

It is the right of survivorship that has made joint tenancy a popular form of ownership among married couples. Married couples often want the surviving spouse to have sole ownership of the marital property. Any property held in joint tenancy goes to the surviving spouse without the delay of probate and usually with less legal expense.

"Poor Man's Will"   Because of the survivorship feature, joint tenancy has loosely been labeled a "poor man's will." However, it cannot replace a properly drawn will as it affects only that property held in joint tenancy. Moreover, a will can be changed if the persons named therein are no longer in one's favor. But once a joint tenancy is formed, title is permanently conveyed and there is no further opportunity for change. As a joint tenant, you cannot will your joint tenancy interest to someone because your interest ends upon your death. Also be aware that ownership in joint tenancy may result in additional estate taxes.

Another important aspect of joint tenancy ownership is that it can be used to defeat dower or curtesy rights. If a married man forms a joint tenancy with someone other than his wife (such as a business partner) and then dies, his wife has no dower rights in that joint tenancy. As a result, courts have begun to look with disfavor upon the right of survivorship. Louisiana, Ohio and Oregon either do not recognize joint tenancy or have abolished it.* Of the remaining states that recognize joint tenancy ownership (see Table 4:1), 14 have abolished the automatic presumption of survivorship. In these states, if the right of survivorship is desired in a joint tenancy, it must be

_____

* In Ohio and Oregon other means are available to achieve rights of survivorship between nonmarried persons. When two or more persons own property together in Louisiana, it is termed an "ownership in indivision" or a "joint ownership." Louisiana law is based on old French civil law.

CONCURRENT OWNERSHIP BY STATES   Table 4:1

	Tenancy in Common	Joint Tenancy	Tenancy by the Entirety	Community Property		Tenancy in Common	Joint Tenancy	Tenancy by the Entirety	Community Property
Alabama	X	X			Missouri	X	X	X	
Alaska	X	X	X		Montana	X	X		
Arizona	X	X		X					
Arkansas	X	X	X		Nebraska	X	X		
					Nevada	X	X		X
California	X	X		X	New Hampshire	X	X		
Colorado	X	X			New Jersey	X	X	X	
Connecticut	X	X			New Mexico	X	X		X
					New York	X	X	X	
Delaware	X	X	X		North Carolina	X	X	X	
District of					North Dakota	X	X		
Columbia	X	X	X						
					Ohio	X		X	
Florida	X	X	X		Oklahoma	X	X	X	
					Oregon	X		X	
Georgia	X	X							
					Pennsylvania	X	X	X	
Hawaii	X	X	X						
					Rhode Island	X	X	X	
Idaho	X	X		X					
Illinois	X	X			South Carolina	X	X		
Indiana	X	X	X		South Dakota	X	X		
Iowa	X	X							
					Tennessee	X	X	X	
Kansas	X	X			Texas	X	X		X
Kentucky	X	X	X						
					Utah	X	X	X	
Louisiana				X					
					Vermont	X	X	X	
Maine	X	X			Virginia	X	X	X	
Maryland	X	X	X						
Massachusetts	X	X	X		Washington	X	X		X
Michigan	X	X	X		West Virginia	X	X	X	
Minnesota	X	X			Wisconsin	X	X		
Mississippi	X	X	X		Wyoming	X	X	X	

clearly stated in the conveyance. For example, a deed might read, "Karen Carson and Judith Johnson, as joint tenants with the right of survivorship and not as tenants in common." Even in those states not requiring it, this wording is often used to ensure that the right of survivorship is intended. In community property states, one spouse cannot take community funds and establish a valid joint tenancy with a third party.

There is a popular misconception that a debtor can protect himself from creditors' claims by taking title to property as a joint tenant. It is true that in a joint tenancy, the surviving joint tenant(s) acquire(s) the property free and clear of any liens against the deceased. However, this can happen only if the debtor dies before the creditor seizes the debtor's interest.

Only a human being can be a joint tenant. A corporation cannot be a joint tenant. This is because a corporation is an artificial legal being and can exist in perpetuity, i.e., never die. Joint tenancy ownership is not limited to the ownership of land; any estate in land and any chattel interest may be held in joint tenancy.

TENANCY BY THE ENTIRETY

Tenancy by the entirety (also called tenancy by the entireties) is a form of joint tenancy specifically for married persons. To the four unities of a joint tenancy is added a fifth: **unity of person.** The basis for this is the legal premise that a husband and wife are an indivisible legal unit. Two key characteristics of a tenancy by the entirety are (1) the surviving spouse becomes the sole owner of the property upon the death of the other, and (2) neither spouse has a disposable interest in the property during the lifetime of the other. Thus, while both are alive and married to each other, both signatures are necessary to convey title to the property. With respect to the first characteristic, tenancy by the entirety is similar to joint tenancy because both feature the right of survivorship. They are quite different, however, with respect to the second characteristic. Whereas a joint tenant can convey to another party without approval of the other joint tenant(s), a tenancy by the entirety can be terminated only by joint action of husband and wife.

States that recognize tenancy by the entirety are listed in Table 4:1. Some of these states automatically assume that a tenancy by the entirety is created when married persons buy real estate. However, it is best to use a phrase such as "John and Mary Smith, husband and wife as tenants by the entirety with the right of survivorship" on deeds and other conveyances. This avoids later questions as to whether their intention might have been to create a joint tenancy or a tenancy in common.

Advantages and Disadvantages

There are several important advantages to tenancy by the entirety ownership: (1) it protects against one spouse conveying or mortgaging the couple's property without the consent of the other, (2) it provides in many states some protection from the forced sale of jointly held property to satisfy a debt judgment against one of the spouses, and (3) it features automatic survivorship. Disadvantages are that (1) tenancy by the entirety provides for no one except the surviving spouse, (2) it may create estate tax problems, and (3) it does not replace the need for a will to direct how the couple's personal property shall be disposed.

Effect of Divorce

In the event of divorce, the parting spouses become tenants in common. This change is automatic, as tenancy by the entirety can exist only when the co-owners are husband and wife. If the ex-spouses do not wish to continue co-ownership, either can sell his or her individual interest. If a buyer cannot be found for a partial interest nor an amicable agreement reached for selling the interests of both ex-spouses simultaneously, either may seek a court action to partition the property.

Note that severalty, tenancy in common, joint tenancy and tenancy by the entirety are called English common law estates because of their historical roots in English common law.

COMMUNITY PROPERTY

Laws and customs acquired from Spain and France when vast areas of the United States were under their control are the basis for the **community property** system of ownership for married persons. Table 4:1 identifies the eight community property states. The laws of each community property state vary slightly, but the underlying concept is that the husband and wife contribute jointly and equally to their marriage and thus should share equally in any property purchased during marriage. Whereas English law is based on the merging of husband and wife upon marriage, community property law treats husband and wife as equal partners, with each owning a one-half interest.

Separate Property   Property owned before marriage, and property acquired after marriage by gift, inheritance or purchase with separate funds, can be exempted from the couple's community property. Such property is called **separate property** and can be conveyed or mortgaged without the signature of the owner's spouse. The owner of a separate property also has full control over naming someone in his or her will to receive the property. All other property acquired by the husband. or wife during marriage is considered community property and requires the signature of both spouses before it can be conveyed or mortgaged. Each spouse can name in his or her will the person to receive his or her one-half interest. It does not have to go to the surviving spouse. If death occurs without a will, in five states (California, Idaho, Nevada, New Mexico and Washington) the deceased spouse's interest goes to the surviving spouse. In Arizona, Louisiana and Texas, the descendants of the deceased spouse are the prime recipients. Neither dower nor curtesy exists in community property states.

Philosophy   The major advantage of the community property system is found in its philosophy: it treats the spouses as equal partners in property acquired through their mutual efforts during marriage. Even if the wife elects to be a full-time homemaker and all the money brought into the household is the result of her husband's job (or vice versa), the law treats them as equal co-owners in any property bought with that money. This is true even if only one spouse is named as the owner.

In the event of divorce, if the parting couple cannot amicably decide how to divide their community property, the courts will usually do so. If the courts do not, the ex-spouses will become tenants in common with each other. If it later becomes necessary, either can file suit for partition.

CAVEAT TO AGENTS   Often while preparing a real estate purchase contract the buyers will ask the real estate agent how to take title. This is an especially common question posed by married couples purchasing a home. If the agent attempts to answer with a specific recommendation, the agent is practicing law and that requires a license to practice law. The agent can describe the ownership methods available in the state, but should then refer the buyers to their lawyer for a specific recommendation. This is important because the choice of ownership method cannot be made in the vacuum of a single purchase. It must be made in the light of the buyers' total financial picture and estate plans by someone well-versed in federal and state estate and tax laws. Meanwhile, on the purchase contract the agent can enter the names of the purchasers and add the words, "vesting to be supplied before closing." This gives the buyers time to decide how to hold title without delaying preparation of the purchase contract. The buyers can then seek legal counsel and advise the closing agent how they want to take title on the deed.

PARTNERSHIP

A **partnership** exists when two or more persons, as partners, unite their property, labor and skill as a business to share the profits created by it. The agreement between the partners may be oral or written. The partners may hold the partnership property either in their own names (as tenants in common or as joint tenants) or in the name of the partnership (which would hold title in severalty). When property is held in the name of the partnership, it is called a **tenancy in partnership.** In that case the name of the partnership and a list of the partners must be published in the public records of each county and state where the partnership owns property. From then on, business may be transacted in the name of the partnership. For convenience, especially in a large partnership, the partners may designate two or three of their group to make contracts and sign documents on behalf of the entire partnership. There are two types of partnerships: general partnerships made up entirely of general partners and limited partnerships composed of general and limited partners.

General Partnership

The **general partnership** is an outgrowth of common law. However, to introduce clarity and uniformity into general partnership laws across the United States, 49 states and the District of Columbia have adopted the **Uniform Partnership Act** either in total or with local modifications. (The exception is Louisiana.) Briefly, the highlights of the act are that (1) title to partnership property may be held in the partnership's name, (2) each partner has an equal right of possession of partnership property—but only for partnership purposes, (3) upon the death of one partner his rights in the partnership property go to the surviving partners—but the deceased's estate must be reimbursed for the value of his interest in the partnership, (4) a partner's right to specific partnership property is not subject to dower or curtesy, and (5) partnership property can only be attached by creditors for debts of the partnership, not for debts of a partner.

As a form of property ownership, the partnership is a method of combining the capital and expertise of two or more persons. It is equally important to note that the profits and losses of the partnership are taxable directly to each individual partner in proportion to his or her interest in the partnership. Although the partnership files a tax return, it is only for informational purposes. The partnership itself does not pay taxes. Negative aspects of this form of ownership center around financial liability, illiquidity and, in some cases, management.

Financial liability means that each partner is personally responsible for all the debts of the partnership. Thus, each general partner can lose not only what he has invested in the partnership, but more, up to the full extent of his personal financial worth. If one partner makes a commitment on behalf of the partnership, all partners are responsible for making good on that commitment. If the partnership is sued, each partner is fully responsible. **Illiquidity** refers to the possibility that it may be very difficult to sell one's partnership interest on short notice in order to raise cash. **Management** means that each general partner is expected to take an active part in the operation of the partnership.

Limited Partnership   Because of unlimited financial liability and management responsibility, an alternative partnership form, the **limited partnership,** has developed. Forty-nine states, plus the District of Columbia, have adopted the **Uniform Limited Partnership Act.** (The exception is Louisiana, which has its own general and limited partnership laws.) This act recognizes the legality of limited partnerships and requires that a limited partnership be formed by a written document.

A limited partnership is composed of general and limited partners. The **general partners** organize and operate the partnership, contribute some capital, and agree to accept the full financial liability of the partnership. The **limited partners** provide the bulk of the investment capital, have little say in the day-to-day management of the partnership, share in the profits and losses, and contract with their general partners to limit the financial liability of each limited partner to the amount he or she invests. Additionally, a well-written partnership agreement will allow for the continuity of the partnership in the event of the death of a general or limited partner.

The advantages of limited liability, minimum management responsibility and direct pass-through of profits and losses for taxation purposes have made this form of ownership popular. However, being free of management responsibility is only advantageous to the investors if the general partners are capable and honest. If they are not, the only control open to the limited partners is to vote to replace the general partners.

Before investing in a limited partnership, one should investigate the past record of the general partners, for this is usually a good indication of how the new partnership will be managed. The investigation should include their previous investments, checking court records for any legal complaints brought against them and talking to past investors. Additionally, the prospective partner should be prepared to stay in for the duration of the partnership as the resale market for limited partnership interests is small.

Registration

Limited partnerships are a very popular method of investing in real estate. The general partners find property, organize and promote the partnership, and invite people to invest money to become limited partners. Such a partnership can be as small as a dozen or so investors or as large as the multimillion-dollar partnerships marketed nationally by major stock-brokerage firms. If a limited partnership consists of more than a few close friends, registration with state and federal securities agencies is required before it can be sold to investors.

JOINT VENTURE

A **joint venture** is an association of two or more persons or firms to carry out a single business project. A joint venture is similar to a partnership and is treated as a partnership for tax purposes. However, whereas a general partner can bind his partnership to a contract, a joint venturer cannot bind the other joint venturers to a contract. Examples of joint ventures in real estate are the purchase of land by two or more persons with the intent of grading it and selling it as lots, the association of a landowner and builder to build and sell, and the association of a lender and builder to purchase land and develop buildings on it to sell to investors. Each member of the joint venture makes a contribution in the form of capital or talent, and all have a strong incentive to make the joint venture succeed. If more than one project is undertaken, the relationship becomes more like a partnership than a joint venture.

SYNDICATION   Although you will often hear the word **syndication** used in such a way as to imply it is a form of ownership, it is not. In other words, there is no such thing as "tenancy by syndication." Rather, syndication is a broad term that simply refers to two or more individuals who have combined to pursue an investment enterprise too large for any of them to undertake individually. The form of ownership might be a tenancy in common, joint tenancy, general or limited partnership, joint venture or a corporation. When people talk about a syndication in the context of real estate investing, it most likely refers to the real estate limited partnership.

CORPORATIONS   Each state has passed laws to permit groups of people to create **corporations** that can buy, sell, own and operate in the name of the corporation. The corporation, in turn, is owned by stockholders who possess shares of stock as evidence of their ownership.

Because the corporation is an entity (or legal being) in the eyes of the law, the corporation must pay income taxes on its profits. What remains after taxes can be used to pay dividends to the stockholders, who in turn pay personal income taxes on their dividend income. This double taxation of profits is the most important negative factor in the corporate form of ownership. On the positive side, the entity aspect shields the investor from unlimited liability. Even if the corporation falls on the hardest of financial times and owes more than it owns, the worst that can happen to the stockholder is that the value of his stock will drop to zero. Another advantage is that shares of stock are much more liquid than any previously discussed form of real estate ownership, even sole ownership. Stockbrokers who specialize in the purchase and sale of corporate stock usually complete a sale in a week or less. Furthermore, shares of stock in most corporations sell for less than $100, thus enabling an investor to operate with small amounts of capital. In a corporation, the stockholders elect a board of directors, who in turn hire the management needed to run the day-to-day operations of the company. As a practical matter, however, unless a person is a major shareholder in a corporation, there is little control over management. The alternative is to buy stock in firms where one likes the management and sell where one does not.

S Corporations

Several large real estate corporations are traded on the New York Stock Exchange, and the corporation is a popular method of organization for real estate brokers and developers. Nevertheless, most real estate investors shun corporations because of the double taxation feature and because the tax benefits of owning real estate are trapped inside the corporation.

In 1958, the Internal Revenue Code first allowed **Subchapter S** corporations that provided the liability protection of a corporation with the profit-and-loss pass-through of a partnership. Although the original 10-stockholder maximum was a drawback, the real problem for real estate investors was that no more than 20% of a Subchapter S's gross receipts could come from passive income. And rent is passive income. In October 1982, Congress revised the rules and eliminated the passive income restriction, increased the maximum number of shareholders to 35 and changed the name to **S corporations.** (Regular corporations are now called C corporations.)

ASSOCIATIONS

An **association** can own property and transact business in its own name. Examples of associations are the homeowner associations found in condominiums and planned unit development. If properly incorporated, an association will shield its members from personal liability in the event of lawsuits against the association. Associations are usually not-for-profit organizations that are nontaxable. However, they must meet guidelines set by the Internal Revenue Service in order to be treated as nontaxable.

REAL ESTATE INVESTMENT TRUSTS

The idea of creating a trust that in turn carries out the investment objectives of its investors is not new. What has changed is that in 1961 Congress passed a law allowing trusts that specialize in real estate investments to avoid double taxation by following strict rules. These **real estate investment trusts (REITs)** pool the money of many investors for the purchase of real estate, much like mutual funds do with stocks and bonds. Investors in a REIT are called **beneficiaries** and they purchase **beneficial interests** somewhat similar to shares of corporate stock. The trust officers, with the aid of paid advisors, buy, sell, mortgage and operate real estate investments on behalf of the beneficiaries. If a REIT confines its activities to real estate investments, and if the REIT has at least 100 beneficiaries and distributes at least 95% of its net income every year, the Internal Revenue Service will collect tax on the distributed income only once—at the beneficiaries' level. Failure to follow the rules results in double taxation.

The REIT is an attempt to combine the advantages of the corporate form of ownership with single taxation status. Like stock, the beneficial interests are freely transferable and usually sell for $100 each or less, a distinct advantage for the investor with a small amount of money to invest in real estate. Beneficial interests in the larger REITs are sold on a national basis, thus enabling a REIT to have thousands of beneficiaries and millions of dollars of capital for real estate purchases.

INTER VIVOS AND TESTAMENTARY TRUSTS

In all states, the trust form of ownership can be used to provide for the well-being of another person. Basically, this is an arrangement whereby title to real and/or personal property is transferred by its owner (the **trustor**) to a trustee. The **trustee** holds title and manages the property for the benefit of another (the **beneficiary**) in accordance with instructions given by the trustor. Two popular trust forms are the inter vivos trust, also called a living trust, and the testamentary trust.

An **inter vivos trust** takes effect during the life of its creator. For example, you can transfer property to a trustee with instructions that it be managed and that income from the trust assets be paid to your children, spouse, relatives or a charity.

A **testamentary trust** takes effect after death. For example, you could place instructions in your will that upon your death, your property is to be placed into a trust. You can name whomever you want as trustee (a bank or trust company or friend, for example) and whom you want as beneficiaries. You can also give instructions as to how the assets are to be managed and how much (and how often) to pay the beneficiaries. Because trusts provide property management and financial control as well as a number of tax and estate planning advantages, this form of property ownership is growing in popularity.

LAND TRUSTS

In several states an owner of real estate may create a trust wherein he is both the trustor and the beneficiary. Called a **land trust,** the landowner conveys his real property to a trustee, who in turn manages the property according to the beneficiary's (owner's) instructions. Since the beneficial interest created by the trust is considered personal property, the land trust effectively converts real property to personal property. Originally, the land trust gained popularity because true ownership could be cloaked in secrecy behind the name of a bank's trust department. Today, however, its popularity is also due to the simplified probate procedures available to a person who lives in one state and owns land in another. The land trust is also a useful vehicle for group ownership and is not subject to legal attachment like real property. Figure 4:1 provides a visual summary of the various forms of ownership described in this chapter.

CAUTION

The purpose of this chapter has been to acquaint you with the fundamental aspects of the most commonly used forms of real estate ownership in the United States. You undoubtedly saw instances where you could apply these. Unfortunately, it is not possible in a real estate principles book to discuss each detail of each state's law (many of which change frequently) nor to take into consideration the specific characteristics of a particular transaction. In applying the principles in this book to a particular transaction, you should add competent legal advice regarding your state's legal interpretation of these principles.

Figure 4:1 **HOLDING TITLE**

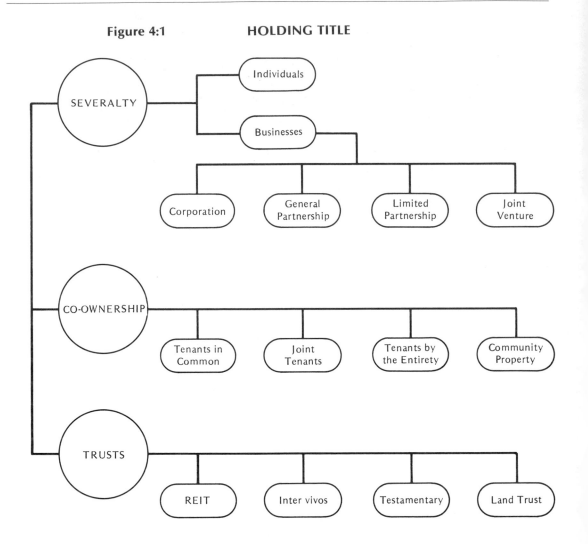

VOCABULARY REVIEW

Match terms **a–r** *with statements* **1–18.**

a. *Association*
b. *Community property*
c. *Estate in severalty*
d. *Financial liability*
e. *General partnership*
f. *Joint tenancy*
g. *Joint venture*
h. *Limited partner*
i. *Partition*

j. *Real estate investment trust*
k. *Right of survivorship*
l. *Separate property*
m. *Syndication*
n. *Tenancy by the entirety*
o. *Tenants in common*
p. *Undivided interest*
q. *Unity of interest*
r. *Unity of time*

1. Owned by one person only. Sole ownership.
2. Each owner has a right to use the entire property.
3. Undivided ownership by two or more persons without right of survivorship; interests need not be equal.
4. The remaining co-owners automatically acquire the deceased's undivided interest.
5. A form of co-ownership in which the most widely recognized feature is the right of survivorship.
6. All co-owners have an identical interest in the property. A requirement for joint tenancy.
7. All co-owners acquired their ownership interests at the same time. A requirement for joint tenancy.
8. Spouses are treated as equal partners with each owning a one-half interest. French and Spanish law origin.
9. An English law form of ownership reserved for married persons. Right of survivorship exists and neither spouse has a disposable interest during the lifetime of the other.
10. Each partner is fully liable for all the debts and obligations of the partnership.
11. A member of a limited partnership whose financial liability is limited to the amount invested.
12. Two or more persons joining together on a single project as partners.
13. Property acquired before marriage in a community property state.
14. A type of mutual fund for real estate investment and ownership wherein a trustee holds property for the benefit of the beneficiaries.
15. A general term that refers to a group of persons who organize to pool their money.
16. Refers to the amount of money a person can lose.
17. To divide jointly held property so that each owner can hold a sole ownership.
18. An organization that can own property and transact business in its own name and is usually operated on a nontaxable, not-for-profit basis.

QUESTIONS AND PROBLEMS

1. What is the key advantage of sole ownership? What is the major disadvantage?
2. Explain what is meant by the term "undivided interest" as it applies to joint ownership of real estate.
3. Name the four unities of a joint tenancy. What requirements do they impose on the joint tenants?
4. What does the term "right of survivorship" mean in real estate ownership?
5. Suppose that a deed was made out to "John and Mary Smith, husband and wife" with no mention as to how they were

taking title. Which would your state assume: joint tenancy, tenancy in common, tenancy by the entirety or community property?

6. Does your state permit the right of survivorship among persons who are not married?

7. If a deed is made out to three women as follows, "Susan Miller, Rhoda Wells, and Angela Lincoln," with no mention as to the form of ownership or the interest held by each, what can we presume regarding the form of ownership and the size of each woman's ownership interest?

8. In a community property state, if a deed names only the husband (or the wife) as the owner, can we assume that only that person's signature is necessary to convey title? Why or why not?

9. List two ways in which a general partnership differs from a limited partnership.

10. What advantages does a real estate investment trust offer a person who wants to invest in real estate?

ADDITIONAL
READINGS

Martindale-Hubble Law Dictionary. (Martindale-Hubble, 1986, 4,500 pages). Contains summaries of law, including real estate, for each state and several foreign countries. Excellent reference material. Published annually.

Origins of the Common Law by **Arthur Hogue.** (Indiana University Press, 1966, 276 pages). Provides a fascinating historical review of the origins of common law in England and how it became transplanted to the United States.

"Real Estate Partnerships: Can They Weather the Storm?" (*Changing Times,* Apr 85, page 48). Article points out that high fees and commissions, pricey properties and tougher tax laws are reducing yields from publicly offered real estate partnerships. This magazine regularly offers very readable and practical articles on real estate ownership.

The Wonderful World of Real Estate by **Emmanuel Halper.** (Warren, Gorham and Lamont, 1975, 203 pages). A delightful and highly readable collection of 17 timeless real estate stories designed to educate and entertain.

*   *   *

The following periodicals may also be of interest to you: *Real Estate Securities Journal, Real Estate Syndication Digest, Realty Stock Review* and *REIT Review.*

Transferring Title

Adverse possession: acquisition of land through prolonged and unauthorized occupation

Bargain and sale deed: a deed that contains no covenants, but does imply that the grantor owns the property being conveyed

Cloud on the title: any claim, lien or encumbrance that impairs title to property

Color of title: some plausible, but not completely clear-cut indication of ownership rights

Consideration: anything of value given to induce another to enter into a contract

Covenant: a written agreement or promise

Deed: a written document that when properly executed and delivered conveys title to land.

Grantee: the person named in a deed who acquires ownership

Grantor: the person named in a deed who conveys ownership

Quitclaim deed: a legal instrument used to convey whatever title the grantor has; it contains no covenants, warranties nor implication of the grantor's ownership

Special warranty deed: grantor warrants title only against defects occurring during the grantor's ownership

Warranty: an assurance or guarantee that something is true as stated

The previous three chapters emphasized how real estate is described, the rights and interests available for ownership, and how title can be held. In this chapter we shall discuss how ownership of real estate is conveyed from one owner to another. We begin with the voluntary conveyance of real estate by deed, and then continue with conveyance after death, and conveyance by occupancy, accession, public grant, dedication and forfeiture.

A **deed** is a written legal document by which ownership of real property is conveyed from one party to another. Deeds were not always used to transfer real estate. In early England, when land was sold, its title was conveyed by inviting the purchaser onto the land. In the presence of witnesses, the seller

DEEDS

picked up a clod of earth and handed it to the purchaser. Simultaneously, the seller stated that he was delivering ownership of the land to the purchaser. In times when land sales were rare, because ownership usually passed from generation to generation, and when witnesses seldom moved from the towns or farms where they were born, this method worked well. However, as transactions became more common and people more mobile, this method of title transfer became less reliable. Furthermore, it was susceptible to fraud if enough people could be bribed or forced to make false statements. In 1677, England passed a law known as the **Statute of Frauds.** This law, subsequently adopted by each of the American states, requires that transfers of real estate ownership be in writing and signed in order to be enforceable in a court of law. Thus, the need for a deed was created.

ESSENTIAL ELEMENTS OF A DEED

What makes a written document a deed? What special phrases, statements and actions are necessary to convey the ownership rights one has in land and buildings? First, a deed must identify the **grantor,** who is the person giving up ownership, and the **grantee,** the person who is acquiring that ownership. The actual act of conveying ownership is known as a **grant.** To be legally enforceable, the grantor must be of legal age (18 years in most states) and of sound mind.

Second, the deed must state that **consideration** was given by the grantee to the grantor. It is common to see the phrase "For ten dollars ($10.00) and other good and valuable consideration," or the phrase "For valuable consideration." These meet the legal requirement that consideration be shown, but retain privacy regarding the exact amount paid. If the conveyance is a gift, the phrase "For natural love and affection" may be used, provided the gift is not for the purpose of defrauding the grantor's creditors.

Words of Conveyance

Third, the deed must contain **words of conveyance.** With these words the grantor (1) clearly states that he is making a grant of real property to the grantee, and (2) identifies the quantity of the estate being granted. Usually the estate is fee simple, but it may also be a lesser estate (such as a life estate) or an easement.

A **land description** that cannot possibly be misunderstood is the fourth requirement. Acceptable legal descriptions are made by the metes and bounds method, by the government survey system, by recorded plat or by reference to another recorded document that in turn uses one of these methods. Street names and numbers are not used as they do not identify the exact boundaries of the land and because street names and numbers can and do change over time. Assessor parcel numbers are not used either. They are subject to change by the assessor, and the maps they refer to are for the purpose of collecting taxes. If the deed conveys only an easement or air right, the deed states that fact along with the legal description of the land. The key point is that a deed must clearly specify what the grantor is granting to the grantee.

Fifth, the grantor executes the deed by signing it. Eight states require that the grantor's signature be witnessed and that the witnesses sign the deed. If the grantor is unable to write his name, he may make a mark, usually an X, in the presence of witnesses. They in turn print his name next to the X and sign as witnesses. If the grantor is a corporation, the corporation's seal is affixed to the deed and two of the corporation's officers sign it.

Signature

Figure 5:1

Witnesseth,   John Stanley , *grantor, for valuable considera-tion given by*   Robert Brenner , *grantee, does hereby grant and release unto the grantee, his heirs and assigns to have and to hold forever, the following described land:* [insert legal description here].

John Stanley
Grantor's signature

Figure 5:1 illustrates the essential elements that combine to form a deed. Notice that the example includes an identification of the grantor and grantee, fulfills the requirement for consideration, has words of conveyance, a legal description of the land involved and the grantor's signature. The words of conveyance are "grant and release" and the phrase "to have and to hold forever" says that the grantor is conveying all future benefits, not just a life estate or a tenancy for years. Ordinarily, the grantee does not sign the deed.

Delivery and Acceptance   For a deed to convey ownership, there must also be **delivery and acceptance.** Although a deed may be completed and signed, it does not transfer title to the grantee until the grantor voluntarily delivers it to the grantee and the grantee willingly accepts it. At that moment title passes. As a practical matter, the grantee is presumed to have accepted the deed if the grantee retains the deed, records the deed, encumbers the title or performs any other act of ownership. This includes the grantee's appointment of someone else to accept and/or record the deed on the grantee's behalf. Once delivery and acceptance have occurred, the deed is evidence that the title transfer has taken place.

COVENANTS AND   Although legally adequate, a deed meeting the preceding
WARRANTIES   requirements can still leave a very important question unanswered in the grantee's mind: "Does the grantor possess all the right, title and interest he is purporting to convey by this deed?" As a protective measure, the grantee can ask the grantor to include certain covenants and warranties in the deed. These are written promises by the grantor that the condition of title is as stated in the deed together with the grantor's guarantee that if title is not as stated he will compensate the grantee for any loss suffered. Five convenants and warranties have evolved over the centuries for use in deeds, and a deed may contain none, some or all of them, in addition to the essential elements already discussed. They are seizin, quiet enjoyment, against encumbrances, further assurance and warranty forever.

Under the **covenant of seizin** (sometimes spelled seisin), the grantor warrants (guarantees) that he is the owner and possessor of the property being conveyed and that he has the right to convey it. Under the **covenant of quiet enjoyment,** the grantor warrants to the grantee that the grantee will not be disturbed, after he takes possession, by someone else claiming an interest in the property.

In the **covenant against encumbrances,** the grantor guarantees to the grantee that the title is not encumbered with any easements, restrictions, unpaid property taxes, assessments, mortgages, judgments, etc., except as stated in the deed. If the grantee later discovers an undisclosed encumbrance, he can sue the grantor for the cost of removing it. The **covenant of further assurance** requires the grantor to procure and deliver to the grantee any subsequent documents that might be necessary to make good the grantee's title. **Warranty forever** is a guarantee to the grantee that the grantor will bear the expense of defending the grantee's title. If at any time in the future someone else can prove that he is the rightful owner, the grantee can sue the grantor for damages up to the value of the property at the time of the sale. Because these warranties and covenants are a formidable set of promises, grantors often back them up with title insurance (see Chapter 6). The grantee is also more comfortable if the deed is backed by title insurance.

Date and Acknowledgment

Although it is customary to show on the deed the **date** it is executed by the grantor, it is not essential to the deed's validity. Remember that title passes upon **delivery** of the deed to the grantee, and that this may not necessarily be the date it is signed.

It is standard practice to have the grantor appear before a notary public or other public officer and formally declare that he signed the deed as a voluntary act. This is known as an **acknowledgment.** Most states consider a deed to be valid even though it is not witnessed or acknowledged, but very few states will allow such a deed to be recorded in the public records. Acknowledgments and the importance of recording deeds will be covered in more detail in Chapter 6. Meanwhile, let us turn our attention to examples of the most commonly used deeds in the United States.

FULL COVENANT AND WARRANTY DEED

The **full covenant and warranty deed,** also known as the **general warranty deed** or **warranty deed,** contains all five covenants and warranties. It is thus considered to be the best deed a grantee can receive, and is used extensively in most states.

Figure 5:2 illustrates in plain language the essential parts of a warranty deed. Beginning at ①, it is customary to identify at the top of the document that it is a warranty deed. At ② the wording begins with "This deed. . . ." These words are introductory in purpose. The fact that this is a deed depends on

Figure 5:2

WARRANTY DEED①

②*THIS DEED, made in the city of* ③Exeter , *state of* XY *on the* ④ 4th *day of* April , *19* xx , *between* ⑤ Henry Odom, a single man , *residing at* ⑥ 1234 Pleasant Rd., Exeter, XY , *herein called the GRANTOR,*⑦ *and* ⑧ Peter Letz and Julie Letz, husband and wife as tenants by the entirety, *residing at* ⑨ 567 Friendly Lane, Exeter, XY , *herein called the GRANTEE.*⑩

WITTNESSETH that in consideration ⑪ *of ten dollars ($10.00) and other valuable consideration, paid by the Grantee to the Grantor, the Grantor does hereby grant* ⑫ *and convey unto the Grantee, the Grantee's* ⑬ *heirs and assigns forever, the following described parcel of land:*

*[legal description of land]*⑭

together with the buildings ⑮ *and improvements thereon and all the estate* ⑯ *and rights pertaining thereto,*

⑰ *TO HAVE AND TO HOLD the premises herein granted unto the Grantee, the Grantee's heirs* ⑱ *and assigns forever.*

The premises are free from encumbrances except as stated herein: ⑲

[note exceptions here]

The Grantee shall not: ⑳

[list restrictions imposed by Grantor on the Grantee]

The Grantor is lawfully seized ㉑ *of a good, absolute, and indefeasible estate in fee simple and has good right, full power, and lawful authority to convey the same by this deed.*

The Grantee, the Grantee's heirs and assigns, shall peaceably ㉒ *and quietly have, hold, use, occupy, possess, and enjoy the said premises.*

Figure 5:2 *continued*

The Grantor shall execute or procure any further ㉓ *necessary assurance of the title to said premises, and the Grantor will forever* ㉔ *warrant and defend the title to said premises.*

IN WITNESS WHEREOF, the Grantor has duly executed this deed the day and year first written above. ㉕

[location of the
acknowledgment:

see Chapter 6]㉘   ㉖   <u>*Henry Odom*</u>
                                  (Grantor's signature)

㉗ (SEAL)

what it contains, not on what it is labeled. A commonly found variation starts with "This indenture" (meaning this agreement or contract) and is equally acceptable. The place the deed was made ③ and the date it was signed ④ are customarily included, but are not necessary to make the deed valid.

At ⑤ and ⑥ the grantor is identified by name and, to avoid confusion with other persons having the same name, by address. Marital status is also stated: husband and wife, single man, single woman, widow, widower, divorced and not remarried. To avoid the inconvenience of repeating the grantor's name each time it is needed, the wording at ⑦ states that in the balance of the deed the word "Grantor" will be used instead. A common variation of this is to call the first party named "the party of the first part." Next appears the name and marital status of the "Grantee" ⑧ and the method by which title is being taken (severalty, tenants in common, joint tenants, etc.). The grantee's address appears at ⑨, and the wording at ⑩ states that the word "Grantee" will now be used instead of the grantee's name. The alternative method is to call the grantee "the party of the second part."

Granting Clause

The legal requirement that consideration be shown is fulfilled at ⑪. Next we come to the **granting clause** at ⑫. Here the grantor states that the intent of this document is to pass ownership to the grantee, and at ⑬ the grantor describes the extent of the estate being granted. The phrase "The grantee's heirs and assigns forever" indicates a fee simple estate. The word **assigns** refers to anyone the grantee may later convey the property to, such as by sale or gift.

The legal description of the land involved is then shown at ⑭. When a grantor is unable or does not wish to convey certain rights of ownership, he can list the exceptions here. For example, a grantor either not having or wishing to hold back oil and gas rights may convey to the grantee the land described, "except for the right to explore and recover oil and gas at a depth below 500 feet beneath the surface." The separate mention at numbers ⑮ and ⑯ of buildings, estate and rights is not an essential requirement as the definition of land already includes these items. Some deed forms add the word **appurtenances** at ⑯. Again, this is not essential wording as appurtenances by definition belong to and pass with the conveyance of the land unless specifically withheld by the grantor. Examples of real estate appurtenances are rights-of-way and other easements, water rights, condominium parking stalls and improvements to land.

Habendum Clause

The **habendum clause,** sometimes called the "To have and to hold clause," begins at ⑰ and continues through ⑱. This clause, together with the statements at ⑫ and ⑬, forms the deed's words of conveyance. For this reason, the words at ⑱ must match those at ⑬. Number ⑲ identifies the covenant against encumbrances. The grantor warrants that there are no encumbrances on the property except as listed here. The most common exceptions are property taxes, mortgages and assessment (improvement district) bonds. For instance, a deed may recite, "Subject to an existing mortgage. . .," and name the mortgage holder and the original amount of the loan, or "Subject to a city sewer improvement district bond in the amount of $1,500."

At ⑳ the grantor may impose restrictions as to how the grantee may use the property. For example, "The grantee shall not build upon this land a home with less than 1,500 square feet of living space."

Special Wording

The covenants of seizin and quiet enjoyment are located at ㉑ and ㉒, respectively. Number ㉓ identifies the covenant of further assurance, and at ㉔ the grantor agrees to warrant and defend forever the title he is granting. The order of grouping of the five covenants is not critical, and in some states there are laws that permit the use of two or three special words to imply the presence of all five covenants. For example, in Alaska, Illinois, Kansas, Michigan, Minnesota and Wisconsin, if the grantor uses the words "convey and warrant" he implies the five covenants even though he does not list them in the deed. The words "warrant generally" accomplish the same purpose in Pennsylvania, Vermont, Virginia and West Virginia, as do "grant, bargain, and sell" in the states of Arkansas, Florida, Idaho, Missouri and Nevada.

At ㉕ the grantor states that he signed this deed on the date noted at ④. This is the **testimony clause;** although customarily included in deeds, it is redundant and could be left out as long as the grantor signs the deed at ㉖. Historically, a seal made with hot wax was essential to the validity of a deed. Today, those few states that require a seal ㉗ accept a hot wax seal, a glued paper seal, an embossed seal, the word "seal" or "L.S." The letters "L.S." are an abbreviation for the Latin words "locus sigilli" (place of the seal). The acknowledgment is placed at ㉘, the full wording of which is given in Chapter 6. If an acknowledgment is not used, this space is used for the signatures of witnesses to the grantor's signature. Their names would be preceded by the words "In the presence of, . . ."

Deed Preparation

The exact style or form of a deed is not critical as long as it contains all the essentials clearly stated and in conformity with state law. For example, one commonly used warranty deed format begins with the words "Know all men by these presents," is written in the first person, and has the date at the end. Although a person may prepare his own deed, the writing of deeds should be left to experts in the field. In fact, some states permit only attorneys to write deeds for other persons. Even the preparation of preprinted deeds from stationery stores and title companies should be left to knowledgeable persons. Preprinted deeds contain several pitfalls for the unwary. First, the form may have been prepared and printed in another state and, as a result, may not meet the laws of your state. Second, if the blanks are incorrectly filled in, the deed will not be legally recognized. This is a particularly difficult problem when neither the grantor nor grantee realizes it until several years after the deed's delivery. Third, the use of a form deed presumes that the grantor's situation can be fitted to the form and that the grantor will be knowledgeable enough to select the correct form.

GRANT DEED   Some states, notably California, Idaho and North Dakota, use a grant deed instead of a warranty deed. In a **grant deed** the grantor covenants and warrants that (1) he has not previously conveyed the estate being granted to another party, (2) he has not encumbered the property except as noted in the deed, and (3) he will convey to the grantee any title to the property he may later acquire. These covenants are fewer in number and narrower in coverage than those found in a warranty deed, particularly the covenant regarding encumbrances. In the warranty deed, the grantor makes himself responsible for the encumbrances of prior owners as well as his own. The grant deed limits the grantor's responsibility to the period of time he owned the property. Figure 5:3 summarizes the key elements of a California grant deed.

Figure 5:3

GRANT DEED①

For a valuable ② consideration, receipt of which is hereby acknowledged, _____③_____ hereby
(name of the grantor)

GRANT(S) ④ to _____⑤_____ the following
(name of the grantee)

ing described real property in the _____⑥_____,
(city, town, etc.)

County of _____, State of California:

[legal description of land here]⑦

Subject to:

[note exceptions and restrictions here]⑧

Dated ⑨_____   _____⑩_____
(Grantor's signature)

⑪[location of the acknowledgment]

Referring to the circled numbers in Figure 5:3, ① labels the document, ② fulfills the requirement that consideration be shown and ③ is for the name and marital status of the grantor. By California statutory law, the single word GRANT(S) at ④ is both the granting clause *and* habendum, *and* it implies the covenants and warranties of possession, prior encumbrances, and further title. Thus, they need not be individually listed.

Number ⑤ is for the name and marital status of the grantee and the method by which title is being taken. Numbers ⑥ and ⑦ identify the property being conveyed. Easements, property taxes, conditions, reservations, restrictions, etc., are noted at ⑧. The deed is dated at ⑨, signed at ⑩ and acknowledged at ⑪.

Why have grantees, in states with more than one-tenth of the total U.S. population, been willing to accept a deed with fewer covenants than a warranty deed? The primary reason is the early development and extensive use of title insurance in these states, whereby the grantor and grantee acquire an insurance policy to protect themselves if a flaw in ownership is later discovered. Title insurance is now available in all parts of the United States and is explained in Chapter 6.

In a **special warranty deed,** the grantor warrants the property's title only against defects occurring during the grantor's ownership and not against defects existing before that time. The special warranty deed is typically used by executors and trustees who convey on behalf of an estate or principal because the executor or trustee has no authority to warrant and defend the acts of previous holders of title. The grantee can protect against this gap in warranty by purchasing title insurance. The special warranty deed is also known in some states as a bargain and sale deed with a covenant against the grantor's acts.

SPECIAL WARRANTY DEED

The basic **bargain and sale deed** contains no covenants and only the minimum essentials of a deed (see Figure 5:4). It has a date, identifies the grantor and grantee, recites consideration, describes the property, contains words of conveyance, and has the grantor's signature. But lacking covenants, what assurance does the grantee have that he is acquiring title to anything? Actually, none. In this deed the grantor only *implies* that he owns the property described in the deed, and that he is granting it to the grantee. Logically, then, a grantee will much prefer a war-

BARGAIN AND SALE DEED

ranty deed over a bargain and sale deed, or require title insurance.

Figure 5:4

BARGAIN AND SALE DEED

THIS DEED made _____ *, between* _____
                              (date)

residing at _____ *, herein called the*
Grantor, and _____ *residing at*
_____ *, herein called the Grantee.*
          WITNESSETH, that the Grantor, in consideration of
_____ *, does hereby grant and release*
unto the Grantee, the Grantee's heirs, successors, and assigns forever, all that parcel of land described as

          [legal description of land]

TOGETHER WITH the appurtenances and all the estate and rights of the Grantor in and to said property.
          TO HAVE AND TO HOLD the premises herein granted together with the appurtenances unto the Grantee.
          IN WITNESS WHEREOF, the Grantor sets his hand and seal the day and year first written above.

                              _____ *L.S.*
                                        (Grantor)

[location of the acknowledgment]

QUITCLAIM DEED   A **quitclaim deed** has no covenants or warranties (see Figure 5:5). Moreover, the grantor makes no statement, nor does he even imply that he owns the property he is quitclaiming to the grantee. Whatever rights the grantor possesses at the time the deed is delivered are conveyed to the grantee. If the grantor has no interest, right or title to the property described in the deed, none is conveyed to the grantee. However, if the grantor possesses fee simple title, fee simple title will be conveyed to the grantee.

The critical wording in a quitclaim deed is the grantor's statement that he "does hereby remise, release, and quitclaim

QUITCLAIM DEED

THIS DEED, made the _____ day of _____ , 19_____ ,
BETWEEN _____ of _____ ,
party of the first part, and _____
of _____ , party of the second part.

WITNESSETH, that the party of the first part, in consideration of ten dollars ($10.00) and other valuable consideration, paid
by the party of the second part, does hereby remise, release, and
quitclaim unto the party of the second part, the heirs, successors
and assigns of the party of the second part forever.

ALL that certain parcel of land, with the buildings and improvements thereon, described as follows,

[legal description of land]

TOGETHER WITH the appurtenances and all the estate
and rights of the Grantor in and to said property.

TO HAVE AND TO HOLD the premises herein granted
unto the party of the second part, the heirs or successors and assigns of the party of the second part, forever.

IN WITNESS WHEREOF, the party of the first part has
duly executed this deed the day and year first above written.

_____
(Grantor)

[location of the acknowledgment]

forever." **Quitclaim** means to renounce all possession, right or
interest. **Remise** means to give up any existing claim one may
have, as does the word **release** in this usage. If the grantor subsequently acquires any right or interest in the property, he is
not obligated to convey it to the grantee.

At first glance it may seem strange that such a deed should
even exist, but it does serve a very useful purpose. Situations
often arise in real estate transactions when a person claims to
have a partial or incomplete right or interest in a parcel of land.

Such a right or interest, known as a **title defect** or **cloud on the title,** may have been due to an inheritance, a dower, curtesy or community property right, or to a mortgage or right of redemption due to a court-ordered foreclosure sale. By releasing that claim to the fee simple owner through the use of a quitclaim deed, the cloud on the fee owner's title is removed. A quitclaim deed can also be used to create an easement as well as release (extinguish) an easement. It can also be used to release remainder and reversion interests.

OTHER TYPES OF DEEDS   A **gift deed** is created by simply replacing the recitation of money and other valuable consideration with the statement, "in consideration of his [her, their] natural love and affection." This phrase may be used in a warranty, special warranty or grant deed. However, it is most often used in quitclaim or bargain and sale deeds as these permit the grantor to avoid being committed to any warranties regarding the property.

A **guardian's deed** is used to convey a minor's interest in real property. It contains only one covenant, that the guardian and minor have not encumbered the property. The deed must state the legal authority (usually a court order) that permits the guardian to convey the minor's property.

Sheriff's deeds and **referee's deeds in foreclosure** are issued to the new buyer when a person's real estate is sold as the result of a mortgage or other court-ordered foreclosure sale. The deed should state the source of the sheriff's or referee's authority and the amount of consideration paid. Such a deed conveys only the foreclosed party's title, and, at the most, carries only one covenant: that the sheriff or referee has not damaged the property's title.

A **correction deed,** also called a deed of confirmation, is used to correct an error in a previously executed and delivered deed. For example, a name may have been misspelled or an error found in the property description. A quitclaim deed containing a statement regarding the error is used for this purpose. A **cession deed** is a form of a quitclaim deed wherein a property owner conveys street rights to a county or municipality. An **interspousal deed** is used in some states to transfer real property between spouses. A **tax deed** is used to convey title to real estate that has been sold by the government because of the nonpayment of taxes. A **deed of trust** is used to convey real estate to a third party as security for a loan and is discussed in Chapter 10.

CONVEYANCE AFTER DEATH

If a person dies without leaving a last will and testament (or leaves one that is subsequently ruled void by the courts because it was improperly prepared), he is said to have died **intestate,** which means without a testament. When this happens, state law directs how the deceased's assets shall be distributed. This is known as a **title by descent** or **intestate succession.** The surviving spouse and children are the dominant recipients of the deceased's assets. The deceased's grandchildren receive the next largest share, followed by the deceased's parents, brothers and sisters, and their children. These are known as the deceased's **heirs** or, in some states, **distributees.** The amount each heir receives, if anything, depends on individual state law and on how many persons with superior positions in the succession are alive. If no heirs can be found, the deceased's property escheats (reverts) to the state.

Testate, Intestate

A person who dies and leaves a valid will is said to have died **testate,** which means that a testament with instructions for property disposal was left behind. The person who made the will is the **testator** (masculine) or **testatrix** (feminine). In the will, the testator names the persons or organizations who are to receive the testator's real and personal property. Real property that is willed is known as a **devise** and the recipient, a **devisee.** Personal property that is willed is known as a **bequest** or **legacy,** and the recipient, a **legatee.** In the will, the testator usually names an **executor** (masculine) or **executrix** (feminine) to carry out the instructions. If one is not named, the court appoints an **administrator.** In some states the person named in the will or appointed by the court to settle the estate is called a **personal representative.**

Notice an important difference between the transfer of real estate ownership by deed and by will: once a deed is made and delivered, the ownership transfer is permanent, the grantor cannot have a change of mind and take back the property. With respect to a will, the devisees, although named, have no rights to the testator's property until the testator dies. Until that time the testator is free to have a change of mind, revoke the old will and write a new one.

Probate or Surrogate Court

Upon death, the deceased's will must be filed with a court having power to admit and certify wills, usually called a **probate** or **surrogate court.** This court determines if the will meets all the requirements of law: in particular, that it is genuine, properly signed and witnessed, and that the testator was of sound mind when the will was made. At this time anyone may step forward and contest the validity of the will. If the court finds the will to be valid, the executor is permitted to carry out its terms. If the testator owned real property, its ownership is conveyed using an **executor's deed** prepared and signed by the executor. The executor's deed is used both to transfer title to a devisee and to sell real property to raise cash. It contains only one covenant, a covenant that the executor has not encumbered the property. An executor's deed is a special warranty deed.

Protecting the Deceased's Intentions

Because the deceased is not present, state laws attempt to ensure that fair market value is received for the deceased's real estate by requiring court approval of proposed sales, and in some cases by sponsoring open bidding in the courtroom. As protection, a purchaser should ascertain that the executor has the authority to convey title.

For a will to be valid it must meet specific legal requirements. All states recognize the **formal** or **witnessed** will, a written document prepared, in most cases, by an attorney. The testator must declare it to be his/her will and sign it in the presence of two to four witnesses (depending on the state), who, at the testator's request and in the presence of each other sign the will as witnesses. A formal will prepared by an attorney is the preferred method, as the will then conforms explicitly to the law. This greatly reduces the likelihood of its being contested after the testator's death. Additionally, an attorney may offer valuable advice on how to word the will to reduce estate and inheritance taxes.

Holographic Will

A **holographic will** is a will that is entirely handwritten, with no typed or preprinted words. The will is dated and signed by the testator; but there are no witnesses. Nineteen states recognize holographic wills as legally binding. Persons selecting this form of will generally do so because it saves the time and expense of seeking professional legal aid, and because it is entirely private. Besides the fact that holographic wills are considered to have no effect in 31 states, they often result in much legal argument in states that do accept them. This can occur when the testator is not fully aware of the law as it pertains to the making of wills. Many otherwise happy families have been torn apart by dissension when a relative dies and the will is opened—only to find that there is a question as to whether or not it was properly prepared, and hence valid. Unfortunately, what follows is not what the deceased intended; those who would receive more from intestate succession will request that the will be declared void and of no effect. Those with more to gain if the will stands as written will muster legal forces to argue for its acceptance by the probate court.

An **oral will,** more properly known as a **nuncupative will,** is a will spoken by a person who is very near death. The witness must promptly put in writing what was heard and submit it to probate. An oral will can only be used to dispose of personal property. Any real estate belonging to the deceased would be disposed of by intestate succession. Some states limit the use of oral wills to those serving in the armed forces.

Oral Will

A **codicil** is a written supplement or amendment made to a previously existing will. It is used to change some aspect of the will or to add a new instruction, without the work of rewriting the entire will. The codicil must be dated, signed and witnessed in the same manner as the original will. The only way to change a will is with a codicil or by writing a complete new will. The law will not recognize cross-outs, notations or other alterations made on the will itself.

Codicil

Through the unauthorized occupation of another person's land for a long enough period of time, it is possible under certain conditions to acquire ownership by **adverse possession.** The historical roots of adverse possession go back many centuries to a time before written deeds were used as evidence of ownership. At that time, in the absence of any claims to the

ADVERSE POSSESSION

contrary, a person who occupied a parcel of land was presumed to be its owner. Today, adverse possession is, in effect, a statute of limitations that bars a legal owner from claiming title to land when he has done nothing to oust an adverse occupant during the statutory period. From the adverse occupant's standpoint, adverse possession is a method of acquiring title by possessing land for a specified period of time under certain conditions.

Courts of law are quite demanding of proof before they will issue a decree in favor of a person claiming title by virtue of adverse possession. The claimant must have maintained actual, visible, continuous, hostile, exclusive and notorious possession and be publicly claiming ownership to the property. These requirements mean that the claimant's use must have been visible and obvious to the legal owner, continuous and not just occasional, and exclusive enough to give notice of the claimant's individual claim. Furthermore, the use must have been without permission (hostile), and the claimant must have acted as though he were the owner, even in the presence of the actual owner. Finally, the adverse claimant must be able to prove that he has met these requirements for a period ranging from 3 to 30 years, as shown in Table 5:1.

Color of Title   The required occupancy period is shortened and the claimant's chances of obtaining legal ownership are enhanced in many states if he has been paying the property taxes and the possession has been under "color of title." **Color of title** suggests some plausible appearance of ownership interest, such as an improperly prepared deed that purports to transfer title to the claimant or a claim of ownership by inheritance. In accumulating the required number of years, an adverse claimant may **tack on** his period of possession to that of a prior adverse occupant. This could be done through the purchase of that right. The current adverse occupant could in turn sell his claim to a still later adverse occupant until enough years were accumulated to present a claim in court.

Although the concept of adverse possession often creates the mental picture of a trespasser moving onto someone else's land and living there long enough to acquire title in fee, this is not the usual application. More often, adverse possession is

ADVERSE POSSESSION: NUMBER OF YEARS OF OCCUPANCY REQUIRED TO CLAIM TITLE*

Table 5:1

	Adverse Occupant Lacks Color of Title & Does Not Pay the Property Taxes	Adverse Occupant Has Color of Title &/or Pays the Property Taxes		Adverse Occupant Lacks Color of Title & Does Not Pay the Property Taxes	Adverse Occupant Has Color of Title &/or Pays the Property Taxes
Alabama	20	3–10	Missouri	10	10
Alaska	10	7	Montana		5
Arizona	10	3	Nebraska	10	10
Arkansas	15	2–7	Nevada		5
California		5	New Hampshire	20	20
Colorado	18	7	New Jersey	30–60	20–30
Connecticut	15	15	New Mexico	10	10
Delaware	20	20	New York	10	10
District of			North Carolina	20–30	7–21
Columbia	15	15	North Dakota	20	10
Florida		7	Ohio	21	21
Georgia	20	7	Oklahoma	15	15
Hawaii	20	20	Oregon	10	10
Idaho	5	5	Pennsylvania	21	21
Illinois	20	7	Rhode Island	10	10
Indiana		10	South Carolina	10–20	10
Iowa	10	10	South Dakota	20	10
Kansas	15	15	Tennessee	20	7
Kentucky	15	7	Texas	10–25	3–5
Louisiana	30	10	Utah		7
Maine	20	20	Vermont	15	15
Maryland	20	20	Virginia	15	15
Massachusetts	20	20	Washington	10	7
Michigan	15	5–10	West Virginia	10	10
Minnesota	15	15	Wisconsin	20	10
Mississippi	10	10	Wyoming	10	10

*As may be seen, in a substantial number of states, the waiting period for title by adverse possession is shortened if the adverse occupant has color of title and/or pays the property taxes. In California, Florida, Indiana, Montana, Nevada and Utah, the property taxes must be paid to obtain the title. Generally speaking, adverse possession does not work against minors and other legal incompetents. However, when the owner becomes legally competent, the adverse possession must be broken within the time limit set by each state's law (the range is 1 to 10 years). In the states of Louisiana, Oklahoma and Tennessee, adverse possession is referred to as title by prescription.

used to extinguish weak or questionable claims to title. For example, if a person buys property at a tax sale, takes possession and pays the property taxes each year afterward, adverse possession laws act to cut off claims to title by the previous owner. Another source of successful adverse possession claims arises from encroachments. If a building extends over a property line and nothing is said about it for a long enough period of time, the building will be permitted to stay.

EASEMENT BY PRESCRIPTION   An easement can also be acquired by prolonged adverse use. This is known as acquiring an **easement by prescription.** Like adverse possession, the laws are strict: the usage must be openly visible, continuous and exclusive, as well as hostile and adverse to the owner. Additionally the use must have occurred over a period of 5 to 20 years, depending on the state. All these facts must be proved in a court of law before the court will issue the claimant a document legally recognizing his ownership of the easement. As an easement is a right to use land for a specific purpose, and not ownership of the land itself, courts rarely require the payment of property taxes to acquire a prescriptive easement.

As may be seen from the foregoing discussion, a landowner must be given obvious notification *at the location* of his land that someone is attempting to claim ownership or an easement. Since an adverse claim must be continuous and hostile, an owner can break it by ejecting the trespassers or by preventing them from trespassing, or by simply giving them permission to be there. Any of these actions would demonstrate the landowner's superior title. Owners of stores and office buildings with private sidewalks or streets used by the public can take action to break claims to a public easement by either periodically barricading the sidewalk or street or by posting signs giving permission to pass. These signs are often seen in the form of brass plaques embedded in the sidewalk or street. In certain states, a landowner may record with the public records office a **notice of consent.** This is evidence that subsequent uses of his land for the purposes stated in the notice are permissive and not adverse. The notice may be later revoked by recording a **notice of revocation.** Federal, state and local governments protect themselves against adverse claims to their lands by passing laws making themselves immune.

The extent of one's ownership of land can be altered by **accession.** This can result from natural or man-made causes. With regard to natural causes, the owner of land fronting on a lake, river or ocean may acquire additional land due to the gradual accumulation of rock, sand and soil. This process is called **accretion** and the results are referred to as alluvion and reliction. **Alluvion** is the increase of land that results when waterborne soil is gradually deposited to produce firm dry ground. **Reliction** (or dereliction) results when a lake, sea or river permanently recedes, exposing dry land. When land is rapidly washed away by the action of water, it is known as **avulsion.** Man-made accession occurs when man attaches personal property to land. For example, when lumber, nails and cement are used to build a house, they alter the extent of one's land ownership.

OWNERSHIP BY ACCESSION

A transfer of land by a government body to a private party is called a **public grant.** Since 1776, the federal government has granted millions of acres of land to settlers, land companies, railroads, state colleges, mining and logging promoters, and any war veteran from the American Revolution through the Mexican War. Most famous was the Homestead Act passed by the U.S. Congress in 1862. That act permitted persons wishing to settle on otherwise unappropriated federal land to acquire fee simple ownership by paying a small filing charge and occupying and cultivating the land for 5 years. Similarly, for only a few dollars, a person may file a mining claim to public land for the purpose of extracting whatever valuable minerals can be found. To retain the claim, a certain amount of work must be performed on the land each year. Otherwise, the government will consider the claim abandoned and another person may claim it. If the claim is worked long enough, a public grant can be sought and fee simple title obtained. In the case of both the homestead settler and the mining claim, the conveyance document that passes fee title from the government to the grantee is known as a **land patent.** In 1976, the U.S. government ended the homesteading program in all states except Alaska.

PUBLIC GRANT

When an owner makes a voluntary gift of his land to the public, it is known as **dedication.** To illustrate, a land developer buys a large parcel of vacant land and develops it into

DEDICATION

streets and lots. The lots are sold to private buyers, but what about the streets? In all probability they will be dedicated to the town, city or county. By doing this, the developer, and later the lot buyers, will not have to pay taxes on the streets, and the public will be responsible for maintaining them. The fastest way to accomplish the transfer is by either statutory dedication or dedication by deed. In **statutory dedication,** the developer prepares a map showing the streets, has the map approved by local government officials, and then records it as a public document. In **dedication by deed** the developer prepares a deed that identifies the streets and grants them to the city.

Common law dedication takes place when a landowner, by his acts or words, shows that he intends part of his land to be dedicated even though he has never officially made a written dedication. For example, a landowner may encourage the public to travel on his roads in an attempt to convince a local road department to take over maintenance.

FORFEITURE

Forfeiture can occur when a deed contains a condition or limitation. For example, a grantor states in the deed that the land conveyed may be used for residential purposes only. If the grantee constructs commercial buildings, the grantor can reacquire title on the grounds that the grantee did not use the land for the required purpose.

ALIENATION

A change in ownership of any kind is known as an **alienation.** In addition to the forms of alienation discussed in this chapter, alienation can result from court action in connection with escheat, eminent domain, partition, foreclosure, execution sales, quiet title suits and marriage. These topics are discussed in other chapters.

VOCABULARY REVIEW

Match terms a–z with statements 1–26.

a. *Accretion*	**h.** *Color of title*
b. *Adverse possession*	**i.** *Consideration*
c. *Alienation*	**j.** *Correction deed*
d. *Alluvion*	**k.** *Covenant and warranties*
e. *Bargain and sale deed*	**l.** *Dedication*
f. *Cloud on the title*	**m.** *Deed*
g. *Codicil*	**n.** *Easement by prescription*

o. *Executor*
p. *Grant*
q. *Grantor*
r. *Holographic will*
s. *Intestate*
t. *Land patent*

u. *Probate*
v. *Quitclaim deed*
w. *Special warranty deed*
x. *Statute of Frauds*
y. *Warranty deed*
z. *Will*

1. A written document that when properly executed and delivered conveys title to land.
2. Requires that transfers of real estate be in writing to be enforceable.
3. Person named in a deed who conveys ownership.
4. The act of conveying ownership.
5. Anything of value given to produce a contract.
6. Promises and guarantees found in a deed.
7. Any claim, lien or encumbrance that impairs title to property.
8. A deed that contains the covenants of seizin, quiet enjoyment, encumbrances, further assurance and warranty forever.
9. A deed that contains no covenants; it only implies that the grantor owns the property described in the deed.
10. A deed with no covenants and no implication that the grantor owns the property he is deeding to the grantee.
11. To die without a will.
12. A will written entirely in one's own handwriting and signed but not witnessed.
13. The process of verifying the legality of a will and carrying out its instructions.
14. A supplement or amendment to a previous will.
15. Acquisition of real property through prolonged and unauthorized occupation.
16. Some plausible but not completely clear-cut indication of ownership rights.
17. Acquisition of an easement by prolonged use.
18. Waterborne soil deposited to produce firm, dry ground.
19. A document for conveying government land in fee to settlers and miners.
20. Private land voluntarily conveyed to the government.
21. The process of land build-up due to the gradual accumulation of rock, sand and soil.
22. A change in ownership of any kind.
23. Used to correct an error in a previously executed and delivered deed.
24. A person named in a will to carry out its instructions.
25. Grantor warrants title only against defects occurring during the grantor's ownership.
26. Instructions stating how a person wants his property disposed of after death.

QUESTIONS AND PROBLEMS

1. Is it possible for a document to convey fee title to land even though it does not contain the word "deed"? If so, why?
2. In the process of conveying real property from one person to another, at what instant in time does title actually pass from the grantor to the grantee?
3. What legal protections does a full covenant and warranty deed offer a grantee?
4. As a real estate purchaser, which deed would you prefer to receive: warranty, special warranty or bargain and sale? Why?
5. What are the hazards of preparing your own deeds?
6. Name five examples of title clouds.
7. What is meant by the term "intestate succession"?
8. With regard to probate, what is the key difference between an executor and an administrator?
9. Does your state consider holographic wills to be legal? How many witnesses are required by your state for a formal will?
10. Can a person who has rented the same building for 30 years claim ownership by virtue of adverse possession? Why or why not?
11. Cite examples from your own community or state where land ownership has been altered by alluvion, reliction or avulsion.

ADDITIONAL READINGS

New Encyclopedia of Real Estate Forms by **Jerome Gross.** (Prentice-Hall, 1983, 701 pages). Chapter 10 contains examples of deeds, including warranty deed, grant deed, special warranty deed, quitclaim deed, executor's deed, life estate deed, correction deed, cession deed and referee deed.

Mastering Real Estate Mathematics, 4th ed. by **William Ventolo, Jr.,** and **Wellington Allaway.** (Real Estate Education Co., 1984, 368 pages). A self-instruction book for percentages, fractions and decimals as they apply to commissions, interest, appraisal, leases, loan points, taxes, proration and price problems.

Plan Your Estate, 4th ed. by **Denis Clifford.** (Nolo Press, 1986, 242 pages). Explains wills, probate avoidance, trusts and taxes. Most bookstores carry a variety of books on this subject.

Real Estate Law, by **Charles Jacobus.** (Reston, 1986, 350 pages). Chapter 8 discusses conveyancing and Chapter 9 the recording of interests in real estate.

Rental Homes: The Tax Shelter that Works and Grows for You by **Vincent Zucchero.** (Reston, 1983, 188 pages). Takes the reader step-by-step through an achievable rental home program from start to finish.

Recordation, Abstracts and Title Insurance

Abstract: a summary of all recorded documents affecting title to a given parcel of land

Acknowledgment: a formal declaration by a person signing a document that he or she, in fact, did sign the document

Actual notice: knowledge gained from what one has actually seen, heard, read or observed

Chain of title: the linkage of property ownership that connects the present owner to the original source of title

Constructive notice: notice given by the public records and by visible possession, coupled with the legal presumption that all persons are thereby notified

Marketable title: title that is free from reasonable doubt as to who the owner is

Public recorder's office: a government-operated facility wherein documents are entered in the public records.

Quiet title suit: court-ordered hearings held to determine land ownership

Title insurance: an insurance policy against defects in title not listed in the title report or abstract

Torrens system: a state-sponsored method of registering land titles

KEY TERMS

In this chapter we shall focus on (1) the need for a method of determining real property ownership, (2) the process by which current and past ownership is determined from public records, (3) the availability of insurance against errors made in determining ownership, (4) the Torrens system of land title registration, and (5) the Uniform Marketable Title Act.

Until the enactment of the Statute of Frauds in England in 1677, determining who owned a parcel of land was primarily a matter of observing who was in physical possession. A landowner gave notice to the world of his claim to ownership by visibly occupying his land. When land changed hands, the old owner moved off the land and the new owner moved onto the land. After 1677 written deeds were required to show transfers

NEED FOR PUBLIC RECORDS

113

of ownership. The problem then became one of finding the person holding the most current deed to the land. This was easy if the deedholder also occupied the land, but was more difficult if he did not. The solution was to create a government-sponsored public recording service where a person could record his deed. These records would then be open free of charge to anyone. In this fashion, an owner could post notice to all that he claimed ownership of a parcel of land.

Constructive Notice   Since 1677 two ways have evolved so that a person can give notice of a claim or right to land. One is by recording documents in the public records that give written notice to that effect. The other is by visibly occupying or otherwise visibly making use of the land. At the same time, the law holds interested parties responsible for examining the public records and looking at the land for this notice of right or claim. This is called **constructive notice.** Constructive notice (also called **legal notice**) charges the public with the responsibility of looking in the public records and at the property itself so as to have knowledge of all who are claiming a right or interest. In other words, our legal system provides an avenue by which a person can give notice (recording and occupancy) *and* makes the presumption that anyone interested in the property has inspected the records and the property.

Inquiry Notice   A person interested in a property is also held by law to be responsible for making further inquiry of anyone giving visible or recorded notice. This is referred to as **inquiry notice** and is notice that the law presumes a reasonably diligent person would obtain by making further inquiry. For example, suppose you are considering the purchase of vacant acreage and, upon inspecting it, see a dirt road cutting across the land that is not mentioned in the public records. The law expects you to make further inquiry. The road may be a legal easement across the property. Another example is that anytime you buy rental property, you are expected to make inquiry as to the rights of the occupants. They may hold substantial rights you would not know about without asking them.

Actual Notice   **Actual notice** is knowledge that one has actually gained based on what one has seen, heard, read or observed. For example, if you read a deed from Jones to Smith, you have actual notice of the deed and Smith's claim to the property. If you go to the property and you see someone in possession, you have actual notice of his/her claim to be there.

Remember that anyone claiming an interest or right is expected to make it known either by recorded claim or visible use of the property. Anyone acquiring a right or interest is expected to look in the public records and go to the property to make a visual inspection for claims and inquire as to the extent of those claims.

All states have passed **recording acts** to provide for the recording of every instrument (i.e., document) by which an estate, interest or right in land is created, transferred or encumbered. Within each state, each county has a **public recorder's office,** known variously as the County Recorder's Office, County Clerk's Office, Circuit Court Clerk's Office, County Registrar's Office, or Bureau of Conveyances. The person in charge is called the recorder, clerk or registrar. Located at the seat of county government, each public recorder's office will record documents submitted to it that pertain to real property in that county. Thus a deed to property in XYZ County is recorded with the public recorder in XYZ County. Similarly, anyone seeking information regarding ownership of land in XYZ County would go to the recorder's office in XYZ County. Some cities also maintain record rooms where deeds are recorded. The recording process itself involves photocopying the documents and filing them for future reference.

Recording Acts

To encourage people to use public recording facilities, laws in each state decree that (1) a deed, mortgage or other instrument affecting real estate is not effective as far as subsequent purchasers and lenders are concerned if it is not recorded, and (2) prospective purchasers, mortgage lenders and the public at large are presumed notified when a document is recorded. Figure 6:1 illustrates the concept of public recording.

Although recording acts permit the recording of any estate, right or interest in land, many lesser rights are rarely recorded because of the cost and effort involved. Month-to-month rentals and leases for a year or less fall into this category. Consequently, only an on-site inspection would reveal their

Unrecorded Leases

Figure 6:1

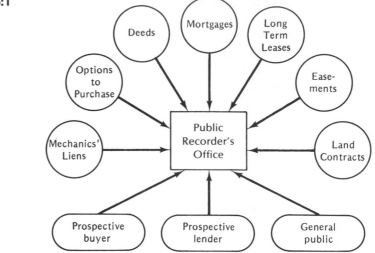

The public recorder's office serves as a central information station for changes in rights, estates, and interests in land.

existence, or the existence of any developing adverse possession or prescriptive easement claim.

Summary   To summarize, if you are a prospective purchaser (or lessee or lender), you are presumed by law to have inspected both the land itself and the public records to determine the present rights and interests of others. If you receive a deed, mortgage or other document relating to an estate, right or interest in land, have it *immediately* recorded in the county in which the land is located. If you hold an unrecorded rental or lease, you should visibly occupy the property.

REQUIREMENTS FOR   Nearly all states require that a document be **acknowledged**
RECORDING   before it is eligible to be recorded. A few states will permit **proper witnessing** as a substitute. Some states require both. The objective of these requirements is to make certain that the person who signs the document is the same person named in the document and that the signing was a free and voluntary act. This is done to reduce the possibility that forged or fraudulently induced documents will enter the public records.

In states that accept witnesses, the person executing the document signs in the presence of at least two witnesses, who in turn sign the document indicating that they are witnesses. To protect themselves, witnesses should not sign unless they know that the person named in the document is the person signing. In the event the witnessed signature is contested, the witnesses would be summoned to a court of law and under oath testify to the authenticity of the signature. An example of a witness statement is shown in Figure 6:2.

Witnesses

Figure 6:2

> *IN WITNESS whereof, the grantor has duly executed this deed in the presence of:*
>
> _____   _____
>   Witness   Grantor
>
> _____
>   Witness

An **acknowledgment** is a formal declaration by a person signing a document that he or she, in fact, did sign the document. Persons authorized to take acknowledgments include notaries public, recording office clerks, commissioners of deeds, judges of courts of record, justices of the peace, and certain others as authorized by state law. Commissioned military officers are authorized to take the acknowledgments of persons in the military; foreign ministers and consular agents can take acknowledgments abroad. If an acknowledgment is taken outside the state where the document will be recorded, either the recording county must already recognize the out-of-state official's authority or the out-of-state official must provide certification that he or she is qualified to take acknowledgments. The official seal or stamp of the notary on the acknowledgment normally fulfills this requirement.

Acknowledgment

An acknowledgment is illustrated in Figure 6:3. Notice the words; the person signing the document must personally appear before the notary *and* the notary states that he or she knows that person to be the person described in the document.

If they are strangers, the notary will require proof of identity. The person acknowledging the document does so by voluntarily signing it in the presence of the notary. Note that it is the signer who does the acknowledging, not the notary. At the completion of the signing, a notation of the event is made in a permanent record book kept by the notary. This record is later given to the state government for safekeeping.

Figure 6:3

ACKNOWLEDGMENT FOR AN INDIVIDUAL

STATE OF _____

COUNTY OF _____ ss

On this _____ *day of* _____ *, 19* _____ *, before me, the undersigned, a Notary Public in and for said State, personally appeared* [name of person executing document] *known to me to be the person whose name is subscribed to the within instrument and acknowledged that he (she) executed the same* [in some states, the words "by his (her) free act and deed" are added here]*. Witness my hand and official seal.*

[space for seal or stamp of the notary public]

_____
Signature of notary public

My commission expires _____
Date

*PUBLIC RECORDS
ORGANIZATION*

Each document brought to a public recorder's office for recordation is photocopied and then returned to its owner. The photocopy is placed in chronological order with photocopies of other documents. These are stamped with consecutive **page numbers** and bound into a **book.** These books are placed in chronological order on shelves that are open to the public for inspection. Before modern-day photocopy machines, public recorders' offices used large cameras with light-sensitive paper (roughly 1920 to 1955). Before that, documents were copied by hand using typewriters (roughly 1900 to 1920), and before that, copying was done in longhand. The current trend is toward entirely paperless systems wherein documents are recorded directly onto microfilm and then returned to their owners. Each document is assigned a book and page number or a reel and frame number. Microfilm readers are made available to anyone wanting to read the microfilms.

Filing incoming documents in chronological order is necessary to establish the chronological priority of documents; however, it does not provide an easy means for a person to locate all the documents relevant to a given parcel of land. Suppose that you are planning to purchase a parcel of land and want to make certain that the person selling it is the legally recognized owner. Without an index to guide you, you might have to inspect every document in every volume. Consequently, recording offices have developed systems of indexing. The two most commonly used are the grantor and grantee indexes, used by all states, and the tract index, used by nine states.

Of the two indexing systems, the **tract index** is the simplest to use. In it, one page is allocated to either a single parcel of land or to a group of parcels, called a tract. On that page you will find listed all the recorded deeds, mortgages and other documents at the recorder's office that relate to that parcel. A few words describing each document are given, together with the book and page where a photocopy of the document can be found.

Tract Indexes

Grantor and grantee indexes are alphabetical indexes and are usually bound in book form. There are several variations in use in the United States, but the basic principle is the same. For each calendar year, the **grantor index** lists in alphabetical order all grantors named in the documents recorded that year. Next to each grantor's name is the name of the grantee named in the document, the book and page where a photocopy of the document can be found, and a few words describing the document. The **grantee index** is arranged by grantee names and gives the name of the grantor and the location and description of the document.

Grantor and Grantee Indexes

Example of
Title Search

As an example of the application of the grantor and grantee indexes to a title search, suppose Robert T. Davis states that he is the owner of Lot 2, Block 2 in the Hilldale Tract in your county, and you would like to verify that statement in the public records. You begin by looking in the grantee index for his name, starting with this year's index and working backward in time. The purpose of this first step is to determine if the property was ever granted to Davis. If it was, you will find his name in the grantee index and, next to his name, a book and page reference to a photocopy of his deed to that parcel.

The Next Step

The next step is to look through the grantor index for the period of time starting from the moment he received his deed up to the present. If he has granted the property to someone else, Davis's name will be noted in the grantor index with a reference to the book and page where you can see a copy of the deed. (Davis could have reduced your efforts by showing you the actual deed conveying the lot to him. However, you would still have to inspect the grantor index for all dates subsequent to his taking title to see if he has conveyed title to a new grantee. If you do not have the name of the property owner, you would first have to go to the property tax office.)

Suppose your search shows that on July 1, 1974, in Book 2324, page 335, a warranty deed from John S. Miller to Davis, for Lot 2, Block 2 of the Hilldale Tract was recorded. Furthermore, you find that no subsequent deed showing Davis as grantor of this land has been recorded. Based on this, it would appear that Davis is the fee owner. However, you must inquire further to determine if Miller was the legally recognized owner of the property when he conveyed it to Davis. In other words, on what basis did Miller claim his right of ownership and, subsequently, the right to convey that ownership to Davis? The answer is that Miller based his claim to ownership on the deed he received from the previous owner.

CHAIN OF TITLE

By looking for Miller's name in the 1974 grantee index and then working backward in time through the yearly indexes, you will eventually find his name and a reference to Lot 2, Block 2 in the Hilldale Tract. Next to Miller's name you will find the name of the grantor and a reference to the book and page where the deed was recorded.

By looking for that name in the grantee index, you will locate the next previous deed. By continuing this process you can construct a chain of title. A **chain of title** shows the linkage of property ownership that connects the present owner to the original source of title. In most cases the chain starts with the original sale or grant of the land from the government to a private citizen. It is used to prove how title came to be **vested** in (i.e., possessed by) the current owner. Figure 6:4 illustrates the chain-of-title concept.

Sometimes, while tracing (running) a chain of title back through time, an apparent break or dead end will occur. This can happen because the grantor is an administrator, executor, sheriff or judge, or because the owner died, or because a mortgage against the land was foreclosed. To regain the title sequence, one must search outside the recorder's office by checking probate court records in the case of a death, or by checking civil court actions in the case of a foreclosure. The chain must be complete from the original source of title to the present owner. If there is a missing link the current "owner" does not have valid title to the property.

In addition to looking for grantors and grantees, a search must be made for any outstanding mortgages, judgments, actions pending, liens and unpaid taxes that may affect the title. With regard to searching for mortgages, states again differ slightly. Some place mortgages in the general grantor and grantee indexes, listing the borrower (mortgagor) as the grantor and the lender (mortgagee) as the grantee. Other states have separate index books for mortgagors and mortgagees. The process involves looking for the name of each owner in each annual **mortgagor index** published while that owner owned the land. If a mortgage is found, a further check will reveal whether or not it has been satisfied and released. If it has been released, the recorder's office will have noted on the margin of the recorded mortgage the book and page where the release is located. When one knows the lender's name, the mortgage location and its subsequent release can also be found by searching the **mortgagee index.**

Title may be clouded by judgments against recent owners, or there may be lawsuits pending that might later affect title. This information is found, respectively, on the **judgment rolls** and in the **lis pendens index** at the office of the county clerk.

Figure 6:4
CHAIN OF TITLE

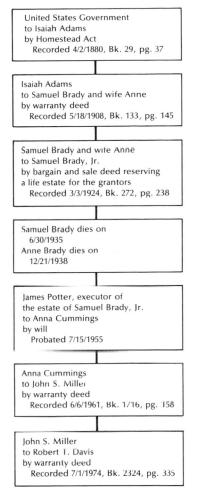

United States Government
to Isaiah Adams
by Homestead Act
    Recorded 4/2/1880, Bk. 29, pg. 37

Isaiah Adams
to Samuel Brady and wife Anne
by warranty deed
    Recorded 5/18/1908, Bk. 133, pg. 145

Samuel Brady and wife Anne
to Samuel Brady, Jr.
by bargain and sale deed reserving
a life estate for the grantors
    Recorded 3/3/1924, Bk. 272, pg. 238

Samuel Brady dies on
    6/30/1935
Anne Brady dies on
    12/21/1938

James Potter, executor of
the estate of Samuel Brady, Jr.
to Anna Cummings
by will
    Probated 7/15/1955

Anna Cummings
to John S. Miller
by warranty deed
    Recorded 6/6/1961, Bk. 1/16, pg. 158

John S. Miller
to Robert T. Davis
by warranty deed
    Recorded 7/1/1974, Bk. 2324, pg. 335

The term "lis pendens" is Latin for pending lawsuits. A separate search is made for **mechanic's liens** against the property by workmen and material suppliers. This step includes both a search of the public records and an on-site inspection of the land for any recent construction activity or material deliveries. A visit is made to the local tax assessor's office to check the tax rolls for unpaid property taxes. This does not exhaust all possible places that must be visited to do a thorough title search. A title searcher may also be found researching birth, marriage, divorce and adoption records, probate records, military files and federal tax liens in an effort to identify all the parties with an interest or potential interest in a given parcel of land and its improvements.

ABSTRACT OF TITLE   Although it is useful for the real estate practitioner to be able to find a name or document in the public records, full-scale title searching should be left to professionals. In a sparsely populated county, title searching is usually done on a part-time basis by an attorney. In more heavily populated counties a full-time **abstracter** will search the records. These persons are experts in the field of title search and for a fee will prepare an abstract of title for a parcel of land.

An **abstract of title** (or abstract) is a complete historical summary of all recorded documents affecting the title of a property. It recites in chronological order all recorded grants and conveyances and recorded easements, mortgages, wills, tax liens, judgments, pending lawsuits, marriages, divorces, etc., that might affect title. The abstracter will summarize each document, note the book and page (or other source) where it was found and give the date it was recorded or entered. In the case of a deed, for example, the abstracter identifies the grantor and grantee and type of deed, and gives a brief description of the property, any conditions or restrictions found in the deed, the date on the deed, the recording date and the book and page. For a mortgage, the abstracter identifies the borrower and lender, gives a brief description of the mortgage contents, and if repaid, the book and page location of the mortgage release document and its date of recordation. The abstract also includes a list of the public records searched, and not searched, in preparing the abstract.

The abstract is next sent to an attorney. Based on the attorney's knowledge of law and the legal history presented in the abstract, the attorney renders an **opinion** as to who the fee owner is and names anyone else with a legitimate right or interest in the property. This opinion, when written, signed by the attorney and attached to the abstract, is known in many states as a **certificate of title.** In some parts of the United States, this certified abstract is so valuable that it is brought up to date each time the property is sold and passed from seller to buyer. Generally speaking, the seller pays the cost of updating the abstract and getting a current attorney's opinion and certificate.

Despite the diligent efforts of abstracters and attorneys to give as accurate a picture of land ownership as possible, there is no guarantee that the finished abstract, or its certification, is completely accurate. Persons preparing abstracts and opinions are liable for mistakes due to their own negligence, and they can be sued if that negligence results in a loss to a client. But what if a recorded deed in the title chain is a forgery? Or what if a married person represented himself on a deed as a single person, thus resulting in unextinguished dower rights? Or what if a deed was executed by a minor or an otherwise legally incompetent person? Or, what if a deed contained an erroneous land description? Or what if a document was misfiled, or there were undisclosed heirs, or a missing will later came to light, or there was confusion because of similar names on documents? These situations can result in substantial losses to a property owner; yet the fault may not lie with the abstracter or attorney. Nor is the recorder's office responsible for verifying the contents of a deed, just that it shows an acceptable acknowledgment. The solution has been the organization of private companies to sell insurance against losses arising from title defects such as these as well as from errors in title examination.

"What Ifs"

Efforts to insure titles date back to the last century and were primarily organized by and for the benefit of attorneys who wanted protection from errors that they might make in the interpretation of abstracts. As time passed, **title insurance** (also called **title guarantee**) became available to anyone wishing to purchase it. The basic principle of title insurance is similar to

TITLE INSURANCE

any form of insurance: many persons pay a small amount into an insurance pool that is then available if any one of them should suffer a loss. In some parts of the United States, it is customary to purchase the title insurance policy through the attorney who reads and certifies the abstract. Elsewhere it is the custom to purchase it from a title company that combines the search and policy in one fee.

Title Report
When a title company receives a request for a title insurance policy, the first step is an examination of the public records. This is usually done by an abstracter or **title searcher** employed by the title company. A company attorney then reviews the findings and renders an opinion as to who the fee owner is and lists anyone else with a legitimate right or interest in the property such as a mortgage lender or easement holder. This information is typed up and becomes the **title report.** An example of a title report is illustrated in plain language in Figure 6:5. Sometimes called a **preliminary title report,** a title report does not commit the title company to insure the property nor is it an insurance policy. It does serve as the basis for a commitment to insure (also called a **binder**) and for the actual title insurance policy.

Notice how a title report differs from an abstract. Whereas an abstract is a chronologically arranged summary of all recorded events that have affected the title to a given parcel of land; a title report is more like a snapshot that shows the condition of title at a specific moment in time. A title report does not tell who the previous owners were; it only tells who the current owner is. A title report does not list all mortgage loans ever made against the land, but only those that have not been removed. The title report in Figure 6:5 states that a search of the public records shows Barbara Baker to be the fee owner of Lot 17, Block M, at the time the search was conducted.

In Part I, the report lists all recorded objections that could be found to Baker's fee estate, in this case, county property taxes, a mortgage and two easements. In Part II, the title company states that there may be certain unrecorded matters that either could not be or were not researched in preparing the report. Note in particular that the title company does not make a visual inspection of the land nor does it make a boundary survey. The buyer is responsible for making the on-site inspection

TITLE REPORT

The following is a report of the title to the land described in your application for a policy of title insurance.

LAND DESCRIPTION: Lot 17, Block M, Atwater's Addition, Jefferson County, State of _____ .

DATE AND TIME OF SEARCH: March 3, 19xx at 9:00 am

VESTEE: Barbara Baker, a single woman

ESTATE OR INTEREST: Fee simple

EXCEPTIONS:

PART I:

1. *A lien in favor of Jefferson County for property taxes, in the amount of $645.00, due on or before April 30, 19xx.*

2. *A mortgage in favor of the First National Bank in the amount of $30,000.00, recorded June 2, 1974, in Book 2975, Page 245 of the Official County Records.*

3. *An easement in favor of the Southern Telephone Company along the eastern five feet of said land for telephone poles and conduits. Recorded on June 15, 1946, in Book 1210, Page 113 of the Official County Records.*

4. *An easement in favor of Coastal States Gas and Electric Company along the north ten feet of said land for underground pipes. Recorded on June 16, 1946, in Book 1210, Page 137 of the Official County Records.*

PART II:

1. *Taxes or assessments not shown by the records of any taxing authority or by the public records.*

2. *Any facts, rights, interests, or claims that, although not shown by the public records, could be determined by inspection of the land and inquiry of persons in possession.*

3. *Discrepancies or conflicts in boundary lines or area or encroachments that would be shown by a survey, but which are not shown by the public records.*

4. *Easements, liens, or encumbrances not shown by the public records.*

5. *Zoning and governmental restrictions.*

6. *Unpatented mining claims and water rights or claims.*

125

and for hiring a surveyor if uncertain as to the land's boundaries. It is also the buyer's responsibility to check the zoning of the land and any other governmental restrictions on the land.

Although an owner may purchase a title insurance policy on his property at any time, it is most often purchased when real estate is sold. In connection with a sale, the title report is used to verify that the seller is indeed the owner. Additionally, the title report alerts the buyer and seller as to what needs to be done to bring title to the condition called for in the sales contract. For example, referring to Figure 6:5, the present owner (Barbara Baker) may have agreed to remove the existing mortgage so that the buyer can get a new and larger loan. Once this is done and the seller has delivered her deed to the buyer, the title company issues a title policy that deletes the old mortgage, adds the new mortgage, and shows the buyer as the owner. Note that title policies are often required by long-term lessees (10 years or more). They too want to know who has property rights superior to theirs.

Policy Premium

In some parts of the United States it is customary for the seller to pay the cost of both the title search and the insurance. In other parts, the seller pays for the search and the buyer for the insurance. In a relatively few instances, the buyer pays for both. Customarily, when a property is sold, it is insured for an amount equal to the purchase price. This insurance remains effective as long as the buyer (owner) or his heirs have an interest in the property.

The insurance premium consists of a single payment. On the average-priced home, the combined charge for a title report and title insurance amounts to about ½ of 1% of the amount of insurance purchased. Each time the property is sold, a new policy must be purchased. The old policy cannot be assigned to the new owner. Some title insurance companies offer reduced **reissue rates** if the previous owner's policy is available for updating.

Lender's Policy

Thus far our discussion of title insurance has centered on what is called an **owner's policy.** In addition, title insurance companies also offer what is called a **lender's policy.** This gives title protection to a lender who has taken real estate as collateral for a loan. There are three significant differences between an owner's title policy and a lender's title policy. First, the owner's policy is good for the full amount of coverage stated on the policy for as long as the insured or the insured's heirs have an interest in the property. In contrast, the lender's policy protects only for the amount owed on the mortgage loan. Thus, the coverage on a lender's policy declines and finally terminates when the loan is fully repaid. The second difference is that the lender's policy does not make exceptions for claims to ownership that could have been determined by physically inspecting the property. The third difference is that the lender's policy is assignable to subsequent holders of that same loan; an owner's policy is not.

The cost of a lender's policy (also known as a mortgagee's title policy or a loan policy) is similar to an owner's policy. Although the insurance company takes added risks by eliminating some exceptions found in the owner's policy, this is balanced by the fact that the liability decreases as the loan is repaid. When an owner's and a lender's policy are purchased at the same time, as in the case of a sale with new financing, the combined cost is only a few dollars more than the cost of the owner's policy alone. Note that the lender's policy covers only title problems. It does not insure that the loan will be repaid by the borrower.

Claims for Losses

The last item in a title policy is a statement as to how the company will handle claims. Although this "Conditions and Stipulations Section" is too lengthy to reproduce here, its key aspects can be summarized as follows. When an insured defect arises, the title insurance company reserves the right to either pay the loss or fight the claim in court. If it elects to fight, any legal costs the company incurs are in addition to the amount of coverage stated in the policy. If a loss is paid, the amount of coverage is reduced by that amount and any unused coverage is still in effect. If the company pays a loss, it acquires the right to collect from the party who caused the loss.

In comparing title insurance to other forms of insurance (e.g., life, fire, automobile), note that title insurance protects against something that has already happened but has not been discovered. A forged deed may result in a disagreement over ownership: the forgery is a fact of history, the insurance is in the event of its discovery. But in some cases the problem will never be discovered. For example, a married couple may be totally unaware of dower and curtesy rights and fail to extinguish them when they sell their property. If neither later claims them, when they die, the rights extinguish themselves, and the intervening property owners will have been unaffected.

Only a small part of the premiums collected by title insurance companies are used to pay claims. This is largely because title companies take great pains to maintain on their own premises complete photographic copies (often computer indexed) of the public records for each county in which they do business. These are called **title plants;** in many cases they are actually more complete and better organized than those available at the public recorder's office. The philosophy is that the better the quality of the title search, the fewer the claims that must be paid.

The Growth of Title Insurance

The title insurance business has mushroomed due to four important reasons. First, in a warranty deed the grantor makes several strongly worded covenants. As you will recall, the grantor covenants that he is the owner, that the grantee will not be disturbed in his possession, that there are no encumbrances except as stated in the deed, that the grantor will procure any necessary further assurance of title for the grantee, and that the grantor will bear the expense of defending the grantee's title and possession. Thus, signing a warranty deed places a great obligation on the grantor. By purchasing title insurance, the grantor can transfer that obligation to an insurance company.

Second, a grantee is also motivated to have title insurance. Even with a warranty deed, there is always the lingering question of whether or not the seller would be financially capable of making good on his covenants and warranties. They are useless if one cannot enforce them. Moreover, title insurance typically provides a grantee broader assurance than a warranty deed. For example, an outsider's claim must produce physical dispossession of the grantee before the covenant of quiet enjoyment is considered broken. Yet the same claim would be covered by title insurance before dispossession took place.

Third, the broad use of title insurance has made mortgage lending more attractive and borrowing a little easier and cheaper for real property owners. This is because title insurance has removed the risk of loss due to defective titles. As a result lenders can charge a lower rate of interest. Secondary market purchasers of loans such as FNMA and FHLMC (Chapter 12) require title insurance on every loan they buy.

Fourth, title insurance has made titles to land much more marketable. In nearly all real estate transactions the seller agrees to deliver **marketable title** to the buyer. Marketable title is title that is free from reasonable doubt as to who the owner is. Even when the seller makes no mention of the quality of the title, courts ordinarily require that marketable title be conveyed. To illustrate, a seller orders an abstract prepared, and it is read by an attorney who certifies it as showing marketable title. The buyer's attorney feels that certain technical defects in the title chain contradict certification as marketable. He advises the buyer to refuse to complete the sale. The line between what is and what is not marketable title can be exceedingly thin, and differences of legal opinion are quite possible. One means of breaking the stalemate is to locate a title insurance company that will insure the title as being marketable. If the defect is not serious, the insurance company will accept the risk. If it is a serious risk, the company may either accept the risk and increase the insurance fee or recommend a quiet title suit.

Marketable Title

When a title defect (also called a **cloud on the title** or a **title cloud**) must be removed, it is logical to remove it by using the path of least resistance. For example, if an abstract or title report shows unpaid property taxes, the buyer may require the seller to pay them in full before the deal is completed. A cloud on the title due to pending foreclosure proceedings can be halted by either bringing the loan payments up to date or negotiating with the lender for a new loan repayment schedule. Similarly, a distant relative with ownership rights might be willing, upon negotiation, to quitclaim them for a price.

QUIET TITLE SUIT

Sometimes a stronger means is necessary to remove title defects. For example, the distant relative may refuse to negotiate, or the lender may refuse to remove a mortgage lien despite pleas from the borrower that it has been paid, or there is a missing link in a chain of title. The solution is a **quiet title suit** (also called a quiet title action). Forty-seven states have enacted legislation that permits a property owner to ask the courts to hold hearings on the ownership of his land. At these hearings anyone claiming to have an interest or right to the land in question may present verbal or written evidence of that claim. A judge, acting on the evidence presented and the laws of his state, rules on the validity of each claim. The result is to legally recognize those with a genuine right or interest and to "quiet" those without.

THE TORRENS SYSTEM

Over a century ago, Sir Robert Torrens, a British administrator in Australia, devised an improved system of identifying land ownership. He was impressed by the relative simplicity of the British system of sailing-ship registration. The government maintained an official ships' registry that listed on a single page a ship's name, its owner, and any liens or encumbrances against it. Torrens felt land titles might be registered in a similar manner. The system he designed, known as the **Torrens system** of land title registration, starts with a landowner's application for registration and the preparation of an abstract. This is followed by a quiet title suit at which all parties named in the abstract and anyone else claiming a right or interest to the land in question may attend and be heard.

Torrens Certificate of Title

Based on the outcome of the suit, a government-appointed **registrar of titles** prepares a **certificate of title.** This certificate names the legally recognized fee owner and lists any legally recognized exceptions to that ownership, such as mortgages, easements, long-term leases, or life estates. The registrar keeps the original certificate of title and issues a duplicate to the fee owner. (Although they sound similar, a Torrens certificate of title is not the same as an attorney's certificate of title. The former shows ownership and claims against that ownership as established by a court of law. The latter is strictly an opinion of the condition of title.)

Once a title is registered, any subsequent liens or encumbrances against it must be entered on the registrar's copy of the certificate of title in order to give constructive notice. When a lien or encumbrance is removed, its notation on the certificate is canceled. In this manner, the entire concept of constructive notice for a given parcel of land is reduced to a single-page document open to public view at the registrar's office. This, Torrens argued, would make the whole process of title transfer much simpler and cheaper.

When registered land is conveyed, the grantor gives the grantee a deed. The grantee takes the deed to the registrar of titles, who transfers the title by canceling the grantor's certificate and issuing a new certificate in the name of the grantee. With a Torrens property this is the point in time when title is conveyed, not when the deed is delivered by the grantor to the grantee. Any liens or other encumbrances not removed at the same time are carried over from the old to the new certificate. The deed and certificate are kept by the registrar; the grantee receives a duplicate of the certificate. If the conveyance is accompanied by a new mortgage, it is noted on the new certificate, and a copy of the mortgage is retained by the registrar. Except for the quiet title suit aspect, the concept of land title registration is quite similar to that used in the United States for registering ownership of motor vehicles.

In the United States, the first state to have a land registration act was Illinois in 1895. Other states slowly followed, but often their laws were vague and cumbersome to the point of being useless. At one point, 20 states had land title registration acts, but since then 9 states have repealed their acts and only 11 remain. They are Hawaii, Illinois, Massachusetts, Minnesota, New York, Colorado, Georgia, North Carolina, Ohio, Virginia and Washington.

Adoption

In all 11 states Torrens co-exists with the regular recording procedures described earlier in this chapter. Thus it is possible for a house on one side of a street to be Torrens registered and a house across the street to be recorded the regular way. Also, it may be customary to use Torrens in just certain areas of the state. In Illinois, use has been concentrated in Cook County (the Chicago area); in Minnesota, in the Minneapolis area; in Massachusetts, the Boston area; and in New York, Suffolk County (eastern Long Island). In Hawaii, Torrens is used statewide, but primarily by large landowners and subdivision developers who want to clear up complex title problems. In the remaining 6 states the public has made relatively little use of land title registration. This limited adoption of Torrens is due, among other things, to the promotion, widespread availability and lower short-run cost of title insurance. (The quiet title suit can be costly.) Note too that although a state-run insurance fund is usually available to cover registration errors, some lenders do not feel this is adequate protection and require title insurance.

MARKETABLE TITLE ACTS

At least 10 states have a **Marketable Title Act.** This is *not* a system of title registration. Rather, it is legislation aimed at making abstracts easier to prepare and less prone to error. This is done by cutting off claims to rights or interests in land that have been inactive for longer than the act's statutory period. In Connecticut, Michigan, Utah, Vermont and Wisconsin, this is 40 years. Thus, in these states, a person who has an unbroken chain of title with no defects for at least 40 years is regarded by the law as having marketable title. Any defects more than 40 years old are outlawed. The result is to concentrate the title search process on the immediate past 40 years. Thus, abstracts can be produced with less effort and expense, and the chance for an error either by the abstracter or in the documents themselves is greatly reduced. This is particularly true in view of the fact that record-keeping procedures in the past were not as sophisticated as they are today.

The philosophy of a marketable title act is that a person has 40 years to come forward and make his claim known; if he does not, then he apparently does not consider it worth pursuing. As protection for a person actively pursuing a claim that is about to become more than 40 years old, the claim can be renewed for another 40 years by again recording notice of the claim in the public records. In certain situations, a title must be searched back more than 40 years (e.g., when there is a lease of more than 40-year duration or when no document affecting ownership has been recorded in over 40 years). In Nebraska the statutory period is 22 years; in Florida, North Carolina and Oklahoma it is 30 years; in Indiana, 50 years.

Marketable title acts do not eliminate the need for legal notice nor do they eliminate the role of adverse possession.

Match terms **a–v** with statements **1–22.**

a. *Abstract*
b. *Acknowledgment*
c. *Actual notice*
d. *Chain of title*
e. *Constructive notice*
f. *Grantor index*
g. *Inquiry Notice*
h. *Lender's title policy*
i. *Lis pendens index*
j. *Marketable title*
k. *Marketable title acts*

l. *Notary public*
m. *Opinion*
n. *Owner's title policy*
o. *Public recorder's office*
p. *Quiet title suit*
q. *Title cloud*
r. *Title insurance*
s. *Title report*
t. *Title searcher*
u. *Torrens system*
v. *Vested*

1. Knowledge gained from what one has seen, heard, read or observed.
2. Notice given by the public records and by visible possession coupled with the legal presumption that all persons are thereby notified.
3. A formal declaration, made in the presence of a notary public or other authorized individual, by a person affirming that he signed a document.
4. A person authorized to take acknowledgments.
5. A place where a person can enter documents affecting title to real estate.
6. A book at the public recorder's office that lists grantors alphabetically by name.
7. The linkage of ownership that connects the present owner to the original source of title.
8. A publicly available index whereby a person can learn of any pending lawsuits that may affect title.
9. A title defect.
10. A complete summary of all recorded documents affecting title to a given parcel of land.
11. Insurance to protect a property owner against monetary loss if his title is found to be imperfect.
12. A report made by a title insurance company showing current title condition.
13. A title policy written to protect a real estate lender.
14. Title that is free from reasonable doubt as to who the owner is.
15. Court-ordered hearings held to determine land ownership.
16. Laws that automatically cut off inactive claims to rights or interests in land.
17. A method of registering land titles that is similar to that of automobile ownership registration.

18. Claims to property rights the law presumes a reasonably diligent person would find through further investigation.
19. A statement as to the ownership of a property that is made by an attorney after reading the abstract.
20. An insurance policy against loss due to errors in title report preparation and inaccuracies in the public records.
21. A person trained and employed to examine the public records.
22. Possessed by; owned by.

QUESTIONS AND PROBLEMS

1. Explain constructive notice.
2. Where is the public recorder's office for your community located?
3. How much does your public recorder's office charge to record a deed? A mortgage? What requirements must a document meet before it will be accepted for recording?
4. What is the purpose of grantor and grantee indexes?
5. Why is it important that a title search be carried out in more places than just the county recorder's office?
6. What is the difference between a certificate of title issued by an attorney and a Torrens certificate of title?
7. How does a title report differ from an abstract?
8. What is the purpose of title insurance?
9. Thorsen sells his house to Williams. Williams moves in but for some reason does not record his deed. Thorsen discovers this and sells the house to an out-of-state investor who orders a title search, purchases an owner's title policy and records his deed. Thorsen then disappears with the money he received from both sales. Who is the loser when this scheme is discovered: Williams, the out-of-state investor or the title company? Why?
10. If you are located near the public recorder's office for your county, examine the records for a parcel of land (such as your home) and trace its ownership back through three owners.

Real Estate Counseling by **James Boykin.** (Prentice-Hall, 1984, 288 pages). Written for those who plan to offer real estate counseling services and those who plan to use those services. Nineteen professional counselors offer advice on real estate analysis and decision making.

Real Estate Law by **Frank Gibson,** et al. (Real Estate Education Co., 1983, 620 pages). Written for persons in or about to be in the real estate business. Includes estates in land, co-ownership, title, title transfer, recording, liens, land descriptions, brokerage, fair housing, purchase contracts, mortgage law, escrow, leaseholds, condominiums and real estate investments.

Title Insurance. Most title insurance companies have booklets explaining title insurance they give free to anyone who asks

"Title Insurance and the Lender" by **Robert Bates**. (*Guarantor,* Jul/Aug 83, page 8). Article points out how title insurance has helped make possible a large and efficient mortgage lending industry in the United States.

"What's Covered in a Title Policy" by **Frederick Romanski**. (*Real Estate Today,* Jul/Aug 83, page 43). Also in the same issue "What You Should Know About Title Insurance" and "Title Insurance: Buyer Security." These three articles explain the need for title insurance with eye-opening cases histories of title problems.

*   *   *

The following periodicals may also be of interest to you: *Lawyers Title News, MGIC Newsletter, National Property Law Digest, Your Public Lands* and *Title News.*

ADDITIONAL READINGS

Contract Law

Breach of contract: failure, without legal excuse, to perform as required by a contract

Competent parties: persons considered legally capable of entering into a binding contract

Consideration: an act or promise given in exchange for something

Contract: a legally enforceable agreement to do (or not to do) a particular thing

Duress: the application of force to obtain an agreement

Fraud: an act intended to deceive for the purpose of inducing another to give up something of value

Liquidated damages: an amount of money specified in a contract as compensation to be paid if the contract is not satisfactorily completed

Power of attorney: a document by which one person authorizes another to act on his behalf

Specific performance: contract performance according to the precise terms agreed upon

Void contract: a contract that has no binding effect on the parties who made it

Voidable contract: a contract that is able to be voided by one of its parties

A **contract** is a legally enforceable agreement to do (or not to do) a specific thing. In this chapter we shall see how a contract is created and what makes it legally binding. Topics covered include offer and acceptance, fraud, mistake, lawful objective, consideration, performance and breach of contract. In Chapter 8 we will turn our attention to the purchase contract, installment contract, lease with option to buy, first right of refusal and trade agreement.

HOW A CONTRACT IS CREATED

A contract may be either expressed or implied. An **expressed contract** occurs when the parties to the contract declare their intentions either orally or in writing. (The word **party** [plural, **parties**] is a legal term that refers to a person or group involved in a legal proceeding.) A lease or rental agreement, for example, is an expressed contract. The lessor (landlord) expresses his intent to permit the lessee (tenant) to use the premises, and the lessee agrees to pay rent in return. A contract to purchase real estate is also an expressed contract.

An **implied contract** is created by neither words nor writing but rather by actions of the parties indicating that they intend to create a contract. For example, when you step into a taxicab, you imply that you will pay the fare. The cab driver, by allowing you in the cab, implies that he will take you where you want to go. The same thing occurs at a restaurant. The presence of tables, silverware, menus, waiters and waitresses implies that you will be served food. When you order, you imply that you are going to pay when the bill is presented.

Bilateral Contract   A contract may be either bilateral or unilateral. A **bilateral contract** results when a promise is exchanged for a promise. For example, in a typical real estate sale, the buyer promises to pay the agreed price, and the seller promises to deliver title to the buyer. In a lease contract the lessor promises the use of the premises to the lessee, and the lessee promises to pay rent in return. A bilateral contract is basically an "I will do this *and* you will do that" arrangement. Depending on its wording, a listing can be a bilateral contract with the broker promising his/her best efforts to locate a buyer and the seller promising to pay a commission when a buyer is found. Or, a listing can be a unilateral contract, discussed next.

Unilateral Contract   A **unilateral contract** results when a promise is exchanged for performance. For instance, during a campaign to get more listings, a real estate office manager announces to the firm's sales staff that an extra $100 bonus will be paid for each saleable new listing. No promises or agreements are necessary from the salespersons. However, each time a salesperson performs by bringing in a saleable listing, he or she is entitled to the promised $100 bonus. An option to purchase is a unilateral contract until it is exercised, at which time it becomes a bilateral contract. A listing can be structured as a unilateral contract wherein the seller agrees to pay a commission if the broker finds a buyer. When the broker produces a buyer for the property the contract becomes bilateral. A unilateral contract is basically an "I will do this *if* you will do that" arrangement.

Forebearance   Most contract agreements are based on promises by the parties involved to act in some manner (pay money, provide services or deliver title). However, a contract can contain a promise to **forebear** (not to act) by one or more of its parties. For example, a lender may agree not to foreclose on a delinquent mortgage loan if the borrower agrees to a new payment schedule.

A **valid contract** is one that meets all the requirements of law. It is binding upon its parties and legally enforceable in a court of law. A **void contract** has no legal effect and, in fact, is not a contract at all. Even though the parties may have gone through the motions of attempting to make a contract, no legal rights are created and any party thereto may ignore it at his pleasure. A **voidable contract** is a contract that is able to be voided by one of its parties. In effect, it is a contract that is not binding on one of its parties. Examples of valid, void and voidable contracts are included throughout this chapter. Let us turn our attention to the requirements of a valid contract. *Valid, Void, Voidable*

For a contract to be **legally valid,** and hence binding and enforceable, the following five requirements must be met: *ESSENTIALS OF A VALID CONTRACT*

1. Legally competent parties.
2. Mutual agreement.
3. Lawful objective.
4. Consideration or cause.
5. Contract in writing when required by law.

If these conditions are met, any party to the contract may, if the need arises, call upon a court of law to either enforce the contract as written or award money damages for nonperformance. In reality, a properly written contract seldom ends in court because each party knows it will be enforced as written. It is the poorly written contract or the contract that borders between enforceable and unenforceable that ends in court. A judge must then decide if a contract actually exists and the obligations of each party. Using the courts, however, is an expensive and time-consuming method of interpreting an agreement. It is much better to have a correctly prepared contract in the first place. Let us look more closely at the five requirements of an enforceable contract.

For a contract to be legally enforceable, all parties entering into it must be legally competent. In deciding competency, the *COMPETENT PARTIES* law provides a mixture of objective and subjective standards. The most objective standard is that of age. A person must reach the age of **majority** to be legally capable of entering into a contract. **Minors** do not have contractual capability. In most states the age for entering into legally binding contracts is 18 years. The purpose of majority laws is to protect minors (also known as "infants" in legal terminology) from entering into contracts that they may not be old enough to understand. Most contracts made with minors, except those for necessities, such as food and clothing, are voidable by the minor at the minor's option. For example, a deed by a minor is voidable, although a minor can be a grantee. A minor wishing to disaffirm a contract must do so while still a minor or within a reasonable time after reaching majority. If not, the contract becomes valid. In some cases a contract with a minor is void. For example, a minor does not have the capacity to appoint someone to sell his property. Any contract to do so (called a power of attorney) is void from the outset. If a contract with a minor is required, it is still possible to obtain a binding contract by working through the minor's legal guardian.

Regarding intoxicated persons, if there was a deliberate attempt to intoxicate a person for the purpose of approving a contract, the intoxicated person, upon sobering up, can call upon the courts to cancel the contract. If the contracting party was voluntarily drunk to the point of incompetence, when he is sober he may ratify or deny the contract if he does so promptly. However, some courts look at the matter strictly from the standpoint of whether the intoxicated person had the capability of formulating the intent to enter into a contract. Obviously, there are some fine and subjective distinctions here, and a judge may interpret them differently than the parties to the contract. The points made in this paragraph also apply to a person who contracts while high on marijuana or other legal or illegal drugs.

Persons of unsound mind who have been declared incompetent by a judge may not make a valid contract, and any attempt to do so results in a void contract. The solution is to contract through the person appointed to act on behalf of the incompetent. If a person has not been judged legally incompetent but nonetheless appears incapable of understanding the transaction in question, he has no legal power to contract. Illegal aliens also lack legal competency. In some states persons convicted of felonies may not enter into valid contracts without the prior approval of the parole board.

An individual can give another person the power to act on his behalf: for example, to buy or sell land or sign a lease. The document that accomplishes this is called a **power of attorney.** The person holding the power of attorney is called an **attorney-in-fact.** With regard to real estate, a power of attorney must be in writing because the real estate documents to be signed must be in writing. Any document signed with a power of attorney should be executed as follows: "Paul Jones, principal, by Samuel Smith, agent, his attorney-in-fact." If the attorney-in-fact is to convey title to land, then the power of attorney must be acknowledged by the principal and recorded. The attorney-in-fact is legally competent to the extent of the powers granted to him by the principal as long as the principal remains legally competent, and as long as both of them are alive. The power of attorney can, of course, be terminated by the principal at any time. A recorded notice of revocation is needed to revoke a recorded power of attorney.

Power of Attorney

Corporations are considered legally competent parties. However, the individual contracting on behalf of the corporation must have authority from the board of directors. Some states also require that the corporate seal be affixed to contracts. A partnership can contract either in the name of the partnership or in the name of any of its general partners. Executors and administrators with court authorization can contract on behalf of estates, and trustees on behalf of trusts.

Corporations, etc.

The requirement of **mutual agreement** (also called **mutual consent,** or **mutual assent,** or **meeting of the minds**) means that there must be agreement to the provisions of the contract by the parties involved. In other words, there must be a mutual willingness to enter into a contract. The existence of mutual agreement is evidenced by the words and acts of the parties indicating that there is a valid offer and an unqualified acceptance. In addition, there must be no fraud, misrepresentation or mistake, and the agreement must be genuine and freely given. Let us consider each of these points in more detail.

MUTUAL AGREEMENT

Offer and Acceptance

Offer and acceptance requires that one party (the **offeror**) make an offer to another party (the **offeree**). The offeree must then communicate to the offeror that he accepts. The means of communication may be spoken or written or an action that implies acceptance. To illustrate, suppose that you own an apartment and want to rent it. You tell a prospective tenant that he can rent it for $495 per month beginning today, and inform him of the house rules, when the rent is due, how much the deposit is, and under what conditions it will be returned. This is the offer, and you, the offeror, have just communicated it to the offeree. One requirement of a valid contract is that the offer be specific in its terms. Mutual agreement cannot exist if the terms of the offer are vague or undisclosed and/or the offer does not clearly state the obligations of each party involved. If you were to say to a prospective tenant, "Do you want to rent this apartment?" without stating the price, and the prospective tenant said "Yes," the law would not consider this to be a contract.

Counteroffer

Upon receiving an offer, the offeree has three options: to agree to it, to reject it or to make a counteroffer. If he agrees, he must agree to every item in the offer. An offer is considered by law to be rejected if the offeree either rejects it outright or makes a change in the terms. If he makes any changes, it is a **counteroffer** and, although it would appear the offeree is only amending the offer before he will accept it, in reality the offeree has rejected it and is making an offer of his own. This now makes him the offeror. To illustrate, suppose that the prospective tenant for your apartment states that he would like to rent the apartment on the terms you offered, but instead of paying $495 per month, he wants to pay $475 per month. This is a rejection of your offer and the making of a counteroffer. You now have the right to accept or reject his offer. If you counter at $485 per month, this rejects his offer and you are again the offeror. If $485 is agreeable with the offeree, he must communicate his acceptance to you. In this case, a spoken "Yes, I'll take it" would be legally adequate.

If the offeree does not wish to accept the offer nor make a counteroffer, how is the offer terminated? He can simply say "No." However, if he says nothing, the passage of time will also terminate the offer. This can happen in two ways. The of-

feror can state how long the offer is to remain open; for example, "You have until 8:00 P.M. tonight to decide if you want the
apartment." If nothing is heard by 8:00 P.M., the offer terminates. When nothing is said as to how long the offer is to remain open, the courts will permit a reasonable amount of time,
depending on the situation. To illustrate, it is reasonable to
presume that if the prospective tenant leaves without accepting
your offer or arranging for time to think about it, your offer
terminates with his departure. This frees you to look for another tenant and make another offer without still being committed to the first offeree. When the offer is for the purchase of
real estate and no termination date is given, law courts have
ruled that a reasonable period of time might be several days or
a week.

The best policy is to state the length of time an offer is
open to avoid the problem of receiving two acceptances. Selecting a time period depends on the amount of time you feel
the offeree needs to decide and the length of time you are willing to tie up your property.

Mutual agreement requires that there be no fraud, misrep-   *Fraud*
resentation or mistake in the contract if it is to be valid. A **fraud**
is an act intended to deceive for the purpose of inducing another to part with something of value. It can be as blatant as
knowingly telling a lie or making a promise with no intention
of performance. For example, you are showing your apartment
and a prospective tenant asks if there is frequent bus service
nearby. There isn't, but you say, "Yes," as you sense this is
important and want to rent the apartment. The prospective
tenant rents the apartment, relying on this information from
you, and moves in. The next day he calls and says there is no
public transportation and he wants to break the rental agreement immediately. Because mutual agreement was lacking, the
tenant can **rescind** (cancel) the contract and get his money
back.

Fraud can also result from failing to disclose important information, thereby inducing someone to accept an offer. For
example, the day you show your apartment to a prospective
tenant the weather is dry. But you know that during every
rainstorm the tenant's automobile parking stall becomes a lake

of water 6 inches deep. This would qualify as a fraud if the prospective tenant was not made aware of the problem before agreeing to the rental contract. Once again, the law will permit the aggrieved party to rescind the contract. However, the tenant does not have to rescind the contract. If he likes the other features of the apartment enough, he can elect to live with the flooded parking stall.

If a real estate agent commits a fraud to make a sale and the deceived party later rescinds the sales contract, not only is the commission lost, but explanations will be necessary to the other parties of the contract. Moreover, state license laws provide for suspension or revocation of a real estate license for fraudulent acts.

Innocent **Innocent misrepresentation** differs from fraud (intentional
Misrepresentation misrepresentation) in that the party providing the wrong information is not doing so to deceive another for the purpose of reaching an agreement. To illustrate, suppose that over the past year you have observed that city buses stop near your apartment building. If you tell a prospective tenant that there is bus service, only to learn the day after the tenant moves in that service stopped last week, this is innocent misrepresentation. Although there was no dishonesty involved, the tenant still has the right to rescind the contract. If performance has not begun on the contract (in this case the tenant has not moved in), the injured party may give notice that he **disaffirms** (revokes) the contract. However, if the tenant wants to break the contract, he must do so in a timely manner; otherwise the law will presume that the situation is satisfactory to the tenant.

Mistake **Mistake** as applied in contract law has a very narrow meaning. It does not include innocent misrepresentation nor does it include ignorance, inability or poor judgment. If a person enters into a contract that he later regrets because he did not investigate it thoroughly enough, or because it did not turn out to be beneficial, the law will not grant relief to him on the grounds of mistake, even though he may now consider it was a "mistake" to have made the contract in the first place. Mistake as used in contract law arises from ambiguity in negotiations and mistake of material fact. For example, you offer to sell your mountain cabin to an acquaintance. He has never seen your cabin, and you give him instructions on how to get there to look at it. He returns and accepts your offer. However, he made a wrong turn and the cabin he looked at was not your cabin. A week later he discovers his error. The law considers this ambiguity in negotiations. In this case the buyer, in his mind, was purchasing a different cabin from the one the seller was selling; therefore, there is no mutual agreement and any contract signed is void.

To illustrate a mistake of fact, suppose that you show your apartment to a prospective tenant and tell him that he must let you know by tomorrow if he wants to rent it. The next day he visits you and together you enter into a rental contract. Although neither of you is aware of it, there has just been a serious fire in the apartment. Since a fire-gutted apartment is not what the two of you had in mind when the rental contract was signed, there is no mutual agreement.

Occasionally, "mistake of law" will be claimed as grounds for relief from a contract. However, mistake as to one's legal rights in a contract is not generally accepted by courts of law unless it is coupled with a mistake of fact. Ignorance of the law is not considered a mistake.

Mutual agreement also requires that the parties express **contractual intent.** This means that their intention is to be bound by the agreement, thus precluding jokes or jests from becoming valid contracts.

Contractual Intent

The last requirement of mutual agreement is that the offer and acceptance be genuine and freely given. **Duress** (use of force), **menace** (threat of violence) or **undue influence** (unfair advantage) cannot be used to obtain agreement. The law permits a contract made under any of these conditions to be revoked by the aggrieved party.

Duress

To be enforceable, a contract cannot call for the breaking of laws. This is because a court of law cannot be called upon to enforce a contract that requires that a law be broken. Such a contract is void, or if already in operation, it is unenforceable in a court of law. For example, a debt contract requiring an interest rate in excess of that allowed by state law would be void. If the borrower had started repaying the debt and then later

LAWFUL OBJECTIVE

stopped, the lender would not be able to look to the courts to enforce collection of the balance. Contracts contrary to good morals and general public policy are also unenforceable.

CONSIDERATION

For an agreement to be enforceable it must be supported by **consideration.** The purpose of requiring consideration is to demonstrate that a bargain has been struck between the parties to the contract. The size, quantity, nature or amount of what is being exchanged is irrelevant as long as it is present. Consideration is usually something of value such as a promise to do something, money, property or personal services. For example, there can be an exchange of a promise for a promise, money for a promise, money for property, goods for services, and the like. Forebearance also qualifies as consideration.

Exchange of Promises

In a typical offer to purchase a home, the consideration is the mutual exchange of promises by the buyer and seller to obligate themselves to do something they were not previously required to do. In other words, the seller agrees to sell on the terms agreed and the buyer agrees to buy the property on those same terms. The earnest money the buyer may put down is not the consideration necessary to make the contract valid. Rather, earnest money is a tangible indication of the buyer's intent and may become a source of compensation (damages) to the seller in the event the buyer does not carry out his promises.

In a deed the consideration requirement is usually met with a statement such as "For ten dollars and other good and valuable consideration." Also, the purchase contract is part of the consideration and is legally merged into the deed. In a lease, the periodic payment of rent is the consideration for the use of the premises.

Valuable Consideration

A contract fails to be legally binding if consideration is lacking from any party to the contract. The legal philosophy is that a person cannot promise to do something of value for someone else without receiving in turn some form of consideration. Stated another way, each party must give up something, i.e., each must suffer a detriment. For example, if I promise to give you my car, the consideration requirement is not met since you promise nothing in return. But if I promise to give you my car when you take me to Hawaii, the consideration requirement is met. As a group, money, plus promises, property, legal rights, services and forebearance, if they are worth money, are classified as **valuable consideration.**

What about outright gifts such as the gift of real property from a parent to a child based solely on love and affection? Although this is not valuable consideration, it is nonetheless **good consideration** and as such fulfills the legal requirement that consideration be present. The law generally will not inquire as to the adequacy of the consideration unless there is evidence of fraud, mistake, duress, threat or undue influence. For instance, if a man gave away his property or sold it very cheaply to keep it from his creditors, the creditors could ask the courts to set aside those transfers.

Good Consideration

If the word "consideration" continues to be confusing to you, it is because the word has three meanings in real estate. The first is consideration from the standpoint of a legal requirement for a valid contract. You may wish to think of this form of consideration as **legal consideration** or **cause.** The second meaning is money. For example, the consideration upon which conveyance taxes are charged is the amount of money exchanged in the transaction. The third meaning is acknowledgment. Thus the phrase "in consideration of ten dollars" means "in acknowledgment of" or "in receipt of."

Multiple Meanings of the Word "Consideration"

In each state there is a law that is commonly known as a **statute of frauds.** Its purpose is to prevent frauds by requiring that all contracts for the sale of land, or an interest in land, be in writing and signed to be enforceable in a court of law. This includes such things as offers, acceptances, binders, land contracts, deeds, escrows and options to purchase. Mortgages and trust deeds (and their accompanying bonds and notes) and leases for more than one year must also be in writing to be enforceable. In addition, most states have adopted the **Uniform Commercial Code** that requires, among other things, that the sale of personal property with value in excess of $500 be in writing. Most states also require that real estate listing contracts be expressed in writing.

CONTRACT IN WRITING

Purpose   The purpose of requiring that a contract be written and signed is to prevent perjury and fraudulent attempts to seek legal enforcement of a contract that never existed. It is not necessary that a contract be a single formal document. It can consist of a series of signed letters or memoranda as long as the essentials of a valid contract are present. Note that the requirement for a written contract relates only to the enforceability of the contract. Thus if Mr. Colby orally agrees to sell his land to Mr. Conan and they carry out the deal, neither can come back after the contract was performed and ask a court to rescind the deal because the agreement to sell was oral.

The most common real estate contract that does not need to be in writing to be enforceable is a month-to-month rental agreement that can be terminated by either landlord or tenant on one-month notice. Nonetheless, most are in writing because people tend to forget oral promises. While the unhappy party can go to court, the judge may have a difficult time determining what oral promises were made, particularly if there were no witnesses other than the parties to the agreement. Hence, it is advisable to put all important contracts in writing and for each party to recognize the agreement by signing it. If a party is a corporation, most states require the signatures of two corporate officers plus the corporate seal. It is also customary to date written contracts, although most can be enforced without showing the date the agreement was reached.

A written contract will supersede an oral one. Thus, if two parties orally promise one thing and then write and sign something else, the written contract will prevail. This has been the basis for many complaints against overzealous real estate agents who make oral promises that do not appear anywhere in the written sales contract.

Parol Evidence Rule   Under certain circumstances the **parol evidence rule** permits oral evidence to complete an otherwise incomplete or ambiguous written contract. However, the application of this rule is quite narrow. If a contract is complete and clear in its intent, the courts presume that what the parties put into writing is what they agreed upon.

Executory, Executed,   A contract which is in the process of being carried out is
Execute   said to be **executory,** i.e., in the process of being performed.

Once completed, it is said to be **executed,** i.e., performance has taken place. This may refer to the signing of the contract or to its completed performance depending on what the contract requires. The word **execute,** a much more frequently used term, refers to the process of completing, performing or carrying out something. Thus, you execute a document when you sign it, and this is the most common use of the term. Once signed, you execute the terms of the contract by carrying out its terms.

PERFORMANCE AND DISCHARGE OF CONTRACTS

Most contracts are discharged by being fully performed by the contracting parties in accordance with the contract terms. However, alternatives are open to the parties of the contract. One is to sell or otherwise **assign** the contract to another party. Unless prohibited by the contract, rights, benefits and obligations under a contract can be assigned to someone else. The original party to the contract, however, still remains ultimately liable for its performance. Note, too, that an assignment is a contract in itself and must meet all the essential contract requirements to be enforceable. A common example of an assignment occurs when a lessee wants to move out and sells his lease to another party. When a contract creates a personal obligation, such as a listing agreement with a broker, an assignment may not be made.

Novation

A contract can also be performed by **novation.** Novation is the substitution of a new contract between the same or new parties. For example, novation occurs when a buyer assumes a seller's loan, *and* the lender releases the seller from the loan contract. With novation the departing party is released from the obligation to complete the contract.

If the objective of a contract becomes legally impossible to accomplish, the law will consider the contract discharged. For example, a new legislative statute may forbid what the contract originally intended. If the parties mutually agree to cancel their contract before it is executed, this too is a form of discharge. For instance, you sign a 5-year lease to pay $900 per month for an office. Three years later you find a better location and want to move. Meanwhile, rents for similar offices in your building have increased to $1,000 per month. Under these conditions the landlord might be happy to agree to cancel your lease.

Deceased Party   If one of the contracting parties dies, a contract is considered discharged if it calls for some specific act that only the dead person could have performed. For example, if you hired a free-lance gardener to tend your landscaping and he died, the contract would be discharged. However, if your contract is with a firm that employs other gardeners who can do the job, the contract would still be valid.

If there is a valid purchase contract and one party dies, the contract is usually enforceable against the estate because the estate has the authority to carry out the deceased's affairs. Similarly, if a person mortgages his or her property and dies, the estate must continue the payments or lose the property.

Property Damage   Under the **Uniform Vendor and Purchaser Risk Act,** if neither possession nor title has passed and there is material destruction to the property, the seller cannot enforce the contract and the purchaser is entitled to his money back. If damage is minor and promptly repaired by the seller, the contract would still be enforceable. If either title or possession has passed and destruction occurs, the purchaser is not relieved of his duty to pay the price, nor is he entitled to a refund of money already paid.

BREACH OF CONTRACT   When one party fails to perform as required by a contract and the law does not recognize the reason for failure to be a valid excuse, there is a **breach of contract.** The wronged or innocent party has six alternatives: (1) accept partial performance, (2) rescind the contract unilaterally, (3) sue for specific performance, (4) sue for money damages, (5) accept liquidated money damages, or (6) mutually rescind the contract. Let us consider each of these.

Partial Performance   **Partial performance** may be acceptable to the innocent party because there may not be a great deal at stake or because the innocent party feels that the time and effort to sue would not be worth the rewards. Suppose that you contracted with a roofing repairman to fix your roof for $400. When he was finished you paid him. A week later you discover a spot that he had agreed to fix, but missed. After many futile phone calls, you accept the breach and consider the contract discharged because it is easier to fix the spot yourself than to keep pursuing the repairman.

Under certain circumstances, the innocent party can **unilaterally rescind** a contract. That is, the innocent party can take the position that if the other party is not going to perform his obligations, then the innocent party will not either. An example would be a rent strike in retaliation to a landlord who fails to keep the premises habitable. Unilateral rescission should be resorted to only after consulting an attorney.

Unilateral Rescission

If the damages to the innocent party can be reasonably expressed in terms of money, the innocent party can sue for **money damages.** For example, you rent an apartment to a tenant. As part of the rental contract you furnish the refrigerator and freezer unit. While the tenant is on vacation, the unit breaks down and $200 worth of frozen meat and other perishables spoil. Since your obligation under the contract is to provide the tenant with a working refrigerator–freezer, the tenant can sue you for $200 in money damages. He can also recover interest on the money awarded to him from the day of the loss to the day you reimburse him.

Lawsuit for Money Damages

A lawsuit for **specific performance** is an action in court by the innocent party to force the breaching party to carry out the remainder of the contract according to the precise terms, price and conditions agreed upon. For example, you make an offer to purchase a parcel of land and the seller accepts. A written contract is prepared and signed by both of you. If you carry out all your obligations under the contract, but the seller has a change of mind and refuses to deliver title to you, you may bring a lawsuit against the seller for specific performance. In reviewing your suit, the court will determine if the contract is valid and legal, if you have carried out your duties under the contract, and if the contract is just and reasonable. If you win your lawsuit, the court will force the seller to deliver title to you as specified in the contract.

Lawsuit for Specific Performance

Note the difference between suing for money damages and suing for specific performance. When money can be used to re-

Comparison

store one's position (as in the case of the tenant who can buy $200 worth of fresh food), a suit for money damages is appropriate. In situations where money cannot provide an adequate remedy, and this is often the case in real estate because no two properties are exactly alike, specific performance is appropriate. Notice, too, that the mere existence of the legal rights of the wronged party is often enough to gain cooperation. In the case of the spoiled food, you would give the tenant the value of the lost food before spending time and money in court to hear a judge tell you to do the same thing. A threat of a lawsuit will often bring the desired results if the defendant knows that the law will side with the wronged party. The cases that do go to court are usually those in which the identity of the wronged party and/or the extent of the damages is not clear.

Liquidated Damages

The parties to a contract may decide in advance the amount of damages to be paid in the event either party breaches the contract. An example is an offer to purchase real estate that includes a statement to the effect that, once the seller accepts the offer, if the buyer fails to complete the purchase, the seller may keep the buyer's deposit (the earnest money) as **liquidated damages.** If a broker is involved, seller and broker usually agree to divide the damages, thus compensating the seller for damages and the broker for time and effort. Another case of liquidated damages occurs when a builder promises to finish a building by a certain date or pay the party that hired him a certain number of dollars per day until it is completed. This impresses upon the builder the need for prompt completion and compensates the property owner for losses due to the delay.

Mutual Rescission

Specific performance, money damages and liquidated damages are all designed to aid the innocent party in the event of a breach of contract. However, as a practical matter the time and cost of pursuing a remedy in a court of law may sometimes exceed the benefits to be derived. Moreover, there is the possibility the judge for your case may not agree with your point of view. Therefore, even though you are the innocent party and you feel you have a legitimate case that can be pursued in the courts, you may find it more practical to agree with the other party (or parties) to simply rescind (i.e., cancel or annul) the contract. To properly protect everyone involved, the agreement to cancel must be in writing and signed by the parties to the original contract. Properly executed, **mutual rescission** relieves the parties to the contract from their obligations to each other.

An alternative to mutual rescission is novation. As noted earlier, this is the substitution of a new contract for an existing one. Novation provides a middle ground between suing and rescinding. Thus the breaching party may be willing to complete the contract provided the innocent party will voluntarily make certain changes in it. If this is acceptable, the changes should be put into writing (or the contract redrafted) and then signed by the parties involved.

The **statute of limitations** limits by law the amount of time a wronged party has to seek the aid of a court in obtaining justice. The aggrieved party must start legal proceedings within a certain period of time or the courts will not help him. The amount of time varies from state to state and by type of legal action involved. However, time limits of 3 to 7 years are typical for breach of contract.

STATUTE OF LIMITATIONS

As was pointed out at the beginning of this chapter, one can incur contractual obligations by implication as well as by oral or written contracts. Home builders and real estate agents provide two timely examples. For many years, if a homeowner discovered poor design or workmanship after he had bought a new home, it was his problem. The philosophy was **caveat emptor,** let the buyer beware *before* he buys. Today, courts of law find that in building a home and offering it for sale, the builder simultaneously implies that it is fit for living. Thus, if a builder installs a toilet in a bathroom, the implication is that it will work. In fact, many states have now passed legislation that makes builders liable for their work for one year.

Similarly, real estate agent trade organizations, such as the National Association of Realtors and state and local Realtor associations, are constantly working to elevate the status of real estate brokers and salespersons to that of a competent professional in the public's mind. But as professional status is gained, there is an implied obligation to dispense professional-quality

IMPLIED OBLIGATIONS

service. Thus, an individual agent is not only responsible for acting in accordance with written laws, but will also be held responsible for being competent and knowledgeable. Once recognized as a professional by the public, the real estate agent will not be able to plead ignorance.

In view of the present trend toward consumer protection, the concept of "Let the buyer beware" is being replaced with "Let the seller beware" and "Let the agent beware."

VOCABULARY REVIEW

Match terms **a–z** *with statements* **1–26.**

a. *Assign*	**n.** *Minor*
b. *Attorney-in-fact*	**o.** *Money damages*
c. *Breach*	**p.** *Mutual agreement*
d. *Competent party*	**q.** *Novation*
e. *Consideration*	**r.** *Offeror*
f. *Contract*	**s.** *Party*
g. *Counteroffer*	**t.** *Rescind*
h. *Disaffirm*	**u.** *Specific performance*
i. *Duress*	**v.** *Statute of frauds*
j. *Execute*	**w.** *Statute of limitations*
k. *Forebear*	**x.** *Unilateral contract*
l. *Fraud*	**y.** *Void contract*
m. *Liquidated damages*	**z.** *Voidable contract*

1. A legally enforceable agreement to do (or not to do) something.
2. A contract in which one party makes a promise or begins performance without first receiving any promise to perform from the other.
3. An act intended to deceive for the purpose of inducing another to part with something of value.
4. A person who is considered legally capable of entering into a contract.
5. A person who is not old enough to enter into legally binding contracts.
6. A contract that is not legally binding on any of the parties that made it.
7. The party who makes an offer.
8. An offer made in response to an offer.
9. To cancel a contract and restore the parties involved to their respective positions before the contract was made.
10. Use of force to obtain contract agreement.

11. Not to act.
12. To transfer one's rights in a contract to another person.
13. Damages that can be measured in and compensated by money.
14. Failure, without legal excuse, to perform any promise called for in a contract.
15. Contract performance according to the precise terms agreed upon.
16. A sum of money called for in a contract that is to be paid if the contract is breached.
17. Laws that set forth the period of time within which a lawsuit must be filed.
18. A person or group involved in a legal proceeding.
19. A contract that is able to be voided by one of its parties.
20. The person holding a power of attorney on behalf of another.
21. A meeting of the minds.
22. To revoke.
23. An act or promise given in exchange for something.
24. Requires all contracts for the sale of land to be in writing to be enforceable in a court of law.
25. To complete, perform or carry out something.
26. The substitution of a new contract for an existing one.

QUESTIONS AND PROBLEMS

1. What is the difference between an expressed contract and an implied contract? Give an example of each.
2. Name the five requirements of a legally valid contract.
3. What is the difference between a void contract and a void-able contract?
4. Give four examples of persons not considered legally competent to enter into contracts.
5. How can an offer be terminated prior to its acceptance?
6. What does the word "mistake" mean when applied to contract law?
7. Why must consideration be present for a legally binding contract to exist? Give examples of three types of consideration.
8. If a contract is legally unenforceable, are the parties to the contract stopped from performing it? Why or why not?
9. If a breach of contract occurs, what alternatives are open to the parties to the contract?
10. Assume that a breach of contract has occurred and the wronged party intends to file a lawsuit over the matter. What factors would he consider in deciding whether to sue for money damages or for specific performance?

ADDITIONAL
READINGS

Homeowners Checklist by **Robert DeHeer.** (Lord Publishing, 1980, 80 pages). Contains numerous checklists, with extra copies, to be used when choosing a house or condominium. Also by the same author and publisher is the *Homeowners Book* which deals with the selection, purchase, financing, taxes, insurance, maintenance, insulation, safety and resale of a home.

Real Estate Law by **Charles Jacobus.** (Reston, 1986, 350 pages). A guide to the legal aspects of sales, mortgages, conveyances, exchanges and leases. Examines broker–lawyer relationship. Identifies various legal entanglements and methods to avoid them.

Real Estate Law by **Marianne Jennings.** (Kent, 1985, 657 pages). Emphasizes real estate law application and how legal problems can be solved. Narrative style followed by numerous court cases to illustrate the points made. Chapter 9 deals with conveyancing and Chapter 11 with purchase contracts.

Real Estate Principles and Practices, 10th ed. by **Alfred Ring** and **Jerome Dasso.** (Prentice-Hall, 1985, 650 pages). A decision-making and analysis approach to real estate from the point of view of the investor. Book covers ownership rights, conveying those rights, financing, markets, investment, ownership and management.

"The Business of Writing" by **Douglas Mueller.** (*Real Estate Today*, Nov/Dec 84, page 34). Article explains techniques of clear writing for the real estate business. Includes explanation of the Fog Index and how to apply it to your writing. Emphasizes the need to express, not impress, when writing.

* * *

The following periodicals may also be of interest to you: *Real Estate Law Journal, Real Estate Law Report, Real Estate Letter, Real Estate Magazine, Real Estate Newsletter* and *Strategic Real Estate.*

Real Estate Sales Contracts

Binder: a short purchase contract used to secure a real estate transaction until a more formal contract can be signed

Counteroffer: an offer made in response to an offer

Default: failure to perform a legal duty; such as failure to carry out the terms of a contract

Deposit receipt: a receipt given for a deposit that accompanies an offer to purchase; also refers to a purchase contract that includes a deposit receipt

Earnest money deposit: money that accompanies an offer to purchase as evidence of good faith

Equitable title: the right to demand that title be conveyed upon payment of the purchase price

Installment contract: a method of selling and financing property whereby the seller retains title but the buyer takes possession while making the payments

"Lease-option": allows the tenant to buy the property at preset price and terms for a given period of time

Right of first refusal: the right to match or better an offer before the property is sold to someone else

"Time is of the essence": a phrase that means that the time limits of a contract must be faithfully observed or the contract is voidable

The present chapter focuses on contracts used to initiate the sale of real estate. Chiefly we will look at the purchase contract, the installment contract and the lease with option to buy. There will also be brief discussions of a real estate binder, letter of intent, first right of refusal and real estate exchange.

PURPOSE OF SALES CONTRACTS

What is the purpose of a real estate sales contract? If a buyer and a seller agree on a price, why can't the buyer hand the seller the necessary money and the seller simultaneously hand the buyer a deed? The main reason is that the buyer needs time to ascertain that the seller is, in fact, legally capable of conveying title. To protect himself, the buyer will enter into a written and signed contract with the seller, promising that the purchase price will be paid only after title has been searched and found to be in satisfactory condition. The seller in turn promises to deliver a deed to the buyer when the buyer has paid his money. This exchange of promises forms the legal consideration of the contract. A contract also gives the buyer time to arrange financing and to specify how such matters as taxes, mortgage debts, existing leases and fire insurance on the property will be discharged.

A properly prepared contract commits each party to its terms. Once a sales contract is in writing and signed, the seller cannot change his mind and sell to another person. He is obligated to convey title to the buyer when the buyer has performed everything required of him by the contract. Likewise, the buyer must carry out his promises, including paying for the property, provided the seller has done everything required by the contract.

PURCHASE CONTRACTS

Variously known as a purchase contract, deposit receipt, offer and acceptance, purchase offer, or purchase and sales agreement, these preprinted forms contain four key parts: (1) provision for the buyer's earnest money deposit, (2) the buyer's offer to purchase, (3) the acceptance of the offer by the seller, and (4) provisions for the payment of a brokerage commission.

Figure 8:1 illustrates in simplified language the highlights of a real estate purchase contract.* The purchase contract begins at ① and ② by identifying the location and date of the deposit and offer. At ③, the name of the buyer is written, and at ④, the name of the property owner (seller). At ⑤, the property for which the buyer is making his offer is described. Although the street address and type of property (in this case a house) are not necessary to the validity of the contract, this information is often included for convenience in locating the property. The legal description that follows is crucial. Care must be taken to make certain that it is correct.

---

* This illustration has been prepared for discussion purposes only and not as a form to copy and use in a real estate sale. For that purpose, you must use a contract specifically legal in your state.

REAL ESTATE PURCHASE CONTRACT

①*City of* ___Riverdale___ *, State of* _____ ,
___October 10, 19xx___ ② .

③ ___Samson Byers___ *(herein called the Buyer) agrees to purchase and* ④___William Ohner and Sarah Ohner___ *(herein called the Seller) agree to sell the following described real property located in the City of* ⑤___Riverdale___ *, County of* ___Lakeside___ ,
State of _____ , _____a single-family dwelling_____
commonly known as ___1704 Main Street___ *, and legally described as* ___Lot 21, Block C of Madison's Subdivision as___ ___per map in Survey Book 10, page 51, in the Office of the___ ___County Recorder of said County___ .

⑥*The total purchase price is* ___ninety thousand___ *Dollars* ___($90,000.00)___, *payable as follows:* ___Three thousand dollars ($3,000.00) is given today as an earnest money deposit, receipt of which is hereby acknowledged. An additional $15,000.00 is to be placed into escrow by the Buyer before the closing date. The remaining $72,000.00 is to be by way of a new mortgage on said property___ .

⑦*Seller will deliver to the Buyer a* ___warranty___ *deed to said property. Seller will furnish to the Buyer at the* ___Seller's___ *expense a standard American Land Title Association title insurance policy issued by* ___First Security Title Company___ *showing title vested in the Buyer and that the Seller is conveying title free of liens, encumbrances, easements, rights and conditions except as follows:* ___People's Gas and Electric Company utility easement along eastern five feet of said lot___ .

⑧*The escrow agent shall be* ___First Security Title Company___ *and escrow instructions shall be signed by the Buyer and Seller and delivered to escrow within five days upon receipt thereof. The close of escrow shall be* ___45___ *days after the date of mutual agreement to this contract.*

⑨*Property taxes, property insurance, mortgage interest, income and expense items shall be prorated as of* ___the close of escrow___ .

Figure 8:1 *continued*

⑩*Any outstanding bonds or assessments on the property shall be* <u>paid by the Seller</u> .

⑪*Any existing mortgage indebtedness against the property is to be* <u>paid by the Seller</u> .

⑫*Seller will provide Buyer with a report from a licensed pest control inspector that the property is free of termites and wood rot. The cost of the report and any corrective work deemed necessary by the report are to be paid for by the* <u>Seller</u> .

⑬*Possession of the property is to be delivered to the Buyer* <u>upon close of escrow</u> .

⑭*Escrow expenses shall be* <u>shared equally by the Buyer and Seller</u> .

⑮*Conveyance tax to be paid by* <u>Seller</u> .

⑯The earnest money deposit is to be held <u>in escrow</u> .

⑰*All attached floor coverings, attached television antenna, window screens, screen doors, storm windows, storm doors, plumbing and lighting fixtures (except floor, standing and swag lamps), curtain rods, shades, venetian blinds, bathroom fixtures, trees, plants, shrubbery, water heaters, awnings, built-in heating, ventilating, and cooling systems, built-in stoves and ranges, and fences now on the premises shall be included unless otherwise noted. Any leased fixtures on the premises are not included unless specifically stated.*

⑱*Other provisions:* <u>The purchase of this property is subject to the Buyer obtaining a mortgage loan on this property in the amount of $72,000.00 or more, with a maturity date of at least 25 years, at an interest rate no higher than 11½% per year and loan fees not to exceed two points. Purchase price to include the refrigerator currently on the premises. Purchase is subject to buyer's approval of a qualified building inspector's report. Said report to be obtained within 7 days at Buyer's expense.</u>

⑲*If the improvements on the property are destroyed or materially damaged prior to the close of escrow, or if the Buyer is unable to obtain financing as stated herein, or if the Seller is unable to deliver title as promised, then the Buyer, at his option, may terminate this agreement and the depo. it made by him shall be re-*

turned to him in full. If the Seller fails to fulfill any of the other agreements made herein, the Buyer may terminate this agreement with full refund of deposit, accept lesser performance, or sue for specific performance.

㉔ If this purchase is not completed by reason of the Buyer's default, the seller is released from his obligation to sell to the Buyer and shall retain the deposit money as his sole right to damages.

㉑ Upon the signature of the Buyer, this document becomes an offer to the Seller to purchase the property described herein. The Seller has until ___11:00 p.m., October 13, 19xx___ to indicate acceptance of this offer by signing and delivering it to the Buyer. If acceptance is not received by that time, this offer shall be deemed revoked and the deposit shall be returned in full to the Buyer.

㉒ Time is of the essence in this contract.

Real Estate Broker ___Riverdale Realty Company___ .

By ㉓ *Shirley Newhouse* .

Address ___1234 Riverdale Blvd.___ Telephone ___333-1234___ .

㉔ The undersigned offers and agrees to buy the above described property on the terms and conditions stated herein and acknowledges receipt of a copy hereof.

Buyer ___Samson Byers___

Address ___2323 Cedar Ave., Riverdale___

Telephone ___666-2468___

Acceptance

㉕ The undersigned accepts the foregoing offer and agrees to sell the property described above on the terms and conditions set forth.

㉖ The undersigned has employed ___Lakeside Realty Company___ as Broker and for Broker's services agrees to pay said Broker as commission the sum of ___fifty-four hundred - - - - - - - - -___ dollars ___($5,400.00)___ payable upon recordation of the deed or if completion of this sale is prevented by the Seller. If completion of this contract is prevented by the Buyer, Broker shall share equally in any damages collected by the Seller, not to exceed the above stated commission.

Figure 8:1 *continued*

㉗ *The undersigned acknowledges receipt of a copy hereof.*

Seller   Sarah Ohner

Seller   William Ohner

Address   1704 Tenth St., Riverdale

Telephone   333-3579   Date   10/10/xx

Notification of Acceptance

㉘ *Receipt of a copy of the foregoing agreement is hereby acknowledged.*

Buyer   Samson Byers   Date   10/10/xx

Earnest Money Deposit

The price that the buyer is willing to pay, along with the manner in which he proposes to pay it, is inserted at ⑥. Of particular importance in this paragraph is the **earnest money deposit** that the buyer submits with his offer. With the exception of court-ordered sales, no laws govern the size of the deposit or even the need for one. Generally speaking though, the seller and his agent will want a reasonably substantial deposit to show the buyer's earnest intentions and to have something for their trouble if the seller accepts and the buyer fails to follow through. The buyer will prefer to make as small a deposit as possible, as a deposit ties up his capital and there is the possibility of losing it. However, the buyer also recognizes that the seller may refuse to even consider the offer unless accompanied by a reasonable deposit. In most parts of the country, a deposit of $2,000 to $5,000 on a $90,000 offer would be considered acceptable. In court-ordered sales, the required deposit is usually 10% of the offering price.

Deed and Condition of Title

At ⑦, the buyer requests that the seller convey title by means of a warranty deed and provide and pay for a policy of title insurance showing the condition of title to be as described here. Before the offer is made, the broker and seller will have told the buyer about the condition of title. However, the buyer has no way of verifying that information until the title is actually searched. To protect himself, the buyer states at ⑦ the condition of title that he is willing to accept. If title to the property is not presently in this condition, the seller is required by the contract to take whatever steps are necessary to place title in this condition before title is conveyed. If, for example, there is an existing mortgage or judgment lien against the property, the seller must have it removed. If there are other owners, their interests must be extinguished. If anyone has a right to use the property (such as a tenant under a lease), or controls the use of the property (such as a deed restriction), or has an easement, other than what is specifically mentioned, the seller must remove these before conveying title to the buyer.

In a growing number of states, escrow agents (described in more detail in Chapter 14) handle the closing. Number ⑧ names the escrow agent, states that the escrow instructions must be signed promptly, and sets the closing date for the transaction. It is on that date that the seller will receive his money and the buyer his deed. The selection of a closing date is based on the estimated length of time necessary to carry out the conditions of the purchase contract. Normally, the most time-consuming item is finding a lender to make the necessary mortgage loan. Typically, this takes from 30 to 60 days, depending on the lender and the availability of loan money. The other conditions of the contract, such as the title search and arrangements to pay off any existing liens, take less time and can be done while arranging for a new mortgage loan. Once a satisfactory loan source is found, the lender makes a commitment to the buyer that the needed loan money will be placed into escrow on the closing date. *Closing Agent*

In regions of the United States where the custom is to use a closing meeting rather than an escrow, this section of the contract would name the attorney, broker or other person responsible for carrying out the paperwork and details of the purchase agreement. A date would also be set for the closing meeting at which the buyer and seller and their attorneys, the lender, and the title company representative would be present to conclude the transaction.

Number ⑨ deals with the question of how certain ongoing expenses, such as property taxes, insurance and mortgage interest, will be divided between the buyer and the seller. For example, if the seller pays $220 in advance for a 1-year fire insurance policy and then sells his house halfway through the *Prorating* policy year, what happens to the remaining 6 months of coverage that the seller paid for but will not use? One solution is to transfer the remaining six months of coverage to the buyer for $110. Income items are also prorated. Suppose that the seller has been renting the basement of his house to a college student for $90 per month. The student pays the $90 rent in advance on the first of each month. If the property is sold part way through the month, the buyer is entitled to the portion of the month's rent that is earned while he owns the property. This process of dividing ongoing expenses and income items is known as **prorating.** More information and examples regarding the prorating process are included in Chapter 14.

At ⑩, the buyer states that, if there are any unpaid assessments or bonds currently against the property, the seller shall pay them as a condition of the sale. Alternatively, the buyer could agree to assume responsibility for paying them off. Since the buyer wants the property free of mortgages so that he can arrange for his own loan, at ⑪ he asks the seller to remove any existing indebtedness. On the closing date, part of the money received from the buyer is used to clear the seller's debts against the property. Alternatively, the buyer could agree to assume responsibility for paying off the existing debt against the property as part of the purchase price.

Termite Inspection

At ⑫, the buyer asks that the property be inspected at the seller's expense for signs of termites and rotted wood (dry rot), and that the seller pay for extermination and repairs. If the property is offered for sale as being in sound condition, a termite and wood rot clause is reasonable. If the property is being offered for sale on an **"as is"** basis in its present condition with no guarantee or warranty of quality and if it has a price to match, then the clause is not reasonable. If the seller is quite sure that there are no termites or wood rot, this condition would not be a major negotiating point, as the cost of an inspection without corrective work is a minor cost in a real estate transaction.

Possession

The day on which possession of the property will be turned over to the buyer is inserted at ⑬. As a rule, this is the same day as the closing date. If the buyer needs possession sooner or the seller wants possession after the closing date, the usual procedure is to arrange for a separate rental agreement between the buyer and seller. Such an agreement produces fewer problems if the closing date is later changed or if the transaction falls through and the closing never occurs.

At ⑭, the purchase contract calls for the buyer and seller to share escrow expenses equally. The buyer and seller could divide them differently if they mutually agreed. Most states charge a conveyance tax when a deed is recorded. At ⑮ the seller agrees to pay this tax. This is in addition to the fee the buyer pays to have the deed recorded in the public records. At ⑯, the buyer and seller agree as to where the buyer's deposit money is to be held pending the close of the transaction. It could be held by the escrow agent, the broker, the seller or an attorney.

The paragraph at ⑰ is not absolutely essential to a valid real estate purchase contract, since what is considered real estate (and is therefore included in the price) and what is personal property (and is not included in the price) is a matter of law. However, because the buyer and seller may not be familiar with the differences between real property and personal property, this statement is often included to avoid misunderstandings. Moreover, such a statement can clarify whether or not an item like a storm window or trash compactor, which may or may not be real property depending on its design, is included in the purchase price. If it is the intention of the buyer and seller that an item mentioned here not be included, that item is crossed out and initialed by all of them.

Loan Conditions

At ⑱, space is left to add conditions and agreements not provided for elsewhere in the preprinted contract. To complete his purchase of this property the buyer must obtain a $72,000 loan. However, what if he agrees to the purchase but cannot get a loan? Rather than risk losing his deposit money, the buyer makes his offer subject to obtaining a $72,000 loan on the property. To further protect himself against having to accept a loan "at any price," he states the terms on which he must be able to borrow. The seller, of course, takes certain risks in accepting an offer subject to obtaining financing. If the buyer is unable to obtain financing on these terms, the seller will have to return the buyer's deposit and begin searching for another buyer. Meanwhile, the seller may have lost anywhere from a few days to a few weeks of selling time. But without such a condition a buyer may hesitate to make an offer at all. The solution is for the seller to accept only those loan conditions that are reasonable in the light of current loan availability. For example, if lenders are currently quoting 12½% interest for loans on similar properties, the seller would not want to accept an offer subject to the buyer obtaining a 10% loan. The possibility is too remote. If the buyer's offer is subject to obtaining a loan at current interest rates, the probability of the transaction collapsing on this condition is greatly reduced. The same principle applies to the amount of loan needed, the number of years to maturity and loan fees: they must be reasonable in light of current market conditions.

In Figure 8:1, the buyer has until the closing date to find the required loan, a period of 45 days. However, to move things along and release the property sooner if the required loan is unavailable, the contract could contain wording that calls for the buyer to obtain within 30 days a letter from a lender stating that the lender will make the required loan at the closing. If this **loan commitment** letter is not obtained, the seller is released from the deal.

Additional Conditions

In the paragraph at ⑱, we also find that the buyer is asking the seller to include an item of personal property in the selling price. While technically a bill of sale is used for the sale of personal property, such items are often included in the real estate purchase contract if the list is not long. If the refrigerator were real property rather than personal, no mention would be required, as all real property falling within the descriptions at ⑤ and ⑰ is automatically included in the price. The third item in the paragraph at ⑱ gives the buyer an opportunity to have the property inspected by a professional building inspector. Most home buyers do not know what to look for in the way of structural deterioration or defects that may soon require expensive repairs. Consequently, in the past several years property inspection clauses in purchase contracts have become more common. The cost of this inspection is borne by the buyer. The inspector's report should be completed as soon as possible so that the property can be returned to the market if the buyer does not approve the findings.

The paragraph at ⑲ sets forth conditions under which the buyer can free himself of his obligations under this contract and recover his deposit in full. It begins by addressing the question of property destruction between the contract signing and the closing date. Fire, wind, rain, earthquake or other damage does occasionally occur during that period of time. Whose responsibility would it be to repair the damage, and could the buyer point to the damage as a legitimate reason for breaking the contract? It is reasonable for the buyer to expect that the property will be delivered to him in as good a condition as when he offered to buy it. Consequently, if there is major damage or destruction, the wording here gives the buyer the option of rescinding the contract and recovering his deposit in full. Note, however, that this clause does not prevent the buyer from accepting the damaged property or the seller from negotiating with the buyer to repair any damage in order to preserve the transaction.

Property Damage

Paragraph ⑲ also states that, if the buyer is unable to obtain financing as outlined at ⑱ or the seller is unable to convey title as stated at ⑦, the buyer can rescind the contract and have his deposit refunded. However, if the buyer is ready to close the transaction and the seller decides he does not want to sell, perhaps because the value of the property has increased between the signing of the contract and the closing date, the buyer can force the seller to convey title through use of a lawsuit for specific performance.

Once the contract is signed by all parties involved, if the buyer fails to carry out his obligations, the standard choices for the seller are to (1) release the buyer and return his deposit in full, (2) sue the buyer for specific performance, or (3) sue the buyer for damages suffered. Returning the deposit does not compensate for the time and effort the seller and his broker spent with the buyer, nor for the possibility that, while the seller was committed to the buyer, the real estate market turned sour. Yet the time, effort and cost of suing for specific performance or damages may be uneconomical. Consequently,

Buyer Default

it has become common practice in many parts of the country to insert a clause in the purchase contract whereby the buyer agrees in advance to forfeit his deposit if he defaults on the contract, and the seller agrees to accept the deposit as his sole right to damages. Thus, the seller gives up the right to sue the buyer and accepts instead the buyer's deposit. The buyer knows in advance how much it will cost if he defaults, and the cost of default is limited to that amount. This is the purpose of paragraph ⑳.

Time Limits

At ㉑, the buyer clearly states that he is making an offer to buy and gives the seller a certain amount of time to accept. If the seller does not accept the offer within the time allotted, the offer is void. This feature is automatic: the buyer does not have to contact the seller to tell him that the offer is no longer open. The offer must be open long enough for the seller to physically receive it, make a decision, sign it and return it to the buyer. If the seller lives nearby, the transaction is not complicated, and the offer can be delivered in person, 3 days is reasonable. If the offer must be mailed to an out-of-town seller, 7 to 10 days is appropriate.

If the buyer wants to offer on another property should the first offer not be accepted, the offer can be made valid for only a day, or even a few hours. A short offer life also limits the amount of time the seller has to hold out for a better offer. If a property is highly marketable, a buyer will want his offer accepted before someone else makes a better offer. Some experienced real estate buyers argue that a purposely short offer life has a psychological value. It motivates the seller to accept before the offer expires. Note too, a buyer can withdraw and cancel his offer at any time before the seller has accepted and the buyer is aware of that acceptance.

"Time is of the Essence"

"Time is of the essence" at ㉒ means that the time limits set by the contract must be faithfully observed or the contract is voidable by the nondefaulting party. Moreover, lateness may give cause for an action for damages. Neither buyer nor seller should expect extensions of time to complete their obligations. This clause does not prohibit the buyer or seller from voluntarily giving the other an extension. But, extensions are neither automatic nor mandatory.

"Time is of the essence" is a very difficult issue to litigate in court, and courts interpret it inconsistently. Generally speaking, courts disfavor automatic cancellation and forfeiture of valuable contract rights after "slight" or "reasonable" delays in performance. This is because unexpected delays are commonplace, and buyers and sellers customarily overlook delays in order to allow a deal to close. As a practical matter the phrase, when used without additional supporting language, seems to be a firm reminder to all parties to keep things moving toward completion. If time is truly an important issue (as in an option contract, for example), the parties must be very explicit in the contract regarding their intentions.

Signatures

The real estate agency and salesperson responsible for producing this offer to buy are identified at ㉓. At ㉔, the buyer clearly states that this is an offer to purchase. If the buyer has any doubts or questions regarding the legal effect of the offer, he should take it to an attorney for counsel before signing it. After he signs, the buyer retains one copy and the rest are delivered to the seller for his decision. By retaining one copy, the buyer has a written record to remind him of his obligations under the offer. Equally important, the seller cannot forge a change on the offer, as he does not have all the copies. Regarding delivery, the standard procedure is for the salesperson who obtained the offer to make an appointment with the agent who obtained the listing, and together they call upon the seller and present the offer.

Acceptance

For an offer to become binding, the seller must accept everything in it. The rejection of even the smallest portion of the offer is a rejection of the entire offer. If the seller wishes to reject the offer but keep negotiations alive, the seller can make a counteroffer. This is a written offer to sell to the buyer at a new price and with terms that are closer to the buyer's offer than the seller's original asking price and terms. The agent prepares the counteroffer by either filling out a fresh purchase contract identical in all ways to the buyer's offer except for these changes, or by writing on the back of the offer (or on another sheet of paper) that the seller offers to sell at the terms the buyer had offered except for the stated changes. The counteroffer is then dated and signed by the seller, and a time limit is given to the buyer to accept. The seller keeps a copy, and the counteroffer is delivered to the buyer for his decision. If the counteroffer is acceptable to the buyer, he signs and dates it, and the contract is complete. Another commonly used, but less desirable practice is to take the buyer's offer, cross out each item unacceptable to the seller, and write above or below it what the seller will accept. Each change is then initialed by the seller and buyer.

Notification   Returning to Figure 8:1, suppose that the sellers accept the offer as presented to them. At ㉕, they indicate acceptance; at ㉖, they state that they employed the Lakeside Realty Company and agree on a commission of $5,400 for brokerage services, to be paid upon closing and recordation of the deed. Provisions are also included as to the amount of the commission if the sale is not completed. At ㉗, the sellers sign and date the contract and acknowledge receipt of a copy. The last step is to notify the buyer that his offer has been accepted, give him a copy of the completed agreement, and at ㉘ have him acknowledge receipt of it. If a party to a purchase contract dies after it has been signed, the deceased's heirs are, as a rule, required to fulfill the agreement. Thus, if a husband and wife sign a purchase contract and one of them dies, the sellers can look to the deceased's estate and the survivor to carry out the terms of the contract. Similarly, if a seller dies, the buyer is still entitled to receive the property as called for in the contract.

If an offer is rejected, it is good practice to have the sellers write the word "rejected" on the offer, followed by their signatures.

Federal Clauses   In two instances, the government requires that specific clauses be included in real estate sales contracts. First, an **amendatory language** clause must be included whenever a sales contract is signed by a purchaser prior to the receipt of an FHA Appraised Value or a VA Certificate of Reasonable Value on the property. The purpose is to assure that the purchaser may terminate the contract without loss when it appears that the agreed purchase price may be significantly above the appraised value. The specific clauses, which must be used verbatim, are available from FHA and VA approved lenders. Second, the Federal Trade Commission (FTC) requires that builders and sellers of new homes include **insulation disclosures** in all purchase contracts. Disclosures, which may be based upon manufacturer claims, must cite the type, thickness and R-value of the insulation installed in the home. The exact clause will be provided by the builder or seller of the home based on model clauses provided by the National Association of Homebuilders as modified by local laws.

Preprinted Clauses

The purchase contract in Figure 8:1 is designed to present and explain the basic elements of a purchase contract for a house. One popular preprinted purchase contract presently for sale to real estate agents consists of four legal-size pages that contain dozens of preprinted clauses. The buyer, seller and agent select and fill in those clauses pertinent to their transaction. For example, if the home is a condominium, there are clauses that pertain to the condominium documents and maintenance reserves. If the home is in a flood zone, there is a clause for disclosing that fact to the buyer and the requirement of flood insurance by lenders. There are four different pest inspection and repair clauses from which the buyer and seller can choose. There are smoke detector clauses and roof inspection clauses as well as detailed contingency and default clauses. There are clauses for personal property included in the sale and guarantees by the seller that electrical, heating, cooling, sewer, plumbing, built-in appliances, etc., are all in normal working order at the closing. Additionally, there may be state-mandated clauses. For example, some states require specific due-on-sale, balloon payment and insulation disclosures. The benefit of preprinted clauses is that much of the language of the contract has already been written for the buyer, seller and agent. But, the buyer, seller and agent must read all the clauses and choose those appropriate to the transaction.

Riders

A **rider** is any addition annexed to a document and made a part of the document by reference. A rider is usually written, typed or printed on a separate piece of paper and stapled to the document. There will be a reference in the document that the rider is a part of the document and a statement in the rider that it is a part of the document. It is good practice to have the parties to the document place their initials on the rider. Riders are also known as addendums or attachments.

Negotiation   One of the most important principles of purchase contracts (and real estate contracts in general) is that nearly everything is negotiable and nearly everything has a price. In preparing or analyzing any contract, consider what the advantages and disadvantages of each condition are to each party to the contract. A solid contract results when the buyer and seller each feel that they have gained more than they have given up. The prime example is the sales price of the property itself. The seller prefers the money over the property, while the buyer prefers the property over the money. Each small negotiable item in the purchase contract has its price too. For example, the seller may agree to include the refrigerator for $200 more. Equally important in negotiating is the relative bargaining power of the buyer and seller. If the seller is confident of having plenty of buyers at the asking price, he can elect to refuse offers for less money, and reject those with numerous conditions or insufficient earnest money. However, if the owner is anxious to sell and has received only one offer in several months, he may be quite willing to accept a lower price and numerous conditions.

THE BINDER   Throughout most of the United States, the real estate agent prepares the purchase contract as soon as the agent is about to (or has) put a deal together. Using preprinted forms available from real estate trade associations, title companies and stationary stores, the agent fills in the purchase price, down payment and other details of the transaction and has the buyer and seller sign it as soon as they reach agreement.

In a few communities, particularly in the northeastern United States, the practice is for the real estate agent to prepare a short-form contract called a **binder.** The purpose of a binder is to hold a deal together until a more formal purchase contract can be drawn by an attorney and signed by the buyer and seller. In the binder the buyer and seller agree to the purchase price, the down payment and how the balance will be financed. The brokerage commission (to whom and how much) is stated along with an agreement to meet again to draw up a more formal contract that will contain all the remaining details of the sale. The agent then arranges a meeting at the office of the seller's attorney. In attendance are the seller and his attorney, the buyer and his attorney, and the real estate agents responsible for bringing about the sale. Together they prepare a written contract which the buyer and seller sign. Note that when the seller's attorney writes the formal contract, the contract will favor the seller. This is because the seller's attorney is expected to protect the seller's best interests at all times. The purchaser, to protect his interests, should not rely on the seller's attorney for advice, but should bring his own attorney.

While it is easy to minimize the importance of a binder because it is replaced by another contract, it does, nonetheless meet all the requirements of a legally binding contract. In the absence of another contract, it can be used to enforce completion of a sale by a buyer or seller. The major weakness of a binder is in what it *does not say.* For example, the binder will likely make no mention of a termite inspection, the type of deed the seller is expected to use or the closing date. Unless the buyer and seller can agree on these matters at the formal contract meeting, a dilemma results. Certainly, the buyer will wonder if his refusal to meet all the seller's demands at the contract meeting will result in the loss of his deposit money. If a stalemate develops, the courts may be asked to decide the termite question, deed type, closing date and any other unresolved points. However, because this is costly and time consuming for all involved, there is give-and-take negotiation at the contract meeting. If a completely unnegotiable impasse is reached, as a practical matter the binder is usually rescinded by the buyer and seller and the buyer's deposit returned.

What the Binder Does Not Say

If two or more parties want to express their mutual intention to buy, sell, lease, develop or invest, and wish to do so without creating any firm, legal obligation, they may use a **letter of intent.** Generally, such a letter contains an outline of the proposal and concludes with language to the effect that the letter is only an expression of mutual intent and that no liability or obligation is created by it. In other words, a letter of intent is neither a contract nor an agreement to enter into a contract. However, it is expected, and usually stipulated in the letter, that the parties signing the letter will proceed promptly and in good faith to conclude the deal proposed in the letter. The letter of intent is usually found in connection with commercial leases, real estate development and construction projects, and with multimillion-dollar real estate sales.

LETTER OF INTENT

PRACTICING LAW

Historically in the United States, the sale of real estate was primarily a legal service. Lawyers matched buyers with sellers, wrote the sales contract and prepared the mortgage and deed. When persons other than lawyers began to specialize in real estate brokerage, the question of who should write the sales contract became important. The lawyer was more qualified in matters of contract law, but the broker wanted something that could be signed the moment the buyer and seller were in agreement. For many years the solution was a compromise. The broker had the buyer and seller sign a binder, and they agreed to meet again in the presence of a lawyer to draw up and sign a more formal contract. The trend today however, is for the real estate agent to prepare a complete purchase contract as soon as there is a meeting of the minds.

The preparation of contracts by real estate agents for their clients has not gone unnoticed by lawyers. The legal profession maintains that preparing contracts for clients is practicing law, and state laws restrict the practice of law to lawyers. This has been, and continues to be, a controversial issue between brokers and lawyers. Resolution of the matter has come in the form of **accords** between the real estate brokerage industry and the legal profession. In nearly all states, courts have ruled that a real estate agent is permitted to prepare purchase, installment and rental contracts provided the agent uses a preprinted form approved by a lawyer and provided the agent is limited to filling in only the blank spaces on the form. (Figure 8:1 illustrates this concept.) If the preprinted form requires extensive cross-outs, changes and riders, the contract should be drafted by a lawyer. A real estate license is *not* a permit to practice law.

INSTALLMENT
CONTRACTS

An installment contract (also known as a **land contract, conditional sales contract, contract for deed** or **agreement of sale**) combines features from a sales contract, a deed and a mortgage. An installment contract contains most all of the provisions of the purchase contract described in Figure 8:1, plus wording familiar to the warranty deed described in Chapter 5, plus many of the provisions of the mortgage described in the next chapter.

The most important feature of an **installment contract** is that the seller does not deliver a deed to the buyer at the closing. Rather, the seller promises to deliver the deed at some future date. Meanwhile, the purchaser is given the right to occupy the property and have for all practical purposes the rights, obligations and privileges of ownership.

The widest use of the installment contract occurs when the buyer does not have the full purchase price in cash or is unable to borrow it from a lender. To sell under these conditions, the seller must accept a down payment plus monthly payments. To carry this out the seller can choose to either (1) deliver a deed to the buyer at the closing and at the same moment take back from the buyer a promissory note and a mortgage secured by the property (a mortgage carryback), or (2) enter into an installment contract wherein the buyer makes the required payments to the seller before the seller delivers a deed to the buyer.

Historically, installment contracts were most commonly used to sell vacant land where the buyer put only a modest amount of money down and the seller agreed to receive the balance as installment payments. When all the installments were made, the seller delivered a deed to the purchaser. The terms of these contracts were usually weighted in favor of the seller. For example, if the buyer (called the **vendee**) fails to make all the payments on time, the seller (called the **vendor**) can rescind the contract and retain payments made to date as rent and retake possession of the land. Additionally, the seller might insert a clause in the installment contract prohibiting the buyer from recording it. The public records would continue to show the seller as owner and the seller could use the land as collateral for loans. That such a one-sided contract would even exist may seem surprising. But, if a buyer did not have all cash, or enough cash down to obtain financing from another source, the buyer was stuck with what the seller offered, or not buy the property. Sellers took the position that if they were selling to buyers who were unwilling or unable to find their own sources of financing, then sellers wanted a quick and easy way of recovering the property if the payments were not made. By selling on an installment contract and not allowing it to be recorded, the seller could save the time and expense of regular foreclosure proceedings. The seller would simply notify the

Vendor, Vendee

buyer in writing that the contract was in default and thereby rescind it. Meanwhile, as far as the public records were concerned, title was still in the seller's name.

Public Criticism   Such strongly worded agreements received much public criticism, as did the possibility that even if the buyer made all the payments, the seller might not be capable of delivering good title. For example, the buyer makes all payments yet the seller may still have the property encumbered with debt, or the seller has gone bankrupt, or the seller is legally incapacitated, or the seller is dead.

Then, in the late 1970s interest rates rose sharply. In order to sell their properties, sellers looked for ways of passing along the benefits of their fixed-rate, low-interest loans to buyers. The installment contract was rediscovered, and it moved from primarily being a contract to sell land to a contract to sell houses and apartment buildings and even office buildings and industrial property. Basically, the seller kept the property and mortgage in the seller's name and made the mortgage payments out of the buyer's monthly payments. This continued until the buyer found alternative financing at which time the seller delivered the deed.

Protections   With its increased popularity, the need for more sophisticated and more protective installment contracts was created. Simultaneously, courts and legislatures in various states were listening to consumer complaints and finding existing installment contract provisions too harsh. One by one, states began requiring that a buyer be given a specified period to cure any default before the seller could rescind. Some states began requiring that installment contracts be foreclosed like regular mortgages. And most states now require that installment contracts be recorded and/or prohibit a seller from enforcing nonrecording clauses.

Buyers have become much more sophisticated also. For example, it is common practice today to require the seller to place the deed (usually a warranty deed) in an escrow at the time the installment contract is made. This relieves a number of the problems noted above regarding the unwillingness or inability of the seller to prepare and deliver the deed later. Additionally, the astute buyer will require that a collection account be used to collect the buyer's payments and make the payments on the underlying mortgage. This is done using a neutral third party such as the escrowholder of the deed, or a bank or a trust company. The seller will likely insist that the buyer place one-twelfth of the annual property taxes and hazard insurance in the escrow account each month to pay for these items. The buyer will want to record the contract so as to establish the buyer's rights to the property. The buyer may also want to include provisions whereby the seller delivers a deed to the buyer and takes back a mortgage from the buyer once the buyer has paid, say, 30% or 40% of the purchase price.

Other provisions found in an installment contract include the names of the buyer and seller, the sales price, the terms of payment, a full legal description of the property, any restrictions on the use of the property, who is to maintain the property and take the risk of loss due to property damage, how the taxes and insurance will be paid, what encumbrances exist and who is responsible, and any prepayment or due-on-sale provisions.

Other Provisions

The installment contract can be the original purchase contract, i.e., a one-step process that combines the offer, acceptance, agreement to finance and provision for delivery of the deed. More likely, especially for improved property, the purchase contract will call for the preparation of a separate installment contract. The buyer and seller sign and acknowledge duplicate copies of the installment contract and each receives a copy at the closing. The buyer then records his copy, or has the person in charge of the closing record it on his behalf.

If an installment contract is used for the purchase of real estate, it should be done with the help of legal counsel to make certain that it provides adequate safeguards for the buyer as well as the seller. In Chapter 11, the installment contract is discussed as a tool to finance the sale of improved property when other sources of financing are not available.

Between the moment that a buyer and seller sign a valid purchase contract and the moment the seller delivers a deed to the buyer, who holds title to the property? Similarly, under an installment contract, until the seller delivers a deed to the buyer, who holds title to the property? The answer in both

EQUITABLE TITLE

cases is the seller. But this is only technically true because the buyer is entitled to receive a deed (and thereby title) once the buyer has completed the terms of the purchase or installment contract. During the period beginning with the buyer and seller signing the contract and the seller delivering the deed, the buyer is said to hold **equitable title** to the property. The concept of equitable title stems from the fact that a buyer can enforce specific performance of the contract in a court of equity to get title. Meanwhile, the seller holds bare or naked title, i.e., title in name only and without full ownership rights.

The equitable title that a purchaser holds under a purchase or installment contract is transferable by subcontract, assignment or deed. Equitable title can be sold, given away or mortgaged, and it passes to the purchaser's heirs and devisees upon the purchaser's death.

It is not unusual to see a property offered for sale wherein the vendee under an installment contract is offering those rights for sale. Barring any due-on-sale clause in the installment contract, this can be done. The buyer receives from the vendee an assignment of the contract and with it the vendee's equitable title. The buyer then takes possession and continues to make the payments called for by the contract. When the payments are completed, the deed and title transfer can be handled in one of two ways. One way is for the original seller to agree to deliver a deed to the new buyer. The other, and most common way, is for the vendee to place a deed to the new buyer in escrow. When the last payment is made, the deed from the original seller to the vendee is recorded and immediately after it the deed from the vendee to the new buyer.

LEASE WITH OPTION TO BUY

An option is an agreement to keep an offer open for a fixed period of time. One of the most popular option contracts in real estate is the **lease with option to buy.** Often simply referred to as a **"lease–option,"** it allows the tenant to buy the property at preset price and terms during the option period. For a residential property, the lease is typically for one year and the option to buy must be exercised during that time. Let us look more closely.

In a lease–option contract all the normal provisions of a lease are present, such as those shown in Figure 15:1. All the normal provisions of a purchase contract are present such as those shown in Figure 8:1. In addition, there will be wording stating that the tenant has the option of exercising the purchase contract provided the tenant notifies the landlord in writing of that intent during the option period. All terms of the purchase contract must be negotiated and in writing when the lease is signed. Both the tenant and landlord must sign the lease. Only the landlord must sign the purchase contract and option agreement, although both parties often do so. If the tenant wants to buy during the option period, the tenant notifies the landlord in writing that the tenant wishes to exercise the purchase contract. Together they proceed to carry out the purchase contract as in a normal sale.

If the tenant does not exercise the option within the option period, the option expires and the purchase contract is null and void. If the lease also expires at the end of the option period, the tenant must either arrange with the landlord to continue renting or move out. Alternatively, they can negotiate a new purchase contract or a new lease–option contract.

Popularity

Lease–options are particularly popular in soft real estate markets where a home seller is having difficulty finding a buyer. One solution is to lower the asking price and/or make the financing terms more attractive. However, the seller may wish to hold out in hopes that prices will rise within a year. Meantime the seller needs someone to occupy the property and provide some income.

The lease–option is attractive to a tenant because the tenant has a place to rent plus the option of buying for the price in the purchase contract anytime during the option period. In other words, the tenant can wait a year and see if he/she likes the property and if values rise to or above the price in the purchase contract. If the tenant does not like the property and/or the property does not rise in value, the tenant is under no obligation to buy. Once the lease expires, the tenant is under no obligation to continue renting either.

Examples

To encourage a tenant to exercise the option to buy, the contract may allow the tenant to apply part or all of the rent paid to the purchase price. In fact, quite a bit of flexibility and negotiation can take place in creating a lease–option. For example, take a home that would rent for $750 per month and sell for $100,000 on the open market. Suppose the owner wants $110,000 and won't come down to the market price. Meanwhile the home is vacant and there are mortgage payments to be made. The owner could offer a one-year lease–option with a rental charge of $750 each month and an exercise price of $110,000. Within a year, $110,000 may look good to the tenant, especially if the market value of the property has risen significantly above $110,000. The tenant can exercise the option or, if not prohibited by the contract, can sell it to someone who intends to exercise it. The owner receives $10,000 more for the property than last year, and the tenant has the benefit of any value increase above that.

Continuing the above example, what if the property rises to $105,000 in value? There is no economic incentive for the tenant to exercise the option at $110,000. The tenant can simply disregard the option and make an offer of $105,000 to the owner. The owner's choice is to sell at that price or continue renting the home, perhaps with another one year lease–option.

Option Fee   The owner can also charge the tenant extra for the privilege of having the option, but it must make economic sense to the tenant. Suppose in the above example the purchase price is set equal to the current market value, i.e., $100,000. This would be a valuable benefit to the tenant and the owner could charge an up-front cash fee for the option and/or charge above-market rent. The amounts would depend on the market's expectations regarding the value of this home a year from now. There is nothing special about a one-year option period, although it is a very popular length of time. The owner and tenant can agree to a three-month, six-month or nine-month option if it fits their needs, and the lease can run longer than the option period. Options for longer than one year are generally reserved for commercial properties. For example, a businessperson just starting out, or perhaps expanding, wants to buy a building but needs a year or two to see how successful the business will be and how much space it will need.

Caveats   Be aware that lease–options may create income tax consequences that require professional tax counseling. Legal advice is also very helpful in preparing and reviewing the lease–option papers. This is because the entire deal (lease, option and purchase contract) must be water-tight from the beginning. One cannot wait until the option is exercised to write the purchase contract or even a material part of it. If a real estate agent puts a lease–option together, the agent is entitled to a leasing commission at the time the lease is signed. If the option is exercised, the agent is due a sales commission on the purchase contract.

Evidence that the option to buy exists should be recorded so as to establish not only the tenant's rights to purchase the property, but also establish those rights back to the date the option was recorded. An option is an example of a unilateral contract. When it is exercised, it becomes bilateral. The lease portion of a lease–option is a bilateral contract. The party giving the option is called the **optionor** (owner in a lease–option). The party receiving the option is the **optionee** (tenant in a lease–option). Sometimes an option to buy is referred to as a **call.** You will see how an option can be used by a home builder to buy land in Chapter 12 and how options can be used to renew leases in Chapter 15.

RIGHT OF FIRST REFUSAL

Sometimes a tenant will agree to rent a property only if given an opportunity to purchase it before someone else does. In other words, the tenant is saying, "Mr. Owner, if you get a valid offer from someone else to purchase this property, show it to me and give me an opportunity to match the offer." This is called a **right of first refusal.** If someone presents the owner with a valid offer, the owner must show it to the tenant before accepting it. If the tenant decides not to match it, the owner is free to accept it.

A right of first refusal protects a tenant from having the property sold out from under him when, in fact, if the tenant knew about the offer he would have been willing to match it. The owner usually does not care who buys, as long as the price and terms are the same. Therefore, an owner may agree to include a right of first refusal clause in a rental contract for little or no additional charge if the tenant requests it. The right of first refusal concept is not limited to just landlord–tenant situations, but that is as deep as we will go here.

EXCHANGE
AGREEMENTS

Most real estate transactions involve the exchange of real estate for monetary consideration. However, among sophisticated real estate investors, exchanging real property for real property has become popular for two important reasons. First, real estate trades can be accomplished without large amounts of cash by trading a property you presently own for one you want. This sidesteps the intermediate step of converting real estate to cash and then converting cash back to real estate. Second, by using an exchange, you can dispose of one property and acquire another without paying income taxes on the profit in the first property at the time of the transaction. As a result, the phrase "tax-free exchange" is often used when talking about trading.

To illustrate, suppose that you own, as an investment, an apartment building. The value on your accounting books is $150,000, but its market value today is $250,000. If you sell for cash, you will have to pay income taxes on the difference between the value of the property on your accounting books and the amount you receive for it. If instead of selling for cash, you find another building that you want and can arrange a trade, then for income tax purposes the new building acquires the accounting book value of the old and no income taxes are due at the time of the trade. Taxes will be due, however, if and when you finally sell rather than trade. Owner-occupied dwellings are treated differently. The Internal Revenue Service permits a homeowner to sell and still postpone paying taxes on the gain provided another home of equal or greater value is purchased within 24 months.

Trading Up

Real estate exchanges need not involve properties of equal value. For example, if you own debt-free a small office building worth $100,000, you could trade it for a building worth $500,000 with $400,000 of mortgage debt against it. Alternatively, if the building you wanted was priced at $600,000 with $400,000 in debt against it, you could offer your building plus $100,000 in cash.

When a simple two-way trade does not leave each party satisfied, exchanges involving several parties can be arranged. In the four-way trade in Figure 8:2A, Fisher would like to own

POSSIBLE TRADING COMBINATIONS   Figure 8:2

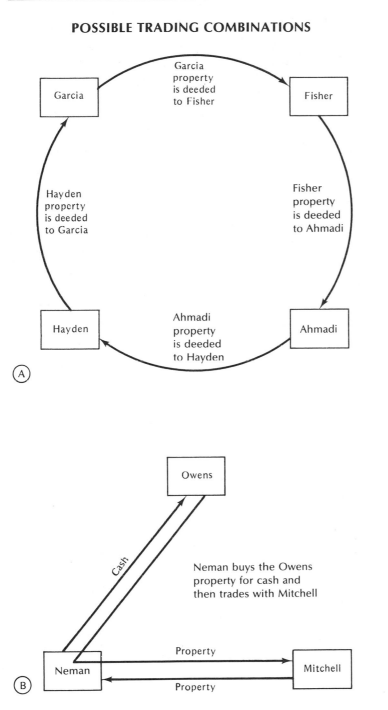

Garcia's property but cannot arrange a trade because Garcia does not want Fisher's property. Fisher then looks for a property Garcia would like to own. He finds one that belongs to Hayden. However, Hayden does not want Fisher's property, and the search must continue to find someone who will take Fisher's property and who has something acceptable to Hayden. Ahmadi holds the missing link, and the four-way trade is possible. Fisher gets Garcia's property, Garcia gets Hayden's property, Hayden gets Ahmadi's property and Ahmadi gets Fisher's property.*

In Figure 8:2B, a combination trade and cash sale is shown. Neman wants Mitchell's property and is willing to pay cash for it. Mitchell refuses to sell for cash because of the income taxes he would have to pay; he will only trade. Owens has a property for sale that Mitchell would like to have. To make the deal, Neman buys it and gives it to Mitchell, receiving Mitchell's property in return. The combination trade and cash sale has become very popular in recent years among sophisticated real estate investors. Correctly applied in an appreciating real estate market, an investor can pyramid his or her wealth with it.

Although trading is a complicated business, it is also very lucrative for real estate agents. Whereas an ordinary sale results in one brokerage commission, a two-party exchange results in two commissions, and a four-party exchange in four commissions.

Delayed Exchanges

The Tax Reform Act of 1984 allows nonsimultaneous exchanges to be tax-deferred under certain circumstances. Such an exchange, commonly called a **delayed exchange,** occurs when property is exchanged for a right to receive property at a future date. It is a helpful technique when one party is willing to exchange out of a property but has not yet chosen a property to exchange into. Meanwhile the other parties to the exchange

---

* Although recent tax developments indicate a "wheel"-type exchange can be carried out tax-free exactly as shown in Figure 8:2A, a few tax experts feel that they are on safer ground by working the trade as a series of two-party exchanges.

are ready and want to close. The delayed exchange allows the closing to take place by giving the party that has not chosen a property the right to designate a property and take title after the closing. The 1984 act specifically allows this provided (1) the designated property is identified within 45 days of the original closing, (2) the title to the designated property is acquired within 180 days of the original closing, and (3) the designated property is received before the designating party's tax return is due. If these rules are not met the transaction will be treated as a sale for the designating party, not an exchange.

Space does not permit a detailed review of a trade contract. However, very briefly, a typical trade contract identifies the traders involved and their respective properties; names the type of deed and quality of title that will be conveyed; names the real estate brokers involved and how much they are to be paid; discusses prorations, personal property, rights of tenants and damage to the property; provides a receipt for the deposit that each trader makes; requires each trader to provide an abstract of title; and sets forth the consequences of defaulting on the contract. If the same broker represents more than one trader, he must disclose this to each trader whom he represents.

Typical Trade Contract

VOCABULARY REVIEW

Match terms **a–r** *with statements* **1–18.**

a. *"As is"*
b. *Bill of sale*
c. *Binder*
d. *Closing date*
e. *Delayed exchange*
f. *Dry rot*
g. *Earnest money deposit*
h. *Equitable title*
i. *Installment sale contract*
j. *"Lease-option"*
k. *Letter of intent*
l. *Loan commitment*
m. *Optionee*
n. *Option fee*
o. *Purchase contract*
p. *Right of first refusal*
q. *"Time is of the essence"*
r. *Vendee*

1. A written and signed agreement specifying the terms at which a buyer will purchase and an owner will sell.
2. A short-form purchase contract to hold a real estate transaction together until a more formal contract can be prepared and signed.
3. Money that accompanies an offer to purchase as evidence of good faith. Also called the deposit.
4. Property offered for sale in its present condition with no guarantee or warranty of quality provided by the seller.
5. Rotted wood; usually the result of alternate soaking and drying over a long period of time.
6. The day on which the buyer pays his money and the seller delivers title.
7. Written evidence of the sale of personal property.
8. A phrase meaning that all parties to a contract are expected to perform on time as a condition of the contract.
9. Also known as a conditional sales contract, land contract, contract for deed or agreement of sale.
10. The buyer under a contract for deed.
11. The right to demand that title be conveyed upon payment of the purchase price.
12. Allows the tenant to buy the property at a preset price for a given period of time.
13. The right to match or better an offer before the property is sold to someone else.
14. Expresses a mutual intention to buy, sell, lease, develop or invest without creating any firm, legal obligation.
15. The party receiving an option.
16. An agreement by a lender to make a loan.
17. Money paid for the privilege of having an option.
18. A nonsimultaneous real estate trade.

1. Why is it necessary to include the extra step of preparing and signing a purchase contract when it would seem much easier if the buyer simply paid the seller the purchase price and the seller handed the buyer a deed?
2. Why is it preferable to prepare a purchase contract that contains all the terms and conditions of sale at the outset rather than to leave some items to be "ironed out" later?
3. What are the advantages and the disadvantages of using pre-printed real estate purchase contract forms?
4. Is it legal for a seller to accept an offer that is not accompanied by a deposit? Why or why not?
5. If a purchase contract for real property describes the land, is it also necessary to mention the fixtures? Why or why not?
6. How will the relative bargaining strengths and weaknesses of the buyer and seller affect the contract negotiation process?
7. Under an installment contract, what is the advantage to the seller if he does not have to deliver title to the buyer until all required payments are made?
8. What position does your state take toward payment forfeiture and nonrecording clauses in land contracts?
9. What are the advantages of trading real estate rather than selling it? What do you consider the disadvantages to be?
10. What is a letter of intent?

QUESTIONS AND PROBLEMS

"Buyer's Personal Inspection" by **Shari Lynn Anderson.** (*First Tuesday*, Jan 85, page 21). Article explains broker's duty of disclosure and includes a sample property inspection agreement form.

"Option to Buy as a Counter Offer" by **Matt Collette.** (*First Tuesday*, Jul 84, page 20). Article suggests sellers may wish to counter with an option to buy when a buyer makes an offer that is laden with contingencies.

Profits from Small-Town Property by **James Koch.** (Van Nostrand Reinhold, 1984, 293 pages). Cites Census study that shows greater growth in rural counties than urban counties for the first time since 1820. Explains the how and where of small-town investing.

Successful Real Estate Negotiation Strategy by **Herbert Holtje** and **Donald Christman.** (Wiley, 1982, 190 pages). A how-to book on behavioral psychology and how this can be applied to real estate sales and negotiations.

ADDITIONAL READINGS

Successful Real Estate Sales Contracts by **Erik Jorgensen.** (Axiom Press, 1983, 336 pages). Shows how to prepare contracts for the sale and exchange of homes, income property and mobile homes. Contains numerous sample contracts.

The Tax Shelter of Real Estate by **Dave Diegelman.** (Real Estate Education Co., 1984, 401 pages). Book teaches exchanging, syndicating, managing and negotiating and how to use tax shelters.

*   *   *

The following periodicals may also be of interest to you: *Real Estate Professional, Real Estate Quarterly, Real Estate Review* and *Real Estate Secrets.*

Mortgage and Note

Acceleration clause: allows the lender to demand immediate payment of entire loan if the borrower defaults

Deficiency judgment: a judgment against a borrower if the foreclosure sale does not bring enough to pay the balance owed

First mortgage: the mortgage loan with highest priority for repayment in the event of foreclosure

Foreclosure: the procedure by which a person's property can be taken and sold to satisfy an unpaid debt

Junior mortgage: any mortgage on a property that is subordinate to the first mortgage in priority

Mortgage: a document which makes property security for the repayment of a debt

Mortgagee: the party receiving the mortgage; the lender

Mortgagor: the party who gives a mortgage; the borrower

Power of sale: allows a mortgagee to conduct a foreclosure sale without first going to court

Promissory note: a written promise to repay a debt

Subordination: voluntary acceptance of a lower mortgage priority than one would otherwise be entitled to

There are two documents involved in a mortgage loan. The first is the promissory note and the second is the mortgage. In 16 states it is customary to use a deed of trust in preference to a mortgage. We begin by describing the promissory note because it is common to both the mortgage and deed of trust. Then we shall discuss the mortgage document at length. This will be followed by an explanation of foreclosure and brief descriptions of the deed of trust, equitable mortgage, security deed and chattel mortgage. (If you either live in or deal with property in a state where the deed of trust is the customary security instrument, you will also want to read Chapter 10 as it deals exclusively with the deed of trust.) Meanwhile, let us begin with the promissory note.

PROMISSORY NOTE   The **promissory note** is a contract between a borrower and a lender. It establishes the amount of the debt, the terms of repayment and the interest rate. A sample promissory note, usually referred to simply as a **note,** is shown in Figure 9:1. Some states use a **bond** to accomplish the same purpose as the promissory note. What is said here regarding promissory notes also applies to bonds.

To be valid as evidence of debt, a note must (1) be in writing, (2) be between a borrower and lender who both have contractual capacity, (3) state the borrower's promise to pay a certain sum of money, (4) show the terms of payment, (5) be signed by the borrower, and (6) be voluntarily delivered by the borrower and accepted by the lender. If the note is secured by a mortgage or trust deed, it must say so. Otherwise, it is solely a personal obligation of the borrower. Although interest is not required to make the note valid, most loans do carry an interest charge; when they do, the rate of interest must be stated in the note. Finally, in some states it is necessary for the borrower's signature on the note to be acknowledged and/or witnessed.

Obligor, Obligee   Referring to Figure 9:1, number ① identifies the document as a promissory note and ② gives the location and date of the note's execution (signing). As with any contract, the location stated in the contract establishes the applicable state laws. For example, a note that says it was executed in Virginia will be governed by the laws of the state of Virginia. At ③, the borrower states that he has received something of value and in turn promises to pay the debt described in the note. Typically, the "value received" is a loan of money in the amount described in the note; it could, however, be services or goods or anything else of value.

The section of the note at ④ identifies to whom the obligation is owed, sometimes referred to as the **obligee,** and where the payments are to be sent. The words "or order" at ⑤ mean that the lender can direct the borrower (the **obligor**) to make payments to someone else if the lender sells the note.

The Principal   The **principal** or amount of the obligation, $60,000, is shown at ⑥. The rate of interest on the debt and the date from which it will be charged is given at ⑦. The amount of the periodic payment at ⑧ is calculated from the loan tables discussed

Figure 9:1

PROMISSORY NOTE SECURED
BY MORTGAGE①

② City, State ___ March 31, 19xx _____

③ *For value received, I promise to pay to* ④ Pennywise Mortgage Company , ⑤ *or order, at* ___ 2242 National Blvd., [City, State] , *the sum of* ⑥ Sixty thousand and no/100- - - - - - - - - - - - - *Dollars, with interest from* March 31, 19xx , *on unpaid principal at the rate of* ⑦ twelve *percent per annum; principal and interest payable in installments of* ⑧ six hundred seventeen and 40/100- - - - - *Dollars on the* first *day of each month beginning* ⑨ May 1, 19xx , *and continuing until said principal and interest have been paid.*

⑩ *This note may be prepaid in whole or in part at any time without penalty.*

⑪ *There shall be a ten-day grace period for each monthly payment. A late fee of $12.50 will be added to each payment made after its grace period.*

⑫ *Each payment shall be credited first on interest then due and the remainder on principal. Unpaid interest shall bear interest like the principal.*

⑬ *Should default be made in payment of any installment when due, the entire principal plus accrued interest shall immediately become due at the option of the holder of the note.*

⑭ *If legal action is necessary to collect this note, I promise to pay such sum as the court may fix.*

⑮ *This note is secured by a mortgage bearing the same date as this note and made in favor of* Pennywise Mortgage Company.

⑰ [this space for witnesses &/or acknowledgment if required by state law]

⑯ *Hap P. Toborrow*
_____
Borrower

in Chapter 11. In this case, $617.40 each month for 30 years will
return the lender's $60,000 plus interest at the rate of 12% per
year on the unpaid portion of the principal. When payments
will begin and when subsequent payments will be due are outlined at ⑨. In this example, they are due on the first day of each
month until the full $60,000 and interest have been paid. The
clause at ⑩ is a **prepayment privilege** for the borrower. It
allows the borrower to pay more than the required $617.40 per
month and to pay the loan off early without penalty. Without
this very important privilege, the note requires the borrower to
pay $617.40 per month, no more and no less, until the $60,000
plus interest has been paid. On some note forms, the prepayment privilege is created by inserting the words "or more" after
the word "dollars" where it appears between ⑧ and ⑨. The
note would then read "six hundred seventeen and 40/100 dollars or more..." The "or more" can be any amount from
$617.41 up to and including the entire balance remaining.

Acceleration Clause   At ⑪, the lender gives the borrower a 10-day grace period
to accommodate late payments. For payments made after that,
the borrower agrees to pay a late charge of $12.50. The clause
at ⑫ states that, whenever a payment is made, any interest due
on the loan is first deducted, and then the remainder is applied
to reducing the loan balance. Also, if interest is not paid, it too
will earn interest at the same rate as the principal, in this example 12% per year. The provision at ⑬ allows the lender to
demand immediate payment of the entire balance remaining
on the note if the borrower misses any of the individual payments. This is called an **acceleration clause,** as it "speeds up"
the remaining payments due on the note. Without this clause,
the lender can only foreclose on the payments that have come
due and not been paid. In this example, that could take as long
as 30 years. This clause also has a certain psychological value:
knowing that the lender has the option of calling the entire loan
balance due upon default makes the borrower think twice
about being late with the payments.

Signature   At ⑭, the borrower agrees to pay any collection costs incurred by the lender if the borrower falls behind in his payments. At ⑮, the promissory note is tied to the mortgage that

secures it, making it a mortgage loan. Without this reference, it would be a personal loan. At ⑯, the borrower signs the note. A person who signs a note is sometimes referred to as a **maker** of the note. If two or more persons sign the note, it is common to include a statement in the note that the borrowers are "jointly and severally liable" for all provisions in the note. This means, the terms of the note and the obligations it creates are enforceable upon the makers as a group and upon each maker individually. If the borrower is married, lenders generally require both husband and wife to sign. Finally, if state law requires the signatures of witnesses or an acknowledgment, this would appear at ⑰. Usually this is not required as it is the mortgage rather than the note that is recorded in public records.

THE MORTGAGE INSTRUMENT

The mortgage is a separate agreement from the promissory note. Whereas the note is evidence of a debt and a promise to pay, the **mortgage** provides security (collateral) that the lender can sell if the note is not paid. The technical term for this is hypothecation. **Hypothecation** means the borrower retains the right to possess and use the property while it serves as collateral. In contrast, **pledging** means to give up possession of the property to the lender while it serves as collateral. An example of pledging is the loan made by a pawn shop. The shop holds the collateral until the loan is repaid. The sample mortgage in Figure 9:2 illustrates in simplified language the key provisions most commonly found in real estate mortgages used in the United States. Let us look at these provisions.

The mortgage begins at ① with the date of its making and the names of the parties involved. In mortgage agreements, the person or party who hypothecates his property and gives the mortgage is the **mortgagor.** The person or party who receives the mortgage (the lender) is the **mortgagee.** For the reader's convenience, we shall refer to the mortgagor as the borrower and the mortgagee as the lender.

At ②, the debt for which this mortgage provides security is identified. Only property named in the mortgage is security for that mortgage. At ③, the borrower conveys to the lender the property described at ④. This will most often be the property that the borrower purchased with the loan money, but this is not a requirement. The mortgaged property need only be

Figure 9:2

MORTGAGE

①*THIS MORTGAGE is made this* 31st *day of* March, 19xx, *between* Hap P. Toborrow *hereinafter called the Mortgagor, and* Pennywise Mortgage Company *hereinafter called the Mortgagee.*

②*WHEREAS, the Mortgagor is indebted to the Mortgagee in the principal sum of* Sixty thousand and no/100- - - - - - - *Dollars, payable* $617.40, including 12% interest per annum, on the first day of each month starting May 1, 19xx, and continuing until paid *, as evidenced by the Mortgagor's note of the same date as this mortgage, hereinafter called the Note.*

③*TO SECURE the Mortgagee the repayment of the indebtedness evidenced by said Note, with interest thereon, the Mortgagor does hereby mortgage, grant, and convey to the Mortgagee the following described property in the County of* Evans *, State of* _____ ;

④*Lot 39, Block 17, Harrison's Subdivision, as shown on Page 19 of Map Book 25, filed with the County Recorder of said County and State.*

⑤*FURTHERMORE, the Mortgagor fully warrants the title to said land and will defend the same against the lawful claims of all persons.*

⑥*IF THE MORTGAGOR, his heirs, legal representatives, or assigns pay unto the Mortgagee, his legal representatives or assigns, all sums due by said Note, then this mortgage and the estate created hereby SHALL CEASE AND BE NULL AND VOID.*

⑦*UNTIL SAID NOTE is fully paid:*

⑧*A. The Mortgagor agrees to pay all taxes on said land.*

⑨*B. The Mortgagor agrees not to remove or demolish buildings or other improvements on the mortgaged land without the approval of the lender.*

⑩*C. The Mortgagor agrees to carry adequate insurance to protect the lender in the event of damage or destruction of the mortgaged property.*

Figure 9:2 *continued*

⑪D. *The Mortgagor agrees to keep the mortgaged property in good repair and not permit waste or deterioration.*

IT IS FURTHER AGREED THAT:

⑫E. *The Mortgagee shall have the right to inspect the mortgaged property as may be necessary for the security of the Note.*

⑬F. *If the Mortgagor does not abide by this mortgage or the accompanying Note, the Mortgagee may declare the entire unpaid balance on the Note immediately due and payable.*

⑭G. *If the Mortgagor sells or otherwise conveys title to the mortgaged property, the Mortgagee may declare the entire unpaid balance on the Note immediately due and payable.*

⑮H. *If all or part of the mortgaged property is taken by action of eminent domain, any sums of money received shall be applied to the Note.*

⑯*IN WITNESS WHEREOF, the Mortgagor has executed this mortgage.*

[this space for witnesses ⑰ and/or acknowledgment if required by state law]

<u>Hap P. Toborrow</u>   (SEAL)
Mortgagor

something of sufficient value in the eyes of the lender; it could just as easily be some other real estate the borrower owns. At ⑤, the borrower states that the property is his and that he will defend its ownership. The lender will, of course, verify this with a title search before making the loan.

Provisions for the defeat of the mortgage are given at ⑥. The key words here state that the "mortgage and the estate created hereby shall cease and be null and void" when the note is paid in full. This is the **defeasance clause.**

As you may have already noticed, the wording of ③, ④ and ⑤ is strikingly similar to that found in a warranty deed. In states taking the **title theory** position toward mortgages, the wording at ③ is interpreted to mean that the borrower is deeding his property to the lender. Sometimes you will see the words "Mortgage Deed" printed at the top of a mortgage for, in fact, a mortgage does technically deed the property to the lender, at least in title theory states. In **lien theory** states, the wording at ③ gives only a lien right to the lender, and the borrower (mortgagor) retains title. In **intermediate theory** states, a mortgage is a lien unless the borrower defaults, at which time it conveys title to the lender. No matter which legal philosophy prevails, the borrower retains possession of the mortgaged property and when the loan is repaid in full, the mortgage is defeated as stated in the defeasance clause.

Covenants

After ⑦, there is a list of covenants (promises) that the borrower makes to the lender. They are the covenants of taxes, removal, insurance and repair. These covenants protect the security for the loan.

In the **covenant to pay taxes** at ⑧, the borrower agrees to pay the taxes on the mortgaged property even though the title may be technically with the lender. This is important to the lender, because if the taxes are not paid they become a lien on the property that is superior to the lender's mortgage.

In the **covenant against removal** at ⑨, the borrower promises not to remove or demolish any buildings or improvements. To do so may reduce the value of the property as security for the lender.

The **covenant of insurance** at ⑩ requires the borrower to carry adequate insurance against damage or destruction of the mortgaged property. This protects the value of the collateral for the loan, for without insurance, if buildings or other improvements on the mortgaged property are damaged or destroyed, the value of the property might fall below the amount owed on the debt. With insurance, the buildings can be repaired or replaced, thus restoring the value of the collateral.

The **covenant of good repair** at ⑪, also referred to as the covenant of preservation and maintenance, requires the borrower to keep the mortgaged property in good condition. The clause at ⑫ gives the lender permission to inspect the property to make sure that it is being kept in good repair and has not been damaged or demolished.

If the borrower breaks any of the mortgage covenants or note agreements, the lender wants the right to terminate the loan. Thus, an **acceleration clause** at ⑬ is included to permit the lender to demand the balance be paid in full immediately. If the borrower cannot pay, foreclosure takes place and the property is sold.

When used in a mortgage, an **alienation clause** (also called   *Alienation Clause*
a **due-on-sale clause**) gives the lender the right to call the entire
loan balance due if the mortgaged property is sold or otherwise
conveyed (alienated) by the borrower. An example is shown at
⑭. The purpose of an alienation clause is twofold. If the mortgaged property is put up for sale and a buyer proposes to assume the existing loan, the lender can refuse to accept that
buyer as a substitute borrower if the buyer's credit is not good.
But, more importantly, lenders have been using it as an opportunity to eliminate old loans with low rates of interest. This
issue, from both borrower and lender perspectives, is discussed
in Chapter 12.

Number ⑮ is a **condemnation clause.** If all or part of the   *Condemnation Clause*
property is taken by action of eminent domain, any money so
received is used to reduce the balance owing on the note.

At ⑯, the mortgagor states that he has made this mortgage.
Actually, the execution statement is more a formality than a
requirement; the mortgagor's signature alone indicates his execution of the mortgage and agreement to its provisions. At ⑰,
the mortgage is acknowledged and/or witnessed as required by
state law for placement in the public records. Like deeds,
mortgages must be recorded if they are to be effective against
any subsequent purchaser, mortgagee or lessee. The reason the
mortgage is recorded, but not the promissory note, is that the
mortgage deals with rights and interests in real property,
whereas the note represents a personal obligation. Moreover,
most people do not want the details of their promissory note in
the public records.

By far, most mortgage loans are paid in full either on or   *MORTGAGE*
ahead of schedule. When the loan is paid, the standard practice   *SATISFACTION*
is for the lender to return the promissory note to the borrower
along with a document called a **satisfaction of mortgage** (or a
release of mortgage). Issued by the lender, this document
states that the promissory note or bond has been paid in full
and the accompanying mortgage may be discharged from the
public records. It is extremely important that this document be
promptly recorded by the public recorder in the same county
where the mortgage is recorded. Otherwise, the records will
continue to indicate that the property is mortgaged. When a

satisfaction or release is recorded, a recording office employee makes a note of its book and page location on the margin of the recorded mortgage. This is done to assist title searchers and is called a **marginal release.**

Partial Release

Occasionally, the situation arises where the borrower wants the lender to release a portion of the mortgaged property from the mortgage after part of the loan has been repaid. This is known as asking for a **partial release.** For example, a land developer purchases 40 acres of land for a total price of $500,000 and finances his purchase with $100,000 in cash plus a mortgage and note for $400,000 to the seller. In the mortgage agreement he might ask that the seller release 10 acres free and clear of the mortgage encumbrance for each $100,000 paid against the loan. This would allow the subdivider to develop and sell those 10 acres without first paying the entire $400,000 remaining balance.

"SUBJECT TO"

If an existing mortgage on a property does not contain a due-on-sale clause, the seller can pass the benefits of that financing along to the buyer. (This is popular when the existing loan carries a lower rate of interest than currently available on new loans.) One method of doing this is for the buyer to purchase the property **subject to the existing loan.** In the purchase contract the buyer states that he is aware of the existence of the loan and the mortgage that secures it, but takes no personal liability for it. Although the buyer pays the remaining loan payments as they come due, the seller continues to be personally liable to the lender for the loan. As long as the buyer faithfully continues to make the loan payments, which he would normally do as long as the property is worth more than the debts against it, this arrangement presents no problem to the seller. However, if the buyer stops making payments before the loan is fully paid, even though it may be years later, in most states the lender can require the seller to pay the balance due plus interest. This is true even though the seller thought he was free of the loan because he sold the property.

ASSUMPTION

The seller is on safer ground if he requires the buyer to **assume the loan.** Under this arrangement, the buyer promises in writing to the seller that he will pay the loan, thus personally obligating himself to the buyer. In the event of default on the loan the lender will first look to the buyer to remedy the problem. If the buyer does not pay, the lender will look to the seller, because the seller's name is still on the original promissory note. The seller will then have to make the payments, but can file suit against the buyer for the money.

The safest arrangement for the seller is to ask the lender to **substitute** the buyer's liability for his. This releases the seller from the personal obligation created by his promissory note, and the lender can now require only the buyer to repay the loan. The lender will require the buyer to prove financial capability to repay by having the buyer fill out a loan application and by running a credit check on the buyer. The lender may also adjust the rate of interest on the loan to reflect current market interest rates. The seller is also on safe ground if the mortgage agreement or state law prohibits deficiency judgments, a topic that will be explained shortly.

NOVATION

When a buyer is to continue making payments on an existing loan, he will want to know exactly how much is still owing. A **certificate of reduction** is prepared by the lender to show how much of the loan remains to be paid. If a recorded mortgage states that it secures a loan for $35,000, but the borrower has reduced the amount owed to $25,000, the certificate of reduction will show that $25,000 remains to be paid. Roughly the mirror image of a certificate of reduction is the **estoppel certificate.** In it, the borrower is asked to verify the amount still owed and the rate of interest. The most common application of an estoppel certificate is when the holder of a loan sells the loan to another investor. It avoids future confusion and litigation over misunderstandings as to how much is still owed on a loan. The word "estoppel" comes from the Latin, "to stop up."

ESTOPPEL

The same property can usually be used as collateral for more than one mortgage. This presents no problems to the lenders involved as long as the borrower makes the required payments on each note secured by the property. The difficulty arises when a default occurs on one or more of the loans, and the price the property brings at its foreclosure sale does not

DEBT PRIORITIES

cover all the loans against it. As a result, a priority system is necessary. The debt with the highest priority is satisfied first from the foreclosure sale proceeds, then the next highest priority debt is satisfied, then the next, and so on until either the foreclosure sale proceeds are exhausted or all debts secured by the property are satisfied.

First Mortgage

In the vast majority of foreclosures, the sale proceeds are not sufficient to pay all the outstanding debt against the property; thus, it becomes extremely important that a lender know his priority position before making a loan. Unless there is a compelling reason otherwise, a lender will want to be in the most senior position possible. This is normally accomplished by being the first lender to record a mortgage against a property that is otherwise free and clear of mortgage debt; this lender is said to hold a **first mortgage** on the property. If the same property is later used to secure another note before the first is fully satisfied, the new mortgage is a **second mortgage,** and so on. The first mortgage is also known as the **senior mortgage.** Any mortgage with a lower priority is known as a **junior mortgage.** As time passes and higher priority mortgages are satisfied, the lower priority mortgages move up in priority. Thus, if a property is secured by a first and a second mortgage and the first is paid off, the second becomes a first mortgage. Note that nothing is stamped or written on a mortgage document to indicate if it is a first or second or third, etc. That can only be determined by searching the public records for mortgages recorded against the property that have not been released.

Subordination

Sometimes a lender will voluntarily take a lower priority position than the lender would otherwise be entitled to by virtue of recording date. This is known as **subordination** and it allows a junior loan to move up in priority. For example, the holder of a first mortgage can volunteer to become a second mortgagee and allow the second mortgage to move into the first position. Although it seems irrational that a lender would actually volunteer to lower his priority position, it is sometimes done by landowners to encourage developers to buy their land.

An interesting situation regarding priority occurs when chattels are bought on credit and then affixed to land that is already mortgaged. If the chattels are not paid for, can the chattel lienholder come onto the land and remove them? If there is default on the mortgage loan against the land, are the chattels sold as fixtures? The solution is for the chattel lienholder to record a **chattel mortgage** or a **financing statement.** This protects the lienholder even though the chattel becomes a fixture when it is affixed to land. A chattel mortgage is a mortgage secured by personal property. If the borrower defaults, the lender is permitted to take possession and sell the mortgaged goods. A more streamlined approach, and one used by most states today, is to file a financing statement as provided by the Uniform Commercial Code to establish lien priority regarding personal property.

Chattel Liens

Although relatively few mortgages are foreclosed, it is important to have a basic understanding of what happens when foreclosure takes place. First, knowledge of what causes foreclosure can help in avoiding it; and, second, if foreclosure does occur, one should know the rights of the parties involved. As you read the material below, keep in mind that to **foreclose** simply means to cut off. What the lender is saying is, "Mr. Borrower, you are not keeping your end of the bargain. We want you out so the property can be put into the hands of someone who will keep the agreements." (What is often unsaid is that the lender has commitments to its savers that must be met. Can you imagine going to your bank or savings and loan and asking for the interest on your savings account and hear the teller say they don't have it because their borrowers have not been making payments?)

THE FORECLOSURE PROCESS

Although noncompliance with any part of the mortgage agreement by the borrower can result in the lender calling the entire balance immediately due, in most cases foreclosure occurs because the note is not being repaid on time. When a borrower runs behind in his payments, the loan is said to be **delinquent.** At this stage, rather than presume that foreclosure is automatically next, the borrower and lender usually meet

Delinquent Loan

and attempt to work out an alternative payment program. Contrary to early motion picture plots in which lenders seemed anxious to foreclose their mortgages, today's lender considers foreclosure to be the last resort. This is because the foreclosure process is time-consuming, expensive and unprofitable. The lender would much rather have the borrower make regular payments. Consequently, if a borrower is behind in his loan payments, the lender prefers to arrange a new, stretched-out, payment schedule rather than immediately declare the acceleration clause in effect and move toward foreclosing the borrower's rights to the property.

If a borrower realizes that stretching out payments is not going to solve his financial problem, instead of presuming foreclosure to be inevitable, he can seek a buyer for the property who can make the payments. More than any other reason, this is why relatively few real estate mortgages are foreclosed. The borrower, realizing he is in, or is about to be in, financial trouble, sells his property. It is only when the borrower cannot find a buyer and when the lender sees no further sense in stretching the payments that the acceleration clause is invoked and the path toward foreclosure taken.

Foreclosure Routes   Basically there are two foreclosure routes: judicial and nonjudicial. **Judicial foreclosure** means taking the matter to a court of law in the form of a lawsuit that asks the judge to foreclose (cut off) the borrower. A **nonjudicial foreclosure** does not go to court and is not heard by a judge. It is conducted by the lender (or by a trustee) in accordance with provisions in the mortgage and in accordance with state law pertaining to nonjudicial foreclosures. Comparing the two, a judicial foreclosure is more costly and more time-consuming, but it does carry the approval of a court of law and it may give the lender rights to collect the full amount of the loan if the property sells for less than the amount owed. It is also the preferred method when the foreclosure case is complicated and involves many parties and interests. The nonjudicial route is usually faster, simpler and cheaper, and it is preferred by lenders when the case is simple and straightforward. Let us now look at foreclosure methods for standard mortgages. (Deed of trust foreclosure will be discussed in Chapter 10.)

The judicial foreclosure process begins with a title search. Next, the lender files a lawsuit naming as defendants the borrower and anyone who acquired a right or interest in the property after the lender recorded his mortgage. In the lawsuit the lender identifies the debt and the mortgage securing it, and states that it is in default. The lender then asks the court for a judgment directing that (1) the defendants' interests in the property be cut off in order to return the condition of title to what it was when the loan was made, (2) the property be sold at a public auction, and (3) the lender's claim be paid from the sale proceeds.

JUDICIAL FORECLOSURE

A copy of the complaint along with a summons is delivered to the defendants. This officially notifies them of the pending legal action against their interests. A junior mortgage holder who has been named as a defendant has basically two choices. One choice is to allow the foreclosure to proceed and file a **surplus money action.** By doing this, the junior mortgage holder hopes that the property will sell at the foreclosure sale for enough money to pay all senior claims as well as his own claim against the borrower. The other choice is to halt the foreclosure process by making the delinquent payments on behalf of the borrower and then adding them to the amount the borrower owes the junior mortgage holder. To do this, the junior mortgage holder must use cash out of his own pocket and decide whether this is a case of "good money chasing bad." In making this decision the junior mortgage holder must consider whether he will have any better luck being paid than did the holder of the senior mortgage.

Surplus Money Action

At the same time that the lawsuit to foreclose is filed with the court, a **notice of lis pendens** is filed with the county recorder's office where the property is located. This notice informs the public that a legal action is pending against the property. If the borrower attempts to sell the property at this time, the prospective buyer, upon making a title search, will learn of the pending litigation. The buyer can still proceed to purchase the property but is now informed of the unsettled lawsuit.

Notice of Lis Pendens

Public Auction   The borrower, or any other defendant named in the lawsuit, may now reply to the suit by presenting his side of the issue to the court judge. If no reply is made, or if the issues raised by the reply are found in favor of the lender, the judge will order that the interests of the borrower and other defendants in the property be foreclosed and the property sold. The sale is usually a **public auction.** The objective is to obtain the best possible price for the property by inviting competitive bidding and conducting the sale in full view of the public. To announce the sale, the judge orders a notice to be posted on the courthouse door and advertised in local newspapers.

Equity of Redemption   The sale is conducted by the **county sheriff** or by a **referee** or **master** appointed by the judge. At the sale, which is held at either the property or at the courthouse, the lender and all parties interested in purchasing the property are present. If the borrower should suddenly locate sufficient funds to pay the judgment, the borrower can, up to the minute the property goes on sale, step forward and redeem the property. This privilege to redeem property anytime between the first sign of delinquency and the moment of foreclosure sale is the borrower's **equity of redemption.** If no redemption is made, the bidding begins. Anyone with adequate funds can bid. Typically, a cash deposit of 10% of the successful bid must be made at the sale, with the balance of the bid price due upon closing, usually 30 days later.

While the lender and borrower hope that someone at the auction will bid more than the amount owed on the defaulted loan, the probability is not high. If the borrower was unable to find a buyer at a price equal to or higher than the loan balance, the best cash bid will probably be less than the balance owed. If this happens, the lender usually enters a bid of his own. The lender is in the unique position of being able to "bid the loan." That is, the lender can bid up to the amount owed without having to pay cash. All other bidders must pay cash, as the purpose of the sale is to obtain cash to pay the defaulted loan. In the event the borrower bids at the sale and is successful in buying back the property, the junior liens against the property are not eliminated. Note however, no matter who the successful bidder is, the foreclosure does not cut off property tax liens against the property. They remain.

If the property sells for more than the claims against it, including any junior mortgage holders, the borrower receives the excess. For example, if a property with $50,000 in claims against it sells for $55,000, the borrower will receive the $5,000 difference, less unpaid property taxes and expenses of the sale. However, if the highest bid is only $40,000, how is the $10,000 deficiency treated? The laws of the various states differ on this question. Forty states allow the lender to request a **deficiency judgment** for the $10,000, with which the lender can proceed against the borrower's other unsecured assets. In other words, the borrower is still personally obligated to the lender for $10,000, and the lender is entitled to collect it. This may require the borrower to sell other assets.

Deficiency Judgment

Only a judge can award a lender a deficiency judgment. If the property sells for an obviously depressed price at its foreclosure sale, a deficiency judgment may be allowed only for the difference between the court's estimate of the property's fair market value and the amount still owing against it. Note that if a borrower is in a strong enough bargaining position, it is possible to add wording in the promissory note that the note is "without recourse." This generally prohibits the lender from seeking a deficiency judgment. But this must be done before the note is signed.

The purchaser at the foreclosure sale receives either a **referee's deed in foreclosure** or a **sheriff's deed.** These are usually special warranty deeds that convey the title the borrower had at the time the foreclosed mortgage was originally made. The purchaser may take immediate possession, and the court will assist him in removing anyone in possession who was cut off in the foreclosure proceedings.

In states with **statutory redemption laws,** the foreclosed borrower has, depending on the state, from one month to one year or more after the foreclosure sale to pay in full the judgment and retake title. This leaves the high bidder at the foreclosure auction in the dilemma of not knowing if he will get the property for certain until the statutory redemption period has run out. Meanwhile, the high bidder receives a **certificate of sale** entitling him to a referee's or sheriff's deed if no redemption is made. Depending on the state, the purchaser may or may not get possession until then. If not, the foreclosed bor-

Statutory Redemption

rower may allow the property to deteriorate and lose value. Knowing this, bidders tend to offer less than what the property would be worth if title and possession could be delivered immediately after the foreclosure sale. In this respect, statutory redemption works against the borrower as well as the lender. This problem can be made less severe if the court appoints a **receiver** (manager) to take charge of the property during the redemption period. Judicial foreclosure with public auction is the predominant method in 21 states, and 9 of them allow a statutory redemption period.

STRICT FORECLOSURE   **Strict foreclosure** is a judicial foreclosure without a judicial sale and usually without a statutory redemption period. Basically, the lender files a lawsuit requesting that the borrower be given a period of time to exercise the equitable right of redemption or lose all rights to the property with title vesting irrevocably in the lender. Although this conjures up visions of a greedy lender foreclosing on a borrower who has nearly paid for the property and misses a payment or two, the court will give the borrower time to make up the back payments or sell the property on the open market. Much more likely is the situation where the debt owed clearly exceeds the property's value. In this case there is little to be gained by conducting a judicial sale. Strict foreclosure is the predominent method of foreclosure in two states and is occasionally used in others. Where the debt exceeds the property's value and the foreclosure prohibits a deficiency judgment, this method may be advantageous to the borrower.

POWER OF SALE   In 27 states the predominent method of foreclosure is by **power of sale,** also known as **sale by advertisement.** This clause, which must be placed in the mortgage before it is signed, gives the lender the power to conduct the foreclosure and sell the mortgaged property without taking the issue to court. The procedure begins when a lender files a **notice of default** with the public recorder. Next is a waiting period that is the borrower's equity of redemption. The property is then advertised and sold at an auction held by the lender and open to the public. The precise procedures the lender must follow are set by state statutes. After the auction, the borrower can still redeem the property if his state offers statutory redemption. The deed the purchaser receives is prepared and signed by the lender or trustee.

A lender foreclosing under power of sale cannot award himself a deficiency judgment. If there is a deficiency as a result of the sale, and the lender wants a deficiency judgment, the lender must go to court for it. Because power of sale foreclosures take place outside the jurisdiction of a courtroom, it is said courts watch them with a jealous eye. If a borrower feels mistreated by power of sale proceedings, the borrower can appeal the issue to a court. Wise lenders know this and keep scrupulous records and follow foreclosure rules carefully. The wise junior mortgage holder will have already filed a **request for notice of default** with the public records office when the junior mortgage was recorded. This requires anyone holding a more senior lien to notify the junior mortgagee if a default notice has been filed. (Usually the junior mortgagee is aware of the problem because if the borrower is not making payments to the holder of the first mortgage, the borrower probably is not making payments to any junior mortgage holders.)

Used as the predominent method of foreclosure in one state and to a lesser degree in three others, **entry and possession** is based on the lender giving notice to the borrower that the lender wants possession of the property. The borrower moves out and the lender takes possession, and this is witnessed and recorded in the public records. If the borrower does not peacefully agree to relinquish possession, the lender will have to use a judicial method of foreclosure.

ENTRY AND POSSESSION

To avoid the hassle of foreclosure proceedings and possible deficiency judgment, a borrower may want to voluntarily deed the mortgaged property to the lender. In turn, the borrower should demand cancellation of the unpaid debt and a letter to that effect from the lender. This method relieves the lender of foreclosing and waiting out any required redemption periods, but it also presents the lender with a sensitive situation. With the borrower in financial distress and about to be foreclosed, it is quite easy for the lender to take advantage of the borrower. As a result, a court of law will usually side with

DEED IN LIEU OF FORECLOSURE

the borrower if he complains of any unfair dealings. Therefore, the lender must be prepared to prove conclusively that the borrower received a fair deal by deeding the property voluntarily to the lender in return for cancellation of the debt. If the property is worth more than the balance due on the debt, the lender must pay the borrower the difference in cash. A **deed in lieu of foreclosure** is a voluntary act by both borrower and lender and hence is sometimes called a "friendly foreclosure." Nonetheless, if either feels he will fare better in regular foreclosure proceedings, he need not agree to it. Note also that a deed in lieu of foreclosure will not cut off the rights of junior mortgage holders. This means the lender will have to make those payments or be foreclosed by the junior mortgage holder(s). Figure 9:3 summarizes through illustration the five methods of mortgage foreclosure that have just been discussed.

INSTALLMENT CONTRACT FORECLOSURE

An installment contract (discussed in Chapter 8) is both a purchase contract and a debt instrument. In years past, if the buyer (vendee) stopped making the payments called for by the contract, the seller (vendor) simply rescinded the contract. The buyer gave up possession; the seller kept all the payments to date; and there was no deficiency judgment. (This effectively is a strict foreclosure without the protection of a court.)

State legislatures found installment contracts too often one-sided in favor of the seller, especially where the buyer had made a substantial number of payments and/or the property had appreciated in value. The need for added consumer protection became even more urgent with increased use of installment contracts in connection with house sales. The result has been that many states have, or are, enacting legislation that requires installment contracts to be foreclosed like regular mortgages.

Deed of Trust

In some states, debts are often secured by trust deeds. Whereas a mortgage is a two-party arrangement with a borrower and a lender, the **trust deed,** also known as a **deed of trust,** is a three-party arrangement consisting of the borrower (the trustor), the lender (the beneficiary) and a neutral third party (a trustee). The key aspect of this system is that the borrower executes a deed to the trustee rather than to the lender. If the borrower pays the debt in full and on time, the lender in-

MORGAGE FORECLOSURE
SIMPLIFIED OVERVIEW

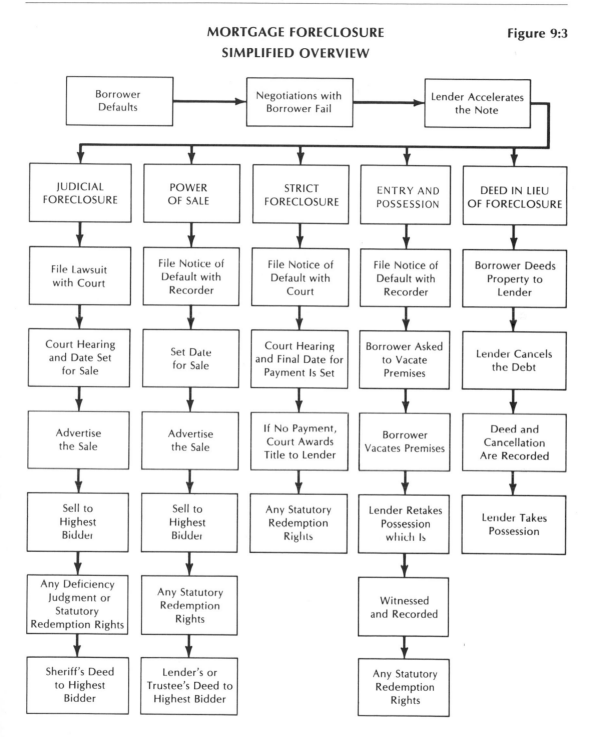

structs the trustee to reconvey title back to the borrower. If the borrower defaults on the loan, the lender instructs the trustee to sell the property to pay off the debt. Trust deeds are covered in more detail in Chapter 10.

Equitable Mortgage   An **equitable mortgage** is a written agreement that, although it does not follow the form of a regular mortgage, is considered by the courts to be one. For example, Black sells his land to Green, with Green paying part of the price now in cash and promising to pay the balance later. Normally, Black would ask Green to execute a regular mortgage as security for the balance due. However, instead of doing this, Black makes a note of the balance due him on the deed before handing it to Green. The laws of most states would regard this notation as an equitable mortgage. For all intents and purposes, it is a mortgage, although not specifically called one. Another example of an equitable mortgage can arise from the deposit money accompanying an offer to purchase property. If the seller refuses the offer and refuses to return the deposit, the courts will hold that the purchaser has an equitable mortgage in the amount of the deposit against the seller's property.

Deed as Security   Occasionally, a borrower will give a bargain and sale or warranty **deed as security** for a loan. On the face of it, the lender (grantee) would appear to own the property. However, if the borrower can prove that the deed was, in fact, security for a loan, the lender must foreclose like a regular mortgage if the borrower fails to repay. If the loan is repaid in full and on time, the lender is obligated to convey the land back to the borrower. Like the equitable mortgage, a deed used as security is treated according to its intent, not its label.

In one state, Georgia, the standard mortgage instrument is the **security deed.** This is a warranty deed with a reconveyance clause. The security deed transfers title to the lender and when all payments have been made on the accompanying note, the lender executes the reconveyance (or cancellation) clause on the reverse of the deed, and it is recorded. If the borrower defaults, a power of sale clause in the deed allows the lender to advertise and sell the property without going through judicial foreclosure.

Generally speaking, a lender will choose, and ask the borrower to sign, whatever security instrument provides the smoothest foreclosure in that state. To illustrate, some states require a statutory redemption period for a mortgage foreclosure but not for a deed of trust foreclosure. Some will allow power of sale for a deed of trust but not for a mortgage. All states allow the use of a deed of trust, but some require that it be foreclosed like a mortgage. More and more states require installment contracts to be foreclosed like mortgages. An analogy for the development of security instrument law is that of a plant growing up through a pile of rocks. Its path up may be twisted and curved, but it reaches its goal—the sunlight. Security instruments follow many paths, but always with one goal in mind—to get money to the borrower who uses it and then returns it to the lender.

Lastly, take a look at Figures 10:1 and 10:5 in the next chapter. These illustrations will help you visualize the differences between a mortgage, deed of trust and land contract at the time of creation, repayment and foreclosure.

CHOICE OF SECURITY INSTRUMENT

VOCABULARY REVIEW

Match terms **a–z** *with statements* **1–26.**

a. *Acceleration clause*
b. *Alienation clause*
c. *Assumption*
d. *Chattel mortgage*
e. *Covenant of insurance*
f. *Deed of trust*
g. *Defeasance clause*
h. *Deficiency judgment*
i. *Delinquent*
j. *Equitable mortgage*
k. *Equity of redemption*
l. *First mortgage*
m. *Foreclosure suit*

n. *Junior mortgage*
o. *Maker*
p. *Mortgage*
q. *Mortgagor*
r. *Partial release*
s. *Power of sale*
t. *Prepayment privilege*
u. *Promissory note*
v. *Public auction*
w. *Satisfaction*
x. *Statutory redemption*
y. *Subject to*
z. *Subordination*

1. A document by which property secures the repayment of a debt.
2. A clause in a mortgage stating that the mortgage is defeated if the borrower repays the accompanying note on time.
3. The borrower's right, prior to the day of foreclosure, to repay the balance due on a delinquent loan.
4. A lawsuit filed by a lender that asks a court to set a time limit on how long a borrower has to redeem his property.
5. An agreement that is considered to be a mortgage in its intent even though it may not follow the usual mortgage wording.
6. A document wherein personal property is used as security for a promissory note.
7. The evidence of debt; contains amount owed, interest rate, repayment schedule and a promise to repay.
8. One who gives a mortgage; the borrower.
9. A clause in a mortgage that allows the lender to call the loan due if the property changes ownership. Also known as a due-on-sale clause.
10. A clause in a mortgage whereby the borrower agrees to keep mortgaged property adequately insured against destruction.
11. Discharge of a mortgage upon payment of the debt owed.
12. Release of a portion of a property from a mortgage.
13. The buyer personally obligates himself to repay an existing mortgage loan as a condition of the sale.
14. The buyer of an already mortgaged property makes the payments but does not take personal responsibility for the loan.
15. Any mortgage lower than a first mortgage in priority.
16. A loan on which the borrower is behind in his payments.

17. A clause in a mortgage that gives the mortgagee the right to conduct a foreclosure sale without first going to court.
18. A judgment against a borrower if the sale of mortgaged property at foreclosure does not bring in enough to pay the balance owing.
19. The right of a borrower, after a foreclosure sale, to reclaim the property by repaying the defaulted loan.
20. Voluntary acceptance of a lower mortgage priority position than one would otherwise be entitled to.
21. A deed given to a trustee as security for a loan.
22. The mortgage loan with highest priority for repayment in the event of foreclosure.
23. A person who signs a promissory note.
24. Allows the borrower to pay more than the required payment.
25. The usual procedure by which foreclosed properties are sold.
26. Allows the lender to speed up the remaining payments on a loan if the borrower defaults.

QUESTIONS AND PROBLEMS

1. Is a prepayment privilege to the advantage of the borrower or the lender?
2. What are the legal differences between lien theory and title theory?
3. How does strict foreclosure differ from foreclosure by sale? Which system does your state use?
4. A large apartment complex serves as security for a first, a second and a third mortgage. Which of these are considered junior mortgage(s)? Senior mortgage(s)?
5. Describe the procedure in your county that is used in foreclosing delinquent real estate loans.
6. What do the laws of your state allow real estate borrowers in the way of equitable and statutory redemption?
7. Do the laws of your state allow a delinquent borrower adequate opportunity to recover his mortgaged real estate? Do you advocate more or less borrower protection than is presently available?
8. In a promissory note, who is the obligor? Who is the obligee?
9. Why does a mortgage lender insist on including mortgage covenants pertaining to insurance, property taxes and removal?
10. What roles do a certificate of reduction and an estoppel certificate play in mortgage lending?

ADDITIONAL
READINGS

Analyzing Real Estate Decisions Using Lotus 1-2-3 by **Austin Jaffee.** (Reston, 1985, 288 pages). Includes introduction, explanation and application of Lotus 1-2-3 to real estate lending, leverage, taxes, brokerage, risk and appraisal problems. Includes templates for creating spreadsheets. This book is also available in a *VisiCalc* edition.

Basic Real Estate Finance and Investments by **Donald Epley** and **James Millar.** (Wiley, 1984, 656 pages). Book takes a decision-making perspective. Includes sources of mortgage money, mortgage documents, alternative financing methods, leverage, capitalization rates, value and risk.

Forced Sale Workbook by **John Beck.** (Impact Publishing Co., 1983, 216 pages). Includes information on how to find and bid on bankrupt properties, VA and FHA repossessed properties, tax lien sales and foreclosures.

Introduction to Real Estate Law, 2nd ed. by **Charles Coit.** (Real Estate Education Co., 1985, 330 pages). Nontechnical style addresses legal issues important to real estate including trust accounts, timesharing, fiduciary duty of the broker, title insurance, etc.

Real Estate Finance by **Jerome Dasso** and **Gerald Kuhn.** (Prentice-Hall, 1983, 464 pages). Provides a comprehensive and practical overview of law, instruments, terminology, institutions and calculations pertinent to real estate finance.

Residential Mortgage Lending by **Marshall Dennis.** (Reston, 1985, 400 pages). Written for students and professionals. Includes mortgage lending techniques, procedures, law and history. Has case studies of actual mortgage transactions.

Deed of Trust

Assignment of rents: establishes the lender's right to take possession and collect rents in the event of loan default

Beneficiary: one for whose benefit a trust is created; the lender in a deed of trust arrangement

Deed of trust: a document that conveys legal title to a neutral third party (a trustee) as security for a debt

Naked title: title that lacks the rights and privileges usually associated with ownership

Reconveyance or release deed: a document used to reconvey title from the trustee back to the property owner once the debt has been paid

Trustee: one who holds property in trust for another

Trustor: one who creates a trust; the borrower in a deed of trust arrangement

The basic purpose of a **deed of trust,** also referred to as a **trust deed,** is the same as a mortgage. Real property is used as security for a debt; if the debt is not repaid, the property is sold and the proceeds are applied to the balance owed. The main legal difference between a deed of trust and a mortgage is diagrammed in Figure 10:1.

PARTIES TO A DEED OF TRUST

Figure 10:1A shows that when a debt is secured by a mortgage the borrower delivers his promissory note and mortgage to the lender, who keeps them until the debt is paid. But when a note is secured by a deed of trust, three parties are involved: the borrower (the **trustor**), the lender (the **beneficiary**), and a neutral third party (the **trustee**). The lender makes a loan to the borrower, and the borrower gives the lender a promissory note (like the one shown in Chapter 9) and a deed of trust. In the deed of trust document, the borrower conveys title to the trustee, to be held in trust until the note is paid in full. (This is the distinguishing feature of a deed of trust.)

The deed of trust is recorded in the county where the property is located and then is given to either the lender or the

Figure 10:1

COMPARING A MORTGAGE WITH
DEED OF TRUST

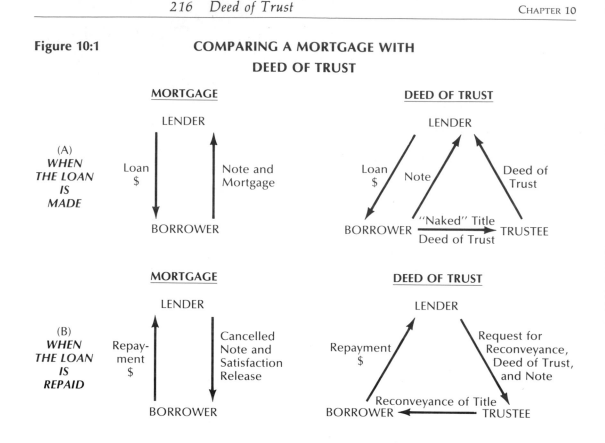

trustee for safekeeping. Anyone searching the title records would find the deed of trust conveying title to the trustee. This would alert the title searcher to the existence of a debt against the property.

The title that the borrower grants to the trustee is sometimes referred to as a **naked title** or **bare title**. This is because the borrower still retains the usual rights of an owner such as the right to occupy and use the property and the right to sell it. The title held by the trustee is limited only to what is necessary to carry out the terms of the trust. In fact, as long as the note is not in default, the trustee's title lies dormant. The lender does not receive title, but only a right that allows the lender to request the trustee to act. Before continuing, take a moment to reread this chapter thus far.

RECONVEYANCE   Referring to Figure 10:1B, we see that when the note is repaid in full under a regular mortgage, the lender cancels the note and returns it to the borrower together with a mortgage satisfaction or release. Upon recordation the mortgage satisfaction or release informs the world at large that the mortgage is nullified and no longer encumbers the property. Under the deed of trust arrangement, the lender sends to the trustee the note, the deed of trust, and a **request for reconveyance.** The trustee cancels the note and issues to the borrower a **reconveyance** or a **release deed** that reconveys title back to the borrower. The borrower records this document to inform the world that the trustee no longer has title. At the recorder's office, a marginal note is made on the record copy of the original deed of trust to show it has been discharged.

If a borrower defaults under a deed of trust, the lender delivers the deed of trust to the trustee with instructions to sell the property and pay the balance due on the note. The trustee can do this because of two important features found in the deed of trust. First, by virtue of signing the deed of trust, the borrower has already conveyed title to the trustee. Second, the power of sale clause found in a deed of trust is designed to give the trustee the authority to sell the property without having to go through a court-ordered foreclosure proceeding.

Default

In nearly all states, a title, trust or escrow company or the trust department of a bank may act as a **trustee.** An individual can be named as a trustee in most jurisdictions. However, this can present a problem if the person dies before reconveyance is made. Therefore, a corporate trustee is preferred because its life span is not limited by the human life span. In a few jurisdictions, Colorado for example, the role of trustee is performed by a government official known as a **public trustee.** Whether public or private, the trustee is expected to be neutral and fair to both the borrower and the lender. To accomplish this, the trustee carefully abides by the agreements found in the deed of trust.

Trustee

Figure 10:2 is a simplified example of a deed of trust that shows the agreements between the borrower and lender and states the responsibilities of the trustee. Beginning at ①, the document is identified as a deed of trust. This is followed by the date of its execution and the names of the trustor, benefi-

DEED OF TRUST DOCUMENT

ciary and trustee. For discussion purposes, this chapter will continue to refer to them as the borrower, lender and trustee, respectively.

At ②, the **promissory note** that accompanies this deed of trust is identified, and it is clearly stated that the purpose of this deed is to provide security for that note. In other words, although this deed grants and conveys title to the trustee at ③, it is understood that the quantity of title the trustee receives is only that which is necessary to protect the note. This permits the borrower to continue to possess and enjoy the use of the property as long as the promissory note is not in default.

Figure 10:2

DEED OF TRUST WITH POWER OF SALE

①*This Deed of Trust, made this* ___15th___ *day of* ___April___ *, 19* ___xx___ *, between* ___Victor Raffaelli and Mary Raffaelli, Husband and Wife___ *, herein called the Trustor, and* ___District Mortgage Company,___ *herein called the Beneficiary, and* ___Safety Title and Trust Co., Inc.___ *herein called the Trustee.*

②*WITNESSETH: To secure the repayment of one promissory note in the principal sum of $* ___70,000___ *executed by the Trustor in favor of the Beneficiary and bearing the same date as this Deed, and to secure the agreements shown below, the Trustor irrevocably* ③ *grants and conveys to the Trustee, in trust, with* ④ *power of sale, the following described real property in the County of* ___Graham___ *, State of* _____ *:*

⑤*Lot 21, Block "A," of Tract 2468, as shown in Map Book 29, Page 17, filed in the Public Records Office of the above County and State.*

⑥*FURTHERMORE: The trustor warrants the title to said property and will defend the same against all claims.*

⑦*UPON WRITTEN REQUEST by the Beneficiary to the Trustee stating that all sums secured hereby have been paid, and upon surrender of this Deed and said Note to the Trustee for cancellation, the Trustee shall reconvey the above described property to the Trustor.*

Figure 10:2 *continued*

⑧*THIS DEED BINDS all parties hereto, their successors, assigns, heirs, devisees, administrators and executors.*

⑨*UNTIL SAID NOTE IS PAID IN FULL:*

A. The Trustor agrees to pay all taxes on said property.

B. The Trustor agrees not to remove or demolish any buildings or other improvements on said property without the approval of the Beneficiary.

C. The Trustor agrees to carry adequate insurance to protect the Beneficiary in the event of damage or destruction of said property.

D. The Trustor agrees to keep the mortgaged property in good repair and not permit waste or deterioration.

E. The Beneficiary shall have the right to inspect said property as may be necessary for the security of the Note.

F. If all or part of said property is taken by eminent domain, any money received shall be applied to the Note.

UPON DEFAULT BY THE TRUSTOR in payment of the debt secured hereby, or the nonperformance of any agreement hereby made, the Beneficiary:

G. May declare all sums secured hereby immediately due and payable.

⑩*H. May enter and take possession of said property and collect the rents and profits thereof.*

⑪*I. May demand the Trustee sell said property in accordance with state law, apply the proceeds to the unpaid portion of the Note, and deliver to the purchaser a Trustee's Deed conveying title to said property.*

⑫*THE TRUSTEE ACCEPTS THIS TRUST when this Deed, properly executed and acknowledged, is made a public record. The Beneficiary may substitute a successor to the Trustee named herein by recording such change in the public records of the county where said property is located.*

⑬ *Victor Raffaelli*
_____
Trustor

⑭ [acknowledgment of
   trustor's signature
   is placed here.]

Mary Raffaelli
_____
Trustor

POWER OF SALE   Under the **power of sale** clause at ④, if the borrower defaults, the trustee has the right to foreclose and sell the property and convey ownership to the purchaser. If the borrower does not default, this power lies dormant. The presence of a power of sale right does not prohibit the trustee from using a court-ordered foreclosure. If the rights of the parties involved, including junior debt holders and other claimants, are not clear, the trustee can request a court-ordered foreclosure.

At ⑤, the property being conveyed to the trustee is described, and at ⑥ the borrower states that he has title to the property and he will defend that title against the claims of others. At ⑦, the procedure that must be followed to reconvey the title is described. State laws require that when the note is paid the lender must deliver a request for reconveyance to the trustee. The lender must also deliver the promissory note and deed of trust to the trustee. Upon receiving these three items, the trustee reconveys title to the borrower and the trust arrangement is terminated. (A simplified request for reconveyance is illustrated in Figure 10:3 and a simplified full reconveyance in Figure 10:4.)

Continuing in Figure 10:2, the sections identified at ⑧ and ⑨ (paragraphs A through G) are similar to those found in a regular mortgage. They were discussed in Chapter 9 and will not be repeated here.

Figure 10:3

REQUEST FOR FULL RECONVEYANCE

To: Safety Title and Trust Company, Inc.,   *trustee.*
The undersigned is the owner of the debt secured by the above Deed of Trust. This debt has been fully paid and you are requested to reconvey to the parties designated in the Deed of Trust, the estate now held by you under same.

Date _____   *District Mortgage*
                                               _____
                                               Beneficiary

    [As a matter of convenience, this form is often printed at the bottom or on the reverse of the trust deed itself.]

FULL RECONVEYANCE

   Safety Title and Trust Company, Inc.   , *the Trustee under a deed of trust executed by*   Victor Raffaelli and Mary Raffaelli, husband and wife   , *Trustors, dated*   April 15, 19xx   *, and recorded as instrument number*   12345   *in Book*   876   *, page*   345   *, in the Official Records of*   Graham   *County, State of* _____ *, having been requested in writing by the holder of the obligation secured by said deed of trust DOES HEREBY RECONVEY WITHOUT WARRANTY to the person(s) legally entitled thereto the estate held by it under said deed of trust.*

(Brief property description)

[Acknowledgment of
trustee's signature
is placed here.]

Safety Title
Trustee

[This document must be recorded to give public notice that the debt has been paid.]

At ⑩, the lender reserves the right to take physical possession of the pledged property, operate it and collect any rents or income generated by it. The right to collect rents in the event of default is called an **assignment of rents** clause. The lender would only exercise this right if the borrower continued to collect rental income from the property without paying on the note. The right to take physical possession in the event of default is important because it gives the lender the opportunity to preserve the value of the property until the foreclosure sale takes place. Very likely, if the borrower has defaulted on the note, his financial condition is such that he is no longer maintaining the property. If this continues, the property will be less valuable by the time the foreclosure sale occurs.

ASSIGNMENT OF RENTS

At ⑪ is the lender's right to instruct the trustee to sell the property in the event of the borrower's default on the note or nonperformance of the agreements in the deed of trust. This

FORECLOSURE

section also sets forth the rules which the trustee is to follow if there is a foreclosure sale. Either appropriate state laws are referred to or each step of the process is listed in the deed of trust. Generally, state laws regarding power of sale foreclosure require that (1) the lender demonstrate conclusively to the trustee that there is reason to cut off the borrower's interest in the property, (2) a notice of default be filed with the public recorder, (3) the notice of default be followed by a 90- to 120-day waiting period before sale advertising begins, (4) advertising of the proposed foreclosure sale occur for at least 3 weeks in public places and a local newspaper, (5) the sale itself be a public auction held in the county where the property is located, and (6) the purchaser at the sale be given a **trustee's deed** conveying all title held by the trustee. This is all the right, title and interest the borrower had at the time he deeded the property to the trustee.

Proceeds

Proceeds from the sale are used to pay (1) the expenses of the sale, (2) the lender, (3) any junior claims, and (4) the borrower, in that order. Once the sale is held, the borrower's equitable right of redemption ends. In some states, statutory redemption may still exist. Anyone can bid at the sale, including the borrower. However, junior claims that would normally be cut off by the sale are not extinguished if the borrower is the successful bidder.

TRUSTEE APPOINTMENT

The wording at ⑫ reflects what is called the **automatic form** of trusteeship. The trustee is named in the deed of trust, but is not personally notified of the appointment. In fact, the trustee is not usually aware of the appointment until called upon to either reconvey or proceed under the power of sale provision. The alternative method is called the **accepted form:** the trustee is notified in advance and either accepts or rejects the appointment. Its primary advantage is that it provides positive acceptance of appointment. The main advantage of the automatic form is that it is faster and easier. In the event the trustee cannot or will not perform when called upon by the lender, the wording at ⑫ permits the lender to name a substitute trustee. This would be necessary if an individual appointed as a trustee had died, or a corporate trustee was dissolved or an appointed trustee refused to perform. Finally, the borrowers sign at ⑬, their signatures are acknowledged at ⑭, and the deed of trust is recorded in the county where the property is located. Figure 10:5 is a summary comparison of a deed of trust, regular mortgage and land contract at creation, repayment and foreclosure.

JURISDICTIONS USING DEEDS OF TRUST

The deed of trust is the customary security instrument in Alaska, Arizona, California, Colorado, the District of Columbia, Idaho, Maryland, Mississippi, Missouri, North Carolina, Oregon, Tennessee, Texas, Virginia and West Virginia. The deed of trust is also used to a certain extent in Alabama, Delaware, Hawaii, Illinois, Montana, Nevada, New Mexico, Utah, Washington and a few other states. The extent of use in a state is governed by the state's attitude toward conveyance of title to the trustee, power of sale, assignment of rents and statutory redemption privileges. Many states not listed here allow the use of a deed of trust, but require that it be foreclosed just like a regular mortgage.

The deed of trust may be the customary security instrument because state law recognizes a power of sale clause in a deed of trust, but not in a regular mortgage. Or, state law may require a statutory redemption period for mortgages but not for a deed of trust. In those states that allow all the provisions of a deed of trust to function without hindrance, the deed of trust has flourished. In California, for example, where it is legally well established that a trust deed does convey title to the trustee, that the trustee has the power of sale, and that there is no statutory redemption on trust deeds, trust deed recordings outnumber regular mortgages by a ratio of more than 500 to 1.

ADVANTAGES OF THE DEED OF TRUST

The popularity of the deed of trust can be traced to the following attributes: (1) if a borrower defaults, the lender can take possession of the property to protect it and collect the rents; (2) the time between default and foreclosure is relatively short, on the order of 90 to 180 days; (3) the foreclosure process under the power of sale provision is far less expensive and complex than a court-ordered foreclosure; (4) title is already in the name of the trustee, thus permitting the trustee to grant title to the purchaser after the foreclosure sale; and (5) once the foreclo-

Figure 10:5   **COMPARING A MORTGAGE, DEED OF TRUST AND LAND CONTRACT**

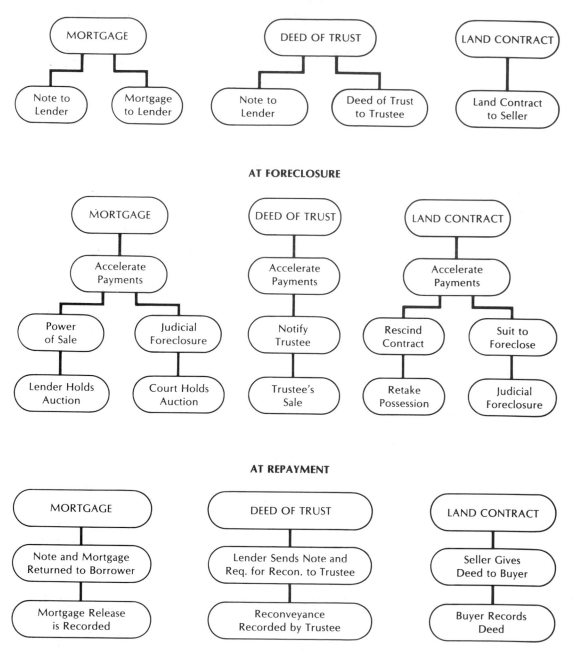

sure sale takes place, there is usually no statutory redemption. These are primarily advantages to the lender, but such advantages have attracted lenders and made real estate loans easier and less expensive for borrowers to obtain. Some states prohibit or restrict the use of deficiency judgments when a deed of trust is used.

Property can be purchased "subject to" an existing deed of trust or it can be "assumed," just as with a regular mortgage. Debt priorities are established as for mortgages: there are first and second, senior and junior trust deeds. Deeds of trust can be subordinated and partial releases are possible.

*Match terms **a–l** with statements **1–12**.*

VOCABULARY REVIEW

a. *Assignment of rents*
b. *Automatic form*
c. *Bare title*
d. *Beneficiary*
e. *Deed of trust*
f. *Power of sale*
g. *Public trustee*
h. *Reconveyance deed*
i. *Request for reconveyance*
j. *Trustee*
k. *Trustee's deed*
l. *Trustor*

1. A document that conveys legal title to a neutral third party as security for a debt.
2. One who creates a trust; the borrower under a deed of trust.
3. The lender.
4. One who holds property in trust for another.
5. Transfers title from the trustee to the trustor.
6. A publicly appointed official who acts as a trustee in some states.
7. The trustee is named in the deed of trust but not personally notified of the appointment.
8. Title in a legal sense only and without the usual rights of ownership.
9. The beneficiary's request to the trustee to deed the secured property to the trustor.
10. A clause in a deed of trust that gives the trustee the right to conduct a foreclosure sale without first going to court.
11. The lender's right to take possession and collect rents in the event of loan default.
12. Conveys to the purchaser at foreclosure the right, title and interest held by the trustee.

QUESTIONS AND
PROBLEMS

1. How does a deed of trust differ from a mortgage?
2. Does possession of a deed of trust give the trustee any rights of entry or use of the property as long as the promissory note is not in default? Explain.
3. What is the purpose of a request for reconveyance?
4. What is the purpose of a power of sale clause in a deed of trust?
5. Explain the purpose of an assignment of rents clause.
6. How does the automatic form of trusteeship differ from the accepted form?
7. What is your state's attitude toward trust deeds, power of sale, statutory redemption and deficiency judgments?

ADDITIONAL
READINGS

Essentials of Real Estate Investment, 3rd ed. by **David Sirota.** (Real Estate Education Co., 1983, 366 pages). Part I of this book deals with the concepts of real estate investment while Part II deals with application. Book covers investing in land, residential and commercial properties, retail stores and industrial property.

Modern Real Estate, 2nd ed. by **Charles Wurtzebach** and **Mike Miles.** (Wiley, 1984, 625 pages). Provides an analytical, decision-making approach to real estate. Includes financing, law, construction, taxation, management, development and marketing.

Real Estate Finance and Investment Tables by **Jack Friedman** and **Peggy Pearson**. (Reston, 1983, 522 pages). Contains tables for loan payments, remaining balance, effective yields at discount, wraparound loan yields, prorations, discount percentages, etc.

Reference Book. (California Department of Real Estate, 1986, 840 pages). Includes a section on trust deeds, trust deed forms, default and foreclosure, and trust deeds compared to mortgages.

Lending Practices

Amortized loan: a loan requiring periodic payments that include both interest and partial repayment of principal

Balloon loan: any loan in which the final payment is larger than the preceding payments

Conventional loans: real estate loans that are not insured by the FHA or guaranteed by the VA

Equity: the market value of a property less the debt against it

Impound or **reserve account:** an account into which the lender places monthly tax and insurance payments

Loan-to-value ratio: a percentage reflecting what a lender will lend divided by the market value of the property

Maturity: the end of the life of a loan

PITI payment: a loan payment that combines principal, interest, taxes and insurance

Point: one percent of the loan amount

Principal: the balance owing on a loan

Section 203(b): FHA's popular mortgage insurance program for houses

Truth in Lending Act: a federal law that requires certain disclosures when extending or advertising credit

Whereas Chapters 9 and 10 dealt with the legal aspects of notes, mortgages and trust deeds, Chapters 11 and 12 will deal with the money aspects of these instruments. We will begin in Chapter 11 with term loans, amortized loans, balloon loans, partially amortized loans, loan-to-value and equity. This will be followed by the functions and importance of the FHA and VA, private mortgage insurance, loan points and Truth In Lending. The last topic in Chapter 11 will be a helpful and informative description of the loan application and approval process you (or your buyer) will experience when applying for a real estate loan. In Chapter 12, we will look at sources and types of financing. This will include where to find mortgage loan money, where mortgage lenders obtain their money, and various types of financing instruments such as the adjustable rate mortgage, equity mortgage, carryback mortgage, wrap-around mortgage and so forth. Note that from here on whatever is said about mortgages applies equally to trust deeds.

TERM LOANS   A loan that requires only interest payments until the last day of its life, at which time the full amount borrowed is due, is called a **term loan** (or straight loan). Until 1930, the term loan was the standard method of financing real estate in the United States. These loans were typically made for a period of 3 to 5 years. The borrower signed a note or bond agreeing (1) to pay the lender interest on the loan every 6 months, and (2) to repay the entire amount of the loan upon **maturity;** that is, at the end of the life of the loan. As security, the borrower mortgaged his property to the lender.

Loan Renewal   In practice, most real estate term loans were not paid off when they matured. Instead, the borrower asked the lender, typically a bank, to renew the loan for another 3 to 5 years. The major flaw in this approach to lending was that the borrower might never own the property free and clear of debt. This left the borrower continuously at the mercy of the lender for renewals. As long as the lender was not pressed for funds, the borrower's renewal request was granted. However, if the lender was short of funds, no renewal was granted and the borrower was expected to pay in full.

The inability to renew term loans caused hardship to hundreds of thousands of property owners during the Great Depression that began in 1930 and lasted most of the decade. Banks were unable to accommodate requests for loan renewals and at the same time satisfy unemployed depositors who needed to withdraw their savings to live. As a result, owners of homes, farms, office buildings, factories and vacant land lost their property as foreclosures reached into the millions. The market was so glutted with properties being offered for sale to satisfy unpaid mortgage loans that real estate prices fell at a sickening pace.

AMORTIZED LOANS   In 1933, a congressionally legislated Home Owner's Loan Corporation (HOLC) was created to assist financially distressed homeowners by acquiring mortgages that were about to be foreclosed. The HOLC then offered monthly repayment plans tailored to fit the homeowner's budget that would repay the loan in full by its maturity date without the need for a balloon payment. The HOLC was terminated in 1951 after rescuing over 1 million mortgages in its 18-year life. However, the use of this stretched-out payment plan, known as an **amortized loan,** took hold in American real estate, and today it is the accepted method of loan repayment.

The amortized loan requires regular equal payments during the life of the loan, of sufficient size and number to pay all interest due on the loan and reduce the amount owed to zero by the loan's maturity date. Figure 11:1 illustrates the contrast between an amortized and a term loan. Figure 11:1A shows a 6-year, $1,000 term loan with interest of $90 due each year of its life. At the end of the sixth year the entire **principal** (the amount owed) is due in one lump sum payment along with the final interest payment. In Figure 11:1B, the same $1,000 loan is fully amortized by making six equal annual payments of $222.92. From the borrower's standpoint, $222.92 once each year is easier to budget than $90 for 5 years and $1,090 in the sixth year.

Furthermore, the amortized loan shown in Figure 11:1 actually costs the borrower less than the term loan. The total

Repayment Methods

REPAYING A 6-YEAR $1,000 LOAN   **Figure 11:1**

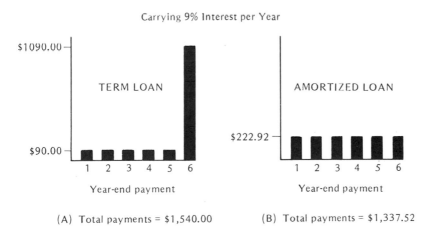

Carrying 9% Interest per Year

(A) Total payments = $1,540.00   (B) Total payments = $1,337.52

payments made under the term loan are $90 + $90 + $90 + $90 + $90 + $1,090 = $1,540. Amortizing the same loan requires total payments of 6 × *$222.92* = $1,337.52. The difference is due to the fact that under the amortized loan the borrower begins to pay back part of the $1,000 principal with his first payment. In the first year, $90 of the $222.92 payment goes to interest and the remaining $132.92 reduces the principal owed. Thus, the borrower starts the second year owing only $867.08. At 9% interest per year, the interest on $867.08 is $78.04; therefore, when the borrower makes his second payment of $222.92, only $78.04 goes to interest. The remaining $144.88 is applied to reduce the loan balance, and the borrower starts the third year owing $722.20. Figure 11:2 charts this repayment program. Notice that the balance owed drops faster as the loan becomes older; that is, as it matures.

Figure 11:2

REPAYING A 6-YEAR $1,000 AMORTIZED LOAN

Carrying 9% Interest per Year

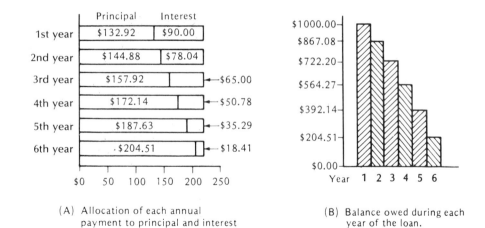

(A) Allocation of each annual payment to principal and interest

(B) Balance owed during each year of the loan.

Monthly Payments   As you have just seen, calculating the payments on a term loan is relatively simple compared to calculating amortized loan payments. As a result, **amortization tables** are published and used throughout the real estate industry. Table 11:1 shows the monthly payments per $1,000 of loan for interest rates from

5% to 25% for periods ranging from 5 to 40 years. (Amortization tables are also published for quarterly, semiannual and annual payments.) When you use an amortization table, notice that there are five variables: (1) frequency of payment, (2) interest rate, (3) maturity, (4) amount of the loan, and (5) amount of the periodic payment. If you know any four of these, you can obtain the fifth variable from the tables. For example, suppose that you want to know the monthly payment necessary to amortize a $60,000 loan over 30 years at 10½% interest. The first step is to look in Table 11:1 for the 10½% line. Then locate the 30-year column. Where they cross, you will find the necessary monthly payment per $1,000: $9.15. Next, multiply $9.15 by 60 to get the monthly payment for a $60,000 loan: $549. If the loan is to be $67,500, then multiply $9.15 by 67.5 to get the monthly payment: $617.63.

Continuing the above example, suppose we reduce the repayment period to 15 years. First look for the 10½% line, then go over to the 15-year column. The number there is $11.06. Next, multiply $11.06 by 60 to get the monthly payment for a $60,000 loan: $663.60. If the loan is to be $67,500, then multiply $11.06 by 67.5 to get the monthly payment: $746.55.

Loan Size

Amortization tables are also used to determine the amount of loan a borrower can support if you know how much the borrower has available to spend each month on loan payments. Suppose that a prospective home buyer can afford monthly principal and interest payments of $650 and lenders are making 30-year loans at 10%. How large a loan can this buyer afford? In Table 11:1 find where the 10% line and the 30-year column meet. You will see 8.78 there. This means that every $8.78 of monthly payment will support $1,000 of loan. To find how many thousands of dollars $650 per month will support, just divide $650 by $8.78. The answer is 74.031 thousands or $74,031. By adding the buyer's down payment, you know what price property the buyer can afford to purchase. If interest rates are 7½%, the number from the table is 7.00 and the loan amount is $92,857. (You can begin to see why the level of interest rates is so important to real estate prices.)

As you have noticed, everything in Table 11:1 is on a monthly payment per thousand basis. With a full book of

Table 11:1

AMORTIZATION TABLE
MONTHLY PAYMENT PER $1,000 OF LOAN

Interest Rate per year	Life of the Loan							
	5 years	10 years	15 years	20 years	25 years	30 years	35 years	40 years
5%	$18.88	$10.61	$ 7.91	$ 6.60	$ 5.85	$ 5.37	$ 5.05	$ 4.83
5½	19.11	10.86	8.18	6.88	6.15	5.68	5.38	5.16
6	19.34	11.11	8.44	7.17	6.45	6.00	5.71	5.51
6½	19.57	11.36	8.72	7.46	6.76	6.32	6.05	5.86
7	19.81	11.62	8.99	7.76	7.07	6.66	6.39	6.22
7½	20.04	11.88	9.28	8.06	7.39	7.00	6.75	6.59
8	20.28	12.14	9.56	8.37	7.72	7.34	7.11	6.96
8½	20.52	12.40	9.85	8.68	8.06	7.69	7.47	7.34
9	20.76	12.67	10.15	9.00	8.40	8.05	7.84	7.72
9½	21.01	12.94	10.45	9.33	8.74	8.41	8.22	8.11
10	21.25	13.22	10.75	9.66	9.09	8.78	8.60	8.50
10½	21.50	13.50	11.06	9.99	9.45	9.15	8.99	8.89
11	21.75	13.78	11.37	10.33	9.81	9.53	9.37	9.29
11½	22.00	14.06	11.69	10.67	10.17	9.91	9.77	9.69
12	22.25	14.35	12.01	11.02	10.54	10.29	10.16	10.09
12½	22.50	14.64	12.33	11.37	10.91	10.68	10.56	10.49
13	22.76	14.94	12.66	11.72	11.28	11.07	10.96	10.90
13½	23.01	15.23	12.99	12.08	11.66	11.46	11.36	11.31
14	23.27	15.53	13.32	12.44	12.04	11.85	11.76	11.72
14½	23.53	15.83	13.66	12.80	12.43	12.25	12.17	12.13
15	23.79	16.14	14.00	13.17	12.81	12.65	12.57	12.54
15½	24.06	16.45	14.34	13.54	13.20	13.05	12.98	12.95
16	24.32	16.76	14.69	13.92	13.59	13.45	13.39	13.36
16½	24.59	17.07	15.04	14.29	13.99	13.85	13.80	13.77
17	24.86	17.38	15.39	14.67	14.38	14.26	14.21	14.19
17½	25.13	17.70	15.75	15.05	14.78	14.67	14.62	14.60
18	25.40	18.02	16.11	15.44	15.18	15.08	15.03	15.02
18½	25.67	18.35	16.47	15.82	15.58	15.48	15.45	15.43
19	25.95	18.67	16.83	16.21	15.98	15.89	15.86	15.85
19½	26.22	19.00	17.20	16.60	16.38	16.30	16.27	16.26
20	26.50	19.33	17.57	16.99	16.79	16.72	16.69	16.68
20½	26.78	19.66	17.94	17.39	17.19	17.13	17.10	17.09
21	27.06	20.00	18.31	17.78	17.60	17.54	17.52	17.51
21½	27.34	20.34	18.69	18.18	18.01	17.95	17.93	17.92
22	27.62	20.67	19.06	18.57	18.42	18.36	18.35	18.34
22½	27.91	21.02	19.44	18.97	18.83	18.78	18.76	18.75
23	28.20	21.36	19.82	19.37	19.24	19.19	19.18	19.17
23½	28.48	21.70	20.20	19.78	19.65	19.61	19.59	19.59
24	28.77	22.05	20.59	20.18	20.06	20.02	20.01	20.01
24½	29.06	22.40	20.97	20.58	20.47	20.43	20.42	20.42
25	29.36	22.75	21.36	20.99	20.88	20.85	20.84	20.84

amortization tables rather than one page, it is possible to look up monthly payments for loans from $100 to $100,000, to determine loan maturities for each year from 1 to 40 years, and to calculate many more interest rates. Amortization books are available from most local bookstores.

An amortization table also shows the impact on the size of the monthly payment when the life of a loan is extended. For example, at 11% interest, a 10-year loan requires a monthly payment of $13.78 per thousand of loan. Increasing the life of the loan to 20 years drops the monthly payment to $10.33 per $1,000. Extending the loan payback to 30 years reduces the monthly payment to $9.53 per thousand. The smaller monthly payment is why 30 years is a popular loan. with borrowers. Note, however, that going beyond 30 years does not significantly reduce the monthly payment. Going from 30 to 35 years reduces the monthly payment by only 16¢ per thousand but adds 5 years of monthly payments. Extending the payback period from 35 to 40 years reduces the monthly payment by just 8¢ per $1,000 ($4 per month on a $50,000 loan) and adds another 60 months of payments at $464.50 per month. As a practical matter, amortized real estate loans are seldom made for more than 30 years.

Change in Maturity Date

The **budget mortgage** takes the amortized loan one step further. In addition to collecting the monthly principal and interest payment (often called P + I), the lender collects one-twelfth of the estimated cost of the annual property taxes and hazard insurance on the mortgaged property. The money for tax and insurance payments is placed in an **impound account** (also called an **escrow** or **reserve account**). When taxes and insurance payments are due, the lender pays them. Thus, the lender makes certain that the value of the mortgaged property will not be undermined by unpaid property taxes or by uninsured fire or weather damage. This form of mortgage also helps the borrower to budget for property taxes and insurance on a monthly basis. To illustrate, if insurance is $240 per year and property taxes are $1,800 per year, the lender collects an additional $20 and $150 each month along with the regular principal and interest payments. This combined principal, interest,

BUDGET MORTGAGE

taxes and insurance payment is often referred to as a **PITI payment.**

BALLOON LOAN

A **balloon loan** is any loan which has a final payment larger than any of the previous payments on the loan. The final payment is called a **balloon payment.** The term loan described at the beginning of this chapter is a type of balloon loan. Partially amortized loans, discussed next, are also a type of balloon loan. In the tight money market of 1979–82, the use of balloon loans increased considerably. Balloon loans with maturities as short as 3 to 5 years were commonplace. This arrangement gives the buyer (borrower) 3 to 5 years to find cheaper and longer-term financing elsewhere. If such financing does not materialize and the loan is not repaid on time, the lender has the right to foreclose. The alternative is for the lender and borrower to agree to an extension of the loan, usually at prevailing interest rates.

PARTIALLY
AMORTIZED LOAN

When the repayment schedule of a loan calls for a series of amortized payments followed by a balloon payment at maturity, it is called a **partially amortized loan.** For example, a lender might agree to a 30-year amortization schedule with a provision that at the end of the tenth year all the remaining principal be paid in a single balloon payment. The advantage to the borrower is that for 10 years the monthly payments will be smaller than if the loan was completely amortized in 10 years. (You can verify this in Table 11:1.) However, the disadvantage is that the balloon payment due at the end of the tenth year might be the borrower's financial downfall. Just how large that balloon payment will be can be determined in advance by using a **loan balance table** (also called a **remaining balance table**). Presuming an interest rate of 11½% and a 30-year loan, at the end of 10 years the loan balance table in Table 11:2 shows that for each $1,000 originally loaned, $929 would still be owed. If the original loan was for $100,000, at the end of 10 years $100 \times \$929 = \$92,900$ would be due as one payment. This qualifies it as a balloon loan.

As you can see from this example, when an amortized loan has a long maturity, relatively little of the debt is paid off during the initial years of the loan's life. Nearly all the early payments go for interest, so that little remains for principal

BALANCE OWING ON A $1,000 AMORTIZED LOAN   Table 11:2

Age of Loan (years)	9½% Annual Interest — Original Life (years)						Age of Loan (years)	11½% Annual Interest — Original Life (years)					
	10	15	20	25	30	35		10	15	20	25	30	35
2	$868	$934	$963	$978	$987	$992	2	$880	$944	$971	$984	$991	$995
4	708	853	918	952	971	983	4	729	873	935	965	981	989
6	515	756	864	921	953	971	6	539	784	889	940	967	982
8	282	639	799	883	930	957	8	300	672	831	909	950	972
10		497	720	837	902	940	10		531	759	870	929	960
12		326	625	781	869	920	12		354	667	821	902	945
14		119	510	714	828	896	14		132	553	759	868	926
16			371	633	780	866	16			409	682	825	903
18			203	535	721	830	18			228	585	772	873
20				416	650	787	20				462	704	836
22				273	564	735	22				308	620	789
24				100	460	671	24				115	513	729
26					335	595	26					380	655
28					183	503	28					211	561
30						391	30						444
32						256	32						296
34						94	34						110

reduction. For example, Table 11:2 shows that even after 16 years of payments on a 30-year, 11½% loan, 82½% of the loan is still unpaid. Not until this loan is about 6 years from maturity will half of it have been repaid.

EARLIER PAYOFF

During the late 1970s when inflation rates exceeded interest rates, the popular philosophy was to borrow as much as possible for as long as possible. Then in the early 1980s inflation rates dropped below interest rates and the opposite philosophy became attractive to many borrowers. This was especially true for those who had borrowed (or were contemplating borrowing) at double-digit interest rates. Let us use as an example an $80,000 loan at 11½% interest. If the loan has a maturity of 30 years, from Table 11:1 we can determine the monthly payments to be $792.80. (Follow this example on your own.)

15-Year Loan

Suppose the maturity of the above loan is changed from 30 to 15 years. Looking at Table 11:1, the monthly payments will now be $935.20. This is $142.40 more per month, but the loan is fully paid in 15 years, not 30 years. The total amount of interest paid on the 15-year loan is (15 × 12 × $935.20) − $80,000 = $88,336. The total amount of interest paid on the 30-year loan is (30 × 12 × $792.80) − $80,000 = $205,408. Thus, for an extra $142.40 per month for 180 months (which amounts to $25,632) the borrower saves the difference between $205,408 and $88,336 (which is $117,072). Many borrowers consider this a very good return on their money. (It is, in fact, an 11½% compounded rate of return.) Lenders are more receptive to making fixed-rate loans for 15 years than for 30 years. This is because the lender is locked into the loan for 15 years, not 30 years. As a result, a lender is usually willing to offer a 15-year loan at a lower rate of interest than a 30-year loan. In view of these benefits to borrower and lender alike, the 15-year loan is becoming a popular home financing tool.

Biweekly Payments   A small but growing number of lenders offer a biweekly repayment plan. The loan is amortized as if it were going to last 30 years. But instead of paying once a month, the borrower makes one-half the monthly payment every two weeks. This may not sound like much difference but the results are eye-opening. Assume you borrow $100,000 at 13% interest, paying (see Table 11:1) $1,107 per month. You will retire the loan in 30 years at a cost of $298,520 in interest. If you decide to pay half of $1,107 every two weeks, the loan will be fully paid in just 18 years and will have cost you $160,023 in interest. This happens because biweekly compounding works in your favor and because you make 26 half-size payments a year, not 24.

Existing Loans   For borrowers with existing loans who want to celebrate with an early mortgage burning, this is done by simply adding a few dollars each month to the required monthly payment. This can be particularly beneficial for persons who borrowed at rates of 13%, 14% and 15% or more. In effect, whatever extra amount is added to the monthly payment will "earn" interest at the loan's interest rate. Thus, if a loan has a 14% rate, early payments "earn" at 14%. If the borrower has no alternative places to invest that will yield 14%, then a few additional dollars each month will work miracles. For example, a 30-year, $100,000 loan at 14% interest requires monthly payments (see

Table 11:1) of $1,185. Voluntarily adding an extra $19 per month will reduce the maturity (payoff) date from 30 years to 25 years (see Table 11:1 again). If an extra $40 is added to the $19, the maturity date shrinks to 20 years. In other words, an extra $59 per month eliminates 10 years of payments.

You may be wondering why borrowers have not thought of this before. There are two key reasons. First, there was a time in 1979 when inflation was 18% per year and 14% to borrow looked cheap by comparison. Second, when interest rates are around 6% and 7% (as they were in the 1960 decade), the mathematics of early payoff is not as impressive.

The relationship between the amount of money a lender is willing to loan and the lender's estimate of the market value of the property that will serve as security is called the **loan-to-value ratio** (often abbreviated **L/V ratio**). For example, a prospective home buyer wants to purchase a house priced at $80,000. A local lender appraises the house, finds it has a market value of $80,000, and agrees to make an 80% L/V loan. This means that the lender will loan up to 80% of the $80,000 and the buyer must provide at least 20% in cash. In dollars, the lender will loan up to $64,000 and the buyer must make a cash down payment of at least $16,000. If the lender appraises the home for more than $80,000 the loan will still be $64,000. If the appraisal is for less than $80,000 the loan will be 80% of the appraised value, and the buyer must pay the balance in cash. The rule is that price or value, whichever is lower, is applied to the L/V ratio. This rule exists to prevent the lender from overlending on a property just because the borrower overpaid for it.

LOAN-TO-VALUE RATIO

The difference between the market value of a property and the debt owed against it is called the owner's **equity.** On a newly purchased $80,000 home with a $16,000 cash down payment, the buyer's equity is $16,000. As the value of the property rises or falls and as the mortgage loan is paid down, equity changes. For example, if the value of the home rises to $90,000 and the loan is paid down to $62,000 the owner's equity will be $28,000. if the owner completely repays the loan so that there is no debt against the home, the owner's equity is equal to the market value of the property.

EQUITY

LOAN POINTS   Probably no single term in real estate finance causes as much confusion and consternation as the word **points.** In finance, the word **point** means one percent of the loan amount. Thus, on a $60,000 loan, one point is $600. On a $40,000 loan, three points is $1,200. On a $100,000 loan, eight points is $8,000.

The use of points in real estate mortgage finance can be split into two categories: (1) loan origination fees expressed in terms of points, and (2) the use of points to change the effective yield of a mortgage loan to a lender. Let us look at these two uses in more detail.

Origination Fee   When a borrower asks for a mortgage loan, the lender incurs a number of expenses, including such things as the time its loan officer spends interviewing the borrower, office overhead, the purchase and review of credit reports on the borrower, an on-site appraisal of the property to be mortgaged, title searches and review, legal and recording fees and so on. For these, some lenders make an itemized billing, charging so many dollars for the appraisal, credit report, title search and so on. The total becomes the **loan origination fee,** which the borrower pays to get his loan. Other lenders do not make an itemized bill, but instead simply state the origination fee in terms of a percentage of the loan amount, for example, one point. Thus, a lender quoting a loan origination fee of one point is saying that, for a $65,000 loan, its fee to originate the loan will be $650.

Discount Points   Points charged to raise the lender's monetary return on a loan are known as **discount points.** A simplified example will illustrate their use and effect. If you are a lender and agree to make a term loan of $100 to a borrower for 1 year at 10% interest, you would normally expect to give the borrower $100 now (disregard loan origination fees for a moment), and 1 year later the borrower would give you $110. In percentage terms, the **effective yield** on your loan is 10% per annum (year) because you received $10 for your 1-year, $100 loan. Now suppose that, instead of handing the borrower $100, you handed him $99 but still required him to repay $100 plus $10 in interest at the end of the year. This is a discount of one point ($1 in this case), and the borrower paid it out of his loan funds. The effect of this financial maneuver is to raise the effective yield (yield to maturity) to you without raising the interest rate itself. Therefore, if you loan out $99 and receive $110 at the end of the year, you effectively have a return of $11 for a $99 loan. This gives you an effective yield of $11 ÷ $99 or 11.1%, rather than 10%.

Calculating the effective yield on a discounted 20- or 30-year mortgage loan is more difficult because the amount owed drops over the life of the loan, and because the majority are paid in full ahead of schedule due to refinancing. Computers and calculators usually make these calculations; however, a useful rule of thumb states that on the typical home loan each point of discount raises the effective yield by ⅛ of 1%. Thus, four discount points would raise the effective yield by approximately ½ of 1% and eight points would raise it by 1%. Discount points are most often charged during periods of **tight money,** that is, when mortgage money is in short supply. During periods of **loose money,** when lenders have adequate funds to lend and are actively seeking borrowers, discount points disappear.

FHA INSURANCE PROGRAMS

The Great Depression caused a major change in the attitude of the federal government toward home financing in the United States. In 1934, one year after the Home Owners Loan Corporation was established, Congress passed the National Housing Act. The act's most far-reaching provision was to establish the Federal Housing Administration (FHA) for the purpose of encouraging new construction as a means of creating jobs. To accomplish this goal, the FHA offered to insure lenders against losses due to nonrepayment when they made loans on both new and existing homes. In turn, the lender had to grant 20-year fully amortized loans with loan-to-value ratios of 80% rather than the 3- to 5-year, 50% to 60% term loans common up to that time.

The FHA did its best to keep from becoming a burden to the American taxpayer. When a prospective borrower approached a lender for an FHA-secured home loan, the FHA reviewed the borrower's income, expenses, assets and debts. The objective was to determine if there was adequate room in the borrower's budget for the proposed loan payments. The FHA also sent inspectors to the property to make certain that it was of acceptable construction quality and to determine its fair market value. To offset losses that would still inevitably occur, the FHA charged the borrower an annual insurance fee of approximately ½ of 1% of the balance owed on his loan. The FHA was immensely successful in its task. Not only did it create construction jobs, but it raised the level of housing quality in the nation and, in a pleasant surprise to taxpayers, actually returned annual profits to the U.S. Treasury. In response to its success, in 1946 Congress changed its status from temporary to permanent.

Current FHA Coverage

The FHA has had a marked influence on lending policies in the real estate industry. Foremost among these is the widespread acceptance of the high loan-to-value, fully amortized loan. In the 1930s, lenders required FHA insurance before making 80% L/V loans. By the 1960s, lenders were readily making 80% L/V loans without FHA insurance. Meanwhile, the FHA insurance program was working so well that the FHA raised the portion it was willing to insure. By 1985, the FHA offered to insure a lender for 97% of the first 50,000 of appraised value and 95% above that to a maximum loan of $67,500 to $90,000. To illustrate, on a $60,000 home the FHA would insure 97% of the first $50,000 and 95% of the remaining $10,000, for a total of $58,000. This means a cash down payment of only $2,000 for the buyer. The borrower is not permitted to use a second mortgage to raise this $2,000. The FHA requires some down payment; otherwise, it is too easy for the borrower to walk away from the debt and leave the FHA to pay the lender's insurance claim. Please be aware that the maximum amount the FHA will insure varies from city to city and is changed from time to time by the FHA.

Assumability

Besides allowing a low down payment, FHA loans are popular because they are 30-year, fixed-rate loans that can be assumed without an increase in interest. Moreover, FHA loans can be repaid early without a prepayment penalty. Thus, in a period of rising interest rates, a seller can pass along the benefits of an existing low-interest rate loan to the buyer. This means the seller can get more money for the property than if the buyer had to completely refinance at a higher rate of interest. If interest rates in the open market fall below the rate on the FHA loan, the borrower can get a new loan and repay the FHA loan ahead of schedule without penalty.

The major disadvantage of an FHA loan is the low loan limit. The FHA's mission is to serve buyers with limited funds who are looking for modestly priced housing. It is possible to get an FHA loan on a more expensive home, but the buyer must make such a large down payment that an FHA loan becomes impractical. You will, however, find existing FHA loans on more expensive homes in the resale market. This is because the loan was written 10 or 20 years ago and the value of the home has risen from modest to expensive since then. Nonetheless, these homes are often eagerly sought by buyers because the existing FHA loan is assumable and may carry an interest rate several percentage points below current market rates. Furthermore, a second mortgage can be used to finance the difference between the existing FHA loan and the buyer's down payment.

Mortgage Insurance

From 1934 until September 1, 1983, the FHA charged an annual insurance premium of approximately ½ of 1% of the balance owing on the loan. This was added to the interest rate and collected each month as part of the borrower's regular monthly payment. Thus, an FHA loan made at 10% interest actually cost approximately 10½% per year once the FHA insurance premium was added. Loans made prior to that date still carry the annual charge.

Effective September 1, 1983, the FHA changed to a one-time lump-sum **mortgage insurance premium (MIP)** that is paid when the loan is made. The amount of the MIP is 3.8% of the loan amount and can be paid in cash or added to the amount borrowed. If borrowed, it can be over and above the FHA ceiling. Thus, if the ceiling is $90,000 and the loan requested is $90,000, the MIP will be $3,420 and the total amount financed will be $93,420. The $93,420 becomes the principal amount of the loan and an amortization table is used to find the monthly payment. If the loan is fully repaid within 11 years, the borrower is entitled to a refund of part of the MIP. After 11 years, there may be a partial refund depending on loan loss experience for the pool of loans that contains the borrower's particular loan. Borrowers under the old annual system may also be entitled to refunds on insurance premiums collected in excess of actual operating experience. In fact, the FHA has several tens of millions of dollars to refund but cannot locate the borrowers on these long-since repaid loans. (FHA borrowers who have repaid in full can contact the FHA to learn if they have a refund coming.)

Interest Rate Ceilings   Another major change in the way the FHA has done business occurred on November 30, 1983. Effective that date, interest rates on FHA loans were freed from government control. Prior to that date the FHA attempted to hold down interest rates by setting ceilings on how much a lender could charge. Whereas this might be a reasonably workable approach in times of stable interest rates, it created nightmares for buyers, sellers, lenders and real estate agents when interest rates spurted upward in the 1970s and early 1980s. What happened was that a seller would put his (or her) home on the market. A buyer would see it and make an acceptable offer subject to obtaining an FHA loan. The FHA would appraise the property, evaluate the borrower and agree to insure a loan. The FHA limited the number of points a borrower could pay to 1 point for existing homes and 2½ points for homes under construction. These were usually consumed by loan origination costs. The FHA required the seller to pay any additional points.

With only two exceptions since 1950, the FHA ceiling was below the prevailing rates on **conventional loans**, i.e., loans not insured by the FHA or guaranteed by the Veterans Administration (VA). When the FHA ceiling was below the market rate on conventional loans, lenders would not make FHA loans unless they were paid discount points. For example, if the open market rate was 12½% and the FHA ceiling was 12%, it was necessary to offer the lender enough discount points to raise the effective yield of the 12% FHA loan to 12½%. This amounted to 4 points. But since the buyer was limited to 1 point and that was used for origination costs, the 4 points came from the seller's pocket. Suppose the loan amount was $60,000. This amounted to $2,400 in points the seller would have to pay so the buyer could enjoy the privilege of obtaining a loan with an interest rate ½ of 1% below the market.

Seller's Position   By placing yourself in the seller's position, you can see the situation this creates. A buyer making an offer under the above conditions is in effect asking you to take a $2,400 cut in price. If you were planning on reducing your price $2,400 anyway, you would accept the offer. However, if you felt you could readily sell at your price to a buyer not requiring seller's points, you would refuse the offer. The alternative is to price the property high enough to allow for anticipated points. However, this is an effective solution only if your price does not exceed the FHA appraisal or VA certificate of reasonable value. If it does, the FHA or VA buyer is either prohibited from buying or must make a larger cash down payment.

Buyers, sellers, lenders and real estate agents can learn to live with the above conditions if interest rates remain fairly stable. But such a system is difficult at best when interest rates change rapidly and/or FHA ceilings change between the date the purchase contract was signed and the day the deed is delivered. Horror stories abound of times when a seller agreed to an FHA sale when the number of points required of the seller was 4 at the time the purchase contract was signed and 8 to 12 by the time the deed was to be delivered. (This would be caused by a market rise without a ceiling increase.) Buyers, meanwhile, would secretly hope the ceiling would not be raised before the closing day.

Floating Interest Rates

Fixed-rate FHA loans are now negotiable and float with the market, and the seller now has a choice in how many points to contribute toward the borrower's loan. This can be none, some, or all the points, and the seller can even pay the borrower's MIP. Typical purchase contract language is, "The seller will pay X points and the buyer will pay not more than Y points and the agreed upon interest rate is Z%" Thus, "X" is the contribution the seller will make, and the seller is protected from having to pay more. The buyer will pay any additional points, but not more than "Y" points. Beyond that, the buyer can cancel the purchase contract. That would happen if the market rates rose quickly while the rate at "Z" is fixed.

Other FHA Programs

Thus far, we have been concentrating on the FHA's most popular program—mortgage insurance on single-family houses. The FHA's authority to offer this is found in **Section 203(b)** of Title II of the National Housing Act. These loans are commonly referred to as "Section 203b" loans. However, the

FHA administers a number of other real estate mortgage insurance programs and several of the better known will be mentioned now.

Under **Section 203(k)** the FHA insures mortgage loans made to finance home improvements. Under **Section 234** the FHA insures loans on condominium units in a manner similar to Section 203(b). **Section 213** insures loans for cooperative housing projects. **Section 235** offers a single-family residence loan subsidy program.

Under **Section 245** the FHA will insure a graduated payment mortgage (GPM). This loan format allows the borrower to make smaller payments initially and to increase payment size gradually over time. The idea is to parallel the borrower's rising earning capacity. (GPMs will receive more coverage in Chapter 12.) The FHA also insures adjustable rate mortgage loans with a program started in mid-1984. These are available to owner-occupants under Section 203(b) and 203(k) and carry an interest rate tied to one-year U.S. Treasury securities. The rate can be adjusted up or down by not more than 1% annually or 5% over the life of the loan. Negative amortization—the addition of unpaid interest to the principal balance—is prohibited. (Adjustable loans will also receive more attention in Chapter 12.)

Loan Qualification

Before leaving the topic of the FHA it is interesting to note that much of what we take for granted as standard loan practice today was the result of FHA innovation years ago. As already noted, standard real estate loan practice called for short-term renewable loans before 1934. Then the FHA boldly offered 20-year amortized loans. Once these were shown to be successful investments for lenders, loans without FHA insurance were made for 20 years. Later, when the FHA successfully went to 30 years, non-FHA-insured loans followed. The FHA also established loan application review techniques that have been widely accepted and copied throughout the real estate industry. The biggest step in this direction was to analyze a borrower's loan application in terms of his earning power. Prior to 1934, emphasis had been placed on how large the borrower's assets were, a measurement that tended to exclude all but the already financially well-to-do from home ownership. Since 1934, the emphasis has shifted primarily to the borrower's ability to meet monthly PITI payments. The rule of thumb today is that no more than 38% of a person's before-tax monthly income should go to the repayment of fixed monthly obligations, including monthly PITI payments.

Since its inception, the FHA has imposed its own minimum construction requirements. Often this was essential where local building codes did not exist or were weaker than the FHA wanted. Before issuing a loan, particularly on new construction, the FHA would impose minimum requirements as to the quantity and quality of building materials to be used. Lot size, street access, landscaping, siting and general house design also were required to fit within broad FHA guidelines. During construction, an FHA inspector would come to the property several times to check if work was being done correctly.

Construction Regulations

The reason for such care in building standards was the FHA recognized that if a building is defective either from a design or construction standpoint, the borrower is more likely to default on the loan and create an insurance claim against the FHA. Furthermore, the same defects will lower the price the property will bring at its foreclosure sale, thus increasing losses to the FHA. Because building codes are now becoming stricter and more standardized in states, counties and cities, the FHA anticipates eliminating its own minimum property standards.

As we leave the FHA and go to the Veterans Administration, keep in mind that the FHA is not a lender. The FHA is an insurance agency. The loan itself is obtained from a savings and loan, bank, mortgage company or similar lender. In addition to principal and interest payments, the lender collects an insurance premium from the borrower which is forwarded to the FHA. The FHA, in turn, guarantees repayment of the loan to the lender. This arrangement makes lenders much more willing to loan to buyers who are putting only 3% to 5% cash down. Thus, when you hear the phrase "FHA loan" in real estate circles, know that it is an FHA-*insured* loan, not a loan from the FHA.

To show its appreciation to servicemen returning from World War II, in 1944 Congress passed far-reaching legislation to aid veterans in education, hospitalization, employment training and housing. In housing, the popularly named G.I. Bill

VETERANS ADMINISTRATION

of Rights empowered the comptroller general of the United States to guarantee the repayment of a portion of first mortgage real estate loans made to veterans. For this guarantee, no fee would be charged to the veteran. Rather, the government itself would stand the losses. The original 1944 law provided that lenders would be guaranteed against losses up to 50% of the amount of the loan, but in no case more than $2,000.

No Down Payment   The objective was to make it possible for a veteran to buy a home with no cash down payment. Thus, on a house offered for sale at $5,000 (houses were much cheaper in 1944) this guarantee enabled a veteran to borrow the entire $5,000. From the lender's standpoint, having the top $2,000 of the loan guaranteed by the U.S. government offered the same asset protection as a $2,000 cash down payment. If the veteran defaulted and the property went into foreclosure, the lender had to net less than $3,000 before suffering a loss.

In 1945, Congress increased the guarantee amount to $4,000 and 60% of the loan and turned the entire operation over to the Veterans Administration (VA). The VA was quick to honor claims, and the program rapidly became popular with lenders. Furthermore, the veterans turned out to be excellent credit risks, bettering, in fact, the good record of FHA-insured homeowners. (The FHA recognizes this and gives higher insurance limits to FHA borrowers who have served in the Armed Forces.) The program blossomed, and to date over 10 million home loans have been guaranteed by the VA, over two-thirds of them with no down payment.

To keep up with the increased cost of homes, the guarantee has been increased several times and in mid-1985 was at $27,500. Generally, a $27,500 guarantee means a veteran can purchase up to a $110,000 home with no down payment, provided, of course, that the veteran has enough income to support the monthly PITI payments. Some lenders will go higher if the borrower makes a down payment. Also, the guarantee amount may increase as it has been several years since the last increase to $27,500.

In the original G.I. Bill of 1944, eligibility was limited to World War II veterans. However, subsequent legislation has broadened eligibility to include any veteran who served for a period of at least 90 days in the armed forces of the United

States, or an ally, between September 16, 1940, and July 25, 1947, or between June 27, 1950, and January 31, 1955. Any veteran of the United States who has served at least 181 days of continuous active duty since January 31, 1955, to the present is also eligible. If service was during the Viet Nam conflict period (August 5, 1964 to May 7, 1975) 90 days is sufficient to qualify. The veteran's discharge must be on conditions other than dishonorable and the guarantee entitlement is good until used. If not remarried, the spouse of a veteran who died as a result of service can also obtain a housing guarantee. Active duty personnel can also qualify. Shorter active duty periods are allowed for service-connected disabilities.

To determine benefits, a veteran should make application to the Veterans Administration for a **certificate of eligibility.** This shows if the veteran is qualified and the amount of guarantee available. It is also one of the documents necessary to obtain a VA-guaranteed loan.

VA Certificates

The VA works diligently to protect veterans and reduce foreclosure losses. When a veteran applies for a VA guarantee, the property is appraised and the VA issues a **certificate of reasonable value.** Often abbreviated **CRV,** it informs the veteran of the appraised value of the property and the maximum VA guaranteed loan a private lender may make. Similarly, the VA establishes income guidelines to make certain that the veteran can comfortably meet the proposed loan payments. Also, the veteran must agree to occupy the property.

The VA will guarantee fixed-rate loans for periods of up to 30 years on homes, and there is no prepayment penalty if the borrower wishes to pay sooner. Moreover, there is no due-on-sale clause that requires the loan to be repaid if the property is sold. The VA will guarantee loans for the purchase of farms and farm equipment, farm buildings and farm capital, to buy or establish a business, or to purchase a mobile home as a residence. A veteran wishing to refinance his existing home or farm can obtain a VA-guaranteed loan provided there is existing debt that will be repaid. The VA will also make direct loans to veterans if there are no private lending institutions nearby.

No matter what loan guarantee program is elected, the veteran should know that in the event of default and subsequent

Financial Liability

foreclosure he is required to eventually make good any losses suffered by the VA on his loan. (This is not the case with FHA-insured loans. There the borrower pays for protection against foreclosure losses that may result from his loan.) Even if the veteran sells the property and the buyer assumes the VA loan, the veteran is still financially responsible if the buyer later defaults. To avoid this, the veteran must arrange with the VA to be released from liability.

A veteran is permitted a full new guarantee entitlement if complete repayment of a previous VA-guaranteed loan has been made. If a veteran has sold and let the buyer assume his VA loan, the balance of the entitlement is still available. For example, if a veteran has used $15,000 of his (her) entitlement to date, the difference between $15,000 and the current VA guarantee amount is still available for use.

Funding Fee   From its inception until October 1, 1982, the VA made loan guarantees on behalf of veterans without a charge. Then starting on that date a ½ of 1% fee was charged at the time of loan funding. In 1984, this **funding fee** was raised to 1% of the loan amount. A major reason has been loan losses. Until the beginning of the 1980 decade, increasing real estate prices coupled with good repayment records of veterans enabled the VA to avoid any sizable losses. But that has changed, and by mid-1985 the VA had thousands of homes that it had to take from lenders because veterans had stopped making payments. The VA has been selling these through price reductions and attractive financing to anyone willing to buy who can make the payments. (The FHA also offers foreclosed properties for sale.)

As of mid-1985, the VA still set interest rate ceilings on the loans it will guarantee. This is nearly the same system as the FHA used until November 30, 1983 at which time the FHA switched to floating rates. If floating rates work well for the FHA, the VA will probably adopt the idea.

As Congress frequently changes eligibility and benefits, a person contemplating a VA or FHA loan should make inquiry to the field offices of these two agencies and to mortgage lenders to ascertain the current status and details of the law, as well as the availability of loan money. Field offices also have information on foreclosed properties that are for sale. Additionally, one should query lenders as to the availability of state veteran benefits. A number of states offer special advantages, including mortgage loan assistance, to residents who have served in the armed forces.

In 1957, the Mortgage Guaranty Insurance Corporation (MGIC) was formed in Milwaukee, Wisconsin, as a privately owned business venture to insure home mortgage loans. Demand was slow but steady for the first 10 years but then grew rapidly and today there are over a dozen private mortgage insurance companies. Like FHA insurance, the object of **private mortgage insurance (PMI)** is to insure lenders against foreclosure losses. But unlike the FHA, PMI insures only the top 20% to 25% of a loan, not the whole loan. This allows a lender to make 90% and 95% L/V loans with about the same exposure to foreclosure losses as a 70% to 75% L/V loan. The borrower, meanwhile, can purchase a home with a cash down payment of either 10% or 5% rather than the 20% to 30% down required by lenders when mortgage insurance is not purchased. For this privilege the borrower pays a PMI fee of 1% or less when the loan is made plus an annual fee of a fraction of 1%. When the loan is partially repaid (for example, to a 70% L/V), the premiums and coverage can be terminated. PMI is also available on apartment buildings, offices, stores, warehouses and leaseholds but at higher rates than on homes.

PRIVATE MORTGAGE INSURANCE

Private mortgage insurers work to keep their losses to a minimum by first approving the lenders with whom they will do business. Particular emphasis is placed on the lender's operating policy, appraisal procedure and degree of government regulation. Once approved, a lender simply sends the borrower's loan application, credit report and property appraisal to the insurer. Based on these documents, the insurer either agrees or refuses to issue a policy. Although the insurer relies on the appraisal prepared by the lender, on a random basis the insurer sends its own appraiser to verify the quality of the information being submitted. When an insured loan goes into default, the insurer has the option of either buying the property from the lender for the balance due or letting the lender foreclose and then paying the lender's losses up to the amount of the insurance. As a rule, insurers take the first option because it is more popular with the lenders and it leaves

Approval Procedure

the lender with immediate cash to re-lend. The insurer is then responsible for foreclosing.

FARMER'S HOME ADMINISTRATION

The **Farmer's Home Administration (FmHA)** is a federal agency under the U.S. Department of Agriculture. Like the FHA, it came into existence due to the financial crises of the 1930s. The FmHA offers programs to help purchase or operate farms. The FmHA will either guarantee a portion of a loan made by a private lender or it will make the loan itself. FmHA loans can also be used to help finance the purchase of homes in rural areas.

TRUTH IN LENDING ACT

The **Federal Consumer Credit Protection Act,** popularly known as the **Truth in Lending Act,** went into effect in 1969. The act, implemented by Federal Reserve Board **Regulation Z,** requires that a borrower be clearly shown how much he is paying for credit in both dollar terms and percentage terms before committing to the loan. The borrower is also given the right to rescind (cancel) the transaction in certain instances. The act came into being because it was not uncommon to see loans advertised for rates lower than the borrower actually wound up paying. Once put into use, several weaknesses and ambiguities of the act and Regulation Z became apparent. Thus, the **Truth in Lending Simplification and Reform Act** (TILSRA) was passed by Congress and became effective October 1, 1982. Concurrently, the Federal Reserve Board issued a **Revised Regulation Z** (RRZ) which details rules and regulations for TILSRA. For purposes of discussion we will refer to all of this as the Truth in Lending Act, or TIL for short.

Advertising

Whether you are a real estate agent or a property owner acting on your own behalf, TIL rules affect you when you advertise just about anything (including real estate) and include financing terms in the ad. If an advertisement contains any one of the TIL list of financing terms (called **trigger terms** and explained below), the ad must also include other required information. For example, an advertisement that reads: "Bargain! Bargain! Bargain! New 3-bedroom townhouses only $499 per month" may or may not be a bargain depending on other financing information missing from the ad.

If an ad contains any of the following trigger terms, five specific disclosures must be included in the ad. Here are the trigger terms: the amount of down payment (for example, nothing down, 10% down $4,995 down, 95% financing); the amount of any payment (for example, monthly payments only $499, buy for less than $650 a month, payments only 1% per month); the number of payments (for example, only 36 monthly payments and you own it, all paid up in 10 annual payments); the period of repayment (for example, 30-year financing, owner will carry for five years, 10-year second available); and the dollar amount of any finance charge (finance this for only $999) or the statement that there is no charge for credit (pay no interest for three years).

Trigger Terms

If any of the above trigger terms is used, then the following five disclosures must appear in the ad. They are (1) the cash price or the amount of the loan; (2) the amount of down payment or a statement that none is required; (3) the number, amount and frequency of repayments; (4) the annual percentage rate; and (5) the deferred payment price or total payments. Item 5 is not a requirement in the case of the sale of a dwelling or a loan secured by a first lien on the dwelling that is being purchased.

The **annual percentage rate** (APR) combines the interest rate with the other costs of the loan into a single figure that shows the true annual cost of borrowing. This is one of the most helpful features of the law as it gives the prospective borrower a standardized yardstick by which to compare financing from different sources.

Annual Percentage Rate

If the annual percentage rate being offered is subject to increase after the transaction takes place (such as with an adjustable rate mortgage), that fact must be stated. For example, "12% annual percentage rate subject to increase after settlement." If the loan has interest rate changes that will follow a predetermined schedule, those terms must be stated. For example, "8% first year, 10% second year, 12% third year, 14% remainder of loan, 13.5% annual percentage rate."

If you wish to say something about financing and avoid triggering full disclosure, you may use general statements. The following would be acceptable: "assumable loan," "financing available," "owner will carry," "terms to fit your budget," "easy monthly payments," or "FHA and VA financing available."

Lending Disclosures   If you are in the business of making loans, the Truth in Lending Act requires you to make 18 disclosures to your borrower. Of these, the four that must be most prominently displayed on the papers the borrower signs are (1) the amount financed, (2) the finance charge, (3) the annual percentage rate and (4) the total payments.

The **amount financed** is the amount of credit provided to the borrower. The **finance charge** is the total dollar amount the credit will cost the borrower over the life of the loan. This includes such things as interest, borrower-paid discount points, loan fees, loan finder's fees, loan service fees, required life insurance and mortgage guarantee premiums. On a long-term mortgage loan, the total finance charge can easily exceed the amount of money being borrowed. For example, the total amount of interest on an 11%, 30-year, $60,000 loan is just over $145,000.

The annual percentage rate was just described. The **total payments** is the amount in dollars the borrower will have paid after making all the payments as scheduled. In the previous 11%, 30-year loan it would be the interest of $145,000 plus the principal of $60,000 for a total of $205,000.

The other 14 disclosures that a lender must make are as follows. (1) The identity of the lender. (2) The payment schedule. (3) Prepayment penalties and rebates. (4) Late payment charges. (5) Any insurance required. (6) Any filing fees. (7) Any collateral required. (8) Any required deposits. (9) Whether the loan can be assumed. (10) The demand feature, if the note has one. (11) The total sales price of the item being purchased if the seller is also the creditor. (12) Any adjustable rate features of the loan. (13) An itemization of the amount financed. (14) A reference to any terms not shown on the disclosure statement but which are shown on the loan contract.

These disclosures must be delivered or mailed to the credit applicant within three business days after the creditor receives the applicant's written request for credit. The applicant must have this information before the transaction can take place, e.g., before the closing can take place.

Any person or firm that regularly extends consumer credit subject to a finance charge (such as interest) or payable by written agreement in more than four installments must comply with the lending disclosures. This includes banks, savings and loans, credit unions, finance companies, etc., and private individuals who extend credit more than five times a year.

Whoever is named on the note as the creditor must make the lending disclosures even if the note is to be resold. A key difference between the old and the new TIL acts is that the new TIL act does not include mortgage brokers or real estate agents as creditors just because they brokered a deal containing financing. This is because they do not appear as creditors on the note. But if a broker takes back a note for part of the commission on a deal, that is the extension of credit and the 18 lending disclosures must be made.

Who Must Comply?

Certain transactions are exempt from the lending disclosure requirement. The first exemption is for credit extended primarily for business, commercial or agricultural purposes. This exemption includes dwelling units purchased for rental purposes (unless the property contains four or less units and the owner occupies one of them, in which case special rules apply).

The second exemption applies to credit over $25,000 secured by personal property unless the property is the principal residence of the borrower. For example, a mobile home that secures a loan over $25,000 qualifies under this exemption if it is used as a vacation home. But it is not exempt if it is used as a principal residence.

Exempt Transactions

If the Federal Trade Commission (FTC) determines that an advertiser has broken the law, the FTC can order the advertiser to cease from further violations. Each violation of that order can result in a $10,000 civil penalty each day the violation continues.

Failure to properly disclose when credit is extended can result in a penalty of twice the amount of the finance charge with a minimum of $100 and a maximum of $1,000 plus court costs, attorney fees and actual damages. In addition the FTC can add a fine of up to $5,000 and/or one year imprisonment. If the required disclosures are not made or the borrower not

Failure to Disclose

given the required 3 days to cancel (see below), the borrower can cancel the transaction at any time within 3 years following the date of the transaction. In that event the creditor must return all money paid by the borrower, and the borrower returns the property to the creditor.

Right to Cancel   A borrower has a limited right to rescind (cancel) a credit transaction. The borrower has 3 business days (counting Saturdays) to back out after signing the loan papers. This aspect of the law was inserted primarily to protect a homeowner from unscrupulous sellers of home improvements and appliances where the credit to purchase is secured by a lien on the home. Vacant lots for sale on credit to buyers who expect to use them for principal residences are also subject to cancellation privileges.

The right to rescind does not apply to credit used for the acquisition or initial construction of one's principal dwelling.

Summary   Truth In Lending regulations are complex and only the highlights have been presented here. If you are involved in transactions that require disclosure, you should seek more information from your local real estate board, lender, attorney or the FTC. Note that the whole topic of truth in lending deals only with disclosure—who must disclose, in what types of situations, what must be disclosed, etc. Truth In Lending legislation does not set the price a lender can charge for a loan. That is determined by supply and demand for funds in the marketplace and, to a lesser degree, by usury laws.

LOAN APPLICATION   When a mortgage lender reviews a real estate loan appli-
AND APPROVAL   cation, the primary concern for both applicant and lender is to approve loan requests that show a high probability of being repaid in full and on time, and to disapprove requests that are likely to result in default and eventual foreclosure. How is this decision made? Figure 11:3 summarizes the key items that a loan officer considers when making a decision regarding a loan request. Let us review these items and observe how they affect the acceptability of a loan to a lender.

In section ①, the lender begins the loan analysis procedure by looking at the property and the proposed financing. Using the property address and legal description, an appraiser is assigned to prepare an appraisal of the property and a title search is ordered. These steps are taken to determine the fair market value of the property and the condition of title. In the event of default, this is the collateral the lender must fall back upon to recover the loan. If the loan request is in connection with a purchase, rather than the refinancing of an existing property, the lender will know the purchase price. As a rule, loans are made on the basis of the appraised value or purchase price, whichever is lower. If the appraised value is lower than the purchase price, the usual procedure is to require the buyer to make a larger cash down payment. The lender does not want to overloan simply because the buyer overpaid for the property.

Continuing in section ①, the year the home was built is requested in order to give the lender some indication of the age of the structure. Note however, chronological age is only part of the loan decision because age must be considered in light of the upkeep and repair of the structure and its construction quality. "No. Units" refers to the number of dwelling units in the structure. For a single-family house this would be 1. For a **duplex,** it's 2; a **triplex,** 3; and a **fourplex,** 4. In a convention that has its roots in FHA history, residential structures containing 1, 2, 3 or 4 units are processed as residential properties. Structures of 5 or more dwelling units are processed as income properties, a topic you will learn more about in Chapter 16 under "Income Approach."

In the past, it was not uncommon for lenders to refuse to make loans in certain neighborhoods regardless of the quality of the structure or the ability of the borrower to repay. This was known as **redlining,** and it effectively shut off mortgage loans in many older or so-called "bad risk" neighborhoods across the country. Today a lender cannot refuse to make a loan simply because of the age or location of a property, or because of neighborhood income level, or because of the racial, ethnic or religious composition of the neighborhood.

Redlining

A lender can refuse to lend on a structure intended for demolition, a property in a known geological hazard area, a single-family dwelling in an area devoted to industrial or commercial use or upon a property that is in violation of zoning laws, deed covenants, conditions or restrictions, or significant health, safety or building codes.

Figure 11:3

RESIDENTIAL MORTGAGE LOAN ANALYSIS

①
Property address _____
Legal description _____
Appraised value $ _____ Purchase price $ _____ Year Built _____ No. Units _____
Down payment $ _____ Total cash required for settlement $ _____
Amount of this mortgage loan $ _____ Other financing $ _____
Loan-to-value ratio: This mortgage loan _____ % All financing for the property _____ %
Source of settlement funds? _____
Purpose of loan? _____
Attitude of borrower _____

② Borrower

Name _____ Marital status _____ School years _____
Age _____
Present address _____ Years _____ Own _____ Rent _____
Former address _____ Years _____ Own _____ Rent _____
Dependents other than co-borrower
Number _____ Ages _____
Employer _____
Years with current employer _____ Years this line of work _____
Position/Title _____
Type of business _____
Self-employed? _____
Previous employer _____
Position _____ Years _____

③ Co-Borrower

Name _____ Marital status _____ School years _____
Age _____
Present address _____ Years _____ Own _____ Rent _____
Former address _____ Years _____ Own _____ Rent _____
Dependents other than co-borrower
Number _____ Ages _____
Employer _____
Years with current employer _____ Years this line of work _____
Position/Title _____
Type of business _____
Self-employed? _____
Previous employer _____
Position _____ Years _____

Occupancy of property? _____

④ Gross Monthly Income

	Borrower	Co-borrower
Base income	$	$
Overtime		
Bonuses		
Commissions		
Interest/Dividends		
Rental income		
Social Security		
Retirement income		
Other		
Total	$	$

⑤ Monthly Housing Expense

	Previous	Proposed
Rent	$	$
First loan (P + I)		
Other loans (P + I)		
Mortgage insurance		
Hazard insurance		
Real estate taxes		
Assessments		
Owners' Assn.		
Utilities		
Total	$	$

Ratio of monthly housing expense to gross monthly income _____ ⑥ _____ %

⑦ Assets

Cash toward purchase	$
Checking and savings	
Stocks and bonds	
Life insurance cash value (Face amount $ ____)	
Sub-total liquid assets	$
Real estate owned	
Retirement fund	
Net worth of business	
Automobiles	
Furniture	
Other assets	
Total Assets	$

⑧ Liabilities

	Mo. Pymt/Mos.	Balance
Installment debts	$ /	$
	/	
	/	
Auto loan		
Real estate loans	/	
Other debts	/	
Alimony/Child support		
Total Mo. Payments	$	
Total Debts		$

Net Worth: *Total assets minus total debts equals $ _____* ⑨

⑩ List credit references _____

Have you declared bankruptcy in the last 7 years? _____ Any pending lawsuits? _____

Any outstanding judgments? _____ Have you ever had property foreclosed upon? _____

Is either applicant a co-maker or endorser on any other loans? _____

Loan-to-Value Ratios   The lender next looks at the amount of down payment the borrower proposes to make, the size of the loan being requested and the amount of other financing the borrower plans to use. This information is then converted into loan-to-value ratios. As a rule, the larger the down payment, the safer the loan is for the lender. On an uninsured loan, the ideal loan-to-value (L/V) ratio for a lender on owner-occupied residential property is 70% or less. This means the value of the property would have to fall more than 30% before the debt owed would exceed the property's value, thus encouraging the borrower to stop making loan payments.

Loan-to-value ratios from 70% through 80% are considered acceptable but do expose the lender to more risk. Lenders sometimes compensate by charging slightly higher interest rates. Loan-to-value ratios above 80% present even more risk of default to the lender, and the lender will either increase the interest rate charged on these loans or require that an outside insurer, such as the FHA or a private mortgage insurer, be supplied by the borrower.

Settlement Funds   Next in section ①, the lender wants to know if the borrower has adequate funds for settlement. Are these funds presently in a checking or savings account, or are they coming from the sale of the borrower's present property? In the latter case, the lender knows the present loan is contingent on closing that escrow. If the down payment and settlement funds are to be borrowed, then the lender will want to be extra cautious as experience has shown that the less money a borrower personally puts into a purchase, the higher the probability of default and foreclosure.

Purpose of Loan   The lender is also interested in the proposed use of the property. Lenders feel most comfortable when a loan is for the purchase or improvement of a property the loan applicant will actually occupy. This is because owner-occupants usually have pride-of-ownership in maintaining their property and even during bad economic conditions will continue to make the monthly payments. An owner-occupant also realizes that losing the home still means paying for shelter elsewhere. It is standard practice for lenders to ask loan applicants to sign a statement stating whether or not they intend to occupy the property.

If the loan applicant intends to purchase a dwelling to rent out as an investment, the lender will be more cautious. This is because during periods of high vacancy, the property may not generate enough income to meet the loan payments. At that point, a strapped-for-cash borrower is likely to default. Note too, that lenders generally avoid loans secured by purely speculative real estate. If the value of the property drops below the amount owed, the borrower may see no further logic in making the loan payments.

Lastly in this section, the lender assesses the borrower's attitude toward the proposed loan. A casual attitude, such as "I'm buying because real estate always goes up," or an applicant who does not appear to understand the obligation being undertaken would bring a low rating here. Much more welcome is the applicant who shows a mature attitude and understanding of the loan obligation and who exhibits a strong and logical desire for ownership.

Borrower Analysis

In sections ② and ③ the lender begins an analysis of the borrower, and if there is one, the co-borrower. At one time, age, sex and marital status played an important role in the lender's decision to lend or not to lend. Often the young and the old had trouble getting loans, as did women and persons who were single, divorced or widowed. Today, the Federal Equal Credit Opportunity Act prohibits discrimination based on age, sex, race and marital status. Lenders are no longer permitted to discount income earned by women from part-time jobs or because the woman is of child-bearing age. If the applicant chooses to disclose it, alimony, separate maintenance and child support must be counted in full. Young adults and single persons cannot be turned down because the lender feels they have not "put down roots." Seniors cannot be turned down as long as life expectancy exceeds the early risk period of the loan and collateral is adequate. In other words, the emphasis in borrower analysis is now focused on job stability, income adequacy, net worth and credit rating.

Thus in sections ② and ③ we see questions directed at how long the applicants have held their present jobs and the stability of those jobs themselves. An applicant who possesses marketable job skills and has been regularly employed with a stable employer is considered the ideal risk. Persons whose income can rise and fall erratically, such as commissioned salespersons, present greater risks. Persons whose skills (or lack of skills) or lack of job seniority result in frequent unemployment are more likely to have difficulty repaying a loan. In these sections the lender also inquires as to the number of dependents the applicant must support out of his or her income. This information provides some insight as to how much will be left for monthly house payments.

Monthly Income   In section ④ the lender looks at the amount and sources of the applicants' income. Quantity alone is not enough for loan approval since the income sources must be stable too. Thus a lender will look carefully at overtime, bonus and commission income in order to estimate the levels at which these may be expected to continue. Interest, dividend and rental income is considered in light of the stability of their sources also. Income from social security and retirement pensions is entered and added to the totals for the applicants. Alimony, child support and separate maintenance payments received need not be revealed. However, such sums must be listed in order to be considered as a basis for repaying the loan.

In section ⑤ the lender compares what the applicants have been paying for housing with what they will be paying if the loan is approved. Included in the proposed housing expense total are principal, interest, taxes and insurance along with any assessments or homeowner association dues (such as in a condominium). Some lenders add the monthly cost of utilities to this list.

At ⑥, proposed monthly housing expense is compared to gross monthly income. A general rule of thumb is that monthly housing expense (PITI) should not exceed 25% to 30% of gross monthly income. A second guideline is that total fixed monthly expenses should not exceed 33% to 38% of income. This includes housing payments plus automobile payments, installment loan payments, alimony, child support and investments with negative cash flows. These are general guidelines, but lenders recognize that food, health care, clothing, transportation, entertainment and income taxes must also come from the applicants' income.

In section ⑦ the lender is interested in the applicants' sources of funds for closing and whether, once the loan is granted, the applicants have assets to fall back upon in the event of an income decrease (a job lay-off) or unexpected expenses (hospital bills). Of particular interest is the portion of those assets that are in cash or are readily convertible into cash in a few days. These are called **liquid assets.** If income drops, they are much more useful in meeting living expenses and loan payments than assets that may require months to sell and convert to cash, that is, assets which are **illiquid.**

Assets and Liabilities

Note in section ⑦ that two values are shown for life insurance. **Cash value** is the amount of money the policyholder would receive if the policy were surrendered to the insurance company or, alternatively, the amount the policyholder could borrow against the policy. **Face amount** is the amount that would be paid in the event of the insured's death. Lenders feel most comfortable if the face amount of the policy equals or exceeds the amount of the proposed loan. Obviously a borrower's death is not anticipated before the loan is repaid, but lenders recognize that its possibility increases the probability of default. The likelihood of foreclosure is lessened considerably if the survivors receive life insurance benefits.

In section ⑧, the lender is interested in the applicants' existing debts and liabilities for two reasons. First, these items will compete each month against housing expenses for available monthly income. Thus high monthly payments in this section may reduce the size of the loan the lender calculates that the applicants will be able to repay. The presence of monthly liabilities is not all negative: it can also show the lender that the applicants are capable of repaying their debts. Second, the applicants' total debts are subtracted from their total assets to obtain their **net worth,** reported at ⑨. If the result is negative (more owed than owned) the loan request will probably be turned down as too risky. In contrast, a substantial net worth can often offset weaknesses elsewhere in the application, such as too little monthly income in relation to monthly housing expense or an income that can rise and fall erratically.

References, etc.   At number ⑩, lenders ask for credit references as an indicator of the future. Applicants with no previous credit experience will have more weight placed on income and employment history. Applicants with a history of collections, adverse judgments, foreclosure or bankruptcy will have to convince the lender that this loan will be repaid on time. Additionally, the applicants may be considered poorer risks if they have guaranteed the repayment of someone else's debt by acting as a comaker or endorser.

Credit Report   As part of the loan application, the lender will order a **credit report** on the applicant(s). The applicant is asked to authorize this and to pay for the report. This provides the lender with an independent means of checking the applicant's credit history. A credit report that shows active use of credit with a good repayment record and no derogatory information is most desirable. The applicant will be asked by the lender to explain any negative information. Because it is possible for inaccurate or untrue information in a credit report to unfairly damage a person's credit reputation, Congress passed the **Fair Credit Reporting Act.** This act gives an individual the right to inspect his or her file at a credit bureau, correct any errors and make explanatory statements to supplement the file.

OVERVIEW   In this chapter you received a good grounding in the mechanics of term loans, amortized loans, balloon loans, partially amortized loans, loan-to-value and equity. Also, you learned something about the functions and importance of the FHA, the VA, private mortgage insurance, loan points and Truth In Lending legislation. Lastly you saw a sample of the type of information a lender requests and considers before granting a real estate loan. In the next chapter you will learn about real estate lenders from whom you can borrow and where those lenders get their money. You will also read about financing techniques that are popular in the United States today.

Match terms **a–x** *with statements* **1–24.**

a. *Amortized loan*
b. *Annual percentage rate*
c. *Balloon payment*
d. *Conventional loan*
e. *CRV*
f. *Equity*
g. *FmHA*
h. *Illiquid assets*
i. *Impound account*
j. *Liquid assets*
k. *Loan balance table*
l. *L/V ratio*

m. *Maturity*
n. *Mortgage insurance*
o. *Origination fee*
p. *Partially amortized loan*
q. *PITI*
r. *Point*
s. *Principal*
t. *Redlining*
u. *Section 203(b)*
v. *Term loan*
w. *Truth In Lending*
x. *Trigger term*

1. Balance owing on a loan.
2. A loan that requires the borrower to pay interest only until maturity, at which time the full amount of the loan must be repaid.
3. Refers to a monthly loan payment that includes principal, interest, property taxes and property insurance.
4. An escrow or reserve account into which the lender places the borrower's monthly tax and insurance payments.
5. The amount a lender will loan on a property divided by the valuation the lender places on the property.
6. A document issued by the Veterans Administration showing the VA's estimate of a property's value.
7. One hundredth of the total amount; 1% of a loan.
8. A real estate loan made without FHA insurance or a VA guarantee.
9. A uniform measure of the annual cost of credit.
10. A loan requiring periodic payments that include both interest and principal.
11. A payment that is larger than any of the previous payments.
12. The market value of a property less the debt against it.
13. A federal law that requires certain disclosures when extending or advertising credit.
14. Assets that may require months to sell and convert to cash.
15. The end of the life of a loan.
16. A loan with a series of amortized payments followed by a balloon payment at maturity.
17. Shows the principal still owing during the life of a loan.
18. Purchased and paid for by the borrower to protect the lender in the event of the borrower's default.
19. FHA's popular mortgage insurance program for houses.
20. The fee charged by a lender to make a loan.
21. Credit information used in advertising that requires additional credit disclosures.

22. Refusal to make a real estate loan based solely on the location of the property.
23. A federal agency under the U.S. Department of Agriculture that will help purchase and operate farms and finance homes in rural areas.
24. Assets that are in cash or are readily convertible to cash in a few days.

QUESTIONS AND PROBLEMS

1. What is the major risk that the borrower takes when he agrees to a loan with a balloon payment?
2. Explain how an amortized loan works.
3. Using Table 11:1, calculate the monthly payment necessary to completely amortize a $65,000, 30-year loan at 11½% interest.
4. A prospective home buyer has a $10,000 down payment and can afford $800 per month for principal and interest payments. If 30-year, 11% amortized loans are available, what price home can the buyer afford?
5. Same problem as in number 4 except that the interest rate has dropped to 9%. What price home can the buyer afford now?
6. Using Table 11:2, calculate the balance still owed on a $90,000, 9½% interest, 30-year amortized loan that is 10 years old.
7. Explain the purpose and operation of the FHA 203(b) home mortgage insurance program.
8. What advantage does the Veterans Administration offer veterans who wish to purchase a home?
9. Explain "points" and their application to real estate lending.
10. What is the basic purpose of the Truth in Lending Act?
11. Why is the monthly income of a loan applicant more important to a lender than the sheer size of the applicant's assets?

ADDITIONAL READINGS

Computers for Real Estate by **Peter Luedtke** and **Rainer Luedtke.** (Harcourt Brace Jovanovich, 1984, 138 pages). Explains benefits of computer systems in real estate and how to choose the right equipment and successfully put it to use.

Monthly Interest Amortization Tables. (Contemporary Books, 1984, 283 pages). Tables cover interest rates from 5% to 28.75%, amounts from $50 to $160,000 and terms up to 40 years. Remaining balance and proration tables are also provided.

Mortgage Lending: Fundamentals and Practices by **Marshall Dennis.** (Reston, 1983, 349 pages). Book includes loan standards and approval, federal regulations, mortgage law, FHA, VA, private mortgage insurance, loan closing and income property financing. Also included are three residential loan case studies.

Sources and Types of Financing

Adjustable rate mortgage: a mortgage on which the interest rate rises and falls with changes in prevailing interest rates

Alienation clause: requires immediate repayment of the loan if ownership transfers; also called a due-on-sale clause

Carryback financing: a note accepted by a seller instead of cash

Equity sharing: an arrangement whereby a party providing financing gets a portion of the ownership

Fannie Mae: a real estate industry nickname for the Federal National Mortgage Association

Mortgage company: a firm that makes mortgage loans and then sells them to investors

Option: a right, for a given period of time, to buy, sell or lease property at specified price and terms

Secondary mortgage market: a market where mortgage loans can be sold to investors

Usury: charging a rate of interest higher than that permitted by law

Wraparound mortgage: a mortgage that encompasses any existing mortgages and is subordinate to them

This chapter will (1) identify various mortgage lenders (the primary market), (2) describe where these lenders get much of their money (the secondary market), and (3) explain mortgage loan instruments and financing techniques currently in use in the United States. Many people consider financing to be the most important of all real estate topics because without financing real estate profits and commissions would be difficult to achieve.

PRIMARY MARKET

The **primary market** (also called the **primary mortgage market**) is where lenders originate loans, i.e., where lenders make funds available to borrowers. Examples are savings and loans (S&Ls), commercial banks, mutual savings banks and mortgage companies. The primary market is what the borrower sees as the source of mortgage loan money. It's the institution with which the borrower has direct and personal contact. It's the place where the loan application is taken, the place where the loan officer interviews the loan applicant, the place where the loan check comes from, and the place to which loan payments are sent by the borrower.

Most borrowers assume that the loan they receive comes from depositors who visit the same bank or S&L to leave their excess funds. This is partly true. But this by itself would be an inadequate source of loan funds in today's market. Thus, primary lenders often sell their loans in what is called the secondary market. Insurance companies, pension funds and individual investors as well as other primary lenders with excess deposits buy these loans for cash. This makes more money available to a primary lender that, in turn, can be loaned to borrowers. The secondary market is so huge that it rivals the entire U.S. corporate bond market in size of annual offerings. We will return to the secondary market later in this chapter. Meanwhile, let us discuss the various lenders a borrower will encounter when looking for a real estate loan.

SAVINGS AND LOAN ASSOCIATIONS

As a group, the nation's 4,000 **savings and loan associations** are the foremost money lenders for residential real estate. Historically, their origin can be traced to early building societies in England and Germany and to the first American building society, the Oxford Provident Building Association, started in 1831 in Pennsylvania. These early building societies were co-operatives where savers were also borrowers. Over time, the emergence of two distinct groups led to the savings and loan associations of today: those who wanted to save and those who wanted to borrow. Today, savings and loan associations (S&Ls) offer interest bearing passbook accounts that allow savers to make deposits at any time and in any amount; and withdrawals, for all practical purposes, are available on demand.

Disintermediation

Savings and loans also offer **certificates of deposit (CDs)** at rates higher than passbook rates in order to attract depositors. This is necessary to compete with higher yields offered by U.S. Treasury bills, notes and bonds and to prevent disintermediation. **Disintermediation** results when depositors take money out of their savings accounts and invest directly in government securities, corporate bonds and money market funds. A major problem, and one that nearly brought the S&L industry to its knees in the late 1970s and early 1980s, was that S&Ls tradi- tionally relied heavily upon short-term deposits from savers and then loaned that money on long-term (often 30-year) loans to borrowers. When interest rates rose sharply in the 1970s, S&Ls either had to raise the interest paid to their depositors or watch depositors withdraw their savings and take the money elsewhere for higher returns. Meanwhile, the S&Ls were hold- ing long-term, fixed-rate mortgage loans, and with interest rates rising, borrowers were not anxious to repay those loans early.

Today, S&Ls are aggressively stretching out their deposit accounts by offering higher rates on longer-term (often 5- and 10-year) certificates of deposit. S&Ls are also aggressively en- forcing due-on-sale clauses in existing mortgage loans, and are encouraging new mortgage loan borrowers to take adjustable rate loans. These actions will help S&Ls to more closely match the rates they must pay depositors with the rates they receive on loans.

COMMERCIAL BANKS

The nation's 15,000 **commercial banks** store far more of the country's money than the S&Ls. However, only one bank dollar in six goes to real estate lending. As a result, in total number of dollars, commercial banks rank second behind S&Ls in importance in real estate lending. Of the loans made by banks on real estate, the tendency is to emphasize short- term maturities since the bulk of a bank's deposit money comes from demand deposits (checking accounts) and a much smaller portion from savings and time deposits. Consequently, banks are particularly active in making loans to finance real es- tate construction as these loans have maturities of 6 months to 3 years. Some banks offer real estate loans up to 30 years. However, a bank will usually sell loans with long maturities rather than keep them in its investment portfolio.

MUTUAL SAVINGS BANKS

Important contributors to real estate credit in several states are the nation's 400 **mutual savings banks**. Started in Philadel- phia in 1816 and in Boston in 1817, mutual savings banks are found primarily in the northeastern United States, where they compete aggressively for the savings dollar. The states of Mas- sachusetts, New York and Connecticut account for 75% of the nation's total. As the word "mutual" implies, the depositors are the owners, and the "interest" they receive is the result of the bank's success or failure in lending. Mutual savings banks offer accounts similar to those offered by S&Ls. To protect depositors, laws require mutual savings banks to place deposits in high-quality investments, including sound real estate mortgage loans.

LIFE INSURANCE COMPANIES

As a group, the nation's 2,200 **life insurance companies** have long been active investors in real estate as developers, owners and long-term lenders. Their source of money is the premiums paid by policyholders. These premiums are invested and ultimately returned to the policyholders. Because premiums are collected in regular amounts on regular dates and because policy payoffs can be calculated from actuarial tables, life insurers are in ideal positions to commit money to long-term investments. Life insurance companies channel their funds primarily into government and corporate bonds and real estate. The dollars allocated to real estate go to buy land and buildings, which are leased to users, and to make loans on commercial, industrial and residential property. Generally, life insurers specialize in large-scale investments such as shopping centers, office and apartment buildings, and million-dollar blocks of home loans purchased in the secondary mortgage market.

Repayment terms on loans made by insurance companies for shopping centers, office buildings and apartment complexes sometimes call for interest and a percentage of any profits from rentals over a certain level. This **participation** feature, or "piece of the action," is intended to provide the insurance company with more inflation protection than a fixed rate of interest.

MORTGAGE COMPANIES

A **mortgage company** makes a mortgage loan and then sells it to a long-term investor. The process begins with locating borrowers, qualifying them, preparing the necessary loan papers, and finally making the loans. Once a loan is made, it is sold for cash on the secondary market. The mortgage company will usually continue to **service the loan,** that is, collect the monthly payments and handle such matters as insurance and property tax impounds, delinquencies, early payoffs and mortgage releases.

Mortgage companies, also known as **mortgage bankers,** vary in size from one or two persons to several dozen. As a rule, they are locally oriented, finding and making loans within 25 or 50 miles of their offices. This gives them a feel for their market, greatly aids in identifying sound loans, and makes loan servicing much easier. For their efforts, mortgage bankers typically receive 1% to 3% of the amount of the loan when it is originated, and from ¼ to ½ of 1% of the outstanding balance each year thereafter for servicing. Mortgage banking, as this business is called, is not limited to mortgage companies. Commercial banks, savings and loan associations, and mutual savings banks in active real estate areas often originate more real estate loans than they can hold themselves, and these are sold on the secondary market. Mortgage companies often do a large amount of their business in FHA and VA loans.

Mortgage brokers, in contrast to mortgage bankers, specialize in bringing together borrowers and lenders, just as real estate brokers bring together buyers and sellers. The mortgage broker does not lend money, and usually does not service loans. The mortgage broker's fee is expressed in points and is usually paid by the borrower. Mortgage brokers are locally oriented and often small firms of from 1 to 10 persons.

MORTGAGE BROKERS

In some cities, **municipal bonds** provide a source of mortgage money for home buyers. The special advantage to borrowers is that municipal bonds pay interest that is tax-free from federal income taxes. Knowing this, bond investors will accept a lower rate of interest than they would if the interest were taxable—as it normally is on mortgage loans. This saving is passed on to the home buyer. Those who qualify will typically pay about 2% less than if they had borrowed through conventional channels.

MUNICIPAL BONDS

The objective of such programs is to make home ownership more affordable for low- and middle-income households. Also, a city may stipulate that loans be used in neighborhoods the city wants to revitalize. The loans are made by local lenders who are paid a fee for originating and servicing these loans. Although popular with the real estate industry, the U.S. Treasury has been less than enthusiastic about the concept because it bears the cost in lost tax revenues. As a result, federal legislation has been passed to limit the future use of this source of money.

OTHER LENDERS

Pension funds and **trust funds** traditionally have channeled their money to high-grade government and corporate bonds and stocks. However, the trend now is to place more money into real estate loans. Already active buyers on the secondary market, pension and trust funds will likely become a still larger source of real estate financing in the future. In some localities, pension fund members can tap their own pension funds for home mortgages at very reasonable rates. This is an often overlooked source of primary market financing.

Finance companies that specialize in making business and consumer loans also provide limited financing for real estate. As a rule, finance companies seek second mortgages at interest rates 2% to 5% higher than the rates prevailing on first mortgages. First mortgages are also taken as collateral; however, the lenders already discussed usually charge lower interest rates for these loans and thus are more competitive.

Credit unions normally specialize in consumer loans. However, real estate loans are becoming more and more important as many of the country's 16,000 credit unions have branched out into first and second mortgage loans. Credit unions are an often overlooked but excellent source of home loan money.

Individuals are sometimes a source of cash loans for real estate, with the bulk of these loans made between relatives or friends. Generally, loan maturities are shorter than those obtainable from the institutional lenders already described. In some cities, persons can be found who specialize in making or buying second and third mortgage loans of up to 10-year maturities. Individuals are beginning to invest substantial amounts of money in secondary mortgage market securities. Ironically, these investments are often made with money that would have otherwise been deposited in a savings and loan.

Individuals are heavily involved in carryback financing. This is where the seller agrees to take payments from the buyer rather than cash. Because of its importance, carryback financing is discussed under its own heading later in this chapter.

SECONDARY MARKET

The **secondary market** (also called the **secondary mortgage market**) provides a way for a lender to sell a loan. It also permits investment in real estate loans without the need for loan origination and servicing facilities. Although not directly encountered by real estate buyers, sellers and agents, the secondary market plays an important role in getting money from those who want to lend to those who want to borrow. In other words think of the secondary market as a pipeline for loan money. Now visualize that pipeline running via the Wall Street financial district in New York City as Wall Street is now a major participant in residential mortgage lending. Figure 12:1 illustrates this pipeline and diagrams key differences between the traditional mortgage delivery system and the secondary market system.

MORTGAGE LOAN DELIVERY SYSTEMS   **Figure 12:1**

Traditional System

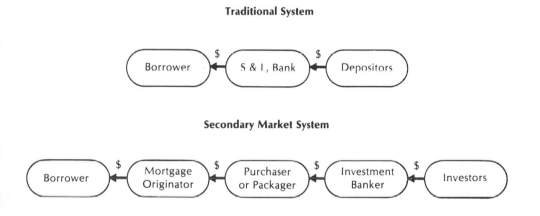

Secondary Market System

Notice in Figure 12:1 that in the traditional system the lender is a local institution gathering deposits from the community and then lending that money as real estate loans in the same community. Traditionally, each lender (S&L, mutual savings bank, commercial bank, credit union) was an independent unit that developed its own appraisal technique, loan application form, loan approval criteria, note and mortgage forms, servicing method and foreclosure policy. Nonetheless, three major problems needed solving. The first was the institution that had an imbalance of depositors and borrowers. Rapidly growing areas of the United States often needed more loan money than their savers were capable of depositing. Stable regions had more depositors than loan opportunities. Thus it was

Traditional Delivery System

common to see correspondent relationships between lenders where, for example, a lender in Los Angeles would sell some of its mortgage loans to a savings bank in Brooklyn. This provided loans for borrowers and interest for savers. The system worked well but required individual correspondent relationships.

The second problem occurs when depositors want to withdraw money from their accounts and invest it elsewhere. To meet withdrawals, lenders need a marketplace in which to convert their loans to cash. Lastly, experience in the 1970s and early 1980s taught S&Ls and mutual savings banks (also called **thrifts**) the hard lessons of borrowing short and lending long. Savers are now encouraged to leave their money on deposit longer, and lenders are looking for ways to better manage the maturities on the loans they make.

Secondary Market Delivery Systems

As shown in Figure 12:1, with the secondary market system the borrower obtains a loan from a mortgage originator. This includes mortgage companies as well as banks and thrifts that originate loans they intend to sell. The mortgage originator packages the loan with other loans and then either sells the package as a whole or keeps the package and sells securities which are backed by the loans in the package. If the originator is not large enough to package its own mortgages, it will sell the loans to someone who can. Next, investment bankers (including some of the largest stockbrokers in the United States) locate investors with money to invest. These investors are pension funds, life insurance companies, trust funds, private individuals and thrifts. Interestingly, the thrifts, especially the S&Ls, are the biggest sellers and the biggest buyers.

Standardized Loan Procedures

A major stumbling block to a highly organized and efficient secondary market has been the uniqueness of both lenders and loans. Traditionally, each lender developed its own special loan forms and procedures. Moreover, each loan is a unique combination of real estate and borrower. No two are exactly alike. How do you package such diversity into an attractive package for investors? A large part of the answer has come through standardized loan application forms, standardized appraisal forms, standardized credit report forms, standardized closing statements, standardized loan approval criteria and standardized promissory notes, mortgages and trust deeds. Loan terms have been standardized into categories, for example, fixed-rate 30-year loans, fixed-rate 15-year loans and various adjustable rate combinations. Additionally, nearly all loans must be insured. This can take the form of FHA or private mortgage insurance, or a VA guarantee, on each loan in the package. Additionally, there will be some form of assurance of timely repayment of the mortgage package as a whole. The net result is a mortgage security that is attractive to investors who in the past have not been interested in investing in mortgages.

Let us now look at some of the key secondary market participants including the three giants of the industry: the FNMA, GNMA and FHLMC.

The **Federal National Mortgage Association (FNMA)** was organized by the federal government in 1938 to buy FHA mortgage loans from lenders. This made it possible for lenders to grant more loans to consumers. Ten years later it began purchasing VA loans. FNMA (fondly known in the real estate business and to itself as **"Fannie Mae"**) was successful in its mission.

FNMA

In 1968 Congress divided the FNMA into two organizations: the Government National Mortgage Association (to be discussed in the next section) and the FNMA as we know it today. As part of that division, the FNMA changed from a government agency to a private profit-making corporation, chartered by Congress but owned by its shareholders and managed independently of the government. There are some 60 million shares of Fannie Mae stock in existence, and it is one of the most actively traded issues on the New York Stock Exchange. Fannie Mae buys FHA and VA loans and, since 1972, conventional whole loans from lenders across the United States. Money to buy these loans comes from the sale of FNMA stock plus the sale of FNMA bonds and notes. FNMA bond and note holders look to Fannie Mae for timely payment of principal and interest on these bonds and notes, and Fannie Mae looks to its mortgagors for principal and interest payments on the loans it owns. Thus, Fannie Mae stands in the middle and, although it is very careful to match interest rates and maturities between the loans it buys and the bonds and notes it sells, it still takes the risk of the middleman. In this respect, it is like a giant thrift institution.

Commitments   Fannie Mae's method of operation is to sell commitments to lenders pledging to buy specified dollar amounts of mortgage loans within a fixed period of time and usually at a specified yield. Lenders are not obligated to sell loans to Fannie Mae if they can find better terms elsewhere. However, Fannie Mae must purchase all loans delivered to it under the terms of the commitments. Loans must be made using FNMA-approved forms and loan approval criteria. The largest loan Fannie Mae would buy in 1985 was $115,300. This limit is adjusted each year as housing prices change. Fannie Mae will also buy loans on duplexes, triplexes and fourplexes all at larger loan limits. Although the FNMA loan limit may seem inadequate for some houses and neighborhoods, the intention of Congress is that Fannie Mae cater to the mid-range of housing prices and leave the upper end of the market to others.

In addition to purchasing first mortgages, Fannie Mae also purchases second mortgages from lenders. FNMA forms and criteria must be followed and the loan-to-value ratio of the combined first and second mortgages cannot exceed 80% if owner-occupied and 70% if not owner-occupied. This is a very helpful program for a person who has watched the value of his or her home increase and wants to borrow against that increase without first having to repay the existing mortgage loan.

Home Seller Program   Another innovation of Fannie Mae to help real estate is the **home seller program.** This is a secondary market for sellers who carryback mortgages. To qualify, the note and mortgage must be prepared by a FNMA-approved lender using standard FNMA loan qualification procedures. The note and mortgage may be kept by the home seller as an investment or sold to a FNMA-approved lender for possible resale to the FNMA.

In other developments, Fannie Mae has standardized the terms of adjustable rate mortgages it will purchase. This is a major step forward in reducing the proliferation of variety in these loans. Fannie Mae is also test marketing mortgage-backed securities in $1,000 increments to appeal to individuals, particularly for Individual Retirement Accounts. Additionally, Fannie Mae has started a collateralized mortgage obligation program and begun a mortgage pass-through program, both of which will be defined momentarily.

The **Government National Mortgage Association** (**GNMA**, popularly known to the industry and to itself as **"Ginnie Mae"**) was created in 1968 when the FNMA was partitioned into two separate corporations. Ginnie Mae is a federal agency entirely within the Department of Housing and Urban Development (HUD). Although Ginnie Mae has some low-income housing functions, it is best known for its mortgage-backed securities (MBS) program. The purpose of the MBS program is to attract new sources of credit to FHA, VA and FmHA mortgages. Ginnie Mae does this by guaranteeing timely repayment of privately issued securities backed by pools of these mortgages.

GNMA

To create a **mortgage-backed security,** the security issuer (such as a bank or S&L) obtains an MBS commitment from Ginnie Mae. The issuer either originates or acquires mortgage loans and creates a pool of mortgages of similar interest rate and maturity. The minimum pool size is $1 million, and the loans are deposited with an independent custodian. Certificates representing undivided ownerships in the pool and carrying Ginnie Mae's guarantee of timely repayment are sold to investors. Minimum purchase is $25,000 and security dealers handle the sales. Each month the investor receives a check from the issuer for a share of the principal and interest scheduled to be made that month and a pro rata share of any prepayments of principal. These are classified as **pass-through securities** as the investors receive a "pass-through" of principal and interest payments due on the pool of mortgages.

Mortgage-Backed Security

The interest rate paid to the investor is ½% less than the interest rate on the loans in the pool. Because this represents a very attractive return and because the individual loans are government insured or guaranteed and because the pool as a whole is guaranteed by Ginnie Mae, these pass-throughs have become very popular investments not only for pension funds and other institutional investors but also for individuals. For an individual who does not have the $25,000 minimum, there are mutual funds that buy Ginnie Mae's and reoffer them in units as small as $1,000.

FHLMC   The **Federal Home Loan Mortgage Corporation (FHLMC**, also known to the industry and to itself as **"Freddie Mac"** or the "Mortgage Corporation") was created by Congress in 1970. Its goal, like that of the FNMA and GNMA, is to increase the availability of financing for residential mortgages. Where it differs is that Freddie Mac deals primarily in conventional mortgages, and it was initially established to serve as a secondary market for S&L members of the Federal Home Loan Bank System. Other differences are that unlike Ginnie Mae, which guarantees securities issued by others, Freddie Mac issues its own securities against its own mortgage pools. These securities are its participation certificates and collateralized mortgage obligations.

Participation   **Participation certificates** (PCs) allow a mortgage originator
Certificates   to deliver to Freddie Mac either whole mortgages or part interest in a pool of whole mortgages. In return, Freddie Mac gives the mortgage originator a PC representing an undivided interest in a pool of investment-quality conventional mortgages created from mortgages and mortgage interests purchased by Freddie Mac. Freddie Mac guarantees that the interest and principal on these PCs will be repaid in full and on time, even if the underlying mortgages are in default. (Freddie Mac reduces its losses by setting strict loan qualification criteria and requiring mortgage insurance on high loan-to-value loans.) The PCs can be kept as investments, sold for cash or used as collateral for loans. PCs are popular investments for S&Ls, pension funds and other institutional investors looking for high-yield investments. Individuals who can meet the $25,000 minimum also find PCs attractive. Freddie Mac also has a collateralized mortgage obligation program and plans to offer a trust for investments in mortgages. These are designed to deal with the unpredictability of mortgage maturities caused by early repayment. This is accomplished by dividing the cash flows from a mortgage pool into separate securities with separate maturities which are then sold to investors.

The financial success of the three giants of the secondary mortgage market (FNMA, GNMA and FHLMC) has brought private mortgage packagers into the marketplace. These are organizations such as MGIC Investment Corporation (a subsidiary of Mortgage Guaranty Investment Corporation); Residential Funding Corporation (a subsidiary of Norwest Mortgage Corp.); financial subsidiaries of such household-name companies as General Electric, Lockheed Aircraft and Sears, Roebuck; and mortgage packaging subsidiaries of state Realtor associations. These organizations both compete with the big three and specialize in markets not served by them. For example, Residential Funding Corp. will package mortgage loans as large as $500,000, well above the limits imposed by FNMA and FHLMC (same as FNMA) and limits on FHA and VA loans. All of these organizations will buy from loan originators who are not large enough to create their own pools. At least one specializes in helping to originate seller carryback loans that can be sold on the secondary market.

PRIVATE CONDUITS

Before leaving the topic of the secondary market, it is important to note that without electronic data transmission and computers, the programs just described would be severely handicapped. There are currently thousands of mortgage pools each containing from $1 million to $500 million (and more) in mortgage loans. Each loan in a pool has its own monthly payment schedule, and each payment must be broken down into its principal and interest components and any property tax and insurance impounds. Computers do this work as well as issue receipts and late notices. The pool, in turn, will be owned by several dozen to a hundred or more investors each with a different fractional interest in the pool. Once a month incoming mortgage payments are tallied, a small fee deducted for the operation of the pool and the balance allotted among the investors, all by computer. A computer will also print and mail checks to investors and provide them with an accounting of the pool's asset level.

COMPUTERIZATION

With advanced computer programs now available, secondary market operators are dispensing with the monthly mailing of checks to large investors. Instead, funds are electronically

Electronic Transfers

transmitted directly to the investor's bank account and the investor receives a notice that this has been done. If an investor is in more than one pool, the computer combines all payments due into one statement and one automatic deposit. Keeping track of the numbers is no small matter when a single large investor can be in as many as 1,000 different pools, and Freddie Mac, for example, is issuing 12 to 40 new pools a day. (By comparison, Fannie Mae does about as much business—$20 billion a year—as Freddie Mac. Ginnie Mae does about $50 billion a year.)

MORTGAGE NETWORKS

Old timers to real estate will remember when a weekly sheet listing mortgage lenders in town with their current loan rates was passed around each real estate office. As interest rates began to fluctuate wildly in the late 1970s, this sheet was updated and circulated more often. In some real estate offices one person was given the job of calling lenders daily for quotes on loan availability and interest rates. Since then, rate changes have become a bit less frequent and, more importantly, the weekly loan sheet is being replaced by a computer terminal. A salesperson simply types in words that request loan information, and the computer screen shows lenders' names plus their current loan offerings and interest rates. A salesperson can shop by computer for the best loan for a buyer and the buyer can watch. The salesperson (or buyer) then makes telephone contact with the lender and arranges for a loan interview.

Some of the more sophisticated mortgage networks go further. The salesperson can touch additional keys, and the computer will prequalify the buyer, match the buyer with a loan and tell the lender to mail loan application papers to that real estate office. If the real estate office has a printer, a loan application and loan agreement can be typed out on the spot.

There are currently a dozen computerized mortgage networks in the United States and more are being formed. Some networks are local and some are national. Some offer information only, and others allow the real estate office to interact with the lender. Some networks will issue a loan commitment by computer in the real estate office. With loan formats becoming more standardized because of the secondary mortgage market, shopping for a mortgage loan by computer is beginning to resemble shopping for generic brands at discount stores. Note that a lender will not be on a computer network unless it chooses to be and pays a fee. Nonmember lenders would still have to be contacted by telephone. The networks also charge real estate offices to be on the network.

Thus far we have been concerned with the money pipelines between lenders and borrowers. Ultimately though, money must have a source. These sources are savings generated by individuals and businesses as a result of their spending less than they earn **(real savings)**, and government-created money, called **fiat money** or "printing press money." This second source does not represent unconsumed labor and materials; instead it competes for available goods and services alongside the savings of individuals and businesses.

In the arena of money and capital, real estate borrowers must compete with the needs of government, business and consumers. Governments, particularly the federal government, compete the hardest when they borrow to finance a deficit. Not to borrow would mean bankruptcy and the inability to pay government employees and provide government programs and services. Strong competition also comes from business and consumer credit sectors. In the face of strong competition for loan funds, home buyers must either pay higher interest or be outbid.

One "solution" to this problem is for the federal government to create more money, thus making competition for funds easier and interest rates lower. Unfortunately, the net result is often "too much money chasing too few goods," and prices are pulled upward by the demand caused by the newly created money. This is followed by rising interest rates as savers demand higher returns to compensate for losses in purchasing power. Many economists feel that the higher price levels and interest rates of the 1970s were due to applying too much of this "solution" to the economy since 1965.

The alternative solution, from the standpoint of residential loans, is to increase real savings or decrease competing demands for available money. A number of plans and ideas have been put forth by civic, business and political leaders. They include proposals to simplify income taxes and balance the federal budget, incentives to increase productive output and incentives to save money in retirement accounts.

AVAILABILITY AND PRICE OF MORTGAGE MONEY

Usury   An old idea that has been tried, but is of dubious value for holding down interest rates, is legislation to impose interest rate ceilings. Known as **usury laws** and found in nearly all states, these laws were originally enacted to prohibit lenders from overcharging interest on loans to individuals. However, since the end of World War II, the ceilings in some states have failed to keep in step with rising interest rates with the result that borrowers are denied loans. Most states have raised usury limits in response to higher interest rates. But the rules and exceptions are so complex that a local attorney must be consulted. Additionally, the U.S. Congress passed legislation in 1980 that exempts from state usury limits most home loans made by institutional lenders.

Price to the Borrower   Ultimately, the rate of interest the borrower must pay to obtain a loan is dependent on the cost of money to the lender, reserves for default, loan servicing costs, and available investment alternatives. For example, go to a savings institution and see what they are paying depositors on various accounts. To this add 2% for the cost of maintaining cash in the tills, office space, personnel, advertising, free gifts for depositors, deposit insurance, loan servicing, loan reserves for defaults and a ¼% profit margin. This will give you an idea of how much borrowers must be charged.

Life insurance companies, pension funds and trust funds do not have to "pay" for their money like thrift institutions. Nonetheless, they do want to earn the highest possible yields, with safety, on the money in their custody. Thus, if a real estate buyer wants to borrow in order to buy a home, the buyer must compete successfully with the other investment opportunities available on the open market. To determine the rate for yourself, look at the yields on newly issued corporate bonds as shown in the financial section of your daily newspaper. Add ½ of 1% to this for the extra work in packaging and servicing mortgage loans and you will have the interest rate home borrowers must pay to attract lenders.

DUE-ON-SALE   From an investment risk standpoint, when a lender makes a loan with a fixed interest rate, the lender recognizes that, during the life of the loan, interest rates may rise or fall. When they rise, the lender remains locked into a lower rate. Most loans contain a **due-on-sale clause** (also called an **alienation clause** or a **call clause**). In the past, these were inserted by lenders so that if the borrower sold the property to someone considered uncreditworthy by the lender, the lender could call the loan balance due. Today lenders use these clauses to increase the rate of interest on the loan when the property changes hands. They enforce the clause by threatening to accelerate the balance of the loan unless the new owner will accept a higher rate of return.

Two important legal events have established lenders' rights to enforce due-on-sale clauses. One occurred in June, 1982, when the U.S. Supreme Court decided the *Fidelity Federal Savings and Loan* vs. *de la Cuesta* case. The Court found in favor of Fidelity Federal ruling that federally chartered savings and loan associations have the right to enforce due-on-sale clauses. In October of the same year, Congress passed the **Garn–St. Germain Depository Institutions Act** (the **Garn Act**). The Garn Act makes all due-on-sale clauses in mortgage loans made by deposit institutions enforceable. In 39 states, this has been less than a major issue because those states have always upheld the enforceability of due-on-sale clauses. Where the Garn Act made a big difference was in the other 11 states: Arkansas, Arizona, California, Colorado, Georgia, Iowa, Michigan, Minnesota, New Mexico, Utah and Vermont. These states had taken legislative or court action to stop due-on-sale clauses from being enforced. The Garn Act reversed this through a "window period" provision that lasted through October 15, 1985. Unless a state legislature acted to preserve its nonenforceability stand before that date, due-on-sale clauses in existing loans are now fully enforceable. Due-on-sale clauses are also enforceable in any mortgage loan made after October 15, 1982, by any deposit institution anywhere in the United States. The Garn Act does not apply to sellers who carryback a loan or to mortgage companies; they are still controlled by state law regarding due-on-sale enforceability.

Garn Act

Why is all this an important issue? The answer is that when interest rates are high, a seller can sell more quickly and for a

The Issue

higher price if the seller is able to pass along to the buyer an existing low-interest rate loan. A lender, however, takes a financial loss whenever the lender receives less interest on a loan than it is paying to borrow money from savers. With enough loans like this a lender can go bankrupt. And if enough lenders go bankrupt, loans will be harder to find. So there is no simple solution. Meanwhile, lenders are writing new loan contracts that specifically allow for interest rate increases upon alienation. Therefore, it is important to understand what constitutes an alienation that will allow a lender to accelerate a loan.

The Garn Act uses the words "sale or transfer" to define alienation and gives the Federal Home Loan Bank Board the power to interpret this very broadly. The obvious example is the sale of a property wherein the seller delivers a deed to the buyer and the buyer records it. But, due-on-sale enforcement can also result from the creation of an installment contract, the creation of a lease with option to buy, the creation of a lease of more than 3 years, the creation or refinancing of a junior lien (owner-occupied single-family homes excluded), the foreclosure of a junior lien, and a transfer into a trust (owner-occupied single-family homes excluded). Before undertaking any of these transactions, the wise real estate owner or investor will obtain a written statement from the lender agreeing not to accelerate the loan. The wise real estate agent will point out the Garn Act to clients and customers before suggesting a deal that would trigger due-on-sale.

PREPAYMENT

If loan rates drop it becomes worthwhile for a borrower to shop for a new loan and repay the existing one in full. To compensate, loan contracts sometimes call for a **prepayment penalty** in return for giving the borrower the right to repay the loan early. A typical prepayment penalty amounts to the equivalent of 6 months interest on the amount that is being paid early. However, this can vary from loan to loan and from state to state. Some loan contracts permit up to 20% of the unpaid balance to be paid in any one year without penalty. Other contracts make the penalty stiffest when the loan is young. In certain states, laws do not permit prepayment penalties on loans more than 5 years old. By federal law, prepayment penalties are not allowed on FHA and VA loans.

As we have already seen, a major problem for savings institutions is that they are locked into long-term loans while being dependent on short-term savings deposits. As a result, savings institutions now prefer to make mortgage loans that allow the interest rate to rise and fall during the life of the loan. To make this arrangement more attractive to borrowers, these loans are offered at a lower rate of interest than a fixed-rate loan of similar maturity.

ADJUSTABLE RATE MORTGAGES

The first step toward mortgage loans with adjustable interest rates came in the late 1970s. The loan was called a **variable rate mortgage** and the interest rate could be adjusted by the lender up or down during the 30-year life of the loan to reflect the rise and fall in interest rates paid to savers by the lender. The Federal Home Loan Bank Board (FHLBB) limited adjustments to no more than ½ of 1% each 6 months and a maximum of 2½% over the life of the loan. Any changes in the interest rate on the loan were reflected each 6 months in the monthly payments on the loan. Then in 1980, the FHLBB approved the use of a **renegotiable rate mortgage** loan. This was a 30-year loan with a requirement that every 1, 3 or 5 years the interest rate be adjusted to reflect current market conditions. Monthly payments were then adjusted up or down accordingly.

In 1981, the FHLBB authorized savings institutions to make the type of adjustable mortgage loan you are most likely to encounter in today's loan marketplace. This loan format is called an **adjustable rate mortgage (ARM)** or **adjustable mortgage loan (AML).** In authorizing ARMs the FHLBB's main requirement is that the interest rate on these loans be tied to some publicly available index that is mutually acceptable to the lender and the borrower. Basically, the concept is the same as the variable rate mortgage: as interest rates rise and fall in the open market, then the interest rate the lender is entitled to receive from the borrower rises and falls. The purpose is to more closely match what the savings institution receives from borrowers to what it must pay savers to attract funds.

Current Format

The benefit of an ARM to a borrower is that ARMs carry an initial interest rate that is lower than the rate on a fixed-rate mortgage of similar maturity. This often makes the difference between being able to qualify for a desired home and not qual-

Figure 12:2

ADJUSTABLE RATE MORTGAGE

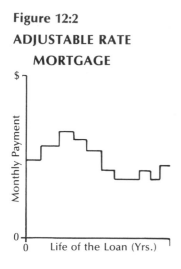

ifying for it. Other advantages to the borrower are that if market interest rates fall, the borrower's monthly payments will fall. (This is done without the cost of prepayment penalties and new loan origination costs as with a fixed-rate loan.) Most ARMs allow assumption by a new buyer at the terms in the ARM, and most allow total prepayment without penalty, particularly if there has been an upward adjustment in the interest rate.

The disadvantage of an ARM to the borrower is that if interest rates rise, the borrower is going to pay more. In periods of rising interest rates, property values and wages presumably will rise. But the possibility of progressively larger monthly payments for the family home is still not attractive. As a result, various compromises have been worked out between lenders and borrowers so that rates can rise on loans, but not by too much. In view of the fact that about one-half of all mortgage loans being originated by thrifts, banks and mortgage companies are now adjustable, let us take a closer look at what a borrower gets with this loan format.

Interest Rate

The interest rate on an ARM is tied to an **index rate.** When the index rate moves up or down, so do the borrower's payments when adjustment time arrives. Lenders and borrowers alike want a rate that genuinely reflects current market conditions for interest rates and which can be easily verified. By far, the most popular index is the interest rate on 1-year U.S. Treasury securities. Next most popular is the cost of funds to thrift institutions as measured by the FHLBB. A few loans use 6-month Treasury bills as an index rate.

Margin

To the index rate is added the margin. The **margin** is for the lender's cost of doing business, risk of loss on the loan and profit. Currently this runs from 2% to 3%, depending on the characteristics of the loan. This is a useful comparison device because if two lenders are offering the same loan terms and the same index, but one loan has a margin of 2% and the other 3%, then the one with the 2% margin will have lower loan payments. As a rule, the margin stays constant during the life of the loan. At each adjustment point in the loan's life, the lender takes the index rate and adds the margin. The total becomes the interest the borrower will pay until the next adjustment occurs.

The amount of time that elapses between adjustments is called the **adjustment period.** By far, the most common adjustment period is 1 year. Less commonly used are 6-month, 3-year and 5-year adjustment periods. When market rates are rising, the longer adjustment periods benefit the borrower. When market rates are falling, the shorter periods benefit the borrower because index decreases will show up sooner in their monthly payments.

Adjustment Period

Many lenders offer an **interest rate cap** or ceiling on how much the interest rate can increase for any one adjustment period during the life of the loan. If the cap is very low, say ½% per year, the lender does not have much more flexibility than if holding a fixed-rate loan. Thus, there would be little reduction of initial rate on the loan compared to a fixed-rate loan. If there is no cap at all, the borrower may feel quite uneasy. Compromises have prevailed, and the two most popular caps are 1% and 2% per year. In other words, the index rate may rise by 3%, but the cap limits the borrower's rate increase to 1% or 2%. Any unused difference may be added the next year, assuming the index rate has not fallen in the meantime.

Interest Rate Cap

Most borrowers also like to have a **lifetime cap** on interest. The purpose is to relieve the borrower's concern of interest rates rising without limit. A popular arrangement is a 5% life-of-loan interest rate cap. Thus, if an ARM is written at 10% interest, the maximum it could go to during its life is 15% interest.

What if a loan's index rate rises so fast that the annual rate cap is reached each year and the lifetime cap is reached soon in the life of the loan? A borrower might be able to handle a modest increase in payments each year, but not big jumps in quick succession. To counteract this possibility, a **payment cap** sets a limit on how much the borrower's monthly payment can increase in any one year. A popular figure now in use is 7½%. In other words, no matter how high a payment is called for by the index rate, the borrower's monthly payment can rise, at the

Payment Cap

most, 7½% per year. For example, given an initial rate of 10% on a 30-year ARM for $100,000, the monthly payment of interest and principal is $878 (see Table 11:1). If the index rate calls for a 2% upward adjustment at the end of 1 year, the payment on the loan would be $1,029. This is an increase of $151 or 17.2%. A 7½% payment cap would limit the increase to 107.5% × $878 = $943.85.

Negative Amortization

Although the 7½% payment cap in the above example protects the borrower's monthly payment from rising too fast, it does not make the difference between what's called for ($1,029) and what's paid ($943.85) go away. The difference ($85.15) is added to the balance owed on the loan and earns interest just like the original amount borrowed. This is called **negative amortization:** instead of the loan balance dropping each month as loan payments are made, the balance owed rises. This can bring concern to the lender who can visualize the day the loan balance exceeds the value of the property. A popular arrangement is to set a limit of 125% of the original loan balance. At that point, either the lender accrues no more negative amortization or the loan is reamortized depending on the wording of the loan contract. Reamortized in this situation means the monthly payments will be adjusted upward by enough to stop the negative amortization.

Choosing Wisely

When a lender makes an ARM loan, the lender must explain to the borrower, in writing, the **worst-case scenario.** In other words, the lender must explain what will happen to the borrower's payments if the index rises the maximum amount each period up to the lifetime interest cap. If there is a payment cap, that and any possibility of negative amortization must also be explained. If the borrower is uneasy with these possibilities, then a fixed-rate loan should be considered. Most lenders offer fixed-rate loans as well as adjustable rate loans. Additionally, FHA and VA loans are fixed-rate loans.

"Teaser rate" adjustables have been offered from time to time by a few lenders and are best avoided. This is an ARM with an enticingly attractive initial rate below the market. For example, the teaser rate may be offered at 2% below market. A borrower who cannot qualify at the market rate might be able to do so at the teaser rate. However, in a year the loan contract calls for a 2% jump followed by additional annual increases. This overwhelms the borrower who, unable to pay, allows foreclosure to take place.

The objective of a **graduated payment mortgage** is to help borrowers qualify for loans by basing repayment schedules on salary expectations. With this type of mortgage, the interest rate and maturity are fixed but the monthly payment gradually rises. For example, a 10%, $60,000, 30-year loan normally requires monthly payments of $527 for complete amortization. Under the graduated payment mortgage, payments could start out as low as $437 per month the first year, then gradually increase to $590 in the eleventh year and then remain at that level until the thirtieth year. Since the interest alone on this $60,000 loan is $500 per month, the amount owed on the loan actually increases during its early years. Only when the monthly payment exceeds the monthly interest does the balance owed on the loan decrease.

The FHA insures graduated payment mortgages under Section 245 and offers five repayment plans. This program is designed to appeal to first-time home buyers in the $15,000 to $25,000 income range because it enables them to tailor their installment payments to their expanding incomes, and thus buy a home sooner than under regular mortgage financing. An **adjustable graduated payment mortgage** combines variable interest with graduated payment features.

A variation of the graduated payment mortgage is the **growing equity mortgage.** This is a 30-year fixed-rate mortgage with monthly payments that are increased 3% to 7% each year. This loan is designed to parallel the borrower's income and fully repay itself in 12 to 15 years.

The basic concept of a **shared appreciation mortgage (SAM)** is that the borrower gives the lender a portion of the property's appreciation in return for a lower rate of interest. To illustrate, a lender who would otherwise charge 12% interest might agree to take 8% interest plus one-third of the appreciation of the property. The lender is accepting what amounts to a speculative investment in the property in return for a reduced

GRADUATED PAYMENT MORTGAGE

Figure 12:3

GRADUATED PAYMENT MORTGAGE

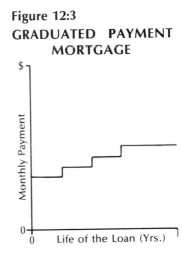

SHARED APPRECIATION MORTGAGE

Figure 12:4
SHARED APPRECIATION
MORTGAGE

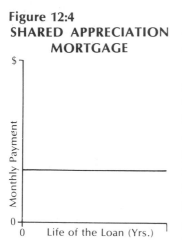

interest rate. The borrower is able to buy and occupy a home that he or she might not otherwise be able to afford, but gives up part of any future price appreciation.

Despite the apparent advantages of the SAM, there are some major pitfalls. For example, at what point in the future is the gain recognized and the lender paid off? If the home is sold, the profits can be split in accordance with the agreement. However, what if the lender feels the home is being sold at too low a price? What if the home is not sold for cash? What if the borrower does not want to sell? One answer to the last situation is that the lender may set a time limit of 10 years on the loan. If the home has not been sold by that time, the home is appraised and the borrower pays the lender the lender's share of the appreciation. At a 10% appreciation rate, a $93,750 house would be worth $243,164 ten years later. If the lender was entitled to one-third of the $149,414 appreciation, the borrower would owe the lender $49,805 in appreciation plus the remaining $70,000 balance on the loan. Unless the borrower can pay cash, this would have to be refinanced at then current rates of interest. On the other hand, if the property experiences no appreciation in value, the borrower will have enjoyed a below-market-rate loan for 10 years and be responsible only for refinancing the remaining loan balance at that time.

EQUITY SHARING

Giving the party that provides the financing a "piece of the action in the deal" is not a new innovation. Insurance companies financing shopping centers and office buildings have long used the idea of requiring part of the rental income and/or part of the profits plus interest on the loan itself. In other words, the lender wants to share in some of the benefits normally reserved for the equity holder in return for providing financing. The equity holder would agree to this either to get a lower rate of interest, such as in the SAM above, or to get financing when financing was scarce, or where the equity holder was not big enough to handle the deal alone. For example, on a $5 million project, the lender might agree to make a loan of $4 million at a very attractive rate if it can buy a half interest in the equity for $500,000.

Equity sharing is also found in residential financing. One

variation is for an enterprising real estate person to find attractive income properties and sell a 50% equity interest to someone who wants to invest in real estate, but who has more money than time. The investor makes half of the down payment and signs for the loan. For this, the investor gets half of the income and profits and all of the tax deductions. The entrepreneur gets the other half in return for the remaining down payment and the effort of finding and managing the property.

A second variation of equity sharing is often called "rich uncle" financing. The investor may be a parent helping a son or daughter buy a home or a son or daughter buying a parent's present home while giving the parent(s) the right to occupy it. A third variation is for an investor to provide most of the down payment for a home buyer, collect rent from the home buyer, pay the mortgage payments and property taxes and claim depreciation. Each party has a right to a portion of any appreciation and the right to buy out the other. The FHLMC now recognizes the importance of equity sharing and will buy mortgage loans on shared-equity properties. The FHLMC requires that the owner-occupant contribute at least 5% of the equity, that the owner-occupant and the owner-investor sign the mortgage and note, that both be individuals and that there be no agreement requiring sale or buy-out within 7 years of the loan date. Equity sharing can provide attractive tax benefits; however, you must seek competent tax advice before involving yourself or someone else.

"Rich Uncle" Financing

Normally, we think of real estate mortgage loans as being secured solely by real estate. However, it is possible to include items classed as personal property in a real estate mortgage, thus creating a **package mortgage.** In residential loans, such items as the refrigerator, clothes washer and dryer can be pledged along with the house and land in a single mortgage. The purpose is to raise the value of the collateral in order to raise the amount a lender is willing to loan. For the borrower, it offers the opportunity of financing major appliances at the same rate of interest as the real estate itself. This rate is usually lower than if the borrower finances the appliances separately.

PACKAGE MORTGAGE

Once an item of personal property is included in a package mortgage, selling it is a violation of the mortgage without the prior consent of the lender.

BLANKET MORTGAGE

A mortgage secured by two or more properties is called a **blanket mortgage.** Suppose you want to buy a house plus the vacant lot next door, financing the purchase with a single mortgage that covers both properties. The cost of preparing one mortgage instead of two is a savings. Also, by combining the house and lot, the lot can be financed on better terms than if it were financed separately, as lenders more readily loan on a house and land than on land alone. Note, however, if the vacant lot is later sold separately from the house before the mortgage loan is fully repaid, it will be necessary to have it released from the blanket mortgage. This is usually accomplished by including a partial release clause in the original mortgage agreement that specifies how much of the loan must be repaid before the lot can be released.

REVERSE MORTGAGE

With a regular mortgage, the lender makes a lump sum payment to the borrower, who in turn repays it through monthly payments to the lender. With a **reverse mortgage,** also known as a reverse annuity mortgage or RAM, the lender makes a monthly payment to the homeowner who later repays in a lump sum. The reverse mortgage can be particularly valuable for an elderly homeowner who does not want to sell, but whose retirement income is not quite enough for comfortable living. The homeowner receives a monthly check, has full use of the property, and is not required to repay until he sells or dies. If he sells the home, money from the sale is taken to repay the loan. If he dies first, the property is sold through the estate and the loan repaid.

CONSTRUCTION LOAN

Under a **construction loan,** also called an interim loan, money is advanced as construction takes place. For example, a vacant lot owner arranges to borrow $60,000 to build a house. The lender does not advance all $60,000 at once because the value of the collateral is insufficient to warrant that amount until the house is finished. Instead, the lender will parcel out the loan as the building is being constructed, always holding a portion until the property is ready for occupancy, or in some cases actually occupied. Some lenders specialize only in construction loans and do not want to wait 20 or 30 years to be repaid. If so, it will be necessary to obtain a permanent long-term mortgage from another source for the purpose of repaying the construction loan. This is known as a permanent commitment or a **take-out loan,** since it takes the construction lender out of the financial picture when construction is completed and allows him to recycle his money into new construction projects.

Many real estate lenders still hold long-term loans that were made at interest rates below the current market. One way of raising the return on these loans is to offer borrowers who have them a **blended-rate loan.** Suppose you owe $50,000 on your home loan and the interest rate on it is 7%. Suppose further that the current rate on home loans is 12%. Your lender might offer to refinance your home for $70,000 at 9%, presuming the property will appraise high enough and you have the income to qualify. The $70,000 refinance offer would put $20,000 in your pocket (less loan fees), but would increase the interest you pay from 7% to 9% on the original $50,000. This makes the cost of the $20,000 14% per year. The arithmetic is as follows: you will now be paying 9% × $70,000 = $6,300 in interest. Before you paid 7% × $50,000 = $3,500 in interest. The difference, $2,800, is what you pay to borrow the additional $20,000. This equates to $2,800 ÷ $20,000 = 14% interest. This is the figure you should use in comparing other sources of financing (such as a second mortgage) or deciding whether you even want to borrow.

A blended-rate loan can be very attractive in a situation where you want to sell your home and you do not want to help finance the buyer. Suppose your home is worth $87,500 and you have the above-described $50,000, 7% loan. A buyer would normally expect to make a down payment of $17,500 and pay 12% interest on a new $70,000 loan. But with a blended loan your lender could offer the buyer the needed $70,000 financing at 9%, a far more attractive rate and one that requires less income in order to qualify. Blended loans are available on FHA, VA and conventional loans held by the FNMA. Other lenders also offer them on fixed-rate assumable loans they hold.

BLENDED-RATE LOAN

BUY-DOWNS

Figure 12:5
BUY-DOWN MORTGAGE

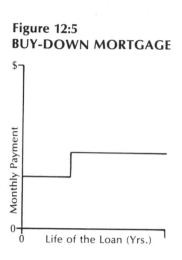

Buy-downs are used to reduce the rate of interest a buyer must pay on a new mortgage loan. For example, suppose a builder has a tract of homes for sale and the current interest rate on home loans is 12%. At that interest rate, there are few buyers. What the builder can do is to arrange with a lender to pay the lender discount points so that the lender can offer a loan at a lower interest to the buyer. This can be done for the life of the loan at the cost of about 8 discount points for every point of interest rate reduction. Or, it can be done for a shorter period, such as the first 3 years of the loan's life. For example, the builder could offer 9% interest for the first 3 years of the loan. Not only is 9% more attractive than 12%, but more buyers can qualify for loans at 9% than at 12%. Although the buy-down is costly to the builder, it will help sell homes that might otherwise go unsold. Moreover, a buy-down will usually boost sales more than a price reduction of like amount. The builder offering the buy-down will usually take a price reduction equal to the discount points if the buyer will forego the buy-down. The disadvantage of a short-term buy-down is that market rates may not drop to allow refinancing and/or the buyer's income may not rise enough.

EQUITY MORTGAGE

An **equity mortgage** is a loan arrangement wherein the lender agrees to extend a line of credit based on the amount of equity in a person's home. The maximum amount of the loan is generally 70% to 80% of the appraised value of the home minus any first mortgage or other liens against the property. The borrower need not take all the credit available, but rather can draw against the mortgage as needed. Some lenders specify a minimum amount per withdrawal. The borrower pays interest only on the amount actually borrowed, not the maximum available. The borrower then has several years to repay the amount borrowed. The interest rate is adjustable and tends to be 1 to 3 percentage points above the "prime rate" paid by large corporations.

The equity mortgage will typically be a second mortgage that is used to tap the increase in equity resulting from rising home prices and first loan paydown. It's all done without having to refinance the first loan and uses the home as an asset against which the homeowner can borrow and repay as needed. Equity mortgages are very popular as a source of home improvement loans, money for college expenses, money to start a business, money for a major vacation and money to buy more real estate.

When a seller is willing to accept part of the property's purchase price in the form of the buyer's promissory note accompanied by a mortgage or deed of trust, it is called **carryback financing.** This allows the buyer to substitute a promissory note for cash, and the seller is said to be "taking back paper." Carryback financing is popular for land sales (where lenders rarely loan), on property where an existing mortgage is being assumed by the buyer, and on property where the seller prefers to receive his money spread out over a period of time, with interest, instead of lump-sum cash. For example, a retired couple sells a rental home they own. The home is worth $120,000, and they owe $20,000. If they need only $60,000 in cash, they might be more than happy to take $60,000 down, let the buyer assume the existing mortgage and accept the remaining $40,000 in monthly payments at current interest rates. Alternatively, the buyer and seller can agree to structure the $40,000 as an adjustable, graduated, partially amortized or interest-only loan.

CARRYBACK FINANCING

If the seller receives the sales price spread out over two or more years, income taxes are calculated using the installment reporting method discussed in Chapter 13. Being able to spread out the taxes on a gain may be an incentive to use seller financing. The seller should be aware, however, that he may not be able to convert his "paper" to cash without a long wait or without having to sell it at a substantial discount to an investor. Additionally, the seller is responsible for servicing the loan and is subject to losses due to default and foreclosure.

Note that some real estate agents and lenders refer to a loan that is carried back by a seller as a **purchase money** loan. Others define a purchase money loan as any loan, carryback or institutional, that is used to finance the purchase of real property.

An alternative method of financing a real estate sale such as the one just reviewed is to use a **wraparound mortgage** or **wraparound deed of trust.** A "wraparound" encompasses ex-

WRAPAROUND MORTGAGE

isting mortgages and is subordinate (junior) to them. The existing mortgages stay on the property and the new mortgage wraps around them.

To illustrate, presume the existing $20,000 loan in the previous example carries an interest rate of 7% and that there are 10 years remaining on the loan. Presume further that current interest rates are 12%. With a wraparound it is possible for the buyer to pay less than 12% and at the same time for the seller to receive more than 12% on the money owed him. This is done by taking the buyer's $60,000 down payment and then creating a new junior mortgage that includes not only the $20,000 owed on the existing first mortgage but also the $40,000 the buyer owes the seller. In other words, the wraparound mortgage will be for $60,000, and the seller continues to remain liable for payment of the first mortgage. If the interest rate on the wraparound is set at 10%, the buyer saves by not having to pay 12% as he would on an entirely new loan. The advantage to the seller is that he is earning 10% not only on his $40,000 equity, but also on the $20,000 loan for which he is paying 7% interest. This gives the seller an actual yield of 11½% on his $40,000. (The calculation is as follows. The seller receives 10% on $60,000, which amounts to $6,000. He pays 7% on $20,000, which is $1,400. The difference, $4,600 is divided by $40,000 to get the seller's actual yield of 11½%.)

Wraparounds are not limited to seller financing. If the seller in the above example did not want to finance the sale, a third-party lender could provide the needed $40,000 and take a wraparound mortgage. The wraparound concept will not work when the mortgage debt to be "wrapped" contains an enforcement due-on-sale clause.

SUBORDINATION

Another financing technique is **subordination.** For example, a person owns a $200,000 vacant lot suitable for building, and a builder wants to build an $800,000 building on the lot. The builder has only $100,000 cash and the largest construction loan available is $800,000. If the builder can convince the lot owner to take $100,000 in cash and $100,000 later, he would have the $1 million total. However, the lender making the $800,000 loan will want to be the first mortgagee to protect its position in the event of foreclosure. The lot owner must be willing to take a subordinate position, in this case a second mortgage. If the project is successful, the lot owner will receive $100,000, plus interest, either in cash after the building is built and sold or as monthly payments. If the project goes into fore-closure, the lot owner can be paid only if the $800,000 first mortgage claim is satisfied in full from the sale proceeds. As you can surmise here, the lot owner must be very careful that the money loaned by the lender actually goes into construction and that whatever is built is worth at least $800,000 in addition to the land.

A **contract for deed,** also called an **installment contract** or **land contract,** enables the seller to finance a buyer by permit-ting him to make a down payment followed by monthly pay-ments. However, title remains in the name of the seller. In addition to its wide use in financing land sales, it has also been a very effective financing tool in several states as a means of selling homes. For example, a homeowner owes $25,000 on his home and wants to sell it for $85,000. A buyer is found but does not have the $60,000 down payment necessary to assume the existing loan. The buyer does have $8,000, but for one rea-son or another cannot or chooses not to borrow from an insti-tutional lender. If the seller is agreeable, the buyer can pay the seller $8,000 and enter into an installment contract with the seller for the remaining $77,000. The contract will call for monthly payments by the buyer to the seller that are large enough to allow the seller to meet the payments on the $25,000 loan plus repay the $52,000 owed to the seller, with interest. Unless property taxes and insurance are billed to the buyer, the seller will also collect for these and pay them. When the final payment is made to the seller (or the property refinanced through an institutional lender), title is conveyed to the buyer. Meanwhile the seller continues to hold title and is responsible for paying the mortgage. In addition to wrapping around a mortgage, an installment contract can also be used to wrap around another installment contract, provided it does not con-tain an enforceable due-on-sale clause. (Please see Chapter 8 for more about the contractual side of installment contracts.)

CONTRACT FOR DEED

When viewed as a financing tool, an **option** provides a method by which the need to immediately finance the full price of a property can be postponed. For example, a developer is

OPTION

offered 100 acres of land for a house subdivision but is not sure that the market will absorb that many houses. The solution is to buy 25 acres outright and take three 25-acre options at preset prices on the remainder. If the houses on the first 25 acres sell promptly, the builder can exercise the options to buy the remaining land. If sales are not good, the builder can let the remaining options expire and avoid being stuck with unwanted acreage.

A popular variation on the option idea is the **lease with option to buy** combination. Under it an owner leases to a tenant who, in addition to paying rent and using the property, also obtains the right to purchase it at a preset price for a fixed period of time. Homes are often sold this way, particularly when the resale market is sluggish. (Please see Chapter 8 for more about a lease with option to buy.)

Options can provide speculative opportunities to persons with limited amounts of capital. If prices do not rise, the optionee loses only the cost of the option; if prices do rise, the optionee exercises the option and realizes a profit.

CREATIVE FINANCING

The decade of the 1980s started with a shortage of money for real estate loans and an abundance of financing ideas. Many of these involved seller-assisted financing. At one point in 1982 it was estimated that 80% of home mortgage financing was by way of assumptions and seller financing.

The wraparound mortgage and installment contract are considered forms of creative financing. Most were designed to pass along the benefits of a low-interest loan in a high-interest market. With the Garn Act and the *de la Cuesta* case fewer loans are suitable for wrapping. If interest rates fall, wrapping will be less attractive and new financing more attractive. Nonetheless, there is plenty of room for creative ideas to solve financing problems. For example, a $400,000 apartment building with a $200,000 first mortgage against it is for sale. The seller wants $120,000 in cash and will carry paper for the rest as long as the loan-to-value ratio does not exceed 80%. A buyer has $40,000 in cash plus a house worth $80,000 with a $20,000 loan against it. The solution is to refinance the apartment building with the lender for 70%. This is a standard L/V ratio for apartment buildings and creates $80,000 in cash. The buyer gives the seller $40,000 in cash, a $40,000 second mortgage against the apartment building and a $40,000 second mortgage against the house.

In another example of creative financing, consider the builder with many unsold homes but plenty of buyers who would like to buy if they could finance buyers for their present homes. The builder offers to help finance the sale of a buyer's property in order to make his own sale. Two parties get the homes they want and the builder is relieved of unsold inventory.

One seller-financing arrangement that deserves special attention because of its traps for the unwary is the **overencumbered property.** Institutional lenders are closely regulated regarding the amount of money they can loan against the appraised value of the property. Individuals are not regulated. The following example will illustrate the potential problem. Suppose you own a house that is realistically worth $100,000 and the mortgage balance is $10,000. A buyer offers to purchase the property with the condition that he be allowed to obtain an $80,000 loan on the property from a lender. The $80,000 is used to pay off the existing $10,000 loan and to pay the broker's commission, loan fees and closing costs. The remaining $62,000 is split $30,000 to the seller and $32,000 to the buyer. The buyer also gives the seller a note, secured by a second mortgage against the property, for $80,000. The seller may feel good about getting $30,000 in cash and an $80,000 mortgage, for this is more than the property is worth, or so it seems.

But the $80,000 second mortgage stands junior to the $80,000 first mortgage. That's $160,000 of debt against a $100,000 property. The buyer might be trying to resell the property for $160,000 or more, but the chances of this are slim. More likely the buyer will wind up walking away from the property. This leaves the seller the choice of taking over the payments on the first mortgage or losing the property completely to the holder of the first.

Although such a scheme sounds crazy when viewed from a distance, the reason it can be performed is that the seller wants more for the property than it's worth. Someone then offers a deal showing that price, and the seller looks the other way from

OVERLY CREATIVE FINANCING?

the possible consequences. Real estate agents who participate in such transactions are likely to find their licenses suspended. State licensing authorities take the position that a real estate agent is a professional who should know enough not to take part in a deal that leaves the seller holding a junior lien on an overencumbered property. This, too, seems logical when viewed from a distance. But when sales are slow and commissions thin, it is sometimes easy to put commission income ahead of fiduciary responsibility. If in doubt about the propriety of a transaction, the Golden Rule of doing unto others as you would have them do unto you still applies. (Or as some restate it: "What goes around, comes around.")

INVESTING IN MORTGAGES   Individuals can invest in mortgages in two ways. One is to invest in mortgage loan pools through certificates guaranteed by Ginnie Mae and Freddie Mac and available from stockbrokers. These yield about ½ of 1% below what FHA and VA borrowers are paying. In 1985, for example, this was approximately 11%, and the certificates are readily convertible to cash at current market prices on the open market if the investor does not want to hold them through maturity.

Individuals can also buy junior mortgages at yields above Ginnie Mae and Freddie Mac certificates. These junior mortgages are seconds, thirds and fourths offered by mortgage brokers. They yield more because they are riskier as to repayment and much more difficult to convert to cash before maturity. "There is," as the wise old adage says, "no such thing as a free lunch." Thus, it is important to recognize that when an investment of any kind promises above-market returns, there is some kind of added risk attached. With junior mortgages, it is important to realize that when a borrower offers to pay a premium above the best loan rates available from banks and thrift institutions, it is because the borrower and/or the property does not qualify for the best rates.

Before buying a mortgage as an investment, one should have the title to the property searched. This is the only way to know for certain what priority the mortgage will have in the event of foreclosure. There have been cases where investors have purchased what they were told to be first and second mortgages only to find in foreclosure that they were actually holding third and fourth mortgages where the amount of debt exceeded the value of the property.

And how does one find the value of a property? By having it appraised by a professional appraiser who is independent of the party making or selling the mortgage investment. This value is compared to the existing and proposed debt against the property. The investor should also run a credit check on the borrower. The investor's final protection is, however, in making certain that the market value of the property is well in excess of the loans against it and that the property is well-constructed, well-located and functional.

RENTAL

Even though tenants do not acquire fee ownership, **rentals** and **leases** are a means of financing real estate. Whether the tenant is a bachelor receiving the use of a $30,000 apartment for which he pays $350 rent per month or a large corporation leasing a warehouse for 20 years, leasing is an ideal method of financing when the tenant does not want to buy, cannot raise the funds to buy or prefers to invest available funds elsewhere. Similarly, **farming leases** provide for the use of land without the need to purchase it. Some farm leases call for fixed rental payment. Other leases require the farmer to pay the landowner a share of the value of the crop that is actually produced—say 25%—and the landowner shares with the farmer the risks of weather, crop output and prices.

Under a **sale and leaseback** arrangement, an owner-occupant sells the property and then remains as a tenant. Thus, the buyer acquires an investment and the seller obtains capital for other purposes while retaining the use of the property. A variation is for the tenant to construct a building, sell it to a prearranged buyer, and immediately lease it back.

LAND LEASES

Although **leased land** arrangements are common throughout the United States for both commercial and industrial users and for farmers, anything other than fee ownership of residential land is unthinkable in many areas. Yet in some parts of the United States (for example, Baltimore, Maryland; Orange County, California; throughout Hawaii; and in parts of Florida) homes built on leased land are commonplace. Typically, these leases are at least 55 years in length and, barring an agreement to the contrary, the improvements to the land become the property of the fee owner at the end of the lease. Rents may be fixed in advance for the life of the lease, renegotiated at preset points during the life of the lease, or a combination of both.

To hedge against inflation, when fixed rents are used in a long-term lease, it is common practice to use **step-up rentals.** For example, under a 55-year house-lot lease, the rent may be set at $400 per year for the first 15 years, $600 per year for the next 10 years, $800 for the next 10 years, and so forth. An alternative is to renegotiate the rent at various points during the life of a lease so that the effects of land value changes are more closely equalized between the lessor and the lessee. For example, a 60-year lease may contain renegotiation points at the fifteenth, thirtieth, and forty-fifth years. At those points the property would be reappraised and the lease rent adjusted to reflect any changes in the value of the property. Property taxes and any increases in property taxes are paid by the lessee.

FINANCING OVERVIEW

If people always paid cash for real estate, the last four chapters would not have been necessary. But 95% of the time they don't; so means have been devised to finance their purchases. This has been true since the beginning of recorded history and will continue into the future. The financing methods that evolve will depend on the problems to be solved. For example, long-term fixed-rate amortized loans were the solution to foreclosures in the 1930s, and they worked well as long as interest rates did not fluctuate greatly. Graduated payment loans were devised when housing prices rose faster than buyer's incomes. Adjustable rate loans were developed so that lenders could more closely align the interest they receive from borrowers with the interest they pay their savers. Extensive use of loan assumptions, wraparounds and seller financing became necessary in the early 1980s because borrowers could not qualify for 16% and 18% loans and sellers were unwilling to drop prices.

With regard to the future, if mortgage money is expensive or in short supply, seller financing will play a large role. With the experience of rapidly fluctuating interest rates fresh in people's minds, loans with adjustable rates will continue to be widely offered. Fixed-rate loans will either have short maturities or carry a premium to compensate the lender for being locked into a fixed rate for a long period. When interest rates turn down again, borrowers with adjustable loans will benefit from lower monthly payments. If rates stay down long enough, fixed-rate loans will become more popular again.

VOCABULARY REVIEW

Match terms **a–z** *with statements* **1–26.**

a. Adjustment period
b. Adjustable rate mortgage
c. Blanket mortgage
d. Blended-rate loan
e. Buy-down
f. Carryback financing
g. Contract for deed
h. Due-on-sale clause
i. Equity mortgage
j. Equity sharing
k. Fannie Mae
l. Graduated payment mortgage
m. Index rate
n. Interest rate cap

o. Mortgage company
p. Negative amortization
q. Option
r. Overencumbered property
s. Package mortgage
t. Payment cap
u. Reverse mortgage
v. Sale and leaseback
w. Secondary mortgage market
x. Subordination
y. Usury
z. Wraparound mortgage

1. The amount of time that elapses between interest rate changes on a loan.
2. A mortgage secured by two or more properties.
3. A mortgage secured by real and personal property.
4. To voluntarily give up a higher mortgage priority for a lower one.
5. A situation where the loans against a property exceed the value of the property.
6. A financing arrangement whereby an owner-occupant sells the property and then remains as a tenant.
7. Results when monthly interest exceeds monthly payment and the difference is added to the principal.
8. A refinanced loan wherein the lender combines the interest rate of the existing loan with a current rate.
9. A mortgage wherein the lender extends a line of credit based on the amount of equity in a person's home.
10. A payment by the seller to the lender in order to reduce the interest rate for the buyer.
11. A loan wherein the lender makes monthly payments to the property owner who later repays in a lump sum.
12. The interest rate, such as on U.S. Treasury securities, to which an adjustable loan is tied.

13. The ceiling to which the interest rate on a loan can rise.
14. A limit on how much a borrower's payment can increase in any one year.
15. Requires immediate repayment of the loan if ownership transfers; also called an alienation clause.
16. A note is accepted by a seller instead of cash.
17. An arrangement whereby a party providing financing gets a portion of the ownership.
18. A right, for a given period of time, to buy, sell or lease property at preset price and terms.
19. A market where mortgage loans can be sold to investors.
20. A firm that makes mortgage loans and then sells them to investors.
21. A method of selling and financing property whereby the buyer obtains possession but the seller retains the title.
22. A lending industry name for the Federal National Mortgage Association.
23. Charging a rate of interest higher than that permitted by law.
24. A mortgage loan on which the rate of interest can rise and fall with changes in prevailing interest rates.
25. A mortgage repayment plan that allows the borrower to make smaller monthly payments at first and larger ones later.
26. A debt instrument that encompasses existing mortgages and is subordinate to them.

QUESTIONS AND PROBLEMS

1. What is the most significant difference between a mortgage broker and a mortgage banker?
2. In the secondary mortgage market, who provides the loan money?
3. What is meant by the term "loan servicing"?
4. What is an adjustable rate mortgage?
5. What was the significance to real estate lending of the *de la Cuesta* case and the Garn Act?
6. By what financing methods do FNMA and GNMA provide money for real estate loans?
7. If a dollar is a dollar no matter where it comes from, what difference does it make if the source of a real estate loan was real savings or fiat money?
8. Regarding adjustable rate mortgage loans, what are the advantages and disadvantages to the borrower and lender?
9. Explain why rentals and leases are considered forms of real estate financing.
10. What is the single most important precaution an investor can make before buying a junior mortgage?

Creative Financing: Avoiding the Pitfalls by **Jeff Wride** and **Richard Ratcliff**. (Reston, 1984, 201 pages). Addresses problems created for the seller by creative financing and shows how to avoid them. Eye-opening reading for anyone considering the use of creative financing.

Real Estate Finance, 4th ed. by **John Wiedemer**. (Reston, 1983, 366 pages). Includes sources of long-term mortgage money, financing instruments, loan procedures, FNMA, FHLMC, GNMA, FHA and VA. Also includes loan analysis, carryback financing and settlement procedures.

Real Estate Finance: A Practical Approach by **Tom Morton**. (Scott-Foresman, 1983, 407 pages). Includes information on creative financing, FHA, VA, FNMA, FHLMC loan guidelines, buyer qualification, etc. With glossary and appendices.

"The Birth of a National Mortgage Network" by **Leanne Lachman**. (*Real Estate Today*, May 85, page 36). Article states that computers installed in real estate offices may form the basis of a national mortgage network. In the same issue is "Computerizing the Loan Process" on page 39.

The Complete Real Estate Math Book, rev. ed. by **Margie Sussex** and **John Stapleton.** (Prentice Hall, 1983, 320 pages). Book provides tools and techniques to pass the math portion of real estate licensing exams in all 50 states.

"The Tax Benefits of Renting to or Owning a Home with a Family Member" by **Thomas Dickens**. (*Real Estate Review*, Spring 84, page 88). Federal tax laws now allow rentals to family members that can shift a home's tax deductions to a higher-tax-bracket family member where they are more valuable.

*   *   *

The following periodicals may also be of interest to you: *Freddie Mac Reports, Federal Reserve Bulletin, FHLBB News, Housing Finance, Housing Finance Review, National Savings and Loan League Journal, Real Estate Finance* and *Real Estate Lenders Report.*

ADDITIONAL READINGS

Taxes and Assessments

Adjusted sales price: the sales price of a property less commissions, fix-up and closing costs

Ad valorem taxes: taxes charged according to the value of a property

Assessed value: a value placed on a property for the purpose of taxation

Assessment appeal board: local governmental body which hears and rules on property owner complaints of overassessment

Basis: the price paid for property; used in calculating income taxes

Capital gain: the gain (profit) on the sale of an appreciated asset

Documentary tax: a fee or tax on deeds and other documents payable at the time of recordation

Mill rate: property tax rate that is expressed in tenths of a cent per dollar of assessed valuation

Tax certificate: a document issued at a tax sale that entitles the purchaser to a deed at a later date if the property is not redeemed

Tax lien: a charge or hold by the government against property to insure the payment of taxes

PROPERTY TAXES

The largest single source of income in America for local government programs and services is the property tax. Schools (from kindergarten through two-year colleges), fire and police departments, local welfare programs, public libraries, street maintenance, parks and public hospital facilities are mainly supported by property taxes. Some state governments also obtain a portion of their revenues from this source.

Property taxes are **ad valorem** taxes. This means that they are levied according to the value of one's property; the more valuable the property, the higher the tax, and vice versa. The underlying theory of ad valorem taxation is that those owning the more valuable properties are wealthier and hence able to pay more taxes.

How does a local government determine the amount of tax to collect each year from each property owner? Step 1 is local budget preparation and appropriation. Step 2 is the appraisal of all taxable property within the taxation district. Step 3 is to allocate the amount to be collected among the taxable properties in the district. Let us look more closely at this process.

Budget and Appropriation   Each taxing body with the authority to tax prepares its **budget** for the coming year. Taxing bodies include counties, cities, boroughs, towns and villages and, in some states, school boards, sanitation districts and county road departments. Each budget along with a list of sources from which the money will be derived is enacted into law. This is the **appropriation process.** Then estimated sales taxes, state and federal revenue sharing, business licenses and city income taxes are subtracted from the budget. The balance must come from property taxes.

Appraisal and Assessment   Next, the valuation of the taxable property within each taxing body's district must be determined. A county or state assessor's office **appraises** each taxable parcel of land and the improvements thereon. In some states this job is contracted out to private appraisal companies. Appraisal procedures vary from state to state. In some, the appraised value is the estimated fair market cash value of the property. This is the cash price one would expect a buyer and a seller to agree upon in a normal open market transaction. Other states start with the fair market value of the land and add to it the cost of replacing the buildings and other improvements on it, minus an allowance for depreciation due to wear and tear and obsolescence.

The appraised value is converted into an assessed value upon which taxes are based. In some states, the **assessed value** is set equal to the appraised value; in others, it is a percentage of the appraised value. Mathematically, the percentage selected makes no difference as long as each property in a taxing district is treated equally. Consider two houses with appraised values of $60,000 and $120,000, respectively. Whether the assessed values are set equal to appraised values or at a percentage of appraised values, the second house will still bear twice the property tax burden of the first.

Tax Rate Calculation   The assessed values of all properties subject to property taxation are added together in order to calculate the tax rate. To explain this process, suppose that a building lies within the taxation districts of the Westside School District, the city of Rostin, and the county of Pearl River. The school district's budget for the coming year requires $800,000 from property taxes, and the assessed value of taxable property within the district is $20,000,000. By dividing $800,000 by $20,000,000, we see that the school district must collect a tax of 4 cents for every dollar of assessed valuation. This levy can be expressed three ways: (1) as a mill rate, (2) as dollars per hundred, or (3) as dollars per thousand. All three rating methods are found in the United States.

As a **mill rate,** this tax rate is expressed as mills per dollar of assessed valuation. Since 1 mill equals one-tenth of a cent, a 4 cent tax rate is the same as 40 mills. Expressed as **dollars per hundred,** the same rate would be $4 per hundred of assessed valuation. As **dollars per thousand,** it would be $40 per thousand.

The city of Rostin also calculates its tax rate by dividing its property tax requirements by the assessed value of the property within its boundaries. Suppose that its needs are $300,000 and the city limits enclose property totaling $10,000,000 in assessed valuation. (In this example, the city covers a smaller geographical area than the school district.) Thus the city must collect 3 cents for each dollar of assessed valuation in order to balance its budget.

The county government's budget requires $2,000,000 from property taxes and the county contains $200,000,000 in assessed valuation. This makes the county tax rate 1 cent per dollar of assessed valuation. Table 13:1 shows the school district, city, and county tax rates expressed as mills, dollars per hundred, and dollars per thousand.

The final step is to apply the tax rate to each property. *Applying the Rate* Applying the mill rate to a home with an assessed value of $20,000, is simply a matter of multiplying the 80 mills (the

EXPRESSING PROPERTY TAX RATES   Table 13:1

	Mill rate	Dollars per hundred	Dollars per thousand
School district	40 mills	$4.00	$40.00
City	30	3.00	30.00
County	10	1.00	10.00
Total	80 mills	$8.00	$80.00

equivalent of 8 cents) by the assessed valuation to arrive at property taxes of $1,600 per year. On a dollars per hundred basis, divide the $20,000 assessed valuation by $100 and multiply by $8. The result is $1,600. To insure collection, a lien for this amount is placed against the property. It is removed when the tax is paid. Property tax liens are superior to other types of liens. A mortgage foreclosure does not clear property tax liens; they still must be paid.

To avoid duplicate tax bill mailings, it is a common practice for all taxing bodies in a given county to have the county collect for them at the same time that the county collects on its own behalf. Property tax years generally fall into two categories: January 1 through December 31, and July 1 through the following June 30. Some states require one payment per year; others collect in two installments. A few allow a small discount for early payment, and all charge penalties for late payments.

Because of the monumental volume of numbers and calculations necessary to budget, appropriate, appraise, assess and calculate property taxes, computers are widely used in property tax offices. Computers also prepare property tax bills, account for property tax receipts and mail computer-generated notices to those who have not paid.

UNPAID PROPERTY TAXES

If you own real estate and fail to pay the property taxes, you will lose the property. In some states, title to delinquent property is transferred to the county or state. A redemption period follows during which the owner, or any lienholder, can redeem the property by paying back taxes and penalties. If redemption does not occur, the property is sold at a publicly announced auction and the highest bidder receives a **tax deed.** In other states, the sale is held soon after the delinquency occurs and the redemption period follows. At the sale, a **tax certificate** or **certificate of sale** in the amount of the unpaid taxes is sold. The purchaser is entitled to a deed to the property provided the delinquent taxpayer, or anyone holding a lien on the property, does not step forward and redeem it during the redemption period that follows. If it is redeemed, the purchaser receives his money back plus interest. The reason that a lienholder (such as a mortgage lender) is allowed to redeem a property is that if the property taxes are not paid, the lienholder's creditor rights in the property are cut off due to the superiority of the tax lien.

The right of government to divorce a property owner from his land for nonpayment of property taxes is well established by law. However, if the sale procedure is not properly followed, the purchaser may find the property's title later successfully challenged in court. Thus, it behooves the purchaser to obtain a title search and title insurance and, if necessary, to conduct a quiet title suit.

By law, assessment procedures must be uniformly applied to all properties within a taxing jurisdiction. To this end, the assessed values of all lands and buildings are made available for public inspection. These are the **assessment rolls.** They permit a property owner to compare the assessed valuation on his property with assessed valuations on similar properties. If an owner feels overassessed, he can then file an appeal before an **assessment appeal board,** or before a board of review, board of equalization or tribunal. Some states also provide further appeal channels or permit appeal to a court of law if the property owner remains dissatisfied with the assessment. Note that the appeal process deals only with the methods of assessment and taxation, not with the tax rate or the amount of tax.

ASSESSMENT APPEAL

In some states, the **board of equalization** performs another assessment-related task: that of equalizing assessment procedures between counties. This is particularly important where county-collected property taxes are shared with the state or other counties. Without equalization, it would be to a county's financial advantage to underassess so as to lessen its contribution. At present, two equalization methods are in common usage: one requires that all counties use the same appraisal procedure and assessed valuation ratio, and the other allows each county to choose its own method and then applies a correction as determined by the board. For example, a state may contain counties that assess at 20%, 24% and 30% of fair market value. These could be equalized by multiplying assessed values in the 20% counties by 1.50, in the 24% counties by 1.25, and in the 30% counties by 1.00.

More than half the land in many cities and counties is exempt from real property taxation. This is because governments and their agencies do not tax themselves or each other. Thus, government-owned offices of all types, public roads and parks,

PROPERTY TAX
EXEMPTIONS

schools, military bases and government-owned utilities are exempt from property taxes. Also exempted are most properties owned by religious and charitable organizations (so long as they are used for religious or charitable purposes), hospitals and cemeteries. In rural areas of many states, large tracts of land are owned by federal and state governments, and these too are exempt from taxation.

Property tax exemptions are used to attract industries. For example, a local government agency buys industrial land and buildings and leases them to industries at a price lower than would be possible if they were privately owned and hence taxed. Alternatively, outright property tax reductions can be granted for a certain length of time to newly established or relocating firms. The rationale is that the cost to the public is outweighed by the economic boost that the new industry brings to the community. A number of states grant assessment reductions to homeowners. This increases the tax burden for households that rent and for commercial properties.

California and several other states have enacted laws that allow elderly homeowners to postpone payment of their property taxes. The state pays the taxes for them and puts a lien on the property. Interest is charged each year on the postponed taxes and postponement can continue indefinitely. The amount due is not payable until the home is sold, or the owners die (in which case the estate or heirs would pay), or the property, for some other reason, ceases to qualify. To qualify, all owners must live in the home and have reached a certain age—62 years, for example. Additionally, there may be a limitation on household income in order to qualify.

PROPERTY TAX VARIATIONS   Property taxes on similarly priced homes within a city or county can vary widely when prices change faster than the assessor's office can reappraise. As a result, a home worth $90,000 in one neighborhood may receive a tax bill of $1,800 per year, while a $90,000 home in another neighborhood will be billed $2,400. When the assessor's office conducts a reappraisal, taxes in the first neighborhood will suddenly rise 33%, undoubtedly provoking complaints from property owners who were unaware that they were previously underassessed. In times of slow-changing real estate prices, reappraisals were made only once every 10 years. Today, assessors are developing computerized appraisal systems that can make adjustments annually.

As an aid to keeping current on property value changes, states are enacting laws that require a real estate buyer to advise the assessor's office of the price and terms of his purchase within 90 days after taking title. This information, coupled with building permit records and on-site visits by assessor's office employees, provides the data necessary to regularly update assessments.

The amount of property taxes a property owner may expect to pay varies from one city to the next and one state to the next. Why is this? The answer is found by looking at the level of services offered, other sources of revenue, taxable property and government efficiency. Generally, cities with low property taxes offer fewer services to their residents. This may be by choice, such as smaller welfare payments, lower school expenditures per student, no subsidized public transportation, fewer parks and libraries, or because the city does not include the cost of some services in the property tax. For example, sewer fees may be added to the water bill and trash may be hauled by private firms. Lower rates can also be due to location. Wage rates are lower in some regions of the country, and a city not subject to ice and snow will have lower street maintenance expenses. Finally, a city may have other sources of revenue, such as oil royalties from wells on city property.

Property tax levels are also influenced by the ability of local tax districts to obtain federal funds and state revenues (especially for schools), and to share in collections from sales taxes, license fees, liquor and tobacco taxes and fines.

The amount and type of taxable property in a community greatly affects local tax rates. Taxable property must bear the burden avoided by tax-exempt property whereas privately owned vacant land, stores, factories and high-priced homes generally produce more taxes than they consume in local government services and help to keep rates lower. Finally, one must look at the efficiency of the city. Has it managed its affairs in prior years so that the current budget is not burdened with large interest payments on debts caused by deficits in previous years? Is the city or county itself laid out in a compact and efficient manner, or does its sheer size make administration expensive? How many employees are required to perform a given service?

Tax Limitation Measures

Unhappy with rising property taxes, particularly when real estate prices were skyrocketing in the 1970s, voters in a number of states went to the polls and voted to limit property tax increases. In some states this has been a limit on the amount of taxes that can be collected. In other states it is a limit on how much government can spend. The cooling off in real estate price increases that began in 1980 has taken much of the urgency out of capping property tax increases. As a result, fewer such measures have been seen on ballots since 1980 and when they do appear, they do not pass as easily as they once did.

SPECIAL ASSESSMENTS

Often the need arises to make local municipal improvements that will benefit property owners within a limited area, such as the paving of a street, the installation of street lights, curbs, storm drains and sanitary sewer lines, or the construction of irrigation and drainage ditches. Such improvements can be provided through **special assessments** on property.

The theory underlying special assessments is that the improvements must benefit the land against which the cost will be charged, and the value of the benefits must exceed the cost. The area receiving the benefit of an improvement is the **improvement district** or **assessment district,** and the property within that district bears the cost of the improvement. This is different from a **public improvement.** A public improvement, such as reconstruction of the city's sewage plant, benefits the general public and is financed through the general (ad valorem) property tax. A local improvement, such as extending a sewer line into a street of homes presently using septic tanks or cesspools, does not benefit the public at large and should properly be charged only to those who directly benefit. Similarly, when streets are widened, owners of homes lining a 20-foot-wide street in a strictly residential neighborhood would be expected to bear the cost of widening it to 30 or 40 feet and to donate the needed land from their frontyards. But a street widening from two lanes to four to accommodate traffic not generated by the homes on the street is a different situation because the widening benefits the public at large. In this case the street widening is funded from public monies and the homeowners are paid for any land taken from them.

An improvement district can be formed by the action of a group of concerned citizens who want and are willing to pay for an improvement. Property owners desiring the improvement take their proposal to the local board of assessors or similar public body in charge of levying assessments. A public notice showing the proposed improvements, the extent of the improvement district and the anticipated costs is prepared by the board. This notice is mailed to landowners in the proposed improvement district, posted conspicuously in the district and published in a local newspaper. The notice also contains the date and place of public hearings on the matter at which property owners within the proposed district are invited to voice their comments and objections.

Forming an Improvement District

If the hearings result in a decision to proceed, then under the authority granted by state laws regarding special improvements, a local government ordinance is passed that describes the project and its costs and the improvement district boundaries. An assessment roll is also prepared that shows the cost to each parcel in the district. Hearings are held regarding the assessment roll. When everything is in order, the roll is **confirmed** (approved). Then the contract to construct the improvements is awarded and work is started.

Confirmation

The proposal to create an improvement district can also come from a city council, board of trustees or board of supervisors. When this happens, notices are distributed and hearings held to hear objections from affected parties. Objections are ruled upon by a court of law and if found to have merit, the assessment plans must be revised or dropped. Once approved, assessment rolls are prepared, more hearings held, the roll confirmed and the contract awarded.

Upon completion of the improvement, each landowner receives a bill for his portion of the cost. If the cost to a landowner is less than $100, the landowner either pays the amount in full to the contractor directly or to a designated public offi-

Bond Issues

cial who, in turn, pays the contractor. If the assessment is larger, the landowner can immediately pay it in full or let it **go to bond.** If he lets it go to bond, local government officials prepare a bond issue that totals all the unpaid assessments in the improvement district. These bonds are either given to the contractor as payment for his work or sold to the public through a securities dealer and the proceeds are used to pay the contractor. The collateral for the bonds is the land in the district upon which assessments have not been paid.

The bonds spread the cost of the improvements over a period of 5 to 10 years and are payable in equal annual (or semi-annual) installments plus accumulated interest. Thus, a $2,000 sewer and street-widening assessment on a 10-year bond would be charged to a property owner at the rate of $200 per year (or $100 each 6 months) plus interest. As the bond is gradually retired, the amount of interest added to the regular principal payment declines.

Like property taxes, special assessments are a lien against the property. Consequently, if a property owner fails to pay his assessment, the assessed property can be sold in the same manner as when property taxes are delinquent.

Apportionment   Special assessments are apportioned according to benefits received rather than by the value of the land and buildings being assessed. In fact, the presence of buildings in an improvement district is not usually considered in preparing the assessment roll; the theory is that the land receives all the benefit of the improvement. Several illustrations can best explain how assessments are apportioned. In a residential neighborhood, the assessment for installation of storm drains, curbs and gutters is made on a **front-foot basis.** A property owner is charged for each foot of his lot that abuts the street being improved.

In the case of a sanitary sewer line assessment, the charge per lot can either be based on front footage or on a simple count of the lots in the district. In the latter case, if there are 100 lots on the new sewer line, each would pay 1% of the cost. In the case of a park or playground, lots nearest the new facility are deemed to benefit more and thus are assessed more than lots located farther away. This form of allocation is very subjective, and usually results in spirited objections at public hearings from those who do not feel they will use the facility in proportion to the assessment that their lots will bear.

We now turn to the income taxes that are due if you sell your personal residence for more than you paid. Income taxes are levied by the federal government, by 44 states (the exceptions are Florida, Nevada, South Dakota, Texas, Washington and Wyoming), and by 48 cities including New York City, Baltimore, Pittsburgh, Philadelphia, Cincinnati, Cleveland and Detroit. The discussion here centers on the federal income tax. State and city income tax laws generally follow the pattern of federal tax laws.

INCOME TAXES ON THE SALE OF ONE'S RESIDENCE

The first step in determining the amount of taxable gain upon the sale of an owner-occupied residence is to calculate the home's **basis.** This is the price originally paid for the home plus any fees paid for closing services and legal counsel, and any fee or commission paid to help find the property. If the home was built rather than purchased, the basis is the cost of the land plus the cost of construction, such as the cost of materials and construction labor, architect's fees, building permit fees, planning and zoning commission approval costs, utility connection charges and legal fees. The value of labor contributed by the homeowner and free labor from friends and relatives cannot be added. If the home was received as compensation, a gift, an inheritance or in a trade, or if a portion of the home was depreciated for business purposes, special rules apply that will not be covered here and the seller should consult the Internal Revenue Service (IRS).

Calculating a Home's Basis

Assessments for local improvements and any improvements made by the seller during his occupancy are added to the original cost of the home. An improvement is a permanent betterment that materially adds to the value of a home, prolongs its life or changes its use. For example, finishing an unfinished basement or upper floor, building a swimming pool, adding a bedroom or bathroom, installing new plumbing or wiring, installing a new roof, erecting a new fence and paving a new driveway are classed as improvements and are added to the home's basis. Maintenance and repairs are not added as they merely maintain the property in ordinary operating condition. Fixing gutters, mending leaks in plumbing, replacing broken windowpanes and painting the inside or outside of the home are considered maintenance and repair items. However, repairs made as part of an extensive remodeling or restoration job may be added to the basis.

Calculating the *Amount Realized*   The next step in determining taxable gain is to calculate the **amount realized** from the sale. This is the selling price of the home less selling expenses. Selling expenses include brokerage commissions, advertising, legal fees, title services, escrow or closing fees and mortgage points paid by the seller. If the sale includes furnishings, the value of those furnishings is deducted from the selling price and reported separately as personal property. If the seller takes back a note and mortgage which are immediately sold at a discount, the discounted value of the note is used, not its face amount.

Calculating Gain *on the Sale*   The **gain on the sale** is the difference between the amount realized and the basis. Table 13:2 illustrates this with an example. Unless the seller qualifies for tax postponement or tax exclusion as discussed next, this is the amount to be reported as gain on the seller's annual income tax forms.

Income Tax Postponement   The income tax law of the United States provides that if a seller purchases another home, the gain on the sale of the first home is automatically postponed if the seller meets two conditions. The first condition is that another home must be purchased and occupied within the time period beginning 24

Table 13:2	CALCULATION OF GAIN	
Buy home for $90,000; closing costs are $500	Basis is	$90,500
Add landscaping and fencing for $3,500	Basis is	$94,000
Add bedroom and bathroom for $15,000	Basis is	$109,000
Sell home for $125,000; sales commissions and closing costs are $8,000	Amount realized	117,000
Calculation of gain:	Amount realized	$117,000
	Less basis	109,000
	Equals gain	$ 8,000

months before the closing date of the old home and ending 24 months after the closing date of the old home. A seller who decides to build has 24 months to finish and occupy the new home. These time limits must be strictly observed or the deferment is lost.

The second condition is that the next home must cost as much or more than the adjusted sales price of the previous home. **Adjusted sales price** is the selling price of the old home less selling expenses and fix-up expenses. Fix-up expenses are for fix-up and repair work performed on the home to make it more salable. For fix-up and repair work to be deductible, the work must be performed during the 90-day period ending on the day the contract to sell is signed, and it must be paid for within another 30 days. Table 13:3 illustrates the method for calculating adjusted sales price.

<table>
<tr><td colspan="2" align="center">**ADJUSTED SALES PRICE**</td><td align="right">Table 13:3</td></tr>
<tr><td>Selling price of old home</td><td align="right">$250,000</td></tr>
<tr><td>Less selling expenses</td><td align="right">−18,000</td></tr>
<tr><td>Less fix-up costs</td><td align="right">−7,000</td></tr>
<tr><td>Equals adjusted sales price</td><td align="right">$225,000</td></tr>
</table>

If the new home costs less than the adjusted sales price of the old, there will be a taxable gain. For example, if the old home had a basis of $150,000 and an adjusted sales price of $225,000, and the new home cost $215,000, then there would be a taxable gain of $10,000 and a postponed gain of $65,000. The basis of the new home is $215,000 minus the postponed gain of $65,000, i.e., $150,000.

Postponement of gain is continued from one home to the next as long as the cost of each subsequent home exceeds the adjusted sales price of the previous home, and as long as 24 months elapses between sales. (A shorter turnover period is usually allowed for work-related moves.) The basis of the first home is simply carried forward and included in the basis of the second home, which in turn is carried forward to the third home, and so on. Note that it is not the amount of cash one puts into a home, or the size of the mortgage that counts, but the sales price. Thus it is possible to move from a home with a small mortgage to a slightly more expensive home with a large mortgage, and finish the transaction with cash in the pocket and postponed taxes. Additionally, the law does not restrict the type of home one may own and occupy. Thus the seller of a single-family residence can buy another house, or a condominium, or a cooperative (or vice versa) and still qualify for postponement. Table 13:4 illustrates a progression of tax-deferred residence replacements.

Table 13:4

TAX-DEFERRED RESIDENCE REPLACEMENT

1. Cost and improvements for first home	$ 50,000
2. Adjusted sales price of first home	80,000
3. Gain on sale of first home	30,000
4. Cost of second home	105,000
5. Basis in second home (line 4 minus line 3)	75,000
6. Adjusted sales price of second home	130,000
7. Gain on sale of second house (line 6 minus line 5)	55,000
8. Cost of third home	160,000
9. Basis in third home (line 8 minus line 7)	105,000

LIFETIME EXCLUSION

The postponement of taxes on gains as one moves from one home to the next works well as long as consistently more expensive homes are purchased. However, there may come a time in the homeowner's life when a smaller and presumably less expensive home is needed. To soften the tax burden that such a move usually causes, Congress has enacted legislation that allows a once-in-a-lifetime election to avoid tax on up to $125,000 of gain on the sale of one's residence. To qualify for this, one must be 55 years of age or older on the date of sale and have owned and occupied the residence for at least 3 of the 5 years preceding the sale. Any profit over $125,000 is taxable, but may be postponed if another residence is purchased in accordance with the rules previously described. For example, a person owning a $225,000 home with a basis of $50,000 could sell and move to a $100,000 home with no taxable gain. A person owning a $175,000 home with a $50,000 basis could sell, rent an apartment rather than buy again, and have no taxable gain. By combining postponement with this $125,000 exclusion it is quite possible to eliminate the taxable gain from a lifetime of homeownership.

The gain on the sale of an appreciated asset is called a **capital gain.** Capital gains are divided into two categories: long-term and short-term. A **short-term capital gain** results when a gain is realized on the sale of a capital asset, such as real estate, which has been owned for one year or less. A **long-term capital gain** results when a gain is realized on the sale of a capital asset which has been owned for more than a year. For assets acquired after January 22, 1984 and before January 1, 1988, the Tax Reform Act of 1984 has reduced the holding period to more than six months. The significance of the distinction between long and short is that long-term capital gains receive more favorable tax treatment than short-term capital gains. Short-term gains are taxed at the same rate as ordinary income. Long-term gains are subject to a 60% exclusion which in effect means they are taxed at only 40% of ordinary income tax rates. Therefore, unless there is a strong reason not to, it is beneficial from a tax standpoint to wait until the long-term holding period has been met before selling an appreciated asset that is subject to taxation. Losses from the sale of capital assets are also classified as long-term and short-term. Because the same 60% exclusion applies, short-term losses are more valuable at tax time than long-term losses.

With regard to owner-occupied residences, any gain not postponed or excluded is taxed as a capital gain—either long-term or short-term depending on the holding period. However, if there is a loss on the sale of a personal residence, it cannot be used as a deduction against other income the taxpayer may have.

With regard to real estate other than an owner-occupied residence, capital losses are deductible against the taxpayer's other capital gains and income. However, it is important to note that no real estate other than owner-occupied residences qualifies for postponement of gains upon sale and for the $125,000 lifetime exclusion. For real estate other than one's personal residence, the choices are to pay the taxes due on the sale, effect a tax-free exchange (discussed in Chapter 8), or elect the installment method of reporting the gain, a topic we consider next.

When a gain cannot be postponed or excluded, a popular method of deferring income taxes is to use the **installment method** of reporting the gain. This can be applied to any kind of real estate, including vacant land and income-producing property, and homeowner gains that do not qualify for postponement or exclusion.

Suppose that your property, which is free and clear of debt, is sold for $100,000. The real estate commission and closing costs are $7,500 and your basis is $40,000. As a result, the gain on this sale is $52,500. If you sell for all cash, you are required to pay all the income taxes due on that gain in the year of sale, a situation that may force you into a higher tax bracket. A solution is to sell to the buyer on terms rather than to send him to a lender to obtain a loan.

For example, if the buyer pays you $20,000 down and gives you a promissory note calling for payments of $5,000 and interest this year, and $25,000 plus interest in each of the next 3 years, your gain is calculated and reported as follows. Of each dollar of sales price received, 52½¢ is reported as gain. Thus, $13,125 is reported this year and in each of the next 3 years. The interest you earn on the promissory note is reported and taxed separately as interest income.

If there is a $30,000 mortgage on the property that the buyer agrees to assume, the $100,000 sales price is reduced by $30,000 to $70,000 for tax-calculating purposes. The portion of each dollar paid to you by the buyer that must be reported as gain is $52,500 divided by $70,000, or 75%. If the down payment is $20,000 followed by $10,000 per year for 5 years, you would report 75% of $20,000, or $15,000 this year and $7,500 in each of the next 5 years. The gain is taxed at the capital gains rates in effect at the time the installment is received.

If you sell by the installment method, that is, you sell property at a gain in one taxable year and receive one or more payments in later taxable years, the installment method of reporting is automatically applied. If this is not suitable, you can elect to pay all the taxes in the year of sale.

Since the federal income tax began in 1913, owners of single-family residences have been permitted to claim as itemized personal deductions money paid out for state and local realty taxes, as well as interest on debt secured by their homes. Subsequently, this deduction was extended to condominium and cooperative apartment owners. The deduction allowed for property taxes does not extend to special assessment taxes for improvement districts. However, if the assessment goes to bond, that portion of each payment attributable to interest is deductible. With regard to mortgages, the IRS also permits the deduction of loan prepayment penalties and the deduction of points on new loans that are clearly distinguishable as interest and not service fees for making the loan. Loan points paid by a seller to help a buyer obtain an FHA or VA loan are not deductible as interest (it is not the seller's debt), but can be deducted from the home's selling price in computing a gain or loss on the sale. FHA mortgage insurance premiums are not deductible nor are those paid to private mortgage insurers.

From an individual taxpayer's standpoint, the ability to deduct property taxes and mortgage interest on one's residence becomes more valuable in successively higher tax brackets. As viewed from a national standpoint, the deductibility of interest and property taxes encourages widespread ownership of the country's land and buildings.

PROPERTY TAX AND INTEREST DEDUCTIONS

When you own real estate for investment purposes, the rental income from that property is fully taxable. However, from this income you can deduct all expenses incurred in earning it, such as property taxes, interest, maintenance, repairs, management, utilities, insurance and depreciation. (In contrast, a homeowner can deduct only property taxes and interest.) Money spent on improvements is not immediately deductible from rental income but must be added to the basis of the property and depreciated. Upon sale, long-term capital gains tax treatment is received if the long-term holding period is met. Alternatively, an investor can structure the sale on an installment basis so as to use the installment method to report gains or arrange a tax-deferred exchange as explained in Chapter 8. (Real estate investing, including the ability of property to

INCOME TAXES ON INVESTMENT PROPERTY

"shelter" other sources of income, is discussed in the last chapter of this book.) If income taxes that are due are not paid, the government may place a lien against the taxpayer's property by issuing a tax warrant. When properly filed, this lien makes the property security for payment of the delinquent taxes.

BELOW-MARKET
INTEREST

In an effort to raise more taxes, in the Tax Reform Act of 1984 Congress enacted legislation requiring sellers to charge market rates of interest or be taxed as if they had. Congress saw that by lowering the rate of interest charged on a carryback loan a seller can increase the selling price. However, an increase in selling price will most likely be a long-term capital gain whereas interest received is ordinary income. The former brings the U.S. government less money than the latter.

For several years federal tax law has required that a minimum 9% interest be charged or the IRS would impute an interest rate of 10% and taxes would be calculated as though the taxpayer had received 10%. However, the 1984 act went further and required minimum rates tied to prevailing rates on federal securities, i.e., U.S. Treasury notes and bonds. This act generated considerable complaint from the real estate industry and in 1985 was changed by Congress. Effective July 1, 1985, if the amount of seller financing in a transaction is $2.8 million or less, the seller must charge no less than 9% interest or a rate equal to the applicable federal rate (AFR). If the amount of seller financing in a transaction is greater than $2.8 million, the seller must charge a rate equal to or greater than the AFR. In the same bill, Congress increased the depreciation period for income producing buildings from 18 to 19 years.

Other rules for real estate may change. There is popular support for tax simplification and reduction of the federal deficit. As a result, some deductions afforded real estate owners in the past may be reduced or eliminated. Possibilities include changes in long-term capital gain treatment and limitations on how much an individual can deduct for mortgage interest on a second home and on investment properties. Additionally, more user fees are likely to be enacted. For example, the FHA mortgage insurance premium is a user fee as is the VA funding fee. There have been proposals to increase the VA funding fee and to enact user fees on mortgage packages insured by the FNMA and GNMA.

Because tax rules for real estate are continually changing, only the major rules least likely to change have been reported and discussed here. As a real estate owner or agent you need a source of more frequent and more detailed information such as the annual income tax guide published by the Internal Revenue Service (free) or the privately published guides available in most bookstores. Additionally, you may wish to subscribe to a tax newsletter for up-to-the-minute tax information.

Please be aware that tax law changes have an impact on real estate values. In the past, tax laws have been very generous to real estate—particularly deductions for depreciation and interest as well as credits for the rehabilitation of old buildings. Many otherwise uneconomic real estate projects have become economically feasible because of tax laws. If those laws change so as to reduce the incentive to buy and hold real estate, this will be taken into consideration by prospective purchasers.

IMPACT ON REAL ESTATE

The real estate industry's desire for professional recognition, coupled with the results of several key court cases, strongly suggests that a real estate agent be reasonably knowledgeable about taxes. This does not mean the agent must have knowledge of tax laws at the level of an accountant or tax attorney. Neither does it mean an agent can plead ignorance of tax laws. Rather it means a real estate agent is now liable for tax advice (or lack of it) if the advice is material to the transaction and to give such advice is common in the brokerage business. What this means is that an agent should have enough general knowledge of real estate tax laws so as to be able to answer basic questions accurately and to warn clients and recommend tax counsel if the questions posed by the transaction are beyond the agent's knowledge. Note that the obligation to inform exists even when a client fails to ask about tax consequences. This is to avoid situations where after the deed is recorded the client says, "Gee, I didn't know I'd have to pay all these taxes, my agent should have warned me," and then sues the agent. Lastly, if the agent tries to fill the role of accountant or tax attorney for the client, then the agent will be held liable to the standards of an accountant or tax attorney.

To summarize, an agent must be aware of tax laws that affect the properties the agent is handling. An agent has a responsibility to alert clients to potential tax consequences,

AGENT'S LIABILITY FOR TAX ADVICE

liabilities and advantages whether they ask for it or not. Lastly, an agent is responsible for the quality and accuracy of tax information given out by the agent.

CONVEYANCE TAXES   Prior to 1968 the federal government required the purchase and placement of federal documentary tax stamps on deeds. The rate was 55¢ for each $500 or fraction thereof computed on the "new money" in the transaction. Thus, if a person bought a home for $75,000 and either paid cash or arranged for a new mortgage, the tax was based on the full $75,000. If the buyer assumed or took title subject to an existing $50,000 loan, then the tax was based on $25,000. Examples of federal documentary tax stamps, which look much like postage stamps, can still be seen on deeds recorded prior to 1968.

Effective January 1, 1968, the federal deed tax program was ended and many states took the opportunity to begin charging a deed tax of their own. Some adopted fee schedules that are substantially the same as the federal government previously charged. Others base their fee on the purchase price without regard to any existing indebtedness left on the property by the seller. Forty-one states, the District of Columbia and some counties and cities charge a transfer tax. The amount ranges from just a few dollars to as much as $4,500 on the sale of a $100,000 property. These fees are paid to the county recorder prior to recording and are in addition to the charge for recording the document itself. Some states also charge a separate tax on the value of any mortgage debt created by a transaction.

VOCABULARY REVIEW

Match terms **a–p** *with statements* **1–16.**

a. *Adjusted sales price*
b. *Ad valorem*
c. *Appropriation process*
d. *Assessed value*
e. *Assessment appeal board*
f. *Assessment roll*
g. *Conveyance tax*
h. *Front-foot basis*

i. *Improvement district*
j. *Installment reporting*
k. *Long-term capital gain*
l. *Mill rate*
m. *Public improvement*
n. *Special assessments*
o. *Tax certificate*
p. *Tax deed*

1. A tax rate expressed in tenths of a cent per dollar of assessed valuation.
2. According to value.

3. A document issued at a tax sale that entitles the purchaser to a deed at a later date if the property is not redeemed.
4. The enactment of a taxing body's budget and sources of money into law.
5. A book that contains the assessed value of each property in the county or taxing district.
6. A document conveying title to property purchased at a tax sale.
7. A value placed on a property for the purpose of taxation.
8. Assessments levied to provide publicly built improvements that will primarily benefit property owners within a small geographical area.
9. A charge or levy based directly on the measured distance that a parcel of land abuts a street.
10. Sales price of a property less fix-up costs and sales commissions, closing and other selling costs.
11. A preferential income tax treatment on the sale of an appreciated asset.
12. Sale of an appreciated property structured to spread out the payment of income taxes on the gain.
13. Hears complaints from property owners regarding their assessments.
14. A state or local tax charged on deeds at the time of recording.
15. The geographical area which will be assessed for a local improvement.
16. An improvement that benefits the public at large and is therefore financed by general property taxes.

QUESTIONS AND PROBLEMS

1. Explain the process for calculating the property tax rate for a taxation district.
2. The Southside School District contains property totaling $120 million in assessed valuation. If the district's budget is $960,000, what will the mill rate be?
3. Continuing with Problem 2 above, if a home situated in the Southside School District carries an assessed valuation of $40,000, how much will the homeowner be required to pay to support the district this year?
4. The Lakeview Mosquito Abatement District levies an annual tax of $0.05 per $100 of assessed valuation to pay for a mosquito control program. How much does that amount to for a property in the district with an assessed valuation of $10,000?
5. In your county, if a property owner wishes to appeal an assessment, what procedure must be followed?
6. If the property taxes on your home were to rise 90% in 1 year, where would you go to protest the increase: to the assessment appeal board, to the city council or to the county government? Explain.

7. How does the amount of tax-exempt real estate in a community affect nonexempt property owners?

8. What methods and techniques are used by your local assessor's office to keep up to date with the changing real estate prices?

9. The Smiths bought a house in 1963 for $21,000, including closing costs. Five years later they made improvements costing $2,000 and 5 years after that more improvements that cost $5,000. Today they sell the house; the sales price is $68,000 and commissions and closing costs total $5,000. For income tax purposes, what is their gain?

10. Continuing with Problem 9, a month after selling, the Smiths purchase a two-bedroom condominium for $58,000, including closing costs. What is their taxable gain now? Will it be taxed as a short-term or a long-term capital gain? (Assume that the Smiths are less than 55 years of age.)

11. What is the conveyance tax rate in your state? What would the conveyance tax be on a $100,000 home?

ADDITIONAL READINGS

"Broker Liability for Tax Advice" by **Michael Hesse.** (*First Tuesday*, Apr 84, page 20). This article points out that a client can collect from a broker if taxes were avoidable in a transaction and the broker failed to alert the client or gave the client wrong information.

"Property Taxation—a Complicated Process" by **Richard Darling.** (*Real Estate Today*, Nov/Dec 84, page 19). Article describes how property owners can challenge their property valuations.

Tax Information for Homeowners. (Internal Revenue Service, Publication 530, 1986, 8 pages). Discusses income tax aspects of settlement costs, itemized deductions, rental and business use, repairs, improvements, buying, selling, record keeping, casualty losses, etc., for owners of houses, condominiums and cooperatives. Published annually and available free from the IRS.

Tax Information on Selling Your Home. (Internal Revenue Service, Publication 523, 1986, 12 pages). Provides instructions on how to report taxable income from the sale of one's residence. Published annually and available free from the IRS.

* * *

The following periodicals may also be of interest to you: *Journal of Taxation, Kiplinger Tax Letter, Monthly Digest of Tax Articles, National Tax Journal, Property Tax Journal, Property Tax Newsletter, Real Estate Tax Digest, Real Estate Tax Ideas, Tax Adviser, Tax Shelter Letter, Tax Shelter Opportunities in Real Estate, Tax Sheltered Investments Law Report* and *Taxes* and *The Tax Magazine.*

Title Closing and Escrow

Closing meeting: a meeting at which the buyer pays for the property and receives a deed to it and all other matters pertaining to the sale are concluded

Escrow agent: the person placed in charge of an escrow

Escrow closing: the deposit of documents and funds with a neutral third party along with instructions as to how to conduct the closing

Prorating: the division of ongoing expenses and income items between the buyer and the seller

Real Estate Settlement Procedures Act (RESPA): a federal law that deals with procedures to be followed in certain types of real estate closings

Settlement statement: an accounting of funds to the buyer and the seller at the completion of a real estate transaction

Title closing: the process of completing a real estate transaction

Walk-through: a final inspection of the property just prior to settlement

Numerous details must be handled between the time a buyer and seller sign a sales contract and the day title is conveyed to the buyer. Title must be searched (Chapter 6), a decision made as to how to take title (Chapter 4), a deed prepared (Chapter 5), loan arrangements made (Chapters 9 through 12), property tax records checked (Chapter 13) and so forth. In this chapter we will look at the final steps in the process, in particular, the buyer's walk-through, the closing meeting or escrow, prorations and the settlement statement.

BUYER'S WALK-THROUGH

To protect both the buyer and the seller, it is good practice for a buyer to make a **walk-through.** This is a final inspection of the property just prior to the settlement date. It is quite possible the buyer has not been on the parcel or inside the structure since the initial offer and acceptance. Now, several weeks later, the buyer wants to make certain that the premises has been vacated, that no damage has occurred, that the seller has left behind personal property agreed upon and that the seller

327

has not removed and taken any real property. If the sales contract requires all mechanical items to be in normal working order, then the seller will want to test the heating and air-conditioning systems, dishwasher, disposer, stove, garage door opener, etc., and the refrigerator, washer and dryer if included. The buyer will also want to test all of the plumbing to be certain the hot water heater works, faucets and showers run, toilets flush and sinks drain. A final inspection of the structure is made, including walls, roof, gutters, driveway, decks, patios, etc., as well as the land and landscaping.

Note that a walk-through is not the time for the buyer to make the initial inspection of the property. That is done before the contract is signed and if there are questions in the buyer's mind regarding the structural soundness of the property, a thorough inspection (possibly with the aid of a professional house inspector) should be conducted within 10 days of signing the purchase contract. The walk-through is for the purpose of giving the buyer the opportunity to make certain that agreements regarding the condition of the premises have been kept. If during the walk-through the buyer notes the walls were damaged when the seller moved out, or the furnace does not function, the buyer (or the buyer's agent) notes these items and asks that funds be withheld at the closing to pay for repairs.

TITLE CLOSING   **Title closing** refers to the completion of a real estate transaction. This is when the buyer pays for the property and the seller delivers the deed. The day on which this occurs is called the **closing date.** Depending on where one resides in the United States, the title closing process is referred to as a **closing, settlement** or **escrow.** All accomplish the same basic goal, but the method of reaching that goal can follow one of two paths.

In some parts of the United States, particularly in the East, and to a certain extent in the Mountain states, the Midwest and the South, the title closing process is concluded at a meeting of all parties to the transaction or their representatives. Elsewhere, title closing is conducted by an escrow agent who is a neutral third party mutually selected by the buyer and seller to carry out the closing. With an escrow, there is no closing meeting; in fact, most of the closing process is conducted by mail. Let us look at the operation of each method.

When a meeting is used to close a real estate transaction, the seller meets in person with the buyer and delivers the deed. At the same time, the buyer pays the seller for the property. To ascertain that everything promised in the sales contract has been properly carried out, it is customary for the buyer and seller each to have an attorney present. The real estate agents who brought the buyer and seller together are also present, along with a representative of the firm that conducted the title search. If a new loan is being made or an existing one is being paid off at the closing, a representative of each lender will be present.

The location of the meeting and the selection of the person responsible for conducting the closing will depend on local custom and the nature of the closing. It is the custom in some states to conduct the closing at the real estate agent's office. In other localities it is conducted in the office of the seller's attorney. An alternative is to have the title company responsible for the title search and title policy conduct the closing at its office. If a new loan is involved, the lender may want to conduct the closing. If the seller is unable to attend the closing meeting, the seller appoints someone, such as his lawyer or real estate agent, to represent him at the meeting. Similarly, a buyer who is unable to attend can appoint a representative to be present at the meeting. Appointment of a representative is accomplished by preparing and signing a power of attorney.

Seller's Responsibilities at Closing

To assure a smooth closing, each person attending is responsible for bringing certain documents. The seller and his attorney are responsible for preparing and bringing the deed together with the most recent property tax bill (and receipt if it has been paid). If required by the sales contract, they also bring the insurance policy for the property, the termite and wood-rot inspection report, deeds or documents showing the removal of unacceptable liens and encumbrances, a title insurance policy, a bill of sale for personal property, a survey map and any needed offset statements or beneficiary statements. An **offset statement** is a statement by an owner or lienholder as to the balance due on an existing lien against the property. A **beneficiary statement** is a statement of the unpaid balance on a note secured by a trust deed. The loan payment booklet, keys to the property, garage door opener and the like are also brought to the meeting. If the property is a condominium, cooperative or planned unit development, the seller will bring such items as the articles of incorporation; bylaws; conditions, covenants and restrictions (CC&Rs); annual budget; reserve fund status report; and management company's name to the closing. If the property produces income, then existing leases, rent schedules, current expenditures and letters advising the tenants of the new owner must also be furnished.

Buyer's Responsibilities at Closing

The buyer's responsibilities include having adequate settlement funds ready, having an attorney present if desired and, if borrowing, obtaining the loan commitment and advising the lender of the meeting's time and place. The real estate agent is present because it is the custom in some localities that the agent be in charge of the closing and prepare the proration calculations. The agent also receives a commission check at that time and, as a matter of good business, will make certain that all goes well.

If a new loan is involved, the lender brings a check for the amount of the loan along with a note and mortgage for the borrower to sign. If an existing loan is to be paid off as part of the transaction, the lender is present to receive a check and release the mortgage held on the property. If a lender elects not to attend, the check and/or loan papers are given to the person in charge of the closing, along with instructions for their distribution and signing. A title insurance representative is also present to provide the latest status of title and the title insurance policy. If title insurance is not used, the seller is responsible for bringing an abstract or asking the abstracter to be present.

Agent's Duties

The seller and the seller's attorney may be unaware of all the things expected of them at the closing meeting. Therefore, it is the duty of the agent who listed the property to make certain that they are prepared for the meeting. Similarly, it is the duty of the agent who found the buyer to make certain that the buyer and the buyer's attorney are prepared for the closing meeting. If the agent both lists and sells the property, the agent assists both the buyer and seller. If more than one agent is involved in the transaction, each should keep the other(s) fully informed so the transaction will go as well as possible. At all times the buyer and seller are to be kept informed as to the status of the closing. An agent should give them a preview of what will take place, explain each payment or receipt and in general prepare the parties for informed participation at the closing meeting.

When everyone concerned has arrived at the meeting place, the closing begins. Those present record each other's names as witnesses to the meeting. The various documents called for by the sales contract are exchanged for inspection. The buyer and his attorney inspect the deed the seller is offering, the title search and/or title policy, the mortgage papers, survey, leases, removals of encumbrances and proration calculations. The lender also inspects the deed, survey, title search and title policy. This continues until each party has a chance to inspect each document of interest.

The Transaction

A settlement statement (also called a closing statement) is given to the buyer and seller to summarize the financial aspects of their transaction. It is prepared by the person in charge of the closing either just prior to or at the meeting. It provides a clear picture of where the buyer's and seller's money is going at the closing by identifying each party to whom money is being paid. (An example of a closing statement is given later in this chapter.)

If everyone involved in the closing has done his or her homework and comes prepared to the meeting, the closing usually goes smoothly. When everything is in order, the seller hands a completed deed to the buyer. Simultaneously, the buyer gives the seller a check that combines the down payment and net result of the prorations. The lender has the buyer sign the mortgage and note and hands checks to the seller and the existing lender, if one is involved. The seller writes a check to his real estate broker, attorney and the abstracter. The buyer writes a check to his attorney. This continues until every document is signed and everyone is paid. At the end, everyone stands, shakes hands and departs. The deed, new mortgage and release of the old mortgage are recorded and the transaction is complete.

Occasionally an unavoidable circumstance can cause delays in a closing. Perhaps an important document, known to

Dry Closing

be in the mail, has not arrived. Yet it will be difficult to reschedule the meeting. In such a situation, the parties concerned may agree to a **dry closing.** In a dry closing, all parties sign their documents and entrust them to the person in charge of the closing for safekeeping. No money is disbursed and the deed is not delivered until the missing paperwork arrives. When it does, the closing attorney completes the transaction and delivers the money and documents by mail or messenger.

ESCROW

The use of an **escrow** to close a real estate transaction involves a neutral third party, called an **escrow agent**, escrow holder, or escrowee who acts as a trusted stakeholder for all the parties to the transaction. Instead of delivering a deed directly to the buyer at the closing meeting, the seller gives the deed to the escrow agent with instructions that it be delivered only after the buyer has completed all of the buyer's promises in the sales contract. Similarly, the buyer hands the escrow agent the money for the purchase price plus instructions that it be given to the seller only after fulfillment of the seller's promises. Let us look closer at this arrangement.

A typical real estate escrow closing starts when a sales contract is signed by the buyer and seller. They select a neutral escrow agent to handle the closing. This may be the escrow department of a bank or savings and loan or other lending agency, an independent escrow company, an attorney or the escrow department of a title insurance company. Sometimes real estate brokers offer escrow services. However, if the broker is earning a sales commission in the transaction, the broker cannot be classed as neutral and disinterested. Because escrow agents are entrusted with valuable documents and large sums of money, most states have licensing and bonding requirements that escrow agents must meet.

Escrow Agent's Duties

The escrow agent's task begins with the deposit of the buyer's earnest money in a special bank trust account and the preparation of a set of escrow instructions based on the signed sales contract. These must be promptly signed by the buyer and seller. The instructions establish an agency relationship between the escrow agent and the buyer, and the escrow agent and the seller. The instructions also detail in writing everything that each party to the sale must do before the deed is delivered to the buyer. In a typical transaction, the escrow instructions will tell the escrow agent to order a title search and obtain title insurance.

If an existing loan against the property is to be repaid as part of the sale, the escrow agent is asked to contact the lender to request a statement of the amount of money necessary to repay the loan and to request a mortgage release. The lender then enters into an agreement with the escrow agent wherein the lender is to give the completed release papers to the escrow agent; but the agent may not deliver them to the seller until the agent has remitted the amount demanded by the lender. If the existing loan is to be assumed, the escrow agent asks the lender for the current balance and any documents that the buyer must sign.

When the title search is completed, the escrow agent forwards it to the buyer or his attorney for approval. The property insurance and tax papers the seller would otherwise bring to the closing meeting are sent to the escrow agent for proration. Leases, service contracts and notices to tenants are also sent to the escrow agent for proration and delivery to the buyer. The deed conveying title to the buyer is prepared by the seller's attorney (in some states by the escrow agent), signed by the seller and given to the escrow agent. Once delivered into escrow, even if the seller dies, marries or is declared legally incompetent before the close of escrow, the deed will still pass title to the buyer.

As the closing date draws near, and provided all the instructions are otherwise complete, the escrow agent requests any additional money the buyer and lender must deposit in order to close. The day before closing the escrow agent calls the title company and orders a last minute check on the title. If no changes have occurred since the first (preliminary) title search, the deed, mortgage, mortgage release and other documents to be recorded as part of the transaction are recorded first thing the following morning. As soon as the recording is confirmed, the escrow agent hands or mails a check to every party to whom funds are due from the escrow (usually the seller, real estate broker and previous lender), along with any

The Closing

papers or documents which must be delivered through escrow (such as the fire insurance policy, copy of the property tax bill and tenant leases). Several days later the buyer and lender will receive a title insurance policy in the mail from the title company. The public recorder's office also mails the documents it recorded to each party. The deed is sent to the buyer, the mortgage release to the seller and the new mortgage to the lender.

Deed Delivery   In the escrow closing method, the closing, delivery of title and recordation usually all take place at the same moment. Technically, the seller does not physically hand a deed to the buyer on the closing day. However, once all the conditions of the escrow are met, the escrow agent becomes an agent of the seller in regard to the money in the transaction and an agent of the buyer in regard to the deed. Thus, the buyer, through an agent, receives the deed and the law regarding delivery is fulfilled.

It is not necessary for the buyer and seller to meet face-to-face during the escrow period or at the closing. This can eliminate personality conflicts that might be detrimental to an otherwise sound transaction. The escrow agent, having previously accumulated all the documents, approvals, deeds and monies prior to the closing date, does the closing alone.

In a brokeraged transaction, the real estate agent is usually the only person who actually meets the escrow agent. All communication can be handled through the broker, by mail or by telephone. If a real estate agent is not involved, the buyer and/or seller can open the escrow, either in person or by mail. The use of an escrow agent does not eliminate the need for an attorney. Although there is no closing meeting for the attorneys to attend, they play a vital role in advising the buyer and seller on each document sent by the escrow agent for approval and signature.

DELAYS AND FAILURE TO CLOSE   When a real estate purchase contract is written, a closing date is also negotiated and placed in the contract. The choice of closing date will depend on when the buyer wants possession, when the seller wants to move out and how long it will take to obtain a loan, title search and termite report and otherwise fulfill the contract requirements. In a typical residential sale this is 30 to 60 days with 45 days being a popular choice when new financing is involved.

Delays along the way are sometimes encountered and may cause a delay in the closing. This is usually not a problem as long as the buyer still intends to buy, the seller still intends to sell and the delay is for a reasonable cause and a justifiable length of time. Many preprinted real estate purchase contracts include a statement that the broker may extend the time for performance including the closing date. Even if the contract contains a "time is of the essence" clause, unless there is supporting evidence in the contract that time really is of the essence, reasonable delays for reasonable causes are usually permitted in law.

Suppose the delay will be quite lengthy. For example, there may be a previously undisclosed title defect that will take months to clear or perhaps there are unusual problems in financing or there has been major damage to the premises. In such cases, relieving all parties from further obligations to each other may be the wisest choice for all involved. If so, it is essential that the buyer and seller sign mutual release papers. These are necessary to rescind the purchase contract and cancel the escrow if one has been opened. The buyer's deposit is also returned. Without release papers the buyer still has a vaguely defined liability to buy and the seller can still be required to convey the property. A mutual release gives the buyer the freedom to choose another property and the seller the chance to fix the problem and remarket the property later.

A stickier problem occurs when one party wants out of the contract and attempts to use any delay in closing as grounds for contract termination. The buyer may have found a preferable property for less money and better terms. The seller may have received a higher offer since signing the purchase contract. Although the party wishing to cancel may threaten with a lawsuit, courts will rarely enforce cancellation of valuable contract rights due to reasonable delays that are not the fault of the other party. Moreover, courts will not go along with a reluctant buyer or seller who manufactures delays so as to delay the closing and then claim default and cancellation of the contract. If the reluctance continues and negotiations to end it fail, the performing party may choose to complete its requirements and then ask the courts to force the reluctant party to the closing table.

LOAN ESCROWS   Escrows can be used for purposes other than real estate sales transactions. For example, a homeowner who is refinancing his property could enter into an escrow with the lender. The conditions of the escrow would be that the homeowner deliver a properly executed note and mortgage to the escrow agent and that the lender deposit the loan money. Upon closing, the escrow agent delivers the documents to the lender and the money to the homeowner. Or, in reverse, an escrow could be used to pay off the balance of a loan. The conditions would be the borrower's deposit of the balance due and the lender's deposit of the mortgage release and note. Even the weekly office sports pool is an escrow—with the person holding the pool money acting as escrow agent for the participants.

PRORATING AT THE CLOSING   Ongoing expenses and income items must be prorated between the seller and buyer when property ownership changes hands. Items subject to proration include property insurance premiums, property taxes, accrued interest on assumed loans, and rents and operating expenses if the property produces income. If heating is done by oil and the oil tank is partially filled when title transfers, that oil can be prorated, as can utility bills when service is not shut off between owners. Several sample prorations common to most closings will help the process.

Hazard Insurance   Hazard insurance policies for such things as fire, wind, storm and flood damage are paid for in advance. At the beginning of each year of the policy's life, the premium for that year's coverage must be paid. When real estate is sold, the buyer may ask the seller to transfer the remaining coverage. The seller usually agrees if the buyer pays for the value of the remaining coverage on a prorated basis.

The first step in prorating hazard insurance is to find out how often the premium is paid, how much it is, and what period of time it covers. Suppose that the seller has a 1-year policy that cost $180 and started on January 1 of the current year.

If the property is sold and the closing date is July 1, the policy is half used. Therefore, if the buyer wants the policy transferred, the buyer pays the seller $90 for the remaining 6 months of coverage.

Because closing dates do not always occur on neat, evenly divided portions of the year, nor do most items that need prorating, it is usually necessary to break the year into months and the months into days to make proration calculations. Suppose in the previous hazard insurance example that prorations are to be made on June 30 instead of July 1. This would give the buyer 6 months and 1 day of coverage. How much does the buyer owe the seller? The first step is to calculate the monthly and daily rates for the policy: $180 divided by 12 is $15 per month. Dividing the monthly rate of $15 by 30 days gives a daily rate of 50¢. The second step is to add 6 months at $15 and 1 day at 50¢. Thus, the buyer owes the seller $90.50 for the unused portion of the policy.

When a buyer agrees to assume an existing loan from the seller, an interest proration is necessary. For example, a sales contract calls for the buyer to assume a 9% mortgage loan with a principal balance of $80,505 at the time of closing. Loan payments are due the tenth of each month, and the sales contract calls for a July 3 closing date, with interest on the loan to be prorated through July 2. How much is to be prorated and to whom?

Loan Interest

First, we must recognize that interest is normally paid in arrears. On a loan that is payable monthly, the borrowers pays interest for the use of the loan at the end of each month he has had the loan. Thus, the July 10 monthly loan payment includes the interest due for the use of $80,505 from June 10 through June 9. However, the seller owned the property through July 2, and from June 10 through July 2 is 23 days. At the closing the seller must give the buyer enough money to pay for 23 days interest on the $80,505. If the annual interest rate is 9%, one month's interest is $80,505 times 9% divided by 12, which is $603.79. Divide this by 30 days to get a daily interest rate of $20.126. Multiply the daily rate by 23 to obtain the interest for 23 days, $462.90.

30-Day Month   In many parts of the country, it is the custom when prorating interest, property taxes, water bills and insurance to use a 30-day month because it simplifies proration calculations. Naturally, using a 30-day month produces some inaccuracy when dealing with months that do not have 30 days. If this inaccuracy is significant to the buyer and seller, they can agree to prorate either by using the exact number of days in the closing month or by dividing the year rate by 365 to find a daily rate. Some states avoid this question altogether by requiring that the exact number of days be used in prorating.

Rents   It is the custom throughout the country to prorate rents on the basis of the actual number of days in the month. Using the July 3 closing date again, if the property is currently rented for $450 per month, paid in advance on the first of each month, what would the proration be? If the seller has already collected the rent for the month of July, he is obligated to hand over to the buyer that portion of the rent earned between July 3 and July 31, inclusive, a period of 29 days. To determine how many dollars this is, divide $450 by the number of days in July. This gives $14.516 as the rent per day. Then multiply the daily rate by 29 days to get $420.96, the portion of the July rent that the seller must hand over to the buyer. If the renter has not paid the July rent by the July 3 closing date, no proration is made. If the buyer later collects the July rent, he must return 2 days rent to the seller.

Property Taxes   Prorated property taxes are common to nearly all real estate transactions. The amount of proration depends on when the property taxes are due, what portion has already been paid and what period of time they cover. Property taxes are levied on an annual basis, but depending on the locality they may be due at the beginning, middle or end of the tax year. In some parts of the country, property owners are permitted to pay in two or more installments.

Suppose you live in a state where the property tax year runs from January 1 through December 31, property tax bills are mailed to property owners in late February and taxes for the full year are due April 10. If a transaction calls for property taxes to be prorated through January 31, how is the calculation made? Since the new bill is not yet available, the old bill is often used as a guide. Suppose it was $1,200 for the year. The proration is from January 1 through January 31, a period of one month. One month's taxes are calculated as one-twelfth of $1,200 or $100. The seller owes the buyer $100 because the seller owned the property through January 31, yet the buyer will later receive and pay the property tax bill for the full year. If it is likely the new tax bill will be substantially different from the previous year, the buyer and seller can agree to make another adjustment between themselves when the new bill is available. If property tax bills had been issued in January and taxes for the full year paid by the seller, the seller would be credited with 11 months × $100/month = $1,100 and the buyer charged $1,100.

Homeowners' Association

If the property being sold is a condominium unit or in a cooperative or a planned unit development, there will be a monthly homeowners' association payment to be prorated. Suppose the monthly fee is $120 and is paid in advance on the first of the month. If the closing takes place on the twentieth, then the buyer owes the seller $40 for the unused portion of the month.

Proration Date

Prorations need not be calculated as of the closing date. In the sales contract, the buyer and seller can mutually agree to a different proration date if they wish. If nothing is said, local law and custom will prevail. In some states it is customary to prorate as of the day before closing, the theory being that the buyer is the new owner beginning on the day the transaction closes. Other states prorate as of the day of closing. If the difference of 1 day is important to the buyer or seller, they should not rely on local custom, but agree in writing on a proration day of their own choosing.

Special assessments for such things as street improvements, water mains and sewer lines are not usually prorated. As a rule, the selling price of the property reflects the added value of the improvements, and the seller pays any assessments in full before closing. This is not an ironclad rule; the buyer and seller in their sales contract can agree to do whatever they want about the assessment.

Table 14:1   **SUMMARY OF COMMON PRORATIONS**

Accumulated interest on existing loan assumed by buyer	Charge seller	Credit buyer	*Prorate backward*
Hazard insurance or mortgage insurance premium paid in advance	Charge buyer	Credit seller	*Prorate forward*
Property taxes paid in advance	Charge buyer	Credit seller	*Prorate forward*
Property taxes in arrears	Charge seller	Credit buyer	*Prorate backward*
Condominium or homeowner fees paid in advance	Charge buyer	Credit seller	*Prorate forward*
Rent paid in advance	Charge seller	Credit buyer	*Prorate forward*
Interest on a new loan	Charge buyer	Credit lender	*Prorate forward*
Interest on a loan to be paid off at the closing	Charge seller	Credit lender	*Prorate backward*

Proration Summary   Table 14:1 summarizes the most common proration situations found in real estate closings. The table also shows who is to be charged and who is to be credited and whether the proration is to be worked forward or backward from the closing date. As a rule, items that are paid in advance are prorated forward from the closing date; for example, prepaid fire insurance. Items that are paid in arrears, such as interest on an existing loan, are prorated backward from the closing date.

SAMPLE CLOSING   To illustrate the arithmetic involved, let us work through a residential closing situation. Note that this example is not particular to any region of the United States, but is rather a composite that shows you how the most commonly encountered residential closing items are handled.

Homer Leavitt has listed his home for sale with List-Rite Realty for $125,000, and the sales commission is to be 6% of the selling price. A salesperson from Quick-Sale Realty learns about the property through the multiple listing service and produces a buyer willing to pay $123,000 with $33,000 down. The offer is conditioned on the seller paying off the existing $48,000, 12% interest mortgage loan and the buyer obtaining a new loan for $90,000. Property taxes, hazard insurance and heating oil in the home's oil tank are to be prorated as of the closing date. The buyer also asks the seller to pay for a termite inspection and repairs if necessary, a title search, an owner's title insurance policy, conveyance taxes and one-half of the closing fee. The seller accepts this offer on August 15, and they agree to close on September 15.

The property tax year for this home runs from January 1 through December 31. Mr. Leavitt has paid the taxes for last year, but not for the current year as yet. Newly issued tax bills show that $1,680 will be due on October 1 for the current year. The hazard insurance policy (fire, windstorm, etc.) that the buyer wishes to assume was purchased by the seller for $240 and covers the period June 15 through the following June 14. The Safety Title Insurance Company will charge the seller $400 for a combined title search, title examination and owner's title policy package.

The buyer obtains a loan commitment from the Ajax National Bank for $90,000. To make this loan, the bank will charge a $900 loan origination fee, $100 for an appraisal and $25 for a credit report on the buyer. The bank also requires a lender's title policy in the amount of $90,000 (added cost $90), 12 months of property tax reserves and 4 months of hazard insurance reserves. The loan is to be repaid in equal monthly installments beginning November 1. The termite inspection by Dead-Bug Pest Company costs $39, and recording fees are $5 for deeds and mortgage releases and $10 for mortgages. The bank charges the buyer and the seller $110 each to conduct the closing plus $10 to prepare a deed for the seller and $2 to notarize it. The state levies a transfer tax on deeds of 50 cents per $500 of sales price, and the seller is leaving $130 worth of heating oil for the buyer.

The buyer and seller have each hired an attorney to advise them on legal matters in connection with the sales contract and closing. They are to be paid $150 and $120, respectively, out of the settlement. List-Rite Realty and Quick-Sale Realty have advised the closing agent they are splitting the $7,380 sales commission equally.

Finally, the $3,000 earnest money deposit that the buyer

Table 14:2   **TRANSACTION SUMARY**

	Amount	Comments
Sale Price	$123,000	
Down Payment	$ 33,000	
Deposit (Earnest Money)	$ 3,000	Credit to buyer's down payment.
Existing Loan	$ 48,000	Seller to pay off through settlement. Interest rate is 12%.
New Loan	$ 90,000	Monthly payments begin Nov. 1. Interest rate is 9.6%.
Loan Origination Fee	$ 900 ⎫	⎧ Paid by buyer in connection
Appraisal Fee	$ 100 ⎬	⎨ with obtaining $90,000 loan.
Credit Report	$ 25 ⎭	⎩
Owner's Title Policy	$ 400	Seller pays Safety Title Co.
Lender's Title Policy	$ 90	Buyer pays Safety Title Co.
County Property Taxes	$ 1,680/yr	Due Oct. 15 for the period Jan. 1 through Dec. 31. Not yet paid.
Hazard Insurance	$ 240/yr	Existing policy with 9 months to run. Transfer to buyer.
Heating Oil	$ 130	Oil in tank. Transfer to buyer.
Pest Inspection	$ 39	Seller pays Dead-Bug Pest Co.
Property Tax Reserves	$ 1,680	12 months at $140 for lender.
Hazard Insurance Reserves	$ 80	4 months at $20 for lender.
Buyer's Attorney	$ 150	
Seller's Attorney	$ 120	
Closing Fee	$ 220	Ajax National Bank charge; buyer & seller each pay $110.
Deed Preparation	$ 10	Seller pays bank.
Notary	$ 4	Seller pays $2 for deed. Buyer pays $2 for mortgage.
Conveyance Tax	$ 123	Seller pays.
Record Deed	$ 5	Buyer pays.
Record Mortgage Release	$ 5	Seller pays.
Record Mortgage	$ 10	Buyer pays.
Brokerage Commission	$ 7,380	Seller pays; to be split equally between List-Rite Realty and Quick-Sale Realty.

Settlement and Proration date is September 15.
All prorations are to be based on a 30-day banker's month.

made with the offer is to be credited toward the down payment. Using this information, which is summarized in Table 14:2 for your convenience, let us see how a settlement statement is prepared.

Figure 14:1 is the most widely used residential settlement form in the United States, and it is filled out to reflect the transaction outlined in Table 14:2. Let us work through this sample transaction in order to see where each item is placed on the settlement statement. (You will notice that the buyer is referred to as the borrower in Figure 14:1. This is not important for the moment and will be explained later.)

Lines 101 and 401 of the settlement statement show the price the buyer is paying and the seller is receiving for the property. Line 103 is the total of the buyer's settlement charges from the reverse side of the form. (The reverse side will be covered in a moment.) Lines 109 and 409 show the hazard insurance proration. The existing policy cost the seller $240 and has 9 months to run. For these 9 months the buyer is being charged $180 (line 109) and the seller is credited the same amount (line 409). The heating oil remaining in the heating system tank is charged to the buyer (line 110) and credited to the seller (line 410). The gross amount due from the buyer is tallied on line 120.

On line 201 the buyer is credited with the earnest money paid at the time the purchase contract was written. On the next line the buyer is credited with the new $90,000 loan. Line 211 shows the property tax proration credit for the buyer; line 511 is the same proration as a charge to the seller. This is because $1,680 in property taxes are due on October 1 for the period January 1 through December 31. Not yet paid for the year, the buyer must pay these taxes on October 1. However, the seller owned the property from January 1 to September 15, a period of 8½ months. At the rate of $140 a month, this means the seller must give the buyer $1,190 as part of the closing.

Line 220 lists the total of the buyer's credits. Line 301 is the total amount due from the buyer for this transaction. The difference, on line 303, is the amount of cash needed from the buyer to close the transaction.

Seller's Side

On the seller's side of the settlement statement, line 420 shows the total dollars due the seller from the sales price and proration credits. Line 502 is the total of the seller's settlement costs from the reverse side of the form. On line 504 the seller is charged for the existing mortgage loan that is being paid off as part of the closing. Accrued interest on that loan for the first half of September is charged the seller (line 506). Line 520 is a total of what must come out of the seller's funds at the closing. This is compared with the gross amount due the seller on line 601 and the difference (line 603) is the cash the seller will receive at the closing.

Settlement Charges

Continuing with Figure 14:1, the real estate commission is handled on lines 700, 701 and 702. Note that if the closing agent is to make a commission split such as shown here, the closing agent must have written instructions to do so from the real estate broker who is being paid by the seller. Otherwise, all the commission goes to the seller's broker, and the seller's broker pays the cooperating broker according to whatever agreement they have.

Lines 801, 803 and 804 indicate charges incurred by the buyer in connection with obtaining the new $90,000 loan. Line 901 shows the interest on the $90,000 loan calculated from the date of closing to the end of September. This brings the loan up to the first day of the next month and simplifies future bookkeeping for the monthly loan payments. At 9.6% the interest on $90,000 is $24.00 a day and the buyer is charged for 15 days.

As a condition for the loan the lender requires impound accounts for hazard insurance and property taxes. In order to have enough on hand to make the October 1 property tax payment, the lender requires (line 1004) an immediate reserve of $1,680. Beginning November 1, one-twelfth of the estimated taxes for next year will be added to the buyer's monthly payment so as to have money in the impound account from which to pay taxes next year. The same concept applies to the hazard insurance. It comes due in 8 months, therefore the lender requires 4 months worth of reserves in advance (line 1001).

Lines 1101, 1105 and 1106 are the closing fee, deed preparation fee and notary fees associated with this closing. Title insurance charges of $400 to the seller for the owner's policy and $90 to the buyer for the lender's policy are itemized on line

A.		B. TYPE OF LOAN

U.S. DEPARTMENT OF HOUSING AND URBAN DEVELOPMENT

SETTLEMENT STATEMENT

B. TYPE OF LOAN

1. ☐ FHA   2. ☐ FmHA   3. ☐ CONV. UNINS.
4. ☐ VA   5. ☐ CONV. INS.

6. FILE NUMBER: 7. LOAN NUMBER:

8. MORTGAGE INSURANCE CASE NUMBER:

c. *NOTE: This form is furnished to give you a statement of actual settlement costs. Amounts paid to and by the settlement agent are shown. Items marked "(p.o.c.)" were paid outside the closing; they are shown here for informational purposes and are not included in the totals.*

D. NAME OF BORROWER:

Neidi Delone
2424 Newpaige Lane
City, State 00000

E. NAME OF SELLER:

Homer Leavitt
1654 West 12th Street
City, State 00000

F. NAME OF LENDER:

Acme National Bank
1111 West 1st Street
City, State 00000

G. PROPERTY LOCATION:

1654 West 12th Street
City, State 00000

H. SETTLEMENT AGENT:

Acme National Bank

PLACE OF SETTLEMENT:

Acme National Bank

I. SETTLEMENT DATE:

Sept. 15, 19xx

J. SUMMARY OF BORROWER'S TRANSACTION		K. SUMMARY OF SELLER'S TRANSACTION	
100. GROSS AMOUNT DUE FROM BORROWER:		*100. GROSS AMOUNT DUE TO SELLER:*	
101. Contract sales price	$123,000	401. Contract sales price	$123,000
102. Personal property		402. Personal property	
103. Settlement charges to borrower *(line 1400)*	3,512	403.	
104.		404.	
105.		405.	
Adjustments for items paid by seller in advance		*Adjustments for items paid by seller in advance*	
106. City/town taxes to		406. City/town taxes to	
107. County taxes to		407. County taxes to	
108. Assessments to		408. Assessments to	
109. Hazard insurance 9/15 to 6/15	180	409. Hazard insurance 9/15 to 6/15	180
110. Heating oil	130	410. Heating oil	130
111.		411.	
112.		412.	
120. GROSS AMOUNT DUE FROM BORROWER	$126,822	420. GROSS AMOUNT DUE TO SELLER	$123,310
200. AMOUNTS PAID BY OR IN BEHALF OF BORROWER:		*500. REDUCTIONS IN AMOUNT DUE TO SELLER:*	
201. Deposit or earnest money	$ 3,000	501. Excess deposit *(see instructions)*	
202. Principal amount of new loan(s)	90,000	502. Settlement charges to seller *(line 1400)*	8,189
203. Existing loan(s) taken subject to		503. Existing loan(s) taken subject to	
204.		504. Payoff of first mortgage loan	48,000
205.		505. Payoff of second mortgage loan	
206.		506. Accrued interest 9/1 to 9/15	240
207.		507.	
208.		508.	
209.		509.	
Adjustments for items unpaid by seller		*Adjustments for items unpaid by seller*	
210. City/town taxes to		510. City/town taxes to	
211. County taxes 1/1 to 9/15	1,190	511. County taxes 1/1 to 9/15	1,190
212. Assessments to		512. Assessments to	
213.		513.	
214.		514.	
215.		515.	
216.		516.	
217.		517.	
218.		518.	
219.		519.	
220. TOTAL PAID BY/FOR BORROWER	$ 94,190	520. TOTAL REDUCTION AMOUNT DUE SELLER	$ 57,619
300. CASH AT SETTLEMENT FROM/TO BORROWER		*600. CASH AT SETTLEMENT TO/FROM SELLER*	
301. Gross amount due from borrower *(line 120)*	$126,822	601. Gross amount due to seller *(line 420)*	$123,310
302. Less amounts paid by/for borrower *(line 220)*	(94,190)	602. Less reductions in amount due seller *(line 520)*	(57,619)
303. CASH (☑ FROM) (☐ TO) BORROWER	$ 32,632	603. CASH (☑ TO) (☐ FROM) SELLER	$ 65,691

L. SETTLEMENT CHARGES		

700. TOTAL SALES/BROKER'S COMMISSION based on price $ 123,000 @ 6 % = $7380	PAID FROM BORROWER'S FUNDS AT SETTLEMENT	PAID FROM SELLER'S FUNDS AT SETTLEMENT
Division of Commission (line 700) as follows:		
701. $ 3,690 to List-Rite Realty		
702. $ 3,690 to Quick-Sale Realty		
703. Commission paid at Settlement		$7,380
704.		
800. ITEMS PAYABLE IN CONNECTION WITH LOAN		
801. Loan Origination Fee %	$ 900	
802. Loan Discount %		
803. Appraisal Fee to	100	
804. Credit Report to	25	
805. Lender's Inspection Fee		
806. Mortgage Insurance Application Fee to		
807. Assumption Fee		
808.		
809.		
810.		
811.		
900. ITEMS REQUIRED BY LENDER TO BE PAID IN ADVANCE		
901. Interest from Sept 15 to Sept 30 @$ 24.00 /day	360	
902. Mortgage Insurance Premium for months to		
903. Hazard Insurance Premium for years to		
904. years to		
905.		
1000. RESERVES DEPOSITED WITH LENDER		
1001. Hazard insurance 4 months @ $ 20 per month	80	
1002. Mortgage insurance months @ $ per month		
1003. City property taxes months @ $ per month		
1004. County property taxes 12 months @ $ 140 per month	1,680	
1005. Annual assessments months @ $ per month		
1006. months @ $ per month		
1007. months @ $ per month		
1008. months @ $ per month		
1100. TITLE CHARGES		
1101. Settlement or closing fee to Acme National Bank	110	110
1102. Abstract or title search to		
1103. Title examination to		
1104. Title insurance binder to		
1105. Document preparation to Acme National Bank		10
1106. Notary fees to Acme National Bank	2	2
1107. Attorney's fees to		
(includes above items numbers;		
1108. Title insurance to Safety Title Insurance Company	90	400
(includes above items numbers;		
1109. Lender's coverage $ 90,000		
1110. Owner's coverage $ 123,000		
1111. Buyer's attorney	150	
1112. Seller's attorney		120
1113.		
1200. GOVERNMENT RECORDING AND TRANSFER CHARGES		
1201. Recording fees: Deed $ 5 ; Mortgage $ 10 ; Releases $ 5	15	5
1202. City/county tax/stamps: Deed $; Mortgage $		
1203. State tax/stamps: Deed $ 123 ; Mortgage $		123
1204.		
1205.		
1300. ADDITIONAL SETTLEMENT CHARGES		
1301. Survey to		
1302. Pest inspection to Dead-Bug Pest Company		39
1303.		
1304.		
1305.		
1400. TOTAL SETTLEMENT CHARGES (enter on lines 103, Section J and 502, Section K)	$3,512	$8,189

1108. Lines 1109 and 1110 show the coverage for each. The amounts paid from settlement funds to the attorneys of the buyer and seller are listed on lines 1111 and 1112. Note that the buyer and seller can choose to pay their attorneys outside of the closing. **Outside of the closing** or **outside of escrow** means a party to the closing has paid someone directly and not through the closing.

Government recording fees and conveyance taxes necessary to complete this transaction are itemized on lines 1201 and 1203 and charged to the buyer and seller as shown. On line 1302 the settlement agent pays the pest inspection company on behalf of the seller. This is another item that is sometimes paid outside of the closing, that is, the seller can write a check directly to the termite company once the inspection has been made. On line 1400 the totals for both the buyer and seller are entered. The same totals are transferred to lines 103 and 502.

Note that Figure 14:1 shows both the buyer's side of the transaction and the seller's side. In actual practice, the seller will receive this settlement statement with lines 100 through 303 blacked out, and the buyer will receive this statement with lines 400 through 603 blacked out.

In response to consumer complaints regarding real estate closing costs and procedures, Congress passed the **Real Estate Settlement Procedures Act** (RESPA) effective June 20, 1975, throughout the United States. The purpose of RESPA, which is administered by the U.S. Department of Housing and Urban Development (HUD), is to regulate and standardize real estate settlement practices when "federally related" first mortgage loans are made on one- to four-family residences, condominiums and cooperatives. Federally related is defined to include FHA or VA or other government-backed or assisted loans, loans from lenders with federally insured deposits, loans that are to be purchased by FNMA, GNMA, FHLMC or other federally controlled secondary mortgage market institutions, and loans made by lenders who make or invest more than $1 million per year in residential loans. As the bulk of all home loans now made fall into one of these categories, the impact of this law is far-reaching.

*REAL ESTATE
SETTLEMENT
PROCEDURES ACT*

Restrictions   RESPA prohibits kickbacks and fees for services not performed during the closing process. For example, in some regions of the United States prior to this act, it was common practice for attorneys and closing agents to channel title business to certain title companies in return for a fee. This increased settlement costs without adding services. Now there must be a justifiable service rendered for each closing fee charge. The act also prohibits the seller from requiring that the buyer purchase title insurance from a particular title company.

The Real Estate Settlement Procedures Act also contains restrictions on the amount of advance property tax and insurance payments a lender can collect and place in an impound or reserve account. The amount is limited to the property owner's share of taxes and insurance accrued prior to settlement, plus one-sixth of the estimated amount that will come due for these items in the 12-month period beginning at settlement. This requirement assures that the lender has an adequate but not excessive amount of money impounded when taxes and insurance payments fall due. If the amount in the reserve account is not sufficient to pay an item when it comes due, the lender must temporarily use its own funds to make up the difference. Then the lender bills the borrower or increases the monthly reserve payment. If there is a drop in the amount the lender must pay out, then the monthly reserve requirement can be reduced.

Considerable criticism and debate have raged over the topic of reserves. Traditionally, lenders have not paid interest to borrowers on money held as reserves, effectively creating an interest-free loan to themselves. This has tempted many lenders to require overly adequate reserves. RESPA sets a reasonable limit on reserve requirements and some states now require that interest be paid on reserves. Although not always required to do so, some lenders now voluntarily pay interest on reserves.

Benefits   Anyone applying for a RESPA-regulated loan will receive several benefits. First is a HUD information booklet explaining RESPA. Second is a good faith estimate of closing costs from the lender. Third, the lender will use the HUD Uniform Settlement Statement shown in Figure 14:1. Fourth, the borrower has

GOOD FAITH ESTIMATES OF CLOSING COSTS   **Figure 14:2**

The charges listed below are our Good Faith Estimate of some of the settlement charges you will need to pay at settlement of the loan for which you have applied. These charges will be paid to the title or escrow company that conducts the settlement. This form does not cover all items you will be required to pay in cash at settlement, for example, deposit in escrow for real estate taxes and insurance. You may wish to inquire as to the amounts of such other items. You may be required to pay other additional amounts at settlement. This is not a commitment to make a loan.

Services		Estimated Fees
801.	Loan Origination Fee _____ % + $ _____	$
802.	Loan Discount %	$
803.	Appraisal Fee	$
804.	Credit Report	$
806.	Mortgage Insurance Application Fee	$
807.	Assumption Fee	$
808.	Tax Service Fee	$
901.	Interest	$
902.	Mortgage Insurance Premium	$
1101.	Settlement or Closing Fee	$
1106.	Notary Fees	$
1109.	Title Insurance, Lender's Coverage	List only those items borrower will pay	$
1110.	Title Insurance, Owner's Coverage		$
1201.	Recording Fees	$
1202.	County Tax/Stamps	$
1203.	City Tax/Stamps	$
1302.	Pest Inspection	$
1303.	Building Inspection	$
↑		$
These numbers correspond to the HUD Settlement Statement	TOTAL	$

the right to inspect the HUD Settlement Statement one business day before the day of closing.

The primary reason lenders are required to promptly give loan applicants an estimate of closing costs is to allow the loan applicant an opportunity to compare prices for the various services his transaction will require. Additionally, these estimates help the borrower estimate closing costs. Figure 14:2 illustrates a good faith estimate form.

RESPA does not require estimates of escrow impounds for property taxes and insurance, although the lender can voluntarily add these items to the form. Note also that RESPA allows lenders to make estimates in terms of ranges. For example, escrow fees may be stated as $150 to $175 to reflect the range of rates being charged by local escrow companies for that service.

HUD Settlement Statement

The HUD Settlement Statement you saw used in Figure 14:1 is required of all federally related real estate lenders. Because it is actually a lender requirement, it uses the word "borrower" instead of buyer. However, if the loan is in connection with a sale, and most are, the buyer and the borrower are one and the same. The case where this is not true is when an owner is refinancing a property.

The HUD Settlement Statement has become so widely accepted that it is now used even when it is not required. Closing agents that handle high volumes of closings use computers with special HUD Settlement Statement programs to fill out these forms. The closing agent types the numbers onto a video screen and a tractor-fed printer with continuous-feed HUD forms takes care of the typing task.

VOCABULARY REVIEW

*Match terms **a–p** with statements **1–16**.*

a. *Beneficiary's statement*
b. *Closing date*
c. *Closing meeting*
d. *Deed delivery*
e. *Dry closing*
f. *Escrow agent*
g. *Escrow closing*
h. *Good faith estimate*
i. *HUD Settlement Statement*
j. *Loan escrow*
k. *Outside of the closing*
l. *Prorate*
m. *RESPA*
n. *Settlement statement*
o. *Title closing*
p. *Walk-through*

1. An accounting of funds to the buyer and seller at the completion of a real estate transaction.
2. Deposit of documents and funds with a neutral third party plus instructions as to how to conduct the closing.
3. The moment at which title passes from the seller to the buyer.
4. To divide the ongoing income and expenses of a property between the buyer and seller.
5. A federal law that deals with procedures to be followed in certain types of real estate closings.
6. The person or firm in charge of an escrow.
7. An escrow for the purpose of financing a property not in connection with a sale.
8. Refers to closing costs paid by the buyer or seller that did not go through the closing agent.
9. A list of anticipated closing costs given to the borrower by the lender as required by RESPA.
10. Federally-related lenders are required to use this particular closing statement format.
11. The day on which the closing is finalized. Also called the settlement date.
12. The process of completing a real estate transaction.
13. A final inspection of the property just prior to the settlement date.
14. A meeting at which the buyer pays for the property and receives a deed for it. Also called a settlement meeting.
15. Shows the unpaid balance on a loan and is provided by the lender.
16. A method to avoid rescheduling a closing meeting when a document, known to be on its way, has not yet arrived.

QUESTIONS AND PROBLEMS

1. What are the duties of an escrow agent?
2. As a means of closing a real estate transaction, how does an escrow differ from a settlement meeting?
3. Is an escrow agent the agent of the buyer or the seller? Explain.
4. The buyer agrees to accept the seller's fire insurance policy as part of the purchase agreement. The policy costs $180, covers the period January 16 through the following January 15 and the settlement date is March 12. How much does the buyer owe the seller (closest whole dollar)?
5. A buyer agrees to assume an existing 8% mortgage on which $45,000 is still owed; the last monthly payment was made on March 1 and the next payment is due April 1. Settlement date is March 12. Local custom is to use a 30-day month and charge the buyer interest beginning with the settlement day. Calculate the interest proration. To whom is it credited? To whom is it charged?

6. In real estate closing, does the buyer or seller normally pay for the following items: conveyance tax, deed preparation, lender's title policy, loan appraisal fee, mortgage recording and mortgage release?

7. Why is it important to have the buyer and seller sign mutual release papers if a transaction does not close?

ADDITIONAL READINGS

California Escrow Procedure: A Blueprint for the Nation. (Prentice-Hall, 1981, 227 pages). Book provides a thorough look at the escrow system of closing and the firms that do it. Valuable reading in other states where escrow closings are becoming popular.

"Going to Escrow" and "Closing Escrow" by **Laura Ann Davis.** (*First Tuesday*, Feb 85, page 6 and Mar 85, page 23). This two-article series explains how escrow works, what documents are required, responsibilities of the parties, modifying escrow instructions, handling delays and cancellations and completing the closing.

"Interim Occupancy" by **Laura Ann Davis.** (*First Tuesday*, Feb 85, page 22). Article discusses how to arrange for occupancy by the buyer before title transfers. Includes sample interim occupancy agreement.

Realty Bluebook by **Robert DeHeer.** (Professional Publishing Co., 1986, 756 pages). Contains 397 pages of amortization tables, 130 pages of financing techniques, 66 pages of checklists, 102 pages of contract clauses and 61 pages of tax information. New editions issued annually.

Settlement Costs and You. (U.S. Department of Housing and Urban Development, 31 pages). Explains borrowers rights under RESPA. Demonstrates sample closings using the HUD settlement forms. Available free from lenders.

*   *   *

Note to readers: Most title insurance companies have booklets describing local settlement procedures and title insurance services that are free for the asking.

Real Estate Leases

KEY TERMS

Assignment: the total transfer of the lessee's rights to another party

CPM, RPA: professional designations for property managers

Gross lease: tenant pays a fixed rent and the landlord pays all property expenses

Lessee: the tenant

Lessor: the landlord

Net lease: tenant pays a base rent plus maintenance, property taxes and insurance

Option: the right at some future time to purchase or lease a property at a predetermined price

Quiet enjoyment: the right of possession and use of property without undue disturbance by others

Reversion: the right to retake possession at a future date

Sublessee: a lessee who rents from another lessee

Sublessor: a lessee who rents to another lessee

Sublet: to transfer only a portion of one's lease rights

Earlier chapters of this book discussed leases as estates in land (Chapter 3) and as a means of financing (Chapter 12). This chapter will look at leases from the standpoint of the tenant, the property owner and the property manager. (During your lifetime you will be in one of these roles and perhaps all three.) Our discussion will begin with some important terminology. Then comes a sample lease document with explanation, plus information on locating, qualifying and keeping tenants. The chapter concludes with information on job opportunities available in professional property management. Emphasis will be on residential property although a number of key points regarding commercial property leases will also be included.

THE LEASEHOLD ESTATE

A lease conveys to the **lessee** (tenant) the right to possess and use another's property for a period of time. During this time the **lessor** (the landlord or fee owner) possesses a **reversion** that entitles him to retake possession at the end of the lease period. Notice that a lease separates the right to use property from the property's ownership. The tenant gets the use of the property during the lease period and pays rent. The property owner is denied use of the property but receives rent in return. At the end of the lease the property owner gets the use of the property back but no more rent. The tenant no longer has the use of the property and no longer pays rent. This chapter describes how this very simple idea is carried out in practice.

A tenant's right to occupy land and/or buildings thereon is called a **leasehold estate.** The two most commonly found leasehold estates are the periodic estate and the estate for years. The **periodic estate** is one that continually renews itself for like periods of time until the tenant or landlord acts to terminate it. A month-to-month lease is an example of this. An **estate for years** is a lease with a specific starting date and a specific ending date. It can be for any length of time, and it does not automatically renew itself. A lease for one year is an example. There are two other leasehold categories: estate at will and tenancy at sufferance. An **estate at will,** rather seldom found, can be terminated by either tenant or landlord at any time. For example, the owner of a rental house decides to sell it upon expiration of the current lease. The owner and tenant agree that the tenant will be able to continue to rent until the house is sold. A **tenancy at sufferance** occurs when a tenant stays beyond his legal tenancy without the consent of the landlord. The tenant is commonly called a **holdover tenant** and no advance notice is required for eviction. He differs from a trespasser only in that his original entry onto the property was legal.

CREATING A
VALID LEASE
A lease is both a conveyance and a contract. As a conveyance it conveys rights of possession to the tenant in the form of a leasehold estate. As a contract it contains provisions for the payment of rent and any other obligations the landlord and tenant have to each other.

For a valid lease to exist, it must meet the usual requirements of a contract as described in Chapter 7. That is to say, the parties involved must be legally competent, and there must be mutual agreement, lawful objective and sufficient consideration. The main elements of a lease are (1) the names of the lessee and lessor, (2) a description of the premises, (3) an agreement to convey (let) the premises by the lessor and to accept possession by the lessee, (4) provisions for the payment of

rent, (5) the starting date and duration of the lease, and (6) signatures of the parties to the lease.

In most states, a lease longer than one year must be in
writing to be enforceable in court. A lease for one year or less
or a month-to-month lease could be oral and still be valid, but
as a matter of good business practice any lease should be put in
writing and signed. This gives all parties involved a written
reminder of their obligations under the lease and reduces
chances for dispute.

Figure 15:1 illustrates a lease document that contains provisions typically found in a residential lease. These provisions
are presented in simplified language to help you more easily
grasp the rights and responsibilities created by a lease.

THE LEASE DOCUMENT

The first paragraph is the conveyance portion of the lease.
At ① and ② the lessor and lessee are identified. At ③ the lessor
conveys to the lessee and the lessee accepts the property. A
description of the property follows at ④ and the **term** of the
conveyance at ⑤. The property must be described so that there
is no question as to the extent of the premises the lessee is
renting. While a tenant, the lessee is entitled to **quiet enjoyment** of the property. This means uninterrupted use of the
property without interference from the owner, the property
manager or any third party.

Conveyance

If the lease illustrated here was a month-to-month lease,
the wording at ⑤ would be changed to read, "commencing
April 15, 19xx and continuing on a month-to-month basis until
terminated by either the lessee or the lessor." A month-to-
month rental is a very flexible arrangement. It allows the owner
to recover possession of the property on one-month notice and
the tenant to leave on one-month notice with no further obligation to the owner. In rental agreements for longer periods of
time, each party gives up some flexibility to gain commitment
from the other. Under a one-year lease the owner commits the
property to the tenant for a year. In return the tenant is committed to paying rent for a full year. In a like manner, the
owner has the tenant's commitment to pay rent for a year but
loses the flexibility of being able to regain possession of the
property until the year is over.

Figure 15:1

LEASE

This lease agreement is entered into the ___10th___ day of ___April___ , 19 _xx_ between ___John and Sally Landlord___ ①(hereinafter called the Lessor) and ___Gary and Barbara Tenant___ ② (hereinafter called the Lessee). The Lessor hereby leases to the Lessee③ and the Lessee hereby leases from the Lessor the premises known as ___Apartment 24, 1234 Maple St., City, State___ ④ for the term of ___one___ ⑤ year beginning 12:00 noon on ___April 15, 19xx___ and ending 12:00 noon on ___April 15, 19xx___ unless sooner terminated as herein set forth.

The rent for the term of this lease is $ ___6,000.00___ ⑥ payable in equal monthly installments of $ ___500.00___ ⑦ on the ___15th___ day of each month beginning on ___April 15, 19xx___. Receipt of the first monthly installment and $ ___500.00___ ⑧ as a security, damage and clean-up deposit is hereby acknowledged. It is furthermore agreed that:

⑨ The use of the premises shall be as a residential dwelling for the above named Lessee only.

⑩ The Lessee may not assign this lease or sublet any portion of the premises without written permission from the Lessor.

⑪ The Lessee agrees to abide by the house rules as posted. A current copy is attached to this lease.

⑫ The Lessor shall furnish water, sewer and heat as part of the rent. Electricity and telephone shall be paid for by the Lessee.

⑬ The Lessor agrees to keep the premises structure maintained and in habitable condition.

⑭ The Lessee agrees to maintain the interior of said premises and at the termination of this lease to return said premises to the Lessor in as good condition as it is now except for ordinary wear and tear.

⑮ The Lessee shall not make any alterations or improvements to the premises without the Lessor's prior written consent. Any alterations or improvements become the property of the Lessor at the end of this lease.

Figure 15:1   *continued*

⑯ *If the premises are not ready for occupancy on the date herein provided, the Lessee may cancel this agreement and the Lessor shall return in full all money paid by the Lessee.*

⑰ *If the Lessee defaults on this lease agreement, the Lessor may give the Lessee three days notice of intention to terminate the lease. At the end of those three days the lease shall terminate and the Lessee shall vacate and surrender the premises to the Lessor.*

⑱ *If the Lessee holds over after the expiration of this lease without the Lessor's consent, the tenancy shall be month to month at twice the monthly rate indicated herein.*

⑲ *If the premises are destroyed or rendered uninhabitable by fire or other cause, this lease shall terminate as of the date of the casualty.*

⑳ *The Lessor shall have access to the premises for the purpose of inspecting for damage, making repairs and showing to prospective tenants or buyers.*

㉑ John Landlord	㉒ Gary Tenant
Lessor	Lessee
Sally Landlord	Barbara Tenant
Lessor	Lessee

Contract

The balance of the lease document is concerned with contract aspects of the lease. At ⑥ the amount of rent that the lessee will pay for the use of the property is set forth. In an estate for years the usual practice is to state the total rent for the entire lease period. This is the total number of dollars the lessee is obligated to pay to the lessor. The lessee can vacate the premises before the lease period expires but is still liable for the full amount of the contract. The method of payment of the obligation is shown at ⑦. Unless the contract calls for rent to be paid in advance, under common law it is not due until the end of the rental period. At ⑧ the lessor has taken a deposit in the form of the first monthly installment and acknowledges receipt of it. The lessor has also taken additional money as security against the possibility of uncollected rent or damage to the premises and for clean-up expenses. (The tenant is supposed to leave the premises clean.) The deposit is refunded, less legitimate charges, when the tenant leaves.

Items ⑨ through ⑳ summarize commonly found lease clauses. At ⑨ and ⑩ the lessor wants to maintain control over the use and occupancy of the premises. Without this he might find the premises used for an entirely different purpose or by people he did not rent to. At ⑪ the tenant agrees to abide by the house rules. These normally cover such things as use of laundry and trash facilities, swimming pool rules, noise rules, etc. Number ⑫ states the responsibility of the lessee and lessor with regard to the payment of utilities.

A strict legal interpretation of a lease as a conveyance means the tenant is responsible for upkeep and repairs unless the lessor promises to do so in the lease contract. The paragraph at ⑬ is that promise. Consumerism has had a profound influence on this matter. As a result courts and legislatures now take the position that the landlord is obligated to keep a residential property repaired and habitable even though this is not specifically stated in the contract. (Commercial property still goes by the strict interpretation, i.e., the landlord has to promise upkeep and repairs or the tenant doesn't get them.)

Number ⑭ is the tenant's promise to maintain the interior of the dwelling. If the tenant damages the property, the tenant must repair or pay for it. Normal wear and tear are considered to be part of the rent. At paragraph ⑮ the landlord protects himself against unauthorized alterations and improvements and then goes on to point out that anything the tenant affixes to the building becomes realty. As realty it remains a part of the building when the tenant leaves.

Paragraphs ⑯ through ⑲ deal with the rights of both parties if the premises are not ready for occupancy, if the lessee defaults after moving in, if the lessee holds over or if the premises are destroyed. The lessor also retains the right (paragraph ⑳) to enter the leased premises from time to time for business purposes.

Finally, at ㉑ and ㉒, the lessor and lessee sign. It is not necessary to have these signatures notarized. That is done only if the lease is to be recorded and then only the lessor's signature is notarized. The purpose of recording is to give constructive notice that the lessee has an estate in the property. Recording is usually done only when the lessee's rights are not apparent from inspection of the property or where the lease is to run for more than three years. From the property owner's standpoint, the lease is an encumbrance on the property. If the owner should subsequently sell the property or mortgage it, the lessee's tenancy remains undisturbed. The buyer or lender must accept the property subject to the lease.

If one of the lessors dies, the lease is still binding on the remaining lessor(s) and upon the estate of the deceased lessor. Similarly, if one of the lessees dies, the lease is still binding on the remaining lessee(s) and upon the estate of the deceased lessee. This is based on common law doctrine that applies to contracts in general (see Chapter 7, "Deceased Party"). The lessee and lessor can, however, agree to do otherwise. The lessee could ask the lessor to **waive** (give up) the right to hold the lessee's estate to the lease in the event of the lessee's death. For example, an elderly tenant about to sign a lease might want to add wording to the lease whereby the tenant's death would allow his estate to terminate the lease early.

Traditionally, courts have been strict interpreters of lease agreements. This philosophy still prevails for leases on commercial property. However, with regard to residential rental property, the trend today is for state legislatures to establish special landlord-tenant laws. The intent is to strike a reasonable balance between the responsibilities of landlords to tenants and vice versa. Typically these laws limit the amount of security deposit a landlord can require, tell the tenant how many days notice he has to give before vacating a periodic tenancy and require the landlord to deliver possession on the date agreed. The landlord must maintain the premises in a fit condition for living, and the tenant is to keep his unit clean and not damage it. The tenant is to obey the house rules, and the landlord must give advance notice before entering an apartment except in legitimate emergencies. Additionally, the laws set forth such things as the procedure for accounting for any deposit money not returned, the right of the tenant to make needed repairs and bill the landlord, the right of the landlord to file court actions for unpaid rent and the proper procedure for evicting a tenant.

LANDLORD-TENANT LAWS

SETTING RENTS

There are several methods for setting rents. The most common is the **gross lease.** Under a gross lease the tenant pays a fixed rent, and the landlord pays all the operating expenses of the property. A tenant paying $450 per month on a month-to-month apartment lease or a person paying $12,000 per year for a one-year house lease are both examples of fixed rents.

A landlord will usually agree to a level rent for one year, but what if the tenant wants a longer lease term such as 2 years, or 5 years, or 10 years, or 25 years, or 99 years? For these situations the following rent setting methods are used in the real estate industry. The simplest is to have a **step-up** or **graduated rent.** For example, a 5-year office lease might call for monthly rents of 90¢ per square foot of floor space the first year, 95¢ the second year, $1.00 the third year, $1.05 the fourth year and $1.10 the fifth. A residential tenant wishing a 2-year lease might find the landlord more receptive if the monthly rent is stepped up the second year.

Office and industrial leases of 5 or more years often include an **escalator** or **participation clause.** This allows the landlord to pass along to the tenant increases in such items as property taxes, utility charges and maintenance. A variation is to have the tenant pay for all property taxes, insurance, repairs, utilities, etc. in addition to the base rent. This arrangement is called a **net lease** or a **triple net lease.** It is commonly used when an entire building is being leased and for long-term ground leases.

Another system for setting rents is the **percentage lease** wherein the owner receives a percentage of the tenant's gross receipts as rent. For example, a farmer who leases land may give the landowner 20% of the value of the crop when it is sold. The monthly rent for a small hardware store might be $600 plus 6% of gross sales above $10,000. A gasoline station may pay $1,000 plus 2¢ per gallon pumped. A supermarket may pay $7,500 plus 1½% of gross above $50,000 per month.

Still another way of setting rents on long-term leases is to **index** the rent to some economic indicator, such as an inflation index. If there is inflation, rents increase; if there is deflation, rents decrease. Arrangements such as step-ups, escalators, percentages, indexes and net leases are all efforts by landlords to protect against rising costs of property operation and declining purchasing power, yet meet tenant's needs to have property committed to them for more than a year.

Option clauses give the tenant the right at some future time to purchase or lease the property at a predetermined price. This gives a tenant flexibility. For example, suppose that a prospective tenant is starting a new business and is not certain how successful it will be. Therefore, in looking for space to rent, he will want a lease that allows an "out" if the new venture does not succeed, but will permit him to stay if the venture is successful. The solution is a lease with options. The landlord could offer a one-year lease, plus an option to stay for 2 more years at a higher rent plus a second option for an additional 5 years at a still higher rent. If the venture is not successful, the tenant is obligated for only one year. But if successful, he has the option of staying 2 more years, and if still successful, for 5 years after that.

Another option possibility is to offer the tenant a lease that also contains an option to buy the property for a fixed period of time at a preset price. This is called a **lease with option to buy** and is discussed in Chapter 8.

OPTION CLAUSES

Unless otherwise provided in the lease contract, a lessee may assign the lease or sublet. An **assignment** is the total transfer of the lessee's rights to another person. These parties are referred to as the **assignor** and the **assignee,** respectively. The assignee acquires all the right, title and interest of the assignor, no more and no less. However, the assignor remains liable for the performance of the contract unless released in writing by the landlord.

To **sublet** means to transfer only a portion of the rights held under a lease. The **sublease** thereby created may be for a portion of the premises, or part of the lease term. The party acquiring those rights is called the **sublessee**. The original lessee is the **sublessor** with respect to the sublessee. The sublessee pays rent to the lessee, who in turn remains liable to the landlord for rent on the entire premises.

ASSIGNMENT & SUBLETTING

A **ground lease** is a lease of land alone. The lessor is the fee simple owner of the land and conveys to the lessee an estate for

GROUND LEASE

years typically lasting from 25 to 99 years. The lessee pays for and owns the improvements. Thus a ground lease separates the ownership of land from the ownership of buildings on that land. The lease rent, called the **ground rent,** is on a net lease basis. As a hedge against inflation, the rent is usually increased every 10 to 25 years. This is done either by a graduated lease or by requiring a reappraisal of the land and then charging a new rent based on that valuation. Ground leases for residential properties can be found in Baltimore, Maryland; Orange County, California; and the state of Hawaii. Mostly, however, they are used for commercial and industrial properties such as office buildings, shopping centers, motels and warehouses.

VERTICAL LEASES

A lease need not be restricted to the use of the earth's surface. In Chapter 2 it was shown that land extends from the center of the earth skyward. Consequently it is possible for one person to own the mineral rights, another the surface rights and a third the air rights. This can also be done with leases. A landowner can lease to an oil company the right to find and extract oil and gas below his land and at the same time lease the surface rights to a farmer. In Chicago and New York City, railroads have leased surface and air rights above their downtown tracks for the purpose of constructing high-rise office buildings.

CONTRACT RENT,
ECONOMIC RENT

The amount of rent that the tenant must pay the landlord for the use of the premises is called the **contract rent.** The rent which a property can command in the competitive open market is called the **economic rent.** When a lease contract is negotiated, the contract rent and economic rent are nearly always the same. However, as time passes, the market value of the right to use the premises may rise above the contract rent. When this occurs, the lease itself becomes valuable. That value is determined by the difference between the contract rent and the economic rent, and how long the lease has to run. An example would be a 5-year lease with 3 years left at a contract rent of $600 per month where the current rental value of the premises is now $800 per month. If the lease is assignable, the fact that it offers a $200 per month savings for 3 years makes it valuable. Similarly, an oil lease obtained for $50 per acre before oil was discovered might be worth millions after its discovery. Conversely, when contract rent exceeds economic rent, the lease takes on a negative value.

Most leases terminate because of the expiration of the term of the lease. The tenant has received the use of the premises and the landlord has received rent in return. However, a lease can be terminated if the landlord and the tenant mutually agree. The tenant surrenders the premises and the landlord releases him from the contract. This should, of course, be done in writing.

LEASE TERMINATION

If a tenant fails to live up to the terms of the lease agreement, the landlord has grounds for eviction. Usually this is for nonpayment of rent, but it can also be for violation of some other aspect of the agreement such as holding over past the term of the lease, bringing animals into a "no pets" apartment, occupancy by more than the number of persons specified in the agreement or operating in an illegal manner on the premises. Called **actual eviction,** the process usually begins with the landlord having a notice served on the tenant requiring the tenant to comply with the lease agreement or move out. If the tenant neither complies not vacates, the landlord takes the matter to court. If the landlord wins the case, either by a preponderance of evidence or because the tenant does not appear to contest the eviction, then the court will terminate the tenant's lease rights and authorize a marshall or sheriff to go on the premises and force the tenant out.

Eviction

A lease agreement may also be terminated through **constructive eviction.** This occurs when the landlord does not keep the premises fit for occupancy and the tenant moves out because of that. For example, the landlord may be continually failing to repair broken plumbing lines or a leaking roof. The tenant's legal remedies are to claim wrongful eviction, move out, stop paying rent and sue the landlord for breach of contract either forcing the landlord to make repairs or terminate the lease, possibly with money damages.

A **retaliatory eviction** is one whereby a landlord evicts a tenant because of a complaint made by the tenant. For example, a tenant may have complained to public health officials or building and safety authorities about conditions on the premises that are in violation of health laws or building codes. The landlord may retaliate or threaten to retaliate with an eviction (or a rent increase or a decrease in services); however, this is illegal.

Eminent Domain   The government, under its right of eminent domain, can also terminate a lease, but must provide just compensation. An example of this would be construction of a new highway that requires the demolition of a building rented to tenants. The property owner and the tenants would be entitled to compensation.

A mortgage foreclosure can also bring about lease termination; it all depends on priority. If the mortgage was recorded before the lease was signed, then foreclosure of the mortgage also forecloses the lease. If the lease was recorded first, then the lease still stands. Because a lease can cloud a lender's title, wording is sometimes inserted in leases that makes them subordinate to any future financing of the property. This is highly technical, but nonetheless a very significant matter in long-term shopping center, office building and industrial leases.

FAIR HOUSING   There are two federal laws that deal with discrimination in housing. They are (1) the Civil Rights Act of 1866 which prohibits discrimination on the basis of race only, and (2) the Fair Housing Act of 1968 which prohibits discrimination based on race, color, religion, sex or national origin.

So far as real estate licensees are concerned, these laws specify that they are not to accept sale or rental listings where they are asked to discriminate, nor are they permitted to make, print or publish any statement or advertisement with respect to a sale or rental of a dwelling which suggests discrimination because of race, color, religion, sex or national origin.

So far as owners are concerned, the 1968 act made exemptions for owners of three or fewer houses or two to four apartment units (one of which must be owner-occupied) provided the sale or lease was arranged without the aid of a real estate agent and without discriminatory advertising. The 1866 act, however, effectively voids these exemptions with respect to racial discrimination. Seeking legal remedy under the 1866 act requires a personal lawsuit and support from government agencies is not provided. Also the property owner faces no statutory penalty for damages and no fine under the 1866 act. The 1968 act does provide for government legal action and support and for financial penalties against a property owner. At the end of Chapter 17 you will find a longer and more detailed discussion of federal fair housing laws including steering, blockbusting and testers. Note too that many states, counties and cities have fair housing laws that go beyond the federal laws. For example, in some jurisdictions it is illegal to discriminate on the basis of age, marital status, presence of children, physical handicaps, sexual orientation and welfare status.

For the most part, until 1970, the concept of residential **rent control** was reserved for wartime use in the United States. During World War I, six states and several major cities and, in World War II, the federal government imposed limits on how much rent an owner could charge for the use of his real property. The purpose was twofold: (1) to discourage the construction of new housing so that the resources could be channeled to war needs, and (2) to set ceilings so that American households would not drive up prices by bidding against each other for available rental housing. With limits on rents, but no price controls on the cost of construction materials and labor, the construction of new housing was slowed without the need for a direct government order to stop building.

RENT CONTROL

Within a few years after World War I, and again after World War II, rent controls disappeared in nearly all parts of the country. The notable exception was New York City, where they have survived since the end of World War II and are still in use. However, beginning in the 1970s a number of other cities enacted rent control laws. This time the major attraction was inflation protection.

Although it is true that since 1956 residential rents in the United States have not risen as rapidly as the general level of consumer prices, any relief from rent increases would nonetheless be welcomed by the 36% of American households that rent. Most tenants recognize that newly constructed properties must command higher rents to meet higher construction, land and interest costs. However, in existing buildings they resent rent increases that have nothing to do with the original cost of the building or the cost of operating it. The argument of rent control supporters is that only increases in such things as property taxes, utilities and maintenance should be passed on to tenants. The tenant's assumption in this argument is that rent alone is enough to attract dollars into housing investments. In reality, rents would have to be even higher if the investor could not also look forward to price appreciation of his property.

Rent Control Experience

Experience to date strongly suggests that rent control creates more problems than it solves. In New York City and Washington, D.C., for example, it is generally agreed that controlled rents have taken existing dwelling units out of circulation. Despite relatively low vacancy rates thousands of dwelling units are abandoned each year by their owner's at a cost of millions of dollars in lost property taxes. With controls on rents but no controls on expenses property owners are often better off abandoning their properties than operating them.

Another problem with controlled rents is that a vacating tenant may demand a substantial cash payment from a tenant who wants to move in. Although this is illegal, the vacating tenant may attempt to circumvent the law by requiring the incoming tenant to purchase his furniture for several times its actual worth. Sometimes this payment is called a "key fee" as to suggest the new tenant is purchasing the key. This places the actual cost of the controlled apartment much closer to the value of the unit on the open market, and the advantage of low, controlled rents is lost to the incoming tenant.

A side effect of rent control has been conversions of existing rental apartments to condominiums since there are no controls on sales prices of dwelling units. Some cities have responded by restricting conversions. Owners began to demolish and build new condominiums; however, laws were then enacted to restrict demolition permits.

Other side effects of rent control in the United States are that lenders prefer not to lend on rent-controlled buildings. This is because lenders do not like to loan unless the investor is assured of reasonable returns. Developers find it hard to attract tenants to new rental units from rent-controlled buildings where they are enjoying below-market rents. Owner-occupied properties and noncontrolled properties are charged higher property taxes to make up for the falling values of controlled properties. Also there is a significant cost to the public to operate the government offices that administer the controls.

One of the ironies of rent control is that although controlled rents are very attractive to the tenant, he soon finds that the number of people like himself who want to buy at controlled prices exceeds the number who want to sell. Consequently a shortage develops. A better solution is to pursue public policies that encourage the construction of housing rather than discourage it.

As real estate becomes a more and more popular investment vehicle, more individuals are buying houses, apartment buildings, offices and stores to rent out. Many choose to operate these themselves thus making themselves property managers. Others hire professional managers as do partnerships and corporations that own real estate. The balance of this chapter will give you a sampling of some of the things you can expect as a manager of residential property as well as an overview of the employment opportunities in this important aspect of real estate.

PROPERTY MANAGEMENT

Successful operation of rental property begins with building or selecting existing buildings that meet the needs of tenants. Although this sounds simple enough, in reality it requires considerable reading, legwork and telephoning. There is no sense in building or buying one-bedroom apartment units when the local demand is for two-bedroom units. A wise investor will conduct an informal survey of existing rents and vacancy rates, plus gather information on the age, household status and numbers of renters in the local rental market. Market rents are then compared with operating costs and the balance capitalized to determine how much to pay for the building. (This process is explained in Chapter 16 under "Income Approach.")

Before Buying

The usual search pattern of a prospective residential tenant is to drive through neighborhoods of interest and to read newspaper classified ads. Thus, advertising money is most effec-

Advertising

tively spent on signs and arrows on and near the property plus newspaper advertising. Ads should tell enough about the property to motivate the prospect to call for an inspection. Signs should be well placed so prospects do not get lost trying to locate the property.

TENANT SELECTION

Just as a prospective tenant qualifies each house or apartment viewed from the tenant's standpoint of suitability, the property manager must also qualify the tenant. If it appears that a prospect, once moved in, will not pay the rent or will be destructive to the premises or will be obnoxious to the neighbors, the time to avoid the problem is before the tenant moves in.

A thorough application form, a personal interview with a seasoned manager and a substantial security deposit are valuable screening tools. A thorough application form acts to discourage prospects who themselves feel only marginally qualified or who prefer not to divulge the information requested. It also provides a basis for checking the tenant's references. This includes talking with former landlords to ask why he left, checking with the local credit bureau to learn if he pays his bills on time and, in some cities, checking with a landlord's reference bureau to find out if he left a previous apartment without paying rent.

The purpose of the interview is to determine if the prospect has the income to support the rental and will be compatible with the other tenants. For example, if the project does not allow pets or disassembled automobiles on the premises, the manager will want to make certain the prospect understands this.

Security Deposit

The requirement of a **security deposit** (against which the manager can deduct for unpaid rent or damage to the building) also serves as a screening device. If, for example, a prospect wants to rent a $400 per month apartment but does not have the money for a $200 security deposit, it is doubtful that he will be able to pay $400 rent each month.

Most states allow a damage deposit equal to one month's rent. In addition, many states also allow the landlord to collect the last month's rent in advance. A prospective tenant who, before moving in, can deposit the first and last month's rent plus a damage deposit not only provides an impressive financial picture but a solid cushion against future unpaid rent and damage.

As noted earlier in this chapter, federal laws have been passed that require owners and managers to disregard matters of race, color, religion, sex or national origin. State and local laws may extend this to age, marital status, presence of children, physical handicaps, sexual orientation and welfare status. These laws cover not only the obvious discrimination of refusing to rent, but also discrimination in such matters as the size of the security deposit, choice of apartment unit, length of lease offered and any number of more subtle discouragements. These laws are designed to give equal access to housing to anyone who can meet the financial requirements and is willing to abide by the lease contract and the house rules.

Rent Concessions

Two methods by which a building owner can attract tenants in an otherwise soft rental market are: (1) reduce the monthly rent, and (2) offer a rent concession. With a **rent concession,** the property owner keeps the rents at the same level, but offers a premium to entice a prospective tenant to move in. Often this is a free month's rent for prospects who will sign a one-year lease. Alternatives are to offer the tenant a cash moving allowance or a free weekend vacation at a nearby resort. The philosophy behind using concessions rather than outright rent reductions is that when the rental market firms up it is easier to stop offering concessions than it is to raise rents.

TENANT RETENTION

Tenant retention begins with finding tenants who will pay the rent and respect their contract agreements. Having once found good tenants, the next task is to keep them as long as possible. Besides the rent lost while the apartment is empty, the costs of apartment clean-up and finding a new tenant are high.

Statistically, about one-third of the units in a typical apartment project must be rerented each year. Certainly, many moves are due to job relocation or the need for larger or smaller quarters. But some moves occur because tenants find something they dislike about the way their apartments are managed. For example, if a building is poorly kept up or the manager gives the impression that he does not care about the tenants or the owner increases the rent with no apparent justification, people will move out. To retain tenants, the property owner and manager should think of them as permanent residents, even though turnover is expected. This begins with using a rental contract that an average tenant can read and understand. A complicated and legalistic contract may be seen by the tenant as the first step in a sparring match with management that will last as long as he resides there. The tenant also expects the property to be clean and properly maintained and repairs to his unit made promptly.

Communications

Good communications between management and tenants is also crucial to tenant retention. If the swimming pool is closed or utilities shut off with no announcement or no apparent reason, tenants become disgusted and add it to their private lists of reasons for ultimately leaving. Tenants expect management to keep them informed through bulletin board announcements or notices placed under their doors. In many larger apartment projects, managers publish newsletters to keep tenants informed and provide a means by which tenants can communicate with each other. For example, one page can explain why rents must go up because of rising property taxes, maintenance and utility costs, while another page announces the formation of a bowling league among project dwellers.

Leases

A very straightforward approach to improving tenant retention is to use leases. Once signed to a one-year lease, a tenant is much less likely to leave after a few months than if on a month-to-month agreement. Similarly, leases for longer than one year will reduce tenant turnover even more, although residential tenants are often wary about committing themselves that far into the future. A tenant can also be encouraged to stay by offering a renewal lease at a slightly lower rate than that being offered to new tenants. Another inducement is to offer long-time tenants free carpet shampooing, drape cleaning and wall painting, all things normally done if the tenant leaves and the apartment must be rented.

COLLECTING RENTS

Ultimately, the success of a rental building depends on the ability of management to collect the rents due from tenants. In accomplishing this, it is generally agreed among property managers that a firm and consistent collection policy, handled in a businesslike manner, is the best approach. Monthly rent statements can be mailed to each tenant. More often though the tenant is told in the rental contract when the rent is due each month and he is expected to pay it on time. Rents can also be collected door to door, but most managers prefer that rent checks be mailed or brought to their office when due. For security reasons some managers do not accept cash.

When a tenant's rent is not received on time, the manager *Late Rents* must decide what action to take. Is the lateness simply a matter of delayed mail or temporary but honest forgetfulness, or is the delay an early sign of a deeper problem, one that may cost the property owner lost rent and ultimately lead to eviction? The accepted procedure is to wait 5 days before sending the tenant a reminder. This avoids generating a negative feeling when the problem was due to a minor delay, for it is a fact that the vast majority of tenants do pay their rent on time. However, if payment is not received by the tenth day after it was due, a second reminder goes out requesting that the tenant personally call on the manager. By meeting with the tenant, the manager may obtain an indication as to what the underlying problem is. If the tenant is suffering from a temporary financial setback, the manager can weigh the humanitarian side and the cost of rerenting the apartment against the possibility that payment will never be received.

When it is apparent that a delinquent tenant will never *Eviction Problems* bring his rent up to date, it is time to ask the tenant to leave and for the manager to rerent the space. What happens if the tenant will neither leave nor pay the rent? Years ago it was not uncommon for an owner to enter a tenant's unit, remove all the tenant's belongings and lock them up. The key to the apartment door was changed and the apartment rerented; if the delinquent tenant wanted his belongings back, he had to pay the back rent. Today a landlord must obtain a court order to move a tenant out. Meanwhile, a nonpaying tenant who is well versed in the law can remain for several rent-free weeks. This is possible because of the time required to go through the legal procedures of eviction. When the delinquent tenant finally leaves a month or two later, he may owe several hundred dollars in back rent. The legal cost of forcing payment may be more than what is owed. The tenant knows this and hopes he will not be pursued.

Manager Remedies   More and more tenants are learning that if they are brash enough they can use the method just described to live rent-free and then move on. Others stop just short of the sheriff knocking on their door and leave on their own. The delinquent tenant hopes the manager or owner will not go to the trouble of pursuing the issue. Tenants are also learning to use the courts to pursue all sorts of real and fancied complaints against management, and managers are learning that judges often favor the tenant in these cases. What can owners and managers do about this? The best defense is careful tenant selection, substantial security deposits, good service and a businesslike policy on rent collection. In other words, the old idea of filling up a building as fast as possible and later weeding out the problem tenants is no longer practical. Beyond that, the presence of a full-time manager means tenants are likely to take better care of the premises and are less likely to leave without paying the rent.

Managers can also make more effective use of the law by using the courts to obtain judgments against those who won't pay, those who move out without paying and those who write bad checks for rent payments. Although a tenant may have left the area and it may not be worth the effort of locating him, the fact that a manager does take a firm stand serves as a deterrent to those planning the same tactics. For the nonpaying tenant, the judgment against him becomes part of his credit record and a warning to the next manager he approaches for an apartment.

ON-SITE   **On-site management** is a term that refers to property man-
MANAGEMENT   agement duties that are performed on the premises. Showing apartment units to prospective tenants, taking applications, conducting interviews, signing leases, maintaining good tenant relations, collecting rents and handling vacancies and evictions are usually handled by a property manager at the rent site. The on-site manager, also called a **resident manager** or **superintendent,** is also responsible for the repair, maintenance and security of the building and grounds. This includes ordering supplies as well as hiring tradespeople, gardeners and a swimming pool maintenance firm. It involves walking through the

entire premises at least once a day for security purposes and to make certain everything is working such as lights in the hallways, security doors, elevators, swimming pool pumps and recreation equipment.

The resident manager is also responsible for keeping the premises clean, the trash collected and supervising hired help. The resident manager is on call in the event of emergencies such as when a tenant or guest becomes boisterous, there are shutdowns in heat or utilities and when the fire alarm goes off. The resident manager is the eyes and ears of the property management company and the owner and makes suggestions as to needed repairs and improvements, needed changes in landlord-tenant policies and ways to better look after the building and its tenants. The resident manager and management company are fiduciaries of the property owner as they hold a position of trust, responsibility, confidence and fidelity toward the owner.

Management–Unit Ratios

A rule of thumb in apartment management is that one on-site manager can handle 50 or 60 units alone. Between 60 and 100 units, the manager needs an assistant to help with management chores and to make it possible to have someone on the property at all times. In projects over 100 units, a popular approach is to hire husband–wife teams, placing both on the payroll and adding assistants in proportion to project size. For example, a 150-unit apartment building would be managed by a husband–wife team and one assistant (usually a full-time custodian). A 200-unit building would have a husband–wife team plus two full-time assistants, and so on, adding an additional employee for each additional 50 to 60 apartment units. Larger projects also mean assistants can specialize. For example, in a 625-unit complex with a husband–wife team and nine assistants, two assistants might run the leasing office, two specialize in cleaning apartments when tenants leave, one acts as a gardener, one as a repairman, one as a custodian, one as a rent collector and bookkeeper and one as a recreational facilities director.

OFF-SITE MANAGEMENT

Off-site management consists of duties that can be accomplished without being on the premises. Examples of off-site management are accounting for rents collected, handling pay-

rolls and paying bills. All of these are well-suited for computerized data processing and property management programs
are available. These programs not only computerize bookkeeping chores, but pinpoint late rental payments, ensure that
lease renewals are mailed promptly, identify upcoming vacancies and make any contract-required rent adjustments. These
systems will also keep track of every item that affects income
and outgo, help manage cash flow so there is always enough
money available to pay bills and the mortgage payment and
even type the checks. Moreover, available programs will generate reports such as tenant directories, rent rolls, tenant led-
gers, upcoming lease expirations and unit vacancies. To further
assist management, these programs will generate operating
statements for each property managed, construct budgets,
make projections and even analyze the financial health of the
management firm.

Although a large part of off-site management is centered
on accounting services, off-site managers have other responsibilities. For example, hazard and liability insurance must be
purchased in the right coverages and for the best rates possible,
resident managers must be hired and trained and bids for contracted services must be taken and contracts awarded. Decisions as to rent policies, rent levels, advertising, major repairs
and capital improvements are made off-site. The off-site manager may even be asked to recommend when to refinance or
sell the property and buy another.

JOB OPPORTUNITIES

In reading this chapter you may have become interested in
a career in real property management. The most successful
apartment managers seem to be those who have had previous
experience in managing people and money and who are handy
with tools. Those with prior military experience or experience
as owners or managers of small businesses are eagerly sought
after. Least successful as on-site property managers are those
who see it as a quiet, peaceful retirement job, those who are
unable to work with and understand people, those who cannot
organize or make decisions, those without a few handyman
skills and those looking for strictly and 8-to-5, Monday-to-
Friday job. Commercial and industrial property management
positions tend to be filled by persons who have had prior prop-

erty management experience and who have a good under-standing of how business and industry make use of real estate.

In a medium-to-large property management firm there will be job opportunities for building service personnel, purchasing agents, bookkeepers, clerks, secretaries, office managers, field supervisors and executive managers. In a small office, one person plus a secretary will be responsible for all the off-site duties.

Finding experienced and capable property managers is not an easy task. Formal education in property management is not widely available in the United States. Instead, most managers learn their profession almost entirely by experience. An individual property owner can place an advertisement in a newspaper and attract a manager from another project, but most professional management firms have found it necessary to develop their own internal training programs. With such a program, a management firm can start a person with no previous property management experience as an assistant manager on a large project. If a person learns the job and enjoys the work, there is a promotion to manager of a 50- or 60-unit building and an increase in salary. If this works well, there is a move to a larger complex with an assistant and another increase in salary. Each step brings more responsibility and more pay. This system provides a steady stream of qualified managers for the management firm. It is also a source of executive-level personnel for the off-site management office. In larger cities executive-level positions pay upward of $100,000 per year.

The dominant professional organization in the property management field is the **Institute of Real Estate Management** (IREM). Established in 1933, the Institute is a division within the National Association of Realtors. Its primary purposes are to serve as an exchange medium for management ideas and to recognize specialists in the field. The Institute awards the designation Certified Property Manager (CPM) to members who successfully complete required educational courses in property management. The Institute also offers an educational program for resident managers of apartment buildings. The designation Accredited Resident Manager (ARM) is awarded upon successful completion. Forty-five percent of all property to be

Training Programs

managed in the United States is managed by IREM members and there are in excess of 10,000 CPMs.

Second in size to IREM is the **Building Owners and Managers Institute** (BOMI). Incorporated in 1970, BOMI provides educational programs aimed primarily at the commercial property management industry. Seven courses are offered ranging from design, operation and maintenance of buildings to accounting, insurance, law, investments and administration. Successful completion of the seven courses leads to the designation of Real Property Administrator (RPA). BOMI also offers eight courses in heating, plumbing, refrigeration, air handling, electrical systems, control systems maintenance, energy management and supervision as they apply to commercial buildings. Completion of these confers the Systems Maintenance Administrator (SMA) designation.

VOCABULARY REVIEW

Match terms **a–z** *with statements* **1–26.**

a. Actual eviction
b. Assignment
c. Assignor
d. Constructive eviction
e. Contract rent
f. CPM, RPA
g. Gross lease
h. Ground rent
i. Holdover tenant
j. Landlord–tenant laws
k. Lessee
l. Lessor
m. Month-to-month rental

n. Net lease
o. On-site management
p. Option
q. Participation clause
r. Percentage lease
s. Quiet enjoyment
t. Rent concession
u. Rent control
v. Reversion
w. Security deposit
x. Step-up rent
y. Sublessee
z. Sublet

1. The landlord.
2. The tenant.
3. Partial transfer of rights held under a lease.
4. Complete transfer of rights held under a lease.
5. One who holds a tenancy at sufferance.
6. Example of a periodic estate.
7. Entitles the landowner to retake possession at the end of the lease.
8. Rent charged for the use of land.
9. Specified rent increases at various points in time during the life of the lease.

10. A lease clause that allows the landlord to add to the tenant's rent any increases in property taxes, maintenance and utilities during the life of the lease.

11. Gives a tenant the opportunity of renewing his lease at a predetermined rental without obligating him to do so.

12. A lease where the amount of rent paid is related to the income the lessee obtains from the use of the premises.

13. Describes leases wherein the tenant pays a fixed rent.

14. Entitles the tenant to uninterrupted use of the property without interference from the owner or third parties.

15. Statutes that set forth the responsibilities and rights of landlords and tenants.

16. A lease wherein a tenant pays a base rent plus maintenance, property taxes and insurance.

17. The party acquiring possession under a sublet agreement.

18. The party who assigns his lease rights to another.

19. Nonpayment of rent would be grounds for this.

20. The amount of rent the tenant must pay the landlord as stated in the lease agreement.

21. An unfit premises would be grounds for this.

22. Government-imposed limits on how much a landlord can charge for space.

23. An advance deposit given by a tenant to a landlord against which the landlord can deduct for unpaid rent or damage.

24. A premium, such as a free month's rent, given to entice a prospective tenant to sign a lease.

25. A resident manager would be in this management category.

26. Professional designations for property managers.

QUESTIONS AND PROBLEMS

1. From the standpoint of the tenant, what are the advantages and disadvantages of a lease versus a month-to-month rental?

2. What remedies does a property manager in your state have when a tenant does not pay his rent and/or refuses to move out?

3. Does your state have a landlord–tenant code? What are its major provisions? If no specific code or act currently exists in your state, where does one look for laws pertaining to landlords and tenants?

4. What is the difference between contract rent and economic rent?

5. On what basis could a tenant claim constructive eviction? What would the tenant's purpose be in doing this?

6. Is an option to renew a lease to the advantage of the lessor or the lessee?

7. What effects do the Civil Rights Act of 1866 and the Fair Housing Act of 1968 have on real estate licensees who handle rentals?

8. Is rent control currently in effect in your community? If so, what effects have these controls had on the sales of investment properties and on the construction of new rental buildings in your community?

9. If you were an apartment building manager interviewing prospective tenants, what questions would you ask?

ADDITIONAL READINGS

Income and Expense Analysis. (Institute of Real Estate Management, Chicago, 1986). Issued annually for apartment buildings and office buildings, these reports show typical rental income and operating expenses across the United States. Very useful for comparing buildings.

Managing Your Rental House for Increased Income by **Doreen Bierbrier.** (McGraw-Hill, 1985, 287 pages). A hands-on, practical guide to renting houses to unrelated single persons on a room-by-room basis. Includes choosing the right house, selecting tenants, rental agreements, record keeping and neighbor relations.

Property Management, 2nd ed. by **Robert Kyle.** (Real Estate Education Co., 1984, 428 pages). Provides practical information on tenant relations, qualifying prospects, leasing procedures, fee setting, negotiating, etc. Covers apartment buildings, cooperatives, condominiums, offices, stores, industrial and subsidized housing. Includes the use of microcomputers and word processing.

"The Rental Resurgence" by **Leanne Lachman.** (*Real Estate Today,* Sep 84, page 23). Article points out that today's housing costs, increased demand and restoration efforts are making rentals a renewed source of investment opportunity.

The Successful On-Site Manager by **Carol King, Gary Langendoen** and **Lyn Hummel.** (Institute of Real Estate Management, 1984, 327 pages). Valuable reading for anyone planning to be an on-site property manager. Covers responsibilities of the manager, planning and budgeting, policies for hiring help, lease writing, collections, property marketing, maintenance and energy conservation.

*   *   *

The following periodicals may also be of interest to you: *Apartment Journal, Apartment Management Newsletter, Apartment News, National Rental Housing Council Newsletter, Real Estate Perspectives, Journal of Property Management, Landlord–Tenant Law Bulletin, Managing Housing Letter* and *Skyscraper Management.*

Real Estate Appraisal

Appraise: to estimate the value of something

Capitalize: to convert future income to current value

Comparables: properties similar to the subject property that have sold recently

Cost approach: land value plus current construction costs minus depreciation

Depreciation: loss in value due to deterioration and obsolescence

Gross rent multiplier (GRM): a number that is multiplied by a property's gross rents to produce an estimate of the property's worth

Highest and best use: that use of a parcel of land which will produce the greatest current value

Income approach: a method of valuing a property based on the monetary returns it can be expected to produce

Market approach: a method of valuing property based on recent sales of similar properties

Market value: the cash price that a willing buyer and a willing seller would agree upon, given reasonable exposure of the property to the marketplace, full information as to the potential uses of the property and no undue compulsion to act

Operating expenses: expenditures necessary to maintain the production of income

Scheduled gross, Projected gross: the estimated rent a fully occupied property can be expected to produce on an annual basis

To **appraise** real estate means to estimate its value. There are three approaches to making this estimate. The first is to locate similar properties that have sold recently and use them as bench marks in estimating the value of the property you are appraising. This is the **market approach** also called the market-data approach or market comparison approach. The second approach is to add together the cost of the individual components that make up the property being appraised. This is the **cost approach;** it starts with the cost of a similar parcel of vacant land and adds the cost of the lumber, concrete, plumbing, wiring, labor, etc., necessary to build a similar building.

Depreciation is then subtracted. The third approach is to consider only the amount of net income that the property can reasonably be expected to produce for its owner plus any anticipated price increase or decrease. This is the **income approach.** For the person who owns or plans to own real estate, knowing how much a property is worth is a crucial part of the buying or selling decision. For the real estate agent, being able to estimate the value of a property is an essential part of taking a listing and conducting negotiations.

MARKET VALUE

In this chapter you will see demonstrations of the market, cost and income approaches and how they are used in determining market value. **Market value,** also called **fair market value,** is the highest price in terms of money that a property will bring if (1) payment is made in cash or its equivalent, (2) the property is exposed on the open market for a reasonable length of time, (3) the buyer and seller are fully informed as to market conditions and the uses to which the property may be put, (4) neither is under abnormal pressure to conclude a transaction, and (5) the seller is capable of conveying marketable title. Market value is at the heart of nearly all real estate transactions.

MARKET COMPARISON APPROACH

Let us being by demonstrating the application of the **market comparison approach** to a single-family residence. The residence to be appraised is called the **subject property** and is described as follows:

> The subject property is a one-story, wood-frame house of 1,520 square feet containing three bedrooms, two bathrooms, a living room, dining room, kitchen, and utility room. There is a two-car garage with concrete driveway to the street, a 300-square-foot concrete patio in the backyard and an average amount of landscaping. The house is located on a 10,200-square-foot, level lot that measures 85 by 120 feet. The house is 12 years old, in good repair and located in a well-maintained neighborhood of houses of similar construction and age.

Comparables

After becoming familiar with the physical features and amenities of the subject property, the next step in the market approach is to locate houses with similar physical features and amenities that have sold recently under market value conditions. These are known as **comparables** or "comps." The more similar they are to the subject property, the fewer and smaller the adjustments that must be made in the comparison process and hence the less room for error. As a rule it is best to use comparable sales no more than 6 months old. During periods of relatively stable prices, this can be extended to 1 year. However, during periods of rapidly changing prices even a sale 6 months old may be out of date.

To apply the market comparison approach, the following information must be collected for each comparable sale: date of sale, sales price, financing terms, location of the property and a description of its physical characteristics and amenities. Recorded deeds at public records offices can provide dates and locations of recent sales. Although a deed seldom states the purchase price, nearly all states levy a deed transfer fee or conveyance tax, the amount of which is shown on the recorded deed. This tax can sometimes provide a clue as to the purchase price.

Sales Records

Records of past sales can often be obtained from title and abstract companies. Property tax assessors keep records on changes in ownership as well as property values. Where these records are kept up to date and are available to the public, they can provide information on what has sold recently and for how much. Assessors also keep detailed records of improvements made to land. This can be quite helpful in making adjustments between the subject property and the comparables. For real estate salespeople, locally operated multiple listing services provide asking prices and descriptions of properties currently offered for sale by member brokers along with descriptions, sales prices and dates for properties that have been sold. In some cities, commercially operated financial services publish information on local real estate transactions and sell it on a subscription basis.

To produce the most accurate appraisal possible, each sale used as a comparable should be inspected and the price and terms verified. An agent who specializes in a given neighborhood will have already visited the comparables when they were

Verification

still for sale. The agent can verify price and terms with the selling broker or from multiple listing service sales records.

Number of Comparables   Three to five comparables usually provide enough basis for reliable comparison. To use more than five, the additional accuracy must be weighed against the extra effort involved. When the supply of comparable sales is more than adequate, one should choose the sales that require the fewest adjustments.

It is also important that the comparables selected represent current market conditions. Sales between relatives or close friends may result in an advantageous price to the buyer or seller, and sales prices that for some other reason appear to be out of line with the general market should not be used. Listings and offers to buy should not be used in place of actual sales. They do not represent a meeting of minds between a buyer and a seller. Listing prices do indicate the upper limit of prices, whereas offers to buy indicate lower limits. Thus, if a property is listed for sale at $80,000 and there have been offers as high as $76,000, it is reasonable to presume the market price lies somewhere between $76,000 and $80,000.

Adjustment Process   Let us now work through the example shown in Table 16:1 to demonstrate the application of the market comparison approach to a house. We being at lines 1 and 2 by entering the address and sale price of each comparable property. For convenience, we shall refer to these as comparables A, B and C. On lines 3 through 10, we make time adjustments to the sale price of each comparable to make it equivalent to the subject property today. **Adjustments** are made for price changes since each comparable was sold, as well as for differences in physical features, amenities and financial terms. The result indicates the market value of the subject property.

Time Adjustments   Returning to line 3 in Table 16:1, let us assume that house prices in the neighborhood where the subject property and comparables are located have risen 5% during the 6 months that have elapsed since comparable A was sold. If it were for sale today, comparable A would bring 5% or $4,590 more. Therefore, we must add $4,590 to bring it up to the present. Comparable B was sold 3 months ago, and to bring it up to the

VALUING A HOUSE BY THE MARKET COMPARISON APPROACH   Table 16:1

Line	Item	Comparable Sale A		Comparable Sale B		Comparable Sale C	
1	Address	1702 Brookside Ave.		1912 Brookside Ave.		1501 18th Street	
2	Sales price		$91,800		$88,000		$89,000
3	Time adjustment	*sold 6 mos. ago, add 5%*	+4,590	*sold 3 mos. ago, add 2½%*	+2,200	*just sold*	0
4	House size	*160 sq ft larger at $40 per sq ft*	−6,400	*20 sq ft smaller at $40/sq ft*	+ 800	*same size*	0
5	Garage/carport	*carport*	+4,000	*3-car garage*	2,000	*2 car garage*	0
6	Other	*larger patio*	− 300	*no patio*	+ 600	*built-in bookcases*	− 500
7	Age, upkeep, & overall quality of house	*superior*	−2,000	*inferior*	+ 400	*equal*	0
8	Landscaping	*inferior*	+1,000	*equal*	0	*superior*	− 700
9	Lot size, features, & location	*superior*	−3,890	*inferior*	+ 900	*equal*	0
10	Terms & conditions of sale	*equal*	0	*special financing*	−1,500	*equal*	0
11	Total adjustments		−3,000		+1,400		−1,200
12	ADJUSTED MARKET PRICE		$88,800		$89,400		$87,800

13   **Correlation process:**

Comparable A	$88,800 × 20%	= $17,760
Comparable B	$89,400 × 30%	= $26,820
Comparable C	$87,800 × 50%	= $43,900

14   **INDICATED VALUE** $88,480

       Round to $88,500

present we need to add 2½% or $2,200 to it sales price. Comparable C was just sold and needs no time correction, as its price reflects today's market.

When using the market comparison approach, all adjustments are made to the comparable properties, not to the subject property. This is because we cannot adjust the value of something for which we do not yet know the value.

House Size

Because house A is 160 square feet larger than the subject house, it is logical to expect that the subject property would sell for less money. Hence a deduction is made from the sales price of comparable A on line 4. The amount of this deduction is based on the difference in floor area and the current cost of similar construction, minus an allowance for depreciation. If we value the extra 160 square feet at $40 per square foot, we must subtract $6,400. For comparable B, the house is 20 square feet smaller that the subject house. At $40 per square foot, we add $800 to comparable B, as it is reasonable to expect that the subject property would sell for that much more because it is that much larger. Comparable C is the same-sized house as the subject property, so no adjustment is needed.

Garage and Patio Adjustments

Next, the parking facilities (line 5) are adjusted. We first look at the current cost of garage and carport construction and the condition of these structures. Assume that the value of a carport is $2,000; a one-car garage, $4,000; a two-car garage, $6,000; and a three-car garage, $8,000. Adjustments would be made as follows. The subject property has a two-car garage worth $6,000 and comparable A has a carport worth $2,000. Therefore, based on the difference in garage facilities, we can reasonably expect the subject property to command $4,000 more than comparable A. By adding $4,000 to comparable A, we effectively equalize this difference. Comparable B has a garage worth $2,000 more than the subject property's garage. Therefore, $2,000 must be subtracted from comparable B to equalize it with the subject property. For comparable C, no adjustment is required, as comparable C and the subject property have similar garage facilities.

At line 6, the subject property has a 300-square-foot patio in the backyard worth $600. Comparable A has a patio worth $900; therefore, $300 is deducted from comparable A's selling price. Comparable B has no patio. As it would have sold for $600 more if it had one, a +$600 adjustment is required. The patio at comparable C is the same as the subject property's. However, comparable C has $500 worth of custom built-in living room bookcases that the subject property does not have. Therefore, $500 is subtracted from comparable C's sales price. Any other differences between the comparables and the subject property such as swimming pools, fireplaces, carpeting, drapes, roofing materials and kitchen appliances would be adjusted in a similar manner.

On line 7 we recognize differences in building age, wear and tear, construction quality and design usefulness. Where the difference between the subject property and a comparable can be measured in terms of material and labor, the adjustment is the cost of that material and labor. For example, the $400 adjustment for comparable B reflects the cost of needed roof repair at the time B was sold. The adjustment of $2,000 for comparable A reflects the fact it has better-quality plumbing and electrical fixtures than the subject property. Differences that cannot be quantified in terms of labor and materials are usually dealt with as lump-sum judgments. Thus, one might allow $1,000 for each year of age difference between the subject and a comparable, or make a lump-sum adjustment of $2,000 for an inconvenient kitchen design.

Building Age, Condition and Quality

Keep in mind that adjustments are made on the basis of what each comparable property was like on the day it was sold. Thus, if an extra bedroom was added or the house was painted after its sale date, these items are not included in the adjustment process.

Line 8 shows the landscaping at comparable A to be inferior to the subject property. A positive correction is necessary here to equalize it with the subject. The landscaping at comparable B is similar and requires no correction; that at comparable C is better and thus requires a negative adjustment. The dollar amount of each adjustment is based on the market value of lawn, bushes, trees and the like.

Landscaping

Line 9 deals with any differences in lot size, slope, view and neighborhood. In this example, all comparables are in the same neighborhood as the subject property, thus eliminating the need to judge, in dollar terms, the relative merit of one neighborhood over another. However, comparable A has a slightly larger lot and a better view than the subject property. Based on recent lot sales in the area, the difference is judged to be $890 for the larger lot and $3,000 for the better view. Comparable B

Lot Features and Location

has a slightly smaller lot judged to be worth $900 less, and comparable C is similar in all respects.

Terms and Conditions
of Sale
Line 10 in Table 16:1 accounts for differences in financing. As a rule, the more accommodating the terms of the sale to the buyer, the higher the sales price, and vice versa. We are looking for the highest cash price the subject property may reasonably be expected to bring, given adequate exposure to the marketplace and a knowledgeable buyer and seller not under undue pressure. If the comparables were sold under these conditions, no corrections would be needed in this category. However, if it can be determined that a comparable was sold under different conditions, an adjustment is necessary. For example, if the going rate of interest on home mortgages is 12% per year and the seller offers to finance the buyer at 9% interest, it is reasonable to expect that the seller can charge a higher selling price. Similarly, the seller can get a higher price if he has a low-interest loan that can be assumed by the buyer. Favorable financing terms offered by the seller of comparable B enabled him to obtain an extra $1,500 in selling price. Therefore, we must subtract $1,500 from comparable B. Another situation that requires an adjustment on line 10 is if a comparable was sold on a rush basis. If a seller is in a hurry to sell, a lower selling price usually must be accepted than if the property can be given more time in the marketplace.

Adjusted Market Price
Adjustments for each comparable are totaled and either added or subtracted from its sale price. The result is the **adjusted market price** shown at line 12. This is the dollar value of each comparable sale after it has gone through an adjustment process to make it the same as the subject property. If it were possible to precisely evaluate every adjustment, and if the buyers of comparables A, B and C had paid exactly what their properties were worth at the time they purchased them, the three prices shown on line 12 would be the same. However, buyers are not that precise, particularly in purchasing a home where amenity value influences price and varies considerably from one person to the next.

Correlation Process
While comparing the properties, it will usually become apparent that some comparables are more like the subject

property than others. The **correlation** step gives the appraiser the opportunity to assign more weight to the more similar comparables and less to the others. At 13, comparable C is given a weight of 50% since it is more like the subject and required fewer adjustments. Moreover, this sameness is in areas where adjustments tend to be the hardest to estimate accurately: time, age, quality, location, view and financial conditions. Of the remaining two comparables, comparable B is weighted slightly higher than comparable A because it is a more recent sale and overall required fewer adjustments.

In the correlation process, the adjusted market price of each comparable is multiplied by its weighting factor and totaled at line 14. The result is the **indicated value** of the subject property. It is customary to round off to the nearest $50 or $100 for properties under $10,000; to the nearest $250 or $500 for properties between $10,000 and $100,000; to the nearest $1,000 or $2,500 for properties between $100,000 and $250,000; and to the nearest $2,500 or $5,000 above that.

CONDOMINIUM, TOWNHOUSE AND COOPERATIVE APPRAISAL

The process for estimating the market value of a condominium, townhouse or cooperative living unit by the market approach is similar to the process for houses except that fewer steps are involved. For example, in a condominium complex with a large number of two-bedroom units of identical floor plan, data on a sufficient number of comparable sales may be available within the building. This would eliminate adjustments for differences in unit floor plan, neighborhood, lot size and features, age and upkeep of the building, and landscaping. The only corrections needed would be those that make one unit different from another. This would include the location of the individual unit within the building (end units and units with better views sell for more), the upkeep and interior decoration of the unit, a time adjustment and an adjustment for terms and conditions of the sale.

When there are not enough comparable sales of the same floor plan within the same building and it is necessary to use different-sized units, an adjustment must be made for floor area. If the number of comparables is still inadequate and units in different condominium buildings must be used, adjustments will be necessary for neighborhood, lot features, management, upkeep, age and overall condition of the building.

MARKET APPROACH
TO VACANT LAND
VALUATION

Subdivided lots zoned for commercial, industrial or apartment buildings are usually appraised and sold on a square foot basis. Thus, if apartment land is currently selling for $3.00 per square foot, a 100,000-square-foot parcel of comparable zoning and usefulness would be appraised at $300,000. Another method is to value on a front-foot basis. For example, if a lot has 70 feet of street frontage and if similar lots are selling for $300 per front foot, that lot would be appraised at $21,000. Storefront land is often sold this way. House lots can be valued either by the square foot, front foot, or lot method. The lot method is useful when one is comparing lots of similar size and zoning in the same neighborhood. For example, recent sales of 100-foot by 100-foot house lots in the $18,000 to $20,000 range would establish the value of similar lots in the same neighborhood.

Rural land and large parcels that have not been subdivided are usually valued and sold by the acre. For example, how would you value 21 acres of vacant land when the only comparables available are 16-acre and 25-acre sales? The method is to establish a per acre value from comparables and apply it to the subject land. Thus, if 16- and 25-acre parcels sold for $32,000 and $50,000, respectively, and are similar in all other respects to the 21-acre subject property, it would be reasonable to conclude that land is selling for $2,000 per acre. Therefore, the subject property is worth $42,000.

4–3–2–1 Rule

The **4–3–2–1 rule** is a depth adjustment that appraisers sometimes use when valuing vacant lots. It states that the land at the back of the lot is worth less than the land at the front. To illustrate, consider a single-family residential lot that has 75 feet of frontage on a street and is 200 feet deep. Across the street and in an equally desirable location are two lots for sale that are each 75 feet on the street and 100 feet deep. Would you pay as much for the single 75′ × 200′ lot as you would for two 75′ × 100′ lots? Let us omit the arithmetic and just remember the principle: the land at the back of a lot is worth less than the land at the front.

COMPETITIVE MARKET
ANALYSIS

A variation of the market comparison approach and one that is very popular with agents who list and sell residential property is the **competitive market analysis (CMA).** This method is based on the principle that value can be estimated not only by looking at similar homes that have sold recently but also by taking into account homes presently on the market plus homes that were listed for sale but did not sell. The CMA is a listing tool that a sales agent prepares in order to show a seller what the home will likely sell for and the CMA helps the agent decided whether or not to accept the listing.

Figure 16:1 shows a competitive market analysis form published by the National Association of Realtors. The procedure in preparing a CMA is to select homes that are comparable to the subject property. The greater the similarity, the more accurate the appraisal will be and the more likely the client will accept the agent's estimate of value and counsel. It is usually best to use only properties in the same neighborhood; this is easier for the seller to relate to and removes the need to compensate for neighborhood differences. The comparables should also be similar in size, age and quality. Although a CMA does not require that individual adjustments be shown as in Table 16:1, it does depend on the agent's understanding of the process that takes place in that table. That is why Table 16:1 and its explanation are important. A residential agent may not be called upon to make a presentation as is done in Table 16:1; nonetheless, all those steps are considered and consolidated in the agent's mind before entering a probable final sales price on the CMA.

Homes for Sale

In section ① of the CMA shown in Figure 16:1, similar homes presently offered for sale are listed. This information is usually taken directly from the agent's multiple listing service (MLS) book, and ideally the agent will already have toured these properties and have first-hand knowledge of their condition. These are the homes the seller's property will compete against in the marketplace.

In section ② the agent lists similar properties that have sold in the past several months. Ideally, the agent will have toured the properties when they were for sale. Sale prices are usually available through MLS sales records. Section ③ is for listing homes that were offered for sale, but did not sell. In other words, buyers were unwilling to take these homes at the prices offered.

In section ④ recent FHA and VA appraisals of comparable

Figure 16:1

COMPETITIVE MARKET ANALYSIS

Property Address _____ Date _____

For Sale Now: (1)	Bed. rms	Baths	Den	Sq. Ft.	1st Loan	List Price	Days on Market	Terms

Sold Past 12 Mos. (2)	Bed. rms	Baths	Den	Sq. Ft.	1st Loan	List Price	Days on Market	Date Sold	Sale Price	Terms

Expired Past 12 Mos. (3)	Bed. rms	Baths	Den	Sq. Ft.	1st Loan	List Price	Days on Market	Terms

(4) F.H.A — V.A. Appraisals

Address	Appraisal	Address	Appraisal

(5) Buyer Appeal   (6) Marketing Position

(Grade each item 0 to 20% on the basis of desirability or urgency)

Buyer Appeal	Marketing Position
1 Fine Location _____ %	1 Why Are They Selling _____ %
2 Exciting Extras _____ %	2 How Soon Must They Sell _____ %
3 Extra Special Financing _____ %	3 Will They Help Finance .... Yes ____ No ____ %
4 Exceptional Appeal _____ %	4 Will They List at Competitive Market Value ... Yes ____ No ____ %
5 Under Market Price _____ Yes ____ No ____ %	5 Will They Pay for Appraisal .... Yes ____ No ____ %

(7) _____ Rating Total _____ %   Rating Total _____ %

Assets _____

Drawbacks _____

Area Market Conditions _____

Recommended Terms _____

(8) Selling Costs

Brokerage	$	Top Competitive Market Value	$ _____
Loan Payoff	$		
Prepayment Privilege	$		
FHA — VA Points	$	(9)	
Title and Escrow Fees: IRS Stamps Recons Recording	$	Probable Final Sales Price	$ _____
Termite Clearance	$		
Misc. Payoffs: 2nd T.D., Pool, Patio, Water Softener, Fence, Improvement Bond.	$	Total Selling Costs	$ _____
	$		
	$	Net Proceeds $ _____	Plus or Minus $ _____
Total	$		

The statements and figures presented herein, while not guaranteed, are secured from sources we believe authoritative   Prepared by _____ homes can be included if it is felt that they will be useful in determining the price at which to list. Two words of caution are in order here. First, using someone else's opinion of value is risky. It is better to determine your own opinion based on actual facts. Second, FHA and VA appraisals often tend to lag behind the market. This means in a rising market they will be too low; in a declining market they will be too high.

In section ⑤ buyer appeal, and in section ⑥ market position, the agent evaluates the subject property from the standpoint of whether or not it will sell if placed on the market. It is important to make the right decision to take or not to take a listing. Once taken, the agent knows that valuable time and money must be committed to get it sold. Factors which make a property more appealing to a buyer include good location, extra features, small down payment, low interest, meticulous maintenance and a price below market. Similarly, a property is more saleable if the sellers are motivated to sell, want to sell soon, will help with financing and will list at or below market. A busy agent will want to avoid spending time on overpriced listings, listings for which no financing is available and listings where the sellers have no motivation to sell. With the rating systems in section ⑤ and ⑥, the closer the total is to zero, the less desirable the listing; the closer to 100%, the more desirable the listing.

Buyer Appeal

Section ⑦ provides space to list the property's high and low points, current market conditions and recommended terms of sale. Section ⑧ shows the seller how much to expect in selling costs. Section ⑨ shows the seller what to expect in the way of a sales price and the amount of cash that can be expected from the sale.

The emphasis in CMA is on a visual inspection of the data on the form in order to arrive at market value directly. No pencil and paper adjustments are made. Instead, adjustments are made in a generalized fashion in the minds of the agent and the seller. In addition to its application to single-family houses, CMA can also be used on condominiums, cooperative apartments, townhouses and vacant lots—provided sufficient comparables are available.

GROSS RENT
MULTIPLIERS

A popular market comparison method that is used when a property produces income is the **gross rent multiplier,** or **GRM.** The GRM is an economic comparison factor that relates the gross rent a property can produce to its purchase price. For apartment buildings and commercial and industrial properties, the GRM is computed by dividing the sales price of the property by its gross annual rent. For example, if an apartment building grosses $100,000 per year in rents and has just sold for $700,000, it is said to have a GRM of 7. The use of a GRM to value single-family houses is questionable since they are usually sold as owner-occupied residences rather than as income properties. Note that if you do work a GRM for a house, it is customary to use the monthly (not yearly) rent.

Where comparable properties have been sold at fairly consistent gross rent multiples, the GRM technique presumes the subject property can be valued by multiplying its gross rent by that multiplier. To illustrate, suppose that apartment buildings were recently sold in your community as shown in Table 16:2. These sales indicate that the market is currently paying seven times gross. Therefore, to find the value of a similar apartment building grossing $24,000 per year, multiply by 7.00 to get an indicated value of $168,000.

Table 16:2   **CALCULATING GROSS RENT MULTIPLIERS**

Building	Sales Price		Gross Annual Rents		Gross Rent Multiplier
No. 1	$245,000	÷	$ 34,900	=	7.02
No. 2	$160,000	÷	$ 22,988	=	6.96
No. 3	$204,000	÷	$ 29,352	=	6.95
No. 4	$196,000	÷	$ 27,762	=	7.06
As a Group:	$805,000	÷	$115,002	=	7.00

The GRM method is popular because it is simple to apply. Having once established what multiplier the market is paying, one need only know the gross rents of a building to set a value. However, this simplicity is also the weakness of the GRM method because the GRM takes into account only the gross rent a property produces. Gross rent does not allow for variations in vacancies, uncollectible rents, property taxes, maintenance, management, insurance, utilities or reserves for replacements.

To illustrate the problem, suppose that two apartment buildings each gross $100,000 per year. However, the first has expenses amounting to $40,000 per year and the second, expenses of $50,000 per year. Using the same GRM, the buildings would be valued the same, yet the first produces $10,000 more in net income for its owner. The GRM also overlooks the expected economic life span of a property. For example, a building with an expected remaining life span of 30 years would be valued exactly the same as one expected to last 20 years, if both currently produce the same rents. One method of partially offsetting these errors is to use different GRMs under different circumstances. Thus, a property with low operating expenses and a long expected economic life span might call for a GRM of 7 or more, whereas a property with high operating expenses or a shorter expected life span would be valued using a GRM of 6 or 5 or even less.

Weakness of GRM

There are times when the market approach is an inappropriate valuation tool. For example, the market approach is of limited usefulness in valuing a fire station, school building, courthouse or highway bridge. These properties are rarely placed on the market and comparables are rarely found. Even with properties that are well-suited to the market approach, there may be times when it is valuable to apply another valuation approach. For example, a real estate agent may find that comparables indicate a certain style and size of house is selling in a particular neighborhood for $150,000. Yet the astute agent discovers through the cost approach that the same house can be built from scratch, including land, for $125,000. The agent builds and sells ten of these and concludes that, yes, there really is money to be made in real estate. Let us take a closer look at the cost approach.

COST APPROACH

Table 16:3 demonstrates the **cost approach.** Step 1 is to estimate the value of the land upon which the building is located. The land is valued as though vacant using the market comparison approach described earlier. In Step 2, the cost of constructing a similar building at today's costs is estimated. These costs include the current prices of building materials, construction wages, architect fees, contractor's services, building permits, utility hookups and the like, plus the cost of financing during the construction stage and the cost of construction equipment used at the project site. Step 3 is the calculation of the amount of money that represents the subject building's wear and tear, lack of usefulness and obsolescence when compared to the new building of Step 2. In Step 4, depreciation is subtracted from today's construction cost to give the current value of the subject building on a used basis. Step 5 is to add this amount to the land value. Let us work through these steps.

Table 16:3

COST APPROACH TO VALUE

Step 1:	Estimate land as vacant		$30,000
Step 2:	Estimate new construction cost of similar building	$120,000	
Step 3:	Less estimated depreciation	−12,000	
Step 4:	Indicated value of building		108,000
Step 5:	Appraised property value by the cost approach		$138,000

Estimating New Construction Costs

In order to choose a method of estimating construction costs, one must decide whether cost will be approached on a reproduction or on a replacement basis. **Reproduction cost** is the cost at today's prices of constructing an *exact replica* of the subject improvements using the same or very similar materials. **Replacement cost** is the cost, at today's prices and using today's methods of construction, for an improvement having the same or *equivalent usefulness* as the subject property. Replacement cost is the more practical choice of the two as it eliminates nonessential or obsolete features and takes full advantage of current construction materials and techniques. It is the approach that will be described here.

Square-Foot Method

The most widely used approach for estimating construction costs is the **square-foot method.** It provides reasonably accurate estimates that are fast and simple to prepare.

The square-foot method is based on finding a newly constructed building that is similar to the subject building in size, type of occupancy, design, materials and construction quality.

The cost of this building is converted to cost per square foot by dividing its current construction cost by the number of square feet in the building.

Cost information is also available from construction cost handbooks. Using a **cost handbook** starts with selecting a handbook appropriate to the type of building being appraised. From photographs of houses included in the handbook along with brief descriptions of the buildings' features, the appraiser finds a house that most nearly fits the description of the subject house. Next to pictures of the house is the current cost per square foot to construct it. If the subject house has a better quality roof, floor covering, heating system, greater or fewer built-in appliances, plumbing fixtures, or has a garage, basement, porch or swimming pool, the handbook provides costs for each of these. Figure 16:2 illustrates the calculations involved in the square-foot method.

Cost Handbooks

Having estimated the current cost of constructing the subject improvements, the next step in the cost approach is to estimate the loss in value due to depreciation since they were built. In making this estimate, we look for three kinds of **depreciation:** physical deterioration, functional obsolescence and economic obsolescence.

Estimating Depreciation

Physical deterioration results from wear and tear through use, such as wall-to-wall carpet that has been worn thin or a dishwasher, garbage disposal or water heater that must be replaced. Physical deterioration also results from the action of nature in the form of sun, rain, heat, cold and wind, and from damage due to plants and animal life such as tree roots breaking sidewalks and termites eating wood. Physical deterioration can also result from neglect (an overflowing bathtub) and from vandalism.

Functional obsolescence results from outmoded equipment (old-fashioned plumbing fixtures in the bathrooms and kitchen), faulty or outdated design (a single bathroom in a three- or four-bedroom house or an illogical room layout), inadequate structural facilities (inadequate wiring to handle today's household appliance loads), and overadequate structural facilities (high ceilings in a home). Functional and physical obsolescence can be separated into curable and incurable

Figure 16:2   SQUARE-FOOT METHOD OF COST ESTIMATING

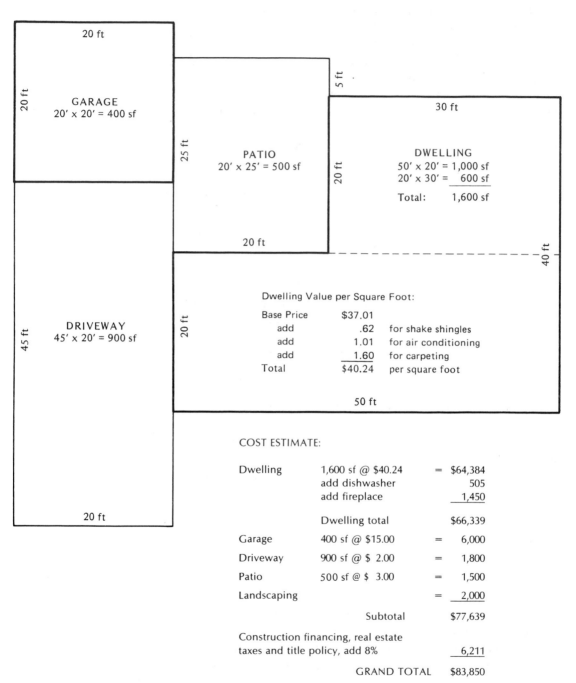

components. **Curable** is something that can be fixed at reasonable cost such as worn carpeting, a leaky roof or outdated faucets in bathrooms. **Incurable** is something that cannot be reasonably fixed and must simply be lived with, for example, an illogical room layout.

Economic obsolescence is the loss of value due to external forces or events. For example, a once-popular neighborhood becomes undesirable because of air or noise pollution or because surrounding property owners fail to maintain their properties. Or, a city that is dependent on a military base finds the base closed and with it a big drop in demand for real estate. Or, the motel district in town loses customers because a new interstate highway is built several miles away. Far more often, however, properties experience economic appreciation and not economic obsolescence. The appreciation can come from new industries moving into town, city growth in a new direction, a shortage of land in beach or waterfront areas, etc. Thus it is quite possible for the economic appreciation of a property to more than offset the depreciation it experiences. The result is a building that is physically and functionally depreciating and at the same time appreciating in value. Consequently, while the chronological age of a building is important to value, what is more important is the remaining economic life of the building and whether it is functionally adequate for use in the future. This is what real estate investors look for.

Final Steps in the Cost Approach

After calculating the current construction cost of the subject improvements and estimating the amount of depreciation, the next step is to subtract the amount of depreciation from the current construction cost to get the depreciated value of the improvements. This is added to the value of the land upon which the subject improvements rest. The total is the value of the property by the cost approach.

INCOME APPROACH

The market approach is very useful in connection with the sale or purchase of a home. The cost approach is very useful for someone planning to build. But what about someone planning to invest? For investors the income approach is the most popular method of valuing a property. The **income approach** considers the monetary returns a property can be expected to produce and converts that into a value the property should sell for if placed on the market today. This is called capitalizing the income stream. To **capitalize** means to convert future income to current value. To illustrate, suppose that an available apartment building is expected to return, after expenses, $18,000 per year. How much would you, as an investor, pay for the building? The answer depends on the return you require on each dollar you invest. Suppose you will accept a return of 9% per year. In that case you will pay $200,000 for this building. The calculation is as follows:

$$\frac{Income}{Rate} = Value \qquad \frac{\$18,000}{.09} = \$200,000$$

This is the basic principle of capitalization. The appraisal work comes in estimating the net income a property will produce and looking at recent sales of similar properties to see what capitalization rates are currently acceptable to investors. Let us look at the techniques one would use in estimating a property's income. Pay close attention because each $1 error in projected annual income or expenses can make a difference of from $8 to $15 in the market value of the property.

Income and Expense Forecasting   The best starting point is to look at the actual record of income and expenses for the subject property over the past 3 to 5 years. Although the future will not be an exact repetition of the past, the past record of a property is usually the best guide to future performance. These historical data are blended with the current operating experience of similar buildings in order to estimate what the future will bring. The result is a projected operating statement, such as the one shown in Table 16:4, which begins with the estimated rents that the property can be expected to produce on an annual basis. This is the **projected gross,** or **scheduled gross,** and represents expected rentals from the subject property on a fully occupied basis. From this, vacancy and collection losses are subtracted. These are based partly on the building's past experience and partly on the operating experience of similar buildings.

PROJECTED ANNUAL OPERATING STATEMENT   Table 16:4
(Also called a Pro Forma Statement)

Scheduled gross annual income	$84,000	
Vacancy allowance and collection losses	4,200	
Effective Gross Income		$79,800
Operating Expenses		
Property taxes	9,600	
Hazard and liability insurance	1,240	
Property management	5,040	
Janitorial services	1,500	
Gardener	1,200	
Utilities	3,940	
Trash pickup	600	
Repairs and maintenance	5,000	
Other	1,330	
Reserves for replacement		
Furniture & furnishings	1,200	
Stoves & refrigerators	600	
Furnace &/or air-conditioning	700	
Plumbing & electrical	800	
Roof	750	
Exterior painting	900	
Total Operating Expenses		$34,400
Net Operating Income		$45,400

Operating Expense Ratio: $34,400 ÷ $79,800 = 43.1%

The next step is to itemize anticipated **operating expenses** for the subject property. These are expenses necessary to maintain the production of income. For an apartment building without recreational facilities or an elevator, the list in Table 16:4 is typical. Again, we must consider both the property's past operating expenses and what we expect those expenses to be in the future. For example, even though a property is currently being managed by its owner and no management fee is being paid, a typical management fee, say 6% of the gross rents, is included.

Not included as operating expenses are outlays for capital improvements, such as the construction of a new swimming pool, the expansion of parking facilities and assessments for

Operating Expenses

street improvements. Improvements are not classified as expenses because they increase the usefulness of the property, which increases the rent the property will generate and therefore the property's value.

Reserves

Reserves for replacement are established for items that do not require an expenditure of cash each year. To illustrate, lobby furniture (and furniture in apartments rented as "furnished") wears out a little each year, eventually requiring replacement. Suppose that these items cost $7,200 and are expected to last 6 years, at which time they must be replaced. An annual $1,200 reserve for replacement not only reflects wear and tear of the furniture during the year, but also reminds us that to avoid having to meet the entire furniture and furnishings replacement cost out of one year's income, money should be set aside each year. In a similar manner, reserves are established for other items that must be replaced or repaired more than once during the life of the building, but not yearly.

Net Operating Income

The operating expense total is then subtracted from the effective gross income. The balance that remains is the **net operating income.** From the net operating income the property owner receives both a return *on* and a return *of* investment. The return *on* investment is the interest received for investing money in the property. The return *of* investment is compensation for the fact that the building is wearing out.

Operating Expense Ratio

At this point, the **operating expense ratio** can be calculated. It is obtained by dividing the total operating expenses by the effective gross income. The resulting ratio provides a handy yardstick against which similar properties can be compared. If the operating expense ratio is out of step compared to similar properties, it signals the need for further investigation. A range of 25% to 45% is typical for apartment buildings. The Institute of Real Estate Management of the National Association of Realtors publishes books and articles that give typical operating ratios for various types of income properties across the United States. Local inquiry to appraisers and brokers who specialize in income properties will also provide typical ratios for buildings in a community.

The final step in the income approach is to capitalize the net operating income. In other words, what price should an investor offer to pay for a property that produces a given net income per year? The solution is: income ÷ rate = value. If the annual net operating income is $45,400 and if the investor intends to pay all cash, expects to receive a 10% return on his investment, and anticipates no change in the value of the property while he owns it, the solution is to divide $45,400 by 10%. However, most investors today borrow much of the purchase price and usually expect an increase in property value. Under these conditions, how much should the investor pay?

The best known method for solving this type of investment question involves using the Ellwood Tables, published in 1959 by L. W. Ellwood, MAI. However, for the person who does not use these tables regularly, the arithmetic involved can prove confusing. As a result **mortgage-equity tables** are now available from bookstores. These allow the user to look up a single number, called an **overall rate,** and divide it into the net operating income to find a value for the property.

For example, suppose an investor who is interested in buying the above property can obtain an 11%, fully amortized 25-year mortgage loan for 75% of the purchase price. He wants an 18% return on his equity in the property, plans to hold it 10 years, and expects it will increase 50% in value (after selling costs) during that time. How much should he offer to pay the seller? In Table 16:5, we look for an interest rate of 11% and for appreciation of 50%. This gives an overall rate of .10756 and the solution is:

$$\frac{\text{Income}}{\text{Overall rate}} = \text{Value} \qquad \frac{\$45,400}{.10756} - \$422,090$$

Further exploration of the numbers in Table 16:5 shows that as loan money becomes more costly, the overall rate rises, and as interest rates fall, so does the overall rate. If the investor can anticipate appreciation in value, the overall rate drops; if he can't, the overall rate climbs. You can experiment by dividing some of the other overall rates in this table into $45,400 to see how the value of this property changes under different circumstances.

Capitalizing Income

Table 16:5

OVERALL RATES—10-YEAR HOLDING PERIOD
25-Year Loan for 75% of the Purchase Price, 18% Investor Return

Appreciation, Depreciation	Loan Interest Rate			
	9%	10%	11%	12%
+100%	.07251	.07935	.08631	.09338
+ 50%	.09376	.10060	**.10756**	.11463
+ 25%	.10439	.11123	.11819	.12526
+ 15%	.10864	.11548	.12244	.12951
+ 10%	.11077	.11761	.12457	.13164
+ 5%	.11289	.11973	.12669	.13376
0	.11502	.12186	.12882	.13589
− 5%	.11715	.12399	.13095	.13802
− 10%	.11927	.12611	.13307	.14014
− 15%	.12140	.12824	.13520	.14227
− 25%	.12565	.13249	.13945	.14652
− 50%	.13628	.14312	.15008	.15715
−100%	.15753	.16437	.17133	.17840

Source: *Financial Capitalization Rate Tables,* Financial Publishing Company, Boston, Mass. By permission.

DEPRECIATION

The pro forma in Table 16:4 provides reserves for replacement of such items as the roof, furnace, air conditioning, plumbing, electrical and exterior paint and so forth. Nonetheless, as the building ages the style of the building will become dated, the neighborhood will change and the structure will experience physical deterioration. Allowance for this is usually accounted for in the selection of the capitalization rate. The less functional, economic and physical obsolescence that is expected to take place, the lower the acceptable "cap" rate and vice versa.

Fictional Depreciation

In contrast to actual depreciation, there is the **fictional depreciation** that the U.S. Treasury allows income property owners to deduct as an expense when calculating income taxes. In late 1985, for example, the Treasury allowed the purchaser of an apartment building to completely depreciate the structure over a period of 19 years regardless of the age or condition of the structure. More often than not, 19 years was an understatement of the remaining life of the structure; but it was chosen by Congress as an incentive to invest in real estate, and not as an accurate gauge of a property's life. Thus it was quite common to see depreciation claimed on buildings that were in reality appreciating because of rising income from rents and/or falling capitalization rates.

For certain types of real property, some approaches are more suitable than others. This is especially true for single-family residences. Here you must rely almost entirely on the market and cost approaches as very few houses are sold on their ability to generate cash rent. Unless you can develop a measure of the "psychic income" in home ownership, relying heavily on rental value will lead to a property value below the market and cost approaches. Applying all three approaches to special-purpose buildings may also prove to be impractical. For example, in valuing a college or university campus or a state capitol building, the income and market approaches have only limited applicability.

CHOICE OF APPROACHES

When appraising a property that is bought for investment purposes such as an apartment building, shopping center, office building or warehouse, the income approach is the primary method of valuation. As a cross-check on the income approach, an apartment building should be compared to other apartment buildings on a price per apartment unit basis or price per square foot basis. Similarly, an office, store or warehouse can be compared to other recent office, store or warehouse sales on a price per square foot basis. Additionally, the cost approach can be used to determine if it would be cheaper to buy land and build rather than buy an existing building.

It is important to realize that the appraised value is the appraiser's best *estimate* of the subject property's worth. Thus, no matter how painstakingly it is done, property valuation requires the appraiser to make many subjective judgments. Because of this, it is not unusual for three highly qualified appraisers to look at the same property and produce three different appraised values. It is also important to recognize that an appraisal is made as of a specific date. It is not a certificate of value, good forever until used. If a property was valued at $115,000 on January 5th of this year, the more time that has elapsed since that date, the less accurate that value is as an indication of the property's current worth.

APPRAISER'S BEST ESTIMATE

An appraisal does not take into consideration the financial condition of the owner, the owner's health, sentimental attachment or any other personal matter. An appraisal does not guarantee the property will sell for the appraised market value. (The buyer and the seller determine the actual selling price.) Nor does buying at the appraised market value guarantee a future profit for the purchaser. (The real estate market can change.) An appraisal is not a guarantee that the roof will not leak, that there are no termites, or that everything in the building works. An appraisal is not an offer to buy, although a buyer can order one made so as to know how much to offer. An appraisal is not a loan commitment, although a lender can order one made so as to apply a loan-to-value ratio when making a loan.

THE APPRAISAL REPORT

There are four methods by which valuation findings and conclusions are reported: oral, letter, form and narrative.

Oral Report

An **oral report** is an appraisal delivered to a client orally without supporting written evidence. It is often given over the telephone or at a meeting. The advantage is that time is saved by not having to write a description of all the comparables and the adjustments made. The disadvantage of an oral report is the lack of written evidence as to what was said. Consequently, it is good practice not to make oral reports without written follow-up as there is too much chance of being misquoted—intentionally or unintentionally.

Appraisal Letter

An **appraisal letter** is a report in the form of a business letter. In it the appraiser identifies the property and the rights being appraised, states his value conclusion and provides highlights of the facts used in drawing that conclusion. An appraisal letter is usually one or two pages long.

Form Appraisal

A **form appraisal** report is an appraisal made on a preprinted form. The objective is to reduce the amount of time the appraiser must spend on reporting findings and conclusions and to standardize the information the lender is seeking. For example, the FHA and VA have developed a form that must accompany all FHA and VA loan applications. Freddie Mac and Fannie Mae also have a jointly developed appraisal form to be used for loans sold to them. Standardized appraisal forms have been a major step in making it possible to have a large secondary mortgage market. Standardized forms also allow greater use of computers in making and preparing appraisals for home loan applications. There are computer programs on the market that allow a person to enter appraisal data on a computer terminal and have the resulting appraisal typed out on appraisal forms that are tractor-fed through a printer.

A **narrative appraisal** is a complete report by the appraiser and typically runs 10 to 100 pages and sometimes longer. In it the appraiser reports on everything pertinent to the property and the market for the property and gives his value conclusion. This thoroughness allows the reader to follow in detail the appraiser's reasoning. After identifying the property and the rights being appraised, a narrative report will include detailed information on the objective of the appraisal assignment; the definition of value as used in the report; regional, city and neighborhood influences on value; economic trends; the physical characteristics of the land and its improvements; the condition of title; the zoning; a survey or map; photographs of the property; and a statement as to the property's highest and best use. Each comparable sale is reported with its sale details and all facts used are identified as to their sources. The appraiser concludes by showing how the information was analyzed in order to value the property.

Narrative Appraisal

Choosing an appraisal format depends on the information needed and how much money can be spent to obtain it. A person desiring to list a home for sale will probably choose a competitive market analysis. A lender asked to make a home loan will want a form appraisal that will satisfy the secondary mortgage market. A prospective buyer who wants to know the value of a four-unit apartment building (fourplex) would probably select an appraisal letter. An out-of-state investor considering a 200-unit apartment building would probably want a narrative report. A government agency purchasing under eminent domain will usually require a narrative report.

Format Choice

If you offer to appraise property for others, make certain you have the training and experience necessary to do the job correctly. Do not imply expertise if you do not possess it. Always conclude an appraisal with a written report of the facts

PROFESSIONAL LIABILITY

you used and your analysis. These are strongly worded statements; however, a real estate practitioner can quickly get into trouble with clients and licensing authorities by giving offhand estimates of value upon which someone relies and thereby suffers a loss. Practitioners who expect to prepare competitive market analysis forms should develop expertise in how to do this accurately.

CHARACTERISTICS OF VALUE

Up to this point we have been concerned primarily with value based on evidence found in the marketplace and how to report it. Before concluding this chapter, let us briefly touch on what creates value, the principles of real property valuation and appraisal for purposes other than market value.

For a good or service to have value in the marketplace it must possess four characteristics: demand, utility, scarcity and transferability. **Demand** is a need or desire coupled with the purchasing power to fill it, whereas **utility** is the ability of a good or service to fill that need. **Scarcity** means there must be a short supply relative to demand. Air, for example, has utility and is in demand, but it is not scarce. Finally, a good or service must be **transferable** to have value to anyone other than the person possessing it.

PRINCIPLES OF VALUE

The **principle of anticipation** reflects the fact that what a person will pay for a property depends on the expected benefits from the property in the future. Thus, the buyer of a home anticipates receiving shelter plus the investment and psychic benefits of home ownership. The investor buys property in anticipation of future income.

The **principle of substitution** states that the maximum value of a property in the marketplace tends to be set by the cost of purchasing an equally desirable substitute property provided no costly delay is encountered in making the substitution. In other words, substitution sets an upper limit on price. Thus, if there are two similar houses for sale, or two similar apartments for rent, the lowest priced one will generally be purchased or rented first. In the same manner, the cost of buying land and constructing a new building sets a limit on the value of existing buildings.

The **highest and best use** of a property is that use which will give the property its greatest current value. This means you must be alert to the possibility that the present use of a parcel of land may not be the use that makes the land the most valuable. Consider a 30-year-old house located at a busy intersection in a shopping area. To place a value on that property based on its continued use as a residence would be misleading if the property would be worth more with the house removed and shopping or commercial facilities built on the land instead.

Principle of Highest and Best Use

The **principle of competition** recognizes that where substantial profits are being made, competition will be encouraged. For example, if apartment rents increase to the point where owners of existing apartment buildings are making substantial profits, builders and investors will be encouraged to build more apartment buildings.

Applied to real estate, the **principle of supply and demand** refers to the ability of people to pay for land coupled with the relative scarcity of land. This means that attention must be given to such matters on the demand side as population growth, personal income and preferences of people. On the supply side, you must look at the available supply of land and its relative scarcity. When the supply of land is limited and demand is great, the result is rising land prices. Conversely, where land is abundant and there are relatively few buyers, supply and demand will be in balance at only a few cents per square foot.

Supply and Demand

The **principle of change** reminds us that real property uses are always in a state of change. Although it may be imperceptible on a day-to-day basis, change can easily be seen when longer periods of time are considered. Because the present value of a property is related to its future uses, the more potential changes that can be identified, the more accurate the estimate of its present worth.

The principle of **diminishing marginal returns,** also called the **principle of contribution,** refers to the relationship between added cost and the value it returns. It tells us that we should invest dollars whenever they will return to us more than

Diminishing Marginal Returns

$1 of value and should stop when each dollar invested returns less than $1 in value.

The **principle of conformity** holds that maximum value is realized when a reasonable degree of homogeneity is present in a neighborhood. This is the basis for zoning laws across the country; certain tracts in a community are zoned for single-family houses, others for apartment buildings, stores and industry. Within a tract there should also be a reasonable amount of homogeneity. For example, a $200,000 house would be out of place in a neighborhood of $90,000 houses.

MULTIPLE MEANINGS OF THE WORD "VALUE"

When we hear the word "value," we tend to think of market value. However, at any given moment in time, a single property can have other values too. This is because value or worth is very much affected by the purpose for which the valuation was performed. For example, **assessed value** is the value given a property by the county tax assessor for purposes of property taxation. **Estate tax value** is the value that federal and state taxation authorities establish for a deceased person's property; it is used to calculate the amount of estate taxes that must be paid. **Insurance value** is concerned with the cost of replacing damaged property. It differs from market value in two major respects: (1) the value of the land is not included, as it is presumed only the structures are destructible, and (2) the amount of coverage is based on the replacement cost of the structures. **Loan value** is the value set on a property for the purpose of making a loan.

Plottage Value

When two or more adjoining parcels are combined into one large parcel it is called **assemblage.** The increased value of the large parcel over and above the sum of the smaller parcels is called **plottage value.** For example, local zoning laws may permit a six-unit apartment building on a single 10,000-square-foot lot. However, if two of these lots can be combined, zoning laws permit 15 units. This makes the lots more valuable if sold together.

Rental value is the value of a property expressed in terms of the right to its use for a specific period of time. The fee simple interest in a house may have a market value of $80,000, whereas the market value of one month's occupancy might be

$600. **Replacement value** is value as measured by the current cost of building a structure of equivalent utility. **Salvage value** is what a structure is worth if it has to be removed and taken elsewhere, either in whole or dismantled for parts. Because salvage operations require much labor the salvage value of most buildings is usually very low.

This list of values is not exhaustive, but it points out that the word "value" has many meanings. When reading an appraisal report, always read the first paragraph to see why the appraisal was prepared. Before preparing an appraisal, make certain you know its purpose and then state it at the beginning of your report.

Whenever supply and demand are unbalanced because of excess supply, a **buyer's market** exists. This means a buyer can negotiate prices and terms more to his liking and a seller, who wants to sell must accept them. When the imbalance occurs because demand exceeds supply, it is a **seller's market** and sellers are able to negotiate prices and terms more to their liking as buyers compete for the available merchandise.

BUYER'S AND SELLER'S MARKETS

A **broad market** means that many buyers and sellers are in the market at the same time. This makes it relatively easy to establish the price of a property and for a seller to find a buyer quickly, and vice versa. A **thin market** is said to exist when there are only a few buyers and a few sellers in the market at the same time. It is oftentimes difficult to appraise a property in a thin market because there are so few sales to use as comparables.

During the 1930s, two well-known professional appraisal societies were organized: The **American Institute of Real Estate Appraisers** (AIREA) and the **Society of Real Estate Appraisers.** Although a person offering services as a real estate appraiser need not be associated with either of these groups, there are advantages in membership. Both organizations have developed designation systems to recognize appraisal education, experience and competence. Within the AIREA, the highest-level designation is the MAI (Member of the Appraisal Institute). To be an MAI requires a 4-year college degree or equivalent education, various AIREA courses, examinations, an

PROFESSIONAL APPRAISAL SOCIETIES

income property demonstration appraisal and at least 5 years of appraisal experience including 3 years in non-single-family real estate. There are about 5,000 MAIs in the United States. Also available is the RM (Residential Member) designation that requires a high school education, appraisal course work, a passing appraisal examination score, a residential demonstration appraisal and 3 years of experience in residential real estate.

The highest designations offered by the Society of Real Estate Appraisers are the SREA (Senior Real Estate Analyst) and SRPA (Senior Real Property Appraiser). For members specializing in residential appraisal, the professional designation is SRA (Senior Residential Appraiser). The SRA designation requires completion of basic courses in real estate appraisal, economics and statistics, an examination on appraising and a residential appraisal demonstration report. To this the SRPA designation adds requirements for advanced course work in real estate appraisal plus an income property demonstration appraisal. For the SREA designation, further advanced course work and written and oral examinations on real estate market analysis are necessary. For all designations, the applicant must have field experience and submit actual appraisals for review by the Society.

In addition to the Institute and the Society there are several other professional appraisal organizations in the United States. They are the National Association of Independent Fee Appraisers, the Farm Managers and Rural Appraisers, the National Society of Real Estate Appraisers and the American Society of Appraisers. All exist to promote and maintain high standards of appraisal services and all offer a variety of appraisal education and designation programs.

Appraisal License　　　Several states require that any person who appraises real estate for a fee must hold a license to do so. Depending on the state, this may be a regular real estate sales or broker license or a special appraiser's license. If you plan to make appraisals for a fee (apart from appraisal in connection with listing or selling a property as a licensed real estate salesperson or broker) make inquiry to your state's real estate licensing department as to appraisal licensing requirements.

Match terms **a–z** *with statements* **1–26.**

a. *Adjustments*
b. *Appraise*
c. *Buyer's market*
d. *Capitalize*
e. *Comparables*
f. *Competitive market analysis*
g. *Cost approach*
h. *Curable depreciation*
i. *Depreciation*
j. *Functional obsolescence*
k. *Gross rent multiplier*
l. *Highest and best use*
m. *Income approach*

n. *Incurable depreciation*
o. *Market approach*
p. *Market value*
q. *Net operating income*
r. *Operating expenses*
s. *Physical deterioration*
t. *Principle of substitution*
u. *Replacement cost*
v. *Reproduction cost*
w. *Scheduled gross*
x. *Square-foot method*
y. *Subject property*
z. *Thin market*

1. Properties similar to the subject property that have sold recently.
2. Cost, at today's prices and using today's methods of construction, to build an improvement having the same usefulness as the subject property.
3. Cost at today's prices of constructing an exact replica of the subject improvements using the same or similar methods.
4. A method of valuing property based on the prices of recent sales of similar properties.
5. Land value plus current construction costs less depreciation.
6. The property that is being appraised.
7. Corrections made to comparable properties to account for differences between them and the subject property.
8. A property valuation and listing technique that looks at properties currently for sale, recent sales and properties that did not sell, and which does not make specific dollar adjustments for differences.
9. Depreciation resulting from wear and tear of the improvements.
10. Depreciation resulting from improvements that are inadequate, overly adequate or improperly designed for today's needs.
11. The estimated rent a fully occupied property can be expected to produce on an annual basis.
12. To convert future income to current value.
13. Gross income less operating expenses, vacancies and collection losses.
14. Expenditures necessary to maintain the production of income.
15. Acts as an upper limit on prices; the lower priced of two similar properties will usually sell first.

16. To estimate the value of something.
17. A method of valuing property based on the monetary return it is expected to produce.
18. A number that is multiplied by a property's gross rents to produce an estimate of its worth.
19. A method for estimating construction costs that is based on the cost per square foot to build a structure.
20. Depreciation that can be fixed at reasonable cost.
21. Depreciation that cannot be fixed at reasonable cost.
22. A market with more sellers than buyers.
23. A market where there are few buyers and few sellers.
24. That use of a parcel of land that will produce the greatest current value for the parcel.
25. Loss in value due to deterioration and obsolescence.
26. The cash price that a willing buyer and a willing seller would agree upon, given reasonable exposure of the property to the marketplace, full information as to the potential uses of the property and no undue compulsion to act.

QUESTIONS AND PROBLEMS

1. When making a market comparison appraisal, how many comparable properties should be used?
2. How useful are asking prices and offers to buy when making a market comparison appraisal?
3. In the market approach, are the adjustments made to the subject property or to the comparables? Why?
4. Why is it important when valuing vacant land that comparable properties have similar zoning, neighborhoods, size and usefulness?
5. Explain the use of gross rent multipliers in valuing real properties. What are the strengths and the weaknesses of this method?
6. What are the five steps used in valuing an improved property by the cost approach?
7. Briefly explain the concept of the income approach to valuing real property.
8. Explain how the competitive market analysis method differs from the standard market approach method. Which method is better? And for what?
9. What precaution does the principle of diminishing marginal returns suggest to a real estate owner?
10. With regard to appraising a single-family house, what type of appraisal format would most likely be requested by a lender? A prospective buyer? An executor of an estate? A highway department?

Appraising Real Property by **Byrl Boyce** and **William Kinnard, Jr.** (The Society of Real Estate Appraisers, 1984, 514 pages). Provides a first exposure to the principles and techniques of real property valuation with special emphasis on residential properties. Follows the Society's Appraisal 101 course.

Base 1000: The Vaughn Method of Appraising Houses by **Charles Vaughn.** (Reston, 1984, 224 pages). Book covers essential factors in appraising houses including site, neighborhood, size, construction, quality, financing, and market conditions. Teaches how to make allowances for positive or negative influences on value and how to arrive at separate values for land and improvements.

Basic Real Estate Appraisal by **Richard Betts** and **Silas Ely.** (Wiley, 1982, 367 pages). A readable and attractively laid-out book that explains appraisal theory and its application in the field. Numerous photographs and illustrations.

Fundamentals of Real Estate Appraisal, 3rd ed. by **William Ventolo, Jr.,** and **Martha Williams.** (Real Estate Education Co., 1983, 338 pages). Book relates appraisal theory to practical application. Generous use of examples to illustrate market, cost and income approaches.

"Pricing Practicalities" by **David Beson.** (*Real Estate Today,* Sep. 84, page 42). Article explains the realities of a competitive market to prospective home sellers.

Residential Cost Handbook. (**Marshall** and **Swift,** 1986, 200 pages). Provides cost of construction information for residential structures. Binder-style book is updated every three months and contains adjustments for various cities in the United States.

The Appraisal of Real Estate, 8th ed. (American Institute of Real Estate Appraisers, Chicago, 1983, 750 pages). Covers the fundamental concepts of real estate value and its estimation by the market, cost and income approaches.

The Appraisal of Rural Property. (American Institute of Real Estate Appraisal, Chicago, 1983, 434 pages). Contains principles, data collection and value estimation for farms, ranches, vineyards, orchards, dairyland, timberland and agricultural land in transition. One of many specialized appraisal books, monographs and articles published by the AIREA.

*   *   *

The following periodicals may also be of interest to you: *Appraisal Journal, Appraisal Review, Appraisal Review Journal, Appraisal Digest, Appraisal Institute Digest, Appraisal Institute Magazine, Boeckh Building Cost Index Numbers, Real Estate Appraiser and Analyst* and *Real Estate Appraiser.*

ADDITIONAL READINGS

The Owner–Broker Relationship

KEY TERMS

Agent: the person empowered to act by and on behalf of the principal

Broker: one who acts as an agent for others in negotiating contracts

Commingling: the mixing of clients' or customers' funds with an agent's personal funds

Dual agency: representation of two or more parties in a transaction by the same agent

Exclusive right to sell: a listing that gives the broker the right to collect a commission no matter who sells the property during the listing period

Listing: a contract wherein a broker is employed to find a buyer or tenant

Middleman: a person who brings two or more parties together but does not conduct negotiations

Principal: a person who authorizes another to act

Puffing: statements a reasonable person would recognize as nonfactual or extravagant

Ready, willing and able buyer: a buyer who is ready to buy at the seller's price and terms and who has the financial capability to do so

Third parties: persons who are not parties to a contract but who may be affected by it

For most owners of real estate the decision to sell means hiring a broker to find a buyer. Although some owners choose to market their properties themselves, most find it advantageous to turn the job over to a real estate broker and pay a commission for the service of finding a buyer and carrying the deal through closing. This chapter and the next are for the owner who plans to use a broker and for the person who plans to be a real estate salesperson or broker. We begin with a simplified real estate listing contract. Next we take a close look at the agency responsibilities a broker has toward a seller together with the seller's obligations toward the broker. Then we discuss seller and broker responsibilities toward persons who are interested in purchasing the listed property. This chapter concludes with property disclosure laws and fair housing laws. Looking ahead, the next chapter focuses on how to enter the

415

real estate profession. Chapter 18 starts with examination and licensing requirements and an overview of how states regulate the real estate profession. This is followed by a section on how to choose a broker with whom to affiliate and a section on professional real estate associations, in particular the National Association of Realtors.

LISTING AGREEMENT

A **real estate listing** is an *employment contract* between a property owner and a real estate broker. By it the property owner appoints the broker as the owner's agent for the specific purpose of finding a buyer or tenant who is willing to meet the conditions set forth in the listing. It does not authorize the broker to sell or convey title to the property or to sign contracts.

Although persons licensed as real estate salespersons perform listing and sales functions, they are actually extensions of the broker. A seller may conduct all aspects of a listing and sale through a salesperson licensee, but it is the broker behind the salesperson with whom the seller has the listing contract and who is legally liable for its proper execution. If you plan to be a salesperson for a broker, be aware of what is legally and ethically required of a broker as you are a broker's eyes, ears, hands and mouth. If your interest is in listing your property with a broker, know that it is the broker with whom you have the listing contract even though your day-to-day contact is with the broker's sales associates. **Sales associates** are the licensed salespersons or brokers who work for a broker.

When a property owner signs a listing, all the essential elements of a valid contract must be present. The owner and broker must be legally capable of contracting, there must be mutual assent, and the agreement must be for a lawful purpose. Nearly all states require that a listing be in writing and signed to be valid and thereby enforceable in a court of law.

Figure 17:1 illustrates a simplified **exclusive right to sell listing** agreement. Actual listing contracts tend to be longer and more complex and vary in detail from one contract to the next. The listing in Figure 17:1 is an educational introduction to listings that provides in plain English commonly found listing contract provisions. Beginning at ①, there is a description of the property plus the price and terms at which the broker is instructed to find a buyer. At ②, the broker promises to make a reasonable effort to find a buyer. The period of time that the listing is to be in effect is shown at ③. It is usually to the broker's advantage to make the listing period for as long as possible as this provides more time to find a buyer. Sometimes, even an overpriced property will become saleable if the listing period is long enough and prices rise fast enough. However, most owners want a balance between their flexibility and the amount of time necessary for a broker to conduct a sales campaign. In residential sales, 3 to 4 months is a popular compromise; farm, ranch, commercial and industrial listings are usually made for 6 months to 1 year.

At ④, the owner agrees not to list the property with any other brokers, permit other brokers to have a sign on the property or advertise it during the listing period. Also, the owner agrees not to revoke the broker's exclusive right to find a buyer as set forth by this contract.

The broker recognizes that the owner may later accept price and terms that are different from those in the listing. The wording at ⑤ states that the broker will earn a commission no matter what price and terms the owner ultimately accepts.

At ⑥, the amount of compensation the owner agrees to pay the broker is established. The usual arrangement is to express the amount as a percentage of the sale or exchange price, although a stated dollar amount could be used if the owner and broker agreed. In any event, the amount of the fee is negotiable between the owner and the broker. An owner who feels the fee is too high can list with someone who charges less or sell the property himself. The broker recognizes that if the fee is too low it will not be worthwhile spending time and effort finding a buyer. The typical commission fee in the United States at present is 5% to 7% of the selling price for houses, condominiums and small apartment buildings and 6% to 10% on farms, ranches and vacant land. On multimillion-dollar improved properties, commissions usually drop to the 2% to 4% range. Brokerage commissions are not set by a state regulatory agency or by local real estate boards. In fact, any effort by brokers to set commission rates among themselves is a violation of federal and state anti-trust laws. The penalty can be as much as triple damages and criminal liability.

Brokerage Commission

Figure 17:1

EXCLUSIVE RIGHT TO SELL
LISTING CONTRACT

① *Property Description:* A single-family house at 2424 E. Main Street, City, State. Legally described as Lot 17, Tract 191, County, State.

Price: $105,000

Terms: Cash

② *In consideration of the services of* ABC Realty Company *(herein called the "Broker"), to be rendered to* Roger Leeving and Mary Leeving *(herein called the "Owner"), and the promise of said Broker to make reasonable efforts to obtain a purchaser, therefore, the Owner hereby grants to the Broker*

③ *for the period of time from noon on* April 1, 19xx *to noon on* July 1, 19xx *(herein called the "listing period")*

④ *the exclusive and irrevocable right to advertise and find a purchaser for the above described property at the price and terms shown*

⑤ *or for such sum and terms or exchange as the owner later agrees to accept.*

⑥ *The Owner hereby agrees to pay Broker a cash fee of* 6% *of the selling or exchange price:*

⑦ *(A) in case of any sale or exchange of the above property within the listing period either by the Broker, the Owner or any person, or*

⑧ *(B) upon the Broker finding a purchaser who is ready, willing, and able to complete the purchase as proposed by the owner, or*

⑨ *(C) in the event of a sale or exchange within 60 days of the expiration of the listing period to any party shown the above property during the listing period by the Broker or his representative and where the name was disclosed to the Owner.*

⑩ *The Owner agrees to give the Broker access to the buildings on the property for the purposes of showing them at reasonable hours and allows the Broker to post a "For Sale" sign on the premises.*

⑪ *The Owner agrees to allow the Broker to place this listing information in any multiple listing organization of which he is a member and to engage the cooperation of other brokers as subagents to bring about a sale.*

⑫ *The Owner agrees to refer to the Broker all inquiries regarding this property during the listing period.*

⑬ *Accepted:*

ABC Realty Company

By: *Kurt Kwiklister*

Owner: *Roger Leeving*

Owner: *Mary Leeving*

Date: April 1, 19xx

The conditions under which a commission must be paid by the owner to the broker appear next. At ⑦, a commission is deemed to be earned if the owner agrees to a sale or exchange of the property no matter who finds the buyer. In other words, even if the owner finds a buyer, or a friend of the owner finds a buyer, the broker is entitled to a full commission fee. If the owner disregards the promise at ④ and lists with another broker who then sells the property, the owner is liable for two full commissions.

The wording at ⑧ is included to protect the broker against the possibility that the owner may refuse to sell after the broker has expended time and effort to find a buyer at the price and terms of the listing contract. The listing itself is not an offer to sell property. It is strictly a contract whereby the owner employs the broker to find a buyer. Thus, even though a buyer offers to pay the exact price and terms shown in the listing, the buyer does not have a binding sales contract until the offer is accepted in writing by the owner. However, if the owner refuses to sell at the listed price and terms, the broker is still entitled to a commission. If the owner does not pay the broker voluntarily, the broker can file a lawsuit against the owner to collect.

Protecting the Broker

Protecting the Owner   At ⑨, the broker is protected against the possibility that the listing period will expire while still working with a prospective purchaser. In fairness to the owner, however, two limitations are placed on the broker. First, a sales contract must be concluded within a reasonable time after the listing expires, and second, the name of the purchaser must have been given to the owner before the listing period expires.

Continuing at ⑩, the owner agrees to let the broker enter the property at reasonable hours to show it and put a "For Sale" sign on the property. At ⑪, the property owner gives the broker specific permission to enter the property into a multiple listing service and to engage the cooperation of other brokers as subagents to bring about a sale.

At ⑫, the owner agrees to refer all inquiries regarding the availability of the property to the broker. The purpose is to discourage the owner from thinking that he might be able to save a commission by personally selling it during the listing period, and to provide sales leads for the broker. Finally, at ⑬, the owner and the broker (or the broker's sales associate if authorized to do so) sign and date the agreement.

EXCLUSIVE RIGHT TO SELL LISTING

The listing illustrated in Figure 17:1 is called an **exclusive right to sell** or **exclusive authorization to sell** listing. Its distinguishing characteristic is that no matter who sells the property during the listing period, the listing broker is entitled to a commission. This is the most widely used type of listing in the United States. Once signed by the owner and accepted by the broker, the primary advantage to the broker is that the money and effort the broker expends on advertising and showing the property will be to the broker's benefit. The advantage to the owner is that the broker will usually put more effort into selling a property if the broker holds an exclusive right to sell than if the broker has an exclusive agency or an open listing.

EXCLUSIVE AGENCY LISTING

The **exclusive agency listing** is similar to the listing shown in Figure 17:1, except that the owner may sell the property himself during the listing period and not owe a commission to the broker. The broker, however, is the only broker who can act as an agent during the listing period; hence the term exclusive agency. For an owner, this may seem like the best of two worlds: the owner has a broker looking for a buyer, but if the owner finds a buyer first, the owner can save a commission fee. The broker is less enthusiastic because the broker's efforts can too easily be undermined by the owner. Consequently, the broker may not expend as much effort on advertising and showing the property as with an exclusive right to sell.

Open listings carry no exclusive rights. An owner can give *OPEN LISTING* an open listing to any number of brokers at the same time, and the owner can still find a buyer and avoid a commission. This gives the owner the greatest freedom of any listing form, but there is little incentive for the broker to expend time and money showing the property as the broker has little control over who will be compensated if the property is sold. The broker's only protection is that if the broker does find a buyer at the listing price and terms, the broker is entitled to a commission. This reluctance to develop a sales effort usually means few, if any, offers will be received and may result in no sale or a sale below market price. Yet, if a broker does find a buyer, the commission earned may be the same as with an exclusive right to sell.

A **net listing** is created when an owner states the price he *NET LISTING* wants for his property and then agrees to pay the broker anything above that price as the commission. It can be written in the form of an exclusive right to sell, an exclusive agency or an open listing. If a homeowner asks for a "net $60,000" and the broker sells the home for $65,000, the commission would be $5,000. By using the net listing method, many owners feel that they are forcing the broker to look to the buyer for the commission by marking up the price of the property. In reality though, would a buyer pay $65,000 for a home that is worth $60,000? Because of widespread misunderstanding regarding net listings, some states prohibit them outright, and most brokers strenuously avoid them even when requested by property owners. There is no law that says a broker must accept a listing; a broker is free to accept only those listings for which the broker can perform a valuable service and earn an honest profit.

Traditionally, real estate brokers charge a fee for their ser- *ADVANCE FEE LISTING* vices based on a percentage of the sales price. Out of this percentage the broker (1) pays all out-of-pocket costs of marketing the property such as advertising and office overhead, (2) pays those who negotiate the transaction, and (3) earns a profit for the firm. If a buyer is not found, the broker receives no money. This means commissions earned from sold properties must also pay for costs incurred by nonsales. Sellers who have marketable property that is priced to sell subsidize sellers whose property is either unattractive or overpriced. As a solution to this inequity, attention is now being given by the real estate industry to the concept of advance fee listings and advance cost listings.

An **advance fee listing** is a listing wherein a broker charges a seller much like an attorney charges a client. In other words, the broker asks for an advance deposit from the seller. Against this the broker charges an hourly fee for time spent selling the property plus out-of-pocket expenses. With the seller paying for services as consumed, the seller becomes much more realistic about marketability and listed price. There is less inclination to price above market in hopes that if the broker works long enough, a buyer might be found who will pay above market or that the market will eventually rise to the asking price.

Advance Cost Listing

An **advance cost listing** covers only out-of-pocket costs incurred by the broker such as advertising, multiple listing fees, flyers, mailings, toll calls, survey, soil report, title report, travel expenses and food served during open houses. With either the advance fee or advance cost arrangement the broker can still charge a commission based on sales price. In this case costs and hourly fees are deducted from the commission at the closing. With the broker receiving payment for costs (and effort) up front, the sales commission can be lowered.

The mechanics of advance fee and advance cost listings must be very clearly explained to the seller before the listing is signed. There must be an accurate accounting of where the seller's money is being spent, a simple example of which is shown in Figure 17:2. (This is an ideal task for a computer.) Moreover, state real estate regulators may have specific rules and prohibitions that must be followed. Watch the advance fee trend in the late 1980s and the 1990s. If it takes hold, it will be an important factor in changing real estate agents from commissioned salespeople to professionals who can command an hourly fee for their time.

ACCOUNTING OF CHARGES   Figure 17:2

For April 1–15

April 1	Consultation and property valuation, 3 hours at $xx	$ yy
April 2	For sale sign deposit and installation	yy
April 2	Prepare newspaper ad and flyer, 1 hour at $xx	yy
April 3	Printing and postage for 300 flyers	yy
April 4	Newspaper advertising costs for April 4–7	yy
April 7	Hold open house, 3 hours at $xx	yy
April 8	Talk to and qualify prospects in office, 1 hour at $xx	yy
April 8	Newspaper advertising for April 8–15	yy
April 9	Talk to and qualify prospects in office, 2 hours at $xx	yy
April 10	Talk to seller about results to date, 1 hour at $xx	yy
April 14	Hold open house, 3 hours at $xx	yy
April 15	Negotiate with buyer and seller, 2 hours at $xx	yy
	Total for April 1–15	$zzz

MULTIPLE LISTING SERVICE

Multiple listing service (MLS) organizations enable a broker with a listing to make a blanket offering of subagency to other brokers, thus broadening the market exposure for a given property. Member brokers are authorized to show each others' properties to their prospects. If a sale results, the commission is divided between the broker who found the buyer and the broker who obtained the listing, less a small deduction for the cost of operating the multiple listing service.

Market Exposure

A property listed with a broker who is a multiple listing service member receives the advantage of greater sales exposure which, in turn, means a better price and a quicker sale. For the buyer it means learning about what is for sale at many offices without having to visit each individually. For a broker or salesperson with a prospect but not a suitable property listed in that office, the opportunity to make a sale is not lost because the prospect can be shown the listings of other brokers.

To give a property the widest possible market exposure and to maintain fairness among its members, most multiple listing organizations obligate each member broker to provide information to the organization on each new listing within three to seven days after the listing is taken. To facilitate the exchange of information, multiple listing organizations have developed customized listing forms. These forms are a combination of an exclusive right-to-sell listing agreement (with authority to place the listing into multiple) plus a data sheet on the property. The data sheet, which describes all the physical and financial characteristics of the property, and a photograph of the property are published weekly in a multiple listing book which is distributed to MLS members. Then, if Broker B has a prospect interested in a property listed by Broker A, Broker B telephones Broker A and arranges to show the property. If Broker B's prospect makes an offer on the property, Broker B contacts Broker A and together they call on the seller with the offer.

Court Issues   MLS organizations have been taken to court for being open only to members of local real estate boards. This has now changed and any licensed broker can join. The role that multiple listing services directly or indirectly play in commission splitting is also being tested in courts. Another idea that will likely be tested in courts is that an MLS be open to anyone who wants to list a property, broker or owner. Proponents say that an owner should be able to advertise in an MLS just like in a newspaper. Opponents feel that owners lacking real estate sophistication would place much inaccurate information in the MLS and this would do considerable harm to MLS members who must rely on that information when describing and showing properties.

Computerized MLS   In addition to publishing MLS books, a number of multiple listing services store their listing information in computers. A salesperson with a briefcase-sized MLS terminal can take any telephone, dial the MLS computer, place the handpiece on the terminal and request up-to-the minute information for any property in the computer. This is a popular system with salespeople who are constantly in the field showing property or in their cars (where they can link up by cellular telephone). It is also quicker than waiting for updated printed MLS information.

Videodisc   Electronic advances now make it possible to give a prospective buyer a visual tour through a neighborhood without leaving the broker's office. A single videodisc can store over 100,000 still photographs of individual properties, neighborhoods, schools, shopping centers, recreation facilities, etc. The discs are professionally shot and duplicated and made available to real estate offices for a fee. So large is the storage capacity of a disc that every property in a community can be photographed and placed on the disc. In the real estate office a salesperson can play back any image on the disc onto a television screen. With an MLS book in hand, the salesperson can show a prospect a color picture of each property for sale along with pictures of the street and neighborhood, plus nearby schools and shopping facilities. Realty offices with computerized access to MLS files can interface the videodisc with the MLS computer.

The broker earns a commission at whatever point in the transaction he and the owner agree upon. In nearly all listing contracts this point occurs when the broker produces a **"ready, willing and able buyer"** at price and terms acceptable to the owner. (See ⑧ in Figure 17:1.) "Ready and willing" means a buyer who is ready to buy at the seller's price and terms. "Able" means financially capable of completing the transaction. An alternative arrangement is for the broker and owner to agree to a "no sale, no commission" arrangement whereby the broker is not entitled to a commission until the transaction is closed.

The difference between the two arrangements becomes important when a buyer is found at price and terms acceptable to the owner, but no sale results. The "ready, willing and able" contract provides more protection for the broker as the commission does not depend on the deal reaching settlement. The "no sale, no commission" approach is to the owner's advantage, for commission payment is not required unless there is a completed sale. Court decisions have tended to blur the clear-cut distinction between the two. For example, if the owner has a "no sale, no commission" agreement, it would appear that if the broker found a ready, willing and able buyer at the listing price and terms and the owner refused to sell, the owner would owe no commission for there was no sale. However, a court of law would find in favor of the broker for the full amount of the

BROKER
COMPENSATION

commission if the refusal to sell was arbitrary and without reasonable cause or in bad faith.

Another change that is taking place is that traditionally it was up to the owner to decide if the buyer was, in fact, financially able to buy. The legal thinking today is that the broker should be responsible because he is in a much better position to analyze the buyer's financial ability than the owner.

PROCURING CAUSE

A broker under an open listing or an exclusive agency listing is entitled to a commission if the broker was the procuring cause of the sale and can prove it. **Procuring cause** means that it was the broker's efforts that originated the sale. Suppose that a broker shows an open-listed property to a prospective buyer and, during the listing period or an extension, the prospect goes directly to the owner and concludes a deal. Even though the owner negotiates his own transaction and prepares his own sales contract, the broker is entitled to a full commission for finding the buyer. This would also be true if the owner and the buyer used a subterfuge or strawman to purchase the property to avoid paying a commission. State laws protect the broker who in good faith has produced a buyer at the request of an owner.

When an open listing is given to two or more brokers, the first one who produces a buyer is entitled to the commission. For example, Broker 1 shows a property to Prospect P, but no sale is made. Later P goes to Broker 2 and makes an offer, which is accepted by the owner. Although two brokers have attempted to sell the property, only one has succeeded, and that one is entitled to the commission. The fact that Broker 1 receives nothing, even though he may have expended considerable effort, is an important reason why brokers dislike open listings.

TERMINATING THE LISTING CONTRACT

The usual situation in a listing contract is that the broker finds a buyer acceptable to the owner. Thus, in most listing contracts the agency terminates because the objective of the contract has been completed. In the bulk of the listings for which a buyer is not found, the agency is terminated because the listing period expires. If no listing period is specified, the listing is considered to be effective for a "reasonable" length of time. A court might consider 3 months to be reasonable for a listing on a home and 6 months reasonable for an apartment building or commercial property. Listing contracts without termination dates are revocable by the principal at any time, provided the purpose of the revocation is not to deprive the broker of an earned commission. A major disadvantage of listings without termination dates is that all too often they evolve into expensive and time-consuming legal hassles.

Even when a listing has a specific termination date, it is still possible for the owner to tell the broker to stop showing the property and not to bring any offers. However, liability for breach of the employment aspect of the contract remains and the broker can demand compensation for effort expended on behalf of the owner to that point. This can be as much as a full commission if the broker has already found a ready, willing and able buyer at the owner's price and terms.

Mutual Agreement

A listing can be terminated by mutual agreement of both the owner and broker without money damages. Because listings are the stock in trade of the brokerage business, brokers do not like to lose listings, but sometimes this is the only logical alternative open as the time and effort in setting and collecting damages can be very expensive. Suppose, however, that a broker has an exclusive right-to-sell listing and suspects that the owner's request to cancel is because he has found a buyer and wants to avoid paying a commission. The broker can stop showing the property, but the owner is still obligated to pay a commission if the property is sold before the listing period expires. Whatever the broker and seller decide, they should put it in writing and sign it.

With an open listing, once the property is sold by anyone, broker or owner, all listing agreements pertaining to the property automatically terminate. Similarly, with an exclusive agency listing if the owner sells the property, the broker's listing automatically terminates.

Abandonment, etc.

A listing can be terminated by improper performance or abandonment by the broker. Thus, if a broker acts counter to the owner's best financial interests, the listing is terminated, no commission is payable and the broker may be subject to a lawsuit for any damages suffered by the owner. If a broker takes a listing and then does nothing to promote it, the owner can assume that the broker abandoned it and thereby has grounds for revocation. The owner should keep written documentation in the event the matter ever goes to court.

A listing is automatically terminated by the death of either the owner or the broker, or if either is judged legally incompetent by virtue of insanity or if either becomes bankrupt. Destruction of the listed property also terminates the listing because the object of the listing no longer exists.

DEPOSIT MONEY DISPOSITION

When an earnest money deposit accompanies an offer to buy, the normal procedure is to apply it to the purchase price if the offer is accepted or to return it to the buyer if the offer is rejected. Suppose, however, that the offer is accepted and subsequently the buyer does not fulfill his obligations and forfeits the deposit to the seller as liquidated damages. If the broker is to share in any part of that money, there must be an agreement between the seller and the broker. Such an arrangement is usually made on the binder or sales contract. The most common one is for the broker and owner to agree to split the deposit equally, but with the limitation that the broker's portion not exceed the amount of the commission earned if the transaction had been completed. Not to have such an agreement may leave the broker with nothing for the effort and the owner with all the forfeited deposit.

BARGAIN BROKERS

The full-service real estate broker who takes a listing and places it in multiple, places and pays for advertising, holds open house, qualifies prospects, shows property, obtains offers, negotiates, opens escrow and follows through until closing is the mainstay of the real estate selling industry. The vast majority of all open-market sales are handled that way. The remainder are sold by owners, some handling everything themselves and some using flat-fee brokers who oversee the transaction but do not do the actual showing and selling.

Flat-Fee Brokers

For a fee that typically ranges from $400 to $1,500, a **flat-fee broker** will list a property, suggest a market price, write advertising, assist with negotiations, draw up a sales contract and turn the signed papers over to an escrow company for closing. The homeowner is responsible for paying for advertising, answering inquiries, setting appointments with prospects, showing the property and applying whatever salesmanship is necessary to induce the prospect to make an offer. Under the flat-fee arrangement, also called self-help brokerage, the homeowner is effectively buying real estate services on an a la carte basis. Some brokerage firms have been very successful offering sellers a choice of a la carte or full service.

A **discount broker** is a full-service broker who charges less than the prevailing commission rates in his community. The discount broker attracts sellers by offering to do the job for less money, for example, 3% or 4% instead of 5% to 7%. Charging less means a discount broker must sell more properties to be successful. Consequently, most discount brokers are careful to take listings only on property that will sell quickly and to reject those that won't.

Discount Broker

Before leaving the topic of listings, it will be valuable to spend a moment on the perceived value of real estate sales services. Several studies have been conducted that show home-sellers feel the fee charged by brokers is too high in relation to time spent selling the property. Those in the real estate business know the amount of time and effort to market a property is extensive and that often it is all for nothing if the property does not sell. However, the public does not see this and believes that very little effort is involved, especially if the home sells at market in 2 or 3 weeks after being shown a handful of times. Ironically, a market value sale within a month and without the inconvenience of dozens upon dozens of showings is what the seller is actually seeking, but once obtained, seems too expensive for the time involved. This leads some sellers to think in terms of selling their property themselves, perhaps with the aid of a self-help brokerage service. For example, if a person is selling a $100,000 house with an $80,000 loan against it, there is but $20,000 in equity to work with. If the broker's commission is 6% of the sales price ($6,000), the seller is actually paying 30% of his equity to the broker.

What stops more people from do-it-yourself selling is they need a broker to evaluate the property, describe current market

PERCEIVED VALUE

and financing conditions, estimate the most probable selling price, write the sales contract and handle the closing. To a considerable degree, a real estate licensee's success will come from providing the services homeowners feel they need, listing property at or near market, emphasizing the value of services rendered and operating in a professional manner to bring about a smooth and speedy sale.

AGENCY

Thus far this chapter has stressed the mechanics of real estate listings. Let us now take a close look at the agency aspects of the owner–broker relationship, i.e., the legal responsibilities of the broker toward the seller and vice versa.

An **agency** is created when one person (called the **principal**) delegates to another person (called the **agent**) the right to act on the principal's behalf. There are three levels of agency: universal, general and specific. In a **universal agency** the principal gives the agent legal power to transact matters of all types on the principal's behalf. An example is an unlimited power of attorney. Universal agencies are rarely encountered in practice, and courts generally frown on them because they are so broad. In a **general agency** the agent is given the power to bind the principal in a particular trade or business. For example, a salesperson is a general agent of his or her employing broker. Another example is that of a property manager for a property owner. In a **special agency** the principal empowers the agent to perform a particular act or transaction. One example is a real estate listing. Another is a power of attorney to sign a deed on behalf of someone who will be out of the country.

The principal in an agency relationship can be either a natural person or a legal person such as a corporation. Likewise, an agent can be either a natural person or a corporation such as a real estate brokerage company. The persons and firms with whom the principal and agent negotiate are called **third parties.** You will also hear these third parties referred to as the broker's **customers** and the principal referred to as the broker's **client.** Sometimes you will see the phrase **"principals only"** in real estate advertisements where property is offered for sale by its owner without the aid of a broker. This means the owner wants to be contacted by persons who want to buy and not by real estate agents who want to list the property.

A written listing agreement outlines the agent's (broker's) authority to act on behalf of the principal (owner) and the principal's obligations to the agent. A written agreement is the preferred method of creating an agency because it provides a document to evidence the existence of the agency relationship.

Agency authority may also arise from custom in the industry, common usage and conduct of the parties involved. For example, the right of an agent to post a "For Sale" sign on the listed property may not be expressly stated in the listing. However, if it is the custom in the industry to do so, and presuming there are no deed covenants or city ordinances to the contrary, the agent has **implied authority** to post the sign. A similar situation exists with regard to showing a listed property to prospects. The seller of a home can expect to have it shown on weekends and evenings whereas a commercial property owner would expect showings only during business hours.

Ostensible authority is conferred when a principal gives a third party reason to believe that another person is his agent even though that person is unaware of the appointment. If the third party accepts this as true, the principal may well be bound by the acts of his agent. For example, you give your house key to a plumber with instructions that when he has finished unstopping the waste lines he is to lock the house and give the key to your next door neighbor. Even though you do not call and expressly appoint your neighbor as your agent to receive your key, once the plumber gives the key to your neighbor, your neighbor becomes your agent with regard to that key. Since you told the plumber to leave the key there, he has every reason to believe that you appointed your neighbor as your agent to receive the key.

An **agency by ratification** is one established after the fact. For example, if an agent secures a contract on behalf of a principal and the principal subsequently ratifies or agrees to it, a court may hold that an agency was created at the time the initial negotiations started. An **agency by estoppel** can result when a principal fails to maintain due diligence over his agent and the agent exercises powers not granted to him. If this causes a third party to believe the agent has these powers, an agency by estoppel has been created. An **agency coupled with an interest** is said to exist when an agent holds an interest in

Establishing the Agent's Authority

the property he is representing. For example, a broker is a part-owner in a property he has listed for sale.

BROKER'S
OBLIGATIONS TO
HIS PRINCIPAL

Anytime an agency is created, such as an attorney for a client, a property manager for an owner, or a broker for a seller, a **fiduciary relationship** is created. The agent (called the **fiduciary**) must be faithful to the principal, exhibit trust and honesty, and exercise good business judgment. In other words, the agent owes fidelity to the principal. For a real estate broker this means the broker must faithfully perform the agency agreement, be loyal to the principal, exercise competence and account for all funds handled in performing the agency. Let us look at these various requirements more closely.

Faithful Performance

Faithful performance (also referred to as **obedience**) means that the agent is to obey all legal instructions given by the principal, and to apply best efforts and diligence to carry out the objectives of the agency. For a real estate broker this means performance as promised in the listing contract. A broker who promises to make a "reasonable effort" or apply "diligence" in finding a buyer and then does nothing to promote the listing gives the owner legal grounds for terminating the listing. Faithful performance also means not departing from the principal's instructions. If the agent does so (except in extreme emergencies not foreseen by the principal), it is at the agent's own risk. If the principal thereby suffers a loss, the agent is responsible for that loss. For example, a broker accepts a personal note from a buyer as an earnest money deposit, but fails to tell the seller that the deposit is not in cash. If the seller accepts the offer and the note is later found to be worthless, the broker is liable for the amount of the note.

Another aspect of faithful performance is that the agent must personally perform the tasks delegated to him. This protects the principal who has selected an agent on the basis of trust and confidence from finding that the agent has delegated that responsibility to another person. However, a major question arises on this point in real estate brokerage, as a large part of the success in finding a buyer for a property results from the cooperative efforts of other brokers and their salespeople.

Therefore, listing agreements usually include a statement that the listing broker is authorized to secure the cooperation of other brokers and pay them part of the commission from the sale.

Once an agency is created, the agent must be loyal to the principal. The law is clear in all states that in a listing agreement the broker (and the broker's sales staff) occupy a position of trust, confidence and responsibility. As such, the broker is legally bound to keep the property owner fully informed as to all matters that might affect the sale of the listed property and to promote and protect the owner's interests.

Loyalty to Principal

Unfortunately, greed and expediency sometimes get in the way. As a result, numerous laws have been enacted for the purpose of protecting the principal and threatening the agent with court action for misplaced loyalty. For example, an out-of-town landowner who is not fully up to date on the value of his land visits a local broker and wants to list it for $30,000. The broker is much more knowledgeable of local land prices and is aware of a recent city council decision to extend roads and utilities to the area of this property. As a result, the broker knows the land is now worth $50,000. The broker remains silent on the matter, and the property is listed for sale at $30,000. At this price the broker can find a buyer before the day is over and have a commission on the sale. However, the opportunity for a quick $20,000 is too tempting to let pass. He buys the property (or to cover up, buys in the name of his wife or a friend) and shortly thereafter resells it for $50,000. Whether he sold the property to a buyer for $30,000 or bought it and resold it for $50,000, the broker did not exhibit loyalty to the principal. Laws and penalties for breach of loyalty are stiff: the broker can be sued for recovery of the price difference and the commission paid, his real estate license can be suspended or revoked, and he may be required to pay additional fines and money damages.

If a licensee intends to purchase a property listed for sale by his agency or through a cooperating broker, he is under both a moral and a legal obligation to make certain that the price paid is the fair market value and that the seller knows who the buyer is.

Protecting the Owner's Interest

Loyalty to the principal also means that when seeking a buyer or negotiating a sale, the broker must continue to protect the owner's financial interests. Suppose that an owner lists his home at $82,000 but confides in the broker, "If I cannot get $82,000, anything over $79,000 will be fine." The broker shows the home to a prospect who says, "Eighty-two thousand is too much. What will the owner really take?" or "Will he take seventy-nine thousand?" Loyalty to the principal requires the broker to say that the owner will take $82,000, for that is the price in the listing agreement. If the buyer balks, the broker can suggest that the buyer submit an offer for the seller's consideration. State laws require that all offers be submitted to the owner, no matter what the offering price and terms. This prevents the agent from rejecting an offer that the owner might have accepted if he had known about it. If the seller really intends for the broker to quote $79,000 as an acceptable price, the listing price should be changed; then the broker can say, "The property was previously listed for $82,000, but is now priced at $79,000."

A broker's loyalty to his principal includes keeping the principal informed of changes in market conditions during the listing period. If after a listing is taken an adjacent landowner is successful in rezoning his land to a higher use and the listed property becomes more valuable, the broker's responsibility is to inform the seller. Similarly, if a buyer is looking at a property priced at $30,000 and tells the broker, "I'll offer $27,000 and come up if need be," it is the duty of the broker to report this to the owner. The owner can then decide if he wants to accept the $27,000 offer or try for more. If the broker does not keep the owner fully informed, he is not properly fulfilling his duties as the owner's agent.

Dual Agency

If a broker represents a seller, it is the broker's duty to obtain the highest price and the best terms possible for the seller. If a broker represents a buyer, the broker's duty is to obtain the lowest price and terms for the buyer. When the same broker represents two or more principals in the same transactions, it is a **dual** or **divided agency** and a conflict of interest results. If the broker represents both principals in the same transaction, to whom is the broker loyal? Does he work equally hard for each principal? This is an unanswerable question; therefore, the law requires that each principal be told not to expect the broker's full allegiance and thus each principal is responsible for looking after his own interest. If a broker represents more than one principal and does not obtain their consent, the broker cannot claim a commission and the defrauded principal(s) may be able to rescind the transaction itself. Moreover, the broker's real estate license may be suspended or revoked. This is true even though the broker does his best to be equally fair to each principal.

Dual agency automatically results when one broker represents two or more parties in a real estate exchange. Consequently, the broker must take care to disclose the dual agency in writing before negotiations begin.

A dual agency also develops when a buyer agrees to pay a broker a fee for finding a property and the broker finds one, lists it and earns a fee from the seller as well as the buyer. Again, both the buyer and seller must be informed of the dual agency in advance of negotiations. If either principal does not approve of the dual agency, he can refuse to participate.

A **middleman** is a person who brings together two or more parties who conduct negotiations between themselves without the help of the middleman. If it is clearly understood by all parties involved that the middleman's only purpose was to bring them together, no one expects the middleman's loyalty. If, however, the middleman assists or influences the negotiations, he becomes an agent and is subject to the laws of agency.

Middleman

The duty of **reasonable care** implies competence and expertise on the part of the broker. It is the broker's responsibility to disclose all knowledge and material facts concerning a property to his principal. Also, the broker must not become a party to any fraud or misrepresentation likely to affect the sound judgment of the principal.

Reasonable Care

Although the broker has a duty to disclose all material facts of a transaction, legal interpretations are to be avoided. Giving legal interpretations of documents involved in a transaction can be construed as practicing law without a license, an act specifically prohibited by real estate licensing acts. Moreover, the broker can be held financially responsible for any wrong legal information he gives to a client.

The duty of reasonable care also requires an agent to take proper care of property entrusted to him by his principal. For example, if a broker is entrusted with a key to an owner's building to show it to prospects, it is the broker's responsibility to see that it is used for only that purpose and that the building is locked upon leaving. Similarly, if a broker receives a check as an earnest money deposit, he must properly deposit it in a bank and not carry it around for several weeks.

Accounting for Funds Received

When a broker obtains an offer on a property, the earnest money that accompanies it belongs to the buyer until the offer is accepted. When the offer is accepted it belongs to the seller. The money does not belong to the broker, even though he possesses a check made out to him. For the purpose of holding clients' and customers' money, laws in nearly all states require a broker to maintain a **trust account.** All monies received by a broker as agent for his principal are to be promptly deposited in this account. Most states now require that this account be a demand deposit (checking account) at a bank or a trust account at a trust company. Some states allow brokers to deposit trust funds in bank accounts that earn interest. The broker's trust account must be separate from his personal bank account and the broker is required by law to accurately account for all funds received into and paid out of the trust account. As a rule, a broker will have one trust account for properties listed for sale and another trust account for rental properties managed by the broker. State-conducted surprise audits are made on broker's trust accounts to ensure compliance with the law. Failure to comply with trust fund requirements can result in the loss of one's real estate license.

Commingling

If a broker places money belonging to a client or customer in his own personal account, it is called **commingling** and is grounds for suspension or revocation of the broker's real estate license. The reason for such severe action is that from commingling, it is a very short step to **conversion**, i.e., the agent's personal use of money belonging to others. Also, clients' and customers' money placed in a personal bank account can be attached by a court of law to pay personal claims against the broker.

If a broker receives a check as an earnest money deposit, along with instructions from the buyer that it remain uncashed, the broker may comply with the buyer's request as long as the seller is informed of this fact when the offer is presented. Similarly, the broker can accept a promissory note, if he informs the seller. The objective is to disclose all material facts to the seller that might influence the decision to accept or reject the offer. The fact that the deposit accompanying the offer is not cash is a material fact. If the broker withholds this information, there is a violation of agency.

A broker's obligations are primarily to the principal who has employed him. State laws nonetheless make certain demands on the broker in relation to the third parties the broker deals with on behalf of the principal. Foremost among these are honesty, integrity and fair business dealing. This includes the proper care of deposit money and offers, responsibility for written or verbal statements, and any impression made by withholding information. Misrepresenting a property by omitting vital information is as wrong as giving false information. Disclosure of such misconduct usually results in a broker losing the right to a commission. Also possible are loss of the broker's real estate license and a lawsuit by any party to the transaction who suffered a financial loss because of the misrepresentation.

BROKER'S OBLIGATIONS TO THIRD PARTIES

In guarding against misrepresentation, a broker must be careful not to make statements not known to be true. For example, a prospect looks at a house listed for sale and asks if it is connected to the city sewer system. The broker does not know the answer, but sensing it is important to making a sale, says, "Yes." If the prospect relies on this statement, purchases the house and finds out that there is no sewer connection, the broker may be at the center of litigation regarding sale cancellation, commission loss, damage lawsuit and state license discipline. The answer should be, "I don't know, but I will find out for you."

Suppose the seller has told the broker that the house is connected to the city sewer system, and the broker, having no reason to doubt the statement, accepts it in good faith and gives that information to prospective buyers. If this statement is not true, the owner is at fault, owes the broker a commission and is subject to legal action for sale cancellation and money damages. When a broker must rely on information supplied by the seller, it is best to have it in writing. However, relying on the seller for information does not completely relieve the broker's responsibility to third parties. If a seller says his house is connected to the city sewer system and the broker knows that is impossible because there is no sewer line on that street, it is the broker's responsibility to correct the erroneous statement.

THIRD-PARTY
LIABILITY

Figure 17:3 pictorially illustrates the disclosure liability of a broker to a third party. Part A illustrates facts that a broker knows about a property he is showing to a prospect. If the broker intentionally misleads a prospect by knowingly making an incorrect statement, or by not stating important information about the property, the broker is guilty of intentional fraud and is subject to litigation and license suspension or revocation. For example, a salesperson for the broker may knowingly underestimate the probable closing costs in a transaction in order to induce the prospect to make an offer to buy. Or, the broker may pass out income and expense statements for a listed apartment building that show rental income based on projected rent increases without mentioning that fact. Or, the statement may leave out or underestimate expenses of running the property.

Most people have a good sense of what constitutes intentional fraud and vigorously avoid it. Not quite so obvious, and yet equally dangerous from the standpoint of dissatisfaction and legal liability, is the area of ignorance. Illustrated in part B

Figure 17:3   **DISCLOSURE LIABILITY**

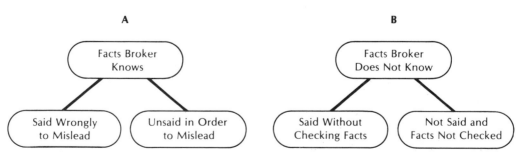

of Figure 17:3, ignorance results from not knowing all the pertinent facts about a property. This may result from the broker not taking time to check the facts or from not knowing what to look for in the first place. This is called "what the agent should have known" and there has been some far-reaching litigation that is forcing real estate brokers and their salespeople to know more about the product they are selling. The 1984 *Easton* vs *Strassburger* case (152 C.A. 3d 90) is explained next to illustrate what is expected of those in the real estate industry.

The *Easton* case involved the sale of a house built on filled land that was not properly engineered and compacted. The sellers did not disclose to the listing broker, or to the broker who found the buyer, or to the buyer that there had been past landslide activity on the property and what corrective measures had been taken. The listing broker's sales associates were aware that (1) the house was built on fill land, (2) there was netting on a slope that had slid and was repaired, and (3) the floor of the guest house was uneven. None of these "red flags" were further investigated or brought to the attention of the buyer. After the buyer closed and took possession, the land problems got worse, virtually destroying the property's value. The buyer sued the seller and the listing broker. The jury awarded the buyer $197,000 and held the seller, listing broker and selling broker liable.

COURT CASE EXAMPLES

In the *Easton* case, the judge stated that a real estate broker has a " . . . duty to conduct a reasonably competent and diligent inspection of the residential property listed for sale and to disclose to prospective purchasers all facts materially affecting the value or desirability of the property that such an investigation would reveal." For the real estate agent, this means a careful inspection of the property to determine obvious defects or red flags. A **red flag** is something that would warn a reasonably observant agent that there may be an underlying problem. The agent is then responsible for disclosing this to the seller and any prospective buyers. The agent is not responsible for knowing the underlying problem that produces the red flag. (In other words, in the *Easton* case the judge did not require the real estate agent to be a soils engineer.) But the case does strongly

Red Flags

suggest that a broker recommend to the seller and/or buyer that a specialist be hired to determine what, if any, problem is causing the red flag.

Although the *Easton* case dealt with soil problems, the careful agent will also want to inspect such things as kitchen appliances, water heater, water supply, swimming pool, sewer hookup, heating and air conditioning systems, electrical capacity, plumbing, roof, walls, ceiling, fireplace, foundation, garage, fences, sidewalks, sprinklers, etc. The broker may also want to have the seller purchase a home warranty for the buyer as a means of reducing legal liability for all involved. What we see in the *Easton* case is the legal system pushing the real estate industry further toward professionalism. When instructing the jury in the *Easton* case the judge said, "A real estate broker is a licensed person or entity who holds himself out to the public as having particular skills and knowledge in the real estate field." In the future you may expect to see more court cases on this issue as well as legislation that defines the standard of care owed by a broker to a prospective purchaser.

Choosing Your Helpers

If you, as an agent, hire someone to look into a question that was raised by a seller, prospect or red flag, make certain you hire someone who is professionally qualified. In the following case the broker listed a house and in due course found a buyer for it. The sale was contingent on getting an inspection and approval of the plumbing, furnace, air conditioning and roof. The buyer asked the broker for someone who could do this, and the broker hired someone they used occasionally to make minor inspections. The inspection was made, the items reported to be in good order and the closing took place. Upon moving in, the buyer found the house lacked water pressure because the pipes were corroded. This was confirmed by the city water department. The buyer had the pipes replaced and sent the broker the bill for $2,200. The broker felt no liability and did not pay. The buyer then sued the broker. At the trial, the buyer introduced evidence that the broker had assured the buyer that the broker would have a man check the plumbing and other items. At the trial the man who made the inspection stated he inspected the house but did not check the water pressure. The court found the broker to be negligent: the broker should have known to hire a competent plumber not a handyman. In deciding for the buyer, the judge expressed the opinion that a real estate agent, like a doctor or lawyer, holds himself out to be an expert in his field.

After reading the above two cases, you may begin to think that selling a property "as is" is a safe way to avoid the liability to disclose. This is not necessarily so. In another case that found its way to the courts, a property had been condemned by local government authorities for building code violations. The broker listed and sold it, making it very clear and in writing to the buyer that the property was sold "as is." Although "as is" means the seller is not going to make repairs, a court found this statement did not excuse the broker from informing the buyer that the building was condemned.

As Is

An agent must be on guard for a principal who wants to do something illegal or unethical. For example, a seller wants to mask a sale so as not to trigger a due-on-sale clause. The broker should advise against this and have no part of it. Otherwise the seller and broker may find themselves defending an expensive lawsuit brought by an innocent buyer when the lender learns about the transfer and calls the loan due. Moreover, the broker may also be sued by the seller on the grounds the broker did not discourage the seller from doing this act.

Masking

Because of the trend in recent years to a more consumer-oriented and more litigious society, the possibility of a broker being sued has risen to the point that **errors and omission insurance** has become very popular. The broker pays an annual fee to an insurance company that in turn will defend the broker and pay legal costs and judgments. E&O, as it is sometimes called, does not cover intentional acts of a broker to deceive, does not cover punitive damages, and does not cover negligence or misrepresentation when buying or selling for one's own account. Other than that, E&O is quite broad in coverage. This includes defending so-called "nuisance cases" in which the broker may not be at fault but must defend anyway. Moreover, E&O covers not only courtroom costs and judgments, but pre-trial conferences and negotiations and out-of-court settlements. Today E&O is simply a cost of the real estate business just like rent, telephone and automobile expenses.

ERRORS AND OMISSION INSURANCE

Sometimes it is hard for a broker to know just what will result in an unhappy buyer and a lawsuit. For example, a broker showed a large house that was listed in the multiple listing service. The MLS card said the house contained 5,400 square feet of living space. The broker told the prospect that 5,400 was an estimate he had not checked and the prospect did not seem concerned or measure the house. The prospect made an offer with a $5,000 deposit and it was accepted by the seller. Several days later in a conversation with the local tax assessor, the buyer learned the tax records listed the house at 4,600 square feet. On the grounds of the square footage discrepancy, the buyer wanted to rescind the contract and retrieve the deposit. The seller rescinded the contract but would not return the deposit. The house was placed back on the market and sold for the original asking price a short time later. A year later the broker who had listed the property, the broker who had found the unhappy buyer, and the seller were sued by the unhappy buyer for return of the $5,000 deposit plus $10,000 in exemplary and punitive damages. In part because the case was not clear-cut, it dragged on for well over a year. In the end, legal expenses amounted to more than anyone gained.

Boundary Stake Case

Another case that a broker had to defend seemed hardly the fault of the broker. An out-of-town lot owner wrote the broker with the lot and tract number and an authorization to find a buyer. The lot was in a mountain subdivision of vacant wooded land. The broker located the boundary stakes, put a sign on the lot and sold it. A year later the problem surfaced: It seems the lot numbers were all marked on the outside of the boundary stakes rather than the inside as was customary. Although the correct lot was very little different, the buyer would not accept it. The buyer wanted his money back plus 25%. In the negotiations that followed, the broker's error and omission insurance company bought the lot and listed it with the broker who resold it.

PUFFING

Puffing (or **puffery**) refers to nonfactual or extravagant statements that a reasonable person would recognize as exaggeration. Thus, a buyer may have no legal complaint against a broker who told him that a certain hillside lot had the most beautiful view in the world or that a listed property had the finest landscaping in the county. Usually a reasonable buyer can see these things and make up his own mind. However, if a broker in showing a rural property says it has "fantastic" well water, there had better be plenty of good water when the buyer moves in. If a consumer believes the broker and relies on the representation, the broker may have a potential liability. The line between puffery and misrepresentation is subjective, but it can be more easily defined by placing oneself in the position of the prospect about to pay a substantial amount of hard-earned money for a property.

OWNER–BROKER OVERVIEW

Because the owner–broker relationship is so important, let us stop for an overview of it. When a seller and a broker enter into a listing agreement, a contract is created that appoints the broker as the special agent of the seller for the purpose of finding a purchaser who is ready, willing and able to buy at the price and terms set forth in the listing. The listing creates a fiduciary relationship between the broker and the owner. The term "**fiduciary**" describes the faithful relationship owed by an agent to his principal. Specifically, these are the duties of faithful performance, loyalty, competence, accounting and disclosure. When a broker breaches these fiduciary responsibilities, the principal can bring a civil suit to recover losses and the broker's license may be revoked or suspended by the state.

Principal's Obligations

The principal also has certain obligations to the agent. Although these do not receive much statutory attention in most states, they are important when the principal fails to live up to those obligations. The principal's primary obligation is **compensation.** Additionally, the agent is eligible for **reimbursement** for expenses not related to the sale itself. For example, if an agent had to pay a plumber to fix a broken pipe for the owner, the agent could expect reimbursement from the owner over and above the sales commission.

The other two obligations of the principal are indemnification and performance. An agent is entitled to **indemnification** upon suffering a loss through no fault of his own, such as when a misrepresentation by the principal to the agent was passed on in good faith to the buyer. The duty of **performance** means the principal is expected to do whatever he reasonably can to accomplish the purpose of the agency such as referring inquiries by prospective buyers to the broker.

Third Parties   Although the broker has no contracts with third parties, the broker is nonetheless responsible for honesty, integrity and fairness of business dealings with them. Courts bend over backwards to protect buyers from misleading or missing information, undisclosed fees and hidden broker identity.

BROKER'S SALES STAFF   A broker's sales associates are general agents of the broker. A sales associate owes the broker the duties of competence, obedience, accounting, loyalty and disclosure. The broker's obligations to the sales associate are compensation, reimbursement, indemnification and performance. In addition, the broker will authorize the extent to which the sales associate can bind the broker. For example, is the sales associate's signature by itself sufficient to bind the broker to a listing or must the broker also sign it? With regard to third parties, the sales associate owes them honesty, integrity and fair business dealings. Because a sales associate is an agent of the broker and the broker is an agent of the principal, the sales associate is sometimes called a **subagent** of the principal.

COOPERATING BROKER   In approximately 70% of all sales made through multiple listing services, the broker who locates the buyer is not the same broker that listed the property. This results in a dilemma: Is the broker who located the buyer (the **cooperating broker**) an agent of the buyer or the seller? There are three schools of thought on this. The traditional one is illustrated in Figure 17:4.

The traditional view is that everyone is an agent (or subagent) of the seller because the seller is paying the commission, and loyalty must follow the money line. A second school of thought is that since the cooperating broker has no contract with the seller (only an agreement to share with the listing broker) and none with the buyer, he is the agent of neither. The third school of thought is that the cooperating broker represents the buyer by virtue of the fact that the cooperating broker is trying to locate a suitable property for the buyer. In fact, a recent Federal Trade Commission study found 71% of buyers surveyed believe this is the case. And buyers come to believe

TRADITIONAL VIEW OF AGENCY   **Figure 17:4**

The vertical links in this illustration must be clearly disclosed to buyers and sellers.

this because it is the cooperating broker that is spending time with them *and* is taking them to see properties *and* will write and present the offer *and*, if needed, come back with a counteroffer. Moreover, the cooperating broker hopes to make a good enough impression that a sale will be made and the buyer in the future will return to that broker for more real estate dealings.

The problem arises when the buyer takes the cooperating broker into confidence not knowing that the cooperating broker's loyalty is to the seller. To avoid becoming a dual agent, the wise course is for the cooperating broker to be very clear with the buyer and the seller as to the cooperating broker's loyalty. If it is with the seller, then the buyer must be informed of this early in the showing process, not at the time the offer is written. If it's with the buyer, then the seller must be aware that although there will be a commission split, the seller is not to expect the cooperating broker's loyalty. In his book on agency relationships, real estate attorney John Reilly concludes that the payment of fees is a matter of contract, not agency, and there is nothing illegal about the seller paying the fee of a broker who is an agent of the buyer. What the law does say is that undisclosed dual agencies are illegal; yet this is what often happens in cooperative sales. The solution is to decide who you

Disclosure

represent, disclose that information to all involved, document it in writing and then do as you say. This will help in knowing what to do if the seller states he will take $115,000 on a $120,000 listing and the buyer is ready to offer $117,500 but wants to start the bidding at $112,500. Expect to see real estate laws and regulations passed that require all brokers to disclose who they represent and to confirm that in writing on the offer and acceptance.

BUYER'S BROKER   Another way out of the representation dilemma is for the buyer to hire a broker whose task is to find properties for sale and present them to the buyer for consideration. In this case it is clear that the **buyer's broker** is loyal to the buyer and working to get the best deal possible for the buyer. Another benefit of buyer representation is that with the present system buyers are shown only "listed properties." A buyer's broker can investigate properties offered for sale by owners and can approach owners who have not put their properties on the market.

The biggest drawback of buyer's brokerage is that most people are accustomed to a system wherein the seller pays the full cost of marketing a property. A solution is for the buyer's broker to present an offer based on the net amount the seller will receive. Consider, for example, a $100,000 property listed at 6% commission and sold the traditional way using a co-operating broker and a 50/50 split. The buyer pays the seller $100,000 and the seller pays the listing broker $6,000 who, in turn, pays $3,000 of that to the cooperating broker. Using a buyer's broker, the buyer pays his broker $3,000 and the seller $97,000. The seller's broker gets $3,000 and splits with no one. The net result is that either way, the seller receives $94,000 and the brokers each get $3,000. The difference is that in the second case, the buyer has a broker whose loyalty and effort are clearly for the buyer.

PROPERTY   The federal government through the Department of Hous-
DISCLOSURE   ing and Urban Development (HUD) has enacted legislation
STATEMENTS   aimed at protecting purchasers of property in new subdivisions from misrepresentation, fraud and deceit. The HUD requirements, administered by the Office of Interstate Land Sales Registration, apply primarily to subdivision lots located in one

state and sold to residents of another state. The purpose of this law, which took effect in 1969 and was amended in 1979, is to require that developers give prospective purchasers extensive disclosures regarding the lots in the form of a **property report.**

The requirement that a property report be prepared according to HUD specifications was the response of Congress to the concern, that all too often, buyers were receiving inaccurate or inadequate information. A color brochure might be handed to prospects picturing an artificial lake and boat marina within the subdivision, yet the developer has not obtained the necessary permits to build either and may never do so. Or, a developer implies that the lots being offered for sale are ready for building when in fact there is no sewer system and the soil cannot handle septic tanks. Or prospects are not told that many roads in the subdivision will not be built for several years, and, when they are, lot owners will face a hefty paving assessment followed by annual maintenance fees because the county has no intention of maintaining them as public roads.

In addition to addressing the above issues, the property report also discloses payment terms, what happens if there is a default, any soil problems, distance to school and stores, any additional costs to expect, availability of utilities, restrictive covenants, oil and mineral rights, etc. The property report must be given to each purchaser before a contract to purchase is signed. Failure to do so gives the purchaser the right to cancel any contract or agreement.

Property Report

The property report is *not* a government approval of the subdivision. It is strictly a disclosure of pertinent facts that the prospective purchaser is strongly encouraged to read before buying. A number of states also have enacted their own disclosure laws. Typically these apply to developers of housing subdivisions, condominiums, cooperatives and vacant lots. In these reports the developer is required to make a number of pertinent disclosures about the lot, structure, owners' association, neighborhood, financing terms, etc., and this must be given to the prospective purchaser before a purchase contract can be signed. Once signed, HUD and most states allow the buyer a "cooling-off" period of from 3 to 7 days during which the buyer can cancel the contract and receive all his money back.

Not an Approval

Like the HUD property report, a state-required property report does not mean the state has approved or disapproved the subdivision. The property report is strictly a disclosure statement designed to help the prospective purchaser make an informed decision about buying.

FAIR HOUSING LAWS   There are two major federal laws that prohibit discrimination in housing. The first is the **Civil Rights Act of 1866.** It states that, "All citizens of the United States shall have the same right in every State and Territory, as is enjoyed by the white citizens thereof to inherit, purchase, lease, sell, hold, and convey real and personal property." In 1968, the U.S. Supreme Court in the case of *Jones* vs. *Mayer* affirmed that the 1866 act prohibits "all racial discrimination, private as well as public, in the sale of real property." The second is the **1968 Fair Housing Law,** officially known as Title VIII of the Civil Rights Act of 1968, as amended. This law makes it illegal to discriminate based on race, color, religion, sex or national origin in connection with the sale or rental of housing and any vacant land offered for residential construction or use.

Specifically, what do these two laws prohibit and what do they allow? The 1968 Fair Housing Law provides protection against the following acts if they are based on race, color, religion, sex or national origin:

1. Refusing to sell or to rent to, deal or negotiate with any person;
2. Discriminating in the terms or conditions for buying or renting housing;
3. Discriminating by advertising that housing is available only to persons of a certain race, color, religion, sex or national origin;
4. Denying that housing is available for inspection, sale or rent when, in fact, it is available;
5. Denying or making differing terms or conditions for home loans by commercial lenders;
6. Denying to anyone the use of or participation in any real estate services, such as brokers' organizations, multiple listing services or other facilities related to the selling or renting of housing;
7. Steering and blockbusting.

Steering   **Steering** is the practice of directing home seekers to particular neighborhoods based on race, color, religion, sex or national origin. Steering includes efforts to exclude minority members from one area of a city as well as to direct them to minority or changing areas. Examples include showing only certain neighborhoods, slanting property descriptions and down-grading neighborhoods. Steering is often subtle, sometimes no more than a word, phrase or facial expression. Nonetheless, steering accounts for the bulk of the complaints filed against real estate licensees under the Fair Housing Act.

Blockbusting (also called **panic-peddling**) is the illegal practice of inducing panic selling in a neighborhood for financial gain. Blockbusting typically starts when one person induces another to sell his property cheaply by stating that an impending change in the racial or religious composition of the neighborhood will cause property values to fall, school quality to decline and crime to increase. The first home thus acquired is sold (at a mark-up) to a minority member. This event is used to reinforce fears that the neighborhood is indeed changing. The process quickly snowballs as residents panic and sell at progressively lower prices. The homes are then resold at higher prices to incoming residents.

Blockbusting

Note that blockbusting is not limited to fears over people moving into a neighborhood. In a Virginia case, a real estate firm attempted to gain listings in a certain neighborhood by playing upon residents' fears regarding an upcoming expressway project.

The 1968 Fair Housing Law applies to the following types of housing:

Housing Covered by the 1968 Fair Housing Law

1. Single-family housing owned by private individuals when (1) a real estate broker or other person in the business of selling or renting dwellings is used and/or (2) discriminatory advertising is used;
2. Single-family housing not owned by private individuals;
3. Single-family houses owned by a private individual who owns more than three such houses or who, in any two-year period, sells more than one in which the individual was not the most recent resident;
4. Multifamily dwellings of five or more units;
5. Multifamily dwellings containing four or fewer units, if the owner does not reside in one of the units.

*Acts Not Prohibited by the
1968 Fair Housing Law*

Not covered by the 1968 Fair Housing Law are the sale or rental of single-family houses owned by a private individual of three or fewer such single-family houses if (1) a broker is not used, (2) discriminatory advertising is not used, and (3) no more than one house in which the owner was not the most recent resident is sold during any two-year period. Not covered by the 1968 act are rentals of rooms or units in owner-occupied dwellings for two to four families, provided discriminatory advertising is not used. Also, the 1968 act does not cover the sale, rental or occupancy of dwellings that a religious organization owns or operates for other than a commercial purpose to persons of the same religion, if membership in that religion is not restricted on account of race, color or national origin. And the 1968 act does not cover the rental or occupancy of lodgings that a private club owns or operates for its members for other than a commercial purpose.

Note, however, the above-listed exemptions in the 1968 Fair Housing Law are not allowed where they violate the 1866 Civil Rights Act.

Fair Housing Enforcement

There are three ways the 1968 act can be enforced by someone who feels discriminated against. The first is to file a written complaint with the Department of Housing and Urban Development in Washington, D.C. The second is to file court action directly in a U.S. District Court or state or local court. The third is to file a complaint with the U.S. Attorney General. If a complaint is filed with HUD, HUD may investigate to see if the law has been broken, may attempt to resolve the problem by conference, conciliation or persuasion, may refer the matter to a state or local fair housing authority, or may recommend the complaint be filed in court. A person seeking enforcement of the 1866 act must file a suit in a Federal Court.

No matter which route is taken, the burden of proving illegal discrimination is the responsibility of the person filing the complaint. If successful, the following remedies are available: (1) an injunction to stop the sale or rental of the property to someone else and make it available to the complainant, (2) money for actual damages caused by the discrimination, (3) punitive damages, and (4) court costs. There are also criminal penalties for those who coerce, intimidate, threaten or interfere with a person's buying, renting or selling of housing.

Agent's Duties

A real estate agent's duties are to uphold the 1968 Fair Housing Act and the 1866 Civil Rights Act. If a property owner asks an agent to discriminate, the agent must refuse to accept the listing. An agent is in violation of fair housing laws by giving a minority buyer or seller less than favorable treatment or by ignoring him or by referring him to an agent of the same minority. Violation also occurs when an agent fails to use best efforts, does not submit an offer, delays submitting an offer, or induces a seller to reject an offer because of race, color, religion, sex or national origin.

Testers

From time to time real estate agents are approached by fair housing testers. These are individuals or organizations that respond to advertising and visit real estate offices to test for compliance with fair housing laws. The tester does not announce himself or herself as such and then ask if the office follows fair housing practices. Rather, the tester plays the role of a person looking for housing to buy or rent and observes if fair housing laws are being followed. If not followed, the tester lodges a complaint with the appropriate fair housing agency.

State Laws

What has been said so far has to do with federal housing laws. In addition, many states, counties and cities have enacted their own fair housing laws. You will need to contact local fair housing authorities as these laws often go beyond the federal laws. For example, within some states it is illegal to discriminate on the basis of age, marital status, presence of children, physical handicap, sexual orientation and welfare status. Within other states, an owner-occupant may discriminate only in his own single-family or two-family home, not the four-family building allowed in the 1968 act.

VOCABULARY REVIEW

Match terms **a–z** *with statements* **1–26.**

a. *Advance fee listing*   **n.** *Net listing*
b. *Agent*   **o.** *Open listing*
c. *Blockbusting*   **p.** *Principal*
d. *Buyer's broker*   **q.** *Procuring cause*
e. *Commingling*   **r.** *Property report*
f. *Dual agency*   **s.** *Puffing*
g. *Exclusive agency*   **t.** *Red flag*
h. *Exclusive right to sell*   **u.** *Sales associate*
i. *Fiduciary relationship*   **v.** *Special agency*
j. *Flat-fee broker*   **w.** *Steering*
k. *Implied authority*   **x.** *Subagent*
l. *Middleman*   **y.** *Third parties*
m. *Multiple listing service*   **z.** *Trust account*

1. A person who authorizes another to act.
2. A listing that gives a broker a nonexclusive right to find a purchaser.
3. Persons who are not parties to a contract but who may be affected by it.
4. An agency created for the performance of specific acts only.
5. A person who brings two or more parties together but does not assist in conducting negotiations.
6. A listing that gives the broker the right to collect a commission no matter who sells the property during the listing period.
7. A listing wherein the owner reserves the right to sell the property himself, but agrees to list with no other broker during the listing period.
8. Person empowered to act by and on behalf of the principal.
9. A listing for which the commission is the difference between the sales price and a minimum price set by the seller.
10. An organization of real estate brokers that exists for the purpose of exchanging listing information.
11. One broker representing two or more parties in a transaction.
12. Mixing of clients' or customers' funds with an agent's personal funds.
13. The broker who is the primary cause of a transaction.
14. Statements that a reasonable person would recognize as nonfactual or extravagant.
15. A licensed salesperson or broker who works for a broker.
16. A listing where the broker charges for time by the hour and for out-of-pocket expenses to market a property.
17. A broker who charges a preset brokerage fee that is collected whether or not the property sells.

18. Agency authority arising from industry custom, common usage and conduct of the parties involved.
19. A relationship that requires trust, honesty and exercise of good business judgment.
20. A separate account for holding clients' and customers' money.
21. Something that would warn a reasonably observant person of an underlying problem.
22. Refers to the agency relationship of a broker's sales associate to the seller.
23. A broker employed by and therefore loyal to the buyer.
24. Government required information that must be given to purchasers in subdivisions.
25. To guide a customer or client away from one neighborhood to another based on race, color, religion, sex or national origin.
26. The illegal practice of inducing panic selling in a neighborhood for financial gain.

QUESTIONS AND PROBLEMS

1. When we speak of the laws of agency, to what are we referring?
2. What is an agency coupled with an interest?
3. What does broker cooperation refer to? How is it achieved?
4. Why do brokers strongly prefer to take exclusive right-to-sell listings rather than exclusive agency or open listings?
5. What is the purpose of errors and omissions insurance?
6. The laws of agency require that the agent be faithful and loyal to the principal. What does this mean to a real estate broker who has just taken a listing?
7. What does the phrase "ready, willing and able buyer" mean in a real estate contract?
8. How are listings terminated?
9. What is the purpose of a property disclosure statement?
10. What is the purpose of fair housing testers?

ADDITIONAL
READINGS

"Avoid Civil Rights Litigation" by **Armin Guggenheim.** (*Real Estate Today*, Sep 84, page 38). Article points out how recent court decisions in civil rights cases are beginning to clarify many of the problems faced by real estate agents.

Classified Secrets: Writing Real Estate Ads that Work by **William Pivar.** (Real Estate Education Co., 1984, 373 pages). Book emphasizes the need to write ads that attract. Includes where to advertise, motivating action, selling special properties, analyzing results, etc.

How to List and Sell Real Estate by **Danielle Kennedy** and **Warren Jamison.** (Reston, 1983, 524 pages). A very popular guide that contains prospecting hints, ideas for letters, role plays, actual situations, time planning, promotions and closing techniques.

Strategies for Success in Real Estate by **Sam Young.** (Reston, 1983, 237 pages). Topics include public relations, creating referral business, listing presentations, telephone techniques, listing property, showing property and closing the sale.

"When the Seller Wants Out" by **Shari Lynn Anderson.** (*First Tuesday*, Apr 85, page 6). Covers the practical and legal aspects of what a broker can do when a seller wants to cancel the listing. Includes sample cancellation form.

Licensing Laws and Professional Affiliation

Broker: a person or legal entity licensed to act independently in conducting a real estate brokerage business

Independent contractor: one who contracts to do work according to his own methods and is responsible to his employer only for the results of that work

License revocation: to recall and make void a license

License suspension: to temporarily make a license ineffective

Licensee: one who holds a license

Principal broker: the broker in charge of a real estate office

Real estate commission: a state board that advises and sets policies regarding real estate licensees and transaction procedures

Realtor: a registered trademark owned by the National Association of Realtors for use by its members

Recovery fund: a state-operated fund that can be tapped to pay for uncollectible judgments against real estate licensees

Sales associate: a salesperson or broker employed by a broker

Salesperson: a person employed by a broker to list, negotiate, sell or lease real property for others

Does the public have a vested interest in seeing that real estate salespersons and brokers have the qualifications of honesty, truthfulness, good reputation and real estate knowledge before they are allowed to negotiate real estate transactions on behalf of others? It was this concern that brought about real estate licensing laws as we know them today. Until 1917, no state required real estate agents to be licensed. Anyone who wanted to be an agent could simply hang up a sign stating that he was an agent. In larger cities there were persons and firms who specialized in bringing buyers and sellers together. In smaller towns, a local banker, attorney or barber would know who had what for sale and be the person a buyer would ask for property information.

The first attempt to require that persons acting as real estate agents be licensed was made by the California legislature in 1917. That law was declared unconstitutional, with the main opposition being that the state was unreasonably interfering with the right of every citizen to engage in a useful and legitimate occupation. Two years later, in 1919, the California legislature passed a second real estate licensing act; this time it was upheld by the Supreme Court. That same year, Michigan, Oregon and Tennessee also passed real estate licensing acts. Today all 50 states and the District of Columbia require that persons who offer their services as real estate agents be licensed.

Loyalty, Honesty and Truthfulness

The first license laws did not require examinations for competency nor did they require real estate education. Those came later. The first laws were aimed at weeding out persons who placed loyalty to themselves above loyalty to those who they were representing. By requiring persons to be licensed, the state had the power to refuse to issue a license to someone with a past record of dishonesty and untruthfulness. Additionally, the state could temporarily or permanently take away a license once it had been issued. To help make licensing laws work, the state refused to allow its courts to enforce claims for commissions by unlicensed persons.

That a real estate license applicant have a good reputation for honesty and truthfulness is still a very important part of real estate licensing today. If you apply for a license, you may be asked to provide a photograph, credit report, fingerprints and/or provide personal character references. The state licensing agency will check for links to any past criminal convictions or other significant infractions of the law. Inquiry may be made of your character references to learn more about your reputation.

In the 1930s and 1940s states began adding the requirement of a license examination in an attempt to determine whether the license applicant also had some level of technical ability in real estate. Then beginning in the 1950s, states began adding the requirement that a person take a certain number of hours of real estate education before being licensed. Thus, what we see today is that a person who plans to be a real estate agent must qualify both ethically and technically before being issued a license.

PERSONS REQUIRED TO BE LICENSED

In what situations does a person need a real estate license? A person who for compensation or the promise of compensation lists or offers to list, sells or offers to sell, buys or offers to buy, negotiates or offers to negotiate either directly or indirectly for the purpose of bringing about a sale, purchase or option to purchase, exchange, auction, lease or rental of real estate, or any interest in real estate, is required to hold a valid real estate license. Some states also require persons offering their services as real estate appraisers, property managers, mortgage bankers or rent collectors to hold real estate licenses.

Property owners dealing with their own property and licensed attorneys conducting a real estate transaction as an incidental part of their duties as an attorney for a client are exempt from holding a license. Also exempt are trustees and receivers in bankruptcy, legal guardians, administrators and executors handling a deceased's estate, officers and employees of a government agency dealing in real estate, and persons holding power of attorney from an owner. However, the law does not permit a person to use the exemptions as a means of conducting a brokerage business without the proper license. That is, an unlicensed person cannot take a listing in the guise of a power of attorney and then act as a real estate broker.

BROKER

Before the advent of licensing laws, there was no differentiation between real estate brokers and real estate salespersons. People who brought about transactions were simply called real estate agents or whatever else they wanted to be called. With licensing laws came two classes of **licensee:** real estate broker and real estate salesperson (for many years called real estate salesman). A **real estate broker** is a person licensed to act independently in conducting a real estate brokerage business. A broker brings together those with real estate to be marketed and those seeking real estate and negotiates a transaction. For those services the broker receives a fee, usually in the form of a commission based on the selling price or lease rent. The broker may represent the buyer or the seller, or, upon full disclosure, both at the same time. The role is more than that of a middleman who puts two interested parties in contact with each other, for the broker usually takes an active role in negotiating price and terms acceptable to both the buyer and seller. A broker can be an actual person or a legal entity, i.e., a business firm. If a business firm, the person in charge must be a broker. The laws of all states permit a real estate broker to hire others for the purpose of bringing about real estate transactions. These persons may be other licensed real estate brokers or they may be licensed real estate salespersons.

SALESPERSON

A **real estate salesperson,** within the meaning of the license laws, is a person employed by a real estate broker to list and negotiate the sale, exchange, lease or rental of real property for others for compensation, under the direction, guidance and responsibility of the employing broker. Only an actual person can be licensed as a salesperson (a business firm cannot be licensed as a salesperson), and a salesperson must be employed by a broker; a salesperson cannot operate independently. Thus, a salesperson who takes a listing on a property does so in the name of his broker, and in some states the broker must sign along with the salesperson for the listing to be valid. In the event of a legal dispute caused by a salesperson, the dispute would be between the principal and the broker. Therefore, some brokers take considerable care to oversee the documents that their salespeople prepare and sign. Other brokers do not, relying instead on the knowledge and sensibility of their salespeople, and accepting a certain amount of risk in the process.

The salesperson is a means by which a broker can expand his sales force. Presumably, the more salespeople a broker employs, the more listings and sales generated, and thus the more commissions earned by the broker. Against this, the broker must pay enough to keep the sales force from leaving, provide sales facilities and personnel management and take ultimate responsibility for any mistakes the salespersons make.

SALES ASSOCIATE

The term **sales associate** is not a license category. Rather it refers to anyone with a real estate license who is employed by a broker. Most often this will be a real estate salesperson. However, a person who holds a broker license can work for another broker. Such a person is a regular member of the employing broker's sales force just like someone with a salesperson license. The salespersons and brokers who work for a broker are known collectively as the broker's sales associates or sales force or sales staff. You will also hear the term real estate agent used in a general sense. Correctly speaking, the broker is a special agent of the property owner and the sales associate is a general agent of the broker. In common language today, real estate agent refers to anyone, broker or salesperson, who negotiates real estate transactions for others.

Of the two license levels, the salesperson's license is regarded as the entry-level license and, as such, requires no previous real estate sales experience. The minimum age is 18 years. By comparison, the broker's license in nearly all states requires 1 to 5 years of experience (2 or 3 years is most common) as a real estate salesperson. Related real estate experience and college education in real estate can sometimes shorten the experience requirement. As a practical matter, however, a person is wise to gain plenty of experience as a salesperson before becoming a broker for the purpose of operating independently.

QUALIFICATIONS FOR LICENSING

Examination of the license applicant's knowledge of real estate law and practices, mathematics, valuation, finance and the like, is required for license granting in all states. Salesperson exams and broker exams typically contain 100 to 140 multiple-choice questions like those shown in Appendices B, C and D. Usually 3 to 4½ hours are allowed to complete the exam. Salesperson exams cover the basic aspects of state license law, contracts and agency, real property ownership, transfer and use, subdivision map reading, fair housing laws, real estate mathematics and the ability to follow written instructions. Broker exams cover the same topics in more depth and test the applicant's ability to prepare listings, offer and acceptance contracts, leasing contracts and closing statements. The applicant's knowledge of real estate finance, appraisal and office management are also tested.

Examination

Nearly all states require that license applicants take real estate education courses at private real estate schools, colleges or through adult education programs at high schools. Table 18:1 shows the education and experience requirements in the United States at the time this book was written. The table is included to give you an overview of the emphasis currently being placed on education and experience by the various states. For up-to-the-minute information on education and experience requirements you should contact the real estate licensing department at your state capital.

Education Requirements

Table 18:1   REAL ESTATE EDUCATION AND EXPERIENCE REQUIREMENTS

| STATE | SALESPERSON LICENSE | | BROKER LICENSE | | |
	Education Requirement	Continuing Education	Education Requirement	Experience Requirement	Continuing Education
Alabama	45 hours	No	45 hours	2 years	No
Alaska	None	No	None	2 years	No
Arizona	45 hours	Yes	180 hours	3 years	Yes
Arkansas	30 hours	No	90 hours *or* 2 yrs.+30 hrs.		No
California	45+90 hours	Yes	360 hours	2 years	Yes
Colorado	48 hours	No	96 hours	2 years	No
Connecticut	30 hours	Yes	90 hours	2 years	Yes
Delaware	126 hours	Yes	201 hours	5 years	Yes
Dist. of Col.	45 hours	Yes	135 hours	2 years	Yes
Florida	63 hours	Yes	135 hours	1 year	Yes
Georgia	24+80 hours	Yes	164 hours	3 years	Yes
Hawaii	40 hours	No	46 hours	2 years	No
Idaho	45 hours	No	135 hours	2 years	No
Illinois	30 hours	No	90 hours	1 year	No
Indiana	40 hours	No	64 hours	1 year	No
Iowa	30 hours	Yes	90 hours	2 years	Yes
Kansas	30 hours	Yes	24 hours	2 years	Yes
Kentucky	96 hours	No	336 hours	2 years	No
Louisiana	90 hours	Yes	150 hours	2 years	Yes
Maine	None	Yes	90 hours *or* 1 year		Yes
Maryland	45 hours	Yes	135 hours	3 years	Yes
Massachusetts	24 hours	No	30 hours	1 year	No
Michigan	40 hours	Yes	90 hours	3 years	Yes
Minnesota	90 hours	Yes	90 hours	2 years	Yes
Mississippi	60+30 hours	No	135 hours	1 year	No

Explanation: Hours are clock-hours in the classroom; experience requirement is experience as a licensed real estate salesperson; continuing education refers to education required for license renewal. Some states credit completed salesperson education toward the broker education requirement. Xns = transactions.

Continuing Education

Licensing authorities in a growing number of states require additional course work each time a license is renewed. This is called **continuing education,** and its purpose is to force licensees to stay up to date in their field as a prerequisite to license renewal. States with continuing education requirements are shown in Table 18:1.

LICENSING PROCEDURE

An application for a real estate salesperson or broker license can be obtained either in person or by mail from a state's real estate licensing department. The application is completed

REAL ESTATE EDUCATION AND EXPERIENCE REQUIREMENTS   **Table 18:1** *continued*

STATE	SALESPERSON LICENSE Education Requirement	SALESPERSON LICENSE Continuing Education	BROKER LICENSE Education Requirement	BROKER LICENSE Experience Requirement	BROKER LICENSE Continuing Education
Missouri	60 hours	Yes	140 hours	None	Yes
Montana	None	No	None	2 years	No
Nebraska	60 hours	Yes	120 hours	2 years	Yes
Nevada	90 hours	Yes	960 hours	2 years	Yes
New Hampshire	None	Yes	None	1 year	Yes
New Jersey	75 hours	No	165 hours	2 years	No
New Mexico	60 hours	No	90 hours	2 years	No
New York	45 hours	Yes	90 hours	2 years	Yes
North Carolina	30 hours	No	120 hours *or* 2 years		No
North Dakota	30 hours	Yes	90 hours	2 years	Yes
Ohio	60+60 hours	Yes	240 hours	2 yrs.+20 Xns	Yes
Oklahoma	45 hours	Yes	90 hours	1 year	Yes
Oregon	90 hours	Yes	150 hours	3 years	Yes
Pennsylvania	60 hours	No	240 hours	3 years	No
Rhode Island	None	No	90 hours	1 year	No
South Carolina	30+30 hours	No	90 hours	3 years	No
South Dakota	30 hours	Yes	90 hours	2 years	Yes
Tennessee	30 hours	Yes	90 hours	2 years	Yes
Texas	180 hours	Yes	900 hours	2 years	No
Utah	90 hours	No	120 hours	3 years	No
Vermont	None	No	None	1 year	No
Virginia	45 hours	No	180 hours	3 years	No
Washington	30+30 hours	Yes	90 hours	2 years	No
West Virginia	90 hours	No	180 hours	2 years	No
Wisconsin	30 hours	Yes	60 hours	None	Yes
Wyoming	30 hours	Yes	60 hours	2 years	Yes

Source: National Association of Real Estate License Law Officials, 50 South Main Street, Suite 600, Salt Lake City, Utah 84144. Check with your state for any subsequent changes.

and returned with the required fee to the department. The character aspects of the applicant are checked and, if approved, an examination date is scheduled. (Some states reverse this and give the exam first and check the references second.) Most states offer their real estate exams monthly. A few offer testing bimonthly or quarterly. Five states offer exams at least once a week.

The applicant is notified of the results in approximately 4 to 6 weeks. If passed, the fee for the license itself is now paid. Also, a salesperson applicant must name the broker he will be working for. This information is usually provided on a form signed by the employing broker. A broker applicant must give the address where he plans to operate his brokerage business. These forms are processed by the department and a license is mailed to the applicant in the case of a broker, or to the employing broker in the case of a salesperson. Upon receipt, the licensee can operate as a real estate salesperson or broker, as the case may be.

If the applicant fails the written examination, the usual procedure is to allow the applicant to repeat it until passed. A fee is charged to retake the exam and the applicant must wait until the next testing date.

Renewal   Once licensed, as long as a person remains active in real estate and meets any continuing education requirements, the license can be renewed by paying the required renewal fee. If a license is not renewed before it expires, most states allow a grace period and charge a late renewal fee. Once the grace period is passed, all license rights lapse and the individual must meet current application requirements and take the current written exam. If a licensee wishes to be temporarily inactive from the business, but does not wish to let the license lapse, some states permit the license to be placed on inactive status. When the licensee wishes to reactive the license, he pays a fee to the department. Then the license is moved from inactive to active status and he can start selling again.

EXAMINATION
SERVICES   Real estate license examinations in approximately four-fifths of the states are administered by the Educational Testing Service (ETS), the American College Testing Program (ACT) or Assessment Systems Incorporated (ASI). The remaining states write and grade their own exams.

As of this writing ETS examinations were being used in the following states: Alaska, Colorado, Connecticut, Delaware, Hawaii, Illinois, Indiana, Kentucky, Louisiana, Michigan, Minnesota, Montana, Nebraska, New Hampshire, New Mexico, North Dakota, Pennsylvania, Rhode Island, South Dakota, Tennessee, Vermont and Wyoming. ACT exams were being used in Alabama, Georgia, Idaho, Iowa, Missouri, Nevada,

Utah, Virginia, Washington and Wisconsin. ASI exams were being used in Arkansas, Kansas, Maryland, Massachusetts, New Jersey and the District of Columbia. The following states used their own exams, in some cases purchasing questions from one of the national services: Arizona, California, Florida, Maine, Mississippi, North Carolina, Ohio, Oklahoma, Oregon, South Carolina, Texas and West Virginia.

Exams written by the national testing services are divided into two parts. Part 1, called the **uniform test,** contains 80 to 100 questions that are relevant to the general principles and practices of real estate that are common or uniform across the country. Part 2, called the **state test,** contains 20 to 40 questions regarding the laws, rules, regulations and practices of the jurisdiction where the examination is being given.

The tests are composed entirely of objective, multiple-choice questions which are constantly being revised and updated to keep them current with the changing practices and laws of real estate. There are many different versions of the tests, but all are equal in difficulty. More details regarding the contents of the ETS, ACT and ASI exams can be found in Appendices B, C and D. Sample exams are available from ETS, ACT and ASI, and their addresses are in the same appendices. Like the national exam services, states that write their own tests have question banks of several thousand questions from which approximately 100 are chosen each time a test is given. Topic coverage and question styles will be substantially similar to the examples shown in Appendices B, C and D.

The general rule regarding license requirements is that a person must be licensed in the state within which he negotiates. Thus, if a broker or one of the broker's sales associates sells an out-of-state property, but conducts the negotiations entirely within the borders of his own state, a license is not needed in the state where the land is located. State laws also permit a broker in one state to split a commission with a broker in another state provided each conducts negotiations only within the state where he is licensed. Therefore, if Broker B, licensed in State B, takes a listing at his office on a parcel of land located in State B, and Broker C in State C sells it conducting

NONRESIDENT LICENSING

the sale negotiations within State C, then Brokers B and C can split the commission. If, however, Broker C comes to State B to negotiate a contract, then a license in State B is necessary.

Many states will issue a **nonresident license** to out-of-state brokers. This is particularly helpful where a broker is located near a state border. In issuing a nonresident license, a state will usually require substantially the same examination and experience requirements as demanded of resident brokers. Some states will give the out-of-state broker credit for the uniform part of a license test already taken, requiring only passage of a test on local law, custom and practice. Others require a complete examination. A few require no examination.

Notice of Consent

When a broker operates outside of his home state, he may be required to file a **notice of consent** in each state in which he intends to operate, usually with the secretary of state. This permits the secretary of state to receive legal summonses on behalf of the nonresident broker and provides a state resident an avenue by which he can sue a broker who is a resident of another state.

Moving to Another State

When a broker or salesperson moves his place of business from one state to another, a license is required in the new state. Many states will give credit for experience and part or all of the examination that was passed in the previous state. This can be particularly helpful for two-income families when one spouse is transferred to another state. Details of what a state will allow as credit are too complex and too changeable to include here. If negotiating across state lines or moving to another state as a real estate agent is of interest to you, you should contact that state's real estate licensing authority.

LICENSING THE BUSINESS FIRM

When a real estate broker wishes to establish a brokerage, the simplest method is a sole proprietorship under the broker's own name, such as David Lee, Real Estate Broker. Some states permit a broker to operate out of his residence. However, operating a business in a residential neighborhood can be bothersome to neighbors, and most states require brokers to maintain a place of business in a location that is zoned for businesses.

When a person operates under a name other than his own, he must register that name by filing a **fictitious business name statement** with the county clerk and the state real estate licensing authority. This statement must also be published in a local newspaper. Thus, if David Lee wishes to call his brokerage business Great Lakes Realty, his business certificate would show "David Lee, doing business as Great Lakes Realty." (Sometimes "doing business as" is shortened to dba or d/b/a.)

Fictitious Business Name

A real estate broker can operate as a sole proprietorship either under the broker's own name or a fictitious name. A broker can also operate in partnership with other brokers or as a corporation. Since a corporation is an artificial being (not an actual person), it cannot take a real estate examination. Therefore, its chief executive officer (usually the president) must be a licensed real estate broker and be responsible for the management of the firm. Other officers and stockholders may include brokers and salespersons and nonlicensed persons. However, only those actually licensed can represent the corporation in activities requiring a real estate license.

If a broker expands by establishing branch offices that are geographically separate from the main or home office, each branch must have a branch office license and a licensed broker in charge. Often referred to as a **principal broker,** this person can be a partner, a corporate owner who is a broker or a sales associate who has a broker's license. A few states allow a sales person licensee to be in charge.

Branch Offices

Thus far we have discussed why and when a real estate license is required and how to obtain one. The next question is, "Who makes these rules and how are they enforced?" The starting point is the state legislature. The legislature of each state has the authority to enact laws to promote the safety, health, morals, order and general welfare of its population. This includes the licensing and regulation of real estate brokers and salespersons. The legislature establishes general requirements. For example, the legislature enacts laws requiring that real estate agents be licensed, that there will be two classes of licenses, that there will be a prelicense education requirement, that there will be a license examination, and that continuing

REAL ESTATE REGULATION

education will be required. The legislature also establishes two bodies to carry out the requirements. One body deals primarily with working out the details of the legislature's intent, for example, how many questions should be on the license exam, what variety should be included and how often the exam should be offered and where. This body or group is called a **real estate commission** in most states and has from 5 to 9 members. Some members are licensees from the real estate community while others are nonlicensed members of the general public. Commission members are volunteers selected by the governor to represent all geographical parts of the state. Meetings are usually held monthly at which members provide input to the state on such matters as the needs of real estate licensees, state policies regarding real estate and the welfare of the general public in dealing with licensees.

The state's real estate **executive director,** or similar title, is appointed by the state to oversee real estate regulation. This person's responsibility is to carry out the wishes of the legislature and the real estate commission on a day-to-day basis. To assist in this, the legislature establishes a second body called a real estate department or real estate division.

Real Estate Department

Staffed by full-time civil service employees, the **real estate department** or **real estate division** answers correspondence, sends out application forms, arranges for examinations, collects fees, issues licenses, approves subdivision reports and so forth. Staff is also available for the investigation of alleged malpractices and for audits of broker trust fund accounts. Additionally, the department publishes a periodic newsletter or magazine to keep licensees informed about changes in real estate law and prints books or leaflets describing the state's license and subdivision laws. In short, it is the real estate department with which licensees have the most contact, but it is the commission, the executive director and the legislature that set license requirements and tell a licensee what he can and cannot do in real estate transactions. Figure 18:1 provides a visual summary of what has just been discussed.

LICENSE SUSPENSION AND REVOCATION

The most important control mechanism a state has over its real estate salespersons and brokers is that it can **suspend** (temporarily make ineffective) or **revoke** (recall and make void) a

REAL ESTATE REGULATION   **Figure 18:1**

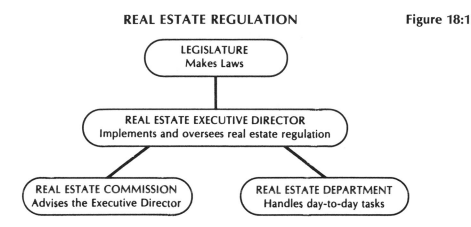

real estate license. Without one, it is unlawful for a person to engage in real estate activities for the purpose of earning a commission or fee. Unless an agent has a valid license, a court of law will not uphold his claim for a commission from a client.

Reasons for license suspension and revocation include any violation of the state's real estate act, misrepresentation or false promises, undisclosed dual agency, commingling and acting as an undisclosed principal. Licenses can also be revoked or suspended for false advertising, obtaining a license by fraud, negligence or incompetence, failure to supervise salespersons, failure to properly account for clients' funds, practicing law without a license, paying commissions to unlicensed persons, conviction of a felony or certain types of misdemeanors, dishonest conduct in general and, in many states, failure to have a fixed termination date on an exclusive listing.

When the real estate commissioner or director receives a complaint from someone who feels he was wronged by a licensee, an investigation is conducted by the real estate department staff. Statements are received from witnesses. Title company records, public records and the licensee's bank records are checked as necessary. The commissioner or director may call an informal conference and invite all parties involved to attend. If it appears the complaint is serious enough and that a violation of the law has occurred, a formal hearing is held in the presence of the full commission. The licensee, the party bringing the complaint and any necessary witnesses appear. Testimony is taken under oath and a written record is made of the proceedings. If the commissioner or director decides to suspend or revoke the respondent's license, the respondent has the right of appeal to the courts.

BONDS AND
RECOVERY FUNDS

The potential of license loss for a wrongdoing strongly encourages licensees to operate within the law. However, suspension or revocation of a license does nothing to provide financial compensation for any losses suffered by a wronged party. This must be recovered from the broker either through a mutually agreed upon monetary settlement or a court judgment resulting from a civil lawsuit brought by the wronged party. But all too often court judgments turn out to be uncollectible because the defendant has no money.

There are two common solutions to the uncollectible judgment problem. Six states (Alabama, Alaska, Massachusetts, Montana, Tennessee and West Virginia) require that a person post a **bond** with the state before a license will be issued. In the event of an otherwise uncollectible court judgment against a licensee, the bond money is used to provide payment. Bond requirements vary from $1,000 to $50,000 with $5,000 to $10,000 being the most popular range. Licensees can obtain these bonds from bonding companies for an annual fee or post the required amount of cash or securities with the state.

The second method of protecting the public is through a state-sponsored **recovery fund.** A portion of the money that each licensee pays for a real estate license is set aside in a fund which is made available for the payment of otherwise uncollectible judgments. Recovery funds offer coverage ranging from $2,000 to $100,000 per licensee with most states in the $25,000 to $50,000 range. The District of Columbia and 33 states use recovery funds. The states are Alabama, Alaska, Arizona, Arkansas, California, Colorado, Connecticut, Delaware, Florida, Georgia, Hawaii, Idaho, Illinois, Kansas, Kentucky, Louisiana, Maryland, Minnesota, Nevada, New Jersey, New Mexico, North Carolina, North Dakota, Ohio, Oklahoma, Pennsylvania, Rhode Island, South Dakota, Tennessee, Texas, Utah, Virginia and Wyoming.

The requirement for bonds and the establishment of recovery funds are not perfect solutions to the problem of uncollectible judgments because the wronged party must expend considerable effort to recover his loss, and it is quite possible that the maximum amount available per transaction or licensee will not fully compensate for the losses suffered. However, either system is better than none at all.

Be aware that there may be times when a real estate salesperson or broker also needs a securities license. This occurs when the property being sold is an investment contract in real estate rather than real estate itself. This investment contract is classified as a **security.** Examples of securities include real estate limited partnerships, rental pools where condominium owners put their units into a pool for a percentage of the pool's income, and some timeshares. Securities licenses are issued by the National Association of Securities Dealers based on successful completion of their examination. Legal counsel is advised if there is the possibility you may be selling securities. Counsel will also advise on state and federal laws requiring the registration of real estate securities before they are sold.

SECURITIES LICENSE

If you plan to enter real estate sales, selecting a broker to work for is one of the most important decisions you must make. The best way to approach it is to carefully consider what you have to offer the real estate business and what you expect in return. And look at it in that order! It is easy to become captivated by the big commission income you visualize coming your way. But if that is your only perspective, you will meet with disappointment. The reason people will pay you money is to receive some product or service in return. Your clients are not concerned with your income goal; it is only incidental to their goals. If you help them attain their goals, you will reach yours.

Before applying for a real estate license, ask yourself if the working hours and conditions of a real estate agent are suitable to you. Specifically, are you prepared to work on a commission-only basis? Evenings and weekends? On your own? With people you've never met before? If you can comfortably answer "Yes" to these questions, then start looking for a broker to sponsor you. (Salesperson license educational requirements can be completed and the examination taken without broker sponsorship, but a salesperson must have a broker to work for before the actual license is issued.)

AFFILIATING WITH A BROKER

Training   Your next step is to look for those features and qualities in a broker that will complement, enhance and encourage your personal development in real estate. If you are new to the industry, training and education will most likely be at the top of your list. Therefore, in looking for a broker you will want to find one that will in one fashion or another teach you the trade. (What you have learned to date from books, classes and license examination preparation will be helpful, but you will need additional specific training.) Real estate franchise operations and large brokerage offices usually offer extensive training. In smaller offices, the broker in charge is usually responsible for seeing that newcomers receive training. An office that offers no training to a newcomer should be avoided.

Compensation   Another question high on your list will be compensation. Very few offices provide a newcomer with a guaranteed minimum wage or even a draw against future commissions. Most brokers feel that one must produce to be paid and the hungrier the salesperson, the quicker the production. A broker who pays salespersons regardless of sales produced simply must siphon the money from those who are producing. The old saying, "There's no such thing as a free lunch" applies to sales commissions.

Compensation for salespersons is usually a percentage of the commissions they earn for the broker. How much each receives is open to negotiation between the broker and each salesperson working for him. A broker who provides office space, extensive secretarial help, a large advertising budget, a mailing program and generous long-distance telephone privileges might take 40% to 50% of each incoming commission dollar for office overhead. A broker who provides fewer services might take 25% or 30%.

Salespersons with proven sales records can usually reduce the portion of each commission dollar that must go to the broker. This is because the broker knows that with an outstanding sales performer, a high volume of sales will offset a smaller percentage for overhead. Conversely, a new and untried salesperson, or one with a mediocre past sales record, may have to give up a larger portion of each dollar for the broker's overhead.

When one brokerage agency lists a property and another locates the buyer, the commission is split according to any agreement the two brokers wish to make. The most common arrangement is a fifty-fifty split. After splitting, each broker pays a portion of the money he receives to the salesperson involved in accordance with their commission agreement.

While investigating commission arrangements, one should also inquire about incentive and bonus plans, automobile expense reimbursement, health insurance, life insurance, errors and omission insurance and retirement plans.

An alternative commission arrangement is the **100% commission** wherein the salesperson does not share his commission with the broker. Instead the salesperson is charged a fee for office space, advertising, telephone, multiple listing and any other expenses the broker incurs on behalf of the salesperson. Generally speaking, 100% arrangements are more popular with proven performers than with newcomers.

Broker Support

Broker support will have an impact on success. Specifically: Does each salesperson have a desk to work from? Are office facilities efficient and modern? Does the broker provide secretarial services? What is the broker's advertising policy and who pays for ads? Who pays for signs, business cards, franchise fees and realty board dues? Does the broker have sources of financing for clients? Does the broker allow his salespersons to invest in real estate? Does the broker have a good reputation in the community?

Finding a Broker

Many licensees associate with a particular broker as a result of friendship or word-of-mouth information. However, there are other ways to find a suitable position. An excellent way to start your search is to decide what geographical area you want to work in. If you choose the same community or neighborhood in which you live, you will already possess a valuable sense and feel for that area.

Having selected a geographical area, look in the Sunday newspaper real estate advertisements section and the telephone book Yellow Pages for names of brokers. Hold interviews with several brokers and as you do, remember that you are interviewing them just as intensively as they are interviewing you.

At your visits with brokers be particularly alert for your feelings. Intuition can be as valuable a guide to a sound working relationship as can a list of questions and answers regarding the job.

As you narrow your choices, revisit the offices of brokers who particularly impressed you. Talk with some of the salespersons who have worked or are working there. They can be very candid and valuable sources of information. Be wary of individuals who are extreme in their opinions: rely instead on the consensus of opinion. Locate clients who have used the firm's services and ask them their opinions of the firm. You might also talk to local appraisers, lenders and escrow agents for candid opinions. If you do all this advance work, the benefits to you will be greater enjoyment of your work, more money in your pocket and less likelihood of wanting to quit or move to another office.

Employment Contract

Having selected a broker with whom to associate, your next step is to make an employment contract. An **employment contract** formalizes the working arrangement between the broker and his salespersons. An oral contract may be satisfactory, but a written one is preferred because it sets forth the relationship with a higher degree of precision and is a written record of the agreement. This greatly reduces the potential for future controversy and litigation.

The employment contract will cover such matters as compensation (how much and under what circumstances), training (how often and if required), hours of work (including assigned office hours and open houses), company identification (distinctive articles of clothing and name tags), fees and dues (license and realty board), expenses (automobile, advertising, telephone), fringe benefits (health and life insurance, pension and profit-sharing plans), withholding (income taxes and social security), territory (assigned area of the community), termination of employment (quitting and firing), and general office policies and procedures (office manual).

INDEPENDENT CONTRACTOR STATUS

Is the real estate sales associate an employee of the broker or an independent contractor? The answer is both. On one hand, the sales associate acts like an **employee** because the associate works for the broker, usually at the broker's place of business and prepares listings and sales documents on forms specified by the broker and upon closing receives payment from the broker. On the other hand, the sales associate acts like an **independent contractor** because the associate is paid only if the associate brings about a sale that produces a commission. An important distinction between the two is whether or not the broker must withhold income taxes and social security from the associate's commission checks. If the sales associate is considered by the Internal Revenue Service (IRS) to be an employee for tax purposes, the broker must withhold. If classed as an independent contractor for tax purposes, the sales associate is responsible for his own income taxes and social security. The IRS prefers employee status because it is easier to collect taxes from an employer than an employee and because the combined social security contribution of employer and employee is greater than that paid by a self-employed person earning the same amount.

As a result of federal legislation that took effect January 1, 1983, the IRS will treat real estate sales associates as independent contractors if they meet all of the following three requirements. First, the associate must be a licensed real estate agent. Second, substantially all of the associate's payment for services as a real estate agent must be directly related to sales and not to hours worked. Third, a written agreement must exist between the associate and the broker stating that the associate will be treated as an independent contractor for tax purposes.

These are highlights of the issue. If you plan to work for a broker, you may find it valuable to have this matter as well as your entire employment contract reviewed by an attorney before you sign it.

FRANCHISED OFFICES

Prior to the early 1970s, real estate brokerage was a small business industry. Most brokerages were one-office firms. A large brokerage was one having four or five offices and selling 200 properties a year. Then real estate franchise organizations entered the real estate business in a big way. **Franchisors** such as Century-21, Red Carpet and Gallery of Homes offered brokerage firms national identification, large-scale advertising, sales staff training programs, management advice, customer referrals, financing help for buyers, and guaranteed sales plans. In return, the brokerage firm (the **franchisee**) paid a fee of from 3% to 8% of gross commission income. The idea became popular and by the mid-1980s approximately half of the real estate licensees affiliated with the National Association of Realtors were working in franchised offices. Meanwhile, the number of franchisors grew to over 60 including such names as Realty World, ERA, International Real Estate Network, Better Homes and Gardens Realty, and Mayflower Realty.

Statistics show that franchising appeals mostly to firms with 10 to 50 sales associates. Larger firms are more capable of providing the advantages of a franchise for themselves. Smaller firms tend to occupy market niches and often consist of one or two licensees who do not bring in additional sales associates. For a newly licensed salesperson wishing to affiliate with a firm, a franchised firm offers immediate public recognition, extensive training opportunities, established office routines, regular sales meetings, and access to a nationwide referral system. Franchise affiliation is not magic however; success still depends on the individual to make sales calls, value property, get listings, advertise, show property, qualify, negotiate and close transactions.

National Real Estate Firms   During the late 1970s a large real estate firm in California—Coldwell Banker—began an expansion program by purchasing multibranch real estate firms in other states. Today, the Coldwell Banker chain has over one thousand offices across the United States. Merrill Lynch, the Wall Street stock brokerage firm, has also entered the real estate brokerage business. It, too, has bought existing real estate brokerage firms to accomplish this and now has more real estate agents than stockbrokers. Other Wall Street firms are looking into the real estate brokerage business, as are several large corporations such as Sears, Roebuck which has purchased Coldwell Banker. Other large national and regional firms include Cushman and Wakefield, Grubb and Ellis, Long and Foster, Shannon and Luchs, Marcus and Millichap, and Rubloff, Inc.

For a newcomer, affiliating with a national or regional real estate firm offers benefits like those of a franchised firm (recognition, training, routines, etc.). The main difference is who owns the firm. A franchised firm will be locally owned and managed, i.e., an independent firm. Regional and national firms are locally managed, but the sales associate will only occasionally, if ever, meet the owner(s).

Even before laws required real estate agents to have licenses, there were professional real estate organizations. Called real estate boards, they joined together agents within a city or county on a voluntary basis. The push to organize came from real estate people who saw the need for some sort of controlling organization that could supervise the activities of individual agents and elevate the profession's status in the public's mind. Next came the gradual grouping of local boards into state associations, and finally, in 1908, the National Association of Real Estate Boards (NAREB) was formed. In 1914, NAREB developed a model license law that became the basis for real estate license laws in many states.

Today the local boards are still the fundamental units of the National Association of Realtors (NAR; the name was changed from NAREB in 1974). Local board membership is open to anyone holding a real estate license. Called boards of Realtors, real estate boards and realty boards, they promote fair dealing among their members and with the public and protect members from dishonest and irresponsible licensees. They also promote legislation that protects property rights, offer short seminars to keep members up to date with current laws and practices and, in general, do whatever is necessary to build the dignity, stability and professionalization of the industry. Local boards often operate the local multiple listing service, although in some communities it is a privately owned and operated business.

State associations are composed of the members of local boards plus sales associates and brokers who live in areas where no local board exists. The purposes of the state associations are to unite members statewide, to encourage legislation that benefits and protects the real estate industry and safeguards the public in their real estate transactions, and to promote economic growth and development in the state. Also, state associations hold conventions to educate members and foster contacts among them.

PROFESSIONAL REAL ESTATE ASSOCIATIONS

Realtor   The NAR is made up of local boards and state associations in the United States. The term **"Realtor"** is a registered trade name that belongs to NAR. Realtor is not synonymous with real estate agent. It is reserved for the exclusive use of members of the National Association of Realtors, who as part of their membership pledge themselves to abide by the Association's Code of Ethics. The term "Realtor" cannot be used by non-members and in some states the unauthorized use of the term is a violation of the real estate law. Prior to 1974, the use of the term "Realtor" was primarily reserved for principal brokers. Then by a national membership vote, the decision was made to create an additional membership class, the **Realtor-Associate,** for salesperson and broker licensees working for members.

CODE OF ETHICS   One of the most important features of the National Association of Realtors is its **Code of Ethics.** First adopted in 1913, the Realtor Code of Ethics has been revised several times since then and now contains 23 articles that pertain to the Realtor's relation to his clients, to other real estate agents, and to the public as a whole. The full Code is reproduced in Figure 18:2.

Although a complete review of each article is beyond the scope of this chapter, it can be seen that some articles parallel existing laws. For example, Article 10 speaks against racial discrimination and Article 12 speaks for full disclosure. However, the bulk of the Code addresses itself to the obligations of a Realtor that are beyond the written law. For example, in Article 2, the Realtor agrees to stay informed regarding laws and regulations, proposed legislation and current market conditions in order to advise clients properly. In Article 5, the Realtor agrees to willingly share with other Realtors the lessons of experience. In other words, to be recognized as a Realtor, one must not only comply with the letter of the law, but also observe the ethical standards by which the industry operates.

In some states, ethical standards such as those in the NAR Code of Ethics have been legislated into law. Called **canons** or **standards of conduct,** their intent is to promote ethical practices by all real estate licensees not just by those who join the National Association of Realtors. Additionally, the National Association of Realtors publishes 34 **Standards of Practice.** These interpret various articles in the Code of Ethics.

CODE OF ETHICS   **Figure 18:2**

Preamble . . .

Under all is the land. Upon its wise utilization and widely allocated ownership depend the survival and growth of free institutions and of our civilization. The REALTOR® should recognize that the interests of the nation and its citizens require the highest and best use of the land and the widest distribution of land ownership. They require the creation of adequate housing, the building of functioning cities, the development of productive industries and farms, and the preservation of a healthful environment.

Such interests impose obligations beyond those of ordinary commerce. They impose grave social responsibility and a patriotic duty to which the REALTOR® should dedicate himself, and for which he should be diligent in preparing himself. The REALTOR®, therefore, is zealous to maintain and improve the standards of his calling and shares with his fellow-REALTORS® a common responsibility for its integrity and honor. The term REALTOR® has come to connote competency, fairness, and high integrity resulting from adherence to a lofty ideal of moral conduct in business relations. No inducement of profit and no instruction from clients ever can justify departure from this ideal.

In the interpretation of his obligation, a REALTOR® can take no safer guide than that which has been handed down through the centuries, embodied in the Golden Rule, "Whatsoever ye would that men should do to you, do ye even so to them."

Accepting this standard as his own, every REALTOR® pledges himself to observe its spirit in all of his activities and to conduct his business in accordance with the tenets set forth below.

ARTICLE 1

The REALTOR® should keep himself informed on matters affecting real estate in his community, the state, and nation so that he may be able to contribute responsibly to public thinking on such matters.

ARTICLE 2

In justice to those who place their interests in his care, the REALTOR® should endeavor always to be informed regarding laws, proposed legislation, governmental regulations, public policies, and current market conditions in order to be in a position to advise his clients properly.

ARTICLE 3

It is the duty of the REALTOR® to protect the public against fraud, misrepresentation, and unethical practices in real estate transactions. He should endeavor to eliminate in his community any practices which could be damaging to the public or bring discredit to the real estate profession. The REALTOR® should assist the governmental agency charged with regulating the practices of brokers and salesmen in his state.

ARTICLE 4

The REALTOR® should seek no unfair advantage over other REALTORS® and should conduct his business so as to avoid controversies with other REALTORS®.

ARTICLE 5

In the best interests of society, of his associates, and his own business, the REALTOR® should willingly share with other REALTORS® the lessons of his experience and study for the benefit of the public, and should be loyal to the Board of REALTORS® of his community and active in its work.

ARTICLE 6

To prevent dissension and misunderstanding and to assure better service to the owner, the REALTOR® should urge the exclusive listing of property unless contrary to the best interest of the owner.

Figure 18:2 *continued*

ARTICLE 7

In accepting employment as an agent, the REALTOR® pledges himself to protect and promote the interests of the client. This obligation of absolute fidelity to the client's interests is primary, but it does not relieve the REALTOR® of the obligation to treat fairly all parties to the transaction.

ARTICLE 8

The REALTOR® shall not accept compensation from more than one party, even if permitted by law, without the full knowledge of all parties to the transaction.

ARTICLE 9

The REALTOR® shall avoid exaggeration, misrepresentation, or concealment of pertinent facts. He has an affirmative obligation to discover adverse factors that a reasonably competent and diligent investigation would disclose.

ARTICLE 10

The REALTOR® shall not deny equal professional services to any person for reasons of race, creed, sex, or country of national origin. The REALTOR® shall not be a party to any plan or agreement to discriminate against a person or persons on the basis of race, creed, sex, or country of national origin.

ARTICLE 11

A REALTOR® is expected to provide a level of competent service in keeping with the Standards of Practice in those fields in which the REALTOR® customarily engages.

The REALTOR® shall not undertake to provide specialized professional services concerning a type of property or service that is outside his field of competence unless he engages the assistance of one who is competent on such types of property or service, or unless the facts are fully disclosed to the client. Any person engaged to provide such assistance shall be so identified to the client and his contribution to the assignment should be set forth.

The REALTOR® shall refer to the Standards of Practice of the National Association as to the degree of competence that a client has a right to expect the REALTOR® to possess, taking into consideration the complexity of the problem, the availability of expert assistance, and the opportunities for experience available to the REALTOR®.

ARTICLE 12

The REALTOR® shall not undertake to provide professional services concerning a property or its value where he has a present or contemplated interest unless such interest is specifically disclosed to all affected parties.

ARTICLE 13

The REALTOR® shall not acquire an interest in or buy for himself, any member of his immediate family, his firm or any member thereof, or any entity in which he has a substantial ownership interest, property listed with him, without making the true position known to the listing owner. In selling property owned by himself, or in which he has any interest, the REALTOR® shall reveal the facts of his ownership or interest to the purchaser.

ARTICLE 14

In the event of a controversy between REALTORS® associated with different firms, arising out of their relationship as REALTORS®, the REALTORS® shall submit the dispute to arbitration in accordance with the regulations of their board or boards rather than litigate the matter.

ARTICLE 15

If a REALTOR® is charged with unethical practice or is asked to present evidence in any disciplinary proceeding or investigation, he shall place all pertinent facts before the proper tribunal of the member board or affiliated institute, society, or council of which he is a member.

Figure 18:2 *continued*

ARTICLE 16

When acting as agent, the REALTOR® shall not accept any commission, rebate, or profit on expenditures made for his principal-owner, without the principal's knowledge and consent.

ARTICLE 17

The REALTOR® shall not engage in activities that constitute the unauthorized practice of law and shall recommend that legal counsel be obtained when the interest of any party to the transaction requires it.

ARTICLE 18

The REALTOR® shall keep in a special account in an appropriate financial institution, separated from his own funds, monies coming into his possession in trust for other persons, such as escrows, trust funds, clients' monies, and other like items.

ARTICLE 19

The REALTOR® shall be careful at all times to present a true picture in his advertising and representations to the public. He shall neither advertise without disclosing his name nor permit any person associated with him to use individual names or telephone numbers, unless such person's connection with the REALTOR® is obvious in the advertisement.

ARTICLE 20

The REALTOR®, for the protection of all parties, shall see that financial obligations and commitments regarding real estate transactions are in writing, expressing the exact agreement of the parties. A copy of each agreement shall be furnished to each party upon his signing such agreement.

ARTICLE 21

The REALTOR® shall not engage in any practice or take any action inconsistent with the agency of another REALTOR®.

ARTICLE 22

In the sale of property which is exclusively listed with a REALTOR®, the REALTOR® shall utilize the services of other brokers upon mutually agreed upon terms when it is in the best interests of the client.

Negotiations concerning property which is listed exclusively shall be carried on with the listing broker, not with the owner, except with the consent of the listing broker.

ARTICLE 23

The REALTOR® shall not publicly disparage the business practice of a competitor nor volunteer an opinion of a competitor's transaction. If his opinion is sought and if the REALTOR® deems it appropriate to respond, such opinion shall be rendered with strict professional integrity and courtesy.

Where the word REALTOR® is used in this Code and Preamble, it shall be deemed to include REALTOR®-ASSOCIATE. Pronouns shall be considered to include REALTORS® and REALTOR®-ASSOCIATES of both genders.

The Code of Ethics was adopted in 1913. Amended at the Annual Convention in 1924, 1928, 1950, 1951, 1952, 1955, 1956, 1961, 1962, 1974 and 1982.

In addition to its emphasis on real estate brokerage, the National Association of Realtors also contains a number of specialized professional groups within itself. These include the American Institute of Real Estate Appraisers, the Farm and Land Institute, the Institute of Real Estate Management, the Realtors National Marketing Institute, the Society of Industrial Realtors, the Real Estate Securities and Syndication Institute, the American Society of Real Estate Counselors, the American Chapter of the International Real Estate Federation and the Women's Council of Realtors. Membership is open to Realtors interested in these specialties.

Realtist   The National Association of Real Estate Brokers (NAREB) is a national trade association representing minority real estate professionals actively engaged in the industry. Founded in 1947, its 5,000 members use the trade name **Realtist.** The organization extends through 14 regions across the country with more than 60 active local boards. NAREB education and certification programs include the Real Estate Management Brokers Institute, National Society of Real Estate Appraisers, Real Estate Brokerage Institute, and United Developers Council. The organization's purposes are to promote high standards of service and conduct and to protect the public against unethical, improper or fraudulent real estate practices.

GRI Designation   To help encourage and recognize professionalism in the real estate industry, state Boards of Realtors sponsor education courses leading to the GRI designation. Course offerings typically include real estate law, finance, appraisal, investments, office management and salesmanship. Upon completion of the prescribed curriculum, the designation, Graduate Realtor's Institute is awarded.

VOCABULARY REVIEW

Match terms **a-x** with statements **1-24.**

a. *Broker*
b. *Code of Ethics*
c. *Continuing education*
d. *Employment contract*
e. *Fictitious business name*
f. *Franchisee*
g. *GRI*

h. *Independent contractor*
i. *Licensee*
j. *Nonresident license*
k. *Notice of content*
l. *Principal broker*
m. *Real estate commission*
n. *Real estate salesperson*

o. *Realtist*　　　　　　　**t.** *Revoke*
p. *Realtor*　　　　　　　**u.** *Sales associate*
q. *Realtor-Associate*　　**v.** *Securities license*
r. *Realty board*　　　　　**w.** *Standards of practice*
s. *Recovery fund*　　　　**x.** *Suspend*

1. One who holds a license.
2. A person who is licensed to bring about real estate transactions for a fee, but who must do so only in the employment of a real estate broker.
3. A registered trademark owned by the National Association of Realtors for exclusive use by its members.
4. Broker in charge of an office.
5. A business operated under any name other than the owner's name.
6. An independent agent who negotiates transactions for a fee.
7. To temporarily make ineffective.
8. To recall and make void.
9. A local trade organization for real estate licensees and other persons allied with the real estate industry.
10. A state-operated fund that can be tapped to pay for uncollectible judgments against real estate licensees.
11. A salesperson or broker employed by a broker.
12. A state board that advises and sets policies regarding real estate licensees and real estate transaction procedures.
13. One who uses his own methods and is responsible only as to the results.
14. A requirement for license renewal in many states, its purpose is to help licensees keep up to date in real estate.
15. Required of a real estate broker in order to conduct negotiations within another state.
16. Permits the secretary of state to receive legal summonses on behalf of a nonresident broker.
17. Required when selling an investment contract.
18. Formalizes the working arrangement between the broker and his salespersons.
19. The party holding a franchise such as a franchised brokerage office.
20. Membership designation for salespersons and broker licensees working for Realtors.
21. Standards by which members of the National Association of Realtors agree to abide.
22. Interpretations of various articles of the Realtors Code of Ethics.
23. A registered trademark for use by members of the National Association of Real Estate Brokers.
24. A designation awarded for completion of real estate courses sponsored by Boards of Realtors.

QUESTIONS AND
PROBLEMS

1. What was the purpose of early real estate license laws?
2. When is a person required to hold a real estate license?
3. What factors does a broker consider when deciding what percentage of commissions should be paid to the salespersons in his office?
4. Does your state subscribe to the ETS, ACT, or ASI exam service or does it write all its own questions? How often are the exams given?
5. What trends are apparent in your state with regard to real estate education requirements?
6. What is the name of the person currently in charge of real estate regulation for your state? What are his (her) duties and responsibilities?
7. How is the real estate commission selected in your state? What are its duties and responsibilities?
8. Under what circumstances are real estate licenses suspended or revoked in your state?
9. What is the purpose of a bond or recovery fund? What does your state require?
10. What is the purpose of the National Association of Realtors?
11. An employment contract between a broker and a salesperson would cover what items?
12. If you were seeking employment as a salesperson for a brokerage firm, how would you decide what firm to associate with?

ADDITIONAL
READINGS

Business Opportunities Brokerage by **Edward Bernd.** (Prentice-Hall, 1983, 169 pages). A practical, readable book on what to do when a client asks you to sell a muffler shop, wine and cheese store, country-western lounge, or yarn and knitting shop, and you don't want to turn down the listing because you don't know how.

Design-a-Day. (Page Unlimited, 1-800-368-5045, 1986). This is a three-ring calendar notebook designed for real estate agents. Has daily pages for appointments, expenses, mileage, notes and important reminders. Also has sections for commission records, telephone numbers, loan tables, appraisal checklist and common abbreviations. Published annually.

Digest of Real Estate License Laws. (National Association of Real Estate License Law Officials, 1986, 165 pages). Contains summaries of real estate license laws for each of the United States and the Canadian Provinces. Published annually.

"Price Competition for Residential Brokerage" by **John Crockett.** (*Real Estate Review*, Winter 84, page 98). Article states that when the commission rate is fixed, the competition among brokerage firms leads to excessive hiring of sales agents who then stay busy by spending significant amounts of time at tasks that add little to the services they produce.

Protecting Your Sales Commission: Professional Liability in Real Estate by **Ronald Friedman** and **Benjamin Henszy.** (Real Estate Education Co., 1982, 280 pages). Book alerts real estate licensees to their professional liability in misrepresentation, conflict of interest, standard of care and fiduciary duties. Also covers broker's right to compensation and what a broker should do if sued.

"The Code of Ethics" (*Real Estate Today*, Feb 85, pages 46–59). This feature section contains the following articles: "Ethics: The Starting Point of Success," "Wait! Let's Arbitrate," "Complaints: Handle With Care," "The Value of Your Reputation" and "How to Create a Client/Customer Relations Department."

"Unlawful, Unethical or Unbusinesslike?" by **Fred Crane** and **Simon Sykes.** (*First Tuesday*, Nov 83 through Jun 84). This is an eight-part series on where the dividing line lies between unlawful, unethical and unbusinesslike behavior for real estate brokers and salespersons.

*   *   *

The following periodicals may also be of interest to you: *Affirmative Action Register, Civil Rights Update, Real Estate Business, Real Estate Perspectives, Real Estate Selling, Real Estate Success Secrets, Real Estate Today* and *Realtor News.*

Condominiums, Cooperatives, PUDs and Timeshares

Bylaws: rules that govern how an owners' association will be run

CC&Rs: covenants, conditions and restrictions by which a property owner agrees to abide

Common elements: those parts of a condominium which are owned by all the unit owners

Condominium: individual ownership of a space of air plus undivided ownership of the common elements

Cooperative: land and building owned or leased by a corporation which, in turn, leases space to its shareholders

Limited common elements: common elements whose use is limited to certain owners

Planned Unit Development: individually owned lots and houses with community ownership of common areas

Proprietary lease: a lease issued by a cooperative corporation to its shareholders

Reserves: money set aside for expenses that do not occur every month

Timesharing: the exclusive use of a property for a specified number of days each year

HISTORY

The idea of combining community living with community ownership is not new. Two thousand years ago, the Roman Senate passed condominium laws that permitted Roman citizens to own individual dwelling units in multiunit buildings. This form of ownership resulted because land was scarce and expensive in Rome. After the fall of the Roman Empire, condominium ownership was used in the walled cities of the Middle Ages. Here it was primarily a defensive measure as residing outside the walls was dangerous due to roving bands of raiders. With the stabilization of governments after the Middle Ages the condominium concept became dormant. Then in the early twentieth century, in response to land scarcity in cities, the idea was revived in Western Europe. From there the concept spread to several Latin American countries and, in 1951, to Puerto Rico. Puerto Rican laws and experience in turn became the basis for passage by Congress in 1961 of Section 234 of the National Housing Act. Designed as a legal model that condominium developers could follow in order to obtain FHA loan

485

insurance, Section 234 also served as a model for state condominium laws now in effect across the United States.

In this chapter we shall begin with a discussion of condominiums, in particular an overview of their organization, operation, benefits and drawbacks. Then we shall turn our attention to cooperatives, planned unit developments and timesharing.

CONDOMINIUM

The first step in creating a **condominium** is for the state to pass laws that create the legal framework for condominium ownership. All states have passed them, and they are variously known as a state's horizontal property act, strata titles act, **condominium act** or by a similar name. They all follow the FHA model plus each state's particular refinements. As the names suggest, these laws address the problem of subdividing the airspace over a given parcel of land. Prior to these acts, the legal framework that made it possible for people to own a cubicle of airspace plus an undivided interest in the shell of the building and the land under and around the building did not exist. Moreover, condominium acts had to be designed to be acceptable to lenders who would be asked to loan on condominiums, property tax authorities who would have to assess them, and income tax authorities who would allow owners to deduct loan interest and property taxes. The lawmakers were successful and today millions of people live in condominiums.

Physically, a condominium can take the shape of a 2-story garden apartment building, a 40-story tower with several living units on each floor, row houses, clustered houses or even detached houses sharing a single parcel of land. Condominiums are not restricted to residential uses. In recent years, a number of developers across the nation have built office buildings and sold individual suites to doctors, dentists and lawyers. The same idea has been applied to shopping centers and industrial space. A condominium does not have to be a new building: many existing apartment houses have been converted from rental status to condominium ownership with only a few physical changes to the building.

Separate and Common Elements

The distinguishing features of a condominium are its separate and common elements and its system of self-government. The separate elements, called **separate property,** are those areas in the condominium that are exclusively owned and used by the individual condominium owners. These are the individual dwelling units in the building. More precisely, the separate property is the airspace occupied by a unit. This is the space lying between the interior surfaces of the unit walls and between the floor and the ceiling. Everything else is a common element in which each unit owner holds an undivided interest. Thus the land and the shell of the building are **common elements** owned by all. Common elements include, for example, the manager's apartment, lobby, hallways, stairways, elevators, recreation areas, landscaping and parking lot. Sometimes you will hear the term **limited common element.** This is a common element the use of which is restricted to a specific unit owner. Examples are assigned parking stalls and individual storage units.

Owners' Association

When a developer wants to create a condominium (either built from the ground up or the conversion of an existing building to condominium ownership), the developer prepares and records with the public recorder what is variously known as an enabling declaration, master deed, plan of condominium ownership or **condominium subdivision.** This document, usually 50 to 150 pages long, converts a parcel of land held under a single deed into a number of individual separate property estates (the condominium units) and an estate composed of all the common elements. Survey maps are included to show the location of each condominium unit plus all the common elements.

The developer also creates a legal framework so that the unit owners can govern themselves. This is the condominium **owner's association** of which each unit purchaser automatically becomes a member. Although the association can be organized as a trust or unincorporated association, most often it will be organized as a corporation so as to provide the legal protections normally afforded by a corporation to its owners. Additionally, it will be organized as not-for-profit so as to avoid income taxes on money collected from members. The main purpose of the owners' association is to control, regulate and maintain the common elements for the overall welfare and benefit of its members. The owners' association is a mini-government by and for the condominium owners.

Bylaws   The rules by which an owners' association operates are called its **bylaws.** They are prepared by the developer's attorney and recorded with the master deed. The bylaws provide the rules by which the association's board of directors is elected and set the standards by which the board must rule. The bylaws set forth how association dues (maintenance fees) will be established and collected, how contracts will be let for maintenance, management and repair work, and how personnel will be hired.

CC&Rs   Finally, the developer must file a list of regulations by which anyone purchasing a unit in the condominium must abide. These are known as **covenants, conditions and restrictions (CC&Rs).** They tell a unit owner such things as not to store personal items on balconies or driveways, what color the exterior of the living room drapes should be, to what extent an owner can alter the exterior of his unit, and whether an owner can install a satellite television dish on the roof. Additional regulations may be embodied in a set of **house rules.** Typically, these govern such things as when the swimming pool and other recreation facilities will be open for use and when quiet hours will be observed in the building.

Deed   Each purchaser of a condominium unit receives a deed from the developer. The deed describes the location of the unit, both in terms of the unit number in the building and its surveyed airspace. The deed will also describe the common elements and state the percentage interest in the common elements that the grantee is receiving. The deed is recorded upon closing just like a deed to a house.

Upon selling, the owner has a new deed prepared that describes the unit and the common element interest and delivers it to the purchaser at closing. If the condominium is on leased land, the developer will deliver a lease (or sublease) to the unit buyer. Upon resale, that lease is assigned to the buyer.

Voting Rules   Once the units in the building have been sold and the association turned over to the unit owners, the unit owners can change the rules. Generally, the bylaws require a three-fourths vote and the CC&Rs require a two-thirds vote from the association members for a change. House rules can be changed with a simple majority or, in some cases, by the board of directors without a vote of the association.

Condominium bylaws provide that a **board of directors** be elected by the association members. The board is authorized to administer the affairs of the condominium including purchasing of hazard and liability insurance for the common elements, arranging for maintenance and repair of common elements, enforcing CC&Rs and house rules, assessing and collecting a sufficient amount of monthly homeowner fees and special assessments, and listening to complaints and suggestions from unit owners as to how the condominium should be run.

Board of Directors

Board members usually are elected at the annual meeting of the association, are unit owners and serve for one year. Typically there will be 5 to 7 members on the board, and one will be elected as president, one as vice-president, one as secretary and one as treasurer. Meetings are held monthly unless added business requires more frequent meetings. Board meetings are usually open to all association members who then can watch the proceedings and provide input. To help spread the work, the board will appoint committees on which owners are asked to serve. Examples are landscaping, architectural, security, clubhouse and social committees. Directors and committee members are not, as a rule, paid for their time.

Once a year the owners' association as a whole will meet for an **annual meeting.** Besides the election of board members for the following year, this is an opportunity for association members to vote on major issues such as changes in the CC&Rs and bylaws, monthly maintenance fee increases, special assessments and any matter the board feels should be put to a general ownership vote rather than handled at a board meeting. Owners also receive an annual report of the fiscal health of the association and other information pertinent to their ownership.

Annual Meetings

Most condominium associations will employ a condominium **management company** to advise the board and take care of day-to-day tasks. The management company is usually responsible for finding, hiring and paying gardeners, trash haulers, janitors, repair personnel and a pool maintenance firm. The management company collects maintenance fees and spe-

CONDOMINIUM MANAGEMENT

cial assessments from unit owners, accounts for condominium expenses, handles the payroll and pays for contracted services.

If the association chooses to hire an on-site manager, that person is usually responsible for enforcing the house rules, handling complaints or problems regarding maintenance, making daily security checks and supervising the swimming pool and recreation areas. The extent of his or her duties and responsibilities is set by the owners' association. The association should also retain the right to fire the resident manager and the management firm if their services are not satisfactory.

MAINTENANCE FEES

The costs of maintaining the common elements in a condominium are allocated among the unit owners in accordance with percentages set forth in the master deed. These are called **maintenance fees** or **association dues** and are collected monthly. Failure to pay creates a lien against the delinquent owner's unit. The amount collected is based on the association's budget for the coming year. This is based on the board of directors estimate of the cost of month-to-month maintenance, insurance, legal and management services, plus reserves for expenses that do not occur monthly.

Reserves

The importance of setting aside **reserves** each month is illustrated by the following example. Suppose it is estimated that the exterior of a 100-unit building will have to be painted every 7 years and that the cost is expected to be $25,200. To avoid a special painting assessment of $252 per unit, the association instead collects $3 per month from each unit owner for 84 months. If the reserves are kept in an interest-bearing savings account, as they should be, less than $3 per month would need to be collected.

PROPERTY TAXES AND INSURANCE

Since condominium law recognizes each condominium dwelling unit as a separate legal ownership, property taxes are assessed on each unit separately. Property taxes are based on the assessed value of the unit which is based on its market value. As a rule, it is not necessary for the taxing authority to assess and tax the common elements separately. The reason is that the market value of each unit reflects not only the value of the unit itself, but also the value of the fractional ownership in the common elements that accompanies the unit.

The association is responsible for purchasing hazard and liability insurance covering the common elements. Each dwelling unit owner is responsible for purchasing hazard and liability insurance for the interior of his dwelling.

Thus, if a visitor slips on a banana peel in the lobby or a hallway of the building, the association is responsible. If the accident occurs in an individual's unit, the unit owner is responsible. In a high-rise condominium, if the roof breaks during a heavy rainstorm and floods several apartments below, the association is responsible. If an apartment owner's dishwasher overflows and soaks the apartments below him, he is responsible. If patio furniture is stolen from the swimming pool area, the association is responsible. If patio furniture (or any personal property for that matter) is stolen from an individual's unit, that is the unit owner's responsibility. Policies designed for associations and policies for condominium owners are readily available from insurance companies.

If a condominium unit is being rented, the owner will want to have landlord insurance, and the tenant, for his own protection, will want a tenant's hazard and liability policy.

CONDOMINIUM FINANCING

Because each condominium unit can be separately owned, each can be separately financed. Thus, a condominium purchaser can choose whether or not to borrow against his unit. If he borrows, he can choose a large or small down payment and a long or short amortization period. If he wants to repay early or refinance, that is his option too. Upon resale, the buyer can elect to assume the loan, pay it off, or obtain new financing. In other words, while association bylaws, restrictions and house rules may regulate the use of a unit, in no way does the association control how a unit may be financed.

Since each unit is a separate ownership, if a lender needs to foreclose against a delinquent borrower in the building, the remaining unit owners are not involved. They are neither responsible for the delinquent borrower's mortgage debt nor are they parties to the foreclosure.

Loan Terms

Loan terms offered condominium buyers are quite similar to those offered on houses. Typically, lenders will make conventional, uninsured loans for up to 80% of value. With private mortgage insurance, this can be raised to 90% or 95%. On

FHA-approved buildings, the FHA offers insurance terms similar to those for detached dwellings. Financing can also be in the form of an installment contract or a seller carryback.

Deposit Practices

If a project is not already completed and ready for occupancy when it is offered for sale, it is common for the developer to require a substantial deposit. The best practice is to place this in an escrow account payable to the developer upon completion. Without this, some developers use deposits to help pay the expenses of construction while the building is being built. Unfortunately, if the deposits are spent by a developer who goes bankrupt before the project is completed, the buyer receives neither a finished unit nor the return of his deposit. If the deposits are held in escrow, the buyers do not receive a unit but they do get their deposits back.

CONDOMINIUM CONVERSIONS

During the late 1970s the idea of condominium ownership became very popular in the United States. Builders constructed new condominiums at a rapid pace, but there were not enough to fill demand. Soon enterprising developers found that existing apartment buildings could be converted to condominiums and sold to the waiting public. Compared to new construction, a condominium conversion is often simpler, faster and more profitable for the developer. The procedure involves finding an attractively built existing building that is well-located and has good floor plans. The developer does a facelift on the outside, adds more landscaping, paints the interior and replaces carpets and appliances. The developer also files the necessary legal paperwork to convert the building and land into condominium units and common elements.

A potential problem area with condominium conversions, and one that a prospective buyer should be aware of, is that converted buildings are used buildings that were not intended as condominiums when built. As used buildings, there may be considerable deferred maintenance, and the building may have thermal insulation suitable to a time when energy costs were lower. If the building was originally built for rental purposes, sound-deadening insulation in the walls, floors and ceilings may be inadequate. Fire protection between units may also be less than satisfactory. In contrast, newly built condominiums must meet current building code requirements regarding thermal and sound insulation, fire-wall construction and so forth.

It is worth noting that not all condominium conversions are carried out by developers. Enterprising tenants have successfully converted their own buildings and saved considerable sums of money. It is not uncommon for the value of a building to double when it is converted to a condominium. Tenants who are willing to hire the legal, architectural and construction help they need can create valuable condominium homes for themselves in the same building where they were previously renters.

Compared to detached dwellings, condominium living offers a number of advantages and some disadvantages. Let's take a look.

ADVANTAGES OF CONDOMINIUM LIVING

On the advantage side, instead of four or five detached dwellings on an acre of land, a condominium builder can place 25 or even 100 living units. This spreads the cost of the site among more dwellings, and the builder does not have the miles of streets, sewers or utility lines that would be necessary to reach every house in a spread-out subdivision. Furthermore, the use of shared walls and foundations, that one dwelling unit's ceiling is another's floor and that one roof can cover many vertically stacked units can produce savings in construction materials and labor. In central city districts where a single square foot of vacant land can cost $100 or more, only a high-rise condominium can make housing units possible. In the suburbs where land is cheaper, a condominium is often the difference between buying and renting.

Other advantages are the lure of "carefree living" wherein such chores as lawn mowing, watering, weeding, snow removal and building maintenance are provided. For some people, it is the security often associated with clustered dwellings and nearby neighbors. Other advantages are extensive recreational and social facilities that are not economically feasible on a single-dwelling basis. It is commonplace to find swimming pools, recreation halls, tennis and volleyball courts, gymnasiums and even social directors at condominiums.

Lastly, we cannot overlook the psychological and financial advantages of ownership. Many large rental apartment projects produce the same economies of scale and amenities just described. Nonetheless, most Americans prefer to own rather than rent their dwellings. Part of this is the pride of owning something. Part comes from a desire for a savings program, the potential for capital appreciation, and income tax laws that favor owners over renters.

DISADVANTAGES OF CONDOMINIUM LIVING

A major disadvantage of condominium living is the close proximity of one's neighbors and the extra level of government. In other words, buying into a condominium means buying into a group of people whose lifestyles may differ from yours and whose opinions as to how to run the association will differ from yours. By way of contrast, if you buy a single-family detached house on a lot, you will have (subject to zoning and legal restrictions) sole control over the use of it. You can choose to remodel or add on. You can choose what color to paint your house and garage, how many people and animals will live there, what type of landscaping to have, from whom to purchase property insurance, whether to rent it out or live in it, and so on. Your next door neighbor will have the same rights over his land. You cannot dictate to him what color to paint his house, what kind of shrubs to grow or from whom to buy hazard insurance if he buys it at all.

In a condominium, the owners have a considerable degree of control over each other in matters that affect the common good of the association. Moreover, certain decisions must be made as a group, such as what kinds of common element hazard and liability insurance to carry, how much to carry and from whom to purchase it. If there is an outdoor swimming pool, a decision must be made as to what months it should be heated and how warm it should be kept. The group as a whole must decide on how the landscaping is to be maintained, who will do it and how much should be spent. If there is to be security service, again there must be a group decision as to how much, when and who should be hired. If a large truck runs into a unit on the other end of the building, it's an association problem because each owner has an undivided interest in the whole building.

All matters affecting the condominium must be brought to the attention of the board of directors, often by way of a committee. All committee and board positions are filled by volunteers from the association. Thus, owning a condominium is not entirely carefree, and there will be times when the board of directors will do things differently than an individual owner would like. Another possibility is that there may be a lack of interested and talented people to serve as directors and on committees. Consequently, things that need to be done may be left undone, possibly posing a hazard to the association. Individual unit owners may be unaware of the management and maintenance requirements for a multimillion-dollar building and may have hired a management firm that knows (or does) even less.

BEFORE BUYING

If you are considering the purchase of a condominium unit, consider the above points with care. Also look closely at the association's finances. The association may not have adequate reserves for upcoming maintenance work such as painting the building and putting on a new roof. If so, existing owners and new buyers will be in for a rude surprise in the form of a special assessment. Check the budget to see if it covers everything adequately and ask about lawsuits against the association that might drain its finances.

Although articles of incorporation, CC&Rs and bylaws make boring reading, if you offer to buy a condominium unit, you should make the offer contingent on your reading and approving them. These are the rules you agree to live by, and it's better to read them before committing to buy than after. You may find prohibitions against your pet cat or dog or against renting your unit while you are temporarily transferred overseas. (At the closing the seller must give you a current set of these documents along with the deed and keys to the unit. When you sell, you must give a current set to your buyer.)

Before buying, pay special attention to construction quality. Will ongoing maintenance be expensive? Is there deferred maintenance? Ask if the clubhouse and recreation facilities are owned by the association or by the developer who will continue to charge you for their use year after year. Is soundproofing between units adequate or will you hear your neighbor's piano, drums and arguments? What is the owner–tenant mix? The most successful condominiums are predominantly owner occupied rather than renter occupied. This is because owners usually take more interest and care in their properties, and this in turn boosts resale values. The list of things to look for and ask about when buying into a condominium is longer than there is space here, and bookstores have good books that will help you. But before moving on, the following two thoughts apply to any purchase of a condominium, cooperative, planned unit development or timeshare. First, keep a balance between your heart and your head. It is easy to be enchanted to the point that no further investigation is made, perhaps knowing in advance it would sour the deal. Second, ask those who have already bought if they would buy again.

COOPERATIVE
APARTMENTS

Now that you have just read about condominiums, take yourself back to the year 1900 in New York City. You've been renting an apartment unit on Manhattan for several years and would like to own it. Your neighbors in the building have expressed the same desire, but condominium legislation is more than half a century in the future. How would you and your neighbors accomplish this given existing legal frameworks? Your answer is the corporate form of ownership, a form of multiperson ownership well established in America by that time. To carry out your collective desires, you form a not-for-profit corporation. Shares in the corporation are sold to the building's tenants and the money used as a down payment to buy the building. Title to the building is placed in the name of the corporation, and each shareholder receives from the corporation a lease to his apartment. Thus, the shareholders own the corporation, the corporation owns the building and the corporation gives its shareholders leases to their apartments. Each month each shareholder makes a payment to the corporation to enable it to make the required monthly payment on the debt against the building and to pay for maintenance and repairs. Government of the building is handled by a board of directors that meets monthly and at an annual meeting of all the shareholders.

This form of residential ownership, which can be found in significant numbers in New York City, Miami, Chicago, San Francisco and Honolulu is called a **cooperative apartment.** The individual shareholders are called **cooperators,** and the lease that the corporation gives to a shareholder is called a **proprietary lease.**

When a cooperator wishes to sell, the cooperator does not sell his apartment but rather the shares of stock that carry with it a proprietary lease on that apartment. Although for all practical purposes the transaction looks like a sale of real estate, from a legal standpoint it is a sale of corporate stock. As such, the listing and selling forms that are used for houses and condominiums are not suitable and special cooperative forms must be used.

Financing a cooperative is different from financing a house or condominium. When a cooperative apartment building is first organized, the entire property is in the name of the cooperative corporation, and there is one mortgage loan on all of it. To illustrate, suppose a 10-unit building will cost the cooperators $1,000,000 and all the units are considered equal in desirability. A lender will finance 70% of the purchase if the cooperators raise the remaining 30%. This requires the cooperators to sell 10 shares of stock, each share for $30,000 and good for one apartment unit in the building. The lender provides the remaining $700,000 to complete the purchase, and the corporation gives the lender a note for $700,000 secured by a mortgage against the building. Suppose the monthly payments on this loan are $7,000; this means each month each cooperator must contribute $700 toward the mortgage plus money to maintain and operate the building, pay the property taxes on it, and keep it insured. *Financing*

What happens if one of the cooperators fails to make his monthly payment to the cooperative? For the cooperative to send the lender anything less than the required $7,000 per month puts the loan in default; this means the remaining cooperators must make up the difference. Meanwhile, they can seek voluntary reimbursement by the tardy cooperator, or, if that does not work, terminate him as a shareholder and resell the share to someone who will make the payments. *Default*

What happens if a shareholder in good standing wants to sell his unit? Since the underlying mortgage is against the entire building, it is impossible to refinance a portion of the building. Only the whole building can be refinanced and that requires approval by the cooperators as a whole. Traditionally, this has forced the cooperator to sell his share for all cash or on an installment sale plan. This is a handicap where the value of *Resale* the share has increased substantially due to property value increase and reduction of the building's mortgage loan. As a solution at least two states, New York and California, have enacted legislation allowing state-regulated lenders to make loans using cooperative stock as collateral.

Government   A cooperative apartment is governed by its articles of incorporation, bylaws, CC&Rs and house rules. The governing body is a board of directors elected by the cooperators. The board hires the services needed to maintain and operate the building just as in a condominium. Annual meetings are also held, just as in a condominium.

Differences   Now that the condominium format is available, relatively few cooperatives are being organized. This is largely because in a condominium the individual apartment unit can be financed separately from the remainder of the building. Moreover, if one condominium unit owner fails to make loan payments, the remaining owners in the building are not responsible for that loan. The condominium unit owner also has the personal choice of whether to have no debt, a little debt or a lot of debt against his unit. Unpaid property taxes are another potential difference. In a condominium, each unit is taxed separately, and nonpayment brings a property tax foreclosure sale against just the delinquent unit, not the entire building.

Similarity   A similarity exists between condominiums and cooperatives with respect to the money collected each month for the general maintenance and upkeep of the building. In either case, nonpayment will bring action against the tardy owner by the association that can result in foreclosure of that owner. Income tax rules effectively allow the same homeowner deductions on cooperatives as on condominiums and houses. However, a strict set of rules must be followed because technically a cooperator does not own real estate, but shares of stock.

New Legislation   Due to the financing difficulty and mutual liability potential associated with cooperatives, several states have enacted legislation that allows new cooperatives to be financed entirely by the sale of stock that in turn is pledged to a lender. This way the failure of one cooperator to make mortgage loan payments does not jeopardize the other cooperators. Also, a county assessor can assess each cooperator individually for property tax purposes if the board of directors so requests. This avoids joint liability. If you are considering the purchase of a cooperative, read the articles of incorporation, bylaws, CC&Rs and house rules before buying. Some operate under old rules, some under new rules, some will have rules you will be comfortable with, and some will not.

Although the opening example in this section on cooperatives was one of tenants banding together to buy their building, cooperatives are also organized and sold by real estate developers. These can be existing buildings converted by developers to cooperative ownership and new buildings built by developers from the ground up. In either case, a prospective purchaser will find it worthwhile to reread earlier paragraphs in this chapter on deposit practices, conversions, advantages, disadvantages and before buying.

If you buy into a condominium, you get a dwelling unit as separate property plus an undivided interest in the land and other common elements. If you buy into a cooperative, you get stock in the corporation that owns the building and a lease on a particular apartment. If you buy into a **planned unit development (PUD),** you get a house and lot as separate property plus ownership in a community association that owns the common areas. Common areas may be as minimal as a few green spaces in open areas between houses or as extensive as to also include parks, pools, clubhouse facilities, jogging trails, boat docks, horse trails and a golf course.

Although you own your lot and house as separate property in a PUD, there will be CC&Rs to follow. The PUD developer will establish an initial set of CC&Rs, then turn them over to the association for enforcement. Thus, your lot and home are not quite all yours to do with as you please because your association can dictate what color you can paint the exterior of your home, what you can and cannot plant in your front yard, and how many people and pets can reside with you. As with condominiums and cooperatives, PUD CC&Rs are not meant to be burdensome for the sake of being burdensome, but rather to

PLANNED UNIT DEVELOPMENT

maintain the attractiveness and tranquility of the development and in doing so keep home values up.

The dwellings in a planned unit development typically take the form of detached houses and houses that share a common wall, such as row houses, townhouses and cluster houses. Because each owner owns his land, vertical stacking of homes is limited to one owner and housing densities to 8 or 10 units per acre. Even though this is twice the density of a typical detached house subdivision, by careful planning a developer can give each owner the feeling of more spaciousness. One way is by taking advantage of uneven terrain. If a parcel contains some flat land, some hilly land, some land covered with trees and a running stream, the dwellings can be clustered on the land best suited for building and thus preserve the stream, woods and steep slopes in their natural state. With a standard subdivision layout the developer would have to remove the groves of trees, fill in the stream and terrace the slopes, and would still be able to provide homes for only half the number of families.

RESORT TIMESHARING

Resort timesharing is a method of dividing up and selling a living unit at a vacation facility for specified lengths of time each year. The idea started in Europe in the 1960s when groups of individuals would jointly purchase ski resort lodgings and summer vacation villas with each owner taking a week or two of exclusive occupancy. Resort developers quickly recognized the market potential of the idea, and in 1969 the first resort timeshare opened in the United States. Since then hotels, motels, condominiums, townhouses, lodges, villas, recreational vehicle parks, campgrounds, houseboats and even a cruise ship have been timeshared.

Right-to-Use

Nearly all timeshares fall into one of two legal formats. The first is the **right-to-use** format. This gives the buyer a contractual right to occupy a living unit at a resort property for one week a year for a specific term of 20 to 40 years. The cost for the entire period is paid in advance. At the end of the contract term all of the buyer's possessory rights terminate unless the contract contains a renewal clause or a right to buy. The developer creates these contracts by either buying or leasing a resort property and then selling 50 one-week-a-year right-to-use contracts on each living unit. (The other two weeks of the year are reserved for maintenance.) Approximately 30% of the timeshare market is right-to-use.

The second format is **fee simple** ownership. Here the timeshare purchaser obtains a fee ownership in the unit purchased. The purchaser owns the property for one week a year in perpetuity, and the sale is handled like a sale of real estate. There will be a formal closing, a title policy, execution of a mortgage and note, and delivery of a recordable deed that conveys the timeshare interest. A developer offers fee timeshares by either building or buying a resort property and then selling 50 one-week-a-year fee simple slices in each unit, with the remaining two weeks for maintenance. Approximately 70% of the timeshare market is fee simple.

Fee Simple

The initial cost of a timeshare week at a resort in the United States is typically $6,000 to $10,000, depending on the quality and location of the resort, the time of year (low season or high season) and form of ownership (right-to-use is usually less expensive). Additionally, there will be an annual maintenance fee of $140 to $280 per timeshare week. Buyers can purchase two or more timeshare weeks if they want a longer vacation. Some buyers purchase one week in the summer and one week in the winter.

Costs

The appeal of timesharing to developers is that a resort or condominium complex that can be bought and furnished for $100,000 per unit can be resold in 50 timeshare slices at $6,000 each, i.e., $300,000 a unit. The primary appeal of timesharing to consumers is having a resort to go to every year at a prepaid price. This is particularly appealing during inflationary times although the annual maintenance fee can change. There may be certain tax benefits if the timeshare is financed and for property taxes paid on fee simple timeshares. There may also be appreciation of the timeshare unit if it is in a particularly popular and well-run resort.
    Then again, some or all of these benefits may not materialize. First, the lump sum paid for a timeshare week does look

Benefits

cheaper than hotel bills year after year. However, the timeshare must be paid for in full in advance (or financed at interest) whereas the hotel is paid as it is used each year. Also, there is a timeshare maintenance fee of $20 to $40 per day that goes for clerk and maid service, linen laundry and replacement, structural maintenance and repairs, swimming pool service, hazard and liability insurance, reservations, collections and accounting services, general management, etc.

Second, going to the same resort for the same week every year for the next 40 years may become wearisome. Yet that is what a timeshare buyer is agreeing to do. And, if the week goes vacant, the maintenance fee must still be paid. To offset this, two large resort exchange services and several smaller ones exist, and some of the larger timeshare developers allow their buyers to exchange weeks among their various projects. There is a cost, however, to exchanging. There may be as many as three fees to pay: an initiation fee, an annual membership fee and a fee when an exchange is made. These can amount to $100 or more for an exchange. Moreover, someone else with a timeshare week they don't want that you do want and at the right time of the year must also be in the exchange bank. Satisfaction is usually achieved in exchanging by being flexible in accepting an exchange. Note too, if you own an off-season week at one resort, do not count on exchanging it for a peak-season vacation somewhere else. Exchange banks require members to accept periods of equal or lesser popularity.

Third, tax laws through 1985 allowed deductions for interest expense on timeshares that are financed and for property taxes on fee timeshares. At the time this book went to press, there were federal tax reform proposals to limit those deductions. Timeshares have occasionally been touted as tax shelter vehicles, however, that has already met the ire of the Internal Revenue Service.

Fourth, although there have been several reported instances of timeshare appreciation, it is generally agreed in the timeshare industry and by consumer groups that the primary reason to purchase a resort timeshare is to obtain a vacation, not appreciation. In fact, a timeshare industry rule-of-thumb is that one-third of the retail price of a timeshare unit goes to marketing costs. This acts as a damper on timeshare resale prices and even suggests a buyer may be able to purchase a timeshare on the resale market for less than from a developer.

Against the comfort of knowing that as a timeshare owner one has a long-term commitment to use a resort, one also has a long-term commitment to its maintenance, repair, refurbishing and management. This is similar to ownership in a condominium, except with ownership split among as many as 50 owners for each unit, will any owner have a large enough stake to want to take an active part in overseeing the management? As a result, management falls to the developer who, having once sold out the project, may no longer have as much incentive to oversee things as carefully as it did during the sales period. The developer can turn the job over to a management firm, but who oversees them to make certain the timeshare owners get good service at a fair price?

Commitment

Approximately 25 states have adopted timeshare regulations. Many of these follow the Model Timeshare Act designed by the National Association of Real Estate License Law Officials and the National TimeSharing Council and endorsed by the National Association of Realtors. Much timeshare legislation is in the form of consumer protection and disclosure (prospectus) requirements. Other legislation deals with how timeshares should be assessed for property taxation and what type of license a person employed to sell timeshares should hold, if any. Due to high-pressure sales techniques observed at some timeshare sales offices, a number of states have enacted mandatory "cooling-off" periods of five days during which a buyer can rescind his contract. Because of multimillion-dollar consumer losses due to uncompleted timeshare projects, the sale of the same timeshare to more than one party, and money collected with deeds never sent, surety bonds and escrows are now required by some states. Meanwhile, any prospective timeshare purchaser or salesperson would do well to take plenty of time in deciding, have all paperwork reviewed by their attorney before signing, and spend time talking to existing purchasers to ask if they would buy again.

State Regulation

VOCABULARY REVIEW

Match terms **a–t** *with statements* **1–20.**

a. Annual meeting
b. Board of directors
c. Bylaws
d. CC&Rs
e. Common elements
f. Condominium
g. Condominium act
h. Condominium subdivision
i. Cooperative
j. Cooperator

k. House rules
l. Maintenance fees
m. Management company
n. Owners' association
o. Proprietary lease
p. PUD
q. Reserves
r. Right-to-use
s. Separate property
t. Timesharing

1. Individual ownership of a space of air plus undivided ownership of the common elements.
2. Ownership by a corporation which in turn leases space to its shareholders.
3. Roof, stairs, elevator, lobby, etc., in a condominium.
4. An organization composed of unit owners in which membership is automatic upon purchase of a unit.
5. Type of lease issued by a cooperative corporation to its shareholders.
6. A document that converts a parcel of land into a stratified subdivision; also called a master deed.
7. Rules that govern how the owners' association will be run.
8. A shareholder in a cooperative apartment.
9. Charges levied against unit owners to cover the costs of maintaining the common areas. Also called association dues.
10. Form of community ownership where the houses and lots are privately owned but title to common areas is held by an owners' association.
11. State legislation that creates the legal framework for condominium subdivisions.
12. That portion of a condominium that is the exclusive property of an individual unit owner.
13. Covenants, conditions and restrictions by which an owner must abide.
14. Rules for the use of the swimming pool and recreation facilities would be found here.
15. A governing body elected by association members.
16. A once-a-year business meeting of the entire association membership.
17. Advises the board of directors and takes care of day-to-day tasks.
18. The exclusive use of a property for a specified number of days each year.

19. A contractual right to occupy a living unit at a timeshare resort.
20. Money set aside from the budget for expenses that do not occur every month.

1. Why are condominiums a popular alternative to single-family houses?
2. Who owns the land in a fee simple condominium project? In a cooperative?
3. What is the key difference between a proprietary lease in a cooperative and a landlord–tenant lease?
4. What is the purpose of the master deed in a condominium project?
5. To whom does the wall between two condominium units belong?
6. What are CC&Rs and what is their purpose?
7. What are maintenance fees? What happens if they are not paid?
8. If the owners' association carries hazard and liability insurance, why is it also advisable for each unit owner to purchase a hazard and liability policy?
9. Briefly explain the concept of right-to-use and fee simple timesharing.
10. Briefly explain how title to land in a PUD is held.

QUESTIONS AND PROBLEMS

Condominium Development Guide, rev. ed. by **Keith Romney** and **Brad Romney**. (Warren, Gorham and Lamont, 1983, 896 pages). Lengthy, legal, readable, practical and detailed. This is the type of information one needs before developing a condominium. Contains procedures, analysis and forms. Annual updates issued.

Real Estate Broker's Guide to Resort Time Sharing by **Richard Lynge** and **Keith Trowbridge**. (Real Estate Education Co., 1984, 262 pages). Book explains the field to anyone considering joining a timeshare sales program. Explains broker-developer relationship, resort quality, sales methods, commissions and management procedures.

"Same Time, Same Place, Next Year." (*Consumer Reports*, Aug 84, page 464). Explains timesharing and swapping timeshares plus economics and pitfalls of timesharing. This magazine frequently has consumer-oriented articles on real estate.

ADDITIONAL READINGS

"The Condominium: A Home For All Seasons." (*Real Estate Today*, Feb 85, pages 10–28). This feature section contains these articles: "Condoeconomics," "Condominium Housing: A Bright Future Ahead," and "Farming Condo Resales."

The Condominium and Cooperative Apartment Buyer's Guide by **David Kennedy.** (Wiley 1983, 314 pages). This is a consumer's guide that includes what to look for, what questions to ask, rights and responsibilities of owners, tax considerations, using a broker, conversions and tips on buying and selling.

The Owner's and Manager's Guide to Condominium Management, rev. ed. (Institute of Real Estate Management, 1984, 323 pages). Readable and helpful for condominium purchasers and the board of directors. Discusses the government, management and human relations that are part of condominium living. Coverage includes association meetings, building maintenance, legal liability, budgeting and taxes.

* * *

The following periodicals may also be of interest to you: *Community Management Report, Condominium Comment, Resort Management, Resort Timesharing Today* and *Timesharing Law Reporter Briefs.*

Property Insurance

All-risks policy: all perils, except those excluded in writing, are covered

Broad-form: an insurance policy that covers a large number of named perils

Endorsement: a policy modification; also called a rider or an attachment

Homeowner policy: a combined property and liability policy designed for residential use

Insurance premium: the amount of money one must pay for insurance coverage

Insured: one who is covered by insurance

Liability: the financial responsibility one has toward others

New for old: policy pays replacement cost

Old for old: policy pays only the depreciated cost

Perils: hazards or risks

If you own real estate, you take the risk that your property may be damaged due to fire or other catastrophe. Additionally, there is the possibility that someone may be injured while on your property and hold you responsible. Insurance to cover losses from either of these occurrences is available and is the topic of this chapter. Let us begin with property damage, then discuss public liability and homeowner insurance. We will conclude with new for old, flood insurance, policy cancellation, policy takeovers and home buyer's insurance.

PROPERTY DAMAGE

Fire insurance is the foundation of property damage policies. Historically, there have been a variety of solutions to the problem of fire damage. Two thousand years ago there was a Roman named Crassus who would bring his firefighters to the scene of a fire and quote a price for putting it out. If the owner refused, Crassus offered cash on the spot for the burning building, and, if accepted, sent in the firefighters to salvage as much as possible.

In Colonial America, fire insurance groups were organized wherein payments by members to the group compensated for fire losses to members and subsidized volunteer firefighting companies. Each member received a plaque to display on the front of his building. Although the volunteer fire companies would answer all calls, they probably put more effort into saving houses displaying the plaque.

Modern Fire Coverage

A major step forward in fire insurance coverage was the enactment in 1886 by the New York legislature of a standardized fire policy. This policy, called the New York fire form, has been revised twice, in 1918 and 1943, and today it serves as the foundation for nearly all property damage policies written in the United States. The 165 lines of court-tested language in the New York fire form cover (1) loss by fire, (2) loss by lightning, and (3) losses sustained while removing property from an endangered premises. A person (called the **insured**) makes a payment (called an **insurance premium**) to an insurance company (called the **insurer**) and the company pays if a loss is suffered.

Endorsements

Although fire is the single most important cause of property damage in the United States, a property owner is also exposed to other **perils** (also called hazards or risks). Examples are hail, tornado, earthquake, riot, windstorm, smoke damage, explosion, glass breakage, waterpipe leaks, vandalism, freezing and building collapse. Coverage for each peril can be purchased with a separate policy or added to the fire form as an **endorsement.** An endorsement, also called a **rider** or **attachment,** is an agreement by the insurer to modify a basic policy. Usually this is to extend coverage to losses by perils not included in the basic policy.

PUBLIC LIABILITY

Public liability (also called **personal liability**) is the financial responsibility one has toward others as a result of one's actions or failure to take action. For example, if you are trimming the limbs from a tall tree in your backyard and a limb falls on your neighbor's roof and damages it, you are liable to your neighbor for damages. If someone is injured on your property, that person may be able to successfully sue you for money damages.

Generally, you are liable when there exists a legal duty to

exercise reasonable care and you fail to do so thereby causing injury to an innocent party. Even though you did not intend for the limb to fall on your neighbor's roof or a house guest to slip on your newly waxed floor, you are not excused from liability. You can be held accountable, in money, for the amount of damage caused.

For major commercial and industrial property owners and users, carefully identifying each risk exposure and then insuring for it is a logical and economic approach to purchasing insurance. But for the majority of homeowners, owners of small apartment and business properties and their tenants, purchasing insurance piecemeal is a confusing process. As a result, package policies have been developed.

HOMEOWNER POLICIES

Of these, the best known and most widely used is the **homeowner policy.** It contains the coverages deemed by insurance experts to be most useful to persons who own the home in which they live. Not only does this approach avoid overlaps and lessen the opportunity for gaps in coverage, but the cost is less than purchasing separate individual policies with the same total coverage. Moreover, homeowner policies also cover certain liability and property losses that occur away from the insured's premises. For renters there is a packaged tenant's policy. Let us take a closer look.

There are seven standardized home insurance policy forms in use in the United States. Five are designed for owners of single-family dwellings, one is for tenants and one is for condominium owners. Each policy contains two sections. Section I deals with loss of, or damage to, the insured's property. Section II deals with liability of the insured and the insured's family. We will proceed in that order.

Policy Formats

A homeowner policy covers your house, garage and other structures on your lot such as a guest house or garden shed. If you are forced to live elsewhere while damage to your residence is being repaired, your homeowner policy will provide for additional living expenses. A homeowner policy also covers much of your personal property. This includes all household

Properties Covered

contents and other personal belongings that are used, owned, worn or carried by you or your family, whether at home or somewhere else.

A homeowner policy does not cover structures on your property that are used for business purposes or rented or leased to others. A homeowner policy does not cover loss of, or damage to, automobiles, business property or pets. Moreover, certain valuables such as jewels, furs and stamp and coin collections may not be covered for full value without additional insurance.

Perils Covered   **Basic form (HO-1)** insures against the first 11 perils shown in Table 20:1. **Broad form (HO-2)** covers all 18 perils in Table 20:1. **Comprehensive form (HO-5)** is called an **all-risks policy** because it covers all perils except those listed in the policy. **Form HO-8** is designed for older homes. It covers the same perils as HO-1. Because it is usually difficult to duplicate an older home for anywhere close to its market value, Form HO-8 insures for actual cash value, not replacement cost. (Actual cash value and replacement cost will be explained momentarily.)

Excluded from all homeowner policies are loss or damage caused by flood, landslide, mudflow, tidal wave, earthquake, underground water, settling, cracking, war and nuclear accident. Some of these can, however, be covered using riders or separate policies.

Special form (HO-3) is a combination form that provides HO-5 coverage on one's dwelling and private structures and HO-2 coverage on one's personal property. Forms HO-3 and HO-5 are the most popular of the four policies designed for single-family homes.

Tenant's Policy   If you rent rather than own your residence, you would choose the **tenant's form (HO-4).** This policy insures your household contents and personal belongings against all of the perils listed in the broad form (HO-2) coverage and provides for additional living expenses. The distinguishing feature in a tenant's policy is that it does not cover damage to the building.

Condominium Policy   In a condominium, the homeowners' association usually buys insurance covering all of the common elements. To cover

HOMEOWNER POLICY COVERAGE   Table 20:1

COMPREHENSIVE (HO-5)	BROAD (HO-2)	BASIC (HO-1)	PERILS COVERED BY INSURANCE
			1. Fire or lightning 2. Losses sustained while removing property from an endangered premises 3. Windstorm or hail 4. Explosion 5. Riot or civil commotion 6. Aircraft 7. Vehicles 8. Smoke 9. Vandalism and malicious mischief 10. Theft 11. Breakage of glass that is part of the building (not in HO-4)
			12. Falling objects 13. Weight of ice, snow, sleet 14. Collapse of building(s) or any part thereof 15. Sudden and accidental tearing asunder, cracking, burning or bulging of a steam or hot water heating system or of appliances for heating water 16. Accidental discharge, leakage or overflow of water or steam from within a plumbing, heating or air-conditioning system or domestic appliance 17. Freezing of plumbing, heating and air-conditioning systems and domestic appliances 18. Sudden and accidental injury from artifically generated currents to electrical appliances, devices, fixtures and wiring
			All perils except flood, landslide, mudflow, tidal wave, earthquake, underground water, settling, cracking, war and nuclear accident. (Check policy for a complete list of perils excluded.)

personal property and any additions or alterations to the unit not insured by the association's policy, a **condominium unit owner's form (HO-6)** is available.

Section II in all seven home insurance forms is a liability policy for you and all family members that live with you. This coverage is designed to protect you from a financially crippling claim or lawsuit. The falling limb and freshly waxed floor examples earlier in this chapter are events that would be covered

Liability Coverage

by this coverage. If a liability claim arises, the insurance company will pay the legal costs of defending you as well as any damages up to the limits of the policy. Note that this section also provides you and your family with liability protection away from your premises. Thus, if you accidentally hit someone with a golf ball on a golf course or your child accidentally kicks a football through a neighbor's window, this part of the policy covers you. If you have a pet and it takes a bite out of a visitor to your home or out of a neighbor's leg while out for a walk, you are covered.

Medical Payments   The cost of treating minor injuries for which you may be liable is paid by **medical payments coverage** found in home insurance policies. The main difference between this and liability coverage is that medical payments coverage provides payment regardless of who is at fault. However, it covers only relatively minor injuries, say $500 or $1,000. Major injuries would come under the liability coverage. The liability and medical payments coverage in a home insurance policy do not apply to your motor vehicles nor your business pursuits. Those require separate policies. Additionally, your home insurance policy does not cover injuries to you or your family. Those must be insured separately.

Endorsements   Any home policy can be endorsed for additional coverage. For example, **inflation guard** endorsements are available that automatically increase property damage coverage by 1½%, 2% or 2½% per quarter, as selected by the insured. Another popular endorsement is **worker's compensation** insurance. This is designed to pay for injuries suffered by persons employed by the insured to do work on the premises such as babysitters and cleaning help. If the property is to be rented out, tenant coverage can be added. Alternatively, a policy specifically designed for rental property can be purchased.

NEW FOR OLD   A special problem in recovering from damage to a building is that, although the building may not be new, any repairs are made new. For example, if a 20-year-old house burns to the ground, it is impossible to put back a used house, even though a used house is exactly what the insured lost. Thus, the question is whether insurance should pay for the full cost of fixing the damage, in effect replace "new for old," or simply pay the actual cash value of the loss. **Actual cash value** is the new price minus accumulated depreciation and is, in effect, **"old for old."** Under "old for old," if the owner rebuilds, he pays the difference between actual cash value and the cost of the repairs. As this can be quite costly to the insured, the alternative is to purchase a policy that replaces **"new for old."**

For the owner of an apartment building, store or other property operated on a business basis, obtaining "new for old" coverage is a matter of substituting the term "replacement cost" for "actual cash value" wherever it appears in the policy. Also, the policyholder must agree to carry coverage amounting to at least 80% of current replacement cost and to use the insurance proceeds to repair or replace the damaged property within a reasonable time.

Most homeowner policies provide that if the amount of insurance carried is 80% or more of the cost to replace the house today, the full cost of repair will be paid by the insurer, up to the face amount of the policy. If the face amount is less than 80% of replacement costs, the insured is entitled to the higher of (1) the actual cash value of the loss or (2) the amount calculated as follows:

$$\frac{\text{Insurance carried}}{\left(\begin{array}{c}80\% \text{ of today's cost} \\ \text{to replace whole structure}\end{array}\right)} \times \left(\begin{array}{c}\text{Today's cost to replace} \\ \text{the damaged portion}\end{array}\right) = \text{Recovery}$$

Real estate lenders such as savings and loans, banks, mortgage companies, etc., require that a borrower carry fire and extended coverage on the mortgaged structures. The reason, of course, is to protect the value of the security for the loan. The lender will be named on the policy along with the property owner, and any checks from the insurance company for damages will be made out to the borrower and the lender jointly. Note that the lender does not require liability and medical payments coverage as the lender is not concerned with that aspect of the borrower's exposure. Nonetheless, most borrowers will choose a homeowner policy that has Section I coverage satisfactory to the lender rather than fire and extended coverage only.

The borrower must have a policy that meets the lender's requirements before the loan is made and must keep the policy

LENDER REQUIREMENTS

in force at all times while the loan is outstanding. Some lenders collect one-twelfth of the annual premium each month and forward the money to the insurer annually. Other lenders allow the homeowner to maintain the policy and each year mail proof of the policy to the lender. The lender on a condominium unit will require proof that the condominium association carries insurance on the common elements.

Guaranteed Replacement Cost

Because of the nearly constant increase in the cost of construction over the past several decades, lenders require either a replacement cost policy that guarantees adequate money to rebuild the entire structure at today's costs or coverage for the full amount of the loan. (The land is not insured as it is assumed it will survive any damage to the structures upon it.) The borrower, for peace of mind, will choose replacement cost coverage. This is especially true where the loan is less than the cost of replacement.

It is difficult to overemphasize the need for a policy review every one to three years. (The insurance agent will do this on request as part of the policy service.) Many a sad tale has been told by a homeowner who bought 20 years ago, has dutifully paid the insurance premium every year, has not revised the coverage to reflect current construction costs, and then has a major loss. Caution is also advised when a seller carries back financing or an individual buys mortgages as investments. If you fall into this category, make certain that any structures on the property serving as collateral are adequately insured so that if the structures are destroyed, there will be enough insurance money to fully pay you off. Also make certain you are named on the policy as a lender and that the borrower renews the policy each year.

FLOOD INSURANCE

In 1968 Congress created the National Flood Insurance Program. This program is a joint effort of the nation's insurance industry and the federal government to offer property owners coverage for losses to real and personal property resulting from the inundation of normally dry areas from (1) the overflow of inland or tidal waters, (2) the unusual and rapid accumulation or runoff of surface waters, (3) mudslides resulting from accumulations of water on or under the ground, and (4) erosion losses caused by abnormal water runoff.

All mortgages in which the federal government is involved (including government-insured lenders and FHA, VA, FNMA, FHLMC and GNMA loans) require either a certificate that the mortgaged property is not in a flood zone, or a policy of flood insurance. Flood insurance is available through insurance agents. Earthquake insurance is also available from insurance agents. Lenders do not, as a rule, require borrowers to carry it. Nonetheless, it is enjoying some popularity in earthquake-prone regions such as California.

LANDLORD POLICIES

If you rent out part of your home to a tenant or if you buy a property and rent it out (such as a house, condominium, apartment building, store, office, warehouse or farm), make certain you purchase adequate property damage and liability coverage. If a loan is involved, the lender will require property damage coverage for the amount of the loan. But the lender is not concerned above the loan amount nor if someone is injured on your property and holds you liable. Landlord coverage can be obtained by endorsement to an existing homeowner policy or by purchasing a landlord package policy that combines property damage, liability, medical expenses and loss of rents. The latter pays you what you would normally collect in rent when damage is severe enough that the tenant has to move out while repairs are made.

Note that if you buy vacant land and do not use it for business purposes and do not rent it out, most standard homeowner policies automatically include liability coverage on the land without additional cost or endorsement. You should, however, verify this with your insurance agent. In any event, do not fail to be adequately insured on any property you own. Reconstruction costs are expensive and liability suits more common and more expensive than in the past.

POLICY CANCELLATION

A property damage or public liability policy can be canceled at anytime by the insured. Since the policy is billed in advance, the insured is entitled to a refund for unused coverage. This refund is computed at short rates which are somewhat higher than a simple pro rata charge. For example, the holder of a 1-year policy who cancels one-third of the way through the year is charged 44% of the 1-year price, not 33⅓%.

The insurer also has the right to cancel a policy. However,

unlike the policyholder who can cancel on immediate notice, the New York fire form requires the insurer to give the policyholder 5-day notice. Also, the cost of the policy, and hence the refund of unused premium, must be calculated on a pro rata basis. For example, the insured would be charged one-half the annual premium for 6 months of coverage.

Policy Suspension   Certain acts of the policyholder will suspend coverage without the necessity of a written notice from the insurer. Suspension automatically occurs if the insured allows the hazard exposure to the insurer to increase beyond the risks normally associated with the type of property being insured, for example, converting a dwelling to a restaurant. Suspension also occurs if the insured building is left unoccupied for more than 60 days (30 days in some states) because unoccupied buildings are more attractive to thieves, vandals and arsonists. If the condition causing the suspension is corrected (returning the restaurant to a dwelling or reoccupying the building) before a loss occurs, the policy becomes effective again.

Willful concealment or misrepresentation by the insured of any material fact or circumstance concerning the policy, the property or the insured, either before or after a loss, will make the policy void. Thus, if a person operates a business in the basement of his house and conceals this from the insurer for fear of being charged more for insurance, the money he pays for insurance could be wasted.

POLICY TAKEOVERS   Oftentimes in a real estate transaction the buyer will ask to assume the seller's existing insurance policy for the property. This way the buyer avoids having to pay a full year's premium in advance and the seller benefits by avoiding a short-rate cancellation charge. To avoid a break in coverage, the insurer must accept the buyer as the new policyholder before the closing takes place. This is done with an endorsement issued by the insurer naming the buyer as the insured party. The reason for this requirement is that an insurance policy does not protect the property, but the insured's financial interest in the property. This is called an **insurable interest.**

Suppose the property is destroyed by fire immediately after the closing. Once title has passed, the seller no longer has an insurable interest in the property. If the insurance company has not endorsed the policy over to the buyer, the company is under no obligation to pay for the damage. If there is doubt that the endorsement to the buyer can be obtained in time for the closing, the buyer should purchase a new policy in his/her own name. Note that anyone holding a mortgage on improved property has an insurable interest.

HOME BUYER'S INSURANCE

A long-standing concern of home buyers has been the possibility of finding structural or mechanical defects in a home after buying it. In new homes the builder can usually be held responsible for repairs and many states require builders to give a one-year warranty. Additional protection is available from builders associated with the Home Owners Warranty Corporation (HOW). Under this program, the first year the builder warrants against defects caused by faulty workmanship or materials and against major structural defects. The second year the builder continues to warrant against major structural defects and against defects in wiring, piping and ductwork. If the builder cannot or will not honor this warranty, the HOW program underwriter will do so. Then for 8 more years the underwriter directly insures the home buyer against major structural defects; less a $250 deductible.

In many cities the buyer, seller or owner of a used house can purchase a home warranty policy for one to three years. Typically these policies cover the plumbing, electrical and heating systems, hot water heater, ductwork, air conditioning and major appliances. The cost ranges from $250 to $400 per year. Some real estate brokers provide this with every home they sell as a way of encouraging people to buy. However, a warranty can also be purchased by the buyer, by the seller or even by a person who does not plan to sell. Insurance plans vary by company and whether the buyer, seller or owner is purchasing the coverage. Some plans require a pre-inspection, some do not. As a rule, the warranty company selects the repair firm, and there may be a service charge or deductible. Coverages, limitations and exclusions in the contract must be read carefully.

VOCABULARY REVIEW

Match terms **a–q** *with statements* **1–17.**

a. *All-risks policy*
b. *Broad-form policy*
c. *Endorsement*
d. *Flood insurance*
e. *Form HO-4*
f. *Form HO-6*
g. *Homeowner policy*
h. *Inflation guard*
i. *Insurable interest*

j. *Insurance premium*
k. *Insured*
l. *Liability*
m. *Medical payments*
n. *New for old*
o. *Old for old*
p. *Perils*
q. *Worker's compensation insurance*

1. Also called hazards or risks.
2. An endorsement that periodically increases insurance coverage.
3. Describes combined property and liability policies designed for residential owner-occupants.
4. Pays current cost of replacement less depreciation.
5. Pays cost of replacing damaged property at current prices.
6. Tenant's policy form.
7. Condominium unit owner's policy form.
8. The financial responsibility one has toward others.
9. The amount of money paid for insurance coverage.
10. Describes a policy where all perils, except those excluded in writing, are covered.
11. Insurance phrase for policies that cover a large number of named perils.
12. An agreement by the insurance company to extend coverage to perils not covered by the basic policy.
13. This would pay for damage from the overflow of inland or tidal waters.
14. A financial interest that can be insured.
15. Insurance coverage for injuries incurred by an employee on the job.
16. One who is covered by insurance.
17. Pays for the treatment of injuries without the need to determine fault.

1. What role does an endorsement or rider play in an insurance policy?
2. What is the purpose of liability insurance?
3. In a homeowner policy, what type of loss does Section I deal with? Section II?
4. How do all-risk insurance policies differ from broad-form policies?
5. What does the phrase "new for old" refer to when talking about insurance policies that cover property damage?
6. Why will an insurer suspend coverage if a property is left vacant too long?

QUESTIONS AND PROBLEMS

"Choosing Tenant or Condo Coverage" by **Richard Lynch.** (*Money*, Jul 84, page 127). Covers finding and buying the right policy to protect you and your possessions as a tenant or condominium owner. Discusses policy costs, coverage, perils, exclusions and personal liability.

"Guarding the Lender's Interest" by **Richard Clarke**. (*Mortgage Banking*, Feb 84, page 37). Mortgage lenders require hazard insurance on property used as collateral. This article explains the how and why of policies that meet this requirement.

"Homeowners Insurance." (*Consumer Reports*, Aug 85, page 473). This excellent 10-page article explains homeowner policies, what they cover and how much they cost. Includes ratings of 23 insurance companies as to accessibility, courtesy, claim handling, speed of payment and customer satisfaction.

Insurance Principles and Practices, 2nd ed. by **F.G. Crane.** (Wiley, 1984, 550 pages). A very readable survey of risk and insurance from a consumer's viewpoint. Includes insurance for the homeowner.

"People and Property: Destruction Clauses Revisited" by Emmanuel Halper. (*Real Estate Review*, Winter 84, page 78 and Spring 84, page 58). This is a delightfully humorous two-part article that deals with the serious business of insurance and property destruction as it pertains to shopping center leases.

*   *   *

The following general interest periodicals may be of interest to you: *Architectural Digest, Better Homes and Gardens, Home and Garden, Homeowner* and *Sunset*.

ADDITIONAL READINGS

Land-Use Control

Building codes: local and state laws that set minimum construction standards

Certificate of occupancy: a government-issued document that states a structure meets local zoning and building code requirements and is ready for use

Downzoning: rezoning of land from a higher-density use to a lower-density use

Environmental impact statement: a report that contains information regarding the effect of a proposed project on the environment of an area

Land-use control: a broad term that describes any legal restriction that controls how a parcel of land may be used

Master plan: a comprehensive guide for the physical growth of a community

Nonconforming use: an improvement that is inconsistent with current zoning regulations

Restrictive covenants: clauses placed in deeds and leases to control how future owners and lessees may or may not use the property

Variance: allows an individual landowner to vary from zoning requirements

Zoning: public regulations that control the specific use of land

Land-use control is a broad term that describes any legal restriction that controls how a parcel of land may be used. Land-use controls can be divided into two broad categories: public controls and private controls. Examples of public controls are zoning, building codes, subdivision regulations and master plans. Private controls come in the form of deed restrictions. Let us explore further.

Rudimentary forms of zoning can be traced back as far as medieval times where regulations prohibited certain activities from taking place within the town wall. In America, colonial cities and towns regulated the location of foul-smelling industries such as tallow rendering and leather tanning. In the late 1880s Boston limited the heights of buildings as did Baltimore, Indianapolis and Washington, D.C. Between 1909 and 1915,

ZONING

521

Los Angeles adopted a complex series of land-use laws. However, credit for the first truly comprehensive and systematic zoning law goes to New York City in 1916. Three years in the making, it went beyond anything up to that time and set a basic pattern that has been followed and refined by American cities, towns and counties ever since.

Zoning laws divide land into zones (districts) and within each zone regulate the purpose for which buildings may be constructed, the height and bulk of the buildings, the area of the lot that they may occupy and the number of persons that they can accommodate. Through zoning a community can protect existing land users from encroachment by undesirable uses, and ensure that future land uses in the community will be compatible with each other. Zoning also can control development so that each parcel of land will be adequately serviced by streets, sanitary and storm sewers, schools, parks and utilities.

The authority to control land use is derived from the basic police power of each state to protect the public health, safety, morals and general welfare of its citizens. Through an enabling act passed by the state legislature, the authority to control land use is also given to individual towns, cities and counties. These local government units then pass zoning ordinances that establish the boundaries of the various land-use zones and determine the type of development that will be permitted in each of them. By going to your local zoning office, you can learn how a parcel of land is zoned. By then consulting the zoning ordinance, you can see the permitted uses for the parcel.

Zoning Symbols   For convenience, zones are identified by code abbreviations such as R (residential), C (commercial), I or M (industrial-manufacturing) and A (agriculture). Within general categories are subcategories, for example, single-family residences, two-family residences, low-rise apartments and high-rise apartments. Similarly, there will usually be several subcategories of commercial ranging from small stores to shopping centers and several subcategories of manufacturing from light, smoke-free to heavy industry.

Additionally, there can be found overlay zoning categories such as RPD (residential planned development) and PUD (planned unit development). These are designed to permit a mixture of land uses within a given parcel. For example, a 640-acre parcel may contain open spaces plus clusters of houses, townhouses and apartments, and perhaps a neighborhood shopping center. Another combination zone is RO (residential-office) that allows apartment buildings alongside or on top of office buildings.

Note that there is no uniformity to zoning classifications in the United States. A city may use "A" to designate apartments while the county uses "A" to designate agriculture. Similarly, one city may use "I" for industrial and another city use "I" for institutional (hospitals and universities, for example).

Besides telling a landowner the use to which he may put his land, the zoning ordinance imposes additional rules. For example, land zoned for low-density apartments may require 1,500 square feet of land per living unit, a minimum of 600 square feet of living space per unit for one bedroom, 800 square feet for two bedrooms and 1,000 square feet for three bedrooms. The zoning ordinance may also contain a set-back requirement which states that a building must be placed at least 25 feet back from the street, 10 feet from the sides of the lot and 15 feet from the rear lot line. The ordinance may also limit the building's height to 2½ stories and require two parking spaces for each dwelling unit. As can be seen, zoning encourages uniformity. *Land-Use Restrictions*

Zoning laws are enforced by virtue of the fact that in order to build, a person must obtain a building permit from his city or county government. Before a permit is issued, the proposed structure must conform with government-imposed structural standards and comply with the zoning on the land. If a landowner builds without a permit, he can be forced to tear down his building. *Enforcement*

When an existing structure does not conform with a new zoning law, it is "grandfathered-in" as a **nonconforming use.** Thus, the owner can continue to use the structure even though it does not conform to the new zoning. However, the owner is not permitted to enlarge or remodel the structure, or to extend its life. When the structure is ultimately demolished, any new use of the land must be in accordance with the zoning law. If *Nonconforming Use* you are driving through a residential neighborhood and see an old store or service station that looks very much out of place, it is probably a nonconforming use that was allowed to stay because it was built before the current zoning on the property went into effect.

Amendment

Once a zoning ordinance has been passed it can be changed by **amendment.** Thus, land previously zoned for agriculture may be changed to residential. Land along a city street that has become a major thoroughfare may change from residential to commercial. An amendment can be initiated by a property owner in the area to be rezoned or by local government. Either way, notice of the proposed change must be given to all property owners in and around the affected area, and a public hearing must be held so that property owners and the public at large may voice their opinions on the matter.

Variance

A **variance** allows an individual landowner to deviate from current zoning requirements for his parcel. For example, a variance might be granted to the owner of an odd-shaped lot to reduce the setback requirements slightly so that he can fit a building on it. Variances usually are granted where strict compliance with the zoning ordinance or code would cause undue hardship. A variance can also be used to change the permitted use of a parcel. However, the variance must not change the basic character of the neighborhood, and it must be consistent with the general objectives of zoning as they apply to that neighborhood.

Conditional Use Permit

A **conditional use permit** allows a land use that does not conform with existing zoning provided the use is within the limitations imposed by the permit. A conditional use permit is usually quite restrictive, and if the conditions of the permit are violated the permit is no longer valid. For example, a neighborhood grocery store operating under a conditional use permit can only be a neighborhood grocery. The structure cannot be used as an auto parts store.

Spot Zoning

Spot zoning refers to the rezoning of a small area of land in an existing neighborhood. For example, a neighborhood convenience center (grocery, laundry, barbershop) might be allowed in a residential neighborhood provided it serves a useful purpose for neighborhood residents and is not a nuisance.

Downzoning means that land previously zoned for higher-density uses (or more active uses) is rezoned for lower-density uses (or less active uses). Examples are downzoning from high-rise commercial to low-rise commercial, apartment zoning to single-family, and single-family to agriculture. Although a landowner's property value may fall as a result of downzoning, there is no compensation to the landowner as there is no taking of land as with eminent domain.

Downzoning

A **buffer zone** is a strip of land that separates one land use from another. Thus, between a large shopping center and a neighborhood of single-family homes, there may be a row of garden apartments. Alternatively, between an industrial park and a residential subdivision, a developer may leave a strip of land in grass and trees rather than build homes immediately adjacent to the industrial buildings. Note that "buffer zone" is a generic term and not necessarily a zoning law category.

Buffer Zone

A zoning law can be changed or struck down if it can be proved in court that it is unclear, discriminatory, unreasonable, not for the protection of the public health, safety and general welfare, or not applied to all property in a similar manner.

Legality, Value

Zoning alone does not create land value. For example, zoning a hundred square miles of lonely desert or mountain land for stores and offices would not appreciably change its value. Value is created by the number of people who want to use a particular parcel of land for a specific purpose. To the extent that zoning channels that demand to certain parcels of land and away from others, zoning does have a powerful impact on property value.

Before a building lot can be sold, a subdivider must comply with government regulations concerning street construction, curbs, sidewalks, street lighting, fire hydrants, storm and sanitary sewers, grading and compacting of soil, water and utility lines, minimum lot size and so on. In addition, the subdivider

SUBDIVISION REGULATIONS

may be required to either set aside land for schools and parks or provide money so that land for that purpose may be purchased nearby. These are often referred to as **mapping requirements** and until the subdivider has complied with all state and local regulations, the subdivision will not be approved. Without approval the plat cannot be recorded which, in turn, means the lots cannot be sold to the public. If the subdivider tries to sell lots without approval, he can be stopped by a government court order and in some states fined. Moreover, permits to build will be refused to lot owners and anyone who bought from the subdivider is entitled to a refund.

BUILDING CODES   Recognizing the need to protect public health and safety against slipshod construction practices, state and local governments have enacted **building codes.** These establish minimum acceptable material and construction standards for such things as structural load and stress, windows and ventilation, size and location of rooms, fire protection, exits, electrical installation, plumbing, heating, lighting and so forth.

Before a building permit is granted, the design of a proposed structure must meet the building-code requirements. During construction, local building department inspectors visit the construction site to make certain that the codes are being observed. Finally, when the building is completed, a **certificate of occupancy** is issued to the building owner to show that the structure meets the code. Without this certificate, the building cannot be legally occupied.

Traditionally, the establishment of building codes has been given by states to individual counties, cities and towns. The result has been a lack of uniformity from one local government to the next, oftimes adding unnecessary construction costs and occasionally leaving gaps in consumer protection. The trend today is toward statewide building codes that overcome these weaknesses and at the same time improve the uniformity of mortgage collateral for the secondary mortgage market.

DEED RESTRICTIONS   Although property owners tend to think of land-use controls as being strictly a product of government, it is possible to achieve land-use control through private means. In fact, Houston, Texas, operates without zoning and relies almost entirely upon private land-use controls to achieve a similar effect.

Private land-use controls take the form of **deed** and **lease restrictions.** In the United States it has long been recognized that the ownership of land includes the right to sell or lease it on whatever legally acceptable conditions the owner wishes, including the right to dictate to the buyer or lessee how he shall or shall not use it. For example, a developer can sell the lots in his subdivision subject to a restriction written into each deed that the land cannot be used for anything but a single-family residence containing at least 1,200 square feet of living area. The legal theory is that, if the buyer or lessee agrees to the re-strictions, he is bound by them. If they are not obeyed, any lot owner in the subdivision can obtain a court order to enforce compliance. The only limit to the number of restrictions that an owner may place on his land is economic. If there are too many restrictions, the landowner may find that no one wants the land.

Deed restrictions, also known as **restrictive covenants,** can be used to dictate such matters as the purpose of the structure to be built, architectural requirements, setbacks, size of the structure and aesthetics. In neighborhoods with view lots, they are often used to limit the height to which trees may be per-mitted to grow. Deed restrictions cannot be used to discrimi-nate on the basis of race, color, religion, sex or national origin; if they do, they are unenforceable by the courts.

PLANNING AHEAD FOR DEVELOPMENT

When a community first adopts a zoning ordinance, the usual procedure is to recognize existing land uses by zoning according to what already exists. Thus, a neighborhood that is already developed with houses is zoned for houses. Undevel-oped land may be zoned for agriculture or simply left unzoned. As a community expands, undeveloped land is zoned for urban uses and a pattern that typically follows the availability of new roads, the aggressiveness of developers and the willingness of landowners to sell. All too often this results in a hodgepodge of land-use districts, all conforming internally because of tightly enforced zoning, but with little or no relationship among them. This happens because they were created over a period of years without the aid of a long-range land-use plan that took a comprehensive view of the entire growth pattern of the city. Since uncoordinated land use can have a negative impact on both the quality of life and economic vitality of a community, more attention is now being directed toward land-use master plans to guide the development of towns and cities, districts, coastlines and even whole states.

Master Plan

To prepare a **master plan** (or **general plan** or **comprehensive plan**), a city or regional planning commission is usually created. The first step is a physical and economic survey of the area to be planned. The physical survey involves mapping existing roads, utility lines, developed land and undeveloped land. The economic survey looks at the present and anticipated economic base of the region, its population and its retail trade facilities. Together the two surveys provide the information upon which a master plan is built. The key is to view the region as a unified entity that provides its residents with jobs and housing, as well as social, recreational and cultural opportunities. In doing so, the master plan uses existing patterns of transportation and land use and directs future growth so as to achieve balanced development. For example, if agriculture is important to the area's economy, special attention is given to retaining the best soils for farming. Waterfront property may also receive special planning protection. Similarly, if houses in an older residential area of town are being converted to rooming houses and apartments, that transition can be encouraged by planning apartment usage for the area. In doing this, the master plan guides those who must make day-to-day decisions regarding zoning changes and gives the individual property owner a long-range idea of what his property may be used for in the future.

Long-Run Continuity

To assure long-run continuity, a master plan should look at least 15 years into the future and preferably 25 years or more. It must also include provisions for flexibility in the event that the city or region does not develop as expected, such as when population grows faster or slower than anticipated. Most importantly, the plan must provide for a balance between the economic and social functions of the community. For example, to emphasize culture and recreation at the expense of adequate housing and the area's economic base will result in the slow decay of the community because people must leave to find housing and jobs.

The purpose of an **environmental impact statement** (EIS), also called an **environmental impact report** (EIR), is to gather into one document enough information about the effect of a proposed project on the total environment so that a neutral decision maker can judge the environmental benefits and costs of the project. For example, a city zoning commission considering a zone change can request an EIS that will show the expected impact of the change on such things as population density, automobile traffic, noise, air quality, water and sewage facilities, drainage, energy consumption, school enrollments, employment, public health and safety, recreation facilities, wildlife and vegetation. The idea is that with this information at hand, better decisions regarding land uses can be made. When problems can be anticipated in advance, it is easier to make modifications or explore alternatives.

At the city and county level, where the EIS requirement has the greatest effect on private development, the EIS usually accompanies the development application that is submitted to the planning or zoning commission. Where applicable, copies are also sent to affected school districts, water and sanitation districts, and highway and flood control departments. The EIS is then made available for public inspection as part of the hearing process on the development application. This gives concerned civic groups and the public at large an opportunity to voice their opinions regarding the anticipated benefits and costs of the proposed development. If the proposed development is partially or wholly funded by state or federal funds, then state or federal hearings are also held.

ENVIRONMENTAL IMPACT STATEMENTS

Because zoning can greatly influence the value of a property, it is absolutely essential that when you purchase real estate you be aware of the zoning for the parcel. You will want to know what the zoning will allow and what it won't; whether the parcel is operating under a restrictive or temporary permit; and what the zoning and planning departments might allow on

PRECAUTIONS

the property in the future. Where there is any uncertainty or where a zone change or variance will be necessary in order to use the property the way you want to, a conservative approach is to make the offer to buy contingent on obtaining planning and zoning approval before going to settlement.

If you are a real estate agent, you must stay abreast of zoning and planning and building matters regarding the properties you list and sell. A particularly sensitive issue that occurs regularly is a property listed for sale which does not meet zoning and/or building code requirements. For example, suppose the current (or previous) owner of a house has converted the garage to a den or bedroom without obtaining building permits and without providing space for parking elsewhere on the parcel. Legally this makes the property unmarketable. If you, as agent, sell this property without telling the buyer about the lack of permits, you've given the buyer grounds to sue you for misrepresentation and the seller for rescission. When faced with a situation like this, you should ask the seller to obtain the necessary permits. If the seller refuses, and the buyer still wants to buy, make the problem very clear to the buyer and have the buyer sign a statement indicating acceptance of title under these conditions. You can also refuse to accept the listing if it looks as though it will create more trouble than it's worth.

Professionals   The point here is that the public has a right to expect real estate agents to be professionals in their field. Thus the agent is expected to be fully aware of the permitted uses for a property and whether or not current uses comply. This is necessary to properly value the property for listing and to provide accurate information to prospective buyers. Even if the seller in the above example was unaware of his zoning and building violations, it is the agent's responsibility to recognize the problem and inform the seller. An agent cannot take the position that if the seller didn't mention it, then the agent needn't worry about it and if the buyer later complains, it's the seller's problem, not the agent's. Recent court decisions clearly indicate that the agent has a responsibility to inform the seller of a problem so that the seller cannot later complain to the agent, "You should have told me about that when I listed the property with you and certainly before I accepted the buyer's offer."

Planning and zoning tend to provide windfall gains for the owners of land that has been authorized for development, while landowners who are prohibited from developing their land suffer financial wipe-outs. This has been a major stumbling block to the orderly utilization of land in America. It is only natural that a landowner will want his land to be zoned for a use that will make it more valuable; however, not all land can be zoned for housing, stores and offices. Some land must be reserved for agriculture and open spaces. If local and state governments embark upon bold land planning programs, how will these financial inequities be resolved?

The past and current position of government and the courts is that if land-use restrictions are for health, safety and general welfare of the community at large, then under the rules of police power, the individual landowner is not compensated for any resulting loss in value. Only when there is an actual physical taking of land is the owner entitled to compensation under the rules of eminent domain. In today's environmentally conscious society, this often results in pitting the landowner who wants to develop his land against those who want to prevent development. For example, a government planning agency in one state stretched the limits of police power to deny an urban landowner a permit to build on his property, and told him he should grow flowers for the public's enjoyment. Many decisions like this could ultimately undermine planning efforts. Yet, government planning agencies do not have the money to buy all the land that they would like to see remain undeveloped.

The solution may come from some radical new thinking about land and the rights to use it. The new planning idea is to eliminate windfalls and wipe-outs by creating **transferable development rights** (TDRs). Previously, the right to develop a parcel of land could not be separated from the land itself. Now planners are exploring the idea of separating the two so that development rights can be transferred to land where greater density will not be objectionable. For example, suppose that within a given planning district there is an area of high-quality farmland that planners feel should be retained for agriculture and not be paved over with streets and covered with buildings.

*WINDFALLS
AND WIPE-OUTS*

*TRANSFERABLE
DEVELOPMENT RIGHTS*

Also in the district is an area deemed more suitable for urban uses and hence an area where government will concentrate on constructing streets, schools, parks, waterlines and other public facilities. To direct growth to the urban area, it is planned and zoned for urban uses. Meanwhile, areas designated for agriculture are forced to remain as farmland. Ordinarily, this would result in windfall gains for the owner of the urban land and a loss in land value for the owner of the farmland.

With the TDR concept in effect, owners of farmland are allowed to sell development rights to the owners of urban land. By purchasing development rights, the urban landowner is permitted to develop his land more intensely than otherwise permissible. This compensates the farmer for the prohibition against developing his land. For the TDR concept to work, there must be a comprehensive regional master plan.

TDRs could be traded on the open market like stocks and bonds. Alternatively, a government agency could pay cash for the value of rights lost. This would be financed by selling those rights to owners in districts to be developed.

Where Used

To date, Chicago and New York City have made use of TDRs for the purpose of protecting historical buildings not owned by the government. An owner who agrees not to tear down his building is given TDRs which can be sold to other nearby landowners. TDRs are also being used to protect open spaces, farm land and environmentally sensitive land in parts of Pennsylvania, Virginia, Florida, Vermont, New Jersey, Maryland and Puerto Rico. In a number of states, the TDR concept is still being tested in court cases. It appears that much of the legal debate centers on the concept of separating the right to develop land from the land itself. The idea is new and has little legal precedence. But, for that matter, neither did zoning when it was new.

Match terms **a–n** with statements **1–14**.

a. *Amendment*
b. *Buffer zone*
c. *Building codes*
d. *Certificate of occupancy*
e. *Downzoning*
f. *EIS or EIR*
g. *Land-use control*

h. *Mapping requirement*
i. *Master plan*
j. *Nonconforming use*
k. *Restrictive covenants*
l. *Spot zoning*
m. *Variance*
n. *Zoning*

1. A broad term used to describe any legal restriction (such as zoning) that controls how a parcel of land may be used.
2. Public regulations that control the specific use of land.
3. An improvement that is inconsistent with current zoning regulations.
4. A comprehensive guide for a community's physical growth.
5. Clauses placed in deeds and leases to control how future owners and lessees may or may not use the property.
6. A government-issued document that states a structure meets zoning and building code requirements and is ready for use.
7. A report that contains information regarding the effect of a proposed project on the environment.
8. Method used to change a zoning ordinance.
9. Allows an individual landowner to vary from a zoning ordinance without changing the ordinance.
10. The rezoning of a small area of land in an existing neighborhood.
11. Local and state laws that set minimum construction standards.
12. A strip of land that separates one land use from another.
13. Rezoning of land from a higher density use to a lower-density use.
14. State and local regulations pertaining to subdivisions that a subdivider must meet before selling lots.

1. For land-use control to be successful, why is it necessary to consider the rights of individual property owners as well as the public as a whole?
2. Explain how a city obtains its power to control land use through zoning.
3. What is the purpose of a variance?
4. In your community, what are the letter/number designations for the following: high-rise apartments, low-rise apartments, single-family houses, stores, duplexes, industrial sites?
5. What is the difference between master planning and zoning?
6. What is the purpose of an environmental impact statement?

7. How would the use of transferable development rights reduce windfalls and wipe-outs for land owners?
8. Does any city or county in your state currently use transferable development rights? What have been the results?

ADDITIONAL READINGS

"America's Innovative Communities" by **Gregg Logan** and **Bonni Hahlbeck.** (*Real Estate Today*, Sep 84, page 31). Article discusses the benefits of master planned communities and the importance of having a variety of housing styles and prices in the same community.

Buying Lots From Developers. (U.S. Department of Housing and Urban Development, 26 pages). This is must reading for anyone planning to buy a vacant lot. Includes what to be wary of, what questions to ask and HUD property report requirements.

"Debunking the Mythology of Zoning" by **Jack Harris** and **William Moore.** (*Real Estate Review*, Winter 84, page 94). Although zoning is accepted as a requisite for a modern city, there may be better methods. Moreover, present zoning laws often add substantially to housing costs.

"Living With Deed Restrictions" by **Judon Fambrough** and **Cindy Dickson.** (*Guarantor*, Nov/Dec 84, page 6). Article shows how deed restrictions have become a popular tool of developers to protect land values thereby making the property more attractive to buyers.

Respectful Rehabilitation. (Preservation Press, 1982, 185 pages). Contains methods and techniques for rehabilitating, preserving and maintaining historic buildings. Generously illustrated with examples.

The Citizens Guide to Zoning, rev. ed. by **Herbert H. Smith.** (Planners Press, 1983, 242 pages). Book stresses the value of citizen involvement in good zoning. Explains zoning and its philosophy and the nuts and bolts of zoning ordinances and administration, variances, hearings, PUDs and TDRs.

Zero Lot Line Housing by **David Jensen.** (Urban Land Institute, 1981, 150 pages). Using a zero lot line is the alternative when people prefer single family houses, yet land is too expensive for large lots. Book discusses site selection, development, building design, landscaping and legal considerations.

*   *   *

The following periodicals may also be of interest to you: *Automation in Housing, Community Development Journal, Journal of the American Planners Association, Land Use Abstracts, Land Use Controls, Land Use Digest, Land Use Law and Zoning Digest* and the *Zoning and Planning Law Report.*

Real Estate and the Economy

Base industry: an industry that produces goods or services for export from the region

Cost-push inflation: higher prices due to increased costs of labor and supplies

Demand-pull inflation: higher prices due to buyers bidding against each other

Economic base: the ability of a region to export goods and services to other regions and receive money in return

Federal Reserve Board: the governing board of the nation's central bank

Monetize the debt: the creation of money by the Federal Reserve to purchase Treasury securities

Real: inflation adjusted

Real-cost inflation: higher prices due to greater effort needed to produce the same product today versus several years ago.

Service industry: an industry that produces goods and services to sell to local residents

Earlier chapters of this book described real estate from the standpoints of what it is, how do you convey it, how do you finance it, how it is taxed, how do you rent it, how do you value it, how do you insure it and how do you brokerage it. In this chapter we will look at the very important role of regional and national economics in giving value to real estate. In particular, this chapter will discuss the need for an economic base to support real estate values, short-run changes in housing demand when a new industry moves into town or an old one closes, long-run effects on housing demand caused by population and income changes, and the impact of federal tax, fiscal and monetary policies. The chapter will conclude with a look at inflation, a review of the 1975–1985 period for real estate, the importance of watching the Federal Reserve and an outlook for the future.

In order to survive, a city (or town or region) must export goods and services so that its residents may purchase goods and services not produced locally. To illustrate, Hollywood

ECONOMIC BASE

535

produces films for theaters and television stations across the country. Income from these films permits residents in Hollywood to purchase things not produced in Hollywood such as cars and trucks made in Detroit. The money Detroit receives is used to buy farm products. A farming region produces farm products in order to generate income with which to buy farm machinery, gasoline, fertilizer, clothing and vacations. In turn, the economy of a resort area is kept alive with the money spent there by vacationers and on and on.

The ability of a city or region to produce a commodity or service that can bring in money from outside its area is called its **economic base.** Industries that produce goods and services for export are called **base, export** or **primary industries.** Thus, film making is a base industry for Hollywood, automobile manufacturing is a base industry for Detroit and agriculture is a base industry in the Midwest. Producers of goods and services that are not exported are called **service, filler** or **secondary industries.** This category includes local school systems, supermarkets, doctors, dentists, drugstores and real estate agents.

Effect on Property Values

Because land is immovable, the existence of base industries is *absolutely essential* to maintaining local real estate values. Unless a region or city exports, it will die economically, and the value of local real estate will fall. An extreme example of this can be found in the abandoned mining towns of yesteryear. Before the discovery of mineral riches, land was often worth but a few dollars an acre for grazing purposes. With the discovery of minerals and subsequent mine development, land that was suitable for townsites zoomed in value. A new and far richer economic base industry than grazing brought wealth and people into the area, and grazing land was suddenly in demand for homesites, stores and offices. Years later, when the mines played out and mineral wealth could no longer be exported from the area, outside money ceased to flow into the town. Miners were laid off and moved to other towns where jobs could be found. Without the miners' money, service industries folded and their employees left. The demand for real estate dropped and real estate prices fell, often all the way back to their value for grazing purposes.

The extent to which regions and cities are vulnerable to changes in economic base depends on how many different kinds of base industries are present and the ability of those industries to consistently export their products. Thus, a city that relies on a single base industry is much more vulnerable than a city with a diversified group of base industries. For example, a city or town that has grown up around a military base will suffer if that base is cut back in size or closed down. In the neighbor cities of Seattle and Tacoma, Washington, real estate prices have been directly influenced by the rise and fall of airplane orders at the area's largest employer, Boeing Aircraft. The economy of Detroit has been hurt by the change in consumer buying preferences to foreign-made cars. The steel-making region that spans Indiana, Ohio, Pennsylvania and West Virginia has been adversely impacted by steel mill shutdowns due to better prices on steel from abroad. Towns that rely heavily on the lumber industry have seen their economies, and real estate prices, hurt by the drop in demand for lumber following the end of the last housing boom. The economies of farm communities and the prices of farm land are tied to the rise and fall of farm product prices.

Vulnerability

Sometimes these events galvanize concerned citizens, property owners and business people into action. Seattle and Tacoma have been busy attracting industries other than aircraft manufacturing so as to smooth out the ups and downs of the aircraft business. Oregon repealed its unitary tax on business firms and is actively courting electronics companies. Some steel mills have been bought by employees determined to keep them open and competitive with foreigners.

Just how important is a base industry job to a local economy? As a rule, for each additional person employed in a base industry, another two persons will be employed in local service industries. Thus, if an electronics firm moves into a community and creates 100 new base industry jobs, opportunities will be created for another 200 persons in jobs such as retail store clerks, restaurant services, gas station operators, gardeners, bankers, doctors, dentists, lawyers, police, fire fighting, school teaching and local government—to name only a few.

Employment Multiplier

If you understand what is happening in local base industries, you can calculate the need for land and housing. For example, the 100 base industry jobs created by the electronics firm result in 200 service jobs, for a total of 300 new job opportunities in the community. If every three jobs require two households (more than one person working in some families) and each household averages 2.9 persons, then 300 jobs will provide income for 200 households containing a total of 580 persons. The ultimate effect of the 300 new jobs on local employment and housing demand will depend on what portion of the jobs can be filled from within the community and the extent of vacant housing. If the community is already operating at full employment and has no vacant housing to speak of, the addition of 100 base jobs will result in a demand for land, building materials and labor necessary to provide 200 new housing units. From the standpoint of local government, 580 more people must be supplied with schools, parks, streets, libraries, water, sewage treatment, police and fire protection.

SHORT-RUN DEMAND FOR HOUSING

Because it takes time to develop raw land into homes, offices and stores, the supply of developed real estate cannot immediately respond to sudden changes in demand. As a result, price changes for developed real property can be rapid and dramatic over short periods of time.

Increase in Demand

To illustrate, suppose that in a given community there are presently 5,000 single-family houses and their average value is $82,000. A new industry moves into the community and increases the demand for houses by 100. Local builders, recognizing the new demand, set to work adding 100 houses to the available housing stock. However, it will take time to acquire land, file subdivision maps, acquire building permits, grade the land and construct the houses. The entire process typically takes 10 to 36 months. Meanwhile the available supply of houses remains fixed. The result will be an increase in house prices as the newly arriving employees bid against each other for a place to live in the existing housing stock. The result is diagrammed in Figure 22:1. Demand Curve 1 represents the demand for houses at various prices before the new employees arrive. Supply and demand are in balance at $82,000 per house, as shown at A.

SHORT-RUN SUPPLY-DEMAND PICTURE   Figure 22:1

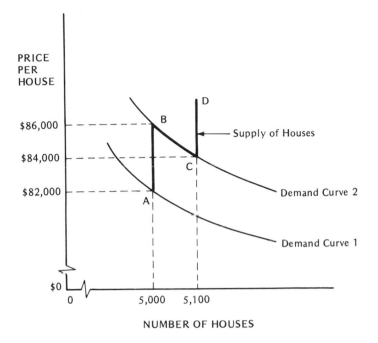

NUMBER OF HOUSES

Next, the new industry moves in. The new employees added to the housing market produces Demand Curve 2. Prices rise owing to competition for the existing houses. This increase literally rations the existing stock of 5,000 houses among 5,100 households. Prices rise until enough existing owners decide to sell and enough new buyers are priced out of the market. Once again, supply and demand are in balance with 5,000 houses occupied by 5,000 families. This is point B at $86,000.

At last, the 100 new houses that were started in response to the new demand are completed and are on the market. At what price must these be offered in order to sell them all? It would appear that $86,000 is the answer, as that is what houses are now selling for. However, the supply–demand relationship in Figure 22:1 shows that only 5,000 houses are in demand at $86,000, not 5,100 houses. To find out at what price the additional 100 houses will be absorbed by the market, we must travel along Demand Curve 2 to 5,100 houses. At point C, the

Increase in Supply

market will absorb 5,100 houses if they are priced at $84,000 each. Thus, a temporary glut of homes causes prices to be reduced slightly. This price softening applies to the builders of the 100 new houses and to the owners of the other 5,000 homes if they wish to sell during this temporary oversupply situation.

Aware of the oversupply of houses on the market, builders will react by halting building activity until those units are sold and demand starts pushing prices upward again to D at which time the process repeats itself. Over a period of years, the supply pattern for houses takes on a stair-step appearance as temporary shortages and temporary excesses alternate.

Decrease in Demand   Just as a short-run increase in demand can cause a quick run-up in prices, a short-run decrease in demand has the opposite effect because supply cannot be decreased as fast as demand falls. This situation is diagrammed in Figure 22:2 with supply and demand in balance at 5,100 houses at $84,000 each. Suppose there is an overnight cutback of jobs and, as a result, 100 homeowners decide to sell and move out of the community. This would cause demand to shift downward from Demand Curve 2 to Demand Curve 1. To sell 100 houses, it is necessary for prices to fall from $84,000 at point C to $80,000 at point E. Without an increase in the economic base of the community, only a reduction in the supply of existing houses through demolition, disasters and conversions to other uses will push prices back up along Demand Curve 1. If supply falls to 5,000 houses, prices will go to $82,000 at point F.

Effect of Inflation   The presence of inflation will cushion the drop in dollar values when demand shifts to Demand Curve 1 in Figure 22:2. Similarly, the drop in prices from B to C in Figure 22:1 will be milder in the presence of moderate inflation. In the presence of high inflation, prices may not drop, but actually rise. However, if you strip away the masking effect of inflation, Figures 22:1 and 22:2 accurately portray what actually happens when demand suddenly changes and supply cannot react fast enough. Although we have been talking in terms of houses, the same concept applies to vacant lots, apartment buildings, townhouses, condominiums, office buildings, factories, hotels and motels, store space and so forth.

SHORT-RUN DROP IN DEMAND   **Figure 22:2**

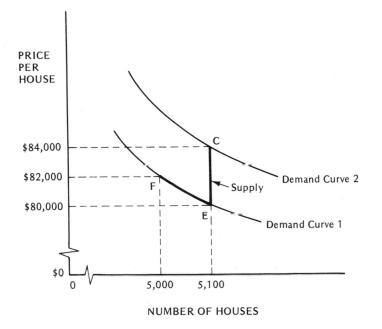

NUMBER OF HOUSES

Future demand for housing in the United States can be seen by looking at the population in terms of age distribution, and the ability of people to obtain income at various age levels. As shown in Figure 22:3, during the first 10 years of life a person earns no income and is dependent on others, usually parents, for sustenance. During junior high school, high school and college (if any) a person has part-time jobs but usually is still dependent on others for financial support.

Upon leaving school and entering the labor market on a full-time basis, a person's income rises quickly, reflecting increased productive capacity in society. As skills increase, income continues to rise rapidly. In another decade the rise stops increasing as rapidly, although it still advances. Then, somewhere between the ages of 40 and 60, depending on a person's skills and the usefulness of those skills in society, health and/or the desire to slow down, the peak earning year occurs. For those with 4 years of college or the equivalent, this occurs

LONG-RUN DEMAND FOR HOUSING

Figure 22:3   **LIFETIME INCOME CURVE**

Based on Median Dollar Income of all Persons
in the United States

around age 55. For the nation as a whole, it occurs in the mid-forties. The peak earning year is followed at first by mild decreases in income and then by more rapid decreases as retirement occurs.

Buying Pattern   With this earning pattern in mind, you can see the progression of housing demand. When a person is young and setting up a household for the first time, income is low and so are accumulated assets. Thus, housing that requires no equity investment at a minimum cost is needed; that is, an inexpensive rental with no frills. During the next decade income increases and the household can increase the quality of its rental unit. At the same time savings accumulate, which, coupled with the ability to make loan payments, enable the household to meet the down payment and loan requirements for a modest housing purchase. As the family grows and income increases, it can move to larger, more expensive quarters. Typically this occurs between the ages of 35 and 45. Another upward move in house size and price usually occurs between 45 and 55 when the family reaches its maximum income.

As the children move out and income peaks and then begins to recede, the household begins to consider a smaller and less expensive dwelling unit. The need for less expensive housing becomes even more compelling upon retirement and a further reduction in income. Retirement income typically is not sufficient to support the large home bought during the peak earning years. However, the household has an equity that it can now consolidate into a smaller residence that is fully or nearly fully paid for.

With the above pattern in mind, let us now turn our attention to Figure 22:4 where the population of the United States is graphed according to its age distribution. The lines labeled 1970 and 1980 are based on the U.S. census; the 1990 and 2000 lines are government-prepared population projections. The 1990 and 2000 lines are based on the fact that persons on the 1980 line will be 10 and 20 years older, respectively, minus losses due to deaths and additions due to immigration.

AGE DISTRIBUTION

There are two peaks in the 1980 age distribution line. The smaller of the two, identified as ①, represents persons aged 50 to 60 years in 1980. These persons were born during the decade of the 1920s, a period of economic prosperity in most parts of the United States. Moving to the left, the dip at ② represents children born during the economic depression that spanned the 1930s. By 1980, they were 40 to 50 years old. Moving again to the left, a substantial upward rise is encountered at ③. This is the famed World War II and postwar "baby boom." It started in 1940 and lasted until 1960. In 1960, the number of births per year began to decline and continued to decline in each subsequent year through 1978. This is shown at ④.

Of particular interest is the huge wave of demand from the 1940–1960 baby boom that is working its way across Figure 22:4. How does this translate into housing demand? Beginning in the early 1960s, the United States experienced a growing demand for inexpensive rentals by persons under 25 years of age. By 1985, that demand peaked as all children born from 1940 to 1960 became 25 years or older. Between 1965 and 1975, the number of persons in the United States aged 25 through 34 increased by 9 million and resulted in the formation of 5 million households. Each household required a housing unit suitable to its income characteristics. Between 1975 and 1985, this age group grew by another 9 million persons and created an addi-

Housing Demand

Figure 22:4   **AGE DISTRIBUTION OF THE U.S. POPULATION FOR**
THE YEARS 1970, 1980, 1990, AND 2000

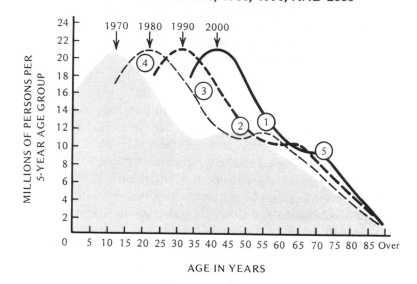

tional 5 million households, each of which required a place to
live.

More Homeowners   In addition to producing new households, the 1940–1960
children are climbing the income ladder and have more money
to spend on housing. And, as they get older they want to own,
not rent. Government statistics show that 60% of all households
aged 35 through 44 are homeowners, and among those 45
through 54 years old, 75% are owners. (The percentages are
even higher if there are children present.) Buying of more expensive homes will continue until the year 2015 at which time
persons born in 1960 will reach the age of 55. Because personal
income patterns decline after that age, a retrenchment into
more modest housing will then be observed.

Over 65   Although the dominant factor in housing demand in the
next several decades will be the maturing members of the
1940–1960 baby boom, we must not overlook the present
steady growth in households over the age of 65 years. Households aged 65 and above are growing in numbers and, as may
be seen at ⑤, will continue to do so until 1995. At that time

there will be a 10-year pause in growth due to persons born during the 1930 decade reaching the age of 65. Following that, the over-65 group will again grow in numbers as those born between 1940 and 1960 reach this age level. As less than one-fifth of the population over 65 remains in the labor force, the housing demand created by these age groups will primarily be the result of their investments, pensions, social security income, public welfare and assets accumulated earlier in life such as the family home.

When the children born after 1960 reach the age at which they want to have a residence of their own (usually 18 to 25 years of age), they will find large amounts of housing available as the persons born between 1940 and 1960 climb the lifetime income curve and upgrade their housing. Unless some of the housing being abandoned by the 1940–1960 group can be used to accommodate households over the age of 65, this situation will probably cause a slowdown in new housing construction. The United States has already experienced a virtual halt in new elementary school construction because of the drop in births after 1960. And this came after a 15-year-long frantic effort to build schoolrooms.

Another Wave

In 1978, the drop in births that began in 1960 began to reverse itself. Now the baby-boom children are having children of their own. This will make a third wave in the age distribution of the U.S. population and, with it, a new wave of housing demand when those children form households.

Thus far we have talked about the requirement of an economic base to support local land values and the effect on housing demand by population age groups and income levels. Now let us look at the influence on real estate caused by the federal government's tax rules, laws, deficits and monetary policies.

GOVERNMENTAL IMPACT

Real estate has long been favored with special income tax treatment. For years, tax laws have allowed homeowners to deduct property taxes and mortgage loan interest when calculating state and federal taxes. To illustrate, for a person in a 40% tax bracket, a 10% interest rate costs, after taxes, only 6%. Similarly, property taxes of $1,500 per year cost, after taxes, only $900.

TAX LAWS

Owners of improved investment property can deduct all costs of operating and maintaining the property plus depreciation on the improvements. For most investment properties since 1940, depreciation expense has been more of an accounting entry than a market reality. This has been a result of rising real estate prices coupled with tax rules that allowed improvements to be depreciated over accounting lives shorter than their useful lives. Moreover, tax rules have allowed depreciation to be accelerated, i.e., taken sooner rather than later. Since depreciation is deductible at tax time and not repaid until years later when the property is sold, tax policies regarding depreciation have made real estate a very, very attractive investment.

There does, however, remain the possibility that what Congress has given real estate owners in special treatment can also be taken away in whole or in part. For example, before the Economic Recovery Tax Act of 1981, improved property bought for business or investment could be depreciated for tax purposes over a life of 20 to 40 years depending on the age and condition of the property. In 1981, the depreciation period was reduced to 15 years for both used and new buildings. In 1984, this was raised to 18 years and in 1985 to 19 years with talk of it going higher. Since a faster depreciation period makes real estate more attractive and a longer period makes it less attractive, you can see how Congress can influence real estate values. The President and Congress have proposed to limit the amount of mortgage interest individuals can deduct on second homes and real estate partnerships. Passage would detract from the attractiveness of these forms of real estate and, in turn, have an impact on values. Other real estate tax areas subject to change are property tax deductions for homeowners, depreciation, capital gains indexing and rehabilitation credits. The key point to remember here is that tax treatment of the expenses and profits from real estate greatly influence what a person can and will pay for a property. Generous tax treatment creates an upward influence on values and vice versa.

FISCAL POLICY   Few home buyers can afford to pay all cash for a place to live; most must borrow. As a result, the housing industry is very sensitive to the price and availability of loan money. Not only does this affect contractors and construction workers, but also appliance and furniture manufacturers, lumber mills, cement factories, real estate appraisers and real estate agents. Anyone connected with the manufacture, sale or resale of housing is directly affected by the price and availability of mortgage loan money to home buyers.

If federal, state or local governments cannot balance their budgets, they too must borrow. When they do, they compete with home buyers and businesses for available savings in the capital markets. Of these, government gets its needs filled first at whatever the interest cost. This is because if a government did not borrow it would not have enough to pay its bills and would be bankrupt. This leaves home buyers and businesses to compete for what is left over. For the most part, state and local governments have learned to live within their budgets. But the federal government has not. Defense spending and social spending in excess of income has produced federal deficits in nearly every year since 1940. Not terribly worrisome at first, by the 1970s financing the federal deficit was taking progressively larger and larger chunks of money out of the capital markets. By the middle of the 1980 decade, annual federal deficits were $200 billion and absorbing that much of the country's, indeed the world's, capital. What was left was available to businesses and home buyers but at high interest rates. In view of this, it is generally agreed among economists that if the federal government will learn to live within its means, interest rates will come down for everyone.

MONETARY POLICY

The Federal Reserve Board through the Federal Reserve Banks has the ability to create and destroy money. This is done by any of the following mechanisms: (1) open-market purchases and sales of Treasury securities, (2) changes in the discount rate charged to banks, and (3) changes in the reserve requirements of banks. We will omit a detailed explanation of each of these and go directly to the point: the Federal Reserve can create money. This is useful because in an economy that grows 3% a year, a 3% increase in the money supply is necessary to keep prices from falling. At the same time, however, there is the temptation to print more money than needed for economic growth because this new money can be used to buy back Treasury securities that were created to fund the federal deficit. The short-term result of such purchases is to drop in interest rates of which the government, business and housing are all beneficiaries. Unfortunately, the longer-run effect (beyond two years) is more inflation as there is now more money in circulation without a corresponding increase in goods and services to buy.

When inflation is apparent, savers become wise and respond by buying equity assets, such as real estate, to hedge against further inflation and by raising the rate of interest they will accept so as to compensate for inflation. Thus, any benefits of creating extra money by the Federal Reserve are lost.

FEDERAL PROGRAMS   A number of federal programs and laws have been enacted to help people buy homes. Two of the oldest and most far-reaching have been the Federal Housing Administration and the Veterans Administration. FHA loan insurance programs have helped persons with modest incomes to qualify for low down payment loans and therefore buy homes they might not otherwise be able to buy. Similarly, the VA has guaranteed loans so that qualifying veterans could buy with as little as no money down. Again, many who might have otherwise not been able to qualify found they could buy a home using the VA's guarantee. To stay abreast of rising home prices, both the FHA and VA have regularly raised their loan limits. Additionally, the FHA offers graduated payment loan programs to squeeze the last ounce of borrowing power out of a loan applicant's income.

Equal Credit   A far-reaching law passed in 1974 was the federal Equal Credit Opportunity Act (ECOA). This law requires that all the income of a woman must be counted in full regardless of marital status or children. Prior to the ECOA, it was common for lenders to refuse to count a married woman's income if she was pregnant and discount it by 50% if she was not pregnant, but in the prime child-bearing years. Coupled with prevailing lower wages for women, the size of loan a couple could get was mainly limited by the husband's income. Additionally, widows, divorcees and singles were considered high-risk borrowers and either did not get credit or did so only in small amounts.

The Equal Credit Opportunity Act created borrowing power that did not exist before. Husband–wife families could qualify for larger loans. Mothers and daughters living together, brothers owning together, single persons, divorced and widowed persons all suddenly found themselves with new and greater borrowing power; and with it, the ability to bid up prices. At the same time, women began to earn more money because of laws requiring equal pay for equal work and laws prohibiting sex discrimination in hiring. Furthermore, more women were going into the labor force and many were choosing higher-paying career-oriented jobs.

A very important influence on real estate activity and prices in the United States has been the secondary mortgage market. Prior to the 1970 decade, home loan money came mostly from savings and loans, mutual savings banks, commercial banks and life insurance companies. This was a relatively limited source of money that tended to keep a lid on real estate prices. With the advent of the Federal National Mortgage Association, the Government National Mortgage Association, the Federal Home Loan Mortgage Corporation and other secondary mortgage market operators, previously untapped sources of loan money were now available to real estate borrowers. Individuals and pension funds that had avoided making mortgage loans because of the work involved could now invest with ease and a guarantee of safety. Additionally, a secondary market provides a place to sell a mortgage that a lender does not want to hold until maturity. Much of the money raised in the secondary market has been used (and will continue to be used) to fund the 1940–1960 baby-boom children as they buy housing. However, a lot of that money also helped fuel real estate speculation and inflation in the late 1970s. (By the way, the secondary market now is producing some drag on prices. Because of substantial foreclosure losses in the early 1980s, loan qualification standards were tightened in 1985.)

SECONDARY MORTGAGE MARKET

In nearly all years since World War II, prices of consumer commodities and real estate have risen. Although inflation is currently not as pressing an issue as it was in the 1970s, there are four concepts with which you should be familiar: cost-push inflation, demand-pull inflation, monetary inflation and real-cost inflation.

TYPES OF INFLATION

Cost-push Inflation   The increasing cost of inputs necessary to manufacture a product or offer a service results in what is called **cost-push inflation.** To illustrate, an automobile manufacturer increases the price of cars because labor and materials cost more. Similarly, a builder of new homes will include any increases in the prices of lumber, bricks, concrete, metal, construction labor, construction loans and government permits.

Demand-pull Inflation   When buyers bid against each other to buy something that has been offered for sale, **demand-pull inflation** results. For example, three buyers for a choice lot may bid $75,000, $76,000 and $77,000, respectively. Demand-pull inflation is basically the result of too much money chasing too few goods. This type of inflation usually has little to do with the actual cost of producing the particular goods or services being sought. Instead, it reflects what buyers feel they would have to pay elsewhere for the same thing.

Monetary Inflation   **Monetary inflation** results from the creation of excessive amounts of money by government. The classic example of this was in Germany during the first 5 years after World War I. In an effort to provide money to solve all the war-torn country's problems at once, the German government created and spent money on a grand scale. However, there was no parallel increase in goods and services to be purchased with that money. The result was demand-pull inflation as millions of people with pockets, and later wheelbarrows, stuffed with newly printed currency fought to buy everything from bread and vegetables to real estate. Within the space of a few short years, prices rose on the order of one million percent before the printing presses were finally shut down.

To a lesser degree monetary inflation is used today by many countries. Allowing the money supply to grow faster than the available supply of goods and services causes a temporary economic stimulus by placing more money in people's hands. But the ultimate result is a reduction in the purchasing power of that money.

Real-cost Inflation   **Real-cost inflation** is inflation caused by the increased effort necessary to produce the same quantity of a good or service. For example, much easy-to-develop land has already been built upon forcing developers to utilize land that requires more effort to bulldoze into usable lots. Another example is water service to new lots. Local water districts that once could supply the town's population from a few wells or a nearby lake or river must now travel many miles to find water. The additional cost of the water system and pumping charges must be added to the user's water bill.

The period from 1975 to 1985 has been one of the most dramatic in American economic history. Real estate prices doubled and tripled between 1975 and 1980. Inflation zoomed upward, interest rates reached record highs and real estate was the favored investment. Then in the early 1980s, inflation fell dramatically, real estate prices stalled and interest rates retreated but still remained historically high. What the country witnessed was a combination of what's been discussed thus far in this chapter at work in the marketplace. Let's take a closer look at what happened then and what may happen in the future. *1975–1985 PERIOD*

In 1975 members of the leading edge of the 1940–1960 baby boom were adults in the market ready for their first housing purchases. Simultaneously, the Equal Credit Opportunity Act made it easier to qualify for loans, and the secondary mortgage market was opening previously untapped sources of loan money. Added to this was the lack of new housing for sale due to a drop in housing starts in connection with a credit crunch and recession in 1974–1975. *1975 to 1980*

As federal spending and money growth policies designed to end the recession took hold, interest rates fell, people regained jobs and the mood of the country turned bullish. People began buying homes again and against a backdrop of limited supply quickly pulled prices upward. Rising prices usually dampen demand. But several other factors were involved that made buying real estate, and in particular buying homes, very attractive.

The first factor was the low **real** (i.e., inflation adjusted) cost of interest. Although interest rates for homes ranged from 8% to 10% between 1975 and 1978, inflation and home prices were rising faster. Thus, it made sense to borrow and buy real *Low Real Interest* estate; in fact, the more the better. Since it was possible to buy with as little as 10% down, buyers were realizing enormous returns on their investments. Persons who received $60,000 for houses bought earlier for $40,000 were now making down payments on $80,000 houses. These sellers were taking their money into $110,000 houses while those sellers were buying $150,000 houses and so on.

Tax Benefits

As already noted, tax laws allow the deduction of interest. During the 1970s, wage increases of 10% per year and more were common. This pushed wage earners into higher tax brackets and made interest deductions even more valuable. Meanwhile, increases from appreciation were not taxable until the property sold and then received preferential long-term capital gains treatment. Thus, despite higher interest and higher home prices, as long as prices continued to rise substantially real estate seemed to be an assured ticket to quick wealth.

Reversal

The boom came to a turning point in late 1979. Politically, high inflation (reaching at one point a rate of 18% per year) became a national issue and something to be halted and reversed. Federal Reserve policy changed from one of generous monetary growth to one of restrained monetary growth. Those who loaned money to real estate buyers were either investing in real estate themselves or charging high enough interest rates to counteract inflation. In the process, mortgage loan rates reached 18% per year and the bank prime rate even higher. Thus, the inflation that had spawned the late 1970s real estate boom was also its downfall. Residential developers who had responded with new construction to meet the market demand now found themselves with homes to sell in the face of 16% to 18% interest rates and few buyers. Many experienced stunning losses, foreclosure and bankruptcy as interest charges on unsold homes bled them financially.

Giveth and Taketh

What was such an irresistible investment from 1975 to 1979 was no longer as attractive by the early 1980s. Inflation rates dropped below interest rates, home prices stopped rising 20% to 30% per year, and higher home prices coupled with higher interest rates now priced many home buyers out of the market. What inflation had given, it was now taking away.

Even the creative financing that kept sales going at successively higher prices was disappearing. Fewer and fewer loans became assumable, a process that the 1982 *de la Cuesta* case and the 1982 Garn Act accelerated. Lenders, stuck badly and some forced out of business, now wanted to loan on adjustable rate terms.

Expectations about inflation (or the lack of it) and interest rates lag the actual changes. At the mid-point of the 1980 decade, much of the home buying public was still unsure what to make of things. House prices, on average, essentially remained stable for the first half of the decade while interest rates were slow to drop. Many investors were left with high-priced properties that could not be sold except at below-market interest rates. More generous depreciation schedules offered by the 1981 tax act did help real estate's attractiveness. But, investors and speculators remained unimpressed with housing and turned to office buildings with depreciation being the carrot. However, even this carrot produced a problem as millions of square feet of office space built between 1981 and 1985 stood vacant at mid-decade while someone was making the interest payments.

Looking Ahead

No longer a speculator's market, the housing market is returning to an owner-occupant market. Owner-occupants receive the benefits of occupancy and the psychic value of owning their home. As such, they are less demanding of appreciation potential compared to investors who, sensing an unrewarding investment, will avoid it or sell out of it and go elsewhere with their capital. Thus, it appears that for the foreseeable future, success in new construction will go to those who appeal best to the owner-occupant's needs, tastes and pocketbook. With falling interest rates, more owner-occupants will be able to qualify for loans and buy homes. This will especially help the resale market and those owners who need to refinance existing loans. Investors, unless they can get a combination of appreciation, tax benefits and rental income that exceeds other investment opportunities will look elsewhere.

Owner-Occupants

During the 1975–1979 period, escalating wage increases, interest rates below inflation, and attractive tax benefits en-

Expensive Housing

couraged home buyers to buy homes larger and more expensive than they otherwise could afford. By the early 1980s, wages were not rising as rapidly, and appreciation was no longer offsetting interest rates. Although persons already owning could usually move to another home of equal value, new entrants to the housing market were much less fortunate. The result has been a demand for smaller houses on smaller lots that has not been seen since the days of the FHA–VA tract houses of the late 1940s and early 1950s. Some of the most dramatic sales success stories of the mid-1980s are coming from developers who are offering single-family detached homes of less than 1,000 square feet. (This is the equivalent of a good-sized 2-bedroom, 2-bath apartment.) Interestingly, developers are finding that although condominiums can provide this size of unit very easily, the American dream is still for a single-family home with its own private backyard; even if the home and yard are both postage-stamp size. Compared with a national median for new houses of 1,600 square feet in the late 1970s, a 1,000 square-foot home costs enough less that even with 10% to 12% interest rates it is affordable for many new home buyers. Given a choice between buying a small house or continuing to rent an apartment unit, the small house is the first-time buyer's choice. To make small houses look bigger than they are, builders and their architects make better use of every square foot. Popular building techniques utilize raised ceilings, sunken floors, blended-space, built-in furniture, more light, more windows and personal touches such as lofts and curved walls.

WATCHING THE FED   If you plan to develop or invest in real estate, it is very helpful to watch Federal Reserve statistics so as to better anticipate changes in interest rates. Although the marketplace is the ultimate decider of interest rates, the actions of the **Federal Reserve Board** can and do provide a powerful push on rates. For example, even though mortgage rates were already rising by 1978 as lenders tried to stay ahead of inflation, Federal Reserve action in 1979 and 1980 to slow money supply growth helped interest rates go higher. By 1985 the Board was carefully increasing the money supply in order to reduce interest rates and thus keep the U.S. economy from falling into another recession.

To understand the Federal Reserve Board, you need to know that the Board has four objectives for the American economy: (1) high employment, (2) stable prices, (3) steady growth in the nation's productive capacity, and (4) a stable foreign exchange value for the dollar. During a recession, employment and economic growth are of primary importance, and the Board adds extra money to the banking system as it did to pull out of the 1974–1975 recession. In the late 1970s, stable prices and a stable dollar were the prime concerns. This required a slowdown in the growth of the money supply, which the Board did. By the end of 1984, inflation was down to 4% and the dollar was very strong. In 1985, the Board was gingerly touching the money accelerator to buoy a banking industry beleaguered by high interest rates, ward off recession and take the edge off what many considered to be an overly strong dollar.

Monetary Base

Week-to-week changes in the results of Federal Reserve monetary policy can be found each Friday in the *Wall Street Journal* under "Federal Reserve Data." Of these, the most important is the **monetary base** figure. This shows the legal reserves of banks at the Federal Reserve plus cash in the hands of the public. If this grows faster than the real (i.e., inflation adjusted) rate of growth of the country's gross national product (GNP), one can assume that the nation's money supply will soon be expanding at a greater rate than real gross national product. This will cause, for the time being, interest rates to fall and economic growth to be stimulated. Two years down the road it will turn to inflation.

THE OUTLOOK

As this material is being written, there are two likely economic scenarios pending and in both the federal deficit plays a leading role. The first scenario is that Congress will not balance its budget. This means the Federal Reserve Board must decide whether or not to expand the money supply in order to buy back the deficit, i.e., **monetize the debt.** Failure to expand the money supply will allow interest rates to rise dramatically and cause a recession worse than the 1981–1982 recession, which itself was the worst since the 1930s. Yet creating money in excess of increases in goods and services will cause inflation and high interest costs just as it did in the 1975–1979 period.

The second scenario is that Congress will bring about a meaningful reduction in the size of the federal deficit. This would reduce the need of the U.S. Treasury to compete with businesses and home buyers for available loan funds. With less competition interest rates will fall. This will attract more loan funds as lenders become confident that rates won't soon be rising. Lower rates will reduce the federal deficit still further as interest paid on existing government debt gradually drops. The cost of this attractive scenario is overall fiscal belt tightening: recipients of social spending programs would have to receive less as would the military. Alternatively, Congress could raise taxes to pay for its spending or it could apply a combination of the two.

A Parallel

There is a very close parallel between the federal government's money problems and the money problems of a free-spending married couple that discovered credit cards. At first, the couple found that a credit card could help them buy a few things that their monthly paychecks would not have covered. But instead of repaying the credit card balance, more items were purchased until the limit on the card was reached. Flushed with the pleasures of living beyond their monthly paychecks, another credit card was obtained. Purchases were made with it until it, too, reached its maximum. Now the first two credit card companies were demanding monthly payments, so a third credit card, this one with cash borrowing privileges, was obtained. This card was used to make payments on the previous two cards and buy still more on credit. Soon all three credit card companies wanted monthly repayments so the couple took out a loan at the bank, mortgaging the appreciation in their house to do so. The buying continued and soon another loan was taken out with a finance company to make payments on the existing loans and buy more things. Then one day, there were simply no more places to borrow, yet the payments on all those loans kept coming due. The couple was advised by a credit counselor that they had two choices: declare bankruptcy or adopt an austerity budget and start repaying the loans. If you were in their shoes, which would you choose? If you were in the U.S. Congress, which would you choose for the country? Or, would you look for one more lender to keep the deficits going a little while longer?

There is no lack of household formation potential in the United States. Additionally there is a large stock of existing housing in the country plus the capacity to build two million new housing units every year. The main question will continue to be who gets what, i.e., how housing will be distributed. Because real estate is so sensitive to the price and availability of loanable funds, the answer will depend heavily on competition from the government.

VOCABULARY REVIEW

Match terms **a–j** *with statements* **1–10.**

a. *Base industry*	**f.** *Monetary inflation*
b. *Cost-push inflation*	**g.** *Monetize the debt*
c. *Demand-pull inflation*	**h.** *Real*
d. *Economic base*	**i.** *Real-cost inflation*
e. *Federal Reserve Board*	**j.** *Service industry*

1. An industry that produces goods or services for export from the region.
2. An industry that produces goods or services to sell to local residents.
3. The ability of a region to export goods and services to other regions.
4. Higher prices due to buyers bidding against each other.
5. Higher prices due to greater effort needed to produce the same product today.
6. Higher prices due to increased costs of labor and supplies.
7. Results from increasing the money supply faster than increases in goods and services to buy.
8. Governing board of the nation's central bank.
9. Inflation adjusted.
10. The creation of money by the Federal Reserve to purchase Treasury securities.

QUESTIONS AND PROBLEMS

1. List and rank in order of importance the base industries that support your community. How stable are they? Are any new ones coming? Are any existing ones leaving?
2. What would be the effect of a new industry creating 500 new jobs in your community? Is there sufficient vacant housing available? What would be the effect of a loss of 500 jobs?
3. Does the population age distribution of your community differ from the United States as a whole? How would this affect demand for housing in your area?
4. What is the after-tax cost of a 15% mortgage loan to a person in a 40% income tax bracket? A 10% loan? A 5% loan?

5. What was the intent of government in passing the Equal Credit Opportunity Act?
6. Identify three specific examples of cost-push inflation that you have personally observed or read about during the past 12 months.
7. Why are large federal deficits considered bad for home buyers?
8. What are the economic goals of the Federal Reserve Board?
9. What is the advantage and the disadvantage of monetizing the federal debt?
10. If money supply grows slower than real gross national product, would the result be rising prices or falling prices?

ADDITIONAL READINGS

"Computers to the Rescue." (*Real Estate Today*, May 85, pages 12–27). This feature section contains the following articles: "Fight Fear of Automation," "Basics of Property Management Software," "Negotiate Before You Automate" and "Practical Protection for Your Software."

Historical Chart Book. (Federal Reserve Board). Published annually, this book contains easy-to-read graphs and charts of money, finance, prices, real estate, production and labor statistics. Most go back 50 years or more to give the reader an excellent historical perspective.

"In Search of Dreams." (*Real Estate Today*, Sep 84, page 8). Looks forward at how Americans will satisfy their housing needs in the 1980s. In the same issue are articles on trends in population shifts, manufactured housing and older homes.

Statistical Abstract of the United States. (Bureau of the Census, 1986, 1,010 pages). Contains statistics on nearly every facet of life in the United States. Includes such real estate related statistics as housing prices, value of construction, construction wages, new housing starts, occupied housing units, occupant characteristics, homes sold and mortgage loans. Published annually.

Savings and Loan Fact Book. (United States League of Savings Associations, 1986). An excellent reference source for statistics on savings, home ownership, residential construction and financing. Published annually.

* * *

The following periodicals may also be of interest to you: *American Real Estate and Urban Economics Association Journal, Business Conditions Digest, Growth and Change, Housing Market Report, Housing Starts (Census), Journal of Housing, Journal of Urban Economics, New One-Family Houses Sold and For Sale (Census), Survey of Current Business, Trends in Housing, Urban Growth* and *Urban Land*.

Investing in Real Estate

Accelerated depreciation: any method of depreciation that achieves a faster rate of depreciation than straight-line

Cash flow: the number of dollars remaining each year after collecting rents and paying operating expenses and mortgage payments

Cash-on-cash: the cash flow produced by a property divided by the amount of cash necessary to purchase it

Downside risk: the possibility that an investor will lose his money in an investment

Equity build-up: the increase of one's equity in a property due to mortgage balance reduction and price appreciation

Investment strategy: a plan that balances returns available with risks that must be taken in order to enhance the investor's overall welfare

Leverage: the impact that borrowed funds have on investment return

Negative cash flow: a condition wherein the cash paid out exceeds the cash received

Prospectus: a disclosure statement that describes an investment opportunity

Straight-line depreciation: depreciation in equal amounts each year over the life of the asset

Tax shelter: the income tax savings that an investment can produce for its owner

There are more millionaires in the United States as a result of real estate investing than from any other source, including oil wells and computers. Moreover, real estate success and wealth has, and is, available to people from all walks of life and all income levels. For most people thinking of making it big financially, real estate is at the top of the list. Considering that real estate provides 235 million people in the United States a place to sleep at night as well as approximately half that number a place to work during the day plus all the other uses we make of real estate, you can begin to see why there are so many opportunities in real estate investing.

The key to your personal success is your time and your intelligence. There are some who say that luck plays the main role in real estate success and that it's all a matter of waiting for the right deal to come along. In reality, however, success results when opportunity and preparedness meet. As you become more knowledgeable as to what makes a good real estate investment and you apply your time to looking for real estate opportunities, you will experience success.

It is impossible to do full justice to the topic of real estate investing in one chapter. There are, however, dozens of entire books on the subject, many of which you can find at your local library and bookstore. What this chapter will do is introduce you to some highlights of real estate investing. We shall begin with the investment benefits of real estate and then look at risks and rewards of various forms of real estate, investment timing, investment strategies and limited partnerships.

BENEFITS OF REAL ESTATE INVESTING

The monetary benefits of investing in real estate come from cash flow, tax shelter, mortgage reduction and appreciation. Let us look at each of these more closely.

CASH FLOW

Cash flow refers to the number of dollars remaining each year after collecting rents and paying operating expenses and mortgage payments. For example, suppose you own an apartment building that generates $30,000 per year in rents when fully occupied. Against this you have an allowance of 5% for vacancies and collection losses, operating expenses (including reserves) of $9,000 per year and mortgage payments of $19,000. Given these facts, your cash flow picture would be as shown in Figure 23:1.

The purpose of calculating cash flow is to show the cash-in-the-pocket effect of owning a particular property. In the Figure 23:1 example, $500 per year is going into your pocket. When money is flowing into your pocket, it is called a **positive cash flow.** If you must dip into your pocketbook to keep a property going, you have a **negative cash flow,** also called an "alligator." For example, if in Figure 23:1, the mortgage payments were $21,000 per year, there would be a negative cash flow. A negative cash flow does not mean a property is a poor investment. There may be tax benefits and appreciation that more than offset this.

Two additional terms you should know are net spendable and cash-on-cash. **Net spendable** is the same thing as cash

Scheduled gross income	**$30,000**
Less allowance for vacancies and collection losses	1,500
Equals effective gross income	28,500
Less operating expenses	9,000
Less mortgage payments	19,000
Equals cash flow	**$ 500**

flow. **Cash-on-cash** is the cash flow that a property produces in a given year divided by the amount of cash required to buy the property. For example, if a property has a cash flow of $5,000 per year and can be purchased with a $50,000 down payment (including closing costs), the cash on cash figure for that property is 10%. For many real estate investors, this is the heart of the investment decision, namely, "How much do I have to put down and how much will I have in my pocket at the end of each year?"

TAX SHELTER

Broadly defined, **tax shelter** describes any tax-deductible expense generated by an investment property. Real estate examples are interest, maintenance, insurance, property taxes and depreciation. You will also hear the term tax shelter refer to long-term capital gain treatment on appreciation. More narrowly defined, real estate tax shelter refers only to the depreciation an improvement can produce for tax purposes. This is because interest, maintenance, insurance and property taxes are all out-of-pocket expenses, and the long-term capital gain treatment comes only when the property is sold. What makes depreciation stand out is that it is allowed as an expense when calculating taxable income from a property, yet it is not an out-of-pocket expense. As such it can shelter from taxes part or all the income earned by the property. If the shelter exceeds the property's income, it can shelter its owner's gains from other investments, business profits and salary income.

To illustrate the benefits of tax shelter, let us continue with the example started in Figure 23:1. Suppose that you are in a combined state and federal income tax bracket of 40%. Suppose further that you can claim depreciation of $10,000 per year on the improvements. Figure 23:2 illustrates the property from the standpoint of income tax consequences.

Figure 23:2

Scheduled gross income	**$30,000**
Less allowance for vacancies and collection losses	1,500
Equals effective gross income	28,500
Less operating expenses	9,000
Less interest	18,000
Less depreciation	10,000
Equals taxable income	**($ 8,500)***

* In accounting language, parentheses indicate a negative or minus amount.

Comparing Figures 23:1 and 23:2, we see two important differences. First, mortgage balance reduction is an out-of-pocket expense, but not a deduction for income tax purposes. Second, depreciation is a deduction against income taxes, but not an out-of-pocket expense. Where does that leave you? The $10,000 depreciation deduction shelters $1,000 of rental income that goes toward principal reduction, $500 in positive cash flow and $8,500 of income you have from other sources.

The value of $10,000 worth of depreciation to you as a 40% bracket taxpayer is $4,000. In other words, you save $4,000 in income taxes by owning this property. Now, if we look at cash flow on an after-tax basis, you actually enjoy a cash flow of $4,500. This makes the property a much more appealing investment, especially if you can also look forward to appreciation. Note that the higher your tax bracket, the more valuable depreciation becomes. If you are in the 50% bracket, $10,000 of depreciation is worth $5,000. If you are in the 20% bracket, it is worth only $2,000.

CALCULATING DEPRECIATION

In theory, all physical property of a business, except land, loses value over time because of wear and tear. **Depreciation expense** is designed to deduct money from income in order to recover the cost of the investment. For example, consider an automobile used by a salesperson to make sales calls. Suppose the vehicle costs $14,000, will be used for 5 years and is expected to have a resale value of $4,000. This amounts to $10,000 of depreciation over 5 years, or an average of $2,000 per year. This reflects the car's actual loss of value and is a deductible expense from income when calculating income taxes.

Now suppose you build a garden-style apartment building that you estimate will have an economic life of 50 years and then be torn down. This would give an average depreciation of 2% per year and for a $1 million building would amount to $20,000 per year. If this were all there was to depreciation, it would not rate much excitement as a tax shelter. But, enter three factors that can make depreciation nearly as valuable as the income a property generates.

First, buildings do not necessarily drop in value as they get older. In fact, because the location of an older building may be superior to new sites, because the building can get rent increases, because new buildings may cost more to build and because of increasing demand for investment properties, buildings, for the most part, have increased in market value even as they are wearing out. This situation gives an investment property owner the best of two worlds: a depreciation expense to claim when calculating taxes and a building that is appreciating in the marketplace.

Short Life

The second factor is that the U.S. Congress has passed tax laws that allow depreciation to be claimed over a much shorter life than the economic life of the building. In other words, an investor does not have to own a building for its entire economic life in order to deduct the entire cost of it. Congress changes the depreciation rules from time to time, but the most extreme example of fast write-off was the 15-year depreciation period available to anyone who bought a new or used building from January 1, 1981 through March 15, 1984.

Accelerated Depreciation

The third factor is that investment property owners may choose accelerated depreciation rather than straight-line depreciation. **Straight-line depreciation** is calculated by taking the total amount of anticipated depreciation and dividing by the number of years. An example is the above-mentioned automobile where $10,000 of depreciation is anticipated over 5 years giving a $2,000 depreciation deduction per year. In contrast, **accelerated depreciation** refers to any method of depreciation that allows depreciation at a rate faster than straight-line depreciation during the first several years of ownership. Since the end of World War II, Congress has allowed

Figure 23:3

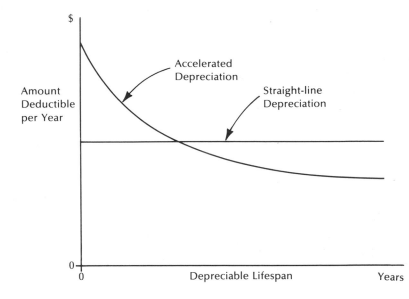

Straight-line depreciation allocates depreciation equally to each year of ownership. Accelerated depreciation allows more depreciation to be claimed sooner and less later.

125%, 150%, 175% and 200% accelerated depreciation depending on the type of property. For example, 125% depreciation means that depreciation is taken one and one-quarter times as fast as straight-line; 200% depreciation means depreciation is taken twice as fast as straight-line. Figure 23:3 illustrates straight-line and accelerated depreciation principles.

Tax rules do not allow an investor to depreciate more than the value of the improvements (and never the land), but if the depreciation can be taken sooner rather than later, it is much more valuable to the investor. After the depreciation has been taken on a property, the investor sells it, buys another and starts the process anew. Meanwhile, the buyer of the property can start the depreciation all over again based on what he paid for the property.

When the building is sold, all the depreciation claimed in excess of actual loss in value comes back to be taxed. (Very briefly explained, upon sale, taxes are due on the difference between the property's basis and the sale price after selling costs. An investment property's **basis** is the purchase price plus improvements minus depreciation claimed since purchase.) However, the tax is not due until the property is sold, and the tax can be postponed if the investor trades or dies rather than sells. Additionally, when taxes are finally paid, with careful advance planning they will be calculated under the preferential long-term capital gain rules rather than higher ordinary income tax rates.

What you can see here is that American tax laws are very favorable in their treatment of real estate. Depending on your viewpoint, this is either an uneconomic and unjustified subsidy for real estate or a national policy that encourages the construction of, and investment in, real property.

MORTGAGE REDUCTION

Mortgage reduction occurs because the investor uses a portion of the property's rental income to reduce the balance owing on the mortgage, thus increasing his equity. At first the reduction may be almost imperceptible because most of the monthly payments are going to interest. But eventually the balance owing begins to fall at a more rapid rate. Some investors invest with the idea that if they hold a rental property for the entire life of the loan, the tenants will have paid for the property. That is to say, the investor acquires the property free and clear of debt for only the cost of the down payment. This presumes the investor is patient and the property does not generate a negative cash flow.

APPRECIATION

Appreciation refers to the increase in property value that the owner hopes will occur while he owns it. Appreciation is the wonder cure of investing. It can overcome a negative cash flow, overestimated income, underestimated expenses and an adjustable rate mortgage that seems to adjust only upward. Without appreciation, real estate becomes less attractive as an investment and people will take their investment money elsewhere, such as into stocks and bonds.

EQUITY BUILD-UP

An owner's **equity** in a property is defined as the market value of the property less all liens or other charges against the property. Thus, if you own a property worth $125,000 and owe

Figure 23:4   **CALCULATING EQUITY BUILD-UP**

Equity at Time of Purchase		Equity 5 Years Later		Equity Build-up	
Purchase price	$200,000	Market value	$220,000	Current equity	$100,000
Mortgage loan	−140,000	Less loan balance	−120,000	Less beginning equity	−60,000
Down payment (equity)	$ 60,000	Equals current equity	$100,000	Equals equity build-up	$ 40,000

$75,000, your equity is $50,000. If you own that property with your brother or sister, each with a one-half interest, your equity is $25,000 and his/her equity is $25,000.

Equity build-up is the change in your equity over a period of time. Suppose you purchase a small apartment building for $200,000, placing $60,000 down and borrowing the balance. Your beginning equity is your down payment of $60,000. If after 5 years you have paid the loan down to $120,000 and you can sell the property for $220,000, your equity is now $100,000. Since you started with $60,000, your equity build-up is $40,000. Figure 23:4 recaps this calculation.

LEVERAGE   **Leverage** is the impact that borrowed funds have on investment return. The purpose of borrowing is to earn more on the borrowed funds than the funds cost. For example, suppose you are an investor and you have $250,000 to invest in an apartment building. If you use all your money to buy a $250,000 building, there is zero leverage. If you use your $250,000 to buy a $500,000 building, there is 50% leverage. If you use your $250,000 to buy a $2,500,000 building there is 90% leverage.

Whether or not to leverage depends on whether the property can reasonably be expected to produce cash flow, tax benefits, mortgage reduction and appreciation in excess of the cost of the borrowed funds. The decision also depends on your willingness to take risk. For example, the $250,000 building would have to fall to zero value before you lost all of your money. Moreover, the building could experience a vacancy rate on the order of 60%, and there would still be enough cash to meet out-of-pocket operating expenses. In other words, with zero leverage there is very little likelihood of a total financial wipe-out.

In contrast, if you buy the $2,500,000 apartment building, a 10% drop in the property's value to $2,250,000 wipes out your entire equity. Moreover, even the slightest drop-off in occupancy from 95% down to 85% will cause great strain on your ability to meet mortgage loan payments and out-of-pocket operating expenses.

But, suppose apartment building values increase by 10%. If you bought the $250,000 building, it will now be worth $275,000, an increase of $25,000 on your investment of $250,000. If you bought the $2,500,000 building, it will now be worth $2,750,000, an increase of $250,000 on your investment of $250,000. As you can see, leverage can work both against you and for you. If the benefits from borrowing exceed the costs of borrowing, it is called **positive leverage.** If the borrowed funds cost more than they are producing, it is called **negative leverage.**

Congress has had a long history of writing and rewriting tax law as applied to real estate. The most generous point for real estate came with the Economic Recovery Tax Act of 1981. Prior to that time a typical residential rental structure was allowed a depreciable life of 20 to 50 years depending on its age, condition and usefulness. Investors were allowed straight-line, 125%, 150%, 175% and 200% depreciation depending on whether the property was residential or commercial and whether it was new or used. The 1981 act allowed nearly all types of buildings, whether new or used, to be fully depreciated in 15 years at 175% accelerated depreciation. This was called the **Accelerated Cost Recovery System** (abbreviated **ACRS** and pronounced "acres"), and the U.S. Treasury published an ACRS table that showed how much depreciation to deduct each year depending on the month of purchase. For taxpayers wanting a slower write-off, the 1981 act also allowed 15-year, 35-year and 45-year straight-line depreciation.

Congress found the 15-year write-off period overly generous and changed it to 18 years in 1984. In 1985 another change was made, this time to 19 years, and there were proposals to

TAX LAW CHANGES

extend still further. (In view of this, your author has purposely not included an ACRS table. This is better left to publishers of tax books and tax newsletters.) Because depreciation rules have experienced so much change, there are those in real estate that now feel the biggest risks in real estate are not in the market-place, but impending tax law changes. The concern is that if real estate loses its long-favored status with Congress it will be less popular as an investment. Therefore, be aware of the tax law change risk and keep your eyes open to it.

Watch List   A partial list of things to watch for are repeal of the 60% exclusion for long-term capital gains, taxation of partnerships with 35 or more limited partners as corporations, limitations and indexing of deductible interest expenses, a lowering of the highest income tax bracket, substitution of economic life de-preciation for ACRS, and extension of "at-risk" rules to real estate. The last item refers to the fact that a real estate investor can claim depreciation on the full value of a building even though a portion of the purchase price was borrowed using a nonrecourse (no personal liability) note. An **"at-risk"** rule would limit depreciation deductions to the amount of money invested plus debt for which the investor is personally liable. Most investment real estate is bought with nonrecourse financ-ing, and at this writing real estate is the only investment to which Congress does not apply an "at-risk" rule.

PROPERTY SELECTION   The real estate market offers a wide selection of properties for investments, including vacant land, houses, condominiums, small, medium and large apartment buildings, office buildings, stores, industrial property and so forth. Selecting a suitable type of property is a matter of matching an investor's capital with his attitudes toward risk taking and the amount of time he is willing to spend on management. Let us look at some of the more popular investments, in particular vacant land, houses, condominiums, apartment buildings and office buildings.

Vacant Land   The major risk of owning vacant land as an investment is that one will have to wait too long for an increase in value. Va-cant land produces no income, yet it consumes the investor's dollars in the form of interest, property taxes, insurance and selling costs. The rule of thumb is that the market value of vacant land must double every 5 years for the investor to break even. If this increase does not occur, the owner will find he has spent more on interest, insurance, property taxes, brokerage fees and closing costs than he has made on the price increase.

Income tax laws improve land speculation benefits because insurance, interest and property taxes plus any other costs of holding the investment are tax deductible at ordinary rates in the year paid. Yet the increase in property value is taxed only after the property is sold, and then usually at much lower long term capital gain rates.

The key to successful land speculating is in outguessing the general public. If the public feels that development of a vacant parcel to a higher use is 10 years in the future, the market price will reflect the discounted cost at current interest rates and property taxes for that waiting period. If the land speculator buys at these prices and the higher use occurs in 5 years, there is a good chance his purchase will be profitable. However, the speculator will lose money if the public expects the higher use to occur in 5 years and it actually takes 10 years.

Finally, land speculators expose themselves to an extra risk that owners of improved property can usually avoid: When it comes time to sell, unless buildings will immediately be placed upon the land by the purchaser, very few lenders will loan the purchaser money to buy the land. This may force the seller to accept the purchase price in the form of a down payment plus periodic payments for the balance. If the interest rate on the balance is below prevailing mortgage rates, as often happens in land sales, the seller is effectively subsidizing the buyer. Furthermore, if the payments are made over several years, the seller takes the risk that the money will have lost some of its purchasing power by the time it is finally received.

Houses and Condominiums

Houses and condominiums are the smallest properties available in income-producing real estate and as such are within the financial reach of more prospective investors than apartment buildings, stores or offices. Moreover, they can usually be purchased with lower down payments and interest rates, because lenders feel that loans on houses and condominiums are less prone to default than on larger buildings. With a small property, the investor can fall back on his salary and other income to meet loan payments in the event rents fall short. With larger buildings, the lender must rely on the rental success of the property and not on the owner's other sources of income.

Houses and condominiums are usually overpriced in relation to the monthly rent they can generate. This is because their prices are influenced by the value of the shelter they provide and the amenity value of home ownership. Thus an investor must pay what prospective owner-occupants are willing to pay; yet when the property is rented, a tenant will pay only for the shelter value. When the investor sells, however, the sale price will be higher than would be justified by rents alone. What this means is that the investor can usually expect a negative cash flow during ownership. Consequently, there must be a substantial increase in property value to offset the monthly negative cash flow and give the investor a good return on his investment.

From time to time substantial appreciation has occurred. During several years of the 1970 decade, house prices rose very rapidly and produced excellent returns. In contrast, during the early 1960s, houses were poorer investments because sufficient new construction kept the prices of existing houses from rising rapidly. In many cities of the United States, condominiums were overbuilt in the early 1970s resulting in unsold new units. Consequently, investors in existing units could not get the appreciation needed to provide a decent return on investment. Later in the decade the supply–demand picture for condominiums changed and more appreciation occurred. Then during the tight money periods of the early 1980s, houses and condominiums again became poor investment performers because of the lack of appreciation.

Small Apartment Buildings

Because considerable appreciation must occur to make house and condominium investments profitable, many investors who start with these move to more income-oriented properties as their capital grows. This reduces investment risk because returns from rental income can be more reliably forecast than changes in prices. Particularly popular with investors who have modest amounts of investment capital are duplexes (two units), triplexes (three units) and fourplexes (four units).

If it were necessary to hire professional management, such small buildings would be uneconomical to own. However, for most owners of two- to four-unit apartment buildings, management is on a do-it-yourself basis and some owners choose to live on the premises. Living on-site eliminates a cash outlay for management and allows the owner to reduce repair and maintenance expenses by handling them himself. Also, with the owner living on the property, tenants are encouraged to take better care of the premises and discouraged from moving out without paying their rent. Finally, the ownership of a residential rental property provides the owner with a wealth of experience and education in property management.

Apartment buildings containing 5 to 24 units also present good investment opportunities for those with sufficient down payment. However, in addition to analyzing the building, rents and neighborhood, thought must be given to the matter of property management before a purchase is made. An apartment building of this size is not large enough for a full-time manager; therefore, the owner must either do the job or hire a part-time manager to live on the property. If the owner does the job, he should be willing to live on or near the property and devote a substantial amount of his time to management, maintenance and upkeep activities. If a part-time manager is hired, the task is to find one who is knowledgeable and capable of maintaining property, showing vacant units, interviewing tenants, collecting rents on time and handling landlord–tenant relations in accordance with local landlord–tenant laws. As the size of an apartment building increases, so does its efficiency. As a rule of thumb, when a building reaches 25 units, it will generate enough rent so that a full-time professional manager can be hired to live on the premises. With a live-in manager, the property owner need not be as involved in day-to-day management chores. This is very advantageous if the owner has another occupation where his or her time is better spent.

Medium-size Buildings

As the number of apartment units increases, the cost of management per unit drops. Beyond 60 units, assistant managers can be hired. This makes it possible to have a representative of the owner on the premises more hours of the day to look after the investment and keep the tenants happy. Size also

Larger Apartment Buildings

means it is possible to add recreational facilities and other amenities that are not possible on a small scale. The cost of having a swimming pool in a 10-unit building might add so much to apartment rents that they would be priced out of the market. The same pool in a 50- or 100-unit building would make relatively little difference in rent. As buildings reach 200 or more units in size, it becomes economical to add such things as a children's pool, gymnasium, game room, lounge and a social director.

Since larger apartment buildings cost less to manage per unit and compete very effectively in the market for tenants, they tend to produce larger cash flows per invested dollar. However, errors in location selection, building design and management policy are magnified as the building grows in size. Also, some lenders, particularly small- and medium-sized banks and savings associations, are simply not large enough to lend on big projects. Finally, the number of investors who can single-handedly invest a down payment of $500,000 or more is limited. This has caused the widespread growth of the limited partnership as a means of making the economies of large-scale ownership available to investors with as little as $5,000 or even $2,000 to invest.

Office Buildings

Office buildings offer the prospective investor not only a higher rent per square foot of floor space than any of the investments discussed thus far, but also larger cash flows per dollar of property worth. This is because office buildings are costlier to build and operate than residential structures and because they expose the owner to more risk.

The higher construction and operating costs of an office building are due to the amenities and services office users demand. To be competitive today, an office building must offer air-conditioning to all tenants on a room-by-room basis thus adding to construction and operating costs. Office users also expect and pay for daily office housecleaning services, such as emptying waste baskets, cleaning ashtrays, dusting and vacuuming. Apartment dwellers neither expect these services nor pay for them.

Tenant turnover is more expensive in an office building than an apartment building because a change in office tenants usually requires more extensive remodeling. To offset this, building owners include the cost of remodeling in the tenant's rent. Another consideration is that it is not unusual for office space to remain vacant for long periods of time. Also, if a building is rented to a single tenant, a single vacancy means there is no income at all. To reduce tenant turnover, incentives such as lower rent may be offered if a tenant agrees to sign a longer lease, such as 5 years instead of 1 or 2 years. Care, however, must be taken on longer leases so that the owner does not become locked into a fixed monthly rent while operating costs escalate.

The risk in properly locating an office building is greater than with a residential property since office users are very particular about where they locate. If a residential building is not well located, the owner can usually drop rents a little and still fill the building. To do the same with an office building may require a much larger drop; then, even with the building full, it may not generate enough rent to pay the operating expenses and mortgage payments. Finally, the tax shelter benefits available from offices may not be as attractive as comparably priced apartments. This is because compared to office buildings, residential properties tend to have a higher percentage of their value in depreciable improvements and less in nondepreciable land.

INVESTMENT TIMING

The potential risks and rewards available from owning improved real estate depend to a great extent on the point in the life of a property at which an investment is made. Should one invest while a project is still an idea? Or is it better to wait until it is finished and fully rented? That depends on the risks one can afford and the potential rewards.

Land Purchase

The riskiest point to invest in a project is when it is still an idea in someone's head. At this point, money is needed to purchase land. But beyond the cost of the land, there are many unknowns, including the geological suitability of the land to support buildings, the ability to obtain the needed zoning and building permits, the cost of construction, the availability of a loan, the rents the market will pay, how quickly the property will find tenants, the expenses of operating the property and finally the return the investor will obtain. Even though the investor may have a feasibility study that predicts success for the project, such a report is still only an educated guess. Therefore, the anticipated returns to an investor entering a project at this point must be high to offset the risks taken. As the project clears such hurdles as zoning approval, building permits, obtaining construction cost bids and finding a lender, it becomes less risky. Consequently, a person who invests after these hurdles are cleared can expect somewhat less potential reward. Nonetheless, the investor is buying into the project at a relatively low price; if it is successful, the investor will enjoy a developer's profit upon which no income tax must be paid until the property is finally sold. Against this, the investor takes the risk that the project may stall along the way or that, once completed, it will lose money.

Project Completion   Another major milestone is reached when the project is completed and opens its doors for business. At this point, the finished cost of the building is known and during the first 12 months of operations the property owners learn what rents the market will pay, what level of occupancy will be achieved and what actual operating expenses will be. As estimates are replaced with actual operating experience, the risk to the investor decreases. As a result, an investor entering at this stage receives a smaller return but is more certain of the return. The tax benefits at this stage are very attractive, but not quite as rewarding as in the earlier stages.

First Decade   A building is new only once, and after its first year it begins to face competition from newer buildings. However, if construction costs are rising on new buildings, existing buildings have the advantage of being able to charge less rent. Furthermore, newer buildings may be forced to use less desirable sites. During the first 10 years, occupancy rates are usually stable, operating expenses are well established, tax benefits are good and the building is relatively free of major repairs or replacements.

Second Decade   As a building passes its tenth birthday, the costs and risks it presents to a prospective investor change. Before buying, the investor must ask whether the neighborhood is still expected to remain desirable to tenants and whether the building's location will increase in value enough to offset wear and tear and obsolescence. A careful inspection must be made of the structure to determine whether poor construction quality will soon result in costly repairs. Also, the investor must be prepared for normal replacements and expenses such as new appliances, water heaters and a fresh coat of paint. As a result, an investor buying a 10-year-old building will seek a larger return than when the building was younger.

Third & Fourth Decades

Larger returns are particularly important as a building reaches its twentieth year and major expense items such as a new roof, replacement of plumbing fixtures, resurfacing of parking areas and remodeling become necessary. As a building approaches and passes its thirtieth year, an investor must consider carefully the remaining economic life of the property and whether rents permit a return on investment as well as a return of investment. Maintenance costs will climb as a building becomes older and decisions will be necessary as to whether or not major restoration and remodeling should be undertaken. If it is, the cost must be recovered during the balance of the building's life. The alternative is to add little or no money to the building, a decision the surrounding neighborhood may already be forcing upon the property owner. Older properties have been a strong magnet to real estate investors who hope to find attractive buys that can be fixed up for a profit. However, care must be taken not to overpay for this privilege in light of the foregoing discussion.

Building Recycling

More buildings are torn down than fall down, and this phase in a building's life also represents an investment opportunity. However, like the first stage in the development cycle, raw land, the risks are high. In effect, when the decision is made to purchase a structure with the intention of demolishing it, the investor is counting on the value of the land being worth more in another use. That use may be a government-sponsored renewal program or the investor may be accumulating adjoining properties with the ultimate intention of creating plottage value by demolishing the structures and joining the lots. Because the risks of capital loss in this phase are high, the potential returns should be too.

Figure 23:5   **"GLITAMAD"**

G = Ground (the raw land stage)

L = Loan (long-term loan commitment)

I = Interim (short-term loan and construction)

T = Tenancy (building filled with tenants)

A = Absorption (second through tenth year)

M = Maturity (eleventh through thirtieth year)

A = Aging (more than 30 years)

D = Demise (demolition, reuse of the land)

Increasing risk, Increasing returns

Least risk, Least returns

Increasing risk, Increasing returns

As the risk that an investor will suffer a loss increases, the expected returns must increase.

Source: Maury Seldin and Richard H. Swesnick, *Real Estate Investment Strategy*, copyright © 1970, John Wiley & Sons, Inc., New York. Used by permission.

GLITAMAD

The acronym GLITAMAD, developed by Maury Seldin and Richard Swesnick, is a helpful way to remember the various phases in the life cycle of improved real estate investments. It is illustrated in Figure 23:5.

DEVELOPING A PERSONAL INVESTMENT STRATEGY

The objective in developing a personal investment strategy is to balance the returns available with the risks that must be taken so that the overall welfare of the investor is enhanced. To accomplish this, it is very helpful to look at lifetime income and consumption patterns.

In Figure 23:6 the broken line represents the income that a person can typically expect to receive at various ages during his or her life. It includes income from wages, pensions and investments and is the same curve that was discussed in Chapter 22. The solid line represents a person's lifetime consumption pattern. Taken together, the two lines show that during the first 20 to 25 years of a person's life, consumption exceeds income. Then the situation reverses itself and income outpaces consumption. If one is planning an investment program, these are the years to carry it out.

Risk Taking

Figure 23:6 shows that a high-risk investment is better suited for a person under the age of 45. Under 45, even if the investment does turn sour, the investor still has a substantial amount of working life remaining to recover financially. An

LIFETIME INCOME AND CONSUMPTION PATTERNS

Figure 23:6

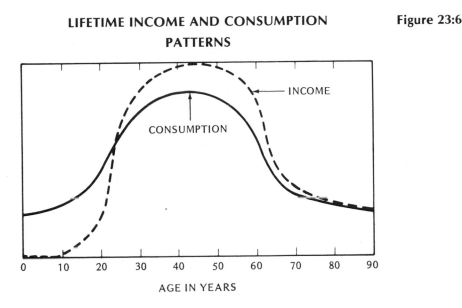

investor between 45 and 55 years of age should be somewhat more cautious in terms of risk taking since there is less time to make a financial recovery if the need arises. Above the age of 55, high-risk investments are even less appropriate for the same reason. Therefore, as a person reaches 55, 60 and 65, there should be a program of moving toward relatively risk-free investments even though the returns will be smaller. Upon retirement, the investor can live off the investments made when younger.

Mortgage debt commitments that require a portion of the investor's personal income should also be considered in light of one's position on the lifetime income and consumption curves. This is done to ascertain whether there will be sufficient income in the future to meet the loan payments. Not to consider the future may force a premature sale, perhaps in the midst of a very sluggish market at a distressed price. For the investor whose income has peaked, financing with less debt and more equity means a higher probability that the properties will generate enough income to meet monthly loan payments. Also, with fewer dollars going to debt repayment, more can be kept by the investor for living expenses. By comparison, a relatively

Debt Repayment

young investor may be handicapped by the lack of starting capital; however, a young investor has the advantages of time and increasing income.

Tax Planning   The income curve in Figure 23:6 provides insight into tax planning using tax shelter investments. During the peak income years, a person is in the highest tax brackets of life. Therefore, a strategy to minimize taxes calls for sound investments that emphasize tax shelter during the peak income years. Later in life when income falls and the investor moves to successively lower tax brackets, there is less concern with finding investments that shelter income, or selling properties in which there is a taxable gain.

Developing a workable tax strategy requires thoughtful advance planning. If a person aged 40 purchases a real estate investment that offers excellent tax shelter for 5 years and then is to be resold at a profit, the income curve shows that while the short-run tax picture is improved, tax problems 5 years hence may be worse. To solve that problem, the investor must either trade for another property in the fifth year or be prepared to invest in another tax shelter investment large enough to shelter the taxable gain from the sale of the first.

The same points made here in connection with investments can also be applied to one's home. If a homeowner can purchase a home with a mortgage and then pay down the mortgage during those years in life when income substantially exceeds consumption, the home can be carried debt free into retirement to provide a place to live without mortgage payments. The home then becomes an investment in every sense of the word.

VALUING AN   Chapter 16, "Real Estate Appraisal," discussed value from
INVESTMENT   the standpoint of an appraiser or listing agent who uses current marketplace facts to estimate the value of a property. An investor's valuation problem is somewhat different. An investor knows the seller's asking price, can find information relating to the current income and expenses of a property and can project future income based on these. Additionally, an investor will have information on how the property can be financed and will have some figure in mind as to how much appreciation to expect. From these, the investor calculates the anticipated return

on investment. If this return is more appealing than alternative investments, the property is purchased. If not, no sale results. Figure 23:7 illustrates the different viewpoints of the appraiser and the investor.

Appraiser's Viewpoint	Investor's Viewpoint
$\text{Value} = \dfrac{\text{Net Income}}{\text{Return}}$	$\text{Return} = \dfrac{\text{Net Income}}{\text{Price}}$
The appraiser solves for value.	The investor solves for return.

LIMITED PARTNERSHIPS

As discussed earlier in this chapter, large investment properties have a number of economic advantages over small ones. Yet the vast majority of investors in the United States do not have the capital to buy a large project single-handedly. Moreover, many persons who would like to own real estate for its yield and tax benefits do not do so because they wish to avoid the work and responsibilities of property management. As a result, the United States has witnessed the widespread use of limited partnerships for real estate investment. This popular form of investment offers investors the following advantages:

1. Management of the property and financial affairs of the partnership by the general partner.
2. Financial liability limited to the amount invested.
3. The opportunity for a small investor to own a part of large projects and to diversify.
4. The same tax benefits as enjoyed by sole owners.

The organizers of a limited partnership are responsible for selecting properties, putting them into a financial package and making it available to investors. As a rule, the organizers are the general partners and the investors are the limited partners. For their efforts in organizing the partnership, the general partners receive a cash fee from the limited partners or a promotional interest in the partnership or both.

Property Purchase Methods

Property is purchased by one of two methods. The organizers can either buy properties first and then seek limited partners, or they can find limited partners first and then buy properties. The first approach is a **specific property offering.** The second is a **blind pool.** The advantage of the specific property offering is that the prospective limited partner knows in advance precisely what properties he will own. However, this approach requires the organizers either to find a seller who is willing to wait for a partnership to be formed or to buy the property in their own names using their own capital. If they use their own capital, the organizers risk the chance of financial loss if limited partners cannot be found.

The advantage of the blind pool is that the organizers do not buy until money has been raised from the limited partners. This requires less capital from the organizers and avoids the problem of holding property but not being able to find sufficient investors. Also, the organizers can negotiate better prices from sellers when they have cash in hand. However, if the organizers are poor judges of property, the investors may wind up owning property that they would not have otherwise purchased.

Property Management

Once property is purchased, the general partners are responsible for managing the property themselves or selecting a management firm to do the job. The general partners also maintain the accounting books and at least once a year remit to each investor a portion of the cash flow, an accounting of the partnership's performance for the year, and profit or loss data for income tax purposes. With regard to selling partnership property, the partnership agreement usually gives the limited partners the right to vote on when to sell, to whom to sell and for how much. In practice, the general partners decide when to put the matter up to a vote, and the limited partners usually follow their advice.

Financial Liability

The word "limited" in limited partnership refers to the limited financial liability of the limited partner. In a properly drawn agreement, limited partners cannot lose more than they have invested. In contrast, the general partners are legally liable for all the debts of the partnership up to the full extent of their entire personal worth. Being a limited partner does not eliminate the possibility of being asked at a later date for more investment money if the properties in the partnership are not financially successful. When this happens, each limited partner must decide between adding more money in hopes the partnership will soon make a financial turnaround or refusing to do so and being eliminated from the partnership. By way of comparison, an individual investor who buys real estate in his own name effectively takes the risks of both the limited and general partner.

Investment Diversification

Investing with others can permit diversification. For example, a limited partnership of 200 members, each contributing $5,000, would raise $1 million. This could be used as a down payment on one property worth $4 million, or on four different properties priced at $1 million each. If the $4 million property is purchased, the entire success or failure of the partnership rides on that one property. With four $1 million properties, the failure of one can be balanced by the success of the others. Even greater diversification can be achieved by purchasing properties in different rental price ranges, in different parts of the same city and in different cities in the country.

Regarding income tax benefits, a very important advantage of the limited partnership is that it allows the investor to be taxed like a sole owner because the partnership itself is not subject to taxation. All income and loss items, including any tax shelter generated by the property, are apportioned to each investor.

Service Fees

If you plan to invest in a limited partnership, you should carefully look at the price the organizers are charging for their services. Is it adequate, but not excessive? To expect good performance from capable people, they must be compensated adequately; but to overpay reduces the returns from the investment that properly belong to those who provide the capital. When is the compensation to be paid? If management fees are paid in advance, there is less incentive for the organizers to provide quality management for the limited partners after the partnership is formed. The preferred arrangement is to pay for management services as they are received and for the limited partners to reserve the right to vote for new management. It is also a good idea to base a substantial portion of the general partner's fee on the success of the investment. By giving the organizers a percentage of the partnership's profits instead of a fixed fee, the organizers have a direct stake in the partnership's success.

Pitfalls   Although the limited partnership form of real estate ownership offers investors many advantages, experience has shown that there are numerous pitfalls that can separate investors from their money. Most importantly, a limited partner should recognize that the success or failure of a limited partnership is dependent on the organizers. Do they have a good record in selecting, organizing and managing real estate investments in the past? Are they respected in the community for prompt and honest dealings? Will local banks and building suppliers offer them credit? What is their rating with credit bureaus? Are they permanent residents of the community in which they operate? Do the county court records show lawsuits or other legal complaints against them?

With reference to the properties in the partnership, are the income projections reasonable and have adequate allowances been made for vacancies, maintenance and management? Overoptimism, sloppy income and expense projections and outright shading of the truth will ultimately be costly to the investor. Unless there is extreme confidence in the promoters, one should personally visit the properties in the partnership and verify the rent schedules, vacancy levels, operating expenses and physical condition of the improvements. Consideration should also be given to the partnership's **downside risk**, i.e., the risk of losing one's money.

The careful investor will consult with a lawyer to make certain that the partnership agreement does limit liability to the amount invested and that the tax benefits will be as advertised. Then there is the question of what will happen if the partnership suffers financial setbacks. Are the partnership's properties to be sold at a loss or at a foreclosure sale, or do the general partners stand ready to provide the needed money? Will the limited partners be asked to contribute? The prospective investor should also investigate to see if the properties are overpriced. Far too many partnerships organized to date have placed so much emphasis on tax shelter benefits that the entire matter of whether the investment was economically feasible has been overlooked. Even to a 50% bracket taxpayer, a dollar wasted before taxes is still 50¢ wasted after taxes.

Finally, to receive maximum benefits from his investment, the investor must be prepared to stay with the partnership until the properties are refinanced or sold. The resale market for limited partnership interests is almost nonexistent and when a buyer is found the price is usually well below the proportional worth of the investor's interest in the partnership. Moreover, the partnership agreement may place restrictions on limited partners who want to sell their interests.

Because investors are vulnerable to unsound investments and exploitation at the hands of limited partnership organizers, state and federal disclosure laws have been passed. Administered by the Securities & Exchange Commission at the federal level and by real estate regulatory departments and commissions at state levels, these laws require organizers and their salespeople to disclose all pertinent facts surrounding the partnership offering. Prospective investors must be told how much money the organizers wish to raise, what portion will go for promotional expenses and organizers' fees, what properties have been (or will be) purchased, from whom they were bought and for how much. Also, prospective investors must be provided with a copy of the partnership agreement and given property income and expense records. They must be told how long the partnership expects to hold its properties until selling, the partnership's policy on cash flow distribution, the right of limited partners to a voice in management, the names of those responsible for managing the partnership properties, and how profits (or losses) will be split when the properties are sold.

DISCLOSURE LAWS

The amount of disclosure detail required by state and federal laws varies with the number of properties and the partners' relationship. For a handful of friends forming a partnership among themselves, there would be little in the way of formal disclosure requirements. However, as the number of investors increases and the partnership is offered to investors across state lines, disclosure requirements increase dramatically. It is not unusual for a disclosure statement, called a **prospectus,** to be 50 to 100 pages long.

The Prospectus

Blue-Sky Laws   The philosophy of disclosure laws is to make information available to prospective investors and let them make their own decisions. Thus, an investor is free to invest in an unsound investment as long as the facts are explained to him in advance. An alternative point of view is that many investors do not read nor understand disclosure statements; therefore, it is the duty of government to pass on the economic soundness of an investment before it can be offered to the public. The result has been the passage of **blue-sky laws** in several states. The first of these was passed by the Kansas legislature in 1911 to protect purchasers from buying into dubious investment schemes that sold them nothing more than a piece of the blue sky. Some states retain these laws and apply them to limited partnerships and other securities offered within their borders.

EFFORT AND COURAGE   As the opening paragraph of this chapter suggested, you can become rich in real estate, very, very rich. But success won't drop in your lap; it takes effort and courage. Good properties and good opportunities are always available, but you will look at 50 properties to find one. And then you will need to know which are the 49 you don't want. That is the part that takes effort. To know what a good opportunity looks like, you need to learn. This book is a step in that direction. From here, start reading articles and books on real estate investing from libraries and bookstores and take coursework in real estate investing. But most important, now is the time to get out and start looking at properties if you have not already done so. Begin to get a sense in the field for what you are learning from your books and classes. Ask questions as you go along. After you've viewed several dozen properties and talked to appraisers, lenders, brokers, property managers, etc., you will begin to get a feel for the market—what's for sale, what a property can earn, how much mortgage money costs, etc. As you do this you will see everything you've learned in this book come to life.

As you continue, you will recognize what a good investment property looks like. At this point, your next big step is to muster the courage to acquire it. All the real estate investment education you've received will not translate into money in your pocket until you make an offer; until you put your money, reputation and good judgment on the line. But once you get the feel of it, it becomes easier and if you stick with it for ten years, you'll probably find it harder not to be a millionaire than it is to be one.

Match terms **a–n** with statements **1–14.**

a. *Accelerated depreciation*   **h.** *Equity build-up*
b. *ACRS*   **i.** *GLITAMAD*
c. *Basis*   **j.** *Leverage*
d. *Blind pool*   **k.** *Negative cash flow*
e. *Cash flow*   **l.** *Prospectus*
f. *Cash-on-cash*   **m.** *Straight-line*
g. *Downside risk*   **n.** *Tax shelter*

1. Number of dollars remaining each year after collecting rents and paying operating expenses and mortgage payments.
2. Requires the investor to dip into his own pocket.
3. Income tax savings that an investment can produce for its owner.
4. Results from mortgage balance reduction and price appreciation.
5. An acronym that refers to the various phases in the life cycle of an improved property.
6. A method of calculating depreciation that takes equal amounts of depreciation each year.
7. Any method of depreciation that achieves a faster rate of depreciation than the straight-line method.
8. A limited partnership wherein properties are purchased after the limited partners have invested their money.
9. The possibility that an investor will lose his money in an investment.
10. A disclosure statement that describes an investment opportunity.
11. The cash flow of a property divided by the amount of cash necessary to purchase it.
12. Purchase price plus improvements minus depreciation claimed since purchase.
13. The impact that borrowed funds have on investment return.
14. Accelerated Cost Recovery System.

1. What is a tax-sheltered real estate investment?
2. What monetary benefits do investors expect to receive by investing in real estate?
3. What is the major risk that a vacant land speculator takes?
4. What advantages and disadvantages do duplexes and triplexes offer to a prospective investor?

5. In an investor better off investing in a project before it is built or after it is completed and occupied? Explain.

6. As a building grows older, why should an investor demand a higher return per dollar invested?

7. How does a person's age affect investment goals and the amount of investment risk that may be taken?

8. An investor is looking at a property that produces a net operating income of $22,000 per year. He expects the property to appreciate 50% in 10 years and plans to finance it with a 25-year, 11% interest, 75% loan-to-value loan. If the property is priced to produce an 18% return on the investor's equity, how much is the seller asking? (Use Table 16:5 in Chapter 16.)

9. Another investor looks at the property described in Problem 8, but feels it will appreciate only 25% in value. How much would he offer to pay the seller?

10. What advantages does the limited partnership form of ownership offer to real estate investors?

11. What can a prospective investor do to increase his chances of joining a limited partnership that will be successful?

ADDITIONAL READINGS

"Don't Get Burned by Securities Laws" by **Anne Hamblin Schiave**. (*Real Estate Today*, May 84). Discusses how to comply with securities laws when selling real estate syndications.

Fundamentals of Real Estate Investing by **Jerry Ferguson**. (Scott-Foresman, 1984, 352 pages). Looks at the selection, acquisition, management and disposition of real estate. Focus is on small properties that can be acquired by individuals.

Real Estate Investment by **John Wiedemer**. (Reston, 1985, 300 pages). Includes financing, depreciation, taxation, property analysis, syndication, charts, tables, glossary, etc.

"Ten Questions to Ask About a Limited Partnership" by **Greg Anrig, Jr.** (*Money*, May 85, page 165). This article provides guidelines to help the investor make a sound decision. (*Money* magazine regularly has articles on real estate for persons with modest amounts to invest.)

*   *   *

The following periodicals may also be of interest to you: *Commercial Investment Journal, Database, Historic Preservation, Investing in Real Estate, National Real Estate Investor, Old House Journal, Preservation News, Property Investment Review, Real Estate Insider Newsletter, Real Estate Investing Letter, Real Estate Investment Digest, Real Estate Investing Ideas, Real Estate Securities Journal, Real Estate Syndication Digest* and *RESSI Review.*

Construction Illustrations and Terminology

COMBINED SLAB AND FOUNDATION (thickened edge slab)Figure A:1

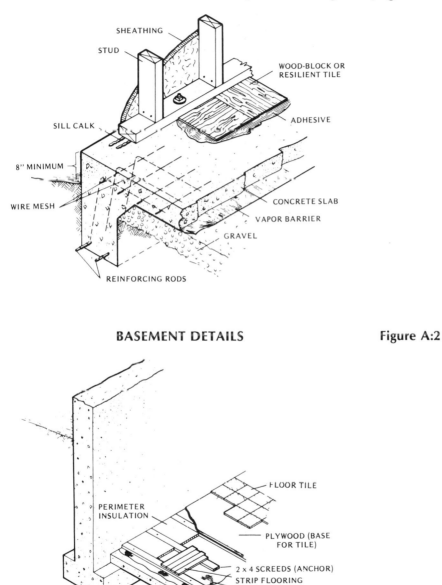

BASEMENT DETAILS   Figure A:2

587

Figure A:3   **FLOOR FRAMING**
1. nailing bridges to joists; 2. nailing board subfloor to joists;
3. nailing header to joists; 4. toenailing header to sill

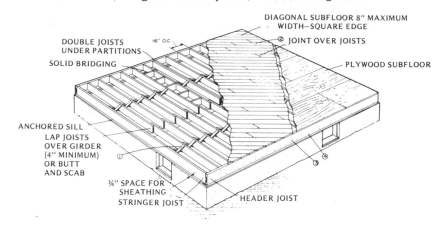

DIAGONAL SUBFLOOR 8" MAXIMUM WIDTH—SQUARE EDGE

② JOINT OVER JOISTS

DOUBLE JOISTS UNDER PARTITIONS

16" O.C.

SOLID BRIDGING

PLYWOOD SUBFLOOR

ANCHORED SILL
LAP JOISTS OVER GIRDER (4" MINIMUM) OR BUTT AND SCAB

¾" SPACE FOR SHEATHING
STRINGER JOIST

HEADER JOIST

Figure A:4   WALL FRAMING USED WITH PLATFORM CONSTRUCTION

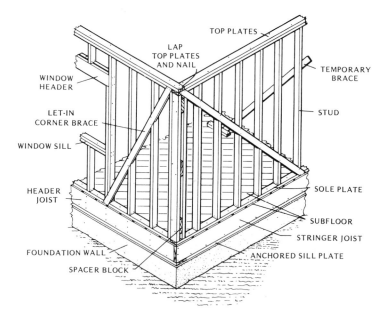

TOP PLATES

LAP TOP PLATES AND NAIL

WINDOW HEADER

TEMPORARY BRACE

LET-IN CORNER BRACE

STUD

WINDOW SILL

HEADER JOIST

SOLE PLATE

SUBFLOOR

STRINGER JOIST

FOUNDATION WALL

ANCHORED SILL PLATE

SPACER BLOCK

HEADERS FOR WINDOWS AND DOOR OPENINGS   Figure A:5

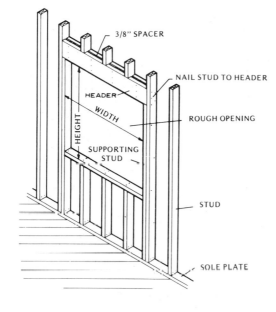

VERTICAL APPLICATION OF PLYWOOD OR STRUCTURAL INSULATING BOARD SHEATHING   Figure A:6

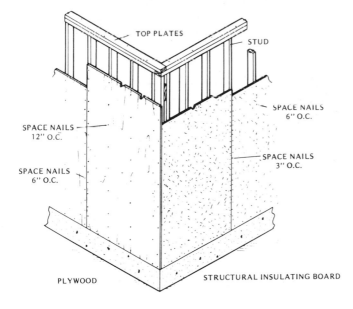

Figure A:7   EXTERIOR SIDING

BEVEL SIDING

NAIL TO STUD OR
WOOD SHEATHING
(TO CLEAR TOP OF
LOWER SIDING COURSE)

PANELING

DROP
OR
RABBETED

BLIND NAIL
(FINISHING NAIL)
FOR WIDTHS GREATER
THAN 6" USE EXTRA FACE
NAIL OR 2 FACE NAILS

2 NAILS FOR
WIDTHS 8" AND OVER
AND WHEN USED
WITHOUT SHEATHING

Figure A:8   VERTICAL BOARD SIDING

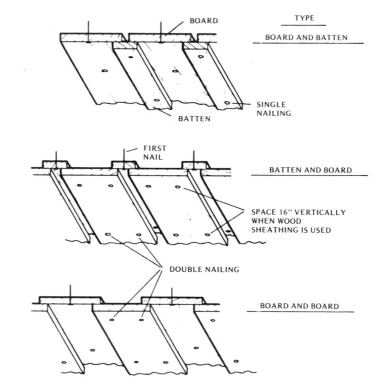

BOARD

TYPE

BOARD AND BATTEN

SINGLE
NAILING

BATTEN

FIRST
NAIL

BATTEN AND BOARD

SPACE 16" VERTICALLY
WHEN WOOD
SHEATHING IS USED

DOUBLE NAILING

BOARD AND BOARD

APPLICATION OF GYPSUM BOARD FINISH
A: vertical application; B: horizontal application

Figure A:9

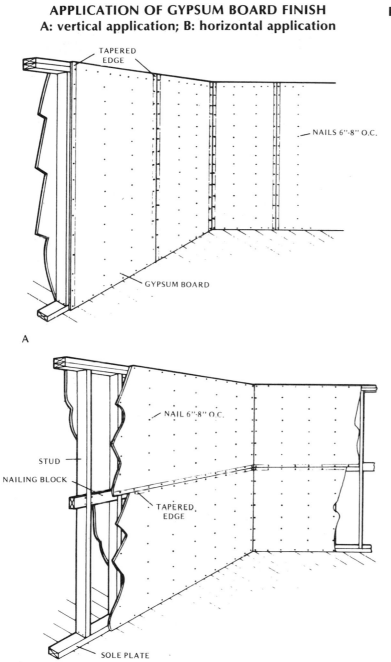

TAPERED EDGE

NAILS 6"-8" O.C.

GYPSUM BOARD

A

NAIL 6"-8" O.C.

STUD

NAILING BLOCK

TAPERED EDGE

SOLE PLATE

B

Figure A:10

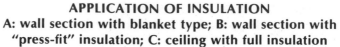

APPLICATION OF INSULATION
A: wall section with blanket type; B: wall section with
"press-fit" insulation; C: ceiling with full insulation

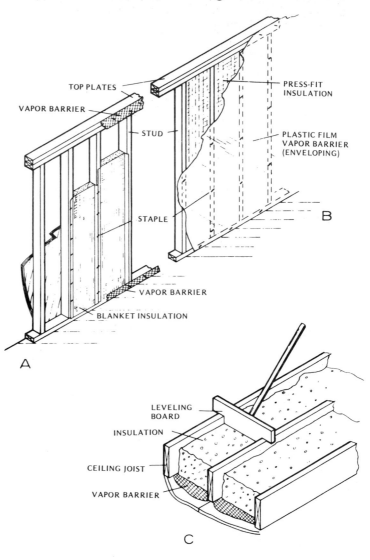

PLACEMENT OF INSULATION
A: in walls, floor and ceiling; B: in 1½ story house;
C: at attic door; D: in flat roof

Figure A:11

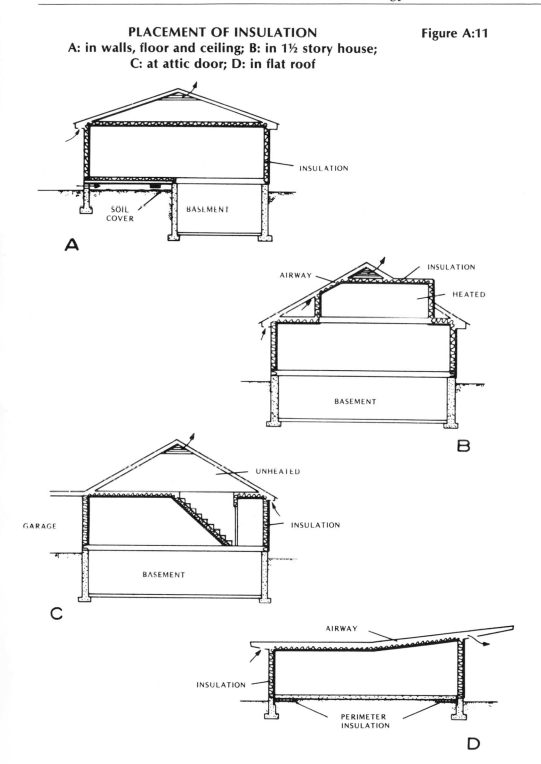

Figure A:12

MASONRY FIREPLACE

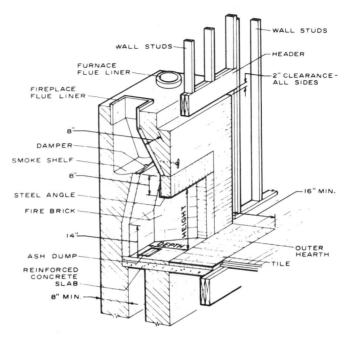

Figure A:13

STAIRWAY DETAILS

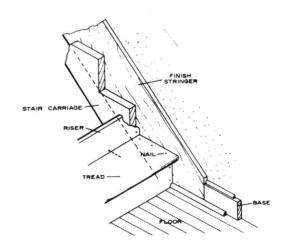

DOOR DETAILS   Figure A:14

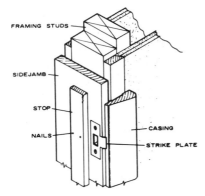

SOUND INSULATION   Figure A:15

WALL DETAIL	DESCRIPTION	STC RATING
16" / 2×4	1/2" GYPSUM WALLBOARD	32
	5/8" GYPSUM WALLBOARD	37
2×4	5/8" GYPSUM WALLBOARD (DOUBLE LAYER EACH SIDE)	45
2×4 / BETWEEN OR "WOVEN"	1/2" GYPSUM WALLBOARD 1 1/2" FIBROUS INSULATION	49
16" / 2×4	RESILIENT CLIPS TO 3/8" GYPSUM BACKER BOARD 1/2" FIBERBOARD (LAMINATED) (EACH SIDE)	52

Figure A:16   **CEILING AND ROOF FRAMING**

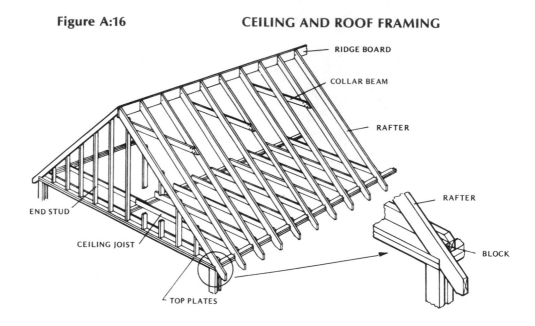

Figure A:17   **INSTALLATION OF BOARD ROOF SHEATHING,**
                       SHOWING BOTH CLOSED AND SPACED TYPES

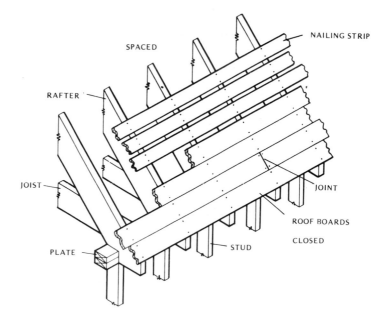

BUILT-UP ROOF FigureA:18

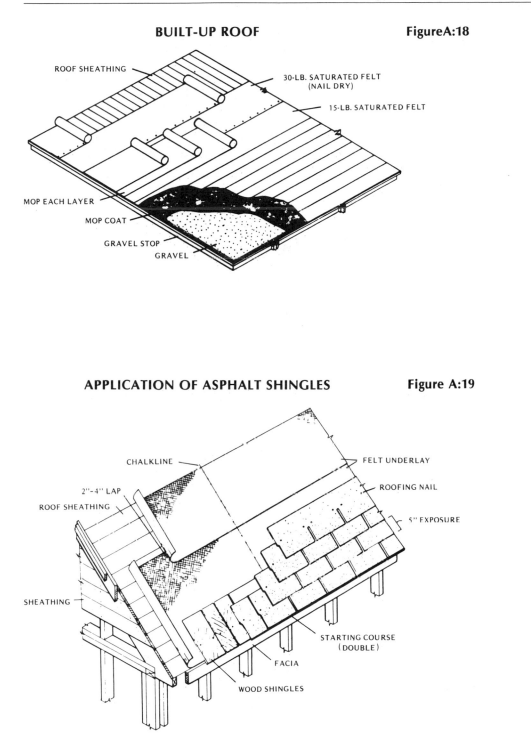

APPLICATION OF ASPHALT SHINGLES Figure A:19

Figure A:20   **ROOFS USING SINGLE ROOF CONSTRUCTION**
A: flat roof; B: low-pitched roof

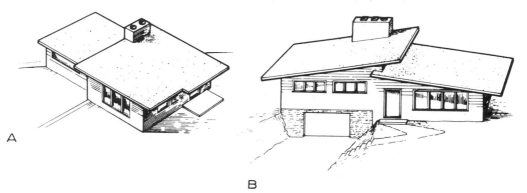

A

B

TYPES OF PITCHED ROOFS
A: gable; B: gable with dormers; C: hip

A

SHED DORMER

GABLE DORMER

B

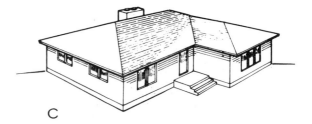

C

Sample ETS-Type Test Questions*

The ETS examination for real estate salespersons, up to four and a half hours long, is made up of 110 to 130 questions. It is divided into two separate tests, the uniform test and the state test.

The Uniform Test (80 questions) contains questions in the subject areas described below. Approximately 20% of the uniform test consists of questions dealing with arithmetic functions. These questions are distributed throughout the test.

1. Real Estate Contracts: (13% of uniform test)

Questions in this area cover the general definition and essential elements of a contract and specific contracts used in real estate, including leases, listing agreements, sales contracts (offer to purchase agreements) and options.

2. Financing: (24% of uniform test)

These questions deal with two major aspects of real estate financing: financing instruments and means of financing. Questions in these areas will cover such topics as sources of financing; governmental agencies and acts pertaining to financing (e.g., Federal Housing Administration, Veterans Administration, Truth-in-Lending Act); basic definitions of the major financing instruments; anatomy of a mortgage loan (including types of mortgages, loan fees, loan placement procedures and term loans); junior finance; default and foreclosure.

3. Real Estate Ownership: (22% of uniform test)

The questions in this subject area cover the following topics:

a. Deeds: the definition of necessary elements for recordation and acknowledgment of various types of deeds.

b. Interests in Real Property: estates (extent of title), private rights to real property (ownership), public powers over real property and special interests in real property (easements, etc.).

c. Condominiums: general information about condominiums, ownership of common and separate elements, and the duties and responsibilities of a condominium owners' association.

d. Federal Fair Housing Act: grievances, penalties, practices and procedures with regard to the federal Fair Housing Act.

---

* The information in Appendix B was adapted and reprinted by permission of Educational Testing Service, the copyright owner.

4. *Real Estate Brokerage:* (24% of uniform test)
   The questions in this area of the test cover the following topics:
   a. Law of Agency: definitions, rights, responsibilities and functions of a principal and an agent.
   b. Property Management: general scope and functions of property management.
   c. Settlement Procedures: title validity, conveyance, settlement charges, credits, adjustments and prorating.

5. *Real Estate Valuation:* (17% of uniform test)
   The questions in this area cover the following topics:
   a. Appraisal: definition of value, approaches to value, the appraisal process, the valuation of partial interest and appraisal terminology.
   b. Planning and Zoning: public land-use control, public planning and zoning, and private subdividing and developing.
   c. Property Description: kinds of property description, plat reading and related terms and concepts.
   d. Taxes and Assessments: real property taxes, special assessments, liens and other tax factors.

The State Test (30 to 50 questions) contains questions dealing with the real estate laws, rules and regulations and other aspects of real estate practice appropriate to the jurisdiction in which the test is being given. Aspects of real estate practice that may be covered in this section include state statutes dealing with condominiums, subdivisions, fair housing and administrative hearing procedures. Other aspects of real estate practice, which are not uniform, may also be included. Be sure to check with your state real estate commission for more details regarding coverage in this section.

License applicants in ETS examination states should send for the free "Bulletin of Information for Applicants for Real Estate Licensing Examinations." Write to: Educational Testing Service, Box 2837, Princeton, N.J. 08541. A Sample Salesperson's Uniform Test can be purchased from ETS at this address.

The following **Sample Questions** illustrate the types of questions in the examination for real estate salespersons. They do not, however, represent the full range of content or the levels of difficulty found in the test. An answer key is provided in Appendix H.

Uniform Test
REAL ESTATE CONTRACTS
1. The party who makes an offer to another is known as the
   A. offeree.   **B.** offeror.   **C.** major.   **D.** minor.

2. An offer that is made in response to an offer is called a(n)
   A. counteroffer.   **B.** antioffer.   **C.** reverse offer.   **D.** defense.

FINANCING

1. When a loan insured by a private insurance company goes into default, the insuror
   I. may buy the property from the lender.
   II. may let the lender foreclose and compensate the lender for his loss.
   (A) I only   **(B)** II only   **(C)** Both I and II   **(D)** Neither I nor II

   When answering this kind of multiple-choice question, read the question and the two statements or possibilities carefully. Determine whether statement (possibility) I is right or wrong; then determine whether statement (possibility) II is right or wrong.
   Next, look at the four choices, (A), (B), (C) and (D). Choice (A) is always "I only." You should pick (A) if you believe statement (possibility) I is right and statement (possibility) II is wrong. Choice (B) is always "II only," and you should pick (B) if you believe statement (possibility) I is wrong and statement (possibility) II is right. Choice (C) is "Both I and II." You should pick (C) when you believe both statements (possibilities) are right, whether or not they happen at the same time. Choice (D) is always "Neither I nor II." You should pick (D) when you believe neither of the two statements (possibilities) is correct.

2. As used in real estate finance, the term "point" means
   I. 1% of the loan.
   II. 1% of the price of the property.
   (A) I only   **(B)** II only   **(C)** Both I and II   **(D)** Neither I nor II

3. All of the following organizations operate in the secondary mortgage market EXCEPT
   A. Fannie Mae   **B.** Freddie Mac   C. Ginnie Mae   **D.** FDIC

REAL ESTATE OWNERSHIP

1. All of the following are essential elements in a valid deed EXCEPT
   A. Consideration   C. Seller's signature
   B. Property description   D. Buyer's signature

2. Characteristic(s) of ownership as tenants by the entireties is (are)
   I. the right of survivorship of a surviving spouse.
   II. any transfer of title requires the signature of husband and wife.
   (A) I only   **(B)** II only   **(C)** Both I and II   **(D)** Neither I nor II

3. A change made to an existing will is known as a(n)
   A. addendum.   C. supplement.
   B. amendment.   D. codicil.

4. The law which requires that transfers of real property ownership be in writing is known as the

A. Law of Evidence.   C. Statute of Frauds.
B. Statute of Liberties. D. Statute of Limitations.

REAL ESTATE BROKERAGE

1. Which of the following will result in the termination of an agency?

I. Insanity
II. Bankruptcy

(A) I only   (B) II only   (C) Both I and II   (D) Neither I nor II

2. Which of the following would not normally be handled by an escrow agent?

A. Ordering title insurance
B. Ordering title examinations
C. Proration of tax and/or insurance
D. Negotiations for and preparation of sales contracts

3. Brown sold his home to Green and closing took place on July 18. Green agreed to assume Brown's prepaid one-year hazard insurance policy which has been in effect beginning December 13 of the previous year. Prorations are made on the basis of 30-day months, with the buyer responsible for the day of closing. The annual premium on the policy was $194.40. Which of the following statements is true?

A. Green would be charged $78.30.
B. Brown would be credited $116.10.
C. Green would be credited $78.30.
D. Green would be charged $194.40.

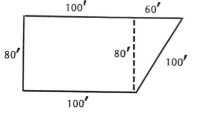

REAL ESTATE VALUATION

1. The lot diagrammed here is sold for $20,800. What is the price per square foot?

(A) $1.00   (B) $1.30   (C) $1.625   (D) $2.00

2. In applying the income approach to real property, the appraiser considers which of the following?

I. The amount of income produced by the property
II. The rate of return demanded by investors

(A) I only   (B) II only   (C) Both I and II   (D) Neither I nor II

3. In valuing houses in a certain neighborhood an appraiser finds that prices have risen at an average of ½ of 1% per month over the past six months. If a house in that neighborhood sold for $100,000 four months ago, how much should it sell for today based on this rate of increase?

A. $101,000   B. $102,000   C. $103,000   D. $104,000

4. All of the following are real estate appraisal approaches EXCEPT
   A. Cost   C. Income
   B. Anticipation   D. Market

State Test
   Note: The following questions are samples of the *type* of question asked in this part of the examination, which is different for each jurisdiction.

1. Which persons are specifically exempt from the real estate licensing act?
   A. War veterans   C. Part-time salespersons
   B. Executors   D. Listers of real estate

2. A Real Estate Salesperson license issued on May 15 is valid until
   A. May 15 the following year.
   B. the end of this year.
   C. January 15 of the following year.
   D. the salesperson's next birthday.

3. An unlicensed secretary in a broker's office may do which of the following?
   I. Give information to a caller about listings available
   II. Take a listing by telephone
   (A) I only   (B) II only   (C) Both I and II   (D) Neither I nor II

BROKER EXAMINATION

The ETS examination for real estate brokers, up to four and a half hours long, is made up of 110 to 130 questions. It is divided into two separate tests, the uniform test and the state test.

   The Uniform Test (80 questions) contains questions in the subject areas outlined below. Approximately 20% of the test consists of questions requiring arithmetic calculations. These questions are distributed throughout the test.

1. *Real Estate Brokerage:* (35% of uniform test)
   The questions in this area cover the following topics:
   a. Listing and Showing Property: the responsibilities of a broker when contracting to list, advertise and show property for sale, lease, trade or exchange; including responsibilities under the law of agency, compliance with federal Fair Housing Act and obligations when entering into written listing agreements.
   b. Settlement Procedures: the responsibilities of a broker in arranging settlement or closing, including recordation procedures; closing costs, charges, credits, adjustments and prorations; and compliance with the Real Estate Settlement Procedures Act.

c. Property Management: the responsibilities of a broker managing property on behalf of an owner, including property maintenance; collecting rents and security deposits in accordance with terms of leases and legal agreements; negotiating leases; and advising on current market conditions.

2. *Contracts and Other Legal Aspects:* (27% of uniform test)
The questions in this area cover the following topics:
a. Contracts: general aspects of contract law; familiarity with listing contracts, contracts for sales, options, leases, installment land contracts and escrow agreements; the referring of clients to legal counsel.
b. Land-Use Controls: zoning; private restrictions; requirements for subdividing and developing; deed restrictions and covenants.
c. Deeds: the general characteristics of various types of deeds and the circumstances under which specific deeds are appropriate.
d. Property Ownership: the rights and interests which may affect ownership of real property; characteristics of various types of ownership (joint tenancy, timesharing, etc.)
e. Condominiums and Cooperatives: the requirements for certification of real property as a condominium or cooperative; types of ownership (individual and common); aspects of property conversion to condominium or cooperative.
f. Other Legal Aspects: the legal implications of public powers over real property (eminent domain, escheat, police power, taxation, etc.); and special interests in real property (easements, party walls, etc.).

3. *Pricing and Valuation:* (15% of uniform test)
a. Appraising the principles of value and approaches to estimating value.
b. Pricing by Comparative Market Analysis: the pricing of real estate for sale, rent or exchange in the absence of an appraisal report.

4. *Finance and Investment:* (23% of uniform test)
a. Financing Arrangements: costs involved in placement of loans; governmental agencies which guarantee or insure mortgages; requirements of the Truth-in-Lending Act regarding advertising financial aspects of a sale.
b. Financing Instruments: characteristics of notes and mortgages, deeds of trust, installment land contracts and other financing instruments.
c. Loans and Mortgages: characteristics of different types of loans or mortgages (amortizing, term, blanket, package, etc.);

essential elements and special clauses of mortgages (prepayment, due on sale clause, variable payment, etc.); sources of junior or secondary loans; conditions and procedures involved in default and foreclosure.

   d. Tax Ramifications: the tax ramifications of home ownership, including interest and property tax deductions, deferred capital gains, etc.; also, the tax ramifications of real estate investments, including depreciation, capital gains and losses, refinancing, etc.

   The State Test (30 to 50 questions) contains questions dealing with the real estate laws, rules and regulations and other aspects of real estate practice appropriate to the jurisdiction in which the test is being given. Aspects of real estate practice that may be covered in this section include state statutes dealing with condominiums, subdivisions, fair housing practices and administrative hearing procedures. Other aspects of real estate practice, which are not uniform from state to state, may also be included. Your state real estate department can give you more details regarding coverage in this section.

   The following **Sample Questions** illustrate the types of questions in the examination for real estate brokers. They do not, however, represent the full range of content or levels of difficulty found in the test. An answer key is provided in Appendix H. A Sample Uniform Broker's Test is available from ETS for a fee.

Uniform Test
REAL ESTATE BROKERAGE
1. A property management contract generally contains which of the following:
   I. A description of the property
   II. An agreement that the property manager will render periodic statements to the owner
   - (A) I only
   - (B) II only
   - (C) Both I and II
   - (D) Neither I nor II

2. Which of the following would be classified as off-site management?
   - (A) Accounting
   - (B) Handling tenant complaints
   - (C) Showing vacant space to prospective tenants
   - (D) Maintenance work

CONTRACTS AND OTHER LEGAL ASPECTS
1. A person who is without heirs may avoid having his property pass to the state by

I. leaving a valid will containing instructions as to the disposition of his property.

II. giving it to a charity prior to death.

(A) I only   **(B)** II only   **(C)** Both I and II   **(D)** Neither I nor II

2. Gift deeds usually take the form of
   (A) sheriff's deeds.   **(C)** warranty deeds.
   (B) bargain and sale deeds.   **(D)** grant deeds.

PRICING AND VALUATION

1. A quarterly tax payment is $657 on a property assessed at 90% of market value. If the annual tax rate is $0.02 per $1 of assessed valuation, then the market value of the property is
   (A) $146,000   **(C)** $36,500
   (B) $87,600   **(D)** $18,250

2. Which of the following would ordinarily be included in the reserves for replacement?
   I. Replacement cost for refrigerators in an apartment unit
   II. Depreciation on the apartment building
   (A) I only   **(B)** II only   **(C)** Both I and II   **(D)** Neither I nor II

3. A contractor estimates he can build a 5,800-square-foot structure for $348,000. This is 10% more than he estimated last year for the same job. How much per square foot did he estimate last year?
   A. $54.00   **C.** $60.00
   B. $54.55   **D.** $66.67

FINANCE AND INVESTMENT

1. An owner's agreement to take a note and mortgage instead of cash from a buyer is known as a
   (A) conventional loan.   **(C)** secondary transaction.
   (B) carryback.   **(D)** bill of sale.

2. FHA mortgage insurance is available for
   I. owner-occupied single-family residences.
   II. multifamily residential buildings.
   (A) I only   **(B)** II only   **(C)** Both I and II   **(D)** Neither I nor II

3. Calculate the balance owing after two $100 monthly payments have been made on a 10-year, $10,000 loan that carries 12% annual interest.
   (A) $10,000.00   **(C)** $10,200.00
   (B) $ 9,800.00   **(D)** $ 9,833.33

State Test
Questions for the state test are similar to those on the salespersons' state test.

Sample ACT-Type Test Questions*

The uniform portions of the ACT salesperson and broker examinations each contain 100 multiple-choice questions. Each question has four alternative responses. The questions are designed to measure the applicant's ability to understand and apply the principles of real estate. The questions are distributed as follows:

Property Ownership, Transfer and Use (36% of the salesperson exam and 25% of the broker exam). Questions in this area deal with the nature and description of real property; parties dealing in real estate (competancy, individuals, corporations and partnerships); land titles (fee simple, life estate, leasehold estates, tenancy in common and tenancy by the entireties); easements, mortgages, mortgage clauses and notes; fixtures, lien priority, encroachments, restrictions, mechanic's liens and attachment of real estate; acquisition and transfer of real estate (contracts, property descriptions, purchase price, standard clauses and contract enforceability); and public land control (planning and zoning, property taxation, eminent domain, water rights and health and building costs).

Brokerage and Laws of Agency (30% on both salesperson and broker exams). Questions in this area deal with real estate agency (types of agency, creation of agency, duties of the agent toward the principal, duties of the agent toward third parties, duties enforced by licensing authorities, rights of an agent relative to principal(s) and termination of agency); federal fair housing laws; the federal Real Estate Settlement Procedures Act; and property management (contracts, rentals, leases, repairs and maintenance).

Valuation and Economics (17% of the salesperson exam and 25% of the broker exam). Topics include concepts and purposes of appraisal, appraisal techniques, depreciation, principles of real property value, the appraisal process, economic trends, neighborhood analysis, site analysis and valuation, principles of capitalization, gross rent multiplier, market data approach, the appraisal report, real estate economics and trends in land use.

Finance (17% of the salesperson exam and 20% of the broker exam). Topics include mortgage lending agencies, government lending insti-

---

* The information in Appendix C was adapted and reprinted by permission of American College Testing, the copyright owner.

tutions, mathematics of financial practice, federal truth-in-lending legislation and principles of finance.

STYLES OF QUESTIONS

The first style of question presents a question or an incomplete statement followed by four different responses which could answer the question or complete the statement. In this style of question, you should choose the one response that answers the question or completes the statement *correctly*. The following example and questions 1 and 3 of the samples which follow illustrate this format.

The Clarks apply for a $30,000 loan to buy a grocery store. Is this transaction covered by Regulation Z?
A. No, because only transactions of $25,000 or less are covered.
B. No, because business loans are not covered.
C. Yes, because all real estate credit transactions are covered.
D. Yes, because the purchase of commercial property by individuals, but not firms, is covered.

The correct answer to this question is B. Response A is incorrect because the $25,000 maximum applies only to credit transactions on personal, family, household or agricultural uses. Responses C and D are incorrect because commercial loans are not covered by Regulation Z.

The second style of question presents a question or an incomplete statement that asks for the *exception*. In this style of question, you should choose the response that is different from the other three responses and is the exception described in the question or statement presented. The following example and question 14 of the samples which follow illustrate this format.

Which of the following is NOT an activity of urban planning boards?
A. Preparing assessed valuations of properties
B. Modifying zoning regulations
C. Controlling the development of land
D. Giving advice on traffic facilities

The correct answer to this question is A. Planning boards regulate the use and development of property and therefore regulate zoning (B), development of land (C) and traffic facilities (D). Assessed valuations (A) are prepared by assessors' offices, not planning boards.

The third style of question presents a question or an incomplete statement followed by several options labeled with Roman numerals. You should select the response that contains the best option or combination of options and that answers the question most adequately. The following example and questions 2 and 5 of the samples which follow illustrate this format.

Which of the following is (are) necessary for a mortgage loan to be enforceable?
  I. An acknowledgment of the borrower's signature on the promissory note.
 II. The borrower's promissory note
III. The borrower's hypothecation of the property to the mortgagee as security for the debt
A. I only   **B.** III only   **C.** II and III only   **D.** I, II and III

   The correct answer to this question is C. Option I (Response A) is incorrect because a promissory note does not need to be acknowledged. Option II is correct because the borrower must create a personal liability for payment. Option III is also correct since there must be a lien on the property as security for the debt. Both II and III must be present for the mortgage to be enforceable; thus, response C is correct.

   The fourth style of question presents a question or an incomplete statement followed by several options labeled with Roman numerals. You should select the *chronological* order of these options that is most appropriate to the context of the item. The following example and question 22 of the samples which follow illustrate this format.

Which of the following is the most appropriate order of steps that a property manager will usually follow in seeking tenants for a residential apartment building?
  I. Determine the means of promotion or the appropriate advertising media to be used
 II. Analyze what the potential market of renters is for the property
III. Evaluate the property and compare it to competitive properties
A. I, II, III   **B.** II, III, I   **C.** III, I, II   **D.** III, II, I

   All three steps are part of the process of seeking tenants. However, response D is the most correct ordering of the steps because a property manager should first evaluate the property's features and then find out what the current demand is for that kind of property. Then the property manager should identify who the potential renters are and direct the advertising strategy to that market.
   When you take the examination, be sure to note whether the question is asking for the *best answer* (question style 1); an *exception* (question style 2); *an option or a combination of options* (question style 3); or the *correct chronological ordering of options* (question style 4). Once you have selected the response that you feel best answers the question or best completes the statement, mark the appropriate response on your answer sheet.

SAMPLE QUESTIONS   The following questions illustrate the types of questions contained in the Salesperson and Broker Examinations. Although the sample questions do not totally represent the full range of content or difficulty levels contained in the examinations, they are intended to help you to become familiar with the types and formats of the questions contained in the examinations. Read each question and decide which answer is best. You may then check your answers with the answer key in Appendix H. A sample real estate examination is available from ACT for a fee. The address is P.O. Box 168, Iowa City, Iowa 52243.

1. Watt bought an industrial lot with a frontage of 244 feet and a depth of 500 feet. Later, Watt bought a lot of the same size next to the first lot. Approximately how many acres are in the two lots combined?
   A. 2.8   B. 3.2   C. 5.6   D. 7.0

2. Farmer Smith sold all of his realty. When Smith moves, which of the following pieces of property will he probably have to leave behind?
   I. The elm trees in the front yard that Smith planted when he purchased the farm
   II. The chicken coop that Smith finished building after signing the sales contract
   III. The apple orchard that Smith planted before signing the sales contract
   IV. The soybean crop that Smith planted before signing the sales contract
     F. I and II only   H. I, II and III only
     G. III and IV only   J. I, II, III and IV

3. In 1947 a judge declared Culp to be mentally incompetent. In 1981 Culp successfully executed a contract to buy a house but did not mention the judgment. Is Culp's contract valid?
   A. Yes, because Culp has successfully executed the contract.
   B. Yes, because incompetency judgments lapse after 25 years.
   C. No, because incompetency judgments lapse after 35 years.
   D. No, because a person who has been declared incompetent does not have the power to make a valid contract.

4. Grace, Harold, John and Hazel formed a partnership to buy a parcel of real estate which they planned to own for 10 years or more. They chose John to be the general partner. What type of partnership did they create?
   F. Limited   H. Corporation
   G. General   J. Syndicate

5. Which of the following leases would be an estate for years?
   I. A lease for 30 days   III. A lease for 2 years
   II. A lease for 90 days   IV. A lease for 99 years
   A. II only   B. III only   C. III and IV only   D. I, II, III and IV

6. Dill and Leitch, both competent adults, formulated a contract for the rental of Dill's home. They made certain the contract clearly stated all the terms agreed upon. To describe the property, they included the street address, city and state of the home. The exact rental price and duration of the rental period were included. Both Dill and Leitch signed and dated the written contract. Is their contract valid?
   F. Yes, it contains everything necessary for a valid contract.
   G. No, it lacks a complete legal description of the property.
   H. No, it must name the insurance company the tenant has chosen to take over the coverage of the property.
   J. No, a notary public's seal must be affixed to the contract.

7. Blake, who owns all of the land surrounding Three-day Lake, posted **"NO TRESPASSING"** signs and built a wall all around the outside boundary of the property. Barnes owns property next to Blake's and wishes to fish in the lake. What type of easement could Blake grant to Barnes to allow Barnes to get to the lake?
   A. Easement in gross   C. Easement by necessity
   B. Party wall easement   D. Easement by prescription

8. Wilkes bought a 100-acre field for a total price of $100,000. Wilkes financed this property with $20,000 in cash and an $80,000 mortgage loan. In the mortgage agreement, Wilkes asked the lender to release one acre free and clear of the mortgage for every $1,000 paid against the loan. Which type of mortgage clause allows this to be done?
   F. Partial release   H. Mortgage release
   G. Marginal release   J. Certificate of reduction

9. Maria inherited from her mother a valuable crystal chandelier that has been in the family for generations. She had a workman install it in the ceiling of her dining room and wire it to a wall switch. Several years later, Maria sold her home without mentioning that the chandelier belonged to the family. When she moved she took the chandelier with her. Can Maria legally do this?
   A. Yes, since the chandelier is a family heirloom.
   B. Yes, since anything Maria chooses to take with her is personal property.
   C. No, since the chandelier was permanently installed at the time the buyer inspected the home and signed the purchase contract.
   D. No, since the chandelier is considered to be a trade fixture.

10. The tenant renting Owner Bonn's house hired a contractor to build an addition onto the house. Owner Bonn discovered the work in progress and told the contractor how good the work was. Upon completion of the work, Bonn refused to pay the contractor. A mechanic's lien was immediately filed. Who must pay the contractor?

    F. Owner Bonn, because she knew about the construction but did not object to the work in progress.

    G. Owner Bonn, because she is liable for the cost of any construction on the house whether or not she is aware of that construction.

    H. The tenant, because he did not tell Owner Bonn about the construction.

    J. No one, because a mechanic's lien is valid only for the construction of an entire house.

11. The Sharps sold their house to the Wards. An hour before closing, the Sharps decided to sell their car to the Wards. In general, which statement about the sale of the car is true?

    A. The broker's commission rate would automatically be extended to the price of the car.

    B. The price of the car would automatically increase the amount of the transfer tax.

    C. The car would be transferred by a bill of sale.

    D. The car must be listed on the estimated closing form required by the federal Real Estate Settlement Procedures Act.

12. A house owned by Cain had been left empty for over five years when the March family moved into it. The March family immediately told Cain of their presence. Cain ordered them to leave but they stayed. If the Marches eventually gain title to the house, they will have most likely done so by

    F. annexation.   H. adverse possession.

    G. condemnation.   J. inverse condemnation.

13. Which of the following actions by a licensed real estate broker would constitute a VIOLATION of his/her fiduciary obligation to his/her principal, the seller?

    A. Advising prospective purchasers of latent structural defects disclosed by the seller in the listing agreement.

    B. Advising prospective purchasers that the seller will accept less than the listing price.

    C. Advising prospective purchasers of standing water in the basement.

    D. Advising prospective purchasers of the lack of nearby public transportation and shopping facilities.

14. In general, a broker who receives earnest money deposits is required to do all of the following EXCEPT:

F. allow the state to conduct an audit of the broker's trust account at any time.

G. accurately account for all earnest money deposits placed in the broker's personal bank accounts.

H. maintain a special account at a bank to be used only for such deposits.

J. keep any checks uncashed at the buyer's request as long as the seller is informed of this when the offer is presented.

15. Broker Grant shows a prospect a house from the multiple listing service files. The prospect later buys the house through Broker Grant. If this house was NOT listed with Broker Grant's agency, what type of commission can Broker Grant expect to receive?

A. All of the commission, as Grant is the selling broker

B. One-half of the commission; the other half goes to the multiple listing service

C. The part of the commission to which the selling broker is entitled according to the agreement with the listing broker

D. The part of the commission to which the selling broker is entitled according to the multiple listing service organization agreement

16. District Four in Lake City is zoned industrial but, except for the Handy Dandy Tool Company, is completely residential because employees have built their homes near the plant. If Lake City decided to rezone the district to residential, the Handy Dandy Tool Company would most likely have to:

F. be paid a fair market value by the city and move the plant.

G. become a nonconforming use but be allowed to continue.

H. become a nonconforming use and undergo condemnation proceedings.

J. allow the city to take over the plant.

17. A portion of the parking lot for Passaway's Mortuary has been condemned by the city so that the land can be used to build a better approach to the municipal hospital's emergency entrance. Which of the following powers is the city exercising?

A. Power of attorney   C. Eminent domain

B. Police power   D. Escheat

18. A house which was exactly the same in design, construction, condition and age as York's house sold recently as a single-family residence for $52,000. The recently sold house sits next to an all-night gasoline station and mini–market while York's house sits next to a new apartment building. If both houses were appraised using the market data approach, one might expect York's house to be appraised at

F. much less than $52,000.   **H.** somewhat more than $52,000.
G. slightly less than $52,000.   **J.** more than $104,000.

19. Daft built a new home and failed to build in a door from the garage to the house. Anyone parking in the garage must go out the overhead garage door and around the house to the front door. This is
   A. physical deterioration.
   B. functional obsolescence.
   C. social obsolescence.
   D. economic obsolescence.

20. When might a gross rent multiplier be used to estimate the market value of a duplex?
   F. When the duplex is being purchased for income purposes
   G. When information about recent sales of similar properties is not available
   H. When information about recent rentals of similar properties is not available
   J. In none of the above circumstances

21. Schell wishes to purchase an investment property that has a gross annual income of $75,000. Schell knows that the monthly expenses equal 3% of the gross annual income. If Schell wants to have a 14% return on the investment, approximately how much should be paid for the property?
   A. $672,000   **B.** $535,714   **C.** $519,643   **D.** $342,857

22. What is the correct sequence of the following tasks when appraising a single-family residence using a market comparison approach?
   I. Inspect the premises of comparable properties to verify the purchase price and adjust for the value of the different characteristics of these properties relative to the subject property
   II. Become familiar with the physical features and amenities of the subject property
   III. Compare and correlate the adjusted market price of each comparable property to arrive at an indicated value of the subject property
   IV. Collect such necessary information as sales price, date of sale, description of physical characteristics and amenities of the comparable properties
   V. Locate houses of similar physical features that have sold recently on the open market
   F. II, I, V, IV, III
   G. II, V, IV, I, III
   H. V, I, IV, III, II
   J. V, IV, III, II, I

23. Biggs purchased May's home with an FHA-insured loan. At closing, the discount for this loan will be paid to the

A. FHA.   C. buyer.
B. broker.   D. lending company.

24. Arnold used his VA guarantee to purchase a home. Later, Arnold sold this home, paid off the mortgage, and made an offer on another, more expensive home. Which statement about the financing of this second home is true?
    F. Arnold may use only one-half of his VA entitlement because VA loans on second homes are guaranteed for one-half of the original entitlement.
    G. Arnold may use a full, new VA guarantee to finance the home because he has repaid the first loan.
    H. Arnold must wait to use a VA-guaranteed loan because he bought and sold the first house within a five-year period.
    J. Arnold may not use a VA-guaranteed loan because they are available only for mortgage loans on first homes.

25. A savings and loan association loaned the owner of a parcel of real property 70% of its appraised valuation. The interest rate was 10.8% per annum. If the first month's interest was $252, what was the appraised value of the property?
    A. $14,000   B. $25,200   C. $28,000   D. $40,000

26. A homebuilder has more prospective buyers than homes to sell and is holding a lottery. There are 60 homes in the tract and 600 prospective buyers have entered their names in the lottery. What chance does a prospective buyer have of getting one of the homes?
    F. 1 in 9   H. 1 in 11
    G. 1 in 10   J. 10 in 1

27. A black prospect asks a broker to show homes to her in a predominately white neighborhood. How should the broker respond to the prospect's request?
    A. "I really don't think there are any homes in that area that you would like."
    B. "I'm sorry, but I cannot be your agent under these circumstances."
    C. "Fine. When would you like to see these homes?"
    D. "I really don't think you'd like this area anyway; let me show you some other homes."

28. The Real Estate Settlement Procedures Act requires that
    F. settlement costs be disclosed in advance of every closing.
    G. the FHA pay legal fees for anyone who cannot afford to hire a lawyer at closing.
    H. the VA guarantee a loan for a property larger than 25 acres.
    J. no acceleration clause be included in a mortgage on a property larger than 25 acres.

APPENDIX D

Sample ASI-Type Test Questions*

ASI examinations consist of 80 general questions for both salesperson and broker examinations. The salesperson examination has an additional 30 state-unique questions, and the broker examination has an additional 40 state-unique questions. Each question is in a four-option multiple-choice format with one correct answer.

CONTENT OUTLINE
GENERAL REAL ESTATE
EXAMINATION

Salesperson 30%
Broker 15%
  I. *Real Estate Law*
    A. Contractual
        1. Encumbrances
          a. Priorities of liens
          b. Encroachments
          c. Restrictions/Easements
          d. Mechanic's liens
          e. Attachments and Agreements
        2. Contracts and Agreements
          a. Characteristics of enforceable real estate contracts
          b. Elements of property descriptions
          c. Purchase price
          d. Standard printed clauses
        3. Options
        4. Deeds
    B. General Practice
        1. Nature of real property
          a. Definitions
          b. Methods of legal description
         2. Parties dealing with interests in real property
          a. Legal capacity   c. Corporations
          b. Individuals   d. Partnerships
    C. Fair housing laws

Salesperson 20%
Broker 25%
 II. *Ownership/Transfer*
    A. Land titles and interest in real property
        1. Estates in land

---

* The information in Appendix D was adapted and reprinted by permission of Assessment Systems, Inc., the copyright owner.

        a. Joint ownership
        b. Severalty ownership
    2. Fixtures/personal property
    3. Insurance
    4. Settlement procedures
    5. Lease and leasehold
B. Voluntary or involuntary alienation
   of real property
    1. Dedication   6. Condemnation
    2. Adverse possession   7. Eminent domain
    3. Sheriff's sale   8. Inheritance
    4. Foreclosure   9. Gifts
    5. Escheat   10. Taxation
C. Public control
    1. Planning
        a. Urban
        b. Rural
    2. Zoning
    3. Property Taxation
    4. Water rights
    5. Health and safety/building codes

Salesperson 20%
Broker 25%
III. Brokerage/Agency
    A. Distinction between agency relationships
    B. Agent responsibilities to principal(s) and/or others
    C. Termination of agency
    D. Listing agreements
    E. Property management (residential/commercial)
        1. Management contracts
        2. Rentals and leases
        3. Repairs and maintenance
    F. Investments

Salesperson 10%
Broker 15%
IV. Concepts of Appraising
    A. Concepts and purposes of appraisal
    B. Appraisal techniques
    C. Elements of depreciation
    D. Principles of real property value
    E. Approaches to value
        1. Cost
        2. Income
        3. Market data
    F. Economic trends
    G. Neighborhood

Broker examination only:
- **H.** Site analysis and valuation
- **I.** Gross rent multiplier
- **J.** Principles in capitalization
- **K.** The appraisal report

Salesperson 20%
Broker 20%

V. *Finance*
- **A.** Methods of financing
    1. Government
    2. Other
- **B.** Truth-in-Lending and RESPA
- **C.** Financing instruments
- **D.** Financing terminology

VI. *Mathematics of Real Estate (included as part of other content areas—approximately 20%) Basic Mathematics to calculate solutions to the following problem areas:*
- **A.** Financing
- **B.** Tax assessment
- **C.** Commissions
- **D.** Area calculations
- **E.** Settlement statements
- **F.** Profit and loss
- **G.** Tax ramifications
- **H.** General

CONTENT OUTLINE
TYPICAL STATE
EXAMINATION

Topics

I. *Duties and Powers of the Real Estate Commission*
- **A.** General powers
- **B.** Examination of records
- **C.** Investigations, hearings and appeals
- **D.** Sanctions
    1. Court actions and imprisonment
    2. License suspension and revocation
- **E.** Real Estate Commission membership

II. *Licensing Requirements*
- **A.** Activities requiring a license
- **B.** Types of licenses
- **C.** Eligibility for licensing
- **D.** License renewal
- **E.** Change in license

III. *Statutory Requirements Governing the Activities of Licensees*
   A. Advertising
   B. Broker/Salesperson relationship
   C. Commissions
   D. Disclosure/conflict of interest
   E. Handling of documents
   F. Handling of monies
   G. Listings
   H. Place of business
   I. Recordkeeping
   J. Unfair inducements
   K. Licensee/public responsibility

IV. *Additional Topics*
   A. Recovery Fund
      1. Purpose of the fund
      2. Licensee's obligations
   B. Requirements Governing Subdivided or out-of-state Land
      1. Registration requirements
      2. Disclosure requirements
   C. Timesharing

SAMPLE QUESTIONS
Only one question format is used in the real estate examinations. An incomplete statement or a question is presented and followed by four choices. The questions are intended to present only one choice out of four as the correct answer. The following examples show question formats.

SALESPERSON

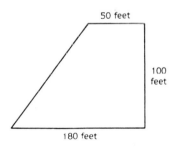

50 feet

100 feet

180 feet

1. Using the dimensions of the lot shown above, how much would the buyer pay per square foot if the total selling price is $37,000?
   (A) $2.34   (C) $3.22
   (B) $2.85   (D) $3.70

2. A broker wanting to list a commercial income property whereby the owner would be obligated to pay a commission no matter who sold the property during the term of the agreement would enter into what type of listing?
(A) Open
(B) Commercial
(C) Exclusive agency
(D) Exclusive right-to-sell

3. Financial advantages of real estate investment include the recovery of all the following amounts **EXCEPT:**
(A) depreciation
(B) real esate tax
(C) mortgage interest
(D) principal

BROKER

1. Using land to its greatest economic advantage is referred to as:
(A) optimization
(B) capitalization
(C) highest and best use
(D) income production

2. A certificate that shows the unpaid principal of a mortgage and the interest on the mortgage is known as a(n):
(A) waiver
(B) estoppel
(C) acknowledgment
(D) warranty deed

3. Property taxes of $1,320 were paid in advance for the full calendar year. The property was sold and closing takes place on November 15 with the seller responsible for the day of closing.
(A) Charge buyer $165, credit seller $165.
(B) Charge seller $1,155, credit buyer $1,155.
(C) Charge seller $165, credit buyer $165.
(D) Charge buyer $165, credit seller $1,155.

Percent (%) means part per hundred. For example, 25% means 25 *PERCENT*
parts per hundred; 10% means 10 parts per hundred. Percentages are
related to common and decimal fractions as follows:

     5% = .05 = 1/20
    10% = .10 = 1/10
    25% = .25 = ¼
    75% = .75 = ¾
    99% = .99 = 99/100

A percentage greater than 100% is greater than 1. For example:

     110% = 1.10 = 1 1/10
     150% = 1.50 = 1½
     200% = 2.00 = 2
  1,000% = 10.0 = 10

To change a decimal fraction to a percentage, move the decimal point
two places to the right and add the % sign. For example:

  .0001 =   .01%
   .01 =   1%
   .06 =   6%
   .35 =   35%
  .356 = 35.6%
 1.15 = 115%

A percentage can be changed to a common fraction by writing it as
hundredths and then reducing it to its lowest common denominator.
For example:

   20% = 20/100 = 1/5
   90% = 90/100 = 9/10
 225% = 225/100 = 2¼

To add decimals, place the decimal point directly over one another. *ADDING AND*
Then place the decimal point for the solutions in the same column *SUBTRACTING DECIMALS*
and add. For example:

   6.25
   1.10
 10.277
 ―――――
 17.627

If you are working with percentages, there is no need to convert to decimal fractions; just line up the decimal points and add. For example:

```
  68.8%
   6.0%
  25.2%
 100.0%
```

When subtracting, the same methods apply. For example:

```
  1.00        100%
 - .80       - 80%
   .20         20%
```

When there is a mixture of decimal fractions and percentages, first convert them all either to percentage or to decimal fractions.

MULTIPLYING AND DIVIDING DECIMALS   Multiplying decimals is like multiplying whole numbers except that the decimal point must be correctly placed. This is done by counting the total number of places to the right of the decimal point in the numbers to be multiplied. Then count off the same number of places in the answer. The following examples illustrate this:

```
  .6        .2       1.01        6          6        .03
 ×.3       ×.2       ×  2       ×.1       ×.11     ×  .02
  .18       .04      2.02        .6        .66      .0006
```

When dividing, the process starts with properly placing the decimal point. A normal division then follows. When a decimal number is divided by a whole number, place the decimal point in the answer directly above the decimal point in the problem. For example:

$$
\begin{array}{r} 1.03 \\ 3\overline{)3.09} \end{array} \qquad \begin{array}{r} .033 \\ 3\overline{).099} \end{array}
$$

To divide by a decimal number, you must first change the divisor to a whole number. Then you must make a corresponding change in the dividend. This is done by simply moving both decimal points the same number of places to the right. For example, to divide .06 by .02, move the decimal point to each to the right two places.

$.02\overline{).06}$ becomes $2\overline{)6}$

$.5\overline{)3}$ becomes $5\overline{)30}$

$.05\overline{)30}$ becomes $5\overline{)3,000}$

When multiplying or dividing with percentages, first convert them to decimal form. Thus 6% of 200 is

$$\begin{array}{r} 200 \\ \times\ .06 \\ \hline 12.00 \end{array}$$

A simple way to solve rate problems is to think of
the word **is** as = (an equal sign).
the word **of** as × (a multiplication sign).
the word **per** as ÷ (a division sign).

PROBLEMS INVOLVING RATES

for example:
"7% of $50,000 is $3,500"
translates:
7% × $50,000 = $3,500"

Problem 1

Beverly Broker sells a house for $60,000. Her share of the com-
mission is to be 2.5% of the sales price. How much does she earn?
Her commission is 2.5% of $60,000
Her commission = .025 × $60,000
Her commission= $1,500

Problem 2

Sam Salesman works in an office which will pay him 70% of the
commission on each home he lists and sells. With a 6% commission,
how much would he earn on a $50,000 sale?
His commission is 70% of 6% of $50,000
His commission = .70 × .06 × $50,000
His commission = $2,100

Problem 3

Newt Newcommer wants to earn $21,000 during his first 12
months as a salesman. He feels he can average 3% on each sale. How
much property must he sell?
3% of sales is $21,000
.03 × sales = $21,000
       sales = $21,000 ÷ .03
       sales = $700,000

> **Note:** An equation will remain an equation as long as you
> make the same change on both sides of the equal sign. If
> you add the same number to both sides, it is still an
> equation. If you subtract the same amount from each
> side, it is still equal. If you multiply both sides by the
> same thing, it remains equal. If you divide both sides by
> the same thing, it remains equal.

Problem 4

An apartment building nets the owners $12,000 per year on their
investment of $100,000. What percent return are they receiving on
their investment?

$12,000 is __% of $100,000
$12,000 = __% × $100,000
$$\frac{\$12,000}{\$100,000} = 12\%$$

Problem 5

Smith wants to sell his property and have $47,000 after paying a 6% brokerage commission on the sales price. What price must Smith get?

$47,000 is 94% of selling price
$47,000 = .94 × selling price
$$\frac{\$47,000}{.94} = \text{selling price}$$
$50,000 = selling price

Problem 6

Miller sold his home for $75,000, paid off an existing loan of $35,000 and paid closing costs of $500. The brokerage commission was 6% of the sales price. How much money did Miller receive? The amount he received is 94% of $75,000 less $35,500

amount = .94 × $75,000 − $35,500
amount = $70,500 − $35,500
amount = $35,000

Problem 7

The assessed valuation of the Kelly home is $10,000. If the property tax rate is $12.50 per $100 of assessed valuation, what is the tax?

The tax is $\frac{\$12.50}{\$100}$ of $10,000

$$\text{tax} = \frac{\$12.50}{\$100} \times \$10,000$$

$$\text{tax} = \$1,250$$

Problem 8

Property in Clark County is assessed at 75% of market value. What should the assessed valuation of a $40,000 property be?

Assessed valuation is 75% of market value
Assessed valuation = .75 × $40,000
Assessed valuation = $30,000

Problem 9

An insurance company charges $.24 per $100 of coverage for a one-year fire insurance policy. How much would a $40,000 policy cost?

Cost is $\dfrac{\$.24}{\$100}$ of $40,000

Cost $= \dfrac{\$.24}{\$100} \times \$40,000$

Cost $= \$96$

The measurement of the distance from one point to another is called *linear* measurement. Usually this is along a straight line, but it can also be along a curved line. Distance is measured in inches, feet, yards and miles. Less commonly used are chains (66 feet) and rods (16 and a half feet). Surface areas are measured in square feet, square yards, acres (43,560 square feet) and square miles. In the metric system, the standard unit of linear measurement is the meter (39.37 inches). Land area is measured in square meters and hectares. A hectare contains 10,000 square meters or 2.471 acres.   *AREA MEASUREMENT*

To determine the area of a square or rectangle, multiply its length times its width. The formula is:
  Area = Length × Width
    A = L × W

Problem 10
  A parcel of land measures 660 feet by 330 feet. How many square feet is this?
    Area = 660 feet × 330 feet
    Area = 217,800 square feet

How many acres does this parcel contain?
    Acres = 217,800 ÷ 43,560
    Acres = 5

If a buyer offers $42,500 for this parcel, how much is the offering per acre?
    $42,500 ÷ 5 = $8,500

To determine the area of a right triangle, multiply one-half of the base times the height:

A = ½ × B × H   A = ½ × B × H
A = ½ × 25 × 50   A = ½ × 40 × 20
A = 625 square feet   A = 400 square feet

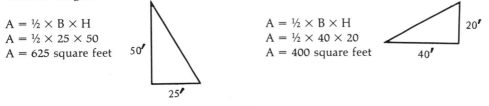

To determine the area of a circle, multiply 3.14 (π) times the square of the radius:

$A = \pi \times r^2$
$A = 3.14 \times 40^2$
$A = 3.14 \times 1,600$
$A = 5,024$ sq ft

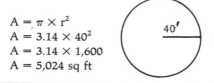

Note: Where the diameter of a circle is given, divide by two to get the radius.

To determine the area of composite figures, separate them into their various components. Thus:

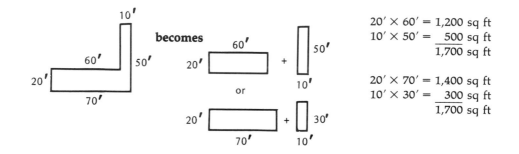

$20' \times 60' = 1,200$ sq ft
$10' \times 50' = \underline{\quad 500}$ sq ft
$ 1,700$ sq ft

$20' \times 70' = 1,400$ sq ft
$10' \times 30' = \underline{\quad 300}$ sq ft
$ 1,700$ sq ft

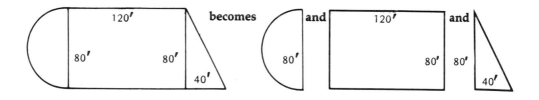

$(3.14 \times 40'^2 \times \tfrac{1}{2}) + (80' \times 120') + (\tfrac{1}{2} \times 40' \times 80') = 13,712$ sq ft

VOLUME MEASUREMENT   Volume is measured in cubic units. The formula is:
Volume = Length $\times$ Width $\times$ Height
$V = L \times W \times H$

For example, what is the volume of a room that is 10 ft by 15 ft with an 8 ft ceiling?
$V = 10' \times 15' \times 8'$
$V = 1,200$ cu ft

> **Caution:** When solving area and volume problems, make certain that all the units are the same. For example, if a parcel of land is one-half mile long and 200 ft wide, convert one measurement so that both are expressed in the same unit; thus the answer will be either in square feet or in square miles. There is no such area measurement as a mile-foot. If a building is 100 yards long by 100 feet wide by 16′ 6″ high, convert to 300 ft by 100 ft by 16.5 before multiplying.

If the label on a five-gallon can of paint says it will cover 2,000 square feet, how many gallons are necessary to cover 3,600 sq ft?

RATIOS & PROPORTIONS

A problem like this can be solved two ways:
One way is to find out what area one gallon will cover. In this case 2,000 sq ft ÷ 5 gallons = 400 sq ft per gallon. Then divide 400 sq ft/gal into 3,600 sq ft and the result is 9 gallons.
The other method is to set up a proportion:

$$\frac{5\ \text{gal}}{2{,}000\ \text{sq ft}} = \frac{Y\ \text{gal}}{3{,}600\ \text{sq ft}}$$

This reads, "5 gallons is to 2,000 sq ft as 'Y' gallons is to 3,600 sq ft." To solve for "Y," multiply both sides of the proportion by 3,600 sq ft. Thus:

$$\frac{5\ \text{gal} \times 3{,}600\ \text{sq ft}}{2{,}000\ \text{sq ft}} = Y\ \text{gal}$$

Divide 2,000 sq ft into 3,600 sq ft and multiply the result by 5 gallons to get the answer.

When land is sold on a front-foot basis, the price is the number of feet fronting on the street times the price per front foot.

FRONT-FOOT CALCULATIONS

Price = front footage × rate per front foot

Thus a 50 ft × 150 ft lot priced at $1,000 per front foot would sell for $50,000. Note that in giving the dimensions of a lot, the first dimension given is the street frontage. The second dimension is the depth of the lot.

Compound Sum of Single Dollar

Year	2%	4%	6%	8%	10%	12%	14%	16%	18%	20%	22%	25%	30%	40%
1	1.020	1.040	1.060	1.080	1.100	1.120	1.140	1.160	1.180	1.200	1.220	1.250	1.300	1.400
2	1.040	1.082	1.124	1.166	1.210	1.254	1.300	1.346	1.392	1.440	1.488	1.563	1.690	1.960
3	1.061	1.125	1.191	1.260	1.331	1.405	1.482	1.561	1.643	1.728	1.816	1.953	2.197	2.744
4	1.082	1.170	1.262	1.360	1.464	1.574	1.689	1.811	1.939	2.074	2.215	2.441	2.856	3.842
5	1.104	1.217	1.338	1.469	1.611	1.762	1.925	2.100	2.288	2.488	2.703	3.052	3.713	5.378
6	1.126	1.265	1.419	1.587	1.772	1.974	2.195	2.436	2.700	2.986	3.297	3.851	4.827	7.530
7	1.149	1.316	1.504	1.714	1.949	2.211	2.502	2.826	3.185	3.583	4.023	4.768	6.275	10.54
8	1.172	1.369	1.594	1.851	2.144	2.476	2.853	3.278	3.759	4.300	4.908	5.960	8.157	14.75
9	1.195	1.423	1.689	1.999	2.358	2.773	3.252	3.803	4.435	5.160	5.987	7.451	10.604	20.66
10	1.219	1.480	1.791	2.159	2.594	3.106	3.707	4.411	5.234	6.192	7.305	9.313	13.786	28.92
11	1.243	1.539	1.898	2.332	2.853	3.479	4.226	5.117	6.176	7.430	8.912	11.642	17.921	40.49
12	1.268	1.601	2.012	2.518	3.138	3.896	4.818	5.936	7.288	8.916	10.872	14.552	23.298	56.6
13	1.294	1.665	2.133	2.720	3.452	4.363	5.492	6.886	8.599	10.699	13.264	18.190	30.287	79.3
14	1.319	1.732	2.261	2.937	3.797	4.887	6.261	7.988	10.147	12.839	16.182	22.737	39.373	
15	1.346	1.801	2.397	3.172	4.177	5.474	7.138	9.266	11.974	15.407	19.742	28.422	51.185	
16	1.373	1.873	2.540	3.426	4.595	6.130	8.137	10.748	14.129	18.488	24.085	35.527	66.541	
17	1.400	1.948	2.693	3.700	5.054	6.866	9.276	12.468	16.672	22.186	29.384	44.409	86.503	
18	1.428	2.026	2.854	3.996	5.560	7.690	10.575	14.462	19.673	26.623	35.849	55.511		
19	1.457	2.107	3.026	4.316	6.116	8.613	12.056	16.776	23.214	31.948	43.735	69.389		
20	1.486	2.191	3.207	4.661	6.727	9.646	13.743	19.461	27.393	38.337	53.357	86.736		
21	1.516	2.279	3.400	5.034	7.400	10.804	15.667	22.574	32.323	46.005	65.096			
22	1.546	2.370	3.603	5.437	8.140	12.100	17.861	26.186	38.142	55.206	79.417			
23	1.577	2.465	3.820	5.871	8.954	13.552	20.361	30.376	45.007	66.247	96.888			
24	1.608	2.563	4.049	6.341	9.850	15.179	23.212	35.236	53.108	79.497				
25	1.641	2.666	4.292	6.848	10.835	17.000	26.462	40.874	62.668	95.396				

Source: John J. Hampton, *Handbook for Financial Decision Makers*, Reston Publishing Company, Reston, Virginia, 1979.

Compound Sum of Annuity of $1

Year	2%	4%	6%	8%	10%	12%	14%	16%	18%	20%	22%	25%	30%	40%
1	1.000	1.000	1.000	1.000	1.000	1.000	1.000	1.000	1.000	1.000	1.000	1.000	1.000	1.000
2	2.020	2.040	2.060	2.080	2.100	2.120	2.140	2.160	2.180	2.200	2.220	2.250	2.300	2.400
3	3.060	3.122	3.184	3.246	3.310	3.374	3.440	3.506	3.572	3.640	3.708	3.813	3.990	4.360
4	4.121	4.246	4.375	4.506	4.641	4.779	4.921	5.066	5.215	5.368	5.524	5.766	6.187	7.104
5	5.204	5.416	5.637	5.867	6.105	6.353	6.610	6.877	7.154	7.442	7.740	8.207	9.043	10.846
6	6.308	6.633	6.975	7.336	7.716	8.115	8.535	8.977	9.442	9.930	10.442	11.259	12.756	16.324
7	7.434	7.898	8.394	8.923	9.487	10.089	10.730	11.414	12.141	12.916	13.740	15.073	17.583	23.853
8	8.583	9.214	9.897	10.637	11.436	12.300	13.233	14.240	15.327	16.499	17.762	19.842	23.858	34.395
9	9.754	10.583	11.491	12.488	13.579	14.776	16.085	17.518	19.086	20.799	22.670	25.802	32.015	49.153
10	10.949	12.006	13.181	14.487	15.937	17.549	19.337	21.321	23.521	25.959	28.657	33.253	42.619	69.814
11	12.168	13.486	14.971	16.645	18.531	20.655	23.044	25.733	28.755	32.150	35.962	42.566	56.405	98.739
12	13.412	15.026	16.870	18.977	21.384	24.133	27.271	30.850	34.931	39.580	44.873	54.208	74.326	
13	14.680	16.627	18.882	21.495	24.522	28.029	32.088	36.786	42.218	48.496	55.745	68.760	97.624	
14	15.973	18.292	21.015	24.215	27.975	32.393	37.581	43.672	50.818	59.196	69.009	86.949		
15	17.293	20.024	23.276	27.152	31.772	37.280	43.842	51.659	60.965	72.035	85.191			
16	18.639	21.824	25.672	30.324	35.949	42.753	50.980	60.925	72.938	87.442				
17	20.011	23.697	28.212	33.750	40.544	48.884	59.117	71.673	87.067					
18	21.412	25.645	30.905	37.450	45.599	55.750	68.393	84.141						
19	22.840	27.671	33.759	41.446	51.158	63.440	78.968	98.603						
20	24.297	29.778	36.785	45.762	57.274	72.052	91.024							
21	25.783	31.969	39.992	50.423	64.002	81.699								
22	27.298	34.248	43.392	55.457	71.402	92.502								
23	28.844	36.618	46.995	60.893	79.542									
24	30.421	39.083	50.815	66.765	88.496									
25	32.029	41.646	54.864	73.106	98.346									

Source: John J. Hampton, *Handbook for Financial Decision Makers,*
Reston Publishing Company, Reston, Virginia, 1979.

Present Value of Single Dollar

Year	2%	4%	6%	8%	10%	12%	14%	16%	18%	20%	22%	24%	25%	30%	40%
1	0.980	0.962	0.943	0.926	0.909	0.893	0.877	0.862	0.847	0.833	0.820	0.806	0.800	0.769	0.714
2	0.961	0.925	0.890	0.857	0.826	0.797	0.769	0.743	0.718	0.694	0.672	0.650	0.640	0.592	0.510
3	0.942	0.889	0.840	0.794	0.751	0.712	0.675	0.641	0.609	0.579	0.551	0.524	0.512	0.455	0.364
4	0.924	0.855	0.792	0.735	0.683	0.636	0.592	0.552	0.516	0.482	0.451	0.423	0.410	0.350	0.260
5	0.906	0.822	0.747	0.681	0.621	0.567	0.519	0.476	0.437	0.402	0.370	0.341	0.328	0.269	0.186
6	0.888	0.790	0.705	0.630	0.564	0.507	0.456	0.410	0.370	0.335	0.303	0.275	0.262	0.207	0.133
7	0.871	0.760	0.665	0.583	0.513	0.452	0.400	0.354	0.314	0.279	0.249	0.222	0.210	0.159	0.095
8	0.853	0.731	0.627	0.540	0.467	0.404	0.351	0.305	0.266	0.233	0.204	0.179	0.168	0.123	0.068
9	0.837	0.703	0.592	0.500	0.424	0.361	0.308	0.263	0.225	0.194	0.167	0.144	0.134	0.094	0.048
10	0.820	0.676	0.558	0.463	0.386	0.322	0.270	0.227	0.191	0.162	0.137	0.116	0.107	0.073	0.035
11	0.804	0.650	0.527	0.429	0.350	0.287	0.237	0.195	0.162	0.135	0.112	0.094	0.086	0.056	0.025
12	0.788	0.625	0.497	0.397	0.319	0.257	0.208	0.168	0.137	0.112	0.092	0.076	0.069	0.043	0.018
13	0.773	0.601	0.469	0.368	0.290	0.229	0.182	0.145	0.116	0.093	0.075	0.061	0.055	0.033	0.013
14	0.758	0.577	0.442	0.340	0.263	0.205	0.160	0.125	0.099	0.078	0.062	0.049	0.044	0.025	0.009
15	0.743	0.555	0.417	0.315	0.239	0.183	0.140	0.108	0.084	0.065	0.051	0.040	0.035	0.020	0.006
16	0.728	0.534	0.394	0.292	0.218	0.163	0.123	0.093	0.071	0.054	0.042	0.032	0.028	0.015	0.005
17	0.714	0.513	0.371	0.270	0.198	0.146	0.108	0.080	0.060	0.045	0.034	0.026	0.023	0.012	0.003
18	0.700	0.494	0.350	0.250	0.180	0.130	0.095	0.069	0.051	0.038	0.028	0.021	0.018	0.009	0.002
19	0.686	0.475	0.331	0.232	0.164	0.116	0.083	0.060	0.043	0.031	0.023	0.017	0.014	0.007	0.002
20	0.673	0.456	0.312	0.215	0.149	0.104	0.073	0.051	0.037	0.026	0.019	0.014	0.012	0.005	0.001
25	0.610	0.375	0.233	0.146	0.092	0.059	0.038	0.024	0.016	0.010	0.007	0.005	0.004	0.001	
30	0.552	0.308	0.174	0.099	0.057	0.033	0.020	0.012	0.007	0.004	0.003	0.002	0.001		
40	0.453	0.208	0.097	0.046	0.022	0.011	0.005	0.003	0.001	0.001					
50	0.372	0.141	0.054	0.021	0.009	0.003	0.001	0.001							

Source: John J. Hampton, *Handbook for Financial Decision Makers,*
Reston Publishing Company, Reston, Virginia, 1979.

Present Value of Annuity of $1

Year	2%	4%	6%	8%	10%	12%	14%	16%	18%	20%	22%	24%	25%	30%	40%
1	0.980	0.962	0.943	0.926	0.909	0.893	0.877	0.862	0.847	0.833	0.820	0.806	0.800	0.769	0.714
2	1.942	1.886	1.833	1.783	1.736	1.690	1.647	1.605	1.566	1.528	1.492	1.457	1.440	1.361	1.224
3	2.884	2.775	2.673	2.577	2.487	2.402	2.322	2.246	2.174	2.106	2.042	1.981	1.952	1.816	1.589
4	3.808	3.630	3.645	3.312	3.170	3.037	2.914	2.798	2.690	2.589	2.494	2.404	2.362	2.166	1.849
5	4.713	4.452	4.212	3.993	3.791	3.605	3.433	3.274	3.127	2.991	2.864	2.745	2.689	2.436	2.035
6	5.601	5.242	4.917	4.623	4.355	4.111	3.889	3.685	3.498	3.326	3.167	3.020	2.951	2.643	2.168
7	6.472	6.002	5.582	5.206	4.868	4.564	4.288	4.039	3.812	3.605	3.416	3.242	3.161	2.802	2.263
8	7.325	6.733	6.210	5.747	5.335	4.968	4.639	4.344	4.078	3.837	3.619	3.421	3.329	2.925	2.331
9	8.162	7.435	6.802	6.247	5.759	5.328	4.946	4.607	4.303	4.031	3.786	3.566	3.463	3.019	2.379
10	8.983	8.111	7.360	6.710	6.145	5.650	5.216	4.833	4.494	4.192	3.923	3.682	3.571	3.092	2.414
11	9.787	8.760	7.887	7.139	6.495	5.937	5.453	5.029	4.656	4.327	4.035	3.776	3.656	3.147	2.438
12	10.58	9.385	8.384	7.536	6.814	6.194	5.660	5.197	4.793	4.439	4.127	3.851	3.725	3.190	2.456
13	11.34	9.986	8.853	7.904	7.103	6.424	5.842	5.342	4.910	4.533	4.203	3.912	3.780	3.223	2.468
14	12.11	10.56	9.295	8.244	7.367	6.628	6.002	5.468	5.008	4.611	4.265	3.962	3.824	3.249	2.477
15	12.85	11.12	9.712	8.559	7.606	6.811	6.142	5.575	5.092	4.675	4.315	4.001	3.859	3.268	2.484
16	13.58	11.65	10.11	8.851	7.824	6.974	6.265	5.669	5.162	4.730	4.357	4.033	3.887	3.283	2.489
17	14.29	12.17	10.48	9.122	8.022	7.120	6.373	5.749	5.222	4.775	4.391	4.059	3.910	3.295	2.492
18	14.99	12.66	10.83	9.372	8.201	7.250	6.467	5.818	5.273	4.812	4.419	4.080	3.928	3.304	2.494
19	15.68	13.13	11.16	9.604	8.365	7.366	6.550	5.877	5.316	4.844	4.442	4.097	3.942	3.311	2.496
20	16.35	13.59	11.47	9.818	8.514	7.469	6.623	5.929	5.353	4.870	4.460	4.110	3.954	3.316	2.497
25	19.52	15.62	12.78	10.68	9.077	7.843	6.873	6.097	5.467	4.948	4.514	4.147	3.985	3.329	2.499
30	22.40	17.29	13.77	11.26	9.427	8.055	7.003	6.177	5.517	4.979	4.534	4.160	3.995	3.332	2.500
40	27.36	19.79	15.05	11.93	9.779	8.244	7.105	6.234	5.548	4.997	4.544	4.166	3.999	3.333	2.500
50	31.42	21.48	15.76	12.23	9.915	8.304	7.133	6.246	5.554	4.999	4.545	4.167	4.000	3.333	2.500

Source: John J. Hampton, *Handbook for Financial Decision Makers,*
Reston Publishing Company, Reston, Virginia, 1979.

Measurement Conversion Table

Mile =
    5,280 feet
    1,760 yards
    320 rods
    80 chains
       = 1.609 kilometers

Square mile =
    640 acres
       = 2.590 sq kilometers

Acre =
    43,560 sq ft
    4,840 sq yds
    160 sq rods
       = 4,047 sq meters

Rod =
    16.5 feet
       = 5.029 meters

Chain =
    66 feet
    4 rods
    100 links
       = 20.117 meters

Meter =
    39.37 inches
       = 1,000 millimeters
    3.281 feet
       = 100 centimeters
    1.094 yards
       = 10 decimeters

Kilometer =
    0.6214 miles
    3,281 feet
    1,094 yards
       = 1,000 meters

Square meter =
    10.765 sq ft
    1.196 sq yds
       = 10,000 sq centimeters

Hectare =
    2.47 acres
    107,600 sq ft
    11,960 sq yds
       = 10,000 sq meters

Square kilometer =
    .3861 sq miles
    247 acres
       = 1,000,000 sq meters

Kilogram =
    2.205 pounds
       = 1,000 grams

Liter =
    1.052 quarts
    .263 gallons
       = 1,000 milliliters

Metric ton =
    2,205 pounds
    1.102 tons
       = 1,000 kilograms

Answers to Questions and Problems

UNIFORM TEST

REAL ESTATE CONTRACTS
1. **B**   2. **A**

FINANCING
1. **C**   2. **A**   3. **D**

REAL ESTATE OWNERSHIP
1. **D**   2. **C**   3. **D**   4. **C**

REAL ESTATE BROKERAGE
1. **C**   2. **D**   3. **A**

REAL ESTATE VALUATION
1. **D**   2. **C**   3. **B**   4. **B**

STATE TEST

1. **B** 2. **Local answer** 3. **D**

UNIFORM TEST
REAL ESTATE BROKERAGE
1. **C**   2. **A**

CONTRACTS AND OTHER LEGAL ASPECTS
1. **C**   2. **B**

PRICING AND VALUATION
1. **A**   2. **A**   3. **B**

FINANCE AND INVESTMENT
1. **B**   2. **C**   3. **A**

1. **C**	7. **A**	13. **B**	19. **B**	25. **D**
2. **H**	8. **F**	14. **G**	20. **F**	26. **G**
3. **D**	9. **C**	15. **C**	21. **D**	27. **C**
4. **F**	10. **F**	16. **G**	22. **G**	28. **F**
5. **D**	11. **C**	17. **C**	23. **D**	
6. **F**	12. **H**	18. **H**	24. **G**	

SALESPERSON: 1. **C**   2. **D**   3. **D**
BROKER: 1. **C**   2. **B**   3. **A**

ETS SALESPERSON EXAMINATION

ETS BROKER EXAMINATION

ACT EXAMINATION

ASI EXAMINATION

ANSWERS TO
CHAPTER QUESTIONS AND PROBLEMS

CHAPTER 2
Nature and Description of Real
Estate

VOCABULARY REVIEW

a. 17	**f.** 15	**j.** 1	**n.** 8	**r.** 6
b. 19	**g.** 21	**k** 22	**o.** 12	**s.** 5
c. 11	**h.** 10	**l.** 13	**p.** 7	**t.** 14
d. 4	**i.** 9	**m.** 16	**q.** 18	**u.** 2
e. 20				**v.** 3

QUESTIONS AND PROBLEMS

1. Requires local answer.

2.

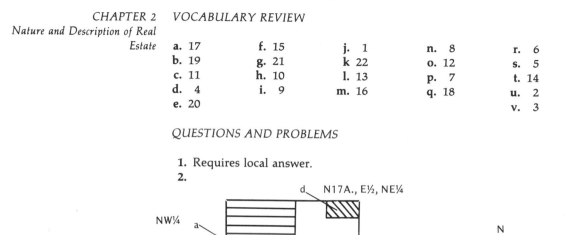

3. (a) 160 acres   (c) 80 acres   (e) 2½ acres
(b) 40 acres   (d) 17 acres

4. (a) NE¼   (d) W½ of the SE¼ of the NW¼
(b) E½ of the SE¼   (e) NE¼ of the SE¼ of the NW¼
(c) SW¼ of the NW¼

5.

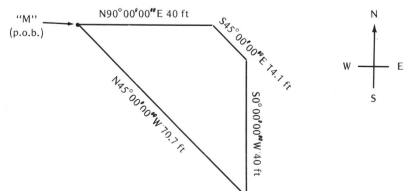

6. No. In the general public interest, laws have been passed that give aircraft the right to pass over land provided they fly above certain altitudes.
7. The key to a door, although highly portable, is adapted to the door and as such is real property.
8. Requires individualized answer. However, as a general rule, anything that is permanently attached is real property and anything that is not attached is personal property.
9. Requires local answer.
10. Unless corrections are made (and they usually are) survey inaccuracies would result.

CHAPTER 3
Rights and Interest in Land

VOCABULARY REVIEW

a. 8	e. 13	i. 6	m. 21	q. 22	u. 24
b. 4	f. 20	j. 11	n. 10	r. 18	v. 17
c. 14	g. 7	k. 9	o. 12	s. 23	w. 15
d. 19	h. 5	l. 1	p. 2	t. 3	x. 16

QUESTIONS AND PROBLEMS

1. For a freehold estate to exist, there must be actual possession of the land (that is, ownership) and the estate must be of unpredictable duration. Leasehold estates do not involve ownership of the land and are of determinate length. Freehold estate cases are tried under real property laws. Leasehold cases are tried under personal property laws.
2. An easement is created when a landowner fronting on a public byway deeds or leases a landlocked portion of his land to another person. This would be an easement by necessity. A second method is by prolonged use and is called an easement by prescription.
3. Requires local answer.
4. England, Spain and France.
5. The holder of an easement coexists side by side with the landowner; that is, both have a shared use of the land in question. The holder of a lease obtains exclusive right of occupancy and the landowner is excluded during the term of the lease.
6. An encumbrance is any impediment to clear title. Examples are: lien, lease, easement, deed restriction and encroachment.
7. Requires local answer. (Answers will likely center around zoning, building codes, general land planning, rent control, property taxation, eminent domain and escheat.)
8. Requires local answer.
9. Requires local answer.

CHAPTER 4
Forms of Ownership

VOCABULARY REVIEW

a. 18	e. 10	i. 17	m. 15	q. 6
b. 8	f. 5	j. 14	n. 9	r. 7
c. 1	g. 12	k. 4	o. 3	
d. 16	h. 11	l. 13	p. 2	

QUESTIONS AND PROBLEMS

1. The key advantage of sole ownership is flexibility—the owner can make all decisions without approval of co-owners. The key disadvantages are responsibility and the high entry cost.
2. Undivided interest means that each co-owner has a right to use the entire property.
3. The four unities are—
   Time: each must acquire ownership at the same moment.
   Title: all must acquire their interests from the same source.
   Interest: each owns an undivided whole of the property.
   Possession: all have the right to use the whole property.
4. Right of survivorship means that upon the death of a joint tenant, his interest in the property is extinguished and the remaining joint tenants are automatically left as the owners.
5. Requires local answer.
6. Requires local answer.
7. The three women would be considered to be tenants in common with each owning an undivided one-third interest.
8. No assumption can safely be made based on name only. Inquiry must be made into whether the land in question was separate or community property.
9. The key differences are in the financial liability of the limited partners, the limited management role of the limited partners and the fact that limited partners are not found in a general partnership.
10. REITs offer investors single taxation, built-in management, small minimum investment and liquidity.

CHAPTER 5
Transferring Title

VOCABULARY REVIEW

a. 21	f. 7	k. 6	q. 3	v. 10
b. 15	g. 14	l. 20	r. 12	w. 25
c. 22	h. 16	m. 1	s. 11	x. 2
d. 18	i. 5	n. 17	t. 19	y. 8
e. 9	j. 23	o. 24	u. 13	z. 26
		p. 4		

QUESTIONS AND PROBLEMS

1. Yes. The fact that a document is a deed depends on the wording it contains, not what it is labeled or not labeled.
2. Title passes upon delivery of the deed by the grantor to the grantee and its willing acceptance by the grantee.
3. The full covenant and warranty deed offers the grantee protection in the form of the grantor's assurances that he is the owner and possessor, that the grantee will not be disturbed after taking possession by someone else claiming ownership, that the title is not encumbered except as stated in the deed, and that the grantor will procure and deliver to the grantee any subsequent documents necessary to make good the title being conveyed.
4. Warranty deed. It provides the grantee with the maximum title protection available from a deed.
5. The hazards of preparing one's own deeds are that any errors made will cause confusion and may make the deed legally invalid. Preprinted deeds may not be suitable for the state where the land is located or for the grantor's purpose. An improperly prepared deed, once recorded, creates errors in the public records.
6. Dower right, curtesy right, community property right, mortgage right of redemption, tax lien, judgment lien, mechanic's lien, undivided interest held by another, inheritance rights and easements are all examples of title clouds.
7. When a person dies without leaving a will, state law directs how that person's assets are to be distributed.
8. An executor is named by the deceased in the will to carry out its terms. In the absence of a will, the state appoints an administrator to settle the deceased's estate.
9. Requires local answer.
10. No. Occupancy on a rental basis is not hostile to the property owner, but rather is by permission.
11. Requires local answer.

CHAPTER 6
Recordation, Abstracts and Title Insurance

VOCABULARY REVIEW

a.	10	e.	2	i.	8	m.	19	q.	9	u.	17
b.	3	f.	6	j.	14	n.	11	r.	20	v.	22
c.	1	g.	18	k.	16	o.	5	s.	12		
d.	7	h.	13	l.	4	p.	15	t.	21		

QUESTIONS AND PROBLEMS

1. By visibly occupying a parcel of land or by recording a document in the public records a person gives constructive notice that he is claiming a right or interest in that parcel of land.

2. Requires local answer.

3. Requires local answer.

4. The grantor and grantee indexes are used to locate documents filed in the public recorder's office.

5. Although the bulk of the information necessary to conduct a title search can be found in the public recorder's office, it may also be necessary to inspect documents not kept there, for example, marriage records, judgment lien files, probate records and the U.S. Tax Court.

6. A certificate of title issued by an attorney is his opinion of ownership, whereas a Torrens certificate of title shows ownership as determined by a court of law.

7. A title report shows the condition of title at a specific moment in time. An abstract provides a complete historical summary of all recorded documents affecting title. From this, an attorney renders an opinion as to the current condition of title.

8. The purpose of title insurance is to protect owners and lenders from monetary loss due to errors in title report preparation and inaccuracies in the public records.

9. Although Williams did not record his deed, his occupancy of the house constitutes legal notice. The out-of-state investor, who probably felt safe because he bought a title insurance policy, apparently did not read the fine print which, in most owner's policies, does not insure against facts, rights, interests or claims that could be ascertained by an on-site inspection or by making inquiry of persons in possession. The out-of-state investor is the loser unless he can recover his money from Thorsen.

10. Requires local answer.

CHAPTER 7
Contract Law

VOCABULARY REVIEW

a. 12	e. 23	i. 10	m. 16	q. 26	u. 15	y. 6
b. 20	f. 1	j. 25	n. 5	r. 7	v. 24	z. 19
c. 14	g. 8	k. 11	o. 13	s. 18	w. 17	
d. 4	h. 22	l. 3	p. 21	t. 9	x. 2	

QUESTIONS AND PROBLEMS

1. An expressed contract is the result of a written or oral agreement. An implied contract is one that is apparent from the actions of the parties involved. (Examples will vary with personal experiences.)

2. A legally valid contract requires: (a) legally competent parties, (b) mutual agreement, (c) lawful objective, (d) sufficient consideration or cause, and (e) a writing when required by law.

3. A void contract has no legal effect on any party to the contract and may be ignored at the pleasure of any party to it. A voidable contract is a contract that is able to be voided by one of its parties.

4. Examples of legal incompetents include: minors, insane persons, drunks and felons. (Exceptions are possible in the latter two.)

5. An offer can be terminated by the passage of time and by withdrawal prior to its acceptance. Passage of time can be in the form of a fixed termination date for the offer or, lacking that, a reasonable amount of time to accept as fixed by a court of law.

6. Mistake as applied to contract law arises from ambiguity in negotiations and mistake of material fact.

7. Consideration is one of the legal requirements of a binding contract. The concept of one party doing something and receiving nothing in return is foreign to contract law. Examples are money, goods, services and forbearance.

8. The parties to a legally unenforceable contract can still voluntarily carry out its terms. However, compliance could not be enforced by a court of law.

9. Alternatives include: mutual rescission, assignment, novation, partial performance, money damages, unilateral rescission, specific performance suit or liquidated damages.

10. His primary concern would be whether money damages would suitably restore his position or whether actual performance is necessary.

VOCABULARY REVIEW

CHAPTER 8
Real Estate Sales Contracts

a. 4	e. 18	i. 9	m. 15	q. 8
b. 7	f. 5	j. 12	n. 17	r. 10
c. 2	g. 3	k. 14	o. 1	
d. 6	h. 11	l. 16	p. 13	

QUESTIONS AND PROBLEMS

1. The purchase contract provides time to ascertain that the seller is capable of conveying title, time to arrange financing and time to carry out the various terms and conditions of the contract.

2. Anything left to be "ironed out" later is an area for potential disagreement and possibly a lost deal. Moreover, the basic contract requirement of a meeting of the minds may be missing.

3. The advantages are convenience (the bulk of the contract is already written) and time (it is faster to fill out a form than construct a contract from scratch). The disadvantages are that a preprinted contract may not adequately fit a given transaction and the blank spaces still leave room for errors.

4. A seller can accept an offer with or without a deposit. (An exception is that some court-ordered sales require a specified deposit.)

5. Most fixtures are considered by law to be a part of the land and therefore do not need separate mention. However, mention is made of any fixture that might be open to a difference of opinion.

6. If a seller is not under pressure to sell quickly and/or there are plenty of buyers in the marketplace, he can hold out for price and terms to his liking. If a buyer is aware of other buyers competing for the same property, he will act quickly and meet (or offer close to) the seller's price and terms. If the seller is in a rush to sell or is afraid that there are few buyers for his property in the market, he will negotiate terms more to the buyer's liking rather than risk not making the sale. If the buyer is aware of this, he can hold out for price and terms to his liking.

7. The advantages to the seller of holding title in an installment contract sale are that the seller still holds title in the event of the buyer's default and may be able to pledge the property as collateral for a loan.

8. Requires local answer.

9. The key advantages of trading are the tax-free exchange possibility and the need for little or no cash to complete the transaction. The disadvantages are in finding suitable trade property for all parties involved and in the fact that there are more transaction details in a trade (compared to a cash sale) that can go awry and ruin the trade.

10. A letter of intent is a mutual expression of interest to carry out some business objective. No firm, legal obligation is created.

CHAPTER 9
Mortgage and Note

VOCABULARY REVIEW

a. 26	e. 10	i. 16	m. 4	q. 8	u. 7	y. 14
b. 9	f. 21	j. 5	n. 15	r. 12	v. 25	z. 20
c. 13	g. 2	k. 3	o. 23	s. 17	w. 11	
d. 6	h. 18	l. 22	p. 1	t. 24	x. 19	

QUESTIONS AND PROBLEMS

1. A prepayment privilege is to the advantage of the borrower. Without it the debt cannot be repaid ahead of schedule.

2. Lien theory sees a mortgage as creating only a lien against a property whereas title theory sees a mortgage as conveying title to the lender subject to defeat by the borrower.

3. Strict foreclosure gives title to the lender whereas foreclosure by sale requires that the foreclosed property be sold at public auction and the proceeds used to repay the lender. (Part two requires local answer.)

4. The first mortgage is the senior mortgage while the second and third mortgages are classed as junior mortgages.

5. Requires local answer.

6. Requires local answer.

7. Requires local answer.

8. The obligor is the party making the obligation, that is, the borrower. The obligee is the party to whom the obligation is owed, that is, the lender.

9. The lender includes mortgage covenants pertaining to insurance, property taxes and removal in order to protect the value of the collateral for the loan.

10. A certificate of reduction is prepared by the lender and shows how much remains to be paid on the loan. An estoppel certificate provides for a borrower's verification of the amount still owed and the rate of interest.

CHAPTER 10
Deed of Trust

VOCABULARY REVIEW

a. 11	d. 3	g. 6	j. 4
b. 7	e. 1	h. 5	k. 12
c. 8	f. 10	i. 9	l. 2

QUESTIONS AND PROBLEMS

1. Under a deed of trust, the borrower gives the trustee title and the lender a promissory note. When the debt is paid, the lender instructs the trustee to reconvey title back to the borrower. With a mortgage, the lender acquires both the note and title (or lien rights) under the mortgage. Upon repayment, the lender releases the mortgage directly. In the event of default under a deed of trust, the trustee conducts the sale and delivers title to the buyer. With a mortgage, the lender is responsible for conducting the sale (if power of sale is present) or carrying out foreclosure proceedings.

2. The trustee's title lies dormant and there is no right of entry or use as long as the promissory note secured by the trust deed is not in default.

3. A request for reconveyance is notification from the beneficiary to the trustee to reconvey (release) the trustee's title to the trustor.

4. The power of sale clause gives the trustee the right to foreclose the borrower's rights, sell the property and convey title to a purchaser without having to go to court.

5. An assignment of rents clause gives the lender the right to operate the property and collect any rents or income generated by it if the borrower is delinquent.

6. In the automatic form, the trustee is not notified of his appointment as trustee and is usually unaware of it until called to perform in the event of default or to reconvey title when the note is paid. In the accepted form, the trustee agrees to his position as trustee at the time the deed of trust is prepared and signed.

7. Requires local answer.

CHAPTER 11
Lending Practices

VOCABULARY REVIEW

a. 10	e. 6	i. 4	m. 15	q. 3	u. 19
b. 9	f. 12	j. 24	n. 18	r. 7	v. 2
c. 11	g. 23	k. 17	o. 20	s. 1	w. 13
d. 8	h. 14	l. 5	p. 16	t. 22	x. 21

QUESTIONS AND PROBLEMS

1. The major risk is that when the balloon payment is due, the borrower will not have the cash to pay it, and will not be able to find a lender to refinance it.
2. An amortized loan requires equal, periodic payments of principal and interest such that the loan balance owing will be zero at maturity. During the life of the loan, payments are first applied to interest owing and then to principal. As the balance owed is reduced, less of each monthly payment is taken for interest and more applied to principal reduction until finally the loan is repaid.
3. $65 \times \$9.91 = \$644.15$ per month
4. $\$800 \div \$9.53 \times \$1,000 + \$10,000 = \$93,945$
5. $\$800 \div \$8.05 \times \$1,000 + \$10,000 = \$109,379$
6. $\$902 \times 90 = \$81,180$
7. The purpose of Section 203b insurance is to qualify buyers of modest-priced homes for low down-payment loans. This is done by insuring lenders against loan default and charging borrowers an insurance premium for this.
8. The VA offers a qualified veteran the opportunity of purchasing a home with no cash down payment.
9. A point is one percent. It is a method of expressing loan origination fees and discounts in connection with lending. Discount points are used to increase the effective rate of interest (yield) to the lender without changing the quoted interest rate.
10. The basic purpose of the Truth in Lending Act is to show the borrower how much he will be paying for credit in percentage terms and in total dollars.
11. As a rule, it is from the borrower's monthly income that monthly loan payments will be made. The assets, although substantial in size may not be available for monthly payments.

CHAPTER 12
Sources of Financing

VOCABULARY REVIEW

a. 1	e. 10	i. 9	m. 12	q. 18	u. 11	y. 23
b. 24	f. 16	j. 17	n. 13	r. 5	v. 6	z. 26
c. 2	g. 21	k. 22	o. 20	s. 3	w. 19	
d. 8	h. 15	l. 25	p. 7	t. 14	x. 4	

QUESTIONS AND PROBLEMS

1. A mortgage broker brings borrowers and lenders together. A mortgage banker makes loans and then resells them.
2. The main source is investors who buy mortgage-backed securities.
3. Loan servicing refers to the care and upkeep of a loan once it is made. This includes payment collection and accounting, handling defaults, borrower questions, loan payoff processing and mortgage releasing.
4. An adjustable rate mortgage is a loan on which the interest rate can be adjusted up or down as current interest rates change.
5. Both the *de la Cuesta* case and the Garn Act allow due on sale clauses to be enforced.
6. FNMA buys, by auction, mortgage loans. These purchases are financed by the sale of FNMA stock and bonds as well as the sale of these loans to investors. GNMA guarantees timely repayment of privately issued securities backed by pools of federally insured mortgages.
7. A loan dollar that is the result of real savings won't cause inflation. That is because the borrower is using goods and services the saver has foregone. But a fiat money dollar does not represent available goods and services; instead it competes with real savings dollars and pushes prices up.
8. Adjustable rate loans share the risk of changing interest rates between the borrower and the lender. The lender feels more comfortable knowing the interest rate charged will change with the cost of money to the lender.
9. Rentals and leases are considered financing forms as they allow a person the use of something without having to first pay the full purchase price.
10. Above all, the investor should make certain that the realistic market value of the property is well in excess of the loans against it.

VOCABULARY REVIEW

CHAPTER 13
Taxes and Assessments

a.	10	e.	13	i.	15	m.	16
b.	2	f.	5	j.	12	n.	8
c.	4	g.	14	k.	11	o.	3
d.	7	h.	9	l.	1	p.	6

QUESTIONS AND PROBLEMS

1. Sources of funds other than property taxes are subtracted from the district budget. The remainder is then divided by the total assessed valuation of property in the district to obtain the tax rate.
2. $960,000 divided by $120,000,000 equals 8 mills

3. $40,000 times $.008 equals $320
4. $10,000 times $0.05 divided by $100 equals $5
5. Requires local answer.
6. Requires local interpretation. However, the point is that the assessor does not set the tax rate. The assessor only applies it. If the complaint is in regard to assessment procedures, the assessment appeal process is taken. If it is in regard to the tax rate, then city, county or state budget makers are responsible.
7. The greater the amount of tax-exempt property in a taxation district, the less taxable property is available to bear the burden of taxation.
8. Requires local answer.
9. $68,000 − $5,000 − ($21,000 + $2,000 + $5,000) = $35,000
10. $68,000 − $5,000 − $58,000 = $5,000
    It will be a long-term capital gain.
11. Requires local answer.

CHAPTER 14
Title Closing and Escrow

VOCABULARY REVIEW

a. 15	e. 16	i. 10	m. 5
b. 11	f. 6	j. 7	n. 1
c. 14	g. 2	k. 8	o. 12
d. 3	h. 9	l. 4	p. 13

QUESTIONS AND PROBLEMS

1. Escrow agent duties include preparation of escrow instructions, holding buyer's earnest money, ordering a title search, obtaining title insurance, making prorations, loan payoffs, loan disbursement, deed and mortgage delivery, and handling papers and paperwork relative to the transaction.
2. The key difference is that an escrow holder is a common agent of the parties to the transaction. This eliminates the need for each party to attend the closing and personally represent himself.
3. The escrow agent is an agent of the buyer with respect to the buyer's role in the transaction and an agent of the seller with respect to the seller's role. The same holds true for the lender, title company, etc.
4. $180 divided by 12 equals $15 per month or 50¢ per day. Using standard 30-day months and presuming the buyer is the owner commencing with the settlement date, there are one month and 26 days used, and 10 months and 4 days remaining. For this remaining coverage, the buyer pays the seller 10 times $15 plus 4 times $.50 equals $152.00.
5. Daily rate equals $45,000 times 8% divided by 360 equals $10. The buyer is credited 11 days times $10 equals $110. The seller is debited the same amount.

6. **Buyer:**   **Seller:**
   lender's title policy   conveyance tax
   loan appraisal fee   deed preparation
   mortgage recording   mortgage release
7. Without release papers the buyer still has a vaguely defined liability to buy and the seller can still be required to sell.

VOCABULARY REVIEW

a. 19	e. 20	i. 5	m. 6	q. 10	u. 22	y. 17
b. 4	f. 26	j. 15	n. 16	r. 12	v. 7	z. 3
c. 18	g. 13	k. 2	o. 25	s. 14	w. 23	
d. 21	h. 8	l. 1	p. 11	t. 24	x. 9	

QUESTIONS AND PROBLEMS

1. A lease assures a tenant space at the rent stated in the lease. But it also requires the tenant to pay for the total time leased. A month-to-month arrangement commits a tenant to one month at a time; however, it also commits the landlord for only one month at a time.
2. Requires local answer.
3. Requires local answer.
4. Contract rent is the amount of rent the tenant must pay the landlord. Economic rent is market value rent.
5. The tenant's basis would be that the premises is unfit to occupy as intended in the lease. The tenant's purpose is to either get the problem fixed or terminate the lease.
6. An option to renew is to the advantage of the lessee.
7. Real estate licensees are not to accept listings where they are asked to discriminate, nor are they permitted to make, print or publish any statement or advertisement with respect to a sale or rental of a dwelling which suggests discrimination because of race, color, religion, sex or national origin.
8. Requires local answer.
9. Questions asked will center on the prospective tenant's ability to pay the rent each month and willingness to abide by the lease contract. Names and addresses of the prospect's current employer and previous landlord would be requested and checked to verify information supplied by the tenant. A credit check would also be run.

VOCABULARY REVIEW

a. 7	e. 1	i. 25	m. 17	q. 13	u. 2	y. 6
b. 16	f. 8	j. 10	n. 21	r. 14	v. 3	z. 23
c. 22	g. 5	k. 18	o. 4	s. 9	w. 11	
d. 12	h. 20	l. 24	p. 26	t. 15	x. 19	

QUESTIONS AND PROBLEMS

1. Enough comparables should be used to reasonably estimate market value but not so many as to involve more time and expense than is gained in added information. For a single-family house, 3 to 5 good comparables are usually adequate, but not excessive.

2. Asking prices are useful in that they set an upper limit on value. Offering prices are useful in that they set a lower limit on value.

3. Adjustments are made to the comparable properties. This is because it is impossible to adjust the value of something for which one does not yet know the value.

4. Using comparables that are not similar to the subject property with respect to zoning, neighborhood characteristics, size or usefulness, requires adjustments that are likely to be very inaccurate or impossible to make.

5. Gross rent times gross rent multiplier equals indicated property value. The strength of this approach is in its simplicity. Its weakness is also in its simplicity as it overlooks anything other than gross rents.

6. The five steps are (1) estimate land value as though vacant, (2) estimate new construction cost of a similar building, (3) subtract estimated depreciation from construction cost to obtain, (4) the indicated value of the structure, and (5) add this to the land value.

7. The income approach values a property based on its expected monetary returns in light of current rates of return being demanded by investors.

8. In the standard market comparison approach, a specific dollar adjustment is made for each item of difference between the comparables and the subject property. With competitve market analysis, adjustments are made in a generalized fashion in the minds of the agent and the seller. The CMA approach is usually preferred for listing homes for sale because there is less room for disagreement. The standard market approach is preferred for appraisal reports as it shows exactly how the appraiser valued the adjustments.

9. The principle of diminishing marginal returns warns against investing more than the capitalized value of the anticipated net returns.

10. **Lender:** form report.
 Buyer: oral or letter report.
 Executor: letter or narrative report.
 Highway department: narrative report.

CHAPTER 17
The Owner–Broker Relationship

VOCABULARY REVIEW

a. 16	e. 12	i. 19	m. 10	q. 13	u. 15	y. 3
b. 8	f. 11	j. 17	n. 9	r. 24	v. 4	z. 20
c. 26	g. 7	k. 18	o. 2	s. 14	w. 25	
d. 23	h. 6	l. 5	p. 1	t. 21	x. 22	

QUESTIONS AND PROBLEMS

1. The laws of agency refer to the legal responsibilities of a broker to his principal and vice versa.
2. An agency coupled with an interest exists when the agent holds an interest in the property he is representing.
3. Broker cooperation refers to the sharing of a single commission fee among the various brokers who brought about a sale. It is achieved by an agreement between the listing broker and the cooperating brokers.
4. An exclusive right to sell listing protects the broker by entitling him to a commission no matter who sells the property. The exclusive agency listing puts the broker in competition with the owner by allowing the owner to find a buyer and owe no commission. The open listing adds other brokers to the competition as any number of brokers can have the listing simultaneously and the owner can still sell it himself and pay no commission.
5. Errors and omissions insurance is designed to defend and pay certain legal costs and judgments arising from business negligence suits.
6. **Faithful:** the broker must perform as promised in the listing contract and not depart from the principal's instructions.
   Loyal: the broker owes his allegiance to the principal and as such works for the benefit of the principal. This means promoting and protecting the principal's best interests and keeping him informed of all matters that might affect the sale of the listed property.
7. "Ready, willing and able buyer" means a buyer who is ready to buy at the seller's price and terms, and who has the financial capacity to do so.
8. Listings are usually terminated with the completion of the agency objective, namely finding a buyer or a tenant. Lacking a buyer, termination usually results when the listing period expires. A listing can also be terminated if the broker fails to perform as agreed in the listing or if the broker and principal mutually agree to terminate.
9. The purpose of a property disclosure statement is to require that sellers of subdivisions provide prospective purchasers with information regarding the property they are being asked to buy.
10. Fair housing testers play the role of prospective buyers and tenants to see if fair housing laws are being followed.

VOCABULARY REVIEW

CHAPTER 18
Licensing Laws and Professional Affiliation

a. 6	e. 5	i. 1	m. 12	q. 20	u. 11
b. 21	f. 19	j. 15	n. 2	r. 9	v. 17
c. 14	g. 24	k. 16	o. 23	s. 10	w. 22
d. 18	h. 13	l. 4	p. 3	t. 8	x. 7

QUESTIONS AND PROBLEMS

1. Early license laws were primarily aimed at protecting the public by qualifying license applicants based on their honesty, truthfulness and good reputation. Real estate examinations and education requirements were added later.

2. Generally speaking, a real estate license is required when a person, who for compensation or the promise of compensation, lists or offers to list, sells or offers to sell, buys or offers to buy, negotiates or offers to negotiate, either directly or indirectly, for the purpose of bringing about a sale, purchase, option to purchase, exchange, auction, lease or rental of real estate. Some states also require that real estate appraisers, property managers, mortgage bankers and rent collectors hold real estate licenses.

3. In deciding on a compensation schedule for his salespersons, a broker must consider office overhead, employee retention and the emphasis he wishes to place on listing versus selling.

4–8. Require local answers.

9. The purpose of a bond requirement or a recovery fund is to have funds available that can be drawn upon in the event a court judgment against a licensee, resulting from a license-related wrongdoing, is uncollectible.

10. The purpose of the National Association of Realtors is to promote the general welfare of the real estate industry by encouraging fair dealing among Realtors and the public, supporting legislation to protect property rights, offering education for members and in general doing whatever is necessary to build the dignity, stability and professionalization of the industry.

11. An employment contract will cover such matters as compensation, training, hours of work, company identification, fees and dues, expenses, use of automobile, fringe benefits, independent contractor status, termination of employment and general office policies and procedures.

12. You would want to consider location, compensation, broker's reputation, working hours, broker support, training opportunities, advertising policy, expense reimbursement and fringe benefits.

CHAPTER 19
Condominiums, Cooperatives,
PUDs and Timeshares

VOCABULARY REVIEW

a.	16	e.	3	i.	2	m.	17	q.	20
b.	15	f.	1	j.	8	n.	4	r.	19
c.	7	g.	11	k.	14	o.	5	s.	12
d.	13	h.	6	l.	9	p.	10	t.	18

QUESTIONS AND PROBLEMS

1. Condominiums are often cheaper to buy than a single-family house, are often better located, may offer better security and maintenance and can be individually financed.
2. Each condominium unit owner holds an undivided interest in the land in a fee simple condominium project. The corporation owns the land in a cooperative.
3. A proprietary lease is a lease issued by a corporation to its stockholders. The lease "rent" is actually the stockholder's share of the cost of operating the building and repaying the debt against it. In a residential lease, the tenant pays for use of the premises, is not responsible for operating expenses nor debt repayment and does not have an ownership interest in the premises.
4. The master deed converts a given parcel of land into a condominium subdivision.
5. The wall between two condominium apartments belongs to the condominium owners as a group.
6. CC&Rs are the covenants, conditions and restrictions by which a property owner agrees to abide. They are established for the harmony and well-being of the owners as a group.
7. Maintenance fees (association dues) pay for common operating costs and are spread among the unit owners. Failure to pay creates a lien against the delinquent owner's unit.
8. The owners' association hazard and liability policy covers only the common elements. To be protected against property loss and accident liability within a dwelling unit, the owner must have his own hazard and liability policy.
9. Right-to-use is a contractual right whereas fee simple is ownership of real estate.
10. In a PUD each owner holds title to the land occupied by his unit and is a member of an owners' association which holds title to the common areas.

VOCABULARY REVIEW

CHAPTER 20
Property Insurance

a. 10	f. 7	j. 9	n. 5
b. 11	g. 3	k. 16	o. 4
c. 12	h. 2	l. 8	p. 1
d. 13	i. 14	m. 17	q. 15
e. 6			

QUESTIONS AND PROBLEMS

1. An endorsement or rider is an agreement by the insurer to modify the coverage found in the basic policy.
2. Liability insurance is concerned with insuring against financial

losses resulting from the responsibility of one person to another.

3. Section I in a home insurance policy covers loss of, and damage to, the insured's property. Section II deals with the liability of the insured.

4. All-risk insurance policies cover loss or damage resulting from any cause not excluded by the policy. A broad-form policy is one that covers a large number of perils that are specifically named in the policy.

5. "New for old" means that the insurer will pay for replacement at today's costs. Thus, although the property lost by the insured was used, he will receive a new replacement from the insurer.

6. Coverage is suspended on vacant buildings because they are more attractive to thieves, vandals and arsonists than are occupied buildings.

CHAPTER 21
Land-Use Control

VOCABULARY REVIEW

a. 8	c. 11	e. 13	g. 1	i. 4	k. 5	m. 9
b. 12	d. 6	f. 7	h. 14	j. 3	l. 10	n. 2

QUESTIONS AND PROBLEMS

1. The individual property owner does not consider his property to be a community resource. Thus, any substantial progress in land planning and control in the future must also consider the right of the individual to develop his land.

2. The authority of government to control land use is derived from the state's right of police power. Through enabling acts, this authority is passed on to the counties, cities and towns in the state.

3. A variance allows an individual landowner to deviate from strict compliance with zoning requirements for his land. A variance must be consistent with the character of the neighborhood and general objectives of zoning as they apply to that neighborhood.

4. Requires local answer.

5. A master plan takes a broad look at the entire land-use picture in a community, county or region. The object is to view the area as a unified entity that provides its residents with jobs and housing as well as social, recreational and cultural activities. In contrast, zoning laws tell a landowner specifically how a parcel of land may be used, and what type and size structures may be placed on it.

6. The purpose of an EIS is to gather information about the effect of a proposed project on the environment so that the anticipated environmental costs and benefits of the project may be considered along with the economic and humanitarian aspects.

7. Transferable development rights would equalize financial windfalls and wipe-outs by requiring those whose land is approved for

urban uses to purchase development rights from those whose land is prohibited from development.

8. Requires local answer.

VOCABULARY REVIEW

a. 1	**c.** 4	**e.** 8	**g.** 10	**i.** 5
b. 6	**d.** 3	**f.** 7	**h.** 9	**j.** 2

QUESTIONS AND PROBLEMS

1. Requires local answer.
2. Requires local answer.
3. Requires local answer.
4. $15\% \times (100\% - 40\%) = 9.0\%$; $10\% \times (100\% - 40\%) = 6\%$; $5\% \times (100\% - 40\%) = 3\%$.
5. The purpose of the Equal Credit Opportunity Act is to require lenders to make credit available without regard to sex or marital status.
6. Requires local answer.
7. Large federal deficits compete against home buyers for available loan funds and in the process push up interest rates.
8. The economic goals of the Federal Reserve Board are high employment, stable prices, steady growth and a stable foreign exchange value for the dollar.
9. The advantage is that in the short-run interest rates can be pushed down which gives the economy a boost. The disadvantage is that inflation will result.
10. Falling prices.

VOCABULARY REVIEW

a. 7	**c.** 12	**e.** 1	**g.** 9	**i.** 5	**k.** 2	**m.** 6
b. 14	**d.** 8	**f.** 11	**h.** 4	**j.** 13	**l.** 10	**n.** 3

QUESTIONS AND PROBLEMS

1. A tax-sheltered investment is one where part or all of the return from a property is not subject to income taxes. The primary source is depreciation, which, although shown as an expense for calculating income taxes, is not an out-of-pocket (cash) expense.
2. Investors in real estate look for cash flow, tax shelter, mortgage reduction and appreciation.
3. The major risk of owning vacant land is having to wait too long for an increase in value.

4. The advantages of duplexes and triplexes are that, compared to larger buildings, the investor's capital, management and risk are on a smaller scale. These buildings are not, however, as efficient to manage and rents are often relatively low per dollar of purchase price.

5. "Better off" must be considered in light of the investor's objectives and ability to take risks. The earlier one invests, the bigger the risks and potential rewards. By waiting, one can lower the risks and the rewards.

6. Higher returns are necessary in an older building to compensate for major replacement, repair and refurbishing costs; for increasing maintenance expenses; for the risk that the neighborhood may decline in popularity; and that the building itself may have limited remaining economic usefulness.

7. A person who has a number of high-income years remaining in life can more comfortably take risks as there is time to recover financially if losses should result. An older person without the time and energy to recover financially would seek to avoid risky investments.

8. $22,000 ÷ .10756 = $204,537. Round to $205,000.

9. $22,000 ÷ .11819 = $186,141. Round to $186,000.

10. Limited partnerships offer the investor the advantages of relatively small minimum investment, built-in property management, limited financial liability, the opportunity to diversify and the same tax benefits as sole owners.

11. A careful investor will check out both the properties and the general partners. Do the general partners have a good record in selecting, organizing and managing real estate investments? Are they honest and creditworthy? Are there lawsuits or other legal complaints against them? Regarding the properties, are the income and expense projections accurate and reasonable? Are the properties in sound physical and financial condition? Are they well located? Are they priced right? Are the tax benefits realistic? Is there financial responsibility or liability for the limited partner in the future? Is the limited partner willing and able to stay in the partnership for its full lifespan?

Agency by estoppel (*continued*)
gence over his agent and the agent exercises powers not granted to him 431

Agency by ratification: one that is established after the fact 431

Agency coupled with an interest: one that results when the agent holds an interest in the property he is representing 431–32

Agent: the person empowered to act by and on behalf of the principal 430, 431–46

Agent's duties at closing 330–31

Agent's liability, appraisal 405–06; for tax advice 323–24; to clients 432–37; to third parties 437–41; zoning 529–30

Agreement of sale, installment contract 174–77; offer to purchase 159–62

Air lot: a designated airspace over a parcel of land 13–14, 32–33

Air right: the right to occupy and use the airspace above the surface of a parcel of land 13–14, 32–33, 63–65

Alienation clause: a clause in a note or mortgage that gives the lender the right to call the entire loan balance due if the property is sold or otherwise conveyed 197, 261–62

Alienation of title: a change in ownership of any kind 110

Allodial system: one in which individuals are given the right to own land 42

All-risks policy: all perils, except those excluded in writing, are covered 510–11

Alluvion: the increase of land when waterborne soil is gradually deposited 109

Amendatory language: government-required clauses in FHA and VA contracts 170

Amendment: the method used to change a zoning ordinance 524

American College Testing: a private firm that writes, administers, and grades real estate examinations 462–63; sample questions in Appendix C 607–15

American Institute of Real Estate Appraisers 409

Amortization table 232

Amortized loan: a loan requiring periodic payments that include both interest and partial repayment of principal 228–33; *illustrated* 229, 230; partially amortized loans 234–35; *table* 232

Amount realized: selling price less selling expenses 316

Annual meeting of the homeowners' association 489

Annual percentage rate (APR): a uniform measure of the cost of credit that includes interest, discount points and loan fees 251–52

Annuity tables, Appendix F 629, 631; monthly payment table 232

Answers to questions and problems, Appendix H 633–52

Apartment buildings, as investments 570–72; management 367–76

Appraisal: an estimate of value 379–409; appraisal report 404–405; competitive market analysis 388–91; cost approach 394–97; for property taxes 306; income approach 398–402; investor's viewpoint 579; market approach 380–88

Appraisal letter: a valuation report in the form of a business letter 404

Appraisal reports, appraisal letter 404; form appraisal 404–405; narrative report 405; oral appraisal 404

Appraise: to estimate the value of something 379

Appraiser organizations 409–10

Appreciation: an increase in property value 565

Appropriation process: the enactment of a taxing body's budget and sources of money into law 306

Appurtenance: a right or privilege or improvement that belongs to and passes

Escrow company: a firm that specializes in handling the closing of a transaction 163–65, 332

Essentials of a valid contract 139

Estate: the extent of one's legal interest or rights in land 46; the extent of one's real and personal property in general 103–104

Estate at will: a leasehold estate that can be terminated by the lessor or lessee at any time 60, 354

Estate for years: any lease with a specific starting time and a specific ending time 59, 354

Estate in severalty: owned by one person, sole ownership 69–70

Estoppel certificate: a document in which a borrower verifies the amount still owed and the interest rate 199

Eviction 363–64, 371–72

Examination for real estate license 459–63; sample test questions in Appendixes B, C and D 599–620

Exchanging real estate 182–85; delayed exchange 184–85; *illustrated* 183

Exclusive agency listing: a listing wherein the owner reserves the right to sell the property himself, but agrees to list with no other broker during the listing period 416–21

Exclusive authority to sell (same as exclusive right to sell) 416–21

Exclusive right to sell: a listing that gives the broker the right to collect a commission no matter who sells the property during the listing period 416–20

Execute: the process of completing, performing, or carrying out something 149

Executed: means that performance has taken place 149

Executive director: the person in charge of real estate regulation in a state 466

Executor: a person named in a will to carry out its instructions (masculine) 103; **executrix** (feminine) 103

Executor's deed: a deed used to convey the real property of a deceased person 104

Executory: in the process of being completed 148

Expressed contract: a contract made orally or in writing 137

Face amount: the dollar amount of insurance coverage 261

Fair Credit Reporting Act 262

Fair housing laws 448–51; blockbusting 449; Civil Rights Act 448–51; discrimination complaints 450; discrimination penalties 450; enforcement 450–51; *Jones* vs. *Mayer* 448; leases 364–65; steering 448–49; Supreme Court 448

Fair market value. *See* **Market value**

Faithful performance: a requirement that an agent obey all legal instructions given to him by his principal 432–33

Fannie Mae: a real estate industry nickname for the Federal National Mortgage Association 273–75

Farm brokerage 7

Farmer's Home Administration (FmHA) 250

Federal clauses: refers to government-required clauses in real estate contracts 170–71

Federal Consumer Credit Protection Act (Truth in Lending Act) 250–54

Federal Home Loan Mortgage Corporation: provides a secondary mortgage market facility for savings and loan associations 276

Federal Housing Administration 239–45; insurance limits 240; programs 243–44

Federal National Mortgage Association: provides a secondary market for real estate loans 273–75

Federal Reserve Board: governing board of the nation's central bank 547–48, 554–55

the state to administer oaths, attest and certify documents and take acknowledgments 93, 117–18

Note: a written promise to repay a debt 190–93; *illustrated* 191

Notice of consent: allows the secretary of state to receive legal summonses for nonresidents 464

Notice of default: public notice that a borrower is in default 206

Notice of lien 54

Notice of lis pendens: notice of a pending lawsuit 203

Novation: the substitution of a new contract or new party for an old one 149, 199

Nuncupative will: a will made orally 105

Obligee: the person to whom a debt or obligation is owed 190

Obligor: the person responsible for paying a debt or obligation 190

Offer 142; acceptance 142–43; counteroffer 142–43; *illustrated* contract 159–61

Offeree: the party who receives an offer 142

Offeror: the party who makes an offer 142

Office buildings as investments 572–73

Office of Interstate Land Sales Registration 446

Offset statement: a statement by an owner or lienholder as to the balance due on an existing lien 329

Off-site management: refers to those property management functions that can be performed away from the premises being managed 373–74

On-site management: refers to those property management functions that must be performed on the premises being managed 372–73

Old for old: insurance policy pays only the depreciated value of damaged property 513

Open listing: a listing that gives a broker a nonexclusive right to find a buyer 421

Operating expense ratio: total operating expenses divided by effective gross income 400

Operating expenses: expenditures necessary to maintain the production of income 399–400

Opinion of title: an attorney's opinion as to the status of title 123

Option: the right at some future time to purchase or lease a property at a predetermined price 178–81, 295–96

Optionee: the party receiving the option 181

Optionor: the party giving the option 181

Oral appraisal report: a spoken estimate of a property's worth 404

Oral contracts 147–48

Oral will 105

Origination fee: a charge for making a loan 238

Ostensible authority: results when a principal gives a third party reason to believe that another person is his agent even though that person is unaware of the appointment 431

Outside of the closing: means that a party to the closing has paid someone directly and not through the closing 347. (*also called* **outside of escrow** 347)

Overall rate: a mortgage-equity factor used to appraise income-producing property 401–402

Overencumbered property: occurs when the market value of a property is exceeded by the loans against it 297–98

Overview of a real estate transaction 3

Owner-broker relationship 415–37; overview 443–44

Owners' association: an administrative association composed of each unit owner in a condominium 487

Owner's policy: a title insurance policy designed to protect the fee owner 126

Statutory redemption: the right of a borrower after a foreclosure sale to reclaim his property by repaying the defaulted loan 205

Steering: the illegal practice of directing minority members to or away from certain neighborhoods 448–49

Step-up rental: a lease that provides for agreed-upon rent increases 300, 360

Straight-line depreciation: depreciation in equal amounts each year over the life of the asset 563

Street numbers, as a means of describing property 18

Strict foreclosure: the lender acquires absolute title without the need for a foreclosure sale 206

Subagent: an agent appointed by an agent to act for the principal's benefit 444

Subdivision regulations 525–26; condominium 487

Subchapter S corporations 83

Subject property: the property that is being appraised 380

Subject to: said of property that is bought subject to the existing loan against it 198

Sublease: a lease given by a lessee 361

Sublessee: one who rents from a lessee 60, 361

Sublessor: a lessee who in turn leases to another 60, 361

Sublet: to transfer only a portion of one's lease rights 361

Subordination: voluntary acceptance of a lower mortgage priority than one would otherwise be entitled to 200; as a financing tool 294

Substitute borrower 199

Subsurface right: the right to use land below the earth's surface 13–14, 32, 64–65

Sunk cost: a cost already incurred that is not subject to revision 37

Superintendant of a building 372–73

Supply and demand for housing 538–41

Surface rights: the right to use the surface of a parcel of land 13–14, 64–66

Surplus money action: a claim for payment filed by a junior mortgage holder at a foreclosure sale 203

Surrogate court: a court of law with the authority to verify the legality of a will and carry out its instructions 104

Survey books: map books 28–29

Survivorship, right of 71–72, 72–73

Suspend: temporarily make ineffective; insurance policies 516; real estate licenses 466

Syndication (syndicate): a group of persons or businesses that combines to undertake an investment 82

T-lot: a lot at the end of a T intersection 34

Tacking: adding successive periods of continuous occupation to qualify for title by adverse possession 106

Take-out loan: a permanent loan arranged to replace a construction loan 291

"Taking back paper": said of a seller who allows a purchaser to substitute a primissory note for cash 293

Tax Acts of 1984 and **1985** 322, 567–68

Tax basis: the price paid for a property plus certain costs and expenses 315–16

Tax certificate: a document issued at a tax sale that entitles the purchaser to a deed at a later date if the property is not redeemed 308

Tax deducations, available to homeowners 321; available to investors 321–22, 561–64

Tax deed: a document that conveys title to property purchased at a tax sale 102, 308

Taxes, conveyance taxes 324; investment property 321–23; impact on real estate 545–46; property taxes 305–15; sale of a residence 315–22; tax-free exchange 182–85